# 2004 Index
# of Economic Freedom

**MARC A. MILES** is Director of the Center for International Trade and Economics (CITE) at The Heritage Foundation.

**EDWIN J. FEULNER** is President of The Heritage Foundation.

**MARY ANASTASIA O'GRADY** is Editor of the "Americas" column and Senior Editorial Page Writer at *The Wall Street Journal*.

**William W. Beach** is John M. Olin Fellow in Economics and Director of the Center for Data Analysis at The Heritage Foundation.

**Brian M. Carney** is an Editorial Page Writer for *The Wall Street Journal Europe*.

**Ana Isabel Eiras** is Senior Policy Analyst in International Economics in the Center for International Trade and Economics at The Heritage Foundation. She is also Editor of the Spanish-language edition of the *Index of Economic Freedom*.

**Paul A. Gigot** is Editor of *The Wall Street Journal* Editorial Page.

**Anthony Kim** is Research Assistant in the Center for International Trade and Economics at The Heritage Foundation.

**Daniel J. Mitchell** is McKenna Senior Fellow in Political Economy in the Thomas A. Roe Institute for Economic Policy Studies at The Heritage Foundation.

**Richard Roll** is Japan Alumni Chair in International Finance in the Anderson School at the University of California, Los Angeles.

**Aaron Schavey** is an Assistant Professor of Economics at Bethel College.

# 2004 Index of Economic Freedom

Marc A. Miles

Edwin J. Feulner

Mary Anastasia O'Grady

with Ana Isabel Eiras and Aaron Schavey

 The Heritage Foundation

THE WALL STREET JOURNAL.

The Heritage Foundation
214 Massachusetts Avenue, NE
Washington, DC 20002
(202) 546-4400
heritage.org

The Wall Street Journal
Dow Jones & Company, Inc.
200 Liberty Street
New York, NY 10281
(212) 416-2000
www.wsj.com

Cover images by photos.com
Cover design by Elizabeth Brewer
ISBN: 0-89195-265-9
ISSN: 1095-7308

# Table of Contents

# Foreword

Three years after the American stock market bubble burst, and two years after September 11, the news is that the global consensus in favor of economic liberalization has held. The trend that gained speed in the 1980s and began to gallop after the Berlin Wall fell can therefore be said to be passing its sternest test. Liberalization is far easier amid prosperity, but the fact that the world did not regress even amid the global trials and slowdown of the past three years may be a larger achievement.

This continuing progress owes much to the proven success of free economies in the past three decades. The rise of the Asian Tigers was a seminal event, shattering the import substitution model of development that had held sway for so many years. China saw their progress and made its own great leap forward from Maoism. Twenty-three years after Deng Xiaoping's decision to open economically, China by 2003 has become one of the world's growth engines. It remains well down the list on our *Index of Economic Freedom* survey at 128, largely because of its trade and regulatory controls, but its rapid growth is being felt everywhere.

To be sure, there were setbacks in the past year, some of them severe. The troubles in South America worsened, with Argentina and Venezuela putting in two of the worst performances in the *Index* survey. Venezuela in particular is tempting long-run decline as President Hugo Chávez takes that oil-rich nation down an anti-democratic path. Argentina is beset by populist democratic gridlock, with political leaders unable or unwilling to champion the reforms that have proven so effective in nearby Chile. The entire Latin American region could use a renewal of U.S. attention and leadership.

The trend toward trade liberalization also seems to be at a crossroads. World trade talks collapsed at Cancun in September, thanks in part to U.S. and especially European refusal to compromise enough on farm subsidies. Yet even this is a sign of some progress, in that the world's developing countries (notably in Africa) now realize they must be attached to global markets to prosper. They are right that First World subsidies hurt Third World farmers, though, as the survey shows, many of them could help themselves by liberalizing their own economic policies.

Rwanda and Ethiopia did precisely that this past year, but too many others regressed.

The United States, for its part, seems headed for one of its periodic national debates about trade. The recession and globalization are again putting pressure on manufacturing jobs, and the issue is emerging in the 2004 presidential contest. Democrats are turning protectionist, with the sole exception of Joe Lieberman, and the Bush Administration isn't helping by making China a target for currency lobbying. Though sound on tax policy, the Bush White House and Treasury seem clueless on international monetary issues. This may not matter if the world economy recovers smartly, but it is a wild card to watch.

It is impossible, since September 11, to discuss world trends without considering the war on terrorism. And on that score, the liberation of Iraq could well prove to be the year's most significant economic event. In the current survey, Iraq remains tied for dead last at 156. But only days after this list was assembled, the new Iraqi Governing Council announced major liberal reforms. They include a flat tax regime with a top marginal rate on individual and corporate income of 15 percent. That is better than Hong Kong. Its trade and foreign ownership laws will also welcome investment capital, both foreign and domestic. Iraq's transition to stability and freedom remains a challenge, but if it succeeds, it may well set off a revolution by example in a Middle East that has been trapped in the statist economics of the past century.

Continued progress on the road from serfdom probably now requires another burst of global growth. As this is being written, that revival seems probable, led by a resurgent United States. Pro-growth tax cuts and monetary reflation appear to be combining to shake the world from its three-year doldrums. Japan and Europe are laggards, as has been the case for most of the past decade, but even they are showing signs of economic life.

One of the great dramas in the coming years will be whether global competition and the rise of the euro force European governments, especially France and Germany, to liberalize their suffocating labor and tax policies. So far the evidence is scant, but public pressure may grow as the population ages and living standards fail to rise. The European Lazarus rose again with a burst of free-market growth after World War II, and the coming decades will see whether it can repeat that miracle. World prosperity would increase enormously if it did.

Paul A. Gigot
Editorial Page Editor
*The Wall Street Journal*
October 2003

# Preface

Economic freedom continues to advance, albeit slowly. For the past 10 years, the *Index of Economic Freedom*, published jointly by The Heritage Foundation and *The Wall Street Journal*, has used 10 factors to measure economic freedom around the world in an effort to trace the path to economic prosperity. This annual volume continues to serve a wide and diverse audience ranging from teachers and students to executives, politicians, and the media.

While progressing more slowly than one might hope, economic freedom nonetheless continues to show significant net gains in two regions. North America and Europe together show the greatest net gain with seven countries. Following close behind, sub-Saharan Africa shows a surprising net gain of six countries.

Sadly, however, this cannot be said for all of the world's regions. North Africa and the Middle East show no net change, Asia and the Pacific show the largest net loss, and Latin America and the Caribbean exhibit a net loss as well.

A loss or relative lack of economic freedom usually calculates into a lower GDP. As the world's freest economy, Hong Kong has a per capita income that differs significantly from that of a country like Zimbabwe. Hong Kong has an attractive environment for business and enterprise, whereas Zimbabwe has an environment that can be characterized fairly as both statist and anti-business.

The benefits of economic freedom are obvious, yet many governments continue to stifle their economies by implementing unsound policies. Obstacles in the form of domestic politics often prevent leaders from taking the actions needed to encourage a climate of economic freedom and overall prosperity. Both developed and developing countries fall into the trap of choosing what is easy over what is economically sound.

While Europe claims the largest number of countries in the top 10, the European Union (EU) continues to burden European economies by heavily subsidizing agriculture through its Common Agricultural Policy (CAP). Brian M. Carney describes the adverse effects of the CAP in his chapter, "The Common Agricultural Policy: How the European Union Distorts Trade with Non-EU Nations." Because of the CAP, farmers in developing countries cannot compete with European goods, and Europeans are forced to pay more for the food they need.

America has likewise pursued this counterproductive approach, both by subsidizing farmers and by protecting items such as sugar with high tariffs. These policies punish the average citizen with higher prices and impede competition. As Adam Smith noted in *The Wealth of Nations*:

> By means of glasses, hotbeds, and hotwalls, very good grapes can be raised in Scotland, and very good wine too can be made of them at about thirty times the expence for which at least equally good can be brought from foreign countries. Would it be a reasonable law to prohibit the importation of all foreign wines, merely to encourage the making of claret and burgundy in Scotland?[1]

Despite the apparent staying power of the CAP, however, there are positive signs in other areas. Tax reductions are sweeping across Europe. Daniel Mitchell's chapter, "The Economics of Tax Competition: Harmonization vs. Liberalization," highlights the encouraging changes in Western Europe and in the former Soviet Union. European countries are starting to realize that Ireland's success does not have to be an isolated phenomenon. Russia is ranked as a "mostly unfree" country, but Russian President Vladimir Putin has still managed to promote enactment of a flat personal income tax and reduced corporate and small business taxes.

By lowering corporate taxes, Putin has given an incentive to investors to hang their hats in Russia. If Russia wants to attract the amount of investment that its Western neighbors are luring, however, more changes need to be implemented. Russia has a large informal market, a high level of restrictions on banking and finance, weak protection of property rights, and a high level of regulation. All of these issues translate into higher business costs and barriers to a higher level of prosperity.

Russia could learn a lot from Estonia and Lithuania. While Estonia's success has been heralded over the past several years, Lithuania has been improving steadily since it was first graded in 1996.

Lithuania is the second freest country in the former Soviet bloc. More than a decade after Ronald Reagan told Mikhail Gorbachev to "tear down this wall," the former Soviet countries continue to advance by tearing down the walls that kept their citizens from prospering. Today, the private sector produces roughly 80 percent of Lithuania's GDP. Foreign banks dominate the banking sector. Lithuania has a very low level of restrictions on banking and finance, and low barriers to foreign investment.

On the other side of the world, sub-Saharan Africa has made great strides this year in raising its level of economic freedom. Five of the countries in this region—Rwanda, Ethiopia, Cape Verde, Senegal, and Mauritania—are among the world's 10 most improved countries. Despite the improvements this year, however, not one of the countries in this region is truly free. Each is held back by such persistent problems as corruption and weak property rights. Though some have made progress, as this year's edition of the *Index of Economic Freedom* demonstrates, each still remains in dire need of investment—but has failed to make the changes in the direction of economic freedom that are needed to attract it.

Most developing countries depend heavily on agriculture. History is telling. Ireland, once a poor country dependent on agriculture, has implemented changes to become a major center for investment. With some changes, many of these developing countries have the potential to become the next Ireland or even the next Hong Kong, and with expanded economic freedom, the citizens of those countries will be able to enjoy long-denied economic prosperity.

Rome wasn't built in a day, and Ireland's success wasn't either. Countries won't see prosperity unless they commit to economic freedom for the long haul. As the saying goes, "good things come to those who wait." Leaders who take the time to fully implement economic reforms will come to see the fruits of their labor. For the citizens living in such a country, the taste of economic freedom will be sweet.

Edwin J. Feulner, President
The Heritage Foundation
October 2003

---

1    Adam Smith, *The Wealth of Nations* (New York: Prometheus Books, 1991), p. 354.

# Acknowledgments

We wish to express our grateful appreciation to the many individuals, especially those at The Heritage Foundation, who have made such valuable contributions to this 10th annual edition of the *Index of Economic Freedom*.

The primary responsibility for producing the *Index* was borne by The Heritage Foundation's Center for International Trade and Economics (CITE). Ana Isabel Eiras and Aaron Schavey did an excellent job in grading the countries this year. Ana also coordinated the complex process of producing the *Index*. In managing the data and the extensive research process, she was ably assisted by Anthony Kim, Ha Nguyen, and Carrie Donovan. In addition to these tasks, Anthony authored the statistical summary that accompanies each country. Sara Fitzgerald made invaluable contributions to the opening chapters.

In the Katheryn and Shelby Cullom Davis Institute for International Studies, Ariel Cohen, Nile Gardiner, John Hulsman, Stephen Johnson, and James Phillips wrote introductory paragraphs and provided their expertise. We are especially grateful for the insightful contributions that Larry Wortzel, Vice President and Director of the Davis Institute, and Helle Dale, Deputy Director of the Davis Institute, made to the content, design, and marketing of this year's *Index*. Yvette Campos and Kathy Gudgel provided valuable production support.

In the Asian Studies Center, Director Peter Brookes, Dana Dillon, Balbina Hwang, John Tkacik, Jr., and Paolo Pasicolan wrote introductions and provided assistance, and Allison Goodman provided valuable production support. We are particularly grateful to William Beach, Director of the Center for Data Analysis, for his continued support and for his contributions to Chapter 5.

We thank Todd Gaziano, Senior Fellow in Legal Studies, for his perceptive comments on the property rights factor and for grading the property rights factor in the United States. In the Information Technology Department, invaluable help was provided by Vice President of Information Technology Michael Spiller, Genevieve Grimes, and Joanna Yu. We are grateful for their professionalism.

We are also grateful to Ted Morgan, Director of Online Communications, and his staff for placing the entire *Index* on the Heritage Web site (*http://www.heritage.org/index/*). They also did an excellent job of developing a searchable database that helps researchers identify key trends over the 10-year history of the *Index*. John Hanley, Melissa Kaiser, and Jason Schryer were likewise indispensable to this project.

Once again, we wish to express our deep appreciation for the work of Senior Editor Richard Odermatt, who was responsible for final review of the entire text, and Senior Copy Editor William T. Poole, who continues to bear the primary responsibility for editing the entire book. Their professionalism, commitment to the project, and attention to detail play a major part in making each year's edition of the *Index* a reality.

In Publishing Services, Director Jonathan Larsen and Elizabeth Brewer were responsible for the extensive design and layout changes that make this 10th edition the most readable and accessible yet published, as well as for developing the regional and country maps and formatting the charts and tables, and Therese Pennefather coordinated the entire production process.

We are especially pleased to include an essay by Richard Roll, who holds the Japan Alumni Chair in Finance at the Anderson School, UCLA, this year. We are also pleased to include essays by Daniel J. Mitchell, McKenna Senior Fellow in Political Economy in the Thomas A. Roe Institute for Economic Policy Studies at the Heritage Foundation, and Brian M. Carney, an editorial page writer for *The Wall Street Journal Europe*. In addition, we thank Ben Goodrich, Philippe Lacoude, Gary Hufbauer, and Richard Roll for their contributions in reviewing and revising the methodology. As always, the editors of *The Wall Street Journal* have helped to guide us with their thoughtful advice and insight on the countries.

Countless individuals serving with various accounting firms, businesses, research organizations, U.S. government agencies, foreign embassies, and other organizations cooperated in providing us with the data used in the *Index*. Their assistance is much appreciated. So, too, is the work of Heritage interns Jaydip Das, John Goodman, Jamie Homer, and Sarah Sanders, who were particularly helpful in producing this edition. Like their predecessors, they did the legwork, compiled the data, and researched hard-to-find information in an unfailingly timely fashion. We wish them the best in their new ventures.

As always, we acknowledge our enduring debt both to Heritage Trustee Ambassador J. William Middendorf II, for originally encouraging us to undertake such a study of global economic freedom, and to the many other people within Heritage who continue to lend their expertise to our effort as they have in past years.

Finally, we would like to express our appreciation to the many people who, year after year, have either praised or criticized the *Index of Economic Freedom* so enthusiastically. The support and encouragement of people in all parts of the world continue to serve as a major source of inspiration for The Heritage Foundation and *The Wall Street Journal* in their ongoing collaboration on this important work. We hope this year's effort matches the expectations of all our supporters, as well as the thoughtful critics who so often have provided the insights that enable us to continue to improve the *Index*.

Marc A. Miles
Edwin J. Feulner
Mary Anastasia O'Grady
October 2003

# Executive Summary

by Marc A. Miles, Edwin J. Feulner, and Mary Anastasia O'Grady

With the publication of this edition, The Heritage Foundation/Wall Street Journal *Index of Economic Freedom* marks its 10th anniversary. The idea of producing a user-friendly "index of economic freedom" as a tool for policymakers and investors was first discussed at The Heritage Foundation in the late 1980s. The goal then, as it is today, was to develop a systematic, empirical measurement of economic freedom in countries throughout the world. To this end, the decision was made to establish a set of objective economic criteria that, since 1994, have been used to study and grade various countries for the annual publication of the *Index of Economic Freedom*.

The *Index*, however, is more than just a dataset based on empirical study; it is a careful theoretical analysis of the factors that most influence the institutional setting of economic growth. Moreover, although there are many theories about the origins and causes of economic development, the findings of this study are straightforward: The countries with the most economic freedom also have higher rates of long-term economic growth and are more prosperous than are those with less economic freedom.

The *2004 Index of Economic Freedom* measures how well 161 countries score on a list of 50 independent variables divided into 10 broad factors of economic freedom. Low scores are more desirable. The higher the score on a factor, the greater the level of government interference in the economy and the less economic freedom a country enjoys.

These 50 variables are grouped into the following categories:

- Trade policy,
- Fiscal burden of government,
- Government intervention in the economy,
- Monetary policy,
- Capital flows and foreign investment,
- Banking and finance,
- Wages and prices,
- Property rights,
- Regulation, and
- Informal market activity.

Chapter 5 explains these factors in detail. Taken together, they offer an empirical depiction of a country's level of economic freedom. A systematic analysis of these factors continues to demonstrate that countries with the highest levels of economic freedom also have the highest living standards.

1

## WORLDWIDE PATTERNS

This year, economic freedom has advanced throughout the world: the scores of 75 countries are better, the scores of 69 are worse, and the scores of 11 are unchanged. Of the 155 countries numerically graded in the *2004 Index*, 16 are classified as "free," 55 as "mostly free," 72 as "mostly unfree," and 12 as "repressed." (Angola, Burundi, Democratic Republic of Congo, Sudan, and Iraq were suspended from grading because of civil unrest or anarchy. Serbia and Montenegro was suspended because reliable data were not available.)

Most of the world's economically repressed countries lie in Asia, which experienced a net loss of economic freedom in five countries. (At the same time, however, the top three countries in this year's rankings are also located in Asia.) Latin America and the Caribbean experienced a net loss of two countries. North Africa and the Middle East had no change.

North America and Europe experienced the largest gain in economic freedom: a net gain of seven countries. Sub-Saharan Africa experienced a net gain of six countries.

By factor, the results were more evenly split. Four factors of the *Index* had a greater net number of countries with expanded freedom, four had less freedom, and two had no net change. The fiscal burden factor marked the greatest number of improvements (57) and the greatest number of losses (71), for an overall net loss of 14. This was the largest net loss. The biggest net gain was in the monetary policy factor, with 30 countries improving and nine worsening for a net gain of 21. The government intervention factor experienced a net gain of 11, with 41 countries improving and 30 countries declining.

Openness to foreign investment had a net setback of 11, with two countries improving and 13 declining. The level of protection that countries maintain in their trade policy is worse, with 15 countries improving and 20 countries declining for a net loss of five. Banking and finance remained the same overall, as 10 countries had freer financial markets but 10 found their freedom slipping. Regulation also remained the same overall

with a gain of one and a loss of one. Wages and prices experienced a net loss of eight, with three countries improving and 11 declining. The informal market experienced a net gain of one country, with 15 countries improving and 14 declining.

For the past three years, we have noted a worldwide trend toward a decline in the protection of property rights. Regrettably, this year is no different. Many countries continue to disregard the important relationship between maintaining strong property rights and attracting investment. The protection of property rights experienced a net loss of seven countries, with seven countries declining in their protection and none demonstrating improvement.

In order to grow, countries must implement policies that attract investors and encourage entrepreneurs. Without strong property rights, an investor cannot be sure of his ability to lay claim to a business he builds; as a result, the level of risk involved in a business venture increases, and investors and entrepreneurs are left reluctant, skeptical, and likely to put their money elsewhere. Hong Kong and Singapore have good investment climates characterized by strong property rights. Both countries have also been magnets for investment and have prospered, each one having a GDP per capita over $24,000.

By contrast, countries that fail to implement strong property rights suffer the consequences of that failure. Zimbabwe, for example, lacks strong property rights and has a GDP per capita of only $559. Governments that refuse to embrace property rights and other economic freedoms sentence their citizens to an impoverished life.

## NORTH AMERICA AND EUROPE

By quantity, North America and Europe continue as the world's most economically free region with seven of the 10 freest countries in this year's *Index*. Most of these countries are European, as Europe claims six of the 10 freest countries.

Seven more countries in this region exhibit an expansion in economic freedom this year than exhibit a decline—one more country than last year. Fiscal burden improves the most, with 18 countries reducing their burdens, yet also declines the most with 18 countries increasing theirs. The region experiences the largest net gain in monetary policy with eight countries improving and none declining. The protection of property rights declined in two countries.

The country that illustrates the most dramatic improvement in its overall score is the Slovak Republic. The Slovak Republic improved by 0.27 point this year, making it the world's 8th most improved country. The government has implemented many positive reforms over the past several years: It has reduced taxes, liberalized prices, accelerated the pace of privatization, and restructured the banking sector. As a result, foreign investment has increased and the banking sector is dominated by foreign capital.

Malta was the world's 10th most improved country with an overall score that is 0.25 point better this year. Like the Slovak Republic, however, Malta still has some distance to cover before it can be classified as a "free" country. Despite its marked improvement, Malta still has high tariffs and high tax rates.

Belarus maintains the stigma of least free country in the region. It remains dependent on Russian economic assistance and self-isolated from the West. Belorussian policies, economic or otherwise, are a disaster: a high level of protectionism, high taxes, high level of government intervention, high level of inflation, high barriers to foreign investment, high level of restrictions to banking and finance, high level of intervention in wages and prices, high level of regulation, and weak protection of property rights.

Overall, however, a number of positive changes are occurring in today's Europe. As Daniel J. Mitchell notes in his chapter on "The Economics of Tax Competition: Harmonization vs. Liberalization," tax reductions are taking place across the continent. "Tax competition has helped drive down corporate taxes in Western Europe's welfare states," for instance, and "[n]umerous nations in the former Soviet bloc have enacted flat taxes."

Ireland remains the second freest country in the region, an accolade that is attributed to its low taxes and pro-business environment.

Ireland's 12.5 percent corporate tax rate is far below the European Union average of 30 percent. As a result, Ireland is a major center for U.S. investment in Europe.

Luxembourg, the freest country in the region, has no restrictions that apply specifically to foreign investors. As a result, it remains a favored destination for both U.S. and European investment. The coalition government has enacted tax reform as a centerpiece of its domestic policy. With a GDP per capita of over $25,000, Luxembourg is a prime example of the fruits of economic freedom.

## LATIN AMERICA AND THE CARIBBEAN

The countries of Latin America and the Caribbean continue to suffer from their own counterproductive policies. Economic freedom in the region has not increased: It has decreased. Of the 26 countries that have been graded this year, 11 have improved in their overall level of economic freedom and 13 are worse. In fact, of the 10 countries with the world's largest declines in economic freedom, two are Latin American: Venezuela and Argentina.

The lack of economic vitality in these two countries reflects the evaporation of economic rights. Argentina's economic plight worsens as it marches toward a closed economy. The downward spiral of its economy has been accompanied by price controls, financial restrictions, high inflation, and a history of violating property rights. Argentina's new President, Nestor Kirchner, aims to jumpstart the economy by financing public works. Inevitably, he will discover that such methods kill economic growth, not create it. The economic history of the former Soviet Union is a telling example.

Venezuela's situation is even darker. President Hugo Chávez has purposely strangled Venezuela's private sector in revenge against entrepreneurs who attempted to force him from power. Chávez has introduced exchange controls that have made it difficult for business, both foreign and domestic, to operate. As a result, 80 percent of Venezuelans live below the poverty level. Venezuela is now ranked as a "repressed" economy and possesses the least amount of economic freedom in the region.

Despite being ranked as "repressed," Cuba is one of the world's 10 most improved countries, entirely because of an improved monetary policy score. Despite this improved score, however, Cuba's significant non-tariff barriers, high taxes, numerous state-owned companies, barriers to investment, high level of restrictions in banking and finance, weak protection of property rights, entirely government-set wages and prices, high level of regulation, and high level of activity in the informal market leave it with much to change before it can even begin to resemble a "free" economy.

With an improved monetary policy score, Chile has shifted from a "mostly free" to a "free" country this year and is by far the freest economy in the region. Chile has completed free trade agreements (FTAs) with the European Union and the United States and will be phasing out complex non-tariff barriers as a result of the FTA with the United States.

El Salvador, ranked as "mostly free," has improved both its government intervention and monetary policy scores this year, making it the region's second freest country. It has made great strides in liberalizing markets, advancing privatization, and deregulating commerce.

## NORTH AFRICA AND THE MIDDLE EAST

North Africa and the Middle East have the same net amount of economic freedom as last year. The scores of eight countries in this region have improved, while those of eight are worse. The region has no countries that are ranked as "free."

Of the 10 factors measured in the *Index*, the fiscal burden factor both improved in the most countries (seven) and worsened in the most (nine), resulting in an overall net loss of two. The trade policy factor experienced the largest net gain, with three countries improving and not a single country declining in openness to trade. The largest net loss was in the wages and prices factor, where no countries improved and three countries declined.

Libya is again ranked as the region's least economically free country and remains a "repressed" economy. Its fiscal burden of government score is worse this year. With the exception of a low inflation rate, Libya needs to show significant improvement in all factors.

Despite a worse score this year, Bahrain remains the most economically free country in this region. It is one of the most advanced economies in the Persian Gulf, and its financial sector has eclipsed oil as the leading source of income. Bahrain maintains a pro-business environment to attract foreign investment. It has strong property rights, low regulation, low barriers to foreign investment, and a low level of activity in the informal market. Yet Bahrain receives over 70 percent of its revenues from state-owned enterprises and could attract more foreign investment if these entities were privatized.

Israel has improved over the past several years and this year is the region's second freest economy. Its fiscal burden of government, for example, is lower. If the views of Finance Minister Benjamin Netanyahu should prevail, public-sector growth will be curbed and a stalled privatization plan will be revived.

While the United Arab Emirates is the third freest economy in the region, its overall score worsened by the third largest margin in the world. The UAE's fiscal burden of government, banking and finance, wages and prices, and informal market scores are worse this year. The UAE has a bloated public employment sector, subsidized services, and government handouts. There is, however, a glimmer of hope: Abu Dhabi is spearheading the privatization of utilities and seeking to attract foreign investment in the power and water sectors.

## SUB-SAHARAN AFRICA

On net, economic freedom continues to improve in sub-Saharan Africa, with 21 countries' economic freedom scores improving and 15 countries' scores declining. The majority of countries—30 out of 42—remain "mostly unfree." Of the 10 factors used to grade countries in the *Index*, government intervention showed the greatest net improvement, with 18 countries improving and only four declining. The largest net loss was in the fiscal burden factor, with 14 countries improving and 21 declining.

Five countries in this region (Rwanda, Ethiopia, Cape Verde, Senegal, and Mauritania) are among the world's 10 most improved. At the same time, four others (Namibia, Madagascar, Lesotho, and Gabon) are among the 10 whose scores worsened by the world's widest margins.

In addition, of all the countries in this year's edition of the *Index*, Rwanda experienced the single greatest degree of improvement overall: an amazing feat when one considers that last year it was one of the countries showing the greatest decline in economic freedom. Rwanda has improved its trade policy, government intervention, monetary policy, and regulation scores.

Zimbabwe continues to be the least free country in the region. Despite improving its fiscal burden of government and government intervention scores, it remains "repressed." As a result, unemployment is at 80 percent, inflation is over 200 percent, and millions of Zimbabweans are facing starvation.

On the other end of the spectrum, Botswana remains the freest country in the region despite a worse score this year. Both its trade policy and fiscal burden of government scores are worse. The second freest is Uganda, which has privatized 74 businesses over the past decade and is targeting 85 more.

Sub-Saharan Africa needs trade liberalization. The trade policy factor improved in only five countries, and 10 countries closed their markets further this year. South Africa has a free trade agreement with the European Union. Additionally, South Africa, Lesotho, Swaziland, and Namibia form the Southern African Customs Union, which, with an average common external tariff rate of 11.4 percent, is currently negotiating a free trade agreement with the United States.

## ASIA–PACIFIC

On net, the scores of the Asia–Pacific region are worse for five countries, with scores for 11 countries improved and scores for 16 countries worse this year. This is drastically different from last year when, on net,

the scores of six countries improved. Of the 10 factors, fiscal burden and monetary policy exhibited the greatest improvement overall, and the greatest number of countries declining in economic freedom occurred in the government intervention factor.

Although most countries in the region are ranked "mostly unfree," the region also contains the world's three freest economies: Hong Kong, Singapore, and New Zealand. Additionally, Fiji and Laos are among the world's 10 most improved countries.

Not surprisingly, Indonesia is among the 10 countries whose scores worsened by the widest margin worldwide. Indonesia's fiscal burden of government, government intervention, capital flows and foreign investment, and wages and prices scores are all worse this year. Indonesia's economy is finally growing, albeit slowly, and the list of changes needed for faster growth includes lower taxes, less government intervention in the economy, lower barriers to investment, lower level of restrictions on banking and finance, stronger protection of property rights, less regulation, and a significant reduction in the informal market. Indonesia continues to suffer from many of the problems that made it so vulnerable to the Asian financial crisis.

North Korea remains the least free country in the region. In addition to earning more revenue from illegal drugs than from legitimate business, North Korea scores poorly on every factor and has nowhere to go but up— if it should ever choose to do so.

Once again, Hong Kong is the poster country for economic freedom, both in the region and around the world. With a duty-free port, Hong Kong is a model for free trade. It also is the world's 10th largest trading entity. Likewise, as the world's second freest country, Singapore has a weighted average tariff rate of approximately 0 percent. Singapore has a high level of government intervention in the economy and a moderate cost of government; Hong Kong has a low level of government intervention in the economy and a low cost of government. In fact, Hong Kong's government intervention score improved this year.

## Table 1: Countries Showing Greatest Improvement Overall Since *2003 Index of Economic Freedom*

| Countries | Score Improvement | Region |
|---|---|---|
| Rwanda | 0.57 | Sub-Saharan Africa |
| Ethiopia | 0.46 | Sub-Saharan Africa |
| Fiji | 0.42 | Asia and the Pacific |
| Cape Verde | 0.39 | Sub-Saharan Africa |
| Cuba | 0.35 | Latin America and the Caribbean |
| Senegal | 0.33 | Sub-Saharan Africa |
| Laos | 0.27 | Asia and the Pacific |
| Slovak Republic | 0.27 | North America and Europe |
| Mauritania | 0.26 | Sub-Saharan Africa |
| Malta | 0.25 | North America and Europe |

Source: Marc A. Miles, Edwin J. Feulner, and Mary Anastasia O'Grady, *2004 Index of Economic Freedom* (Washington, D.C.: The Heritage Foundation and Dow Jones & Company, Inc., 2004).

## Table 2: Countries Showing Greatest Decline Overall Since *2003 Index of Economic Freedom*

| Countries | Score Deterioration | Region |
|---|---|---|
| Venezuela | 0.47 | Latin America and the Caribbean |
| Argentina | 0.44 | Latin America and the Caribbean |
| United Arab Emirates | 0.40 | North Africa and Middle East |
| Honduras | 0.34 | Latin America and the Caribbean |
| Indonesia | 0.34 | Asia and the Pacific |
| Namibia | 0.31 | Sub-Saharan Africa |
| Madagascar | 0.29 | Sub-Saharan Africa |
| Lesotho | 0.26 | Sub-Saharan Africa |
| Gabon | 0.26 | Sub-Saharan Africa |
| Panama | 0.24 | Latin America and the Caribbean |

Source: Marc A. Miles, Edwin J. Feulner, and Mary Anastasia O'Grady, 2004 *Index of Economic Freedom* (Washington, D.C.: The Heritage Foundation and Dow Jones & Company, Inc., 2004).

## COUNTRY TREND TABLES

Table 1 lists the countries whose scores have improved the most since publication of the 2003 edition of the *Index*. Cuba once again has made this list with an even larger improvement than last year. Cuba's monetary score is 4 points better this year.

Rwanda is the most improved country, with improved trade policy, government intervention, monetary policy, and regulation scores. Ethiopia, the second most improved country, improved its score in four factors: trade policy, capital flows and foreign investment, fiscal burden of government, and government intervention.

Despite such marked improvements, both countries remain "mostly unfree," but if they continue to improve at this pace, they could achieve a ranking of "free" within two years, creating the environment for higher GDP per capita. Ethiopia has a GDP per capita of only $121, and Rwanda has a GDP per capita of only $253.

Table 2 lists the countries experiencing the greatest decline in economic freedom during the past year. With a president who is trying to punish the business sector, Venezuela's overall level of economic freedom fell the most. Its fiscal burden of government, government intervention, monetary policy, banking and finance, and capital flows and foreign investment scores are all worse. As a result, its overall score is 0.47 point worse this year, causing Venezuela to be classified as "repressed."

Last year, Argentina experienced the greatest decline in economic freedom. This year, it is the second country on the list. Argentina's monetary policy, wages and prices, and informal market scores are all worse. As a result, its overall score is 0.44 point worse this year.

Honduras and Indonesia are tied for fourth place on this list. Honduras's fiscal burden of government, capital flows and foreign investment, wages and prices, and property rights scores are all worse this year, as are Indonesia's fiscal burden of government, government intervention, capital flows and foreign investment, and wages and prices scores.

Table 3 shows the countries that have made the largest overall improvement over the entire history of the *Index*. Azerbaijan has improved the most with a score change of 1.39 since it was first graded in 1996. Bosnia and Lithuania are tied for the second most improved with a change of 1.31 in their scores. As this year's most improved country, Rwanda has made the third largest overall improvement with a score change of 1.24 since it was first graded in 1997. Nicaragua has made the greatest improvement since the inception of the *Index*.

Table 4 shows the countries that have exhibited the greatest decline in economic freedom over the entire history of the *Index*. Venezuela has declined the most, both this year and over the entire 10 years of the *Index*. President Hugo Chávez can begin to reverse this pattern only if he recognizes his country's long-standing, dire need of economic freedom.

Malaysia's economic freedom not only declined this year, but also exhibited the second greatest decline over the history of the *Index* with a score change of 0.71. Malaysia is ranked as "mostly unfree." Argentina is also on this list with the third greatest decline in economic freedom and a cumulative score change of 0.63.

## GLOBAL FREE TRADE ASSOCIATION COUNTRIES

In the 2001 edition of the *Index*, three Heritage analysts proposed a plan for a global free trade association (GFTA).[1] This year, 12 countries qualify, while 19 are in the "near-miss" category, falling short in only one factor by 1 point.[2]

The qualifying countries, based on *2004 Index of Economic Freedom* data, are Australia, Denmark, Estonia, Finland, Hong Kong, Iceland, Ireland, Luxembourg, New Zealand, Singapore, the United Kingdom, and the United States. All of these countries qualified last year as well.

Among the near-miss countries are examples that range from Switzerland to Bahrain. Regulation continues to be the most common reason for a near miss. Trinidad and Tobago's trade policy score improved this year, moving the country into the near-miss category. Burdensome regulation is keeping the country from qualifying.

Of the 19 near-miss countries, 14 fail to qualify because of their regulation scores; two (Canada and Cyprus) do not qualify because of their foreign investment scores; two (Bahrain and Botswana) do not qualify because of restrictions on trade; and one (El Salvador) does not qualify because of weak property rights.

Although all liberalization in the past year has been accomplished through bilateral free trade agreements, such agreements include only two parties, thereby creating trade diversion for those who are left out. A GFTA would not be a substitute for a comprehensive World Trade Organization (WTO) agreement, but would seek to advance liberalization while the WTO round is being negotiated.

A GFTA would limit trade diversion by welcoming all those who are truly free traders into the fold. Additionally, a GFTA

### Table 3: Countries Showing Greatest Improvement in Economic Freedom Since the *1995 Index of Economic Freedom*\*

| Country | Score Improvement | Region |
|---|---|---|
| Azerbaijan (1996) | 1.39 | Asia and the Pacific |
| Bosnia (1998) | 1.31 | North America and Europe |
| Lithuania (1996) | 1.31 | North America and Europe |
| Rwanda (1997) | 1.24 | Sub-Saharan Africa |
| Nicaragua (1995) | 1.14 | Latin America and the Caribbean |
| Mozambique (1995) | 1.11 | Sub-Saharan Africa |
| Armenia (1996) | 1.06 | North America and Europe |
| Moldova (1995) | 1.01 | North America and Europe |
| Haiti (1995) | 1.01 | Latin America and the Caribbean |
| Slovenia (1996) | 0.99 | North America and Europe |
| Mauritania (1996) | 0.99 | Sub-Saharan Africa |

\* Number in parentheses indicates the first year country was included in the *Index*.

**Source:** Marc A. Miles, Edwin J. Feulner, and Mary Anastasia O'Grady, *2004 Index of Economic Freedom* (Washington, D.C.: The Heritage Foundation and Dow Jones & Company, Inc., 2004).

### Table 4: Countries Showing Greatest Decline in Economic Freedom Since the *1995 Index of Economic Freedom*\*

| Country | Score Improvement | Region |
|---|---|---|
| Venezuela (1995) | 0.91 | Latin America and the Caribbean |
| Malaysia (1995) | 0.71 | Asia and the Pacific |
| Argentina (1995) | 0.63 | Latin America and the Caribbean |
| Nigeria (1995) | 0.53 | Sub-Saharan Africa |
| Japan (1995) | 0.47 | Asia and the Pacific |
| Paraguay (1995) | 0.45 | Latin America and the Caribbean |
| Zimbabwe (1995) | 0.45 | Sub-Saharan Africa |
| Turkey (1995) | 0.44 | North America and Europe |
| Belarus (1995) | 0.39 | North America and Europe |
| Zambia (1995) | 0.35 | Sub-Saharan Africa |
| France (1995) | 0.33 | North America and Europe |

\* Number in parentheses indicates the first year country was included in the *Index*.

**Source:** Marc A. Miles, Edwin J. Feulner, and Mary Anastasia O'Grady, *2004 Index of Economic Freedom* (Washington, D.C.: The Heritage Foundation and Dow Jones & Company, Inc., 2004).

would motivate other countries to liberalize their markets in order to join.

Market liberalization should be voluntary, and the GFTA would operate under this concept. Membership in the GFTA would be open only to countries that have demonstrated their commitment to free trade *and* free markets.

## Table 5: Membership in a Global Free Trade Association

| Qualifying Countries | Next in Line: Country | Policy Blocking Membership |
|---|---|---|
| 1 Australia | 1 Austria | Regulation |
| 2 Denmark | 2 Bahrain | Trade |
| 3 Estonia | 3 Belgium | Regulation |
| 4 Finland | 4 Canada | Foreign Investment |
| 5 Hong Kong | 5 Chile | Regulation |
| 6 Iceland | 6 Cyprus | Foreign Investment |
| 7 Ireland | 7 Germany | Regulation |
| 8 Luxembourg | 8 Netherlands | Regulation |
| 9 New Zealand | 9 Sweden | Regulation |
| 10 Singapore | 10 Switzerland | Regulation |
| 11 United Kingdom | 11 Botswana | Trade Policy |
| 12 United States | 12 El Salvador | Property Rights |
| | 13 France | Regulation |
| | 14 Israel | Regulation |
| | 15 Italy | Regulation |
| | 16 Portugal | Regulation |
| | 17 Spain | Regulation |
| | 18 Trinidad and Tobago | Regulation |
| | 19 Uruguay | Regulation |

**Source:** Marc A. Miles, Edwin J. Feulner, and Mary Anastasia O'Grady, *2004 Index of Economic Freedom* (Washington, D.C.: The Heritage Foundation and Dow Jones & Company, Inc., 2004).

# Criteria for Membership in a Global Free Trade Association

**Freedom to Trade.** Countries must maintain an open trade policy, with minimal barriers to imports and minimal subsidies to domestic industries. This means an average tariff rate not greater than 9 percent as well as few or no non-tariff barriers, which include import quotas or licensing requirements that restrict trade. Countries that generally set low tariff barriers, do not impose excessive non-tariff barriers, and do not put serious impediments in the way of foreign investment demonstrate their fundamental commitment to free trade.

**Freedom to Invest.** Countries must maintain liberal policies regarding capital flows and investment. Specifically, this means a transparent and open foreign investment code, impartial treatment of foreign investments, and an efficient approval process. Restrictions on foreign investment must be few in number and not significant economically.

**Freedom to Operate a Business (Low Regulatory Burden).** Countries must maintain an open environment for business. Overly burdensome regulations can deter trade and investment. Investors may choose not to enter a country because of the difficulties involved in opening a business or because the cost of doing business in that country is excessive. Countries must maintain simple licensing procedures, apply regulations uniformly, and be nondiscriminatory in their treatment of foreign-owned business.

**Secure Property Rights.** A country with a well-established rule of law protects private property and provides an environment in which business transactions can take place with a degree of certainty. Investors are likely to engage in economic transactions when they know the judicial system protects private property and is not subject to outside influence. Secure property rights help to ensure that efforts to expand trade with a GFTA country can be successful.

## Endnotes

1   John C. Hulsman, Gerald P. O'Driscoll, Jr., and Denise H. Froning, "The Free Trade Association: A Trade Agenda for the New Global Economy," in Gerald P. O'Driscoll, Jr., Kim R. Holmes, and Melanie Kirkpatrick, 2001 *Index of Economic Freedom* (Washington, D.C.: The Heritage Foundation and Dow Jones & Company, Inc., 2001), pp. 33–41.

2   See Table 5, "Membership in a Global Free Trade Association," above.

# Index of Economic Freedom Rankings

| 2004 Rank | Country | 2004 Scores | 2003 Scores | 2002 Scores | 2001 Scores | 2000 Scores | 1999 Scores | 1998 Scores | 1997 Scores | 1996 Scores | 1995 Scores | Trade Policy | Fiscal Burden | Govt. Intervention | Monetary Policy | Foreign Investment | Banking & Finance | Wages & Prices | Property Rights | Regulation | Informal Market |
|---|---|---|---|---|---|---|---|---|---|---|---|---|---|---|---|---|---|---|---|---|---|
| 1 | Hong Kong | 1.34 | 1.44 | 1.39 | 1.29 | 1.40 | 1.51 | 1.40 | 1.54 | 1.50 | 1.51 | 1.0 | 1.9 | 2.0 | 1.0 | 1.0 | 1.0 | 2.0 | 1.0 | 1.0 | 1.5 |
| 2 | Singapore | 1.61 | 1.61 | 1.69 | 1.66 | 1.59 | 1.54 | 1.54 | 1.68 | 1.63 | 1.68 | 1.0 | 2.6 | 3.5 | 1.0 | 1.0 | 2.0 | 2.0 | 1.0 | 1.0 | 1.0 |
| 3 | New Zealand | 1.70 | 1.68 | 1.68 | 1.71 | 1.75 | 1.71 | 1.83 | 1.75 | 1.74 | n/a | 2.0 | 4.0 | 2.0 | 1.0 | 1.0 | 1.0 | 2.0 | 1.0 | 2.0 | 1.0 |
| 4 | Luxembourg | 1.71 | 1.68 | 1.88 | 1.79 | 1.84 | 1.95 | 1.96 | 1.96 | 1.99 | n/a | 2.0 | 4.1 | 2.0 | 1.0 | 1.0 | 1.0 | 2.0 | 1.0 | 2.0 | 1.0 |
| 5 | Ireland | 1.74 | 1.73 | 1.73 | 1.60 | 1.81 | 1.88 | 1.91 | 2.14 | 2.14 | 2.15 | 2.0 | 2.4 | 2.0 | 1.0 | 1.0 | 1.0 | 2.0 | 1.0 | 2.0 | 2.0 |
| 6 | Estonia | 1.76 | 1.68 | 1.73 | 1.89 | 2.19 | 2.29 | 2.43 | 2.46 | 2.44 | 2.40 | 1.0 | 2.1 | 2.0 | 2.0 | 1.0 | 1.0 | 2.0 | 2.0 | 2.0 | 2.5 |
| 7 | United Kingdom | 1.79 | 1.88 | 1.83 | 1.78 | 1.85 | 1.81 | 1.85 | 1.95 | 1.85 | 1.75 | 2.0 | 3.9 | 3.0 | 1.0 | 1.0 | 1.0 | 2.0 | 1.0 | 2.0 | 1.0 |
| 8 | Denmark | 1.80 | 1.71 | 1.79 | 2.10 | 2.29 | 2.13 | 2.11 | 1.98 | 2.13 | n/a | 2.0 | 4.0 | 2.0 | 1.0 | 2.0 | 1.0 | 2.0 | 1.0 | 2.0 | 1.0 |
| 9 | Switzerland | 1.84 | 1.88 | 1.80 | 1.89 | 1.91 | 1.88 | 1.91 | 1.91 | 1.94 | n/a | 2.0 | 3.4 | 2.0 | 1.0 | 2.0 | 1.0 | 2.0 | 1.0 | 3.0 | 1.0 |
| 10 | United States | 1.85 | 1.86 | 1.84 | 1.78 | 1.84 | 1.89 | 1.89 | 1.88 | 1.94 | 1.99 | 2.0 | 4.0 | 2.0 | 1.0 | 2.0 | 1.0 | 2.0 | 1.0 | 2.0 | 1.5 |
| 11 | Australia | 1.88 | 1.88 | 1.91 | 1.91 | 1.90 | 1.94 | 1.95 | 2.19 | 2.08 | 2.09 | 2.0 | 3.8 | 2.0 | 2.0 | 2.0 | 1.0 | 2.0 | 1.0 | 3.0 | 2.0 |
| 12 | Sweden | 1.90 | 1.90 | 1.88 | 2.03 | 2.15 | 2.20 | 2.24 | 2.25 | 2.53 | 2.63 | 2.0 | 4.0 | 3.0 | 1.0 | 2.0 | 2.0 | 2.0 | 1.0 | 3.0 | 1.0 |
| 13 | Chile | 1.91 | 2.01 | 1.88 | 2.03 | 2.04 | 2.13 | 2.10 | 2.26 | 2.61 | 2.60 | 2.0 | 2.6 | 2.0 | 1.0 | 1.0 | 2.0 | 2.0 | 1.0 | 3.0 | 1.5 |
| 14 | Cyprus | 1.95 | 2.09 | 2.13 | 2.11 | 2.68 | 2.66 | 2.64 | 2.63 | 2.64 | n/a | 2.0 | 2.5 | 2.0 | 1.0 | 3.0 | 2.0 | 2.0 | 1.0 | 2.0 | 2.0 |
| 14 | Finland | 1.95 | 1.85 | 1.89 | 2.04 | 2.06 | 2.19 | 2.09 | 2.18 | 2.34 | n/a | 2.0 | 3.5 | 3.0 | 1.0 | 2.0 | 2.0 | 2.0 | 1.0 | 2.0 | 1.0 |
| 16 | Canada | 1.98 | 2.00 | 1.90 | 2.01 | 2.06 | 2.04 | 2.09 | 2.08 | 2.08 | 2.10 | 2.0 | 2.8 | 3.0 | 1.0 | 2.0 | 2.0 | 2.0 | 1.0 | 2.0 | 1.0 |
| 17 | Iceland | 2.00 | 1.93 | 2.18 | 2.16 | 2.11 | 2.20 | 2.20 | 2.30 | n/a | n/a | 2.0 | 3.0 | 3.0 | 2.0 | 2.0 | 3.0 | 1.0 | 1.0 | 2.0 | 1.0 |
| 18 | Germany | 2.03 | 2.03 | 2.00 | 2.04 | 2.24 | 2.26 | 2.36 | 2.25 | 2.26 | 2.15 | 2.0 | 3.8 | 2.0 | 1.0 | 1.0 | 2.0 | 2.0 | 1.0 | 3.0 | 1.5 |
| 19 | Netherlands | 2.04 | 2.00 | 2.03 | 1.84 | 2.03 | 2.01 | 2.03 | 1.88 | 1.89 | n/a | 2.0 | 4.4 | 3.0 | 2.0 | 1.0 | 1.0 | 2.0 | 1.0 | 3.0 | 1.0 |
| 20 | Austria | 2.08 | 2.08 | 2.08 | 2.03 | 1.98 | 2.08 | 2.08 | 2.03 | 2.06 | 2.09 | 2.0 | 4.3 | 2.0 | 1.0 | 2.0 | 2.0 | 2.0 | 1.0 | 3.0 | 1.5 |
| 20 | Bahrain | 2.08 | 2.04 | 2.10 | 2.01 | 1.88 | 1.81 | 1.90 | 1.80 | 1.75 | 1.78 | 3.0 | 1.8 | 4.0 | 1.0 | 2.0 | 1.0 | 3.0 | 3.0 | 2.0 | 2.0 |
| 22 | Belgium | 2.19 | 2.10 | 2.10 | 2.10 | 2.14 | 2.06 | 2.05 | 2.03 | 2.06 | n/a | 2.0 | 4.4 | 2.5 | 1.0 | 1.0 | 2.0 | 3.0 | 1.0 | 3.0 | 2.0 |
| 22 | Lithuania | 2.19 | 2.21 | 2.35 | 2.53 | 2.84 | 2.90 | 2.98 | 3.05 | 3.50 | n/a | 2.0 | 2.4 | 2.5 | 2.0 | 2.0 | 1.0 | 2.0 | 3.0 | 3.0 | 3.0 |
| 24 | El Salvador | 2.24 | 2.35 | 2.23 | 2.16 | 2.15 | 2.38 | 2.61 | 2.60 | 2.68 | 2.94 | 2.0 | 3.4 | 1.5 | 1.0 | 2.0 | 2.0 | 2.0 | 3.0 | 2.0 | 3.5 |
| 25 | Bahamas | 2.25 | 2.15 | 2.06 | 2.23 | 2.23 | 2.16 | 2.16 | 2.05 | 2.09 | 2.36 | 5.0 | 1.5 | 2.0 | 2.0 | 3.0 | 3.0 | 1.0 | 2.0 | 2.0 | 2.0 |
| 26 | Italy | 2.26 | 2.31 | 2.28 | 2.21 | 2.21 | 2.24 | 2.34 | 2.41 | 2.56 | 2.58 | 2.0 | 4.1 | 2.0 | 1.0 | 2.0 | 2.0 | 2.0 | 2.0 | 3.0 | 2.5 |
| 27 | Spain | 2.31 | 2.31 | 2.41 | 2.49 | 2.51 | 2.41 | 2.40 | 2.50 | 2.73 | 2.54 | 2.0 | 4.1 | 2.0 | 2.0 | 2.0 | 2.0 | 2.0 | 2.0 | 3.0 | 2.0 |
| 28 | Norway | 2.35 | 2.28 | 2.40 | 2.44 | 2.25 | 2.28 | 2.28 | 2.39 | 2.39 | n/a | 2.0 | 4.0 | 3.5 | 1.0 | 3.0 | 3.0 | 2.0 | 1.0 | 3.0 | 1.0 |
| 29 | Israel | 2.36 | 2.40 | 2.55 | 2.60 | 2.70 | 2.68 | 2.65 | 2.64 | 2.81 | 2.90 | 2.0 | 4.6 | 2.5 | 1.0 | 2.0 | 3.0 | 2.0 | 2.0 | 3.0 | 1.5 |
| 29 | Latvia | 2.36 | 2.30 | 2.49 | 2.49 | 2.69 | 2.74 | 2.84 | 2.91 | 3.24 | n/a | 2.0 | 2.6 | 2.5 | 1.0 | 2.0 | 2.0 | 3.0 | 3.0 | 3.0 | 3.5 |
| 31 | Portugal | 2.38 | 2.40 | 2.30 | 2.33 | 2.34 | 2.31 | 2.41 | 2.41 | 2.60 | 2.80 | 2.0 | 3.8 | 2.0 | 2.0 | 2.0 | 3.0 | 3.0 | 2.0 | 3.0 | 2.0 |
| 32 | Czech Republic | 2.39 | 2.35 | 2.29 | 2.10 | 2.20 | 2.14 | 2.43 | 2.29 | 2.33 | 2.38 | 3.0 | 3.9 | 2.5 | 1.0 | 2.0 | 1.0 | 2.0 | 2.0 | 3.0 | 3.5 |
| 33 | Barbados | 2.41 | 2.29 | 2.53 | 2.64 | 2.74 | 2.86 | 2.63 | 2.93 | 3.15 | n/a | 4.0 | 4.6 | 2.5 | 1.0 | 3.0 | 2.0 | 2.0 | 1.0 | 3.0 | 2.0 |
| 34 | Taiwan | 2.43 | 2.29 | 2.38 | 2.18 | 1.98 | 2.09 | 2.24 | 2.21 | 2.23 | 2.26 | 2.0 | 3.3 | 2.5 | 1.0 | 3.0 | 3.0 | 2.0 | 2.0 | 3.0 | 2.5 |
| 35 | Slovak Republic | 2.44 | 2.71 | 2.76 | 2.85 | 3.18 | 3.38 | 3.31 | 3.18 | 3.18 | 2.88 | 3.0 | 2.9 | 2.0 | 2.0 | 2.0 | 1.0 | 2.0 | 3.0 | 3.0 | 3.5 |
| 36 | Trinidad and Tobago | 2.45 | 2.54 | 2.54 | 2.64 | 2.48 | 2.49 | 2.60 | 2.68 | 2.69 | n/a | 2.0 | 4.0 | 2.5 | 2.0 | 2.0 | 2.0 | 2.0 | 2.0 | 3.0 | 3.0 |
| 37 | Malta | 2.51 | 2.76 | 2.78 | 2.84 | 3.09 | 3.14 | 3.15 | 3.25 | 3.24 | 3.44 | 4.0 | 4.1 | 3.0 | 1.0 | 3.0 | 2.0 | 2.0 | 3.0 | 3.0 | 3.0 |
| 38 | Japan | 2.53 | 2.36 | 2.34 | 2.04 | 2.06 | 2.11 | 2.16 | 2.16 | 2.18 | 2.06 | 2.0 | 4.3 | 2.0 | 1.0 | 3.0 | 4.0 | 2.0 | 2.0 | 2.0 | 3.0 |
| 39 | Botswana | 2.55 | 2.49 | 2.99 | 2.95 | 2.93 | 2.91 | 2.90 | 2.75 | 3.09 | 3.38 | 3.0 | 3.0 | 4.5 | 3.0 | 2.0 | 2.0 | 2.0 | 2.0 | 2.0 | 2.0 |

# Index of Economic Freedom Rankings

| 2004 Rank | Country | 2004 Scores | 2003 Scores | 2002 Scores | 2001 Scores | 2000 Scores | 1999 Scores | 1998 Scores | 1997 Scores | 1996 Scores | 1995 Scores | Trade Policy | Fiscal Buden | Govt. Intervention | Monetary Policy | Foreign Investment | Banking & Finance | Wages & Prices | Property Rights | Regulation | Informal Market |
|---|---|---|---|---|---|---|---|---|---|---|---|---|---|---|---|---|---|---|---|---|---|
| 39 | Uruguay | 2.55 | 2.45 | 2.51 | 2.30 | 2.50 | 2.60 | 2.59 | 2.60 | 2.85 | 3.03 | 2.0 | 3.5 | 2.0 | 3.0 | 2.0 | 3.0 | 2.0 | 2.0 | 3.0 | 3.0 |
| 41 | Bolivia | 2.59 | 2.59 | 2.66 | 2.31 | 2.61 | 2.61 | 2.61 | 2.56 | 2.61 | 3.21 | 3.0 | 2.9 | 2.0 | 1.0 | 1.0 | 2.0 | 2.0 | 4.0 | 4.0 | 4.0 |
| 42 | Hungary | 2.60 | 2.55 | 2.23 | 2.38 | 2.43 | 2.89 | 2.94 | 3.04 | 2.98 | 2.93 | 3.0 | 3.0 | 2.0 | 3.0 | 2.0 | 2.0 | 3.0 | 2.0 | 3.0 | 3.0 |
| 42 | United Arab Emirates | 2.60 | 2.20 | 2.28 | 2.16 | 2.20 | 2.30 | 2.35 | 2.35 | 2.40 | n/a | 2.0 | 2.0 | 4.0 | 1.0 | 3.0 | 4.0 | 3.0 | 2.0 | 3.0 | 2.0 |
| 44 | Armenia | 2.63 | 2.59 | 2.78 | 3.03 | 3.21 | 3.50 | 3.50 | 3.50 | 3.69 | n/a | 2.0 | 2.3 | 3.0 | 2.0 | 2.0 | 1.0 | 3.0 | 3.0 | 4.0 | 4.0 |
| 44 | France | 2.63 | 2.74 | 2.85 | 2.49 | 2.44 | 2.34 | 2.34 | 2.33 | 2.31 | 2.30 | 2.0 | 4.3 | 5.0 | 1.0 | 2.0 | 3.0 | 2.0 | 2.0 | 3.0 | 2.0 |
| 46 | Belize | 2.69 | 2.74 | 2.79 | 2.69 | 2.84 | 2.76 | 2.96 | 2.71 | 2.74 | 2.85 | 4.0 | 2.9 | 2.0 | 1.0 | 3.0 | 3.0 | 2.0 | 3.0 | 3.0 | 3.0 |
| 46 | Korea, South | 2.69 | 2.75 | 2.49 | 2.35 | 2.50 | 2.38 | 2.30 | 2.31 | 2.49 | 2.41 | 4.0 | 3.4 | 2.5 | 2.0 | 2.0 | 3.0 | 2.0 | 2.0 | 3.0 | 3.0 |
| 48 | Kuwait | 2.70 | 2.58 | 2.71 | 2.48 | 2.45 | 2.40 | 2.50 | 2.39 | 2.50 | n/a | 2.0 | 1.5 | 4.5 | 1.0 | 4.0 | 3.0 | 3.0 | 3.0 | 3.0 | 2.0 |
| 48 | Uganda | 2.70 | 2.95 | 3.15 | 3.15 | 3.15 | 2.64 | 2.64 | 2.75 | 2.89 | 3.10 | 3.0 | 3.0 | 2.0 | 1.0 | 3.0 | 2.0 | 2.0 | 3.0 | 4.0 | 4.0 |
| 50 | Costa Rica | 2.71 | 2.71 | 2.73 | 2.84 | 2.88 | 3.00 | 3.00 | 3.03 | 3.00 | 3.04 | 3.0 | 3.1 | 2.0 | 3.0 | 2.0 | 3.0 | 2.0 | 3.0 | 3.0 | 3.0 |
| 51 | Jordan | 2.73 | 2.80 | 2.73 | 2.85 | 2.95 | 2.96 | 2.99 | 2.85 | 3.10 | 2.90 | 4.0 | 3.8 | 3.5 | 3.0 | 2.0 | 2.0 | 2.0 | 3.0 | 3.0 | 3.0 |
| 52 | Slovenia | 2.75 | 2.86 | 3.25 | 3.01 | 3.20 | 3.05 | 3.15 | 3.45 | 3.74 | n/a | 3.0 | 3.5 | 2.5 | 3.0 | 3.0 | 3.0 | 2.0 | 3.0 | 2.0 | 2.5 |
| 53 | South Africa | 2.79 | 2.58 | 2.79 | 3.00 | 3.01 | 2.98 | 2.88 | 2.99 | 3.25 | 3.23 | 4.0 | 3.9 | 2.0 | 3.0 | 2.0 | 2.0 | 2.0 | 3.0 | 3.0 | 3.0 |
| 54 | Greece | 2.80 | 2.79 | 2.84 | 2.69 | 2.69 | 2.88 | 2.89 | 2.81 | 2.95 | 3.15 | 2.0 | 4.0 | 2.0 | 2.0 | 3.0 | 3.0 | 3.0 | 3.0 | 3.0 | 3.0 |
| 54 | Oman | 2.80 | 2.75 | 2.78 | 2.60 | 2.93 | 2.80 | 2.69 | 2.79 | 2.85 | 2.70 | 3.0 | 1.5 | 4.5 | 1.0 | 3.0 | 3.0 | 4.0 | 3.0 | 2.0 | 2.0 |
| 56 | Jamaica | 2.81 | 2.73 | 3.01 | 3.01 | 2.61 | 2.91 | 2.89 | 2.86 | 2.99 | 3.16 | 4.0 | 4.1 | 2.5 | 3.0 | 1.0 | 2.0 | 2.0 | 3.0 | 3.0 | 3.5 |
| 56 | Poland | 2.81 | 2.83 | 2.60 | 2.64 | 2.84 | 2.83 | 2.91 | 3.09 | 3.24 | 3.46 | 3.0 | 3.6 | 2.0 | 2.0 | 3.0 | 2.0 | 3.0 | 3.0 | 3.0 | 3.5 |
| 58 | Panama | 2.83 | 2.59 | 2.68 | 2.58 | 2.56 | 2.43 | 2.45 | 2.54 | 2.60 | 2.70 | 3.0 | 3.8 | 3.5 | 1.0 | 2.0 | 2.0 | 2.0 | 4.0 | 3.0 | 4.0 |
| 58 | Peru | 2.83 | 2.86 | 2.88 | 2.61 | 2.64 | 2.66 | 2.96 | 3.03 | 3.06 | 3.59 | 4.0 | 3.3 | 2.5 | 1.0 | 2.0 | 2.0 | 2.0 | 4.0 | 4.0 | 3.5 |
| 60 | Cape Verde | 2.86 | 3.25 | 3.30 | 3.56 | 3.66 | 3.81 | 3.74 | 3.80 | 3.60 | n/a | 5.0 | 3.6 | 2.0 | 3.0 | 3.0 | 3.0 | 2.0 | 2.0 | 2.0 | 4.0 |
| 60 | Qatar | 2.86 | 2.78 | 3.03 | 3.18 | 3.18 | 3.11 | n/a | n/a | n/a | n/a | 3.0 | 3.1 | 4.5 | 3.0 | 3.0 | 3.0 | 2.0 | 3.0 | 4.0 | 2.0 |
| 60 | Thailand | 2.86 | 2.71 | 2.46 | 2.29 | 2.76 | 2.58 | 2.56 | 2.58 | 2.58 | 2.59 | 4.0 | 3.6 | 2.5 | 1.0 | 3.0 | 3.0 | 2.0 | 3.0 | 3.0 | 3.5 |
| 63 | Cambodia | 2.90 | 2.68 | 2.78 | 3.00 | 3.14 | 3.13 | 3.24 | 3.68 | n/a | n/a | 4.0 | 2.5 | 2.5 | 1.0 | 3.0 | 2.0 | 3.0 | 4.0 | 4.0 | 3.0 |
| 63 | Mexico | 2.90 | 2.81 | 2.96 | 3.05 | 3.09 | 3.25 | 3.41 | 3.35 | 3.31 | 3.10 | 2.0 | 4.0 | 3.5 | 3.0 | 3.0 | 2.0 | 2.0 | 3.0 | 3.0 | 3.5 |
| 63 | Mongolia | 2.90 | 3.01 | 2.98 | 3.03 | 3.06 | 3.18 | 3.14 | 3.23 | 3.60 | 3.50 | 2.0 | 4.5 | 2.5 | 2.0 | 3.0 | 2.0 | 2.0 | 4.0 | 3.0 | 3.0 |
| 66 | Morocco | 2.93 | 2.96 | 3.15 | 2.80 | 3.05 | 2.95 | 3.08 | 3.00 | 2.89 | 3.03 | 5.0 | 3.8 | 2.0 | 1.0 | 2.0 | 3.0 | 2.0 | 4.0 | 3.0 | 3.5 |
| 67 | Mauritania | 2.94 | 3.20 | 3.46 | 3.89 | 4.00 | 4.00 | 3.96 | 4.03 | 3.93 | n/a | 3.0 | 2.9 | 2.5 | 2.0 | 3.0 | 2.0 | 3.0 | 4.0 | 4.0 | 4.0 |
| 67 | Nicaragua | 2.94 | 3.09 | 3.23 | 3.54 | 3.70 | 3.75 | 3.68 | 3.80 | 3.70 | 4.08 | 2.0 | 2.9 | 2.5 | 2.0 | 3.0 | 2.0 | 3.0 | 4.0 | 4.0 | 4.0 |
| 67 | Tunisia | 2.94 | 2.91 | 2.89 | 3.04 | 2.94 | 3.01 | 2.90 | 2.89 | 2.83 | 2.98 | 5.0 | 3.9 | 2.5 | 1.0 | 3.0 | 3.0 | 2.0 | 3.0 | 3.0 | 3.0 |
| 70 | Namibia | 2.96 | 2.65 | 2.84 | 2.93 | 2.98 | 2.84 | 2.99 | 2.80 | n/a | n/a | 4.0 | 4.1 | 3.0 | 3.0 | 2.0 | 3.0 | 2.0 | 2.0 | 3.0 | 3.0 |
| 71 | Mauritius | 2.99 | 2.96 | 2.95 | 2.98 | 2.90 | 2.68 | 2.99 | n/a | n/a | n/a | 5.0 | 2.9 | 3.0 | 2.0 | 3.0 | 2.0 | 4.0 | 2.0 | 3.0 | 2.5 |
| 72 | Senegal | 3.00 | 3.33 | 3.45 | 3.33 | 3.34 | 3.41 | 3.51 | 3.64 | 3.81 | n/a | 3.0 | 4.5 | 2.0 | 1.0 | 3.0 | 3.0 | 3.0 | 3.0 | 3.0 | 3.0 |
| 73 | Macedonia | 3.04 | 3.23 | 3.35 | n/a | n/a | n/a | n/a | n/a | n/a | n/a | 4.0 | 2.4 | 3.5 | 2.0 | 3.0 | 2.0 | 2.0 | 4.0 | 4.0 | 3.5 |
| 74 | Philippines | 3.05 | 2.95 | 3.05 | 3.16 | 3.00 | 2.98 | 2.84 | 3.06 | 3.14 | 3.35 | 2.0 | 3.5 | 2.0 | 2.0 | 3.0 | 3.0 | 3.0 | 4.0 | 4.0 | 3.0 |
| 74 | Saudi Arabia | 3.05 | 3.09 | 3.16 | 3.35 | 3.15 | 3.11 | 2.89 | 2.95 | 2.95 | n/a | 4.0 | 2.0 | 4.5 | 1.0 | 4.0 | 4.0 | 2.0 | 3.0 | 3.0 | 3.0 |
| 76 | Fiji | 3.06 | 3.48 | 3.54 | 3.50 | 3.29 | 3.29 | 3.23 | 3.23 | 3.24 | 3.49 | 4.0 | 3.6 | 2.0 | 1.0 | 4.0 | 2.0 | 3.0 | 4.0 | 3.0 | 4.0 |
| 76 | Sri Lanka | 3.06 | 3.05 | 2.89 | 2.84 | 2.91 | 2.81 | 2.76 | 2.61 | 2.94 | 3.06 | 3.0 | 3.6 | 2.5 | 3.0 | 3.0 | 3.0 | 3.0 | 3.0 | 3.0 | 3.5 |
| 78 | Bulgaria | 3.08 | 3.26 | 3.28 | 3.28 | 3.35 | 3.49 | 3.60 | 3.53 | 3.50 | 3.56 | 4.0 | 1.8 | 2.5 | 4.0 | 3.0 | 2.0 | 2.0 | 4.0 | 4.0 | 3.5 |

# Index of Economic Freedom Rankings

| 2004 Rank | Country | 2004 Scores | 2003 Scores | 2002 Scores | 2001 Scores | 2000 Scores | 1999 Scores | 1998 Scores | 1997 Scores | 1996 Scores | 1995 Scores | Trade Policy | Fiscal Burden | Govt. Intervention | Monetary Policy | Foreign Investment | Banking & Finance | Wages & Prices | Property Rights | Regulation | Informal Market |
|---|---|---|---|---|---|---|---|---|---|---|---|---|---|---|---|---|---|---|---|---|---|
| 79 | Moldova | 3.09 | 3.13 | 3.30 | 3.75 | 3.35 | 3.49 | 3.48 | 3.65 | 3.50 | 4.10 | 2.0 | 2.4 | 2.5 | 3.0 | 4.0 | 3.0 | 3.0 | 3.0 | 4.0 | 4.0 |
| 80 | Albania | 3.10 | 3.28 | 3.24 | 3.48 | 3.78 | 3.51 | 3.53 | 3.59 | 3.58 | 3.48 | 4.0 | 3.0 | 3.0 | 2.0 | 2.0 | 3.0 | 2.0 | 3.0 | 3.0 | 4.0 |
| 80 | Brazil | 3.10 | 3.01 | 3.06 | 3.21 | 3.46 | 3.19 | 3.36 | 3.28 | 3.56 | 3.46 | 4.0 | 2.5 | 4.0 | 3.0 | 3.0 | 3.0 | 2.0 | 3.0 | 3.0 | 3.5 |
| 82 | Croatia | 3.11 | 3.06 | 3.29 | 3.39 | 3.49 | 3.55 | 3.63 | 3.56 | 3.53 | n/a | 4.0 | 3.1 | 2.5 | 2.0 | 3.0 | 2.0 | 3.0 | 4.0 | 4.0 | 3.5 |
| 83 | Colombia | 3.13 | 3.10 | 2.94 | 3.00 | 3.14 | 2.99 | 3.19 | 3.23 | 3.15 | 3.10 | 4.0 | 4.3 | 3.5 | 3.0 | 2.0 | 2.0 | 2.0 | 4.0 | 3.0 | 3.5 |
| 83 | Guyana | 3.13 | 3.20 | 3.28 | 3.35 | 3.35 | 3.30 | 3.55 | 3.35 | 3.38 | 3.70 | 4.0 | 3.8 | 3.5 | 2.0 | 3.0 | 2.0 | 2.0 | 3.0 | 4.0 | 4.0 |
| 83 | Lebanon | 3.13 | 3.09 | 3.01 | 2.65 | 3.06 | 3.03 | 3.06 | 2.78 | 2.96 | n/a | 4.0 | 2.3 | 3.0 | 1.0 | 3.0 | 2.0 | 3.0 | 4.0 | 4.0 | 5.0 |
| 86 | Madagascar | 3.14 | 2.85 | 3.29 | 3.29 | 3.39 | 3.45 | 3.51 | 3.44 | 3.55 | 3.74 | 3.0 | 4.4 | 1.5 | 4.0 | 3.0 | 3.0 | 2.0 | 3.0 | 3.0 | 4.5 |
| 87 | Guatemala | 3.16 | 3.01 | 3.00 | 2.88 | 2.91 | 2.89 | 2.91 | 2.89 | 3.15 | 3.36 | 3.0 | 3.6 | 2.0 | 3.0 | 4.0 | 2.0 | 2.0 | 4.0 | 4.0 | 4.0 |
| 87 | Malaysia | 3.16 | 3.14 | 3.23 | 3.05 | 2.76 | 2.64 | 2.64 | 2.85 | 2.63 | 2.45 | 3.0 | 3.6 | 4.0 | 1.0 | 4.0 | 4.0 | 3.0 | 3.0 | 3.0 | 3.0 |
| 89 | Ivory Coast | 3.18 | 3.16 | 3.00 | 3.08 | 3.68 | 3.73 | 3.74 | 3.80 | 3.83 | 3.43 | 4.0 | 4.3 | 1.5 | 2.0 | 3.0 | 2.0 | 3.0 | 4.0 | 4.0 | 4.0 |
| 89 | Swaziland | 3.18 | 3.00 | 3.21 | 3.05 | 3.16 | 3.06 | 3.13 | 3.31 | 3.30 | 3.16 | 4.0 | 3.8 | 2.0 | 3.0 | 3.0 | 3.0 | 3.0 | 3.0 | 3.0 | 4.0 |
| 91 | Georgia | 3.19 | 3.40 | 3.48 | 3.68 | 3.80 | 3.85 | 3.78 | 3.88 | 3.94 | n/a | 4.0 | 2.4 | 1.5 | 3.0 | 3.0 | 3.0 | 3.0 | 4.0 | 4.0 | 4.0 |
| 92 | Djibouti | 3.23 | 3.30 | 3.16 | 3.38 | 3.38 | 3.28 | 3.29 | 3.18 | n/a | n/a | 5.0 | 2.8 | 3.5 | 1.0 | 3.0 | 3.0 | 2.0 | 4.0 | 4.0 | 4.0 |
| 93 | Guinea | 3.24 | 3.26 | 3.45 | 3.21 | 3.34 | 3.19 | 3.11 | 3.39 | 3.13 | 3.29 | 5.0 | 4.4 | 1.0 | 2.0 | 4.0 | 2.0 | 2.0 | 3.0 | 4.0 | 4.5 |
| 94 | Kenya | 3.26 | 3.21 | 3.28 | 3.26 | 3.05 | 3.09 | 3.06 | 3.26 | 3.54 | 3.45 | 5.0 | 3.6 | 2.5 | 2.0 | 3.0 | 3.0 | 2.0 | 3.0 | 4.0 | 4.5 |
| 95 | Burkina Faso | 3.28 | 3.35 | 3.33 | 3.45 | 3.61 | 3.63 | 3.80 | 3.81 | 3.96 | n/a | 4.0 | 3.8 | 3.0 | 1.0 | 3.0 | 3.0 | 3.0 | 4.0 | 4.0 | 4.0 |
| 95 | Egypt | 3.28 | 3.39 | 3.53 | 3.53 | 3.58 | 3.35 | 3.31 | 3.49 | 3.40 | 3.69 | 4.0 | 4.3 | 3.0 | 1.0 | 3.0 | 4.0 | 3.0 | 3.0 | 3.0 | 3.5 |
| 95 | Mozambique | 3.28 | 3.40 | 3.15 | 3.40 | 3.94 | 3.95 | 4.15 | 4.15 | 4.11 | 4.39 | 4.0 | 3.9 | 2.0 | 4.0 | 2.0 | 2.0 | 3.0 | 4.0 | 4.0 | 4.0 |
| 98 | Tanzania | 3.29 | 3.54 | 3.56 | 3.65 | 3.58 | 3.36 | 3.48 | 3.46 | 3.73 | 3.79 | 5.0 | 3.9 | 2.0 | 2.0 | 3.0 | 2.0 | 3.0 | 4.0 | 4.0 | 5.0 |
| 99 | Bosnia | 3.30 | 3.49 | 3.89 | 4.04 | 4.40 | 4.61 | 4.61 | n/a | n/a | n/a | 3.0 | 2.5 | 2.5 | 1.0 | 4.0 | 2.0 | 3.0 | 5.0 | 5.0 | 5.0 |
| 100 | Algeria | 3.31 | 3.39 | 3.05 | 3.40 | 3.40 | 3.59 | 3.64 | 3.63 | 3.70 | 3.68 | 5.0 | 4.1 | 4.0 | 1.0 | 2.0 | 4.0 | 3.0 | 4.0 | 3.0 | 3.0 |
| 101 | Ethiopia | 3.33 | 3.79 | 3.70 | 3.88 | 3.70 | 3.68 | 3.70 | 3.80 | 3.80 | 3.90 | 4.0 | 3.8 | 3.0 | 1.0 | 3.0 | 4.0 | 3.0 | 4.0 | 4.0 | 3.5 |
| 102 | Mali | 3.34 | 3.20 | 3.10 | 3.15 | 3.13 | 3.24 | 3.33 | 3.50 | 3.44 | 3.53 | 3.0 | 4.4 | 4.0 | 2.0 | 3.0 | 4.0 | 2.0 | 3.0 | 3.0 | 5.0 |
| 103 | Kyrgyzstan | 3.36 | 3.41 | 3.65 | 3.80 | 3.78 | 3.73 | 4.00 | n/a | n/a | n/a | 4.0 | 3.1 | 2.5 | 3.0 | 3.0 | 3.0 | 3.0 | 4.0 | 4.0 | 4.0 |
| 103 | Rwanda | 3.36 | 3.93 | 3.73 | 3.94 | 4.28 | 4.29 | 4.60 | 4.60 | n/a | n/a | 3.0 | 4.6 | 2.0 | 1.0 | 4.0 | 3.0 | 3.0 | 4.0 | 4.0 | 5.0 |
| 105 | Central African Rep. | 3.38 | 3.28 | 3.31 | n/a | n/a | n/a | n/a | n/a | n/a | n/a | 5.0 | 3.8 | 4.0 | 1.0 | 2.0 | 3.0 | 3.0 | 4.0 | 4.0 | 4.0 |
| 106 | Azerbaijan | 3.39 | 3.50 | 3.58 | 3.93 | 4.33 | 4.29 | 4.35 | 4.58 | 4.78 | n/a | 3.0 | 3.4 | 3.0 | 4.0 | 4.0 | 4.0 | 3.0 | 4.0 | 4.0 | 4.5 |
| 106 | Paraguay | 3.39 | 3.40 | 3.28 | 3.39 | 3.01 | 3.00 | 3.04 | 2.91 | 2.89 | 2.94 | 3.0 | 3.4 | 3.0 | 1.0 | 3.0 | 3.0 | 3.0 | 4.0 | 4.0 | 4.5 |
| 106 | Turkey | 3.39 | 3.50 | 3.33 | 2.93 | 2.73 | 2.80 | 2.66 | 2.70 | 3.00 | 2.95 | 3.0 | 3.9 | 2.5 | 5.0 | 3.0 | 3.0 | 3.0 | 3.0 | 4.0 | 3.5 |
| 109 | Ghana | 3.40 | 3.54 | 3.59 | 3.29 | 3.24 | 3.29 | 3.29 | 3.53 | 3.54 | 3.54 | 4.0 | 4.0 | 3.5 | 4.0 | 3.0 | 3.0 | 3.0 | 3.0 | 3.0 | 3.5 |
| 109 | Pakistan | 3.40 | 3.44 | 3.44 | 3.50 | 3.50 | 3.50 | 3.31 | 3.29 | 3.26 | 3.34 | 5.0 | 4.0 | 3.0 | 1.0 | 3.0 | 4.0 | 3.0 | 4.0 | 3.0 | 4.0 |
| 111 | Gabon | 3.43 | 3.18 | 3.33 | 3.38 | 3.26 | 3.09 | 3.18 | 3.31 | 3.40 | 3.19 | 5.0 | 4.8 | 3.5 | 3.0 | 3.0 | 3.0 | 3.0 | 3.0 | 4.0 | 3.5 |
| 111 | Niger | 3.43 | 3.61 | 3.74 | 3.78 | 4.09 | 3.91 | 4.01 | 4.19 | 4.25 | n/a | 4.0 | 4.3 | 3.0 | 1.0 | 3.0 | 3.0 | 3.0 | 4.0 | 4.0 | 5.0 |
| 113 | Benin | 3.44 | 3.56 | 3.46 | 3.23 | 3.16 | 3.89 | 3.35 | 3.44 | 3.53 | n/a | 4.0 | 4.4 | 4.0 | 1.0 | 3.0 | 3.0 | 3.0 | 4.0 | 4.0 | 4.0 |
| 114 | Malawi | 3.46 | 3.63 | 3.64 | 3.76 | 3.84 | 3.89 | 3.96 | 3.86 | 3.64 | 3.74 | 3.0 | 4.1 | 2.5 | 4.0 | 3.0 | 4.0 | 3.0 | 3.0 | 4.0 | 4.0 |
| 114 | Russia | 3.46 | 3.54 | 3.74 | 3.79 | 3.75 | 3.60 | 3.54 | 3.83 | 3.65 | 3.55 | 3.0 | 2.6 | 2.0 | 5.0 | 3.0 | 3.0 | 3.0 | 4.0 | 4.0 | 4.0 |
| 116 | Argentina | 3.48 | 3.04 | 2.58 | 2.29 | 2.23 | 2.28 | 2.53 | 2.75 | 2.63 | 2.85 | 4.0 | 3.8 | 2.0 | 4.0 | 3.0 | 4.0 | 3.0 | 4.0 | 3.0 | 4.0 |
| 117 | Ukraine | 3.49 | 3.59 | 3.84 | 3.88 | 3.75 | 3.75 | 3.83 | 3.83 | 3.75 | 4.05 | 3.0 | 3.9 | 3.0 | 3.0 | 4.0 | 3.0 | 3.0 | 4.0 | 4.0 | 4.0 |

# Index of Economic Freedom Rankings

| 2004 Rank | Country | 2004 Scores | 2003 Scores | 2002 Scores | 2001 Scores | 2000 Scores | 1999 Scores | 1998 Scores | 1997 Scores | 1996 Scores | 1995 Scores | Trade Policy | Fiscal Buden | Govt. Intervention | Monetary Policy | Foreign Investment | Banking & Finance | Wages & Prices | Property Rights | Regulation | Informal Market |
|---|---|---|---|---|---|---|---|---|---|---|---|---|---|---|---|---|---|---|---|---|---|
| 118 | Lesotho | 3.50 | 3.24 | 3.39 | 3.44 | 3.44 | 3.48 | 3.69 | 3.70 | 3.78 | n/a | 4.0 | 3.5 | 3.5 | 3.0 | 4.0 | 3.0 | 3.0 | 3.0 | 4.0 | 4.0 |
| 118 | Zambia | 3.50 | 3.50 | 3.30 | 3.25 | 2.94 | 2.96 | 2.94 | 2.88 | 3.08 | 3.15 | 4.0 | 4.0 | 2.0 | 5.0 | 3.0 | 3.0 | 3.0 | 3.0 | 4.0 | 4.0 |
| 120 | Dominican Republic | 3.51 | 3.29 | 3.19 | 3.04 | 3.03 | 3.20 | 3.26 | 3.24 | 3.39 | 3.63 | 5.0 | 3.1 | 1.5 | 3.0 | 3.0 | 4.0 | 4.0 | 4.0 | 4.0 | 3.5 |
| 121 | Honduras | 3.53 | 3.19 | 3.33 | 3.50 | 3.51 | 3.71 | 3.51 | 3.58 | 3.58 | 3.58 | 3.0 | 3.3 | 4.0 | 3.0 | 4.0 | 3.0 | 3.0 | 4.0 | 4.0 | 4.0 |
| 121 | India | 3.53 | 3.58 | 3.61 | 3.91 | 3.93 | 3.93 | 3.83 | 3.88 | 3.93 | 3.93 | 5.0 | 3.8 | 3.5 | 2.0 | 3.0 | 4.0 | 3.0 | 3.0 | 4.0 | 4.0 |
| 121 | Nepal | 3.53 | 3.63 | 3.51 | 3.60 | 3.79 | 3.54 | 3.76 | 3.89 | 3.86 | n/a | 5.0 | 3.3 | 2.0 | 1.0 | 4.0 | 4.0 | 3.0 | 4.0 | 4.0 | 5.0 |
| 124 | Chad | 3.54 | 3.59 | 3.75 | 3.74 | 4.00 | 4.06 | 4.24 | 4.24 | n/a | n/a | 5.0 | 4.4 | 3.0 | 3.0 | 3.0 | 2.0 | 2.0 | 4.0 | 4.0 | 5.0 |
| 124 | Gambia | 3.54 | 3.49 | 3.34 | 3.59 | 3.64 | 3.60 | 3.66 | 3.55 | n/a | n/a | 4.0 | 4.4 | 4.0 | 2.0 | 3.0 | 3.0 | 3.0 | 3.0 | 4.0 | 5.0 |
| 126 | Ecuador | 3.60 | 3.58 | 3.60 | 3.51 | 3.14 | 3.09 | 3.10 | 3.21 | 3.33 | 3.39 | 4.0 | 3.0 | 3.0 | 5.0 | 3.0 | 3.0 | 3.0 | 4.0 | 4.0 | 4.0 |
| 127 | Cameroon | 3.63 | 3.54 | 3.45 | 3.50 | 3.73 | 3.70 | 3.96 | 3.95 | 4.08 | 3.51 | 5.0 | 4.8 | 3.5 | 2.0 | 3.0 | 3.0 | 3.0 | 4.0 | 4.0 | 4.0 |
| 128 | China, PRC | 3.64 | 3.54 | 3.56 | 3.55 | 3.49 | 3.56 | 3.69 | 3.73 | 3.78 | 3.78 | 5.0 | 4.4 | 3.5 | 1.0 | 4.0 | 4.0 | 3.0 | 4.0 | 4.0 | 3.5 |
| 129 | Romania | 3.66 | 3.71 | 3.78 | 3.59 | 3.20 | 3.20 | 3.21 | 3.30 | 3.40 | 3.60 | 4.0 | 3.1 | 2.5 | 5.0 | 4.0 | 3.0 | 3.0 | 4.0 | 4.0 | 4.0 |
| 130 | Equatorial Guinea | 3.69 | 3.73 | 4.15 | 4.13 | 4.18 | 4.26 | n/a | n/a | n/a | n/a | 5.0 | 2.9 | 2.0 | 3.0 | 3.0 | 4.0 | 4.0 | 4.0 | 4.0 | 5.0 |
| 131 | Bangladesh | 3.70 | 3.69 | 4.00 | 4.05 | 4.04 | 3.98 | 3.80 | 3.76 | 3.79 | 3.79 | 5.0 | 4.0 | 3.5 | 1.0 | 3.0 | 4.0 | 3.0 | 4.0 | 5.0 | 4.5 |
| 131 | Kazakhstan | 3.70 | 3.55 | 3.70 | 3.85 | 3.90 | 4.14 | 4.23 | n/a | n/a | n/a | 4.0 | 3.5 | 2.5 | 3.0 | 5.0 | 4.0 | 3.0 | 4.0 | 4.0 | 4.0 |
| 131 | Yemen | 3.70 | 3.73 | 3.74 | 3.98 | 3.94 | 4.19 | 4.15 | 3.95 | 3.88 | 3.79 | 3.0 | 4.0 | 4.0 | 3.0 | 3.0 | 4.0 | 3.0 | 4.0 | 4.0 | 5.0 |
| 134 | Sierra Leone | 3.73 | 3.95 | n/a | n/a | 4.04 | 3.96 | 3.70 | 3.79 | 3.65 | 3.90 | 5.0 | 4.3 | 2.0 | 1.0 | 4.0 | 4.0 | 2.0 | 5.0 | 5.0 | 5.0 |
| 134 | Togo | 3.73 | 3.86 | 3.88 | 4.00 | 4.05 | 4.14 | n/a | n/a | n/a | n/a | 3.0 | 4.3 | 3.0 | 2.0 | 4.0 | 4.0 | 3.0 | 4.0 | 5.0 | 4.5 |
| 136 | Indonesia | 3.76 | 3.43 | 3.49 | 3.60 | 3.60 | 3.14 | 3.00 | 3.05 | 3.00 | 3.58 | 3.0 | 4.1 | 3.0 | 3.0 | 4.0 | 4.0 | 3.0 | 4.0 | 5.0 | 4.5 |
| 137 | Haiti | 3.78 | 3.86 | 4.08 | 4.13 | 4.33 | 4.26 | 4.43 | 4.35 | 4.64 | 4.79 | 4.0 | 3.8 | 3.0 | 3.0 | 4.0 | 3.0 | 3.0 | 5.0 | 5.0 | 5.0 |
| 138 | Syria | 3.88 | 3.88 | 4.11 | 4.00 | 4.05 | 4.04 | 4.01 | 4.14 | 4.15 | n/a | 4.0 | 3.3 | 4.5 | 1.0 | 4.0 | 5.0 | 4.0 | 4.0 | 4.0 | 5.0 |
| 139 | Congo, Rep. | 3.90 | 3.80 | 3.90 | 3.95 | 4.20 | 4.26 | 4.71 | 4.33 | 4.39 | n/a | 5.0 | 5.0 | 4.0 | 1.0 | 4.0 | 4.0 | 3.0 | 4.0 | 4.0 | 5.0 |
| 139 | Guinea–Bissau | 3.90 | 3.90 | 4.15 | 4.19 | 4.40 | 4.50 | n/a | n/a | n/a | n/a | 5.0 | 3.5 | 2.5 | 2.0 | 3.0 | 5.0 | 3.0 | 5.0 | 5.0 | 5.0 |
| 141 | Vietnam | 3.93 | 3.90 | 3.98 | 4.24 | 4.49 | 4.48 | 4.33 | 4.46 | 4.50 | 4.60 | 5.0 | 4.3 | 4.0 | 1.0 | 4.0 | 4.0 | 3.0 | 5.0 | 5.0 | 4.0 |
| 142 | Nigeria | 3.95 | 4.04 | 3.79 | 3.49 | 3.39 | 3.40 | 3.40 | 3.43 | 3.53 | 3.43 | 5.0 | 3.5 | 4.5 | 4.0 | 3.0 | 4.0 | 3.0 | 4.0 | 4.0 | 4.5 |
| 143 | Suriname | 3.96 | 4.06 | 4.03 | 3.98 | 3.98 | 4.08 | 4.08 | 4.00 | 4.10 | n/a | 5.0 | 3.6 | 4.0 | 5.0 | 3.0 | 4.0 | 3.0 | 3.0 | 4.0 | 5.0 |
| 144 | Cuba | 4.08 | 4.43 | 4.88 | 4.88 | 4.88 | 4.90 | 4.95 | 4.90 | 5.00 | 4.95 | 3.0 | 4.3 | 4.5 | 1.0 | 4.0 | 5.0 | 5.0 | 5.0 | 5.0 | 5.0 |
| 145 | Belarus | 4.09 | 4.24 | 4.21 | 4.10 | 4.13 | 4.14 | 4.15 | 3.95 | 3.45 | 3.70 | 4.0 | 3.4 | 3.5 | 5.0 | 4.0 | 4.0 | 4.0 | 4.0 | 5.0 | 3.0 |
| 146 | Tajikistan | 4.15 | 4.10 | 4.09 | 4.11 | 4.21 | 4.15 | 4.30 | n/a | n/a | n/a | 3.0 | 3.5 | 4.0 | 5.0 | 4.0 | 5.0 | 4.0 | 5.0 | 4.0 | 5.0 |
| 147 | Venezuela | 4.18 | 3.71 | 3.88 | 3.78 | 3.43 | 3.48 | 3.43 | 3.58 | 3.63 | 3.28 | 4.0 | 4.3 | 3.5 | 5.0 | 5.0 | 4.0 | 4.0 | 4.0 | 4.0 | 4.0 |
| 148 | Iran | 4.26 | 4.30 | 4.63 | 4.84 | 4.69 | 4.56 | 4.76 | 4.80 | 4.79 | n/a | 2.0 | 3.6 | 5.0 | 4.0 | 4.0 | 5.0 | 4.0 | 5.0 | 5.0 | 4.0 |
| 149 | Uzbekistan | 4.29 | 4.29 | 4.39 | 4.61 | 4.56 | 4.64 | 4.68 | n/a | n/a | n/a | 5.0 | 2.9 | 4.0 | 5.0 | 4.0 | 5.0 | 4.0 | 4.0 | 5.0 | 4.0 |
| 150 | Turkmenistan | 4.31 | 4.21 | 4.39 | 4.39 | 4.40 | 4.39 | 4.50 | n/a | n/a | n/a | 5.0 | 3.1 | 5.0 | 4.0 | 4.0 | 5.0 | 4.0 | 4.0 | 4.0 | 5.0 |
| 151 | Burma | 4.45 | 4.35 | 4.33 | 4.45 | 4.28 | 4.15 | 4.31 | 4.38 | 4.45 | n/a | 5.0 | 3.0 | 3.5 | 5.0 | 5.0 | 4.0 | 4.0 | 4.0 | 4.0 | 5.0 |
| 151 | Laos | 4.45 | 4.73 | 4.81 | 4.75 | 4.80 | 4.75 | 4.63 | 4.70 | 4.51 | n/a | 5.0 | 4.0 | 3.5 | 4.0 | 3.0 | 5.0 | 4.0 | 5.0 | 4.0 | 5.0 |
| 153 | Zimbabwe | 4.54 | 4.63 | 4.39 | 4.21 | 4.04 | 3.89 | 4.16 | 3.69 | 3.79 | 4.09 | 5.0 | 3.4 | 4.0 | 5.0 | 5.0 | 5.0 | 5.0 | 5.0 | 4.0 | 4.0 |
| 154 | Libya | 4.55 | 4.48 | 4.60 | 4.90 | 4.85 | 4.95 | 4.95 | 4.95 | 4.95 | n/a | 5.0 | 4.5 | 5.0 | 1.0 | 5.0 | 5.0 | 5.0 | 5.0 | 5.0 | 5.0 |
| 155 | Korea, North | 5.00 | 5.00 | 5.00 | 5.00 | 5.00 | 5.00 | 5.00 | 5.00 | 5.00 | 5.00 | 5.0 | 5.0 | 5.0 | 5.0 | 5.0 | 5.0 | 5.0 | 5.0 | 5.0 | 5.0 |
| **Not Ranked** | | | | | | | | | | | | | | | | | | | | | |
| n/a | Angola | n/a | n/a | n/a | n/a | 4.48 | 4.50 | 4.48 | 4.43 | 4.38 | 4.38 | n/a | n/a | n/a | n/a | n/a | n/a | n/a | n/a | n/a | n/a |
| n/a | Burundi | n/a | n/a | n/a | n/a | 4.00 | 4.20 | 4.38 | 4.20 | n/a | n/a | n/a | n/a | n/a | n/a | n/a | n/a | n/a | n/a | n/a | n/a |
| n/a | Congo, Dem. Rep. | n/a | n/a | n/a | n/a | 4.60 | 4.59 | 4.29 | 4.39 | 4.29 | 3.89 | n/a | n/a | n/a | n/a | n/a | n/a | n/a | n/a | n/a | n/a |
| n/a | Iraq | n/a | n/a | 5.00 | 4.90 | 4.90 | 4.85 | 4.85 | 4.85 | 4.85 | n/a | n/a | n/a | n/a | n/a | n/a | n/a | n/a | n/a | n/a | n/a |
| n/a | Serbia and Montenegro | n/a | 4.28 | 4.21 | n/a | 4.05 | 4.39 | 4.29 | 4.30 | 4.29 | 4.30 | n/a | n/a | n/a | n/a | n/a | n/a | n/a | n/a | n/a | n/a |
| n/a | Sudan | n/a | n/a | n/a | 1.00 | 4.05 | 4.39 | 4.29 | 4.10 | 4.10 | 4.30 | n/a | n/a | n/a | n/a | n/a | n/a | n/a | n/a | n/a | n/a |

# Asia and the Pacific Index of Economic Freedom Scores (30 Economies)

| 2004 Rank | Country | 2004 Scores | 2003 Scores | 2002 Scores | 2001 Scores | 2000 Scores | 1999 Scores | 1998 Scores | 1997 Scores | 1996 Scores | 1995 Scores |
|---|---|---|---|---|---|---|---|---|---|---|---|
| 1 | Hong Kong | 1.34 | 1.44 | 1.39 | 1.29 | 1.40 | 1.51 | 1.40 | 1.54 | 1.50 | 1.51 |
| 2 | Singapore | 1.61 | 1.61 | 1.69 | 1.66 | 1.59 | 1.54 | 1.54 | 1.68 | 1.63 | 1.68 |
| 3 | New Zealand | 1.70 | 1.68 | 1.68 | 1.71 | 1.75 | 1.71 | 1.83 | 1.75 | 1.74 | n/a |
| 11 | Australia | 1.88 | 1.90 | 1.91 | 1.91 | 1.90 | 1.94 | 1.95 | 2.19 | 2.08 | 2.09 |
| 34 | Taiwan | 2.43 | 2.29 | 2.38 | 2.18 | 1.98 | 2.09 | 2.24 | 2.21 | 2.23 | 2.26 |
| 38 | Japan | 2.53 | 2.36 | 2.34 | 2.04 | 2.06 | 2.11 | 2.16 | 2.16 | 2.18 | 2.06 |
| 46 | Korea, South | 2.69 | 2.75 | 2.49 | 2.35 | 2.50 | 2.38 | 2.30 | 2.31 | 2.49 | 2.41 |
| 60 | Thailand | 2.86 | 2.71 | 2.46 | 2.29 | 2.76 | 2.58 | 2.56 | 2.58 | 2.58 | 2.59 |
| 63 | Cambodia | 2.90 | 2.68 | 2.78 | 3.00 | 3.14 | 3.13 | 3.24 | 3.68 | n/a | n/a |
| 63 | Mexico | 2.90 | 2.81 | 2.96 | 3.05 | 3.09 | 3.25 | 3.41 | 3.35 | 3.31 | 3.10 |
| 74 | Philippines | 3.05 | 2.95 | 3.05 | 3.16 | 3.00 | 2.98 | 2.84 | 3.06 | 3.14 | 3.35 |
| 76 | Fiji | 3.06 | 3.48 | 3.54 | 3.50 | 3.29 | 3.29 | 3.23 | 3.23 | 3.24 | 3.49 |
| 76 | Sri Lanka | 3.06 | 3.05 | 2.89 | 2.84 | 2.91 | 2.81 | 2.76 | 2.61 | 2.94 | 3.06 |
| 87 | Malaysia | 3.16 | 3.14 | 3.23 | 3.05 | 2.76 | 2.64 | 2.64 | 2.85 | 2.63 | 2.45 |
| 103 | Kyrgyzstan | 3.36 | 3.41 | 3.65 | 3.80 | 3.78 | 3.73 | 4.00 | n/a | n/a | n/a |
| 106 | Azerbaijan | 3.39 | 3.50 | 3.58 | 3.93 | 4.33 | 4.29 | 4.35 | 4.58 | 4.78 | n/a |
| 109 | Pakistan | 3.40 | 3.44 | 3.44 | 3.50 | 3.50 | 3.50 | 3.31 | 3.29 | 3.26 | 3.34 |
| 121 | India | 3.53 | 3.58 | 3.61 | 3.91 | 3.93 | 3.93 | 3.83 | 3.88 | 3.93 | 3.93 |
| 121 | Nepal | 3.53 | 3.63 | 3.51 | 3.60 | 3.79 | 3.54 | 3.76 | 3.89 | 3.86 | n/a |
| 128 | China, PRC | 3.64 | 3.54 | 3.56 | 3.55 | 3.49 | 3.56 | 3.69 | 3.73 | 3.78 | 3.78 |
| 131 | Bangladesh | 3.70 | 3.69 | 4.00 | 4.05 | 4.04 | 3.98 | 3.80 | 3.76 | 3.79 | 3.79 |
| 131 | Kazakhstan | 3.70 | 3.55 | 3.70 | 3.85 | 3.90 | 4.14 | 4.23 | n/a | n/a | n/a |
| 136 | Indonesia | 3.76 | 3.43 | 3.49 | 3.60 | 3.60 | 3.14 | 3.00 | 3.05 | 3.00 | 3.58 |
| 141 | Vietnam | 3.93 | 3.90 | 3.98 | 4.24 | 4.49 | 4.48 | 4.33 | 4.46 | 4.50 | 4.60 |
| 146 | Tajikistan | 4.15 | 4.10 | 4.09 | 4.11 | 4.21 | 4.15 | 4.30 | n/a | n/a | n/a |
| 149 | Uzbekistan | 4.29 | 4.29 | 4.39 | 4.61 | 4.56 | 4.64 | 4.68 | n/a | n/a | n/a |
| 150 | Turkmenistan | 4.31 | 4.21 | 4.39 | 4.39 | 4.40 | 4.39 | 4.50 | n/a | n/a | n/a |
| 151 | Burma | 4.45 | 4.35 | 4.33 | 4.45 | 4.28 | 4.15 | 4.31 | 4.38 | 4.45 | n/a |
| 151 | Laos | 4.45 | 4.73 | 4.81 | 4.75 | 4.80 | 4.75 | 4.63 | 4.70 | 4.51 | n/a |
| 155 | Korea, North | 5.00 | 5.00 | 5.00 | 5.00 | 5.00 | 5.00 | 5.00 | 5.00 | 5.00 | 5.00 |

**Mongolia**, not **Mexico**, should be listed as ranked 63rd on this page.
The figures for Mongolia are:

| | 2004 | 2003 | 2002 | 2001 | 2000 | 1999 | 1998 | 1997 | 1996 | 1995 |
|---|---|---|---|---|---|---|---|---|---|---|
| **Mongolia** | 2.90 | 3.01 | 2.98 | 3.03 | 3.06 | 3.18 | 3.14 | 3.23 | 3.60 | 3.50 |

# North America and Europe Index of Economic Freedom Scores (45 Economies)

| 2004 Rank | Country | 2004 Scores | 2003 Scores | 2002 Scores | 2001 Scores | 2000 Scores | 1999 Scores | 1998 Scores | 1997 Scores | 1996 Scores | 1995 Scores |
|---|---|---|---|---|---|---|---|---|---|---|---|
| 4 | Luxembourg | 1.71 | 1.68 | 1.88 | 1.79 | 1.84 | 1.95 | 1.96 | 1.96 | 1.99 | n/a |
| 5 | Ireland | 1.74 | 1.73 | 1.73 | 1.60 | 1.81 | 1.88 | 1.91 | 2.14 | 2.14 | 2.15 |
| 6 | Estonia | 1.76 | 1.68 | 1.73 | 1.89 | 2.19 | 2.29 | 2.43 | 2.46 | 2.44 | 2.40 |
| 7 | United Kingdom | 1.79 | 1.88 | 1.83 | 1.78 | 1.85 | 1.81 | 1.85 | 1.95 | 1.85 | 1.75 |
| 8 | Denmark | 1.80 | 1.71 | 1.79 | 2.10 | 2.29 | 2.13 | 2.11 | 1.98 | 2.13 | n/a |
| 9 | Switzerland | 1.84 | 1.88 | 1.80 | 1.89 | 1.91 | 1.88 | 1.91 | 1.91 | 1.94 | n/a |
| 10 | United States | 1.85 | 1.86 | 1.84 | 1.78 | 1.84 | 1.89 | 1.89 | 1.88 | 1.94 | 1.99 |
| 12 | Sweden | 1.90 | 1.88 | 1.88 | 2.03 | 2.15 | 2.20 | 2.24 | 2.25 | 2.53 | 2.63 |
| 14 | Cyprus | 1.95 | 2.09 | 2.13 | 2.11 | 2.68 | 2.66 | 2.64 | 2.63 | 2.64 | n/a |
| 14 | Finland | 1.95 | 1.85 | 1.89 | 2.04 | 2.06 | 2.19 | 2.09 | 2.18 | 2.34 | n/a |
| 16 | Canada | 1.98 | 2.00 | 1.90 | 2.01 | 2.06 | 2.04 | 2.09 | 2.08 | 2.08 | 2.10 |
| 17 | Iceland | 2.00 | 1.93 | 2.18 | 2.16 | 2.11 | 2.20 | 2.20 | 2.30 | n/a | n/a |
| 18 | Germany | 2.03 | 2.03 | 2.00 | 2.04 | 2.24 | 2.26 | 2.36 | 2.25 | 2.26 | 2.15 |
| 19 | Netherlands | 2.04 | 2.00 | 2.03 | 1.84 | 2.03 | 2.01 | 2.03 | 1.88 | 1.89 | n/a |
| 20 | Austria | 2.08 | 2.08 | 2.08 | 2.03 | 1.98 | 2.08 | 2.08 | 2.03 | 2.06 | 2.09 |
| 22 | Belgium | 2.19 | 2.10 | 2.10 | 2.10 | 2.14 | 2.06 | 2.05 | 2.03 | 2.06 | n/a |
| 22 | Lithuania | 2.19 | 2.21 | 2.35 | 2.53 | 2.84 | 2.90 | 2.98 | 3.05 | 3.50 | n/a |
| 26 | Italy | 2.26 | 2.31 | 2.28 | 2.21 | 2.21 | 2.24 | 2.34 | 2.41 | 2.56 | 2.58 |
| 27 | Spain | 2.31 | 2.31 | 2.41 | 2.49 | 2.51 | 2.41 | 2.40 | 2.50 | 2.73 | 2.54 |
| 28 | Norway | 2.35 | 2.28 | 2.40 | 2.44 | 2.25 | 2.28 | 2.28 | 2.39 | 2.39 | n/a |
| 29 | Latvia | 2.36 | 2.30 | 2.49 | 2.49 | 2.69 | 2.74 | 2.84 | 2.91 | 3.24 | n/a |
| 31 | Portugal | 2.38 | 2.40 | 2.30 | 2.33 | 2.34 | 2.31 | 2.41 | 2.41 | 2.60 | 2.80 |
| 32 | Czech Republic | 2.39 | 2.35 | 2.29 | 2.10 | 2.20 | 2.14 | 2.43 | 2.29 | 2.33 | 2.38 |
| 35 | Slovak Republic | 2.44 | 2.71 | 2.76 | 2.85 | 3.18 | 3.38 | 3.31 | 3.18 | 3.18 | 2.88 |
| 37 | Malta | 2.51 | 2.76 | 2.78 | 2.84 | 3.09 | 3.14 | 3.15 | 3.25 | 3.24 | 3.44 |
| 42 | Hungary | 2.60 | 2.55 | 2.23 | 2.38 | 2.43 | 2.89 | 2.94 | 3.04 | 2.98 | 2.93 |
| 44 | Armenia | 2.63 | 2.59 | 2.78 | 3.03 | 3.21 | 3.50 | 3.50 | 3.50 | 3.69 | n/a |
| 44 | France | 2.63 | 2.74 | 2.85 | 2.49 | 2.44 | 2.34 | 2.34 | 2.33 | 2.31 | 2.30 |
| 52 | Slovenia | 2.75 | 2.86 | 3.25 | 3.01 | 3.20 | 3.05 | 3.15 | 3.45 | 3.74 | n/a |
| 54 | Greece | 2.80 | 2.79 | 2.84 | 2.69 | 2.69 | 2.88 | 2.89 | 2.81 | 2.95 | 3.15 |
| 56 | Poland | 2.81 | 2.83 | 2.60 | 2.64 | 2.84 | 2.83 | 2.91 | 3.09 | 3.24 | 3.46 |
| 63 | Mongolia | 2.90 | 3.01 | 2.98 | 3.03 | 3.06 | 3.18 | 3.14 | 3.23 | 3.60 | 3.50 |
| 73 | Macedonia | 3.04 | 3.23 | 3.35 | n/a | n/a | n/a | n/a | n/a | n/a | n/a |
| 78 | Bulgaria | 3.08 | 3.26 | 3.28 | 3.28 | 3.35 | 3.49 | 3.60 | 3.53 | 3.50 | 3.56 |
| 79 | Moldova | 3.09 | 3.13 | 3.30 | 3.75 | 3.35 | 3.49 | 3.48 | 3.65 | 3.50 | 4.10 |
| 80 | Albania | 3.10 | 3.28 | 3.24 | 3.48 | 3.78 | 3.51 | 3.53 | 3.59 | 3.58 | 3.48 |
| 82 | Croatia | 3.11 | 3.06 | 3.29 | 3.39 | 3.49 | 3.55 | 3.63 | 3.56 | 3.53 | n/a |
| 91 | Georgia | 3.19 | 3.40 | 3.48 | 3.68 | 3.80 | 3.85 | 3.78 | 3.88 | 3.94 | n/a |
| 99 | Bosnia | 3.30 | 3.49 | 3.89 | 4.04 | 4.40 | 4.61 | 4.61 | n/a | n/a | n/a |
| 106 | Turkey | 3.39 | 3.50 | 3.33 | 2.93 | 2.73 | 2.80 | 2.66 | 2.70 | 3.00 | 2.95 |
| 114 | Russia | 3.46 | 3.54 | 3.74 | 3.79 | 3.75 | 3.60 | 3.54 | 3.83 | 3.65 | 3.55 |
| 117 | Ukraine | 3.49 | 3.59 | 3.84 | 3.88 | 3.75 | 3.75 | 3.83 | 3.83 | 3.75 | 4.05 |
| 129 | Romania | 3.66 | 3.71 | 3.78 | 3.59 | 3.20 | 3.20 | 3.21 | 3.30 | 3.40 | 3.60 |
| 145 | Belarus | 4.09 | 4.24 | 4.21 | 4.10 | 4.13 | 4.14 | 4.15 | 3.95 | 3.45 | 3.70 |
| n/a | Serbia and Montenegro | n/a | 4.28 | 4.21 | n/a | n/a | n/a | n/a | n/a | n/a | n/a |

**Mexico**, not **Mongolia**, should be listed as ranked 63rd on this page.
The figures for Mexico are:

| | 2004 | 2003 | 2002 | 2001 | 2000 | 1999 | 1998 | 1997 | 1996 | 1995 |
|---|---|---|---|---|---|---|---|---|---|---|
| **Mexico** | 2.90 | 2.81 | 2.96 | 3.05 | 3.09 | 3.25 | 3.41 | 3.35 | 3.31 | 3.10 |

*2004 Index of Economic Freedom*

# North Africa and Middle East Index of Economic Freedom Scores (18 Economies)

| 2004 Rank | Country | 2004 Scores | 2003 Scores | 2002 Scores | 2001 Scores | 2000 Scores | 1999 Scores | 1998 Scores | 1997 Scores | 1996 Scores | 1995 Scores |
|---|---|---|---|---|---|---|---|---|---|---|---|
| 20 | Bahrain | 2.08 | 2.04 | 2.10 | 2.01 | 1.88 | 1.81 | 1.90 | 1.80 | 1.75 | 1.78 |
| 29 | Israel | 2.36 | 2.40 | 2.55 | 2.60 | 2.70 | 2.68 | 2.65 | 2.64 | 2.81 | 2.90 |
| 42 | United Arab Emirates | 2.60 | 2.20 | 2.28 | 2.16 | 2.20 | 2.30 | 2.35 | 2.35 | 2.40 | n/a |
| 48 | Kuwait | 2.70 | 2.58 | 2.71 | 2.48 | 2.45 | 2.40 | 2.50 | 2.39 | 2.50 | n/a |
| 51 | Jordan | 2.73 | 2.80 | 2.73 | 2.85 | 2.95 | 2.96 | 2.99 | 2.85 | 3.10 | 2.90 |
| 54 | Oman | 2.80 | 2.75 | 2.78 | 2.60 | 2.93 | 2.80 | 2.69 | 2.79 | 2.85 | 2.70 |
| 60 | Qatar | 2.86 | 2.78 | 3.03 | 3.18 | 3.18 | 3.11 | n/a | n/a | n/a | n/a |
| 66 | Morocco | 2.93 | 2.96 | 3.15 | 2.80 | 3.05 | 2.95 | 3.08 | 3.00 | 2.89 | 3.03 |
| 67 | Tunisia | 2.94 | 2.91 | 2.89 | 3.04 | 2.94 | 3.01 | 2.90 | 2.89 | 2.83 | 2.98 |
| 74 | Saudi Arabia | 3.05 | 3.09 | 3.16 | 3.35 | 3.15 | 3.11 | 2.89 | 2.95 | 2.95 | n/a |
| 83 | Lebanon | 3.13 | 3.09 | 3.01 | 2.65 | 3.06 | 3.03 | 3.06 | 2.78 | 2.96 | n/a |
| 95 | Egypt | 3.28 | 3.39 | 3.53 | 3.53 | 3.58 | 3.35 | 3.31 | 3.49 | 3.40 | 3.69 |
| 100 | Algeria | 3.31 | 3.39 | 3.05 | 3.40 | 3.40 | 3.59 | 3.64 | 3.63 | 3.70 | 3.68 |
| 131 | Yemen | 3.70 | 3.73 | 3.74 | 3.98 | 3.94 | 4.19 | 4.15 | 3.95 | 3.88 | 3.79 |
| 138 | Syria | 3.88 | 3.88 | 4.11 | 4.00 | 4.05 | 4.04 | 4.01 | 4.14 | 4.15 | n/a |
| 148 | Iran | 4.26 | 4.30 | 4.63 | 4.84 | 4.69 | 4.56 | 4.76 | 4.80 | 4.79 | n/a |
| 154 | Libya | 4.55 | 4.48 | 4.60 | 4.90 | 4.85 | 4.95 | 4.95 | 4.95 | 4.95 | n/a |
| n/a | Iraq | n/a | n/a | 5.00 | 4.90 | 4.90 | 4.85 | 4.85 | 4.85 | 4.85 | n/a |

# Sub-Saharan Africa Index of Economic Freedom Scores (42 Economies)

| 2004 Rank | Country | 2004 Scores | 2003 Scores | 2002 Scores | 2001 Scores | 2000 Scores | 1999 Scores | 1998 Scores | 1997 Scores | 1996 Scores | 1995 Scores |
|---|---|---|---|---|---|---|---|---|---|---|---|
| 39 | Botswana | 2.55 | 2.49 | 2.99 | 2.95 | 2.93 | 2.91 | 2.90 | 2.75 | 3.09 | 3.38 |
| 48 | Uganda | 2.70 | 2.95 | 3.15 | 3.15 | 3.15 | 2.64 | 2.64 | 2.75 | 2.89 | 3.10 |
| 53 | South Africa | 2.79 | 2.58 | 2.79 | 3.00 | 3.01 | 2.98 | 2.88 | 2.99 | 3.25 | 3.23 |
| 60 | Cape Verde | 2.86 | 3.25 | 3.30 | 3.56 | 3.66 | 3.81 | 3.74 | 3.80 | 3.60 | n/a |
| 67 | Mauritania | 2.94 | 3.20 | 3.46 | 3.89 | 4.00 | 4.00 | 3.96 | 4.03 | 3.93 | n/a |
| 70 | Namibia | 2.96 | 2.65 | 2.84 | 2.93 | 2.98 | 2.84 | 2.99 | 2.80 | n/a | n/a |
| 71 | Mauritius | 2.99 | 2.96 | 2.95 | 2.98 | 2.90 | 2.68 | n/a | n/a | n/a | n/a |
| 72 | Senegal | 3.00 | 3.33 | 3.45 | 3.33 | 3.34 | 3.41 | 3.51 | 3.64 | 3.81 | n/a |
| 86 | Madagascar | 3.14 | 2.85 | 3.29 | 3.29 | 3.39 | 3.45 | 3.51 | 3.44 | 3.55 | 3.74 |
| 89 | Ivory Coast | 3.18 | 3.16 | 3.00 | 3.08 | 3.68 | 3.73 | 3.74 | 3.80 | 3.83 | 3.43 |
| 89 | Swaziland | 3.18 | 3.00 | 3.21 | 3.05 | 3.16 | 3.06 | 3.13 | 3.31 | 3.30 | 3.16 |
| 92 | Djibouti | 3.23 | 3.30 | 3.16 | 3.38 | 3.38 | 3.28 | 3.29 | 3.18 | n/a | n/a |
| 93 | Guinea | 3.24 | 3.26 | 3.45 | 3.21 | 3.34 | 3.19 | 3.11 | 3.39 | 3.13 | 3.29 |
| 94 | Kenya | 3.26 | 3.21 | 3.28 | 3.26 | 3.05 | 3.09 | 3.06 | 3.26 | 3.54 | 3.45 |
| 95 | Burkina Faso | 3.28 | 3.35 | 3.33 | 3.45 | 3.61 | 3.63 | 3.80 | 3.81 | 3.96 | n/a |
| 95 | Mozambique | 3.28 | 3.40 | 3.15 | 3.40 | 3.94 | 3.95 | 4.15 | 4.15 | 4.11 | 4.39 |
| 98 | Tanzania | 3.29 | 3.54 | 3.56 | 3.65 | 3.58 | 3.36 | 3.48 | 3.46 | 3.73 | 3.79 |
| 101 | Ethiopia | 3.33 | 3.79 | 3.70 | 3.88 | 3.70 | 3.68 | 3.70 | 3.80 | 3.80 | 3.90 |
| 102 | Mali | 3.34 | 3.20 | 3.10 | 3.15 | 3.13 | 3.24 | 3.33 | 3.50 | 3.44 | 3.53 |
| 103 | Rwanda | 3.36 | 3.93 | 3.73 | 3.94 | 4.28 | 4.29 | 4.60 | 4.60 | n/a | n/a |
| 105 | Central African Rep. | 3.38 | 3.28 | 3.31 | n/a | n/a | n/a | n/a | n/a | n/a | n/a |
| 109 | Ghana | 3.40 | 3.54 | 3.59 | 3.29 | 3.24 | 3.29 | 3.29 | 3.53 | 3.54 | 3.54 |
| 111 | Gabon | 3.43 | 3.18 | 3.33 | 3.38 | 3.26 | 3.09 | 3.18 | 3.31 | 3.40 | 3.19 |
| 111 | Niger | 3.43 | 3.61 | 3.74 | 3.78 | 4.09 | 3.91 | 4.01 | 4.19 | 4.25 | n/a |
| 113 | Benin | 3.44 | 3.56 | 3.46 | 3.23 | 3.16 | 3.29 | 3.35 | 3.44 | 3.53 | n/a |
| 114 | Malawi | 3.46 | 3.63 | 3.64 | 3.76 | 3.84 | 3.89 | 3.96 | 3.86 | 3.64 | 3.74 |
| 118 | Lesotho | 3.50 | 3.24 | 3.39 | 3.44 | 3.44 | 3.48 | 3.69 | 3.70 | 3.78 | n/a |
| 118 | Zambia | 3.50 | 3.50 | 3.30 | 3.25 | 2.94 | 2.96 | 2.94 | 2.88 | 3.08 | 3.15 |
| 124 | Chad | 3.54 | 3.59 | 3.75 | 3.74 | 4.00 | 4.06 | 4.24 | 4.24 | n/a | n/a |
| 124 | Gambia | 3.54 | 3.49 | 3.34 | 3.59 | 3.64 | 3.60 | 3.66 | 3.55 | n/a | n/a |
| 127 | Cameroon | 3.63 | 3.54 | 3.45 | 3.50 | 3.73 | 3.70 | 3.96 | 3.95 | 4.08 | 3.51 |
| 130 | Equatorial Guinea | 3.69 | 3.73 | 4.15 | 4.13 | 4.18 | 4.26 | n/a | n/a | n/a | n/a |
| 134 | Sierra Leone | 3.73 | 3.95 | n/a | n/a | 4.04 | 3.96 | 3.70 | 3.79 | 3.65 | 3.90 |
| 134 | Togo | 3.73 | 3.86 | 3.88 | 4.00 | 4.05 | 4.14 | n/a | n/a | n/a | n/a |
| 139 | Congo, Rep. | 3.90 | 3.80 | 3.90 | 3.95 | 4.20 | 4.26 | 4.71 | 4.33 | 4.39 | n/a |
| 139 | Guinea–Bissau | 3.90 | 3.90 | 4.15 | 4.19 | 4.40 | 4.50 | n/a | n/a | n/a | n/a |
| 142 | Nigeria | 3.95 | 4.04 | 3.79 | 3.49 | 3.39 | 3.40 | 3.40 | 3.43 | 3.53 | 3.43 |
| 153 | Zimbabwe | 4.54 | 4.63 | 4.39 | 4.21 | 4.04 | 3.89 | 4.16 | 3.69 | 3.79 | 4.09 |
| n/a | Angola | n/a | n/a | n/a | n/a | 4.48 | 4.50 | 4.48 | 4.43 | 4.38 | 4.38 |
| n/a | Burundi | n/a | n/a | n/a | n/a | 4.00 | 4.20 | 4.38 | 4.20 | n/a | n/a |
| n/a | Congo, Dem. Rep. | n/a | n/a | n/a | n/a | 4.60 | 4.59 | 4.29 | 4.39 | 4.29 | 3.89 |
| n/a | Sudan | n/a | n/a | n/a | 1.00 | 4.05 | 4.39 | 4.29 | 4.30 | 4.10 | 4.30 |

# Latin America and the Caribbean Index of Economic Freedom Scores (26 Economies)

| 2004 Rank | Country | 2004 Scores | 2003 Scores | 2002 Scores | 2001 Scores | 2000 Scores | 1999 Scores | 1998 Scores | 1997 Scores | 1996 Scores | 1995 Scores |
|---|---|---|---|---|---|---|---|---|---|---|---|
| 13 | Chile | 1.91 | 2.01 | 1.88 | 2.03 | 2.04 | 2.13 | 2.10 | 2.26 | 2.61 | 2.60 |
| 24 | El Salvador | 2.24 | 2.35 | 2.23 | 2.16 | 2.15 | 2.38 | 2.61 | 2.60 | 2.68 | 2.94 |
| 25 | Bahamas | 2.25 | 2.15 | 2.06 | 2.23 | 2.23 | 2.16 | 2.16 | 2.05 | 2.09 | 2.36 |
| 33 | Barbados | 2.41 | 2.29 | 2.53 | 2.64 | 2.74 | 2.86 | 2.63 | 2.93 | 3.15 | n/a |
| 36 | Trinidad and Tobago | 2.45 | 2.54 | 2.54 | 2.64 | 2.48 | 2.49 | 2.60 | 2.68 | 2.69 | n/a |
| 39 | Uruguay | 2.55 | 2.45 | 2.51 | 2.30 | 2.50 | 2.60 | 2.59 | 2.60 | 2.85 | 3.03 |
| 41 | Bolivia | 2.59 | 2.59 | 2.66 | 2.31 | 2.61 | 2.61 | 2.61 | 2.56 | 2.61 | 3.21 |
| 46 | Belize | 2.69 | 2.74 | 2.79 | 2.69 | 2.84 | 2.76 | 2.96 | 2.71 | 2.74 | 2.85 |
| 50 | Costa Rica | 2.71 | 2.71 | 2.73 | 2.84 | 2.88 | 3.00 | 3.00 | 3.03 | 3.00 | 3.04 |
| 56 | Jamaica | 2.81 | 2.73 | 3.01 | 3.01 | 2.61 | 2.91 | 2.89 | 2.86 | 2.99 | 3.16 |
| 58 | Panama | 2.83 | 2.59 | 2.68 | 2.58 | 2.56 | 2.43 | 2.45 | 2.54 | 2.60 | 2.70 |
| 58 | Peru | 2.83 | 2.86 | 2.88 | 2.61 | 2.64 | 2.66 | 2.96 | 3.03 | 3.06 | 3.59 |
| 67 | Nicaragua | 2.94 | 3.09 | 3.23 | 3.54 | 3.70 | 3.75 | 3.68 | 3.80 | 3.70 | 4.08 |
| 80 | Brazil | 3.10 | 3.01 | 3.06 | 3.21 | 3.46 | 3.19 | 3.36 | 3.28 | 3.56 | 3.46 |
| 83 | Colombia | 3.13 | 3.10 | 2.94 | 3.00 | 3.14 | 2.99 | 3.19 | 3.23 | 3.15 | 3.10 |
| 83 | Guyana | 3.13 | 3.20 | 3.28 | 3.35 | 3.35 | 3.30 | 3.55 | 3.35 | 3.38 | 3.70 |
| 87 | Guatemala | 3.16 | 3.01 | 3.00 | 2.88 | 2.91 | 2.89 | 2.91 | 2.89 | 3.15 | 3.36 |
| 106 | Paraguay | 3.39 | 3.40 | 3.28 | 3.39 | 3.01 | 3.00 | 3.04 | 2.91 | 2.89 | 2.94 |
| 116 | Argentina | 3.48 | 3.04 | 2.58 | 2.29 | 2.23 | 2.28 | 2.53 | 2.75 | 2.63 | 2.85 |
| 120 | Dominican Republic | 3.51 | 3.29 | 3.19 | 3.04 | 3.03 | 3.20 | 3.26 | 3.24 | 3.39 | 3.63 |
| 121 | Honduras | 3.53 | 3.19 | 3.33 | 3.50 | 3.51 | 3.71 | 3.51 | 3.58 | 3.58 | 3.58 |
| 126 | Ecuador | 3.60 | 3.58 | 3.60 | 3.51 | 3.14 | 3.09 | 3.10 | 3.21 | 3.33 | 3.39 |
| 137 | Haiti | 3.78 | 3.86 | 4.08 | 4.13 | 4.33 | 4.26 | 4.43 | 4.35 | 4.64 | 4.79 |
| 143 | Suriname | 3.96 | 4.06 | 4.03 | 3.98 | 3.98 | 4.08 | 4.10 | 4.00 | 4.10 | n/a |
| 144 | Cuba | 4.08 | 4.43 | 4.88 | 4.88 | 4.88 | 4.90 | 4.95 | 4.90 | 5.00 | 4.95 |
| 147 | Venezuela | 4.18 | 3.71 | 3.88 | 3.78 | 3.43 | 3.48 | 3.43 | 3.58 | 3.63 | 3.28 |

# Economic Freedom and Income

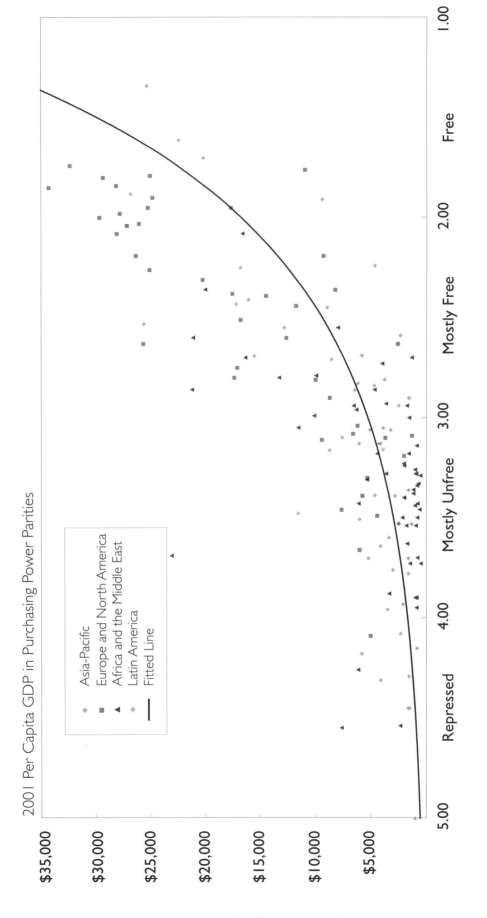

2001 Per Capita GDP in Purchasing Power Parities

Legend:
- Asia-Pacific
- Europe and North America
- Africa and the Middle East
- Latin America
- Fitted Line

$35,000
$30,000
$25,000
$20,000
$15,000
$10,000
$5,000

5.00   Repressed   4.00   Mostly Unfree   3.00   Mostly Free   2.00   Free   1.00

2004 Index of Economic Freedom Score

**Sources:** *World Bank, World Development Indicators Online,* available by subscription at *www.worldbank.org/data;* Central Intelligence Agency, *The World Factbook 2002,* for the following countries: Bahamas, Burma, Cuba, Iraq, Israel, North Korea, Libya, Mozambique, Nicaragua, Qatar, Taiwan, Serbia and Montenegro, United Arab Emirates; and Marc A. Miles, Edwin J. Feulner, and Mary Anastasia O'Grady, *2004 Index of Economic Freedom* (Washington, D.C.: The Heritage Foundation and Dow Jones & Company, Inc., 2004).

# Chapter 1

# **Introduction**

## by Marc A. Miles

The 10th anniversary of The Heritage Foundation/Wall Street Journal *Index of Economic Freedom* provides an opportunity to reflect on past editions and ask some tough questions. We are trying to measure the degree of economic freedom in a vast array of countries around the globe, but does our methodology accurately capture this important concept? We are pleased to announce that after a rigorous statistical evaluation of several aspects of our measurement approach, the conclusion is clear: The *Index* works!

Such a rigorous analysis is possible only because we have nine editions behind us. Only with sufficient data can we examine past trends, take a critical look at what we are doing, and zero in on how better to measure our concept. Each year's edition is like a "snapshot" of economic freedom at a given time. However, with the passage of time, these snapshots can be combined into a "motion picture" of how economic freedom is shifting within and among the world's countries.

And what a tumultuous 10 years it has been. Former Eastern bloc countries are now among the most economically free, and former leaders of the industrialized world have slipped in the standings. A country in South America and another one in the Baltic States have become textbook examples of how to make the transition from economic restrictions and deprivation to economic freedom and prosperity.

But how well have we captured these shifts? Specifically:

- Are we correct in weighting the 10 factors of the *Index* equally?
- Does the fiscal burden factor accurately measure the impact of current and future taxes?
- Does the government intervention factor accurately access the degree to which the government controls economic resources?
- Implied in each question, of course, is another equally important one: If the answer is "no," how could we do it better?

## WEIGHTING THE FACTORS

The question of how best to weight each of the 10 factors is examined in Chapter 3 by Professor Richard Roll of UCLA. He compares the nine years of experience from the *Index*, which uses a simple equal weighting approach, to a more sophisticated, statistical "optimal" weighting approach. The bottom line: Our approach is correct. Equal

> After a rigorous statistical evaluation of several aspects of our measurement approach, the conclusion is clear: *The Index* works!

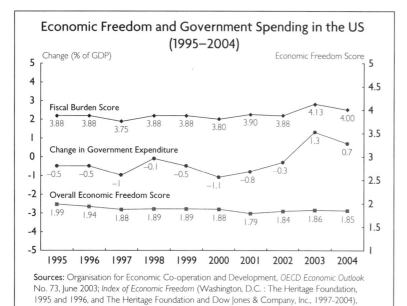

## Economic Freedom and Government Spending in the US (1995–2004)

Change (% of GDP) | Economic Freedom Score

Fiscal Burden Score
3.88  3.88  3.75  3.88  3.88  3.80  3.90  3.88  4.13  4.00

Change in Government Expenditure
−0.5  −0.5  −1  −0.1  −0.5  −1.1  −0.8  −0.3  1.3  0.7

Overall Economic Freedom Score
1.99  1.94  1.88  1.89  1.89  1.88  1.79  1.84  1.86  1.85

1995  1996  1997  1998  1999  2000  2001  2002  2003  2004

**Sources:** Organisation for Economic Co-operation and Development, *OECD Economic Outlook* No. 73, June 2003; *Index of Economic Freedom* (Washington, D.C. : The Heritage Foundation, 1995 and 1996, and The Heritage Foundation and Dow Jones & Company, Inc., 1997-2004), available at *www.heritage.org/index.*

weighting works as well as the most sophisticated system he constructed.

The fact that each factor should be equally weighted in turn has an important policy implication. It is often asked which of the 10 policy factors is most important for achieving economic freedom. The answer from Professor Roll's research is that all 10 of the factors are equally important.

In other words, achieving economic freedom is like building a car. What is the most important component of the car: the powerful engine, the transmission, the seats, the steering wheel, the brakes, or the tires? The question defies an answer, because without any one of these components, the car is unlikely to reach the desired destination. In similar fashion, ignore any one of the 10 factors of economic freedom, and abundant prosperity is likely to remain elusive.

That is why we often refer to the 10 factors of the *Index* as a "10-step plan to end dependency." The 10 factors provide a road map, and only by sticking to the highlighted route can a country achieve economic freedom, prosperity, and self-sufficiency.

A wonderful example of the power of this 10-step plan is Chile. Over the past 30 years, it has stuck to the road map by establishing the rule of law; knocking down tax rates, regulation, and foreign trade barriers; freeing the banking system and capital flows; and reducing the burden and scope of govern-

ment. In the 10 years of the *Index*, Chile has moved steadily from a rank of 24th out of the 101 countries covered in 1995 to 13th out of the 161 analyzed this year.

Compare the experience of Chile to those of the other Latin American countries, which have at most resorted to picking a couple of tires, a passenger seat, maybe a steering wheel, and some brakes. Over the past 10 years, economic growth has been notably better in Chile than among its neighbors, and Chile has been largely immune from the latest round of South American economic disasters.[1]

## CAPTURING FISCAL BURDEN

The issue of appropriately capturing fiscal burden was equally interesting. Professor Roll notes in Chapter 3 that the fiscal burden measure seemed not to add much information to the *Index*. A statistical analysis of the factor's components quickly revealed why.[2] While the top marginal tax rates for both individuals and corporations were good measures, the marginal rate for the average taxpayer and the share or percentage of GDP that is government expenditure were not.

The solution became obvious. The marginal rate for the average taxpayer—a dubious concept—was dropped, and the data showed that *changes* in government expenditure's share of GDP is an excellent measure. In the end, therefore, the components of the fiscal burden factor became the top tax rates faced by individuals and corporations today and the changing rate at which future taxes (government expenditure share) were increasing. Consistent with economic theory, decisions apparently are made on the margin. The revised measure is used in the 2004 rankings, as well as in historical comparisons.

Policy implications also become immediately apparent. Take the case of the United States. As government surpluses began to pile up in the past few years, Congress and the President saw them as potential resources for all types of new government programs. The share of government expenditure as a percentage of GDP began to rise at a faster rate starting around the year 2000. (See chart above.) Under the new measurement, this worsened the fiscal burden score for the U.S., and hence its overall score (a higher score means less freedom). In other words, bigger government increased the fiscal burden imposed on Americans and reduced their economic freedom.

## MEASURING GOVERNMENT INTERVENTION

Similarly, the historical data revealed that the government intervention factor was not adding as much information to the *Index* as one might have hoped.[3] The data, however, also revealed the solution: more symmetrical measurement scales for the two components—government consumption and the percentage of government revenues from state-owned enterprises.

The two numbers derived from these scales for each country in turn are equal-weighted to produce the ultimate government consumption score. This revised scoring is also used in the 2004 rankings and historical comparisons.

## ECONOMIC FREEDOM AND GROWTH

As more years of data become available, we gain new insights into other aspects of the *Index*. For several years, we have published a graph showing that a country's *Index* score is positively related to per capita GDP.[4] In other words, economically free countries have higher per capita incomes.

But there is another dimension to that relationship: one that involves the evolution of the score and of incomes over time. The chart above demonstrates that (seven-year average) growth rates in countries are positively related to (seven-year) improvements in their *Index* scores.[5]

The 142 countries with available data were divided into fifths according to how much their *Index* scores had improved over the seven years. The countries with the most improvement are in the first quintile, and those with the least improvement (or most deterioration) are in the fifth quintile. Comparing the average growth rates of these two groups, the countries in the top quintile had almost twice as much growth (4.9 percent) as those in the bottom quintile (2.5 percent). Even for the middle three quintiles,

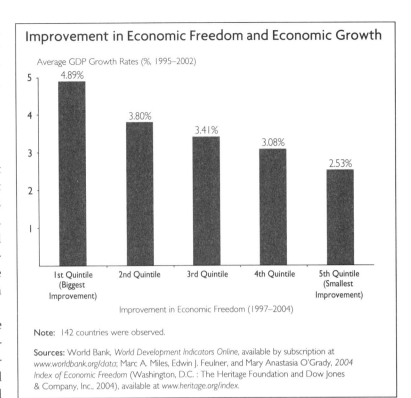

**Improvement in Economic Freedom and Economic Growth**

Average GDP Growth Rates (%, 1995–2002)

Improvement in Economic Freedom (1997–2004)

**Note:** 142 countries were observed.

**Sources:** World Bank, *World Development Indicators Online*, available by subscription at *www.worldbank.org/data*; Marc A. Miles, Edwin J. Feulner, and Mary Anastasia O'Grady, *2004 Index of Economic Freedom* (Washington, D.C. : The Heritage Foundation and Dow Jones & Company, Inc., 2004), available at *www.heritage.org/index*.

growth rises and falls with changes in the *Index* score.

In other words, countries moving down the road map toward economic freedom have higher growth rates. As long as they keep progressing along the road map, their growth rate tends to be above the average for all countries. The faster they move (the greater the improvement in score), the higher the growth rate.

Once countries decide to stop by the roadside or to retrace their steps, growth plummets. So the important message to the countries of the world is that they can help themselves just by starting to adopt economic freedom. The more economic freedom they adopt, the faster they grow or the longer they have superior growth. More growth in turn means that the average level of prosperity is increasing.

## ECONOMIC FREEDOM AND TAXES

The two other chapters in this year's *Index* elaborate further on the theme of how the 10 steps work. From the foregoing discussion of fiscal burden, it is clear that marginal tax rates are an important potential barrier to economic freedom. In Chapter 2, Daniel J. Mitchell contrasts two tax movements among European countries: tax harmonization, which "eliminate[s] fiscal competition, much as a price-fixing agreement among gas stations destroys competition for gasoline," and tax competition, which "facilitates economic growth by encouraging policymakers to adopt sensible tax policy."[6]

Tax harmonization invokes images of tax cartels with minimum tax levels, and of punishing those citizens who try to avoid tax barriers. Mitchell describes recent attempts by some European Union (EU) countries and international institutions to punish people who vote with their feet and leave high-tax states by taxing them on worldwide income (income earned in any country) instead of territorial income (income earned only within the country's borders).

In contrast, tax competition invokes images of innovation. The tax cuts of the Thatcher and Reagan eras in Great Britain and the United States and the Irish Miracle of the later 1980s all reduced the barrier of high marginal tax rates and helped to restore vitality and growth to countries with weak economies. The more contemporary movement is competition among countries of Eastern Europe to see which one can establish the lowest flat tax.

In last year's *Index*, for example, former Estonian Prime Minister Mart Laar wrote about how his country made the transition from a Soviet satellite to a successful free-market economy, in part by adopting a flat tax.[7] Now Mr. Laar's Estonia is competing against Russia's successful 13 percent flat tax. Mr. Laar has said that, as a result, Estonia may be forced to lower its tax barriers further.

## ECONOMIC FREEDOM AND TRADE

Another barrier to economic freedom is trade restrictions, and a tenacious stumbling block on the road to freer global trade is agricultural subsidies. In Chapter 4, Brian M. Carney, an editorial page writer for *The Wall*

*Street Journal Europe*, describes how the European system of agricultural subsidies known as the Common Agricultural Policy (CAP) distorts decisions not only in Europe, but also around the world.[13] The CAP consumes half of the annual EU budget, costs the average European family 1,200 euros a year, has led in the past to lakes of European excess milk and mountains of European excess butter, and lowers income in countries throughout the world. Worst of all, it stands in the way of successful completion of the Doha Round of World Trade Organization negotiations, threatening to unleash retaliation particularly in the developing world.

Carney recounts the history of CAP from its origin in 1957 as "the price French President Charles de Gaulle exacted for France's membership" in the pre-EU European Economic Community to the EU's inability in 2003 to negotiate meaningful reforms even under world pressure. Today, French farmers produce about 2 percent of France's GDP but receive about 20 percent of the entire EU-wide CAP budget.

The CAP has become an immovable object in the bizarre world of EU politics. France, bogged down in a tie for 44th place in this year's *Index of Economic Freedom*, has developed a reputation for policies inconsistent with economic freedom. That the EU or France wants to retain policies that retard its own growth is one thing. That either would stand in the way of the rest of the world improving their growth is quite another.

Thus, a lesson in the fundamentals of the 10-step program, or that the *Index* works, is not important just to developing or transitional countries. Clearly, there are some older economic powers that need to learn the lessons as well. It is with these goals in mind that The Heritage Foundation and *The Wall Street Journal* are pleased to present readers with the *2004 Index of Economic Freedom*.

Another barrier to
economic freedom is
trade restrictions, and
a tenacious stumbling
block on the road to
freer global trade is
agricultural subsidies.

# Endnotes

1    For more details, see Ana I. Eiras, "Chile: Ten Steps for Abandoning Aid Dependency for Prosperity," Heritage Foundation *Backgrounder* No. 1654, May 20, 2003.

2    Philippe J. Lacoude, "Study—Fiscal Burden Component, Index of Economic Freedom of the Heritage Foundation," unpublished, April 15, 2003.

3    Philippe J. Lacoude, "Study—Government Intervention Component, Index of Economic Freedom of the Heritage Foundation," unpublished, May 15, 2003.

4    See Executive Summary, *supra*.

5    The graph shows changes in *Index* scores and average growth rates over a seven-year period. The intervals seem to differ slightly because of the way the data are reported. The 2004 *Index* uses primarily 2002 GDP data, since they were the most recent data available as the *Index* was being prepared. The 1997 *Index* would have used 1995 data.

6    See Daniel J. Mitchell, Chapter 2, "The Economics of Tax Competition: Harmonization *vs.* Liberalization," *infra*.

7    See Mart Laar, Chapter 3, "How Estonia Did It," in Gerald P. O'Driscoll, Jr., Edwin J. Feulner, and Mary Anastasia O'Grady, *2003 Index of Economic Freedom* (Washington, D.C.: The Heritage Foundation and Dow Jones & Company, Inc., 2003), pp. 35–37.

8    See Brian M. Carney, Chapter 4, "The Common Agricultural Policy: How the European Union Distorts Trade With Non-EU Nations," *infra*.

Chapter 2

# The Economics of Tax Competition: Harmonization vs. Liberalization

by Daniel J. Mitchell

*An inquisition into every man's private circumstances, and an inquisition which, in order to accommodate the tax to them, watched over all the fluctuations of his fortunes, would be a source of such continual and endless vexation as no people could support…. The proprietor of stock is properly a citizen of the world, and is not necessarily attached to any particular country. He would be apt to abandon the country in which he was exposed to a vexatious inquisition, in order to be assessed to a burdensome tax, and would remove his stock to some other country where he could either carry on his business, or enjoy his fortune more at his ease. By removing his stock he would put an end to all the industry which it had maintained in the country which he left. Stock cultivates land; stock employs labour. A tax which tended to drive away stock from any particular country would so far tend to dry up every source of revenue both to the sovereign and to the society. Not only the profits of stock, but the rent of land and the wages of labour would necessarily be more or less diminished by its removal.*

—Adam Smith, *An Inquiry into the Nature & Causes of the Wealth of Nations*, 1776.

Like other forms of competition, fiscal rivalry generates positive results.

Tax competition exists when people can reduce tax burdens by shifting capital and/or labor from high-tax jurisdictions to low-tax jurisdictions. This migration disciplines profligate governments and rewards nations that lower tax rates and engage in pro-growth tax reform.

Like other forms of competition, fiscal rivalry generates positive results. People get to keep more of the money they earn, and economic performance is enhanced because of lower tax rates on work, saving, and investment. The capital mobility that defines tax competition also protects against government abuses. People can guard against corruption and protect their human rights more effectively when they know that they and/or their capital can flee across national borders.

The thought of losing sources of tax revenue scares government officials from high-tax nations, who vociferously condemn tax competition and would like to see it reduced or eliminated. Working through international bureaucracies like the European Union (EU), the United Nations (UN), and the Organisation for Economic Co-operation and Development (OECD), high-tax governments are promoting various tax harmonization schemes to inhibit the flow of jobs and capital from high-tax jurisdictions to low-tax jurisdictions.

These proposals are fundamentally inconsistent with good tax policy. Tax harmonization means higher tax rates, but it also means discriminatory and destructive double taxation of income that is saved and invested. It also means extraterritorial taxation since most tax harmonization schemes are designed to help governments tax economic activity outside their borders.

Tax competition should be celebrated, not persecuted. It is a powerful force for economic liberalization that has helped promote good tax policy in countries around the world. Even OECD economists have admitted that "the ability to choose the location of economic activity offsets shortcomings in government budgeting processes, limiting a tendency to spend and tax excessively."[1]

Fiscal rivalry among governments has produced an amazingly desirable impact on fiscal policy in the past 25 years. For instance:

- Nations across the globe felt compelled to lower personal income tax rates following the Thatcher and Reagan tax rate reductions.
- Tax competition has helped drive down corporate tax rates in Western Europe's welfare states.
- Numerous nations in the former Soviet bloc have enacted flat taxes, a process greatly aided by tax competition.

Protecting and preserving the right to engage in tax competition should be a key goal for economic policymakers, particularly those interested in promoting economic development in poorer nations. If international bureaucracies succeed in destroying or limiting tax competition, governments will have much less incentive to behave responsibly. The absence of competition would undermine countries' opportunities for cre-

ative economic reform and reduce individual freedom.

People throughout the world should be allowed to benefit from lower tax rates. The OECD, EU, and UN should not limit the options of investors and workers by creating a cartel that benefits high-tax nations. An "OPEC for politicians" would insulate government officials from market discipline, and the resulting deterioration in economic policy would slow global economic performance.

## WHAT IS TAX COMPETITION?

When a town has only one gas station, consumers have very little leverage. In the absence of competition, the gas station is much more likely to charge high prices, maintain inconvenient hours, and provide inferior service. But when there are several gas stations, their owners must pay attention to the needs of consumers in order to stay in business. This means market prices, better hours, and improved service.

More important, competition enhances economic performance. Businesses of all kinds—if they face competitive pressure—are constantly driven to improve quality and offer new products in order to attract and hold the interest of consumers. Competitive pressure encourages better allocation of resources and boosts economic efficiency. This is why market-based economies tend to grow faster and provide higher living standards.

Competition between governments has similarly desirable economic effects. Nations with less inhibiting policies will enjoy more job creation and investment, much as gas stations with better service and prices will attract more motorists. But jurisdictional competition is not just about tax policy. Regulatory policy, monetary policy, trade policy, and legal policy can also erect roadblocks that affect the flow of jobs and capital across national borders.

Tax competition is just one slice of this competition among countries, but it is increasingly important because of the growing mobility of capital and labor. Workers and people with money to invest want to obtain the best after-tax reward (or rate of return), and their search for profitable opportunities is not limited by national borders. Not surprisingly, investors and workers tend to leave (or avoid) nations with punitive tax burdens and onerous tax codes. Instead, these resources gravitate toward nations that reward private-sector wealth creation— much as motorists gravitate to gas stations that provide good value for the money.

No wonder politicians from high-tax nations dislike tax competition. Fiscal rivalry restricts their ability to overtax (and therefore overspend). Just as the owner of a town's only gas station is unhappy when competitors set up shop, politicians do not like competitive neighbors who force them to behave responsibly in order to attract economic activity—or to keep economic activity from fleeing to a lower-tax environment.

The tax competition battle revolves largely around the tax treatment of capital. Investment funds can cross national borders at the click of a mouse, and this mobility makes it very difficult to maintain high tax rates or to impose discriminatory taxes on income that is saved and invested. The charts at right show the dramatic increase in cross-border capital flows in recent years. This also helps explain why high-tax governments are so eager to get the ability to track—and tax—fleeing capital.

Where borders are relatively open for immigration, the taxation of workers and entrepreneurial talent is beginning to attract more attention from greedy governments. Many French move to the lower-tax United Kingdom. People from Canada move to the United States, as do many talented professionals from Third World nations. And similar tax-motivated migrations take place in other parts of the world. The phenomenon of workers "voting with their feet" has caused considerable angst among high-tax nations and has even led to proposals that would give governments permanent taxing authority over their citizens no matter where they live.

## WHAT IS TAX HARMONIZATION?

Tax harmonization exists when taxpayers face similar or identical tax rates no matter where they work, save, shop, or invest. Harmonized tax rates eliminate fiscal competi-

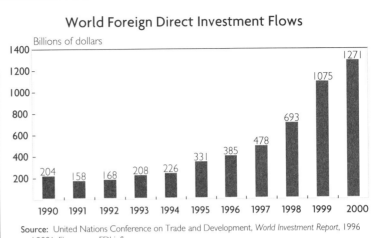

### World Foreign Direct Investment Flows

Billions of dollars

1990: 204
1991: 158
1992: 168
1993: 208
1994: 226
1995: 331
1996: 385
1997: 478
1998: 693
1999: 1075
2000: 1271

**Source:** United Nations Conference on Trade and Development, *World Investment Report*, 1996 and 2001. Figures are FDI inflows.

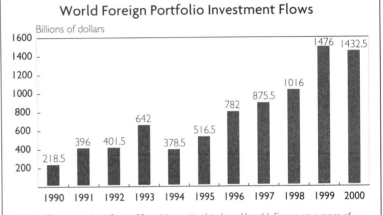

### World Foreign Portfolio Investment Flows

Billions of dollars

1990: 218.5
1991: 396
1992: 401.5
1993: 642
1994: 378.5
1995: 516.5
1996: 782
1997: 875.5
1998: 1016
1999: 1476
2000: 1432.5

**Note:** These are private flows of financial securities (stocks and bonds). Figures are average of inflows and outflows.

**Source:** International Monetary Fund, *Balance of Payments Statistics*, 2001.

tion, much as a price-fixing agreement among gas stations destroys competition for gasoline.

Tax harmonization can be achieved two different ways:

■ Explicit tax harmonization occurs when nations agree to set minimum tax rates or decide to tax at the same rate. The European Union, for instance, requires that member nations impose a value-added tax (VAT) of at least 15 percent.2 The EU also has harmonized tax rates for fuel, alcohol, and tobacco, and there are ongoing efforts to harmonize the taxation of personal and corporate income tax rates.

Under this *direct* form of tax harmonization, taxpayers are unable to benefit from better tax policy in other nations, and governments are insulated from market discipline.

■ Implicit harmonization occurs when governments tax the income their citizens earn in other jurisdictions. This policy of "worldwide taxation" requires governments to collect financial information on nonresident investors and to share that information with tax collectors from foreign governments. This "information exchange" system tends to be a one-way street since jobs and capital generally flow from high-tax nations to low-tax nations.

Under this *indirect* form of tax harmonization, just as under the direct form outlined above, taxpayers are unable to benefit from better tax policy in other nations, and governments are insulated from market discipline.[3]

Both forms of tax harmonization have similarly counterproductive economic consequences. In each case, tax competition is emasculated, encouraging higher tax rates. This hinders the efficient allocation of capital and labor, slowing overall economic performance.

Currently, international bureaucracies are pursuing three major tax harmonization initiatives:

**1.** The Paris-based Organisation for Economic Co-operation and Development launched a "harmful tax competition" initiative in the 1990s, identifying more than 40 so-called tax havens.[4] The OECD is threatening these jurisdictions with financial protectionism if they do not agree to weaken their tax and privacy laws so that high-tax nations could more easily track—and tax—flight capital. Ironically, the OECD did not blacklist any of its member nations even though at least four of them—Switzerland, Luxembourg, the United States, and the United Kingdom—qualify as tax havens according to the OECD's own definition.

**2.** The European Union is a major advocate of tax harmonization, and the Brussels-based bureaucracy has had some success. Value-added taxes, energy taxes, and excise taxes all have been subject to some level of direct harmonization among EU nations. The EU's current initiative is the "savings tax directive," an indirect form of tax harmonization that would require member nations—as well as six non-EU nations—

either to impose a special tax on nonresident investors (and give the lion's share of the revenue to the investor's government) or to collect information about the investment earnings of nonresidents and forward it to their respective governments (which would then tax the income).[5]

**3.** The United Nations has a "Financing for Development" proposal that calls for the creation of an International Tax Organization. This new bureaucracy supposedly would have the power to override the tax policy of sovereign nations and would be specifically responsible for curtailing tax competition. Equally worrisome, the UN proposes to give nations the power to tax emigrant income, which would have particularly adverse effects on the United States because of the large numbers of skilled immigrants.[6]

As of this writing, all of these tax harmonization schemes have been stymied. The OECD did convince many blacklisted jurisdictions to sign so-called commitment letters, which ostensibly obligate low-tax governments to obey OECD dictates, but most of these letters include "level playing field" clauses stating that the blacklisted nations have no intention of emasculating their tax and privacy laws unless all OECD nations agree to impose the same misguided policies.

As originally conceived, with its automatic collection and sharing of information regarding nonresident investors, the EU savings tax directive would have created the "level playing field." The EU was forced to withdraw that proposal, however, and the replacement scheme clearly results in unequal treatment.

But this may be a moot point since the watered-down directive still faces a number of obstacles. Several nations—most notably the United States—have refused to join the EU's proposed cartel. This presumably is a death knell for the directive since it is predicated on unanimous participation from all 15 EU nations and six non-EU nations.

Finally, the United Nations' proposed International Tax Organization almost surely will never materialize. The right to tax—and the right to control the taxation of economic

# WORLDWIDE TAXATION VS. TERRITORIAL TAXATION

Direct harmonization of income taxes is not the biggest threat to the global economy, even among European Union nations.[1] Instead, the threat to tax competition comes from the indirect harmonization proposals being advanced by the OECD and EU. This is why the issue of worldwide taxation vs. territorial taxation is so important. "Worldwide taxation" undermines the flow of resources from high-tax nations to low-tax nations by preventing the taxpayers in one jurisdiction from benefiting from lower tax rates in another jurisdiction.

*Worldwide taxation* occurs when a government taxes the income its citizens earn in other nations (often referred to as foreign-source income). Foreign governments, of course, have the primary right to tax income earned inside their borders. A government that imposes worldwide taxation therefore generally allows taxpayers to reduce their tax bills on foreign-source income by subtracting—using a foreign tax credit—taxes paid to the foreign government.

Worldwide taxation forces taxpayers to pay the highest possible tax rate when engaging in cross-border economic activity. If a foreign government has a higher tax rate than their domestic government, for instance, taxpayers must pay that high rate on their foreign-source income. (The foreign tax credit should cancel any domestic liability on that income.) But if a foreign country has a lower tax rate than their domestic government, taxpayers are required to pay the foreign tax—and then to pay more tax to their own government until the overall tax is equal to their domestic tax rate.

In other words, taxpayers face a "heads-you-win, tails-I-lose" situation. Countries that impose worldwide taxation also put their companies at a competitive disadvantage, as seen from the table below, which compares the tax burden on companies from three nations competing for business in Ireland.

*Territorial taxation* occurs when governments tax income only that is earned inside national borders. Territorial taxation respects sovereignty and automatically reduces conflicts between governments. It is good tax policy, and it rewards nations that enact policies that encourage economic growth. Territorial taxation dramatically reduces complexity and allows more privacy for law-abiding people.[2]

## Worldwide Taxation Punishes U.S. Company Competing in Ireland

|  | Profit | Irish Tax | Additional Tax | Total Tax |
|---|---|---|---|---|
| U.S. company | $100 | $12.5 | $22.50 to IRS | $35 |
| Local company | $100 | $12.5 | 0 | $12.5 |
| Dutch company | $100 | $12.5 | 0 | $12.5 |

1    Currently, EU tax harmonization proposals can be implemented only if all member nations agree. High-tax nations resent this "national veto" policy because nations like Ireland, Luxembourg, and England have attractive tax policies for certain forms of economic activity and generally use their veto powers to block further harmonization. High-tax nations also worry that tax competition will become even stronger when 10 new nations join the EU in May 2004, particularly since many of these new member nations have relatively attractive tax systems. Uncompetitive nations such as France and Germany would like to abolish the national veto so that a mere majority of nations can impose tax harmonization policies on all EU nations, and the ongoing effort to create a new constitution for the EU has created an opportunity to weaken or abolish the national veto.

2    For more information comparing worldwide taxation and territorial taxation, see Daniel J. Mitchell, "Making American Companies More Competitive," Heritage Foundation *Backgrounder* No. 1691, September 25, 2003.

## Top Personal Income Tax Rates, 1980—2000
### (Includes national and state/provincial taxes)

| Country | 1980 | 1985 | 1990 | 1995 | 2000 | Change 1980-2000 |
|---|---|---|---|---|---|---|
| Australia | 62 | 60 | 49 | 47 | 47 | -15 |
| Austria | 62 | 62 | 50 | 50 | 50 | -12 |
| Belgium | 76 | 76 | 55 | 58 | 58 | -18 |
| Canada | 60 | 50 | 44 | 44 | 44 | -16 |
| Denmark | 66 | 73 | 68 | 64 | 59 | -7 |
| Finland | 65 | 64 | 63 | 55 | 52 | -13 |
| France | 60 | 65 | 53 | 51 | 54 | -6 |
| Germany | 65 | 65 | 65 | 66 | 59 | -6 |
| Greece | 60 | 63 | 50 | 45 | 43 | -17 |
| Iceland | 63 | 56 | 40 | 47 | 45 | -18 |
| Ireland | 60 | 65 | 58 | 48 | 42 | -18 |
| Italy | 72 | 81 | 66 | 67 | 51 | -21 |
| Japan | 75 | 70 | 65 | 65 | 50 | -25 |
| Korea | 89 | 65 | 60 | 48 | 44 | -45 |
| Luxembourg | 57 | 57 | 56 | 50 | 49 | -8 |
| Mexico | 55 | 55 | 40 | 35 | 40 | -15 |
| Netherlands | 72 | 72 | 72 | 60 | 52 | -20 |
| New Zealand | 62 | 66 | 33 | 33 | 39 | -23 |
| Norway | 75 | 64 | 54 | 42 | 48 | -27 |
| Portugal | 84 | 69 | 40 | 40 | 40 | -44 |
| Spain | 66 | 66 | 56 | 56 | 48 | -18 |
| Sweden | 87 | 80 | 72 | 58 | 51 | -36 |
| Switzerland | 31 | 33 | 33 | 35 | 31 | 0 |
| Turkey | 75 | 63 | 50 | 55 | 45 | -30 |
| United Kingdom | 83 | 60 | 40 | 40 | 40 | -43 |
| United States | 70 | 50 | 33 | 42 | 42 | -28 |
| Average for 26 OECD countries | 67 | 63 | 53 | 50 | 47 | -20 |

Note: Figures include the lowest state or provincial tax rate, as applicable.

Source: James Gwartney and Robert Lawson with Walter Park and Charles Skipton, *Economic Freedom of the World: 2001 Annual Report*(Vancouver: Fraser Institute, 2001); data retrieved from http://www.freetheworld.com.

poses, advocates of tax harmonization are seeking to stop the downward pressure on tax rates that is caused by competition.

The history of corporate tax rates in the European Union is a good example. As early as 1962 and 1970, official reports were calling for harmonization of corporate tax systems. In 1975, the European Commission sought a minimum corporate tax of 45 percent. This initiative failed, as did a similar effort in the early 1990s to require a minimum corporate tax rate of 30 percent.[9] Today, the average corporate tax rate in the European Union is less than 30 percent.

The European Union's treatment of Ireland also bolsters the view that tax harmonization is a one-way street designed to keep tax rates high. In an unprecedented move, EU finance ministers voted two years ago to reprimand Ireland for its fiscal policy—even though Ireland at the time had the EU's biggest budget surplus, second lowest amount of debt, greatest reduction in government debt, lowest level of government spending, and lowest total tax burden.[10] Most observers felt that politicians from other nations were upset that Ireland's 12.5 percent corporate tax rate was putting pressure on them to implement similar reforms.[11] Interestingly, there has never been a reprimand for a country because its taxes were too high.

The benefits of tax competition can be appreciated by looking at tax policy changes that have swept the world in the past 25 years. Obviously, tax competition should not be seen as the only factor leading to the following tax changes. In some cases, it may not even be the driving force. But in each case, tax competition has encouraged the shift to tax policy that creates more growth and opportunity.[12]

■ **The Thatcher–Reagan Tax Rate Reductions.** Margaret Thatcher became Prime Minister of the United Kingdom in 1979, and Ronald Reagan became President of the United States in 1981. Both leaders inherited weak economies but managed to restore growth and vitality with free-market reforms.

Sweeping reductions in personal income tax rates were a significant component of

activity inside national borders—is the very essence of national sovereignty, and it is very unlikely that powerful nations will ever surrender that right.[7]

The proposal to give governments permanent taxing authority over emigrants also faces daunting obstacles. Policymakers may not fully understand why it is misguided to tax flight capital, but they do seem to realize that it is wrong to tax flight labor.

## BENEFITS OF TAX COMPETITION

Tax competition is desirable for a number of reasons. Most important, it facilitates economic growth by encouraging policymakers to adopt sensible tax policy. Tax harmonization, by contrast, usually is associated with higher fiscal burdens.[8] For all intents and pur-

both the Thatcher and Reagan agendas. The top tax rate was 83 percent when Thatcher took office, and she reduced the top rate to 40 percent.[13] The top tax rate in the United States was 70 percent when Reagan was inaugurated, and he lowered the top rate to 28 percent.[14]

The United Kingdom and the United States both benefited from tax rate reductions, but other nations also profited because they were compelled to lower tax rates—and this shift to better tax policy is an ongoing process. The table on previous page shows the sweeping tax rate reductions that have occurred since 1980.

Tax competition surely played a role in this global shift to lower tax rates, and lower tax rates unambiguously have helped the world economy to grow faster. Even the OECD, which is hardly sympathetic to pro-growth tax policy, has estimated that economies grow one-half of 1 percent (0.5 percent) faster for every 10-percentage-point reduction in marginal tax rates.[15]

■ **The Irish Miracle and Corporate Rate Reduction in Europe.** In addition to reductions in tax rates on personal income, tax competition has helped to encourage lower tax rates on corporate income. The Reagan tax rate reductions once again deserve credit for starting the process, and the table on this page demonstrates that corporate tax rates have fallen dramatically since 1986.

But the Irish Miracle is perhaps the most impressive evidence of how tax competition advances good tax policy. Less than 20 years ago, Ireland was an economic "basket case" with double-digit unemployment and an anemic economy. This weak performance was caused, at least in part, by an onerous tax burden. The top tax rate on personal income in 1984 was 65 percent, the capital gains taxes reached a maximum of 60 percent, and the corporate tax rate was 50 percent.[16]

Although these rates were slightly reduced later in the 1980s, the top rates in 1991 were still very high: 52 percent on personal income, 50 percent on capital gains, and 43 percent on corporate income. At this point, Irish leaders decided that tinkering with the tax code was not a recipe for success. Over the next 10 years, tax rates—especially

### Top Corporate Income Tax Rates, 1986—2000
(Includes national level taxes only)

| Country | 1986 | 1991 | 1995 | 2000 | Change 1986-2000 |
|---|---|---|---|---|---|
| Australia | 49 | 39 | 33 | 34 | -15 |
| Austria | 30 | 30 | 34 | 34 | 4 |
| Belgium | 45 | 39 | 39 | 39 | -6 |
| Canada | 36 | 29 | 29 | 28 | -8 |
| Denmark | 50 | 38 | 34 | 32 | -20 |
| Finland | 33 | 23 | 25 | 29 | -4 |
| France | 45 | 42 | 33 | 33 | -12 |
| Germany | 56 | 50 | 45 | 40 | -16 |
| Greece | 49 | 46 | 40 | 40 | -9 |
| Iceland | 51 | 45 | 33 | 30 | -21 |
| Ireland | 50 | 43 | 40 | 24 | -26 |
| Italy | 36 | 36 | 36 | 37 | 1 |
| Japan | 43 | 38 | 38 | 27 | -16 |
| Korea | 30 | 34 | 32 | 28 | -2 |
| Luxembourg | 40 | 33 | 33 | 37 | -3 |
| Mexico | 34 | 34 | 34 | 35 | 1 |
| Netherlands | 42 | 35 | 35 | 35 | -7 |
| New Zealand | 45 | 33 | 33 | 33 | -12 |
| Norway | 28 | 27 | 19 | 28 | 0 |
| Portugal | 47 | 36 | 36 | 32 | -15 |
| Spain | 35 | 35 | 35 | 35 | 0 |
| Sweden | 52 | 30 | 28 | 28 | -24 |
| Switzerland | 10 | 10 | 10 | 8 | -2 |
| Turkey | 46 | 49 | 25 | 33 | -13 |
| United Kingdom | 35 | 34 | 33 | 30 | -5 |
| United States | 46 | 34 | 35 | 35 | -11 |
| Average for 26 OECD countries | 41 | 35 | 33 | 32 | -9 |

Source: Cato Institute based on OECD data.

on capital gains and corporate income—were slashed dramatically.[17] Today, the personal income tax rate is 42 percent, the capital gains tax rate is just 20 percent, and the corporate income tax rate is only 12.5 percent.

These aggressive "supply-side" tax rate reductions have yielded enormous benefits. The Irish economy has experienced the strongest growth of all industrialized nations, expanding at an average of 7.7 percent annually during the 1990s.[18] The late 1990s were particularly impressive, as Ireland enjoyed annual growth rates in excess of 9 percent.[19] In a remarkably short period of time, the "sick man of Europe" has become the "Celtic Tiger." Unemployment has dropped dramatically, and investment has boomed.[20]

The Irish people have been the big winners. Once a relatively poor nation, Ireland now enjoys the second highest standard of living in the European Union. Even the gov-

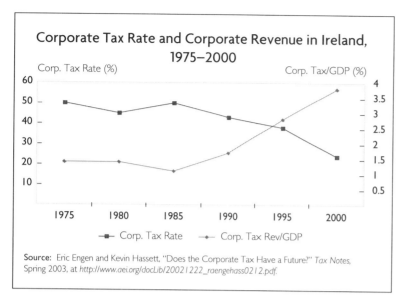

### Corporate Tax Rate and Corporate Revenue in Ireland, 1975–2000

Corp. Tax Rate (%)    Corp. Tax/GDP (%)

**Source:** Eric Engen and Kevin Hassett, "Does the Corporate Tax Have a Future?" *Tax Notes*, Spring 2003, at *http://www.aei.org/docLib/20021222_raengehass0212.pdf*.

ernment has reaped benefits. In the mid-1980s, when the corporate income tax rate was close to 50 percent, it raised revenue barely in excess of 1 percent of gross domestic product (GDP). As the chart on this page illustrates, however, today's 12.5 percent corporate tax raises revenue totaling nearly 4 percent of GDP.[21]

Thanks to tax competition, Ireland's tax rate reductions have had a positive effect on the rest of Europe. The Irish Miracle has motivated other EU nations to reduce their tax rates significantly in recent years. These lower tax rates will improve economic performance and should encourage European policymakers to make reductions in other tax rates as well.

■ **Tax Reform in Eastern Europe.** One of the most amazing fiscal policy developments is the adoption of flat taxes in former Soviet bloc nations. The three Baltic nations—Estonia, Lithuania, and Latvia—adopted flat tax systems in the 1990s,[22] and tax reform in the Baltics triggered a virtuous cycle of tax competition. Russia followed with a 13 percent flat tax that took effect in January 2001. Ukraine recently approved a 13 percent flat tax, and Slovakia is implementing a 19 percent flat tax.[23] Even Serbia has a variant of a flat tax.[24]

These flat tax regimes, by themselves, will not solve all the problems that exist in post-communist nations, but the evidence already shows that good tax policy is having a desirable impact. The Baltic nations, for instance, are the most prosperous of the nations that emerged from the former Soviet Union.[25] The Russian Federation was the next to adopt a flat tax. Not surprisingly, it is the next most prosperous of the former Soviet "Republics."[26]

The evidence from Russia, where the 13 percent flat tax has produced dramatic results, is particularly striking: Russia's economy has expanded by about 10 percent since 2001.[27] That may not sound like much, but it is rather noteworthy considering t e slowdown in the global economy. The Russian economy certainly has performed better than the U.S. economy and has easily outpaced the anemic growth rates elsewhere in Europe.

In addition to faster growth, Russia's tax reform has had a dramatic effect on tax compliance, something even *The New York Times* was forced to concede.[28] Over the past two and one-half years, inflation-adjusted income tax revenue in Russia has grown by about 60 percent, demonstrating that people are willing to produce more and pay their taxes when the system is fair and tax rates are low.[29]

Tax competition has played a role in each of these success stories. In some cases, the benefits accrue because policymakers want to mimic success in other nations. In other cases, governments enact good tax policy because they fear that jobs and capital will leave. Irrespective of motives, however, good tax policy in one jurisdiction has a positive spillover effect on other jurisdictions.

It is also worth noting that tax competition is a successful tool for economic development. Hong Kong is perhaps the best example. Extremely poor after World War II, Hong Kong used market-based policy—including a low-rate flat tax—to boost economic performance. The results have been dramatic: Hong Kong has been the world's fastest growing economy in the post–World War II era and currently ranks as the 15th richest jurisdiction, according to the World Bank.[30]

The World Bank's rankings are in fact very instructive. Many of the world's wealthiest jurisdictions, including 11 of the top 16

# FRINGE BENEFITS OF TAX COMPETITION

**Privacy.** The indirect form of tax harmonization requires the automatic collection and unlimited sharing of personal financial information. This is a troublesome development for those who believe that individuals should have a presumptive right to keep their personal matters confidential. Equally troubling, the "information exchange" policies advocated by many high-tax governments would suspend many due process legal protections—including the right to be notified of government investigations, the right to contest government information requests, and the right to appeal government decisions.

**Human Rights.** For some people, the loss of financial privacy can be a matter of life and death. Many overseas Chinese in places like Indonesia use "offshore" financial centers to protect themselves from ethnic persecution. Many businessmen from Latin America put their money in tax havens to protect their families from kidnapping and extortion. Many citizens of repressive regimes use low-tax jurisdictions to protect themselves and their assets from oppression. All of these people will be at risk if governments create a global network of tax police to collect and swap private financial data.

**Sovereignty.** All forms of tax harmonization presume that there should be a one-size-fits-all rule for tax policy. Low-tax jurisdictions are being told that they must make sweeping changes in their tax and privacy laws solely for the benefit of tax collectors from high-tax nations. These demands run roughshod over the rights of nations, especially smaller jurisdictions that are being bullied by the OECD. Another aspect of the sovereignty debate is whether nations are obliged to enforce the laws of other nations. Traditionally, jurisdictions are free to decide for themselves whether to help other jurisdictions. The United States, for instance, did not help China investigate and prosecute Tiananmen Square protestors. Likewise, many European nations refuse to assist the United States in cases that could result in the death penalty. As a general rule, under the "dual criminality" principle, nations do assist each other when an alleged offense violates the laws of both nations. The OECD and EU want to dismantle this sovereign right.

Note: For more information on issues of privacy, human rights, and sovereignty, see Task Force on Information Exchange and Financial Privacy, *Report on Financial Privacy, Law Enforcement, and Terrorism*, March 25, 2002, at *http://www.freedomandprosperity.org/task-force-report.pdf.*

(see table at right), are "tax havens" based on the OECD definition. This raises an interesting question: If international bureaucracies are supposed to be promoting growth, would it not make sense for them to publicize so-called tax havens instead of persecuting them?

## POISON PILL FOR TAX REFORM?

There is a strong effort in the United States to enact a flat tax, and President George W. Bush's 2001 and 2003 tax cuts move the tax code in that direction by lowering rates and reducing double taxation of income that is saved and invested.[31] These policies help to make America a magnet for global capital.

## World's Wealthiest Jurisdictions

*(Tax Havens in Bold)*

| | |
|---|---|
| 1. **Bermuda** | 9. Denmark |
| 2. **Luxembourg** | 10. Iceland |
| 3. **Switzerland** | 11. San Marino |
| 4. Norway | 12. **Cayman Islands** |
| 5. **Liechtenstein** | 13. United Kingdom |
| 6. United States | 14. Sweden |
| 7. Japan | 15. **Hong Kong** |
| 8. **Channel Islands** | 16. **Monaco** |

Source: Gross national income per capita, 2002, Atlas Method, in World Bank, *World Development Indicators*, July 2003.

## HARMONIZATION DOES NOT MEAN MORE TAX REVENUE

Even if the OECD, EU, and other international bureaucracies succeed in destroying tax competition, it is not likely that this will result in a surge of new tax revenue. Many taxpayers simply will shift resources to the underground economy. Indeed, the underground economy already accounts for one-fourth to one-third of GDP in many of Europe's welfare states.[1]

Interestingly, even the OECD recognizes that high tax rates are the real problem. Staff economists have written that tax evasion "can be attributed to higher tax burdens."[2] OECD economists have even outlined the solution, writing that "lowering statutory corporate tax rates and rates on personal capital income in countries where these are particularly high, may increase the domestic tax base as there are less incentives to shift taxable profits and capital income abroad."[3]

1. Friedrich Schneider and Dominik Enste, "Shadow Economies Around the World: Size, Causes, and Consequences," International Monetary Fund, Working Paper No. WP/00/26, February 2000.
2. Organisation for Economic Co-operation and Development, *Economic Outlook*, No. 63 (June 1998).
3. Willi Leibfritz, John Thornton, and Alexandra Bibbee, "Taxation and Economic Performance," Organisation for Economic Co-operation and Development, Economics Department, Working Paper No. 176, 1997.

---

Tax competition promotes tax reform by helping to drive down marginal tax rates.

---

Indeed, tax competition is completely consistent with fundamental tax reform. For instance:

- Tax reform envisions a system with low tax rates on productive behavior. Tax competition promotes tax reform by helping to drive down marginal tax rates.
- Tax reform envisions a system in which income is taxed only one time. Tax competition promotes tax reform by helping to eliminate double taxation of income that is saved and invested.
- Tax reform envisions a system in which governments do not tax income earned in other nations. Tax competition promotes tax reform by rewarding territorial taxation, the common-sense notion that governments tax only income earned inside national borders.
- The tax harmonization agenda, however, is a distinct threat to the right of nations to reform their tax codes and enact single-rate, consumption-based tax systems.[32] The tax harmonization agenda certainly means that tax reform would be very unlikely.
- The flat tax, for instance, is a territorial system. Yet the OECD and other international bureaucracies believe that territorial taxation is a form of "harmful" competition. The flat tax also eliminates double taxation,

but the OECD initiative is designed to help governments discriminate against income that is saved and invested.

## WHICH PATH FOR EUROPE?

High-tax European welfare states are the biggest supporters of tax harmonization. Germany and France even want European-wide taxes imposed and collected by Brussels. Along with a handful of additional nations, they also advocate harmonization of personal and corporate income tax rates. Other European nations are not quite so anxious to harmonize rates, but they certainly seem sympathetic to indirect forms of tax harmonization such as the EU savings tax directive.

The outcome of the push for a savings tax directive could determine whether Europe's high-tax nations are able to cripple tax competition. If the savings tax directive is implemented, it will be more difficult for taxpayers in high-tax nations to benefit from better tax regimes outside their borders—especially if the EU manages to convince the United States and Switzerland to participate in the proposed cartel.

At this stage, it is not clear whether the EU will succeed. Austria, Belgium, and Luxembourg probably would like the initiative to die. Switzerland has not embraced the pro-

# THE SINGLE-MARKET TAX HARMONIZATION MYTH

European supporters of tax harmonization frequently assert that tax rates must be harmonized to permit the functioning of a single market. This is a rather odd claim. The United States has had a single market for more than 200 years, notwithstanding the vigorous tax competition that takes place between American states.

Critics may claim that state taxes are dwarfed by federal taxes, but this argument is not very convincing because states still account for one-third of government taxes and spending. Moreover, for much of U.S. history, the federal government was considerably smaller than the combined size of state and local governments.

**Note:** For more information, see Daniel J. Mitchell, "The Single-Market Tax Harmonization Myth," *Tax Notes International*, May 6, 2002, at *http://www.freedomandprosperity.org/articles/tni05-06-02.pdf.*

posal, and the Bush Administration already has announced that the United States does not support the savings tax directive.

The EU has responded to these obstacles by weakening its proposal. To appease Switzerland, the EU has offered to permit withholding tax regimes instead of automatic information-sharing of tax data. The EU also has tried to sidestep U.S. opposition by asserting that America already is in compliance—a rather odd claim since interest and capital gains paid to foreigners are neither taxed nor reported.[33]

Europe's high-tax nations may be fighting a losing battle. In May 2004, 10 new nations will join the EU. These countries include many jurisdictions with tax laws that are designed to boost growth and attract economic activity. Some of these new member nations, such as Slovakia, Lithuania, Estonia, and Latvia, have (or will have) flat tax regimes. Other new members, such as Hungary, Malta, Cyprus, and Slovenia, have elements of their tax systems that are very attractive (such as Hungary's 18 percent tax rate on corporate income). And more changes are on the way. Poland has announced that it will reduce its corporate rate to 19 percent, and the Czech Republic plans to lower its corporate tax rate to 24 percent.

Once these new nations are part of the EU, the competitive pressure on Europe's welfare states will increase because many investors and entrepreneurs will shift economic activity to take advantage of more favorable tax laws. Equally important, it will be much hard-

er for the EU to pursue additional tax harmonization schemes once 10 new nations have voting power. This is especially true if the national veto for tax matters is not eroded as part of the EU's constitutional deliberations.

## CONCLUSION

The battle between tax competition and tax harmonization is really a fight about whether government will control the factors of production. Supporters of tax harmonization would like to hinder the flow of workers and investments from high-tax nations to low-tax nations. The debate has focused primarily on capital, particularly on whether governments can track—and tax—flight capital; there are, however, even proposals that would allow government to tax the other factor of production—labor—when it crosses national borders.

Some assert that tax harmonization policies are needed to reduce evasion, but there are two ways to improve tax compliance. The international bureaucracies want to create a system of automatic and unlimited information exchange among governments—a system that former House Majority Leader Richard Armey (R–TX) said would create a "global network of tax police."[34] Fundamental tax reform, by contrast, would reduce incentives to evade while simultaneously reducing opportunities to evade (because capital income would be taxed at the source).

Ironically, the OECD's staff economists know the answer. They write that "legal tax avoidance can be reduced by closing loopholes

> The battle between tax competition and tax harmonization is really a fight about whether government will control the factors of production.

and illegal tax evasion can be contained by better enforcement of tax codes. But the root of the problem appears in many cases to be high tax rates."[35]

Ultimately, this is a debate about the size of government. Harmonization means higher tax rates and bigger government. Freed from the rigor of competition, politicians would cater to special interests and resist much-needed fiscal reforms. This is why the residents of high-tax nations have the most to lose if governments create an "OPEC for politicians."

Tax competition is the only realistic hope for German taxpayers, French taxpayers, and Swedish taxpayers. It is quite likely that politicians from those nations will be fiscally responsible only if they know that labor and capital have the right to escape fiscal oppression.

# Endnotes

1 Organisation for Economic Co-operation and Development, *Economic Outlook*, No. 63 (June 1998).

2 European Parliament, "Value Added Tax (VAT)," *Fact Sheet* No. 3.4.5, October 19, 2000, at *http://www.europarl.eu.int/factsheets/3_4_5_en.htm*.

3 For more information on information exchange and its harmful effects on economic growth, see Daniel J. Mitchell, "An OECD Proposal to Eliminate Tax Competition Would Mean Higher Taxes and Less Privacy," Heritage Foundation *Backgrounder* No. 1395, September 18, 2000, at *http://www.heritage.org/library/backgrounder/bg1395.html*.

4 The OECD is a Paris-based bureaucracy representing 30 industrialized nations. Most of its members are high-tax European nations. For the text of the OECD's report, *Harmful Tax Competition: An Emerging Global Issue*, see *http://www.oecd.org/daf/fa/harm_tax/Report_En.pdf*. Many people assume that so-called tax havens are money-laundering centers. Several government agencies and one international bureaucracy, however, have analyzed the problem of money laundering and have concluded unambiguously that low-tax jurisdictions are neither the source nor the destination for a disproportionate share of the world's "dirty" money. See Daniel J. Mitchell, "U.S. Government Agencies Confirm that Low-Tax Jurisdictions Are Not Money Laundering Havens," *Journal of Financial Crime*, Vol. 11, No. 2 (Fall 2003).

5 The European Union is a Brussels-based bureaucracy representing the 15-member European Community. For a description of the EU's "Savings Tax Directive," see *http://europa.eu.int/comm/taxation_customs/publications/official_doc/IP/ip011026/memo0 1266_en.pdf*.

6 The United Nations is based in New York and professes to represent the entire world. For the text of the UN proposal, see *http://www.un.org/esa/ffd/a55-1000.pdf*.

7 For more information on the UN scheme, see Daniel J. Mitchell, "United Nations Seeks Global Tax Authority," *Prosperitas*, Vol. I, No. II (August 2001), at *http://www.freedomandprosperity.org/Papers/un-report/un-report.shtml*.

8 It is possible that harmonization could be used to limit tax rates. In the European Union, for instance, value-added taxes may not exceed 25 percent.

9 European Parliament, "Personal and Company Taxation," *Fact Sheet* No. 3.4.8, October 19, 2000, at *http://www.europarl.eu.int/factsheets/3_4_8_en.htm*.

10 "International Commentary: Bully Europe," *The Wall Street Journal Europe*, March 6, 2001, at *http://www.freedomandprosperity.org/Articles/wsje03-06-01/wsje03-06-01.shtml*.

11 Therese Raphael, "Irish Economy Creates a Pot of Gold," *The Wall Street Journal*, December 30, 1998.

12 Researchers have discovered that tax competition is a primary cause of lower tax rates. See Michael P. Devereux, Ben Lockwood, and Michela Redoano, "Do Countries Compete Over Corporate Tax Rates?" mimeo, University of Warwick, 2002.

13 Jim Gwartney and Robert Lawson with Walter Park and Charles Skipton, *Economic Freedom of the World: 2001 Annual Report* (Vancouver: Fraser Institute, 2001); data retrieved from *http://www.freetheworld.com*.

14 For more information on the Reagan tax cuts, see Daniel J. Mitchell, "Lowering Marginal Tax Rates: The Key to Pro-Growth Tax Relief," Heritage Foundation *Backgrounder* No. 1443, May 22, 2001, at *http://www.heritage.org/Research/Taxes/BG1443.cfm*.

15 Willi Leibfritz, John Thornton, and Alexandra Bibbee, "Taxation and Economic Performance," Organisation for Economic Co-operation and Development, Economics Department, *Working Paper* No. 176, 1997.

16 Historical tax data provided by e-mail from the Economic and Budget Division of the Irish Finance Department, March 29, 2001.

17 For a thorough history of Irish economic reform, see James B. Burnham, "Why Ireland Boomed," *The Independent Review*, Vol. VII, No. 4 (Spring 2003), pp. 537–556, at *http://www.independent.org/tii/media/pdf/tir74burnham.pdf*.

18 Organisation for Economic Co-operation and Development, *OECD in Figures*, 2002, at *http://www1.oecd.org/publications/e-book/0102071E.PDF*.

19 Burnham, "Why Ireland Boomed."

20 Benjamin Powell, "Economic Freedom and Growth: The Case of the Celtic Tiger," *The Cato Journal*, Vol. 22, No. 3 (Winter 2003), at *http://www.cato.org/pubs/journal/cj22n3/cj22n3-3.pdf*.

21 Eric Engen and Kevin Hassett, "Does the Corporate Tax Have a Future?" *Tax Notes*, Spring 2003, at *http://www.aei.org/docLib/20021222_raengehass0212.pdf.*

22 "Eastern Tax Enlightenment," *The Wall Street Journal Europe*, July 7, 2003.

23 Alvin Rabushka, "The Flat Tax in Russia and the New Europe," National Center for Policy Analysis, *Brief Analysis* No. 452, September 3, 2003, at *http://www.ncpa.org/pub/ba/ba452/ba452.pdf.*

24 Republic of Serbia, Ministry of Finance and the Economy, Individual Income Tax Law, at *http://www.mfin.sr.gov.yu/html/modules.php?op=modload&name=Subjects&file=index&req=view-page&pageid=213.*

25 Gross national income per capita, 2002, Atlas Method, in World Bank, *World Development Indicators*, July 2003.

26 *Ibid.*

27 Alvin Rabushka, "The Flat Tax at Work in Russia: Year Two," *The Russian Economy*, February 18, 2003, at *http://www.russiaeconomy.org/comments/021803.html.*

28 Sabrina Tavernese, "Russia Imposes Flat Tax on Income, and Its Coffers Swell," *The New York Times*, March 23, 2002.

29 Alvin Rabushka, "The Flat Tax at Work in Russia: Year Three, January–June 2003," *The Russian Economy*, August 13, 2003, at *http://www.russiaeconomy.org/comments/081303.html.*

30 Gross national income per capita, 2002, Atlas Method, in World Bank, *World Development Indicators*, July 2003.

31 For more information on tax reform, see Daniel J. Mitchell, "Jobs, Growth, Freedom, and Fairness: Why America Needs a Flat Tax," Heritage Foundation *Backgrounder* No. 1035, May 25, 1995.

32 For a comprehensive analysis of this issue, see Daniel J. Mitchell, "Tax Reform: The Key to Preserving Privacy and Competition in the Global Economy," Institute for Policy Innovation, *Policy Report* No. 171, February 7, 2002, at *http://www.ipi.org/ipi/IPIPublications.nsf/PublicationLookupFullText/C9BD6A1A962A316D06256B590025A9A9.*

33 For more information on America's status as a tax haven, see Marshall Langer, "Who Are the Real Tax Havens," *Tax Notes International*, December 18, 2000, at Center for Freedom and Prosperity, *http://www.freedomandprosperity.org/Articles/tni12-18-00.pdf.* See also Daniel Mitchell, "The Adverse Impact of Tax Harmonization and Information Exchange on the U.S. Economy," *Prosperitas*, Vol. I, No. IV, November 2001, at *http://www.freedomandprosperity.org/Papers/taxharm/taxharm.shtml.*

34 Letter to Treasury Secretary Paul O'Neill, March 16, 2001, at *http://www.freedomandprosperity.org/ltr/armey/armey.shtml.*

35 Organisation for Economic Co-operation and Development, *Economic Outlook*, No 63 (June 1998).

Chapter 3

# Weighting the Components of the *Index of Economic Freedom*

## by Richard Roll

Every index attempts to capture unobservable attributes in a summary number by averaging measurements of observable, related numbers. A classic example is IQ, an index based on the fraction of correct answers from a standardized test. The unobservable attribute is a person's innate intelligence, and the observable numbers are the test answers. Many questions are administered because no single question is likely to measure intelligence perfectly. IQ tests weigh every question equally, but equal weighting need not provide the most precise index because some questions could reveal more about intelligence than others.

The Heritage Foundation faces a similar problem. Its *Index of Economic Freedom* is intended to capture, in a single number, the *actual* level of economic freedom in a country. Economic freedom is a conceptual attribute about which everyone has an intuitive notion, yet for which there is no obvious, universally accepted quantitative measure. Most would agree, however, that economic freedom is correlated with various indicators, such as strong property rights and low taxes, two attributes within the 10 Heritage ratings. But how should such indicators be weighted to obtain the most precise index?

For nine years, The Heritage Foundation has adopted the eminently sensible method of averaging its 10 country ratings equally to obtain the overall *Index* number for each country. But while this is a reasonable approach and there is no obviously superior procedure, there is also no evidence that equal weights are best. There is no *a priori* reason to think that foreign investment is more or less important than property rights to economic freedom or that monetary policy measures freedom more or less accurately than taxes. On the other hand, there seems every reason to think that some components, such as property rights, *might* be more closely related and more important to freedom than others.

Improving the precision of an index could seem a formidable problem; after all, the attribute being indexed is unobservable. Over the years, however, statisticians, psychologists, economists, and other social scientists have developed some highly effective methods for allowing the data themselves to speak about the best weighting scheme. Instead of imposing a number, the data point the researcher in the right direction.

The *Index of Economic Freedom* is intended to capture, in a single number, the actual level of economic freedom in a country.

These methods recognize that each component of an index captures (albeit imperfectly) an important aspect of the targeted attribute. In other words, each index component is correlated with the targeted attribute, though the degree of correlation probably varies across components. Presumably, both variability in the components and how they are related to each other contain information about how to construct an optimal index.

As an example, suppose we want to quantify the level of economic freedom in, say, 100 different countries and we possess ratings of property rights and informal market activity for each country on the same scale; e.g., 1 through 5 from best to worst. We notice that the informal market rating varies roughly twice as much across countries as the property rights rating. This greater variation in one component cannot be caused by cross-country variation in true economic freedom. Economic freedom varies the same for both components. Instead, the cause of the greater observed cross-country variation must be a larger measurement error in the informal market rating as compared to the property rights rating.

In other words, in this example, property rights are better correlated (more closely related) across countries with true economic freedom. If the mission were to construct an index of economic freedom with just the informal market and property rights ratings, the latter would properly be weighted more heavily.

The remaining question is how much *more* heavily property rights should be weighted in the index. It turns out there is a scientific answer to this question. The technical details are beyond the scope of this discussion, but the most accepted method for determining the weighting is called the method of "principal components." This method provides a set of weights that maximizes variation in the *Index* across countries and allows the clearest discrimination of economic freedom among the countries considered.

The method of principal components (PC) can detect more than a single unobserved attribute from a set of components. Consider the difference between economic freedom and political freedom. For example, Hong Kong under British rule had no elections but was one of the world's most economically free nations.

Perhaps property rights reflect both types of freedoms while voting rights are more political. Principal components could conceivably produce two indexes, one for political liberty and another for economic freedom; property rights and voting rights would both be weighted in each index, but differently weighted. Voting rights would have heavier weight in the Political Liberty Index and lower weight in the Economic Freedom Index. From the perspective of constructing the most precise Economic Freedom Index, the dependence of voting rights on political liberty represents a measurement error.

## AN ALTERNATIVE HERITAGE FOUNDATION *INDEX OF ECONOMIC FREEDOM*

This year, The Heritage Foundation asked me to examine this weightings issue to ascertain whether the *Index of Economic Freedom* could be improved. The question was, "Is equal weighting of the factors appropriate?" My charge was to answer by applying annually the method of principal components to the data. This process produces a set of component weights that effectively define an alternative Index. How closely the two indexes resemble each other reveals whether equal weighting is appropriate.

The *Index of Economic Freedom* has been published for nine years (1995–2003) and involves 10 different country attributes or factors. In the earlier years, some countries were missing certain ratings or were missing entirely, so the number of available countries ranged from 98 to 161 over the nine calendar years.

The chart on the next page plots the resulting principal components weights for each of the 10 factors for each of the nine years. These weightings can be compared against equal weights (the 10 percent line in the graph) for each of the 10 factors every year.

For most of the 10 factors, the PC weights are not very far from 10 percent (i.e., equal weighting). Moreover, although each year's computation was done independently, the weights are similar or stable within each rating category across the 10 years. The weights of capital flows, banking and finance, and property rights have trended slightly upward over the nine years, while the weight of monetary policy has trended modestly downward.

Some points of difference are as follows:

- Compared to equal weights, the following attributes are weighted more heavily in all years by the PC method: trade policy, monetary policy, property rights, and informal market activity.
- Compared to equal weights, the following attributes are weighted less heavily in all years by the PC method: fiscal burden, government intervention, and wages and prices.
- Compared to equal weights, the following attributes are weighted similarly by the PC method but exhibit some minor variation from year to year: capital flows, banking and finance, and regulation.

One can offer some conjectures on why the PC method weights some attributes more heavily and others less heavily. It seems intuitively plausible that property rights and informal market activity should be strongly correlated with economic freedom (the former positively and the latter negatively). It also seems that a higher fiscal burden and more government intervention can occur in both totalitarian and democratic countries, which suggests that the character of these factors is different from that of classic indicators of economic freedom such as strong property rights.

The Heritage fiscal burden attribute is particularly surprising. It is composed of four elements: the highest income tax rate, the average income tax rate, the corporate tax rate, and government expenditures as a share of GDP. Fiscal burden actually has negative weights under the PC method in most years, though they are very small in absolute magnitude. This suggests that a country's fiscal burden rating is virtually uncorrelated with the ratings in other categories.

Evidently, *some* high-tax/high-spending countries have strong property rights, etc., while other countries with strong property rights, etc., have low taxes and low spending. There is simply little connection between fiscal burden and everything else. Perhaps fis-

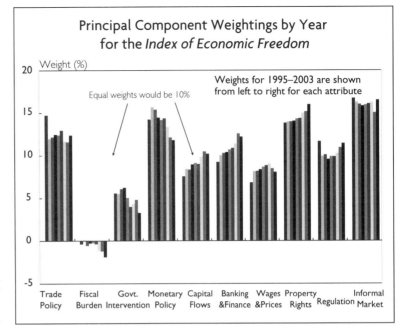

cal burden is a proxy for some characteristic *other* than economic freedom. Admittedly, this is not all that intuitive because high taxes are typically regarded, at least by the wealthy, as an infringement on freedom.

## DOES THE WEIGHTING SCHEME MAKE A MATERIAL DIFFERENCE?

Although the PC method produces weights similar to equal weights for many, but not all, country attributes, the bottom line is whether the two weighting schemes produce indexes with materially different country rankings of economic freedom.

A standard measure of how similar the PC and Heritage rankings are is the correlation across countries between the rankings in the two indexes in a given year. This correlation turns out to be very high; it is above 98 percent in the last seven of the nine sample years and is above 97 percent in 1995 and 1996. Such high correlation is a good argument in favor of preserving equal weights because they have the advantage of simplicity while also providing an accurate depiction of economic freedom.

The two alternative indexes do, however, generate somewhat different country rankings.[2] For example, in 2003, Guatemala moved down (had a lower index of economic freedom) by 32 positions when using the PC method compared to equal weighting. In the same year, Egypt moved up 26 positions in ranking. Quite a few countries changed in rank by at least 10 positions, though most countries moved less.

At the extremes, among the freest and the least free countries, there is some minor shuffling of position between the two indexes. For example, Hong Kong fell from first place under the equally weighted method to second place under the PC method in 1995, replaced at the top by Singapore. In 2003, Denmark rose from sixth to second, overtaking Singapore.

According to the equally weighted index, North Korea ranks last in every year. However, the PC method rated Libya as even worse in 1997–2001 and Cuba worse in 1997–1999.

## CONCLUSION

The equally weighted *Index* reported annually by The Heritage Foundation does, I believe, provide an accurate measure of economic freedom. Alternative weighting schemes produced by standard statistical methods induce some changes, particularly in country rankings, but the differences are minor. The gain in precision from non-equal weights seems hardly worth the complexity involved in computing them, not to mention their substantially greater opacity.

## Endnotes

1  The fiscal burden factor was re-evaluated separately. The new formulation makes more sense economically and eliminates the strange behavior noted in this chapter. For a brief description of the changes, see Chapter 5.

2  A technical paper with complete country rankings under both indexes is available from the author.

# Chapter 4

# The Common Agricultural Policy: How the European Union Distorts Trade with Non-EU Nations

## by Brian M. Carney

The European Union (EU)—or, more precisely, its predecessor, the European Economic Community (EEC)—was founded on the idea that war in Europe could be stopped through free trade and open borders. It is a cruel irony, therefore, that the EU in its various forms has spent most of its 46-year history waging economic war on others, and most particularly on the world's developing nations.

The predominant form that this warfare has taken is known as the Common Agricultural Policy, an anti-competitive combination of subsidies designed to give the European farmer an edge. Written into the EEC's founding documents in 1957, CAP was the price French President Charles de Gaulle exacted for France's membership. It has grown inexorably ever since and now eats up approximately half of the EU's 90 billion euro annual budget.

Nor does the cost to European taxpayers end with government-funded subsidies to farmers. CAP also entails market interventions and tariffs on imports, which keep the prices of most of the goods it subsidizes artificially high for consumers in Europe. This means Europeans pay for CAP twice—once at the supermarket and a second time at the

taxman's till. It is estimated that this double whammy costs the average European family of four some 1,200 euros a year, a socially regressive bill that hits Europe's least-well-off especially hard.

It may be surprising to learn that fully half of the funds spent each year by Brussels takes the form of handouts to farmers—that is, supports the CAP. Yet, apart from the direct costs of the EU subsidies, there is another cost that exacts a terrible toll on world economic prosperity and development. That is the cycle of global protectionism that EU agricultural policy perpetuates. CAP is harming European consumers and taxpayers, Europe's manufacturers and service providers, and—just as important—consumers in the developing world because it is a major stumbling block to further world trade liberalization, as was vividly demonstrated at the WTO ministerial meeting in Cancun in September 2003.

### A ROADBLOCK TO DOHA

The World Trade Organization launched a new round of trade liberalization talks in Doha, Qatar. At those meetings, developed countries acknowledged that by subsidizing

The EU in its various forms has spent most of its 46-year history waging economic war on others, and most particularly on the world's developing nations.

and protecting agriculture, they were blocking market access to the developing world's agricultural producers. They also made it clear that they wanted greater access to markets in the developing world.

On the other side of the table, developing countries suggested they would sign onto the idea of guaranteeing intellectual property rights protection and market access for manufacturing and services, but only if they won market access for their products in the developed world. Many developing countries feel they made concessions in the Uruguay WTO round but were not rewarded reciprocally by gaining market access in agriculture. At the Cancun ministerial, the developing world made agricultural liberalization—and actual cuts in rich-country subsidies to farmers—the keys to any deal, and the EU decided to walk away rather than countenance any real reductions in subsidies, bringing negotiations on a broader trade liberalization package to a halt.

The developing countries' emphasis on reciprocal liberalization—"I'll open my markets if you open yours"—makes little sense economically. Any country is better off with open markets regardless of whether its trading partners are protectionist or not, and the economic costs of tariffs and other trade barriers are always borne chiefly by the country that implements them, not by its trading partners. Politically, however, it may be nearly impossible to open Third World markets for European manufacturers and service providers without a *quid pro quo*. Practically speaking, therefore, the developed world has to reform its distorting subsidies in agriculture if world trade liberalization is to advance.

## ASTONISHING RESILIENCE

Of all the redistribution schemes that come from Brussels, CAP is easily the largest and most important. Its resilience is astonishing. Perhaps never before has a program that cost so much and harmed so many while helping so few persisted for so long.

When the Treaty of Rome that founded the European Economic Community was signed in 1957, 25 percent of the French workforce worked the land. De Gaulle

required assurance that trade liberalization among France, Germany, Italy, the Netherlands, Belgium, and Luxembourg (the six founding members of the EEC) would not hurt the interests of French farmers, so a resource-pooling scheme was devised. Farmers across the EEC would be subsidized from a common pool and according to common rules. This had the advantage of preventing a "subsidy war" between member states, in which countries that are unable to defend their agricultural sector from fellow members through tariffs or other trade barriers ratchet up direct support for farmers in response to perceived threats from their neighbors' own farm policies.

This threat is raised to this day in defense of CAP. The possibility of scrapping CAP and replacing it with nothing, as countries such as Australia and New Zealand have done to their benefit (and the benefit of their farmers), is dismissed out of hand.

The resilience of the Franco–German pact that gave birth to both the EEC, which would later become the EU, and CAP is remarkable, but in recent years it has become positively mind-boggling. Today, less than 5 percent of France's workforce remains on the farm, and those farmers produce some 2 percent of France's gross domestic product. Yet France continues to receive 9 billion euros a year in agricultural aid from Brussels, or about 20 percent of CAP's total budget.

Germany, meantime, remains the single largest net contributor to CAP. Yet, despite the occasional grumble about the need for reform, German Chancellor Gerhard Schröder has been a reliable ally of French President (and former Agriculture Minister) Jacques Chirac in standing athwart meaningful changes in the EU's agricultural subsidies.

In October 2002, on the eve of a summit of EU leaders to work out a framework budget for the post-enlargement EU, Chirac and Schröder announced a backroom deal to freeze CAP spending through the end of the EU's current budget cycle in 2006. Without the deal, CAP spending could have been put in play as the EU figured out how to pay for the accession of 10 new members in May 2004. The deal assured not only that France would continue to receive its farm subsidies through 2006, but also that between 2007 and 2014, CAP funding would continue to rise at the rate of inflation. This in effect foreclosed any reduction in overall farm spending even in the coming budget cycle, negotiations for which have not even officially started.

The deal was met with initial outrage from those cut out of the negotiations, but anger soon gave way to resignation, and the rest of the EU more or less acquiesced to the *fait accompli* by Paris and Berlin.

This act was repeated in June 2003, on the eve of another summit, this time to discuss a wide-ranging reform of CAP proposed by Franz Fischler, the EU's Agriculture Commissioner. Before that summit, Schröder once again agreed to support France in opposing meaningful reform. While Commissioner Fischler eventually got some of what he wanted, many of the proposed reforms were agreed to on a voluntary basis, meaning France can effectively opt out of the changes—exactly as it is expected to do.

Why Germany continues to bend to France's will 45 years after the initial deal was struck is an abiding mystery. But how the system works and its damaging effects on international trade are well-known even to its defenders.

## A CAP PRIMER

Prior to 1993, when the current cycle of reforms began, nearly the entire CAP budget was spent on three items: market interventions, export subsidies, and storage of surplus.

Market interventions were triggered by a floor price set in Brussels. If the price within the EU fell below the floor, the EU would step in to buy as much as necessary to bring the price back above the intervention price. This artificial price was always well above the prevailing world price for the product in question, keeping agricultural prices higher in Europe than elsewhere. This was essential to maintaining the viability of farming in many sectors because the EU is a high-cost producer of almost everything agricultural.

But the EU's high prices also meant that agricultural products could not be exported without farmers suffering a loss, so if a buyer could be found outside the EU, Brussels would compensate the farmer for the differ-

ence between the world price of a good and the internal EU price.

Because the EU was a massive buyer of domestic farm products, it had to store whatever products it bought until they could be resold. At its peak, this combination of policies led the EU to spend a full 17 percent of the CAP budget on storage for its famous "mountains" of butter and "lakes" of milk and wine.

Finally, all of this was held together, predictably, by high tariffs and low quotas on non-EU goods to minimize the effects of international competition on Europe's artificially high prices.

By the end of the 1990s, it was clear even in Brussels that the policy of guaranteeing above-market prices and subsidizing exports had led to massive overproduction in pursuit of subsidy, and a reform was attempted to bring agricultural practice back into line with economic reality. Since 1993, the EU has been moving toward a system of direct payment to farmers and retreating from its role as a market actor. This is supposed both to allow agricultural prices to fall without damaging farmers' incomes and to reduce the amount of goods the EU has to purchase directly.

In addition to the old system's manifest unsustainability, this change in tactics was driven as well by the then-ongoing Uruguay round of trade negotiations. As the EU likes to point out, the system put in place then helped bring the EU into compliance with Uruguay round commitments concerning which forms of subsidy were "trade distorting" and which were not.

Over the course of the 1990s, the percentage of the CAP budget spent on export subsidies fell to 14 percent from 33 percent, according to the commission's own numbers. This compliance has not led to an elimination of the distortions, however. Far from it.

For the past decade, Brussels has increasingly been paying farmers directly on the basis of what they produce but allowing them to sell what they can on the market. This is not a free market, however. Farmers in many crops are still guaranteed a minimum price and still rewarded for overproduction by increased production-linked payments.

By the end of the 1990s, it was clear even in Brussels that the policy of guaranteeing above-market prices and subsidizing exports had led to massive overproduction in pursuit of subsidy.

This distortion has led to the Fischler reforms of 2003, due to take effect in 2005 (although member states retain the option of putting them off for their own country until 2007). Franz Fischler's original proposal was to "decouple" subsidies from production, in effect paying farmers whether they produce crops and bring them to market or not. This was designed to encourage European farmers to match production to demand rather than chasing money from Brussels. The level of de-linked payment would be set based on how much a farm produced in the "reference years" of 2000–2002. Under French pressure at the June 2002 summit, this proposal was watered down so that only some of the aid would be decoupled from production, with the percentages varying somewhat from crop to crop and certain sensitive crops excluded altogether. But even this rather Byzantine attempt to get around the problem of paying for overproduction is likely to fail.

## A SWEET DEAL FOR FARMERS

To understand how the current system works—and why it is likely that the latest reform will fail to eliminate the distortions—take the example of sugar (which is excluded from the 2003 reforms). The EU likes to trumpet that it is the world's biggest importer of sugar, and this is true; but it is also the biggest exporter. Europe's overproduction of sugar keeps world prices 30 percent–40 percent lower than they would otherwise be, according to some estimates. Not that Europeans benefit from these low prices: The price of sugar in the EU—a price guaranteed by Brussels—is fixed at a level 200 percent–300 percent above the world price. This odd fact is the direct result of the EU's subsidy regime.

Commissioner Fischler likes to paint opposition to CAP as restricted to some zealous free-market fringe, but this is far from the truth. In 2003, for example, Oxfam issued *The Great EU Sugar Scam*, a scathing report on the EU's sugar subsidy regime in which the organization contends that "nothing more powerfully demonstrates the insanity of the CAP than sugar." Oxfam's report explains how the EU, despite being perhaps the world's highest-cost producer of sugar, came

to be its largest exporter as well, dumping mountains of sugar on world markets.

In 2001, the EU produced 17 million tons of sugar domestically and imported a further 2.3 million tons. Most of those imports come from former colonies that are allotted special quotas under which they can sell raw sugar into the EU at Europe's inflated prices. 12.7 million tons were consumed domestically, and the remaining 7 million tons were then dumped on the world market at a price about 60 percent below the EU's guaranteed minimum price, which is over $600 per ton. Of those exports, 3.1 million tons were eligible for export subsidies to make up the full difference between the world price and the EU price. The remainder was sold at the world price (around $300 per ton in 2001) without export subsidy. These unsubsidized exports are made possible because the subsidized production helps Europe's sugar beet farmers cover their fixed costs and allows them to profit from even unsubsidized exports.

In 2000, the Institute for Economic Affairs (IEA) in London published a report titled "Global Economic Effects of the EU Common Agricultural Policy." Using a computer-driven economic model to calculate the trade-distorting effects of European agricultural subsidies, the authors estimated that eliminating Europe's sugar subsidies would increase the EU's sugar imports by some 7 million tons (in other words, the EU would import substantially *all* of its annual sugar consumption), while its exports would basically disappear. The result, according to the authors of the study, would be an increase of between 30 percent and 38 percent in the world price of sugar even as the price of sugar in the EU was cut by half.

In order to sustain a domestic sugar industry, the EU fixes the price of sugar internally and keeps out imports through quotas and high tariffs. But even these high walls fail to keep the EU's subsidies from disrupting international trade in sugar. The amount of sugar for which the EU guarantees both a minimum price and a fixed export subsidy is capped at a level approximately equal to the EU's annual sugar consumption. Yet, despite this cap, the EU still produces some 7 million

The EU, despite being perhaps the world's highest-cost producer of sugar, came to be its largest exporter as well, dumping mountains of sugar on world markets.

tons of sugar each year beyond what it actually needs.

## A REFORM THAT WASN'T

In other words, eliminating or capping production-linked subsidies is not enough to ensure that production matches demand within the EU; whatever the WTO's rules may say, the mere existence of an industry sustained entirely by subsidy is in itself trade-distorting.

Moreover, this is not just internally relevant. As Paul Goodison of the European Research Office in Brussels notes in his 2001 report "The Future of CAP," even direct payments decoupled from production (a goal that is realized only partially in most agricultural sectors and not at all in sugar) help to maintain whole industries that then become potential exporters on the world market. They also foreclose potential imports into Europe from the developing world by allowing farmers to sell crops below their actual cost. This does allow prices in the EU to drop toward prevailing commodity prices, but it also boosts production in ways that cannot but distort.

This is of vital interest to the developing world, much of which depends heavily on the exporting of agricultural products—but has been prevented from exporting these products to some of the world's biggest markets both by CAP and by agricultural protectionism in the U.S. On this point, Commissioner Fischler acknowledges that EU policies have been destructive, but his response has been sanguine if not downright callous. "It is every country's right to respect the sustainability of agriculture, and environmental, food quality and animal-welfare objectives which cannot be reached via market forces alone," he wrote in *The Wall Street Journal* in July 2003. This is Brussels-speak for "We can't be bothered to worry about whether we are destroying the economies of some of the poorest countries in the world."

The EU has, it is true, taken some steps to facilitate market access for poorer countries. The 2.3 million tons of sugar the EU imports annually comes in mostly under a deal struck in the 1970s to allow former colonies of EU countries to maintain their historical trade ties with Europe. But as the IEA paper on CAP's trade distortions points out, this arrangement is itself distorting; the countries that "benefit" from it have cost structures in the sugar industry similar to Europe's, just as the guarantee of above-market prices has also encouraged inefficiency in the exporting countries.

Moreover, the 2001 "Everything But Arms" initiative that the EU likes to trot out as proof of its commitment to the world's 49 "least developed countries" (LDCs) largely excludes sugar until at least 2009. In the meantime, limited imports are allowed under the program, but the quotas assigned to the LDCs come at the expense of other countries' (the ex-colonies') quotas, so the total amount of imports between now and 2009 remains unchanged.

In both cases, the imports are limited to raw sugar, foreclosing the possibility of developing (or using) higher-value-added industries such as refining (or branding) their sugar. That remains the exclusive domain of Europe's largely monopolistic refining industry, which benefits from fixed costs of purchasing and guaranteed minimum resale prices as part of CAP's sugar regime.

This is particularly egregious, as protecting the EU's refiners cannot be excused with any of the standard European agricultural justifications—protecting the countryside, environmental protection, etc.—that are normally put forward in defense of CAP. All it does is provide a steady and profitable business for the monopolists it shelters.

## PROTECTING THE PAST

Paul Johnson, in his history of Europe, *Modern Times*, explains the birth of CAP. At the heart of the EEC, according to Johnson, was a compact between the French and the Germans; France would open its markets to German industrial goods, and Germany in turn would bankroll French agriculture. This view of things has the advantage of throwing into stark relief an essential truth about Europe's 50-year-long road toward internal trade liberalization: At every step along the way, progress has been made only when every side could be assured that what

Whatever the WTO's rules may say, the mere existence of an industry sustained entirely by subsidy is in itself trade-distorting.

already existed would not undergo change—in other words, that the status quo would remain untouched.

This reflects the sad truth that at the heart of Europe's great experiment in trade liberalization, guarantees that liberalization would not disrupt traditional industries and ways of life have always been the norm. It is not for nothing that close to 90 percent of the EU's budget is spent not on enforcing the voluminous body of law that is supposed to guarantee fair play among its members, but on redistributing wealth among those members. Often, as with CAP, this is done not in the name of competition, but with the express purpose of reducing or eliminating it, and thereby attenuating the promise of free trade even within the EU.

But while the EU bears most of the cost of its own agricultural protectionism in absolute terms, in relative terms the deleterious effects on the prosperity of non-EU nations that are its trading partners, and on Europe's more competitive industries that are reciprocally blocked from international markets, are far greater. Cane sugar, which can be produced more cheaply and efficiently than Europe's beet sugar, is a tropical crop. It is, therefore, potentially one of huge economic importance to some of the world's poorest countries, many of which lie in climates, unlike Europe's, that are well-suited to its production. European manufacturers and consumers in the underdeveloped world are also harmed by the fact that CAP is met with Third World protectionism in retaliation.

## OUTLOOK

Europe has come under pressure recently to reform its ways. The 2003 reform was motivated in part by a desire to give the EU room to maneuver in the Doha round of WTO negotiations, just as the so-called McSharry reforms in 1992 were in part the result of the pressures of the Uruguay round. But the outcome of the Cancun ministerial made it clear that the "flexibility" offered by the Fischler reforms was not nearly good enough to satisfy the developing world that Europe is serious about agricultural reform. The poor countries that are most dependent on agriculture want to see actual reductions in European and U.S. farm subsidies, not just a shifting of funds from one form of support for farmers to another.

Given Europe's long budgeting cycles for agriculture, as well as the staunch unwillingness of France to contemplate further reform before 2007 at the earliest (and quite possibly through 2013, the end of the *next* CAP budget cycle), the near-term prospects for major change look bleak. To date, each reform proposal has merely found ways to shift around the money given to Europe's farmers, and many of the changes have resulted in major *increases* in payments to certain sectors to compensate for the loss or reduction of price floors and other indirect forms of aid.

But Europe has long fancied itself a champion of the world's poor, and it is perhaps here that the greatest leverage can be applied. A freer world trading system in agriculture might both offer evidence of the potential benefits to the developing world and serve to increase the pressure on Europe not to undercut those countries by dumping its surpluses abroad.

A system that has lasted this long for the benefit of so few is not likely to go down without a fight now, but the Soviet Union eventually collapsed under its own weight. The Common Agricultural Policy may yet do so too.

The poor countries that are most dependent on agriculture want to see actual reductions in European and U.S. farm subsidies, not just a shifting of funds from one form of support for farmers to another.

# Chapter 5

# Explaining the Factors of the *Index of Economic Freedom*

## by William W. Beach and Marc A. Miles

Since 1995, the *Index of Economic Freedom* has offered the international community an annual in-depth examination of the factors that contribute most directly to economic freedom and prosperity. As the first comprehensive study of economic freedom ever published, the 1995 *Index* defined the method by which economic freedom can be measured in such vastly different places as Hong Kong and North Korea. Since then, other studies have joined the effort, analyzing such issues as trade or government intervention in the economy.[1]

There is overlapping coverage among these indices, but the *Index of Economic Freedom* includes the broadest array of institutional factors determining economic freedom:

- **Corruption** in the judiciary, customs service, and government bureaucracy;
- **Non-tariff barriers to trade,** such as import bans and quotas as well as strict labeling and licensing requirements;
- **The fiscal burden of government,** which encompasses income tax rates, corporate tax rates, and trends in government expenditures as a percent of output;
- **The rule of law,** efficiency within the judiciary, and the ability to enforce contracts;

- **Regulatory burdens** on business, including health, safety, and environmental regulation;
- **Restrictions on banks** regarding financial services, such as selling securities and insurance;
- **Labor market regulations,** such as established work weeks and mandatory separation pay; and
- **Informal market activities,** including corruption, smuggling, piracy of intellectual property rights, and the underground provision of labor and other services.

Analyzing economic freedom annually permits the authors of the *Index* to include the most recent information on these factors as it becomes available country by country. Not surprisingly, changes in government policy are occurring at a rapid rate in many less-developed countries. The *Index of Economic Freedom*, because it is published each year, enables readers around the world to see how recent changes in government policy affect economic freedom in any one of 161 specific countries. The historical score graph on each country page also permits readers to discriminate among those countries where economic freedom and opportunities are expanding and those where they are not. (This year, numerical grading was suspended for six countries: Angola, Burundi, Democratic Republic of Congo, Iraq, Sudan, all five of which are in a state of civil unrest or anarchy, and Serbia–Montenegro, for which data necessary to grade the country are not available. Information is provided, however, even for these countries.)

## MEASURING ECONOMIC FREEDOM

Economic freedom is defined as *the absence of government coercion or constraint on the production, distribution, or consumption of goods and services beyond the extent necessary for citizens to protect and maintain liberty itself.* In other words, people are free to work, produce, consume, and invest in the ways they feel are most productive.

All government action involves coercion. Some minimal coercion is necessary for the citizens of a community or nation to defend themselves, promote the evolution of civil society, and enjoy the fruits of their labor. This Lockean idea was embodied in the U.S. Constitution. For example, citizens are taxed to provide revenue for the protection of person and property as well as for a common defense. Most political theorists also accept that certain goods—what economists call "public goods"—can be supplied most conveniently by government.

When government coercion rises beyond that minimal level, however, it risks trampling on freedom. When it starts interfering in the market beyond the protection of person and property, it risks undermining economic freedom. Exactly where that line is crossed is open to reasoned debate. The goal in the scoring of economic freedom is not to define these extremes—either anarchy or utopia—but to describe the world's economies as they are.

Throughout history, governments have imposed a wide array of constraints on economic activity. Many constraints can be measured by assessing the impact on economic choices. Constraining economic choice distorts and diminishes the production, distribution, and consumption of goods and services (including, of course, labor services).[2]

One fact is overridingly true: When governments restrict people, their behavior changes, and probably not for the best. Coercion alters choices that ordinary people make. Economic freedom is diminished, and economic growth suffers.

To measure economic freedom and rate each country, the authors of the *Index* study 50 independent economic variables. These variables fall into 10 broad categories, or factors, of economic freedom:

- Trade policy,
- Fiscal burden of government,
- Government intervention in the economy,
- Monetary policy,
- Capital flows and foreign investment,
- Banking and finance,
- Wages and prices,
- Property rights,
- Regulation, and
- Informal market activity.

A detailed discussion of each of these factors and their component variables follows this overview.

**Weighting.** In the *Index of Economic Freedom*, all 10 factors are equally important to the level of economic freedom in any country. Thus, to determine a country's overall score, the factors are weighted equally.

This is a common-sense approach. It is also consistent with the purpose of the *Index*: to reflect the economic environment in every country. The *Index* is not designed to measure how much each factor adds to economic growth; that is ably done in the many empirical studies of economic growth. Rather, the authors of the *Index* identify institutional factors that, taken together, determine the degree of economic freedom in a society. It is this institutional environment that allows economies to grow.

While our approach appeals to common sense, some recent research on the determinants of growth indicates that some factors are statistically more important than others. In Chapter 3 of this year's *Index*, however, Professor Richard Roll illustrates that equally weighting the *Index* factors reveals as true a picture of economic freedom in a country as the best weighting system that statistics can devise.[3] In any event, it is clear that for a country to succeed in achieving long-term growth and economic well-being, it must perform well in *all 10* factors.

**The Grading Scale.** Each country receives its overall economic freedom score based on the simple average of the 10 individual factor scores. Each factor is graded according to a unique scale. The scales run from 1 to 5: A score of 1 signifies an economic environment or set of policies that are most conducive to economic freedom, while a score of 5 signifies a set of policies that are least conducive to economic freedom.

In addition, following each factor score is a description—"better," "worse," or "stable"—to indicate, respectively, whether that factor of economic freedom has improved, worsened, or stayed the same compared with the country's score last year.

Finally, the 10 factors are added and averaged, and an overall score is assigned to the country.

The four broad categories of economic freedom in the *Index* are:

- **Free**—countries with an average overall score of 1.99 or less;
- **Mostly Free**—countries with an average overall score of 2.00 to 2.99;
- **Mostly Unfree**—countries with an average overall score of 3.00 to 3.99; and
- **Repressed**—countries with an average overall score of 4.00 or higher.

**Previous Scores.** The *Index of Economic Freedom* includes a comprehensive listing of 161 countries with their scores for each of the 10 factors. This year, each country's section also includes a graph of its overall score for each year the country has been graded since 1995. With this history, readers can easily discern whether a country's economic freedom has improved or diminished over time, or simply become stuck in the mud.

**Transparency.** The authors endeavor to make their scoring as transparent as possible to the reader. This chapter explains why each factor is an important element of economic freedom, how the five levels of economic freedom are broken down and scored, and what sources of data and information were used for this analysis.

Factor scoring is straightforward and consistent across countries. If a country's banking system received a score of 3, for example, this means that its banking and financial system displays most of the characteristics for level 3, which are spelled out on page 61: The government exercises substantial influence on banks; the government owns or operates some banks; the government significantly influences credit allocation; and there are significant barriers to the formation of domestic banks. Similarly, a country receiving a score of 5 in trade policy has the characteristics explained on page 53: either an average tariff rate that is greater than 19 percent or a lower tariff but very high nontariff barriers that, for all practical purposes, close its markets to imports.

**Period of Study.** For the *2004 Index of Economic Freedom*, the authors generally examined data for the period covering the second half of 2002 through the first half of 2003. To the extent possible, the information considered for each factor was current as of June 30, 2003.

It is important to understand, however, that some factors are based on historical information. For example, the monetary policy factor is a 10-year weighted average inflation rate from January 1, 1993, to December 31, 2002. Other factors are current for the year in which the *Index* is published. For example, the taxation variable for this *Index* considers tax rates that apply to the taxable year 2003.

Occasionally, because the *Index* is published several months after the cutoff date for evaluation, major economic events occur that cannot be factored into the scores. In the past, such occurrences have been uncommon and isolated to one region of the world. The Asian financial crisis, for example, erupted as the *1998 Index of Economic Freedom* was ready to go to print. As a result, the effects of policy changes in response to that crisis were not considered in that year's scoring; however, they were considered in later editions. In the country write-ups, the authors and editors also note major events that might have a substantial impact on a country's score in the future.

**Sources.** In evaluating the criteria for each factor, the authors have used a range of authoritative sources. For example, a statement about the level of corruption in a country's customs service may be followed by a supporting quote from a source of demonstrated reliability. There also are innumerable lesser sources of information, including conversations with government officials and visits to Internet sites. These sources are indicated in the narrative where appropriate. It would be unnecessarily cumbersome to cite all the sources used in scoring every single variable of each factor; therefore, unless otherwise noted, the major sources used in preparing the country summaries may be found below, in the introduction to Chapter 6, and in the list of Major Works.

## A SUMMARY OF FACTOR VARIABLES

To grade each country's level of economic freedom for the *Index*, the authors examined 50 independent variables. The information collected was analyzed to determine for each of the 10 factors which of the five grade levels most closely resembles that country's environment. Even though all of the variables were studied, not all are given an individual score or specific mention in the text. For example, it is not necessary to mention cases in which corruption in the judiciary is virtually nonexistent; in general, it is necessary to discuss judicial corruption only when it is a documented problem.

In other words, what is most important is accurately grading each of the 10 broad factors of economic freedom, not necessarily each of the 50 variables, of the 155 countries that are scored in this year's edition. Such a system keeps the *Index* to a manageable length. The independent variables used to evaluate each factor are summarized in the callout box within the factor's description.

## FACTORS OF ECONOMIC FREEDOM

### Factor #1: Trade Policy

 Trade policy is a key factor in measuring economic freedom. The degree to which government hinders access to and the free flow of foreign

commerce can have a direct bearing on the ability of individuals to pursue their economic goals.

For example, when a government directly taxes the importation of a product through tariffs, or impedes it through non-tariff barriers, incentives are distorted. Some group of people in that country now have an incentive to produce that product instead of another one they may be better suited to produce. The import limitation reduces opportunities or economic freedom by discouraging individuals from applying their talents and skills in a manner that they know or believe will be better for them. In addition, it limits consumers' choices, thereby also limiting their well-being.

**Methodology.** The trade policy score is based on a country's weighted average tariff rate—weighted by imports from the country's trading partners. The higher the rate, the worse (or higher) the score. Gathering data on tariffs to make a consistent cross-country comparison can be a challenging task. Unlike data on inflation, for instance, countries do not report their weighted average tariff rate or simple average tariff rate every year; in some cases, the last time a country reported its tariff data could have been as far back as 1993. To preserve consistency in grading the trade policy factor, the authors have decided to use the most recently reported weighted average tariff rate for a country from our primary source. If another reliable source reports more updated information on the country's tariff rate, the authors note this fact and may review the grading of this factor if there is strong evidence that the last reported weighted average tariff rate is outdated.

The World Bank produces the world's most comprehensive and consistent information on weighted average applied tariff rates. When the weighted average applied tariff rate is not available, the authors utilize the country's applied average tariff rate; and when the country's average applied tariff rate is not available, the authors utilize the weighted average or the simple average of most favored nation (MFN) tariff rates.[4] If neither applied tariff nor MFN tariff data are available, the

## Trade Policy Grading Scale

| Score | Levels of Protectionism | Criteria |
|---|---|---|
| 1 | Very low | Weighted average tariff rate less than or equal to 4 percent. |
| 2 | Low | Weighted average tariff rate greater than 4 percent but less than or equal to 9 percent. |
| 3 | Moderate | Weighted average tariff rate greater than 9 percent but less than or equal to 14 percent. |
| 4 | High | Weighted average tariff rate greater than 14 percent but less than or equal to 19 percent. |
| 5 | Very high | Weighted average tariff rate greater than 19 percent. |

authors base their grading on the revenue raised from tariffs and duties as a percentage of total imports of goods. The data for customs revenues and total imports may not be consolidated in just one source. In addition, in the very few cases in which data on duties and customs revenues are not available, the authors use data on international trade taxes instead. In all cases, the authors clarify the type of data used and the different sources for those data in the corresponding write-up for the trade policy factor. Sometimes, when none of this information is available, the authors simply analyze the overall tariff structure and estimate an effective tariff rate.

Tariffs, however, are not the only barriers to trade. Many countries impose import quotas, licensing requirements, and other mandates—known collectively as non-tariff barriers (NTBs)—to restrict imports. The trade analysis also considers corruption within the customs service. This is an important consideration because, even though countries may have low published tariff rates and no official NTBs, their customs officials may be corrupt and may require bribes to allow products to enter their ports. Alternatively, customs officials may steal goods for themselves, creating a cost or barrier to trade.

The circumstances are analyzed and documented whenever possible. If NTBs

## Variables for Factor #1

• Weighted average tariff rate
• Non-tariff barriers
• Corruption in the customs service

exist in sufficient quantity, or if there is ample evidence of corruption, a country's score based solely on tariff rates receives an additional point on the scale (representing decreased economic freedom).

**Sources.** Unless otherwise noted, the authors used the following sources to determine scores for trade policy, in order of priority: World Bank, *World Development Indicators 2003*; World Trade Organization, *Trade Policy Reviews*, 1995 to June 2003; and official government publications of each country.

For all the European Union countries, the authors have based the score on data reported by the World Bank; Office of the U.S. Trade Representative, *2003 National Trade Estimate Report on Foreign Trade Barriers*; U.S. Department of State, *Country Commercial Guide*,[5] 2002 and 2003; Economist Intelligence Unit, *Country Report* and *Country Commerce*, 2003; and International Monetary Fund, *Government Finance Statistics Yearbook 2002* and *International Financial Statistics Online*.

# Individual Income Tax Grading Scale

This scale lists a score from 1 through 5. The higher the tax rate, the higher the score.

| Score | Tax Rates | Criteria |
|-------|-----------|----------|
| 1 | Very low | Top marginal income tax rate less than 10 percent. |
| 1.5 | Low | Top marginal income tax rate equal to or greater than 10 percent and less than 20 percent. |
| 2 | Low | Top marginal income tax rate equal to or greater than 20 percent and less than 25 percent. |
| 2.5 | Moderate | Top marginal income tax rate equal to or greater than 25 percent and less than 30 percent. |
| 3 | Moderate | Top marginal income tax rate equal to or greater than 30 percent and less than 35 percent. |
| 3.5 | High | Top marginal income tax rate equal to or greater than 35 percent and less than 40 percent. |
| 4 | High | Top marginal income tax rate equal to or greater than 40 percent and less than 45 percent. |
| 4.5 | Very high | Top marginal income tax rate equal to or greater than 45 percent and less than 50 percent. |
| 5 | Very high | Top marginal income tax rate equal to or greater than 50 percent. |

## Factor #2: Fiscal Burden of Government

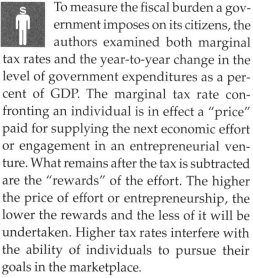 To measure the fiscal burden a government imposes on its citizens, the authors examined both marginal tax rates and the year-to-year change in the level of government expenditures as a percent of GDP. The marginal tax rate confronting an individual is in effect a "price" paid for supplying the next economic effort or engagement in an entrepreneurial venture. What remains after the tax is subtracted are the "rewards" of the effort. The higher the price of effort or entrepreneurship, the lower the rewards and the less of it will be undertaken. Higher tax rates interfere with the ability of individuals to pursue their goals in the marketplace.

The year-to-year change in the share of output diverted to government expenditures captures the incremental increase or decrease of the true cost of government in a society. When a government expends money, it acquires resources, diverting them away from potentially more productive private choices and goals. This is true whether the expenditure is to acquire resources for its own purposes (government consumption) or for transfer payments among citizens. As a government increases (decreases) its expenditures, it necessarily reduces (increases) the level of economic freedom in a society.

The government's need to finance these year-to-year changes in expenditures creates a burden. The choice is whether to tax the public now or in the future. No matter how a given level of government expenditure is financed—by current taxation, or future (debt issuance or money creation), or varying amounts of each—resources are going to be diverted from the private sector. Hence, the expenditures reflect the total fiscal burden.

# Corporate Tax Grading Scale

This scale lists a score from 1 through 5. The higher the tax rate, the higher the score.

| Score | Tax Rates | Criteria |
|---|---|---|
| 1 | Very low | Top marginal corporate tax rate less than 15 percent. |
| 1.5 | Low | Top marginal corporate tax rate equal to or greater than 15 percent and less than 18 percent. |
| 2 | Low | Top marginal corporate tax rate equal to or greater than 18 percent and less than 21 percent. |
| 2.5 | Moderate | Top marginal corporate tax rate equal to or greater than 21 percent and less than 24 percent. |
| 3 | Moderate | Top marginal corporate tax rate equal to or greater than 24 percent and less than 27 percent. |
| 3.5 | High | Top marginal corporate tax rate equal to or greater than 27 percent and less than 30 percent |
| 4 | High | Top marginal corporate tax rate equal to or greater than 30 percent and less than 33 percent. |
| 4.5 | Very high | Top marginal corporate tax rate equal to or greater than 33 percent and less than 36 percent. |
| 5 | Very high | Top marginal corporate tax rate equal to or greater than 36 percent. |

This perspective underlies Milton Friedman's belief that government expenditures are the most complete measure of a state's burden on the economy. Government expenditures capture the possibility of spending in excess of tax revenues, financed either by increased borrowing or by the printing of money, which imposes further costs on an economy.[6]

**Methodology.** The score for the fiscal burden of government has three components: the top marginal income tax rate, the top marginal corporate tax rate, and the year-to-year change in government expenditures as a share of GDP. The authors followed several steps in scoring this factor. First, a country's individual income tax score was assigned a score between 1 and 5 based on the top marginal income tax rate (see table on page 54). Second, a country's corporate tax score was assigned a score between 1 and 5 based on the top marginal

## Variables for Factor #2

- Top marginal income tax rate
- Top marginal corporate tax rate
- Year-to-year change in government expenditures as a percent of GDP

corporate tax rate (see table on page 55). Third, a country was assigned a score between 1 and 5 based on the year-to-year change in government expenditures as a percent of GDP (see table on page 56).

The authors then calculated a weighted average of the three components of the fiscal burden of government factor to arrive at a final score. The top income tax rate was assigned a 25 percent weight, the top corporate tax rate a 50 percent weight, and the year-to-year change in the share of government expenditures a 25 percent weight. The authors conducted a statistical analysis of the relationship between the individual components of the fiscal burden factor and the overall level of economic freedom and found that the correlation between the top corporate tax rate and overall economic freedom was about twice as great as the correlation between economic freedom and either the top income tax rate or the year-to-year change in government spending as a share of GDP. Thus, the authors chose to place the double weight on the top corporate tax rate.

**Sources.** Unless otherwise noted, the authors used the following sources for information on taxation, in order of priority: Ernst & Young, *2003 The Global Executive* and *2003 Worldwide Corporate Tax Guide*; International Monetary Fund, Staff Country Report, *Selected Issues and Statistical Appendix*, 2000 to 2003; Economist Intelligence Unit, *Country Commerce*, *Country Profile*, and *Country Report*, 2002 and 2003; U.S. Department of State,

*Country Commercial Guide*,[7] 2002 and 2003; and official government publications of each country. Sources other than Ernst & Young are noted in the text.

For information on government expenditures, the authors' primary sources were Organisation for Economic Co-operation and Development data (for member countries); International Monetary Fund, *Government Finance Statistics Yearbook for 2002*, and International Monetary Fund, Staff Country Report, *Selected Issues and Statistical Appendix*, 2000 to 2003; Asian Development Bank, *Key Indicators 2002: Population and Human Resource Trends and Challenges*; African Development Bank, *African Indicators: Selected Statistics on African Countries—2003*; European Bank for Reconstruction and Development, *Country Strategies*; U.S. Department of State, *Country Commercial Guide*,[8] 2002 and 2003; and official government publications of each country. Sources other than the OECD and the IMF are noted in the text.

## Change in Government Expenditures Scale

This scale lists a score from 1 through 5. The more the level of government expenditures as a percent of GDP increases, the higher the score.

| Score | Year-to year Change in Government Expenditures as Percent of GDP | Criteria |
| --- | --- | --- |
| 1 | Very high decrease | Equal to or greater than −4 percent. |
| 1.5 | High decrease | Equal to or greater than −3 percent and less than −4 percent. |
| 2 | Moderate decrease | Equal to or greater than −2 percent and less than −3 percent. |
| 2.5 | Low decrease | Equal to or greater than −1 percent and less than −2 percent. |
| 3 | Very low decrease | Equal to or greater than 0 percent and less than −1 percent. |
| 3.5 | Low increase | Greater than 0 percent and less than or equal to 1 percent. |
| 4 | Moderate increase | Greater than 1 percent and less than or equal to 2 percent. |
| 4.5 | High increase | Greater than 2 percent and less than or equal to 3 percent. |
| 5 | Very high increase | Greater than 3 percent. |

## Government Consumption Grading Scale

This scale lists a score from 1 through 5. The higher the level of government consumption as a percent of GDP, the higher the score.

| Score | Level of Government Consumption in the Economy | Criteria |
|---|---|---|
| 1 | Very low | Less than or equal to 5 percent of GDP. |
| 2 | Low | Greater than 5 percent but less than or equal to 10 percent of GDP. |
| 3 | Moderate | Greater than 10 percent but less than or equal to 20 percent of GDP. |
| 4 | High | Greater than 20 percent but less than or equal to 40 percent of GDP. |
| 5 | Very high | Greater than 40 percent of GDP. |

## Factor #3: Government Intervention in the Economy

 This factor measures government's direct use of scarce resources for its own purposes and government's control over resources through ownership. The measure comprises both government consumption and government production. Transfer payments (the difference between government expenditure and government consumption), which consist of compulsory exchange of the rights to resources from the Peters to the Pauls, are excluded from this measure.

Government consumption totals net purchases of goods, services, and structures (for example, bridges and buildings); wages paid to government employees; net purchases of fixed assets; and inventory changes in government enterprises.[9] Government production is described below. The government intervention factor is distinct from government's regulatory role and complements the measure of fiscal burden.[10]

**Methodology.** Government consumption as a percentage of GDP is evaluated separately from government production. First, the level of government intervention in the economy is determined. The higher the rate of government consumption as a percentage of GDP,

### Variables for Factor #3

• Government consumption as a percentage of the economy
• Government ownership of businesses and industries
• Share of government revenues from state-owned enterprises and government ownership of property
• Economic output produced by the government

the more resources the government is pulling from the private or free market and, therefore, the lower its level of economic freedom and the higher its *Index* score (lower ranking).

Governments intervene in the economy not only by consuming scarce resources, but also to engage in business activities that generally could be carried out more efficiently in the private sector. Governments that operate state-owned enterprises crowd out private initiative and investment, and the resultant inefficiency deters economic growth. Economic freedom and the economy suffer. The authors measure the size of the state-owned sector using the share of revenues a country receives from both state-owned enterprises and government-owned property.

# Share of Revenues from State-Owned Enterprises and Property

This scale lists a score from 1 through 5. The higher the share of revenues from state-owned enterprises as a percent of total government revenues, the higher the score.

| Score | Share of Revenues Received from State-Owned Enterprises and Property | Criteria |
| --- | --- | --- |
| 1 | Very low | Less than or equal to 5 percent of GDP. |
| 2 | Low | Greater than 5 percent but less than or equal to 10 percent of GDP. |
| 3 | Moderate | Greater than 10 percent but less than or equal to 20 percent of GDP. |
| 4 | High | Greater than 20 percent but less than or equal to 40 percent of GDP. |
| 5 | Very high | Greater than 40 percent of GDP. |

Grading employs two tables that assign one score for each level of government consumption as a percentage of GDP and one score for each level of the share of revenues from state-owned enterprises and property. The two scores are then averaged to obtain the final government intervention score for each country.

The main source for revenues from state-owned enterprises is the International Monetary Fund's *Government Finance Statistics Yearbook*. When these data are not available, the authors rely on the country's Economic or Finance Minister's Web site, the International Monetary Fund's statistical appendix, or the country's embassy in the United States. When the authors obtain the data on revenues from state-owned enterprises from more than one place, they note this fact in the country's write-up.

For countries in which the share of total revenues from state-owned enterprises and government ownership of property were not available, 1 point was added to the government intervention score (with a variety of sources used in making this judgment) when evidence of many state-owned enterprises was found.

The government intervention factor also examines the state of privatization programs. If a country's state-owned sector is being aggressively privatized, the authors note this fact, which puts into context any statements about the size of the state-owned sector. If the privatization program has stalled or if one is not in place, however, the authors note that as well.

Additionally, in a few cases, there is strong reason to doubt either the reported measure of government consumption or the reported share of enterprise income. In these cases, when compelling evidence of heavy government involvement in the economy was found, the authors added 1 or more points to the score (making it worse).[11]

The final consideration is whether or not the government intervenes in the stock market. When a government intervenes in the stock market, it contravenes the choices of millions of individuals. It does so by interfering with the pricing of capital—the most critical function of a market economy. Equity markets measure, on a continual basis, the expected profits and losses in publicly held companies. This measurement is essential in allocating capital resources to their highest-valued uses and thereby satisfying consumers' most urgent wants. When the authors find evidence of government intervention in the stock market, they note this fact in the country's write-up.

## Monetary Policy Grading Scale

| Score | Inflation Rate | Criteria |
|---|---|---|
| 1 | Very low | Weighted inflation less than or equal to 3 percent. |
| 2 | Low | Weighted inflation greater than 3 percent but less than or equal to 6 percent. |
| 3 | Moderate | Weighted inflation greater than 6 percent but less than or equal to 12 percent. |
| 4 | High | Weighted inflation greater than 12 percent but less than or equal to 20 percent. |
| 5 | Very high | Weighted inflation greater than 20 percent. |

**Sources.** Unless otherwise noted, the authors used the following sources for information on government intervention in the economy, in order of priority: World Bank, *World Development Indicators 2003*; official government publications of each country; Economist Intelligence Unit, *Country Report* and *Country Profile*, 2003; International Monetary Fund, *Government Finance Statistics Yearbook 2002*; and U.S. Department of State, *Country Commercial Guide*,[12] 2002 and 2003.

Sometimes, data for the share of total revenues from state-owned enterprises and government ownership of property are not readily available. In these cases, the authors look both for data on total revenues from state-owned enterprises and property and for data on total government revenues, and then calculate the percentage of total revenues that is attributable to revenues from state-owned enterprises and property.

## Factor #4: Monetary Policy

The value of a country's currency is shaped largely by its monetary policy. With a stable monetary policy, people can rely on market prices for the foreseeable future. Hence, investment, savings, and other longer-term plans are easier to make, and individuals enjoy greater economic freedom. John Maynard Keynes observed about the opposite of stable money that "by a continuing process of inflation, governments can confiscate, secretly and unob-

## Variable for Factor #4

• Average inflation rate from 1993 to 2002

served, an important part of the wealth of their citizens."[13] Inflation not only confiscates wealth, but also distorts pricing, misallocates resources, raises the cost of doing business, and undermines a free society.

There is no singularly accepted theory of the right monetary institutions for a free society. At one time, the gold standard enjoyed widespread support, but this is no longer the case (though some continue to support that system). What characterizes almost all monetary theorists today, however, is support for low or zero inflation. A good way to gauge the influence of monetary policy on economic freedom is to analyze the inflation rate over a period of time.

**Methodology.** This factor's score is based on a country's weighted average annual rate of inflation from 1993 to 2002. First, the authors weighted inflation rates for each of the past 10 years, giving the year farthest from the present the least weight and the current year the greatest weight. Then they calculated an average of these weighted rates.[14] In some cases, data were not available for all 10 years; for these countries, the authors used as many years of data as were available.[15] The reader should be aware that when governments have comprehensive price and wage controls, measured inflation probably is distorted.

## Capital Flows and Foreign Investment Grading Scale

| Score | Barriers to Foreign Investment | Criteria |
| --- | --- | --- |
| 1 | Very low | Open and impartial treatment of foreign investment; accessible foreign investment code; almost no restrictions on foreign investments except for fields related to national security; no restrictions on capital transactions. |
| 2 | Low | Restrictions on investments in few sectors, such as utilities, companies vital to national security, and natural resources; limited, efficient approval process; minimal restrictions on capital transactions. |
| 3 | Moderate | Restrictions on many investments, but official policy conforms to established foreign investment code; bureaucratic approval process; extensive use of capital controls. |
| 4 | High | Investment permitted on a case-by-case basis; possible presence of bureaucratic approval process and corruption; capital flows are prohibited. |
| 5 | Very high | Government seeks actively to prevent foreign investment and prohibits all capital flows; widespread corruption. |

**Sources.** Unless otherwise noted, the authors used the following sources for data on monetary policy, in order of priority: International Monetary Fund, *International Financial Statistics On-line*; International Monetary Fund, *2003 World Economic Outlook*, available at *http://www.imf.org/external/pubs/ft/weo/2003/ 01/data/index.htm*; and Economist Intelligence Unit, *Country Report*, 1996 to 2003. Sources other than the IMF *International Financial Statistics* are noted in the text.

### Factor #5: Capital Flows and Foreign Investment

 Restrictions on foreign investment limit the inflow of capital and thus hamper economic freedom. By contrast, little or no restriction of foreign investment enhances economic freedom because foreign investment provides funds for economic expansion. For this factor, the more restrictions a country imposes on foreign investment, the lower its level of economic freedom and the higher its score.

## Variables of Factor #5

- Foreign investment code
- Restrictions on foreign ownership of business
- Restrictions on industries and companies open to foreign investors
- Restrictions and performance requirements on foreign companies
- Foreign ownership of land
- Equal treatment under the law for both foreign and domestic companies
- Restrictions on repatriation of earnings
- Restrictions on capital transactions
- Availability of local financing for foreign companies

**Methodology.** This factor scrutinizes each country's policies toward foreign investment in order to determine its overall investment climate. Policies examined include the presence of a foreign investment code that defines the country's investment laws and

## Banking and Finance Grading Scale

| Score | Restrictions on Banks | Criteria |
| --- | --- | --- |
| 1 | Very low | Negligible government involvement in the financial sector; very few restrictions on foreign financial institutions; banks may engage in all types of financial services. |
| 2 | Low | Minimal government involvement in the financial sector; few limits on foreign banks; country may maintain some limits on financial services; domestic bank formation may face some barriers. |
| 3 | Moderate | Substantial government influence on banks; government owns or controls some banks; government controls credit; domestic bank formation may face significant barriers. |
| 4 | High | Heavy government involvement in the financial sector; banking system in transition; banks tightly controlled by government; possible corruption; domestic bank formation virtually nonexistent. |
| 5 | Very high | Financial institutions in chaos; banks operate on primitive basis; most credit controlled by government and goes only to state-owned enterprises; corruption widespread. |

procedures; whether the government encourages foreign investment through fair and equitable treatment of investors; whether there are restrictions on access to foreign exchange; whether foreign firms are treated the same as domestic firms under the law; whether the government imposes restrictions on payments, transfers, and capital transactions; and whether specific industries are closed to foreign investment. This analysis helps to develop an overall description of the country's investment climate. The authors then grade each country based on those variables.

**Sources.** Unless otherwise noted, the authors used the following sources for data on capital flows and foreign investment, in order of priority: International Monetary Fund, *Annual Report on Exchange Arrangements and Exchange Restrictions 2002*; official government publications of each country; Economist Intelligence Unit, *Country Commerce, Country Profile,* and *Country Report,* 2002 and 2003; Office of the U.S. Trade Representative, *2002 National Trade Estimate Report on Foreign Trade Barriers;* and U.S.

## Variables for Factor #6

- Government ownership of financial institutions
- Restrictions on the ability of foreign banks to open branches and subsidiaries
- Government influence over the allocation of credit
- Government regulations
- Freedom to offer all types of financial services, securities, and insurance policies

Department of State, *Country Commercial Guide,*[16] 2002 and 2003.

### Factor #6: Banking and Finance

 In most countries, banks provide the essential financial services that facilitate economic growth; they lend money to start businesses, purchase homes, and secure credit that is used to buy durable consumer goods, in addition to furnishing a safe place in which individuals can store their earnings. The more banks are controlled by the government, the less free they are to engage in these activities. Hence, heavy bank regulation reduces opportunities and restricts economic freedom; therefore, the more a government restricts its banking sector, the lower its level of economic freedom and the higher its score.

In developed economies, commercial banks are relatively less important because a higher proportion of credit is supplied in organized securities markets. Over the years, the authors have devoted more attention to the non-banking part of the financial services industry (insurance and securities).

It should be noted that virtually all countries provide some type of prudential supervision of banks and other financial services. This supervision serves two major purposes: ensuring the safety and soundness of the financial system and ensuring that financial services firms meet basic fiduciary responsibilities. Ultimately, this task falls under a government's duty to enforce contracts and protect its citizens against fraud.

The marketplace provides some protection of this sort through such institutions as independent auditors and firms providing information services, and arguably could take over even more of this oversight responsibility. The key point, however, is that markets demand independent oversight of financial services firms because of the high standards of fiduciary duty required in that industry. Such oversight is distinguished from burdensome government regulation, which interferes with market provision of financial services to consumers. It is the latter, not the former, that interferes with economic freedom and causes a country's grade on this factor to be better or worse.

**Methodology.** The banking and finance factor measures the relative openness of a country's banking and financial system. The authors score this factor by determining, specifically, whether foreign banks and financial services firms are able to operate freely, how difficult it is to open domestic banks and other financial services firms, how heavily regulated the financial system is, the presence of state-owned banks, whether the government influences the allocation of cred-

it, and whether banks are free to provide customers with insurance and invest in securities (and vice versa). The authors use this analysis to develop a description of the country's financial climate.

**Sources.** Unless otherwise noted, the authors used the following sources for data on banking and finance, in order of priority: Economist Intelligence Unit, *Country Commerce, Country Profile,* and *Country Report,* 2002 and 2003; official government publications of each country; and U.S. Department of State, *Country Commercial Guide,*[17] 2002 and 2003.

## Factor #7: Wages and Prices

 In a free-market economy, prices allocate resources to their highest use. A firm that needs more employees may signal this need to the market by offering a higher wage; an individual who greatly values a home on the market offers a higher price to purchase it. Prices also act as signals to producers and consumers by conveying information that otherwise would be prohibitively costly to obtain. For example, if the demand for a good increases, it is reflected in the price of the product and is a signal to producers to increase production.

When prices are determined freely, resources go to their most productive use for satisfying consumers. As Nobel Laureate Friedrich A. Hayek put it, "We must look at the price system as…a mechanism for communicating information if we want to understand its real function—a function which, of course, it fulfills less perfectly as prices grow more rigid."[18]

Some governments mandate wage and price controls. By so doing, they inhibit information, restrict economic activity, and curtail economic freedom. Government control can emanate not only from explicit price controls, but also from heavy involvement in the economy, which distorts pricing. Therefore, the more a government intervenes and controls prices and wages, the lower its level of economic freedom and the higher its score.

**Methodology.** The authors score this factor by the extent to which a government allows the market to set wages and prices. Specifically, this factor looks at which products have prices set by the government and

# Wages and Prices Grading Scale

| Score | Wage and Price Controls | Criteria |
|---|---|---|
| 1 | Very low | The market sets prices of goods and services, and either the country does not have a minimum wage or the evidence indicates that the minimum wage applies to a small portion of the work force and is therefore not relevant in wage setting. The government may participate in collective bargaining as long as it does not impose those wage agreements on other sectors or on workers that are not immediate parties to the agreement. |
| 2 | Low | The government controls prices on some goods and services, but controls do not apply to a significant portion of national output. The government either has a minimum wage that applies to a significant portion of the work force or extends collective bargaining agreements across industries or sectors and on workers that are not immediately party to the agreement. |
| 3 | Moderate | The government controls prices of goods and services that constitute a significant portion of national output, and/or government-set wages apply to a large portion of the work force. |
| 4 | High | The government determines most prices of goods and services and most wages. |
| 5 | Very high | Wages and prices of goods and services are almost completely controlled by the government. |

## Variables for Factor #7

- Minimum wage laws
- Freedom to set prices privately without government influence
- Government price controls
- Extent to which government price controls are used
- Government subsidies to businesses that affect prices

whether the government has a minimum wage policy or otherwise influences wages. The factor's scale measures the relative degree of government control over wages and prices. A "very low" score of 1 represents wages and prices that are set almost completely by the market, whereas a "very high" score of 5 means that wages and prices are set almost completely by the government.

**Sources.** Unless otherwise noted, the authors used the following sources for data on wages and prices, in order of priority: Economist Intelligence Unit, *Country Commerce*, *Country Profile*, and *Country Report*, 2002 and 2003; official government publications of each country; and U.S. Department of State, *Country Commercial Guide*[19] and *Country Reports on Human Rights Practices*, 2002 and 2003.

## Factor #8: Property Rights

 The ability to accumulate private property is the main motivating force in a market economy, and the rule of law is vital to a fully functioning free-market economy. Secure property rights give citizens the confidence to undertake commercial activities, save their income, and make long-term plans because they know that their income and savings are safe from expropriation. This factor examines the extent to which the government protects private property by

## Property Rights Grading Scale

| Score | Protection of Private Property | Criteria |
|---|---|---|
| 1 | Very high | Private property guaranteed by the government; court system efficiently enforces contracts; justice system punishes those who unlawfully confiscate private property; corruption nearly nonexistent and expropriation unlikely. |
| 2 | High | Private property guaranteed by the government; court system suffers delays and is lax in enforcing contracts; corruption possible but rare; expropriation unlikely. |
| 3 | Moderate | Court system inefficient and subject to delays; corruption may be present; judiciary may be influenced by other branches of government; expropriation possible but rare. |
| 4 | Low | Property ownership weakly protected; court system inefficient; corruption present; judiciary influenced by other branches of government; expropriation possible. |
| 5 | Very low | Private property outlawed or not protected; almost all property belongs to the state; country in such chaos (for example, because of ongoing war) that property protection is nonexistent; judiciary so corrupt that property is not effectively protected; expropriation frequent. |

## Variables for Factor #8

- Freedom from government influence over the judicial system
- Commercial code defining contracts
- Sanctioning of foreign arbitration of contract disputes
- Government expropriation of property
- Corruption within the judiciary
- Delays in receiving judicial decisions
- Legally granted and protected private property

enforcing the laws and how safe private property is from expropriation. The less protection private property receives, the lower a country's level of economic freedom and the higher its score.

**Methodology.** This factor scores the degree to which a country's laws protect private property rights and the degree to which its government enforces those laws. It also accounts for the possibility that private property will be expropriated. In addition, it analyzes the independence of the judiciary, the existence of corruption within the judiciary, and the ability of individuals and businesses to enforce contracts. The less legal protection of property, the higher a country's score; similarly, the greater the chances of government expropriation of property, the higher a country's score.

**Sources.** Unless otherwise noted, the authors used the following sources for information on property rights, in order of priority: Economist Intelligence Unit, *Country Commerce*, 2002 and 2003, and U.S. Department of State, *Country Commercial Guide*[20] and *Country Reports on Human Rights Practices*, 2002 and 2003.

## Factor #9: Regulation

 Regulations and restrictions are in effect a form of taxation that makes it difficult for entrepreneurs to cre-

## Regulation Grading Scale

| Score | Levels of Regulation | Criteria |
|---|---|---|
| 1 | Very low | Existing regulations straightforward and applied uniformly to all businesses; regulations not much of a burden for business; corruption nearly nonexistent. |
| 2 | Low | Simple licensing procedures; existing regulations relatively straightforward and applied uniformly most of the time, but burdensome in some instances; corruption possible but rare. |
| 3 | Moderate | Complicated licensing procedures; regulations impose substantial burden on business; existing regulations may be applied haphazardly and in some instances are not even published by the government; corruption may be present and poses minor burden on businesses. |
| 4 | High | Government-set production quotas and some state planning; major barriers to opening a business; complicated licensing process; very high fees; bribes sometimes necessary; corruption present and burdensome; regulations impose a great burden on business. |
| 5 | Very high | Government impedes the creation of new businesses; corruption widespread; regulations applied randomly. |

ate and/or maintain new businesses. In some countries, government officials frown on any private-sector initiatives; in a few, they even make them illegal. Although many regulations hinder business, the most important are associated with licensing new companies and businesses. In some countries, as well as many states in the United States, the procedure for obtaining a business license can be as simple as mailing in a registration form with a minimal fee. In Hong Kong, for example, obtaining a business license requires filling out a single form, which can be completed in a few hours.[21] In other countries, such as India and countries in parts of South America, the process involved in obtaining a business license requires endless trips to government offices and can take a year or more.

Once a business is open, government regulation does not always subside; in some cases, it increases. Interestingly, two countries with the same set of regulations can impose different regulatory burdens. If one

## Variables for Factor #9

- Licensing requirements to operate a business
- Ease of obtaining a business license
- Corruption within the bureaucracy
- Labor regulations, such as established workweeks, paid vacations, and parental leave, as well as selected labor regulations
- Environmental, consumer safety, and worker health regulations
- Regulations that impose a burden on business

of them, for instance, applies its regulations evenly and transparently, it lowers the regulatory burden since businesses can make long-term plans. If the other applies regulations inconsistently, it raises the regulatory burden on businesses by creating an unpredictable business environment. For example, in some countries, an environmental regulation may be used to shut down one business but not another. Business owners are uncertain about which regulations they must obey. In addition, the existence of excessive regulation can support corruption as confused and harassed business owners attempt to navigate the red tape.

**Methodology.** This factor measures how easy or difficult it is to open and operate a business. The more regulations are imposed on business, the harder it is to establish one. The factor also examines the degree of corruption in government and whether regulations are applied uniformly to all businesses. Another consideration is whether the country has state planning agencies that set production limits and quotas. The scale establishes a set of conditions for each of the five possible grades. These conditions also include such items as the extent of government corruption, how uniformly regulations are applied, and the extent to which regulations impose a burden on business. A "very low" score of 1 indicates that corruption is virtually nonexistent and regulations are minimal and applied uniformly; a "very high" score of 5 indicates that corruption is widespread, regulations are applied randomly, and the general level of regulation is very high. A country need only meet a majority of the conditions for a particular score to receive that score.

**Sources.** Unless otherwise noted, the authors used the following sources for data on regulation, in order of priority: Economist Intelligence Unit, *Country Commerce* and *Country Report*, 2002 and 2003; official government publications of each country; U.S. Department of State, *Country Commercial Guide*,[22] 2002 and 2003; and Office of the U.S. Trade Representative, *2003 National Trade Estimate Report on Foreign Trade Barriers*.

## Factor #10: Informal Market

 At times, the existence of an informal market is positive: There is some ability to engage in entrepreneurship or to obtain scarce goods and services that otherwise would not exist. "In some circumstances," notes Harvard economist Robert Barro, "corruption may be preferable to honest enforcement of bad rules. For example, outcomes may be worse

if a regulation that prohibits some useful economic activity is thoroughly enforced rather than circumvented through bribes."[23] Alejandro Chafuen and Eugenio Guzmán, however, point out that "corruption is the cost of obtaining privileges that only the State can 'legally' grant, such as favoritism in taxation, tariffs, subsidies, loans, government contracting, and regulation."[24]

Informal markets are the direct result of some kind of government intervention in the marketplace. An informal market activity is one that the government has taxed heavily, regulated in a burdensome manner, or simply outlawed in the past. This factor captures the effects of government interventions not always fully measured elsewhere.

Many societies, of course, outlaw such activities as trafficking in illicit drugs, but others frequently limit individual liberty by outlawing such activities as private transportation and construction services. A government regulation or restriction in one area may create an informal market in another. For example, a country with high barriers to trade may have laws that protect its domestic market and prevent the import of foreign goods, but these barriers create incentives for smuggling and an informal market for the barred products. In addition, governments that do not have strong property rights protection for items like intellectual property, or that do not enforce existing laws, encourage piracy and theft of these products.

For the purposes of this *Index*, the informal market reflects restrictions, taxes, or imperfections in the private market. Hence, the larger the informal market, the lower the country's level of economic freedom; and the more prevalent informal market activities are, the worse the country's score. Conversely, the smaller the informal market, the higher the country's level of economic freedom; and the less prevalent these activities are, the better the country's score.

**Methodology.** This factor relies on Transparency International's Corruption Perceptions Index (CPI), which measures the level of corruption in 102 countries, to determine the informal market scores of countries that are also listed in the *Index of Economic Freedom*.[25] As the level of corruption increases,

# Informal Market Grading Scale

| Score | Informal Market Activity | Criteria |
|---|---|---|
| 1 | Very low | Country has a free-market economy with informal market in such things as drugs and weapons. |
| 2 | Low | Country may have some informal market involvement in labor or pirating of intellectual property. |
| 3 | Moderate | Country may have some informal market activities in labor, agriculture, and transportation, and moderate levels of intellectual property piracy. |
| 4 | High | Country may have substantial levels of informal market activity in such areas as labor, pirated intellectual property, and smuggled consumer goods, and in such services as transportation, electricity, and telecommunications. |
| 5 | Very high | Country's informal market is larger than its formal economy. |

the level of informal market activity rises as well. Citizens often engage in corrupt activity, such as bribing an official, so that they can enter the informal market.

Because the CPI is based on a 10-point scale in which 10 equals very little corruption and 1 equals a very corrupt government, it was necessary to transform the CPI to a five-point scale consistent with the other nine factors graded in the *Index*. To do this, the authors regressed the CPI on the informal market *Index of Economic Freedom* score. After estimating the relationship between the two variables, the authors substituted the CPI into the equation to arrive at a number between 1 and 5. They then rounded the numbers to the nearest half point (0.5 point).[26] If 2002 Transparency International data were not available and 2001 TI data were available, the authors used the 2001 TI data.

For countries that are not covered in the CPI, the informal market score is determined by using the same procedure as in previous years. (See text box.) This procedure considers the extent to which informal market activities occur. Although information on the size of informal markets in less-developed countries is difficult to obtain, information on the extent of smuggling, piracy of intellec-

## Variables for Factor #10

- Smuggling
- Piracy of intellectual property in the informal market
- Agricultural production supplied on the informal market
- Manufacturing supplied on the informal market
- Services supplied on the informal market
- Transportation supplied on the informal market
- Labor supplied on the informal market

tual property, and informal labor can be found. When such information is available, the authors use it to determine the extent of informal market activities. The higher the level of informal market activity, the lower the level of overall economic freedom and the higher a country's score. As newer data become available, it may become possible to document the percentage of informal market activity in a country's overall economy.

Although this factor measures informal market activity in the production, distribution, or consumption of goods and services, it does not measure such things as informal market exchange rates or illegal provision of "vices," such as gambling, narcotics, prostitution, and related activities. Such activities are very difficult to quantify with objectivity.

**Sources.** Unless otherwise noted, the authors used the following sources for information on informal market activities, in order of priority: Transparency International, *Corruption Perceptions Index*, 2000, 2001, and 2002; U.S. Department of State, *Country Commercial Guide*,[27] 2002 and 2003; Economist Intelligence Unit, *Country Commerce*, *Country Profile*, and *Country Report*, 2003; Office of the U.S. Trade Representative, *2003 National Trade Estimate Report on Foreign Trade Barriers*; and official government publications of each country.

# Endnotes

1   See also James D. Gwartney and Robert A. Lawson with Chris Edwards, Walter Park, Veronique de Rugy, and Smita Wagh, *Economic Freedom of the World, 2002 Annual Report* (Vancouver, Canada: Fraser Institute, 2002), and Richard E. Messick, *World Survey of Economic Freedom: 1995–1996* (New Brunswick, N.J.: Transaction Publishers, 1996).

2   "The property which every man has in his own labour, as it is the original foundation of all other property, so it is the most sacred and inviolable." Adam Smith, *An Inquiry into the Nature and Causes of the Wealth of Nations* (New York: The Modern Library, 1937), pp. 121–122; first published in 1776.

3   See Chapter 3, "Weighting the Components of the *Index of Economic Freedom*."

4   The most favored nation tariff rate is the "normal," non-discriminatory tariff charged on imports of a good. In commercial diplomacy, exporters seek MFN treatment; that is, the promise that they get treated as well as the most favored exporter. The MFN rule requires that the concession be extended to all other members of the World Trade Organization.

5   The *Country Commercial Guides* are published by the U.S. Commercial Service but are based on data from U.S. embassies, the U.S. Department of State, and the U.S. Department of Commerce. Quotes from this publication are cited as originating with the U.S. Department of State in the country write-ups.

6   Walter Block, ed., *Economic Freedom: Toward a Theory of Measurement* (Vancouver, Canada: Fraser Institute, 1991).

7   See note 5.

8   See note 5.

9   U.S. Department of Commerce, Bureau of Economic Analysis, *Survey of Current Business*, March 1998, p. 31.

10  In a few cases, data on government consumption were not available for a country, but data on government expenditures were available, or vice versa. When information on government consumption was not available for the government intervention factor and data on government expenditure were available, the authors used government expenditures as a proxy for government consumption. Similarly, when data on government expenditure were not available for the fiscal burden of government factor and data on government consumption were available, the authors used government consumption as a proxy for government expenditures.

11  The countries for which data correction points were added include Armenia, Bangladesh, Burkina Faso, Burma, Belarus, Cuba, China, Djibouti, Indonesia, Iran, Macedonia, Niger, Romania, Romania, Syria, Tajikistan, Turkmenistan and Vietnam.

12  See note 5.

13  John Maynard Keynes, *The Economic Consequences of the Peace* (London: Macmillan and Co., Ltd., 1919), pp. 102–103.

14  The weights were generated using an exponential weighting procedure. The weights are as follows: The most recent year received a weight of 1.0, followed by 0.36788, 0.13534, 0.04979, 0.01832, 0.00674, 0.00248, 0.00091, 0.00034, and 0.00012.

15  In his cross-country study on growth, Robert J. Barro found that relatively recent inflation had the main explanatory power for growth. Robert J. Barro, *Determinants of Economic Growth: A Cross-Country Empirical Study* (Cambridge, Mass.: MIT Press, 1997).

16  See note 5.

17  See note 5.

18  Friedrich A. Hayek, "The Use of Knowledge in Society," in *Individualism and Economic Order* (Chicago: University of Chicago Press, 1948), p. 86.

19  See note 5.

20  See note 5.

21 John Stossel, "Is America Number One?" ABC News, aired September 19, 1999.
22 See note 5.
23 Robert J. Barro, "Rule of Law, Democracy, and Economic Performance," in Gerald P. O'Driscoll, Jr., Kim R. Holmes, and Melanie Kirkpatrick, *2000 Index of Economic Freedom* (Washington, D.C.: The Heritage Foundation and Dow Jones & Company, Inc., 2000), p. 36.
24 Alejandro A. Chafuen and Eugenio Guzmán, "Economic Freedom and Corruption," in O'Driscoll, Holmes, and Kirkpatrick, *2000 Index of Economic Freedom*, p. 53.
25 This year, the authors graded the informal market factor using Transparency International's 2001 and 2002 *Corruption Perceptions Index* (CPI) reports.
26 The equation the authors estimated is as follows: informal market = 5.227 − 0.4771*CPI. The authors then substituted the CPI score back into the equation to arrive at a number between 1 and 5. For example, substituting Denmark's CPI score of 9.5 back into the equation yields an informal market score of 0.695 (which rounds up to a score of 1).
27 See note 5.

Chapter 6

# The *2004 Index of Economic Freedom:* The Countries

by Ana Isabel Eiras, Aaron Schavey, and Anthony Kim

This chapter is a compilation of 161 countries, each graded in all 10 factors of the *Index of Economic Freedom*. (For this year's edition of the *Index*, numerical grading was suspended for six countries: Angola, Burundi, Democratic Republic of Congo, Iraq, and Sudan, all five of which are in a state of civil unrest or anarchy, and Serbia–Montenegro, for which data necessary to grade the country are not available. Information is provided, however, even for these countries.)

Each country is given a score ranging from 1 through 5 for all 10 factors, and these scores are then averaged (using equal weights) to get its final *Index of Economic Freedom* score. Countries with a score between 1 and 2 have the freest economies; those with a score around 3 are less free; those with a score near 4 are excessively regulated and will need significant economic reform to achieve sustained increases in economic growth; and those with a score of 5 are the most economically repressed.[1]

In addition to these factor scores and an overall score, each country summary includes a brief introduction describing the country's political and economic background, as well as the principal challenges that it currently faces, and a statistical profile with the main economic indicators. These statistics and their sources are outlined in detail below.

To assure consistency and reliability for each of the 10 factors on which the countries are graded, every effort has been made to use the same source for each country; when data are unavailable from the primary source, secondary sources are used as indicated in Chapter 5. The information included reflects the most recent data available at the time of publication.

## GUIDE TO STATISTICS

Unless otherwise indicated, the data in each country's statistical profile are for 2001 and in constant 1995 U.S. dollars. As of *2004 Index* production time, data for 2002 were available for only 42 countries: Argentina, Australia, Austria, Belgium, Brazil, Canada, Chile, China, Croatia, the Czech Republic, Denmark, Estonia, Finland, France, Germany, Greece, Hong Kong, Hungary, Iceland, Ireland, Israel, Italy, Japan, Lithuania, Luxembourg, Mexico, the Netherlands, New Zealand, Norway, Poland, Portugal, Singapore, the Slovak Republic, Slovenia, the

Republic of Korea, Spain, Sweden, Switzerland, Taiwan, Turkey, the United Kingdom, and the United States. The few cases in which no statistical data were available are indicated by "n/a."

The sources for each country's statistical profile include the following:

**Population:** 2001 estimate from World Bank, *World Development Indicators 2003* on-line. For some countries, the source is the country's statistical agency and/or central bank and U.S. Central Intelligence Agency, *The World Factbook 2002.*

**Total area:** Both land and sea area, expressed in square kilometers. From U.S. Central Intelligence Agency, *The World Factbook 2002.*

**GDP:** Gross domestic product—total production of goods and services—expressed in constant 1995 U.S. dollars. The primary source for GDP data is World Bank, *World Development Indicators 2003* on-line. Other sources include Economist Intelligence Unit, *Country Reports*, 2003, and *Country Profiles*, 2001–2002 and 2002–2003; the country's statistical agency; and the country's central bank. For some countries, 2002 GDP estimates were calculated by applying the real 2002 GDP growth rate to real 2001 GDP data in constant 1995 U.S. dollars. The data used in this calculation are from Organisation for Economic Co-operation and Development, *Main Economic Indicators*; Economist Intelligence Unit, *Country Reports*, 2003; International Monetary Fund, *World Economic Outlook: Growth and Institutions*, April 2003; the country's statistical agency; and the country's central bank.

**GDP growth rate:** Annual percentage growth rate of GDP at market prices based on constant local currency. The primary sources for 2001 data are World Bank, *World Development Indicators 2003* on-line, and Economist Intelligence Unit, *Country Reports*, 2002 and 2003. 2002 growth rate data are from Organisation for Economic Co-operation and Development, *Main Economic Indicators*; the country's statistical agency; the country's central bank; and International Monetary Fund, *World Economic Outlook: Growth and Institutions*, April 2003.

**GDP per capita:** Gross domestic product expressed in constant 1995 U.S. dollars divided by total population. The sources for these data are World Bank, *World Development Indicators 2003* on-line; Economist Intelligence Unit, *Country Reports*, 2003; Organisation for Economic Co-operation and Development, *Main Economic Indicators*; and the country's statistical agency.

**Major exports:** The country's six to eight principal export products. Data for major exports are from U.S. Central Intelligence Agency, *The World Factbook 2002*, and Economist Intelligence Unit, *Country Reports*, 2002 and 2003, and *Country Profiles*, 2001–2002 and 2002–2003.

**Exports of goods and services:** The value of all goods and other market services. Included is the value of merchandise, freight, insurance, travel, and other non-factor services. Factor and property income, such as investment income, interest, and labor income, is excluded. Data are in constant 1995 U.S. dollars. 2001 data are from World Bank, *World Development Indicators 2003* on-line, and Economist Intelligence Unit, *Country Reports*, 2002 and 2003, and *Country Profiles*, 2001–2002 and 2002–2003. Other sources include the country's statistical agency and/or ministry of economy and trade. Data necessary for this calculation are from Economist Intelligence Unit, *Country Reports*, 2002 and 2003; World Bank, *World Development Indicators 2003* on-line; and the country's statistical agency.

**Major export trading partners:** Main destination of exports from each country and percentage of overall exports. From Economist Intelligence Unit, *Country Reports*, 2002 and 2003, and *Country Profiles*, 2001–2002 and 2002–2003.

**Major imports:** The country's six to eight principal import products. From U.S. Central Intelligence Agency, *The World Factbook 2002*, and Economist Intelligence Unit, *Country Reports*, 2002 and 2003, and *Country Profiles*, 2001–2002 and 2002–2003.

**Imports of goods and services:** The value of all goods and other market services. Included is the value of merchandise, freight, insurance, travel, and other non-factor services. Factor and property income, such as investment income, interest, and labor income, is excluded. Data are in constant 1995 U.S. dollars. The primary source is World Bank, *World Development Indicators 2003* on-line. Other sources include Economist Intelligence Unit, *Country Reports*, 2002 and 2003, and *Country Profiles*, 2001–2002 and 2002–2003; the country's statistical agency; and the country's ministry of economy and trade. Data necessary to carry out this calculation are from Economist Intelligence Unit, *Country Reports*, 2002 and 2003; World Bank, *World Development Indicators 2003* on-line; and the country's statistical agency.

**Major import trading partners:** Principal countries from which imports originate and percentage of overall imports. From Economist Intelligence Unit, *Country Reports*, 2002 and 2003, and *Country Profiles*, 2001–2002 and 2002–2003.

**Foreign direct investment (net):** Net inflows of investment to acquire a lasting management interest (10 percent or more of voting stock) in an enterprise operating in an economy other than that of the investor. It is the sum of equity capital, reinvestment of earnings, other long-term capital, and short-term capital as shown in the balance of payments. This series indicates total net; that is, net FDI in the reporting economy (inflows) less net FDI by the reporting economy (outflows). Data are in constant 1995 U.S. dollars. The 1995 GDP deflator was used to convert net FDI from current U.S. dollars to constant 1995 U.S. dollars. Data for 2001 are from World Bank, *World Development Indicators 2003* on-line; United Nations Conference on Trade and Development, *World Investment Report 2002*; United Nations Economic Commission for Latin America and the Caribbean, *Statistical Yearbook for Latin America and the Caribbean*; the country's statistical agency; and the country's central bank. Data for 2002 are from the country's central bank; the country's statistical agency; and Organisation for Economic Co-operation and Development, *Trends and Recent Developments in Foreign Direct Investment*.

## TERMS USED IN IMPORT–EXPORT STATISTICS

**CARICOM:** Caribbean Community and Common Market, consisting of the Bahamas, Barbados, Belize, Guyana, Haiti, Jamaica, Suriname, Trinidad and Tobago, and the Windward and Leeward Islands in the Eastern Caribbean.

**CIS:** Commonwealth of Independent States, consisting of Azerbaijan, Armenia, Belarus, Georgia, Kazakhstan, Kyrgyzstan, Moldova, Russia, Tajikistan, Turkmenistan, Uzbekistan, and Ukraine.

**EU:** European Union, consisting of Austria, Belgium, Denmark, Finland, France, Germany, Greece, Ireland, Italy, Luxembourg, the Netherlands, Portugal, Spain, Sweden, and the United Kingdom.

**SACU:** Southern African Customs Union, consisting of Botswana, Lesotho, Namibia, South Africa, and Swaziland.

## Endnote

1    For a detailed explanation of the scoring procedure used in this year's *Index*, see Chapter 5.

# ALBANIA

ALBANIA

Rank: 80

Score: 3.10

Category: Mostly Unfree

Present & Past Scores

(Best) 1
2
3
4
(Worst) 5

3.48 3.58 3.59 3.53 3.51 3.78 3.48 3.24 3.28 3.10

'95 '96 '97 '98 '99 '00 '01 '02 '03 '04

P olitical instability, the pyramid collapse of 1997, the Kosovo crisis of 1999, and corruption in government institutions and the electoral process have held back the rule of law in Albania. Since coming to power in July 2002, the government of socialist Fatos Nano has moved to reverse this trend, arresting significantly larger numbers of high-level officials such as the deputy governor of the Bank of Albania and the director of the Public Order Police (although, to the displeasure of Albania's Greek and Italian neighbors, it has failed to crack down on smuggling and illegal drug trafficking). As a result of these renewed efforts, during the first half of 2003, the European Union resumed negotiations with Tirana for an EU association agreement. In addition to corruption, a crumbling infrastructure and the fact that most major privatizations have been put on hold cause Albania to attract very small amounts of foreign direct investment. Inflation remains at relatively high levels: over 4 percent per year at the end of 2002. These shortcomings explain why nearly half of Albanians live on less than $2 per capita per day and up to 25 percent of Albanians of working age have left the country since the demise of communism. Albania's fiscal burden of government score is 0.2 point worse this year, but its trade policy and informal market scores are 1 point better. As a result, Albania's overall score is 0.18 point better this year.

## TRADE POLICY
### Score: **4**–Better (high level of protectionism)

According to the World Bank, Albania's weighted average tariff rate in 2001 (the most recent year for which World Bank data are available) was 11.8 percent, down from the 14.4 percent reported in the 2003 *Index*. As a result, Albania's trade policy score is 1 point better this year. Non-tariff barriers take the form of corruption in customs clearance and licensing. According to the U.S. Department of State, "businesses decry governmental corruption, particularly in the tendering and licensing processes...." The Economist Intelligence Unit reports that "public administration in Albania remains weak and prone to corruption.... The area most affected is customs...."

## FISCAL BURDEN OF GOVERNMENT
Score—Income Taxation: **2.5**–Stable (moderate tax rates)
Score—Corporate Taxation: **3**–Stable (moderate tax rates)
Score—Change in Government Expenditures: **3.5**–Worse (low increase)
### Final Score: **3**–Worse (moderate cost of government)

Albania's top income tax rate is 25 percent. The top corporate tax rate is 25 percent. In 2001, government expenditures as a percentage of GDP rose 0.1 percentage point to 31.5 percent, compared to a 1.3 percentage point decline the previous year. As a result, Albania's fiscal burden of government score is 0.2 point worse this year.

## GOVERNMENT INTERVENTION IN THE ECONOMY
### Score: **3**–Stable (moderate level)

The World Bank reports that the government consumed 10.9 percent of GDP in 2001. In the same year, based on data from the International Monetary Fund, Albania received 12.16 percent of its revenues from state-owned enterprises and government ownership of property.

## MONETARY POLICY
### Score: 2–Stable (low level of inflation)

From 1993 to 2002, Albania's weighted average annual rate of inflation was 4.64 percent.

## CAPITAL FLOWS AND FOREIGN INVESTMENT
### Score: 2–Stable (low barriers)

Foreign and domestic firms are treated equally under the law and are guaranteed safety from expropriation or nationalization. The government does not screen foreign investments, and nearly all sectors of the economy, with the exception of agricultural land, are open to foreign investment. Political instability, crime, corruption, and a thriving informal market continue to discourage foreign investment and undermine the implementation of reform. The International Monetary Fund reports that both residents and non-residents may hold foreign exchange accounts. Payments and transfers exceeding a specified amount require supporting documentation but face no other restrictions. The Bank of Albania must approve the purchase of capital and money market instruments, outward direct investment, most credit operations, and the purchase of real estate abroad by residents.

## BANKING AND FINANCE
### Score: 3–Stable (moderate level of restrictions)

Albania's banking sector is rudimentary, and most transactions are still carried out in cash. There are 13 commercial banks, of which 10 were foreign-owned at the end of 2001. The share of banking assets held by foreign entities increased sharply from 60 percent in 1999 to 84 percent in 2001, while that of state-owned banks dropped from 38 percent to 13 percent, according to the Economist Intelligence Unit. The government privatized the second-largest bank, the National Commercial Bank, in June 2000 and plans to privatize the Savings Bank of Albania, which currently accounts for 80 percent of all deposits, by 2004.

## WAGES AND PRICES
### Score: 2–Stable (low level of intervention)

Most prices have been liberalized. The Economist Intelligence Unit reports that the government affects prices for water, education, railway transport, and electricity through subsidies. The government also directly controls the price of electricity. A minimum wage applies to all workers over 16 years old.

## PROPERTY RIGHTS
### Score: 4–Stable (low level of protection)

Albania's legal system does not protect private property sufficiently. According to the U.S. Department of State, "The Constitution provides for an independent judiciary; however, because of political pressure, intimidation, endemic corruption, bribery, and limited resources, the judiciary was unable to function independently and efficiently." In addition, "Property rights established under Albanian law are not adequately protected; enforcement is generally left to the owner. Intellectual property rights [laws]…generally are not enforced and violations of copyright, trademark, and other intellectual property rights are widespread and blatant."

## REGULATION
### Score: 4–Stable (high level)

Albania has made some progress toward streamlining its bureaucracy. Nevertheless, according to the U.S. Department of State, "Businesses have complained that in some instances bureaucracy and corruption made obtaining a business license a lengthy and/or costly process. Other companies have lost licenses without any prior notice or due process." In addition, "The regulatory system is far from transparent. Businesses have difficulty obtaining copies of laws and regulations. Laws and regulations are sometimes inconsistent, leading to unreliability of interpretation. Corruption also means that laws and regulations are applied inconsistently."

## INFORMAL MARKET
### Score: 4–Better (high level of activity)

Transparency International's 2002 score for Albania is 2.5. Therefore, Albania's informal market score is 4 this year.

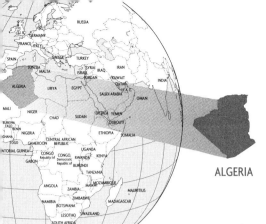

# ALGERIA

ALGERIA

Rank: 100

Score: 3.31

Category: Mostly Unfree

**Present & Past Scores**

(Best) 1
2
3
4
(Worst) 5

3.68 3.70 3.63 3.64 3.59 3.40 3.40 3.05 3.39 3.31

'95 '96 '97 '98 '99 '00 '01 '02 '03 '04

## QUICK STUDY

### SCORES

| | |
|---|---|
| Trade Policy | 5 |
| Fiscal Burden | 4.1 |
| Government Intervention | 4 |
| Monetary Policy | 1 |
| Foreign Investment | 2 |
| Banking and Finance | 4 |
| Wages and Prices | 3 |
| Property Rights | 4 |
| Regulation | 3 |
| Informal Market | 3 |

**Population:** 30,835,000

**Total area:** 2,381,740 sq. km

**GDP:** $49.8 billion

**GDP growth rate:** 2.1%

**GDP per capita:** $1,616

**Major exports:** petroleum, natural gas, and petroleum products

**Exports of goods and services:** $14.8 billion

**Major export trading partners:** Italy 22.8%, France 14.6%, Spain 13.9%, US 13.9%

**Major imports:** capital goods, food and beverages, consumer goods

**Imports of goods and services:** $12.6 billion

**Major import trading partners:** France 37.3%, US 11.3%, Italy 10.0%, Spain 7.6%

**Foreign direct investment (net):** $1 billion

2001 Data (in constant 1995 US dollars)

Algeria, primarily a one-party socialist state since gaining its independence from France in 1962, has been embroiled in a brutal civil war that has claimed the lives of more than 100,000 Algerians since 1992. Although the intensity of the civil war has declined since its peak in the mid-1990s, when President Abdelaziz Bouteflika negotiated a peace accord with the Islamic Salvation Front (FIS), years of economic mismanagement, high unemployment, housing shortages, and disenfranchisement have led to a resurgence of civil unrest, particularly in the Berber community. In response to mounting social tensions, the government launched a five-year spending program to target funds for public infrastructure projects aimed at stimulating the economy and reducing unemployment, but implementation has been slow. The government has encountered difficulty building political support for its economic reform policy, which includes important deregulation measures. Political pressure from the military elite and labor unions, which share a vested interest in the current system, has stalled privatization initiatives in the oil and gas sector. Hydrocarbons remain the backbone of the economy, accounting for 30 percent of GDP and 95 percent of export earnings. The key legislative battle this year involved the hydrocarbons reform bill, aimed at liberalization of the energy sector, which was scrapped in the face of political pressure from labor unions. The upcoming presidential election, coupled with the dismissal of the pro-reform participation and investment promotion minister Hamid Temmar, makes it highly unlikely that any meaningful progress on privatization will occur until after the 2004 presidential election. Algeria's fiscal burden of government score is 0.2 point worse this year, but its monetary policy score is 1 point better. As a result, Algeria's overall score is 0.08 point better this year.

## TRADE POLICY
### Score: **5–Stable** (very high level of protectionism)

According to the World Bank, Algeria's weighted average tariff rate in 2001 (the most recent year for which World Bank data are available) was 15 percent, down from the 17.3 percent reported in the 2003 *Index*. Non-tariff barriers take the form of bureaucratic customs clearance procedures. According to the U.S. Department of State, the customs process "remains time-consuming and the source of many complaints." In addition, "Certain imports are subject to prior authorization by some ministries. For example, the Ministry of Health and Population must clear medical products, the Ministry of Defense and National Security Directorate must clear hunting weapons, and the Ministry of Information and Culture must clear books and magazines."

## FISCAL BURDEN OF GOVERNMENT
Score—Income Taxation: **4–Better** (high tax rates)
Score—Corporate Taxation: **4–Stable** (high tax rates)
Score—Change in Government Expenditures: **4.5–Worse** (high increase)
### Final Score: **4.1–Worse** (high cost of government)

According to the International Monetary Fund, Algeria's top income tax rate is 40 percent, down from the 50 percent reported in the 2003 *Index*. The top corporate tax rate is 30 percent. Government expenditures as a percentage of GDP increased 2.7 percentage points to 31.6 percent in 2001, compared to a decline of 1.1 percentage points the previous year. On net, Algeria's overall fiscal burden of government score is therefore 0.2 point worse this year.

## GOVERNMENT INTERVENTION IN THE ECONOMY
### Score: **4**–Stable (high level)

The World Bank reports that the government consumed 14.9 percent of GDP in 2001. In the same year, according to the Economist Intelligence Unit, Algeria received 60.49 percent of its total revenues solely from state-owned enterprises in the hydrocarbon sector. The EIU reports that the government owns a monopoly in the energy sector, particularly in gas and oil, and employs approximately 16 percent of the labor force. The scrapping of the hydrocarbons reform bill, which would have ended the monopoly position of the state-owned energy firm, Sonatrach, demonstrated the power of Algeria's military elite and restive union movement.

## MONETARY POLICY
### Score: **1**–Better (very low level of inflation)

From 1993 to 2002, Algeria's weighted average annual rate of inflation was 2.13 percent, down from the 3.37 percent from 1992 to 2001 reported in the 2003 *Index*. As a result, Algeria's monetary policy score is 1 point better this year.

## CAPITAL FLOWS AND FOREIGN INVESTMENT
### Score: **2**–Stable (low barriers)

In 1993, Algeria revised its investment code to provide equal and nondiscriminatory treatment for all investors. In August 2001, a new law created the National Investment Development Agency (ANDI) to simplify investment procedures. Liberalization of oil and natural gas exploration has led to greater foreign investment. Foreign ownership of pipelines, however, is prohibited. The International Monetary Fund reports that both residents and non-residents may hold foreign exchange accounts. Payments and transfers are subject to various limits, approvals, surrender requirements, and restrictions. According to the IMF, "Capital transfers to any destination abroad are subject to individual approval by the Bank of Algeria." Purchase, sale, or issue of capital market securities is permitted through an authorized intermediary.

## BANKING AND FINANCE
### Score: **4**–Stable (high level of restrictions)

Société Générale and Natexis of France, the Arab Banking Corporation, EFG–Hermes of Egypt, and Citibank of the United States have subsidiaries or branches in Algeria. A new private bank, Compagnie Algérienne de Banque, opened its first branch in 2001. According to the Economist Intelligence Unit, "Algeria's banking sector is dominated by six state-owned banks, which together account for between 90–95% of all deposits and assets. These banks have financed, and continue to finance, loss-making public-sector enterprises, and consequently non-performing loans account for a large chunk of the banks' 'assets'.... In short, the banks tend to lend to failing public firms or regime cronies with little or no credit risk assess-

ment of the projects involved." The EIU further reports that privatization of state-owned banks is unlikely in the near term.

## WAGES AND PRICES
### Score: **3**–Stable (moderate level of intervention)

Although the government has removed some price controls, it still influences prices through subsidies and direct controls on some commodities such as tobacco. According to the Economist Intelligence Unit, basic agricultural products such as dairy products and wheat, as well as public transport and energy services, are still subsidized. In 2001, Algeria increased its monthly minimum wage to $100 from $60.

## PROPERTY RIGHTS
### Score: **4**–Stable (low level of protection)

Government expropriation is unlikely. The constitution provides for an independent judiciary; according to the U.S. Department of State, however, "executive branch decrees restricted the judiciary's authority. The Minister of Justice appoints the judges.... The Government reportedly may remove judges at will. In August 2000, the President announced a massive reorganization of the judiciary. He changed approximately 80 percent of the heads of the 187 lower courts and all but three of the presidents of the 37 higher-level courts." In addition, "The judicial environment is inefficient and, in fields like the adjudication of intellectual property disputes, suffers from a lack of trained magistrates."

## REGULATION
### Score: **3**–Stable (moderate level)

Labor regulations and red tape are moderately burdensome. According to the U.S. Department of State, "Algeria's bureaucracy remains powerful thanks to complex regulations and licensing requirements." Also, "Algerian commercial law can be complex and technical, with more than 400 legislative and regulatory texts. Many investors consider it blurry and rely on local counsel and agents to ensure that all procedures and rules are followed." Lack of transparent rules also affects businesses. According to the Economist Intelligence Unit, "The shadowy military elite have an enormous influence on political and economic decisions, but remain accountable only to themselves" and "can influence the bureaucracy and the judiciary, resulting in a situation where only businessmen that are connected can prosper."

## INFORMAL MARKET
### Score: **3**–Stable (moderate level of activity)

According to a study on the size of the informal economy done by Friedrich Schneider of the University of Linz, Algeria's informal economy accounted for 34 percent of GNP in 1999–2000. The Economist Intelligence Unit reports that "stringent and unsuitable regulations and lengthy administrative procedures have led to the emergence of a large informal sector."

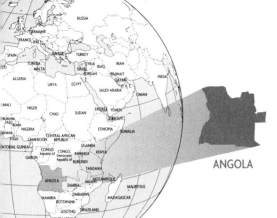

ANGOLA

# ANGOLA

Rank: Suspended

Score: n/a

Category: n/a

**Present & Past Scores**

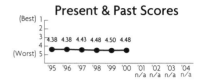

(Best) 1
2
3
4.38  4.38  4.43  4.48  4.50  4.48
4
(Worst) 5

'95  '96  '97  '98  '99  '00  '01  '02  '03  '04
                          n/a  n/a  n/a  n/a

T he death of Jonas Savimbi, leader of the National Union for the Total Independence of Angola (UNITA), in February 2002 presented an opportunity for UNITA and the ruling Popular Movement for the Liberation of Angola (MPLA) to negotiate the fourth peace agreement since the beginning of the civil war in 1975. It now looks likely that the peace will hold. However, many serious problems, including the difficult task of demobilizing large numbers of armed men on both sides of the conflict, still need to be resolved. Post-conflict priorities include combating extensive corruption and mismanagement, creating an effective legal system, and enforcing the rule of law, as well as establishing a representative government that incorporates UNITA supporters. Angola faces enormous economic problems. Over 4 million Angolans depend on emergency assistance, and the specter of starvation hangs over much of the country. Nearly half a million refugees living in Angola have yet to be repatriated to their home countries. Top officials of the MPLA regime, led by former Marxist Jose Eduardo dos Santos, have looted vast sums of state money. The International Monetary Fund estimates that over $4 billion was removed illegally from state coffers over the past five years. There are some bright spots on the horizon, however. Oil output is expected to double in the next five years due to the discovery of rich offshore fields, and the Economist Intelligence Unit estimates real GDP growth of 6 percent in 2003 and 2004.

## QUICK STUDY

### SCORES

Trade Policy                    n/a
Fiscal Burden                   n/a
Government Intervention   n/a
Monetary Policy              n/a
Foreign Investment          n/a
Banking and Finance        n/a
Wages and Prices             n/a
Property Rights                n/a
Regulation                       n/a
Informal Market               n/a

**Population:** 13,512,450

**Total area:** 1,246,700 sq. km

**GDP:** $7.1 billion

**GDP growth rate:** 3.2%

**GDP per capita:** $525

**Major exports:** diamonds, timber, cotton, crude oil, refined petroleum

**Exports of goods and services:** $5.1 billion

**Major export trading partners:** US 44.2%, China 18.7%, France 9.0%, Belgium 8.8%, Spain 2.1%

**Major imports:** electrical equipment and machinery, medicines, food, textiles

**Imports of goods and services:** $4.7 billion

**Major import trading partners:** Portugal 14.6%, South Africa 12.4%, US 10.3%, France 4.8%, Brazil 4.1%

**Foreign direct investment (net):** $1 billion

2001 Data (in constant 1995 US dollars)

## TRADE POLICY
### Score: Not graded

There are no accurate data on Angola's tariffs and non-tariff barriers. "On March 10th," according to the Economist Intelligence Unit, "the Angolan government formally ratified the Southern African Development Community (SADC) trade protocol, an agreement that will reduce tariff and non-tariff trade barriers with the SADC community over eight years." The U.S. Department of State reports that "Foreign exchange is authorized only by the central bank at a foreign exchange sale called a 'fixing', held at irregular intervals.... All imports must be made through the central bank, even if foreign exchange is held in another bank." According to Xinhua News Agency, "The British company Crowns Agents, one of the Angolan partners in the customs service, has been operating in Angola for over a year in charge of customs administrative works, and is currently involved in professional training of Angolan customs officers." This new customs management should help to increase the efficiency in Angola's customs.

## FISCAL BURDEN OF GOVERNMENT
### Score—Income Taxation: Not graded
### Score—Corporate Taxation: Not graded
### Score—Change in Government Expenditures: Not graded
### Final Score: Not graded

Angola's official top income tax rate is 15 percent. The top corporate tax rate is 35 percent. Government expenditures as a percentage of GDP decreased by less in 2001 (10.6 percentage points to 45.1 percent) than they did in 2000 (30.7 percentage points). However, these figures are very unreliable. Decades of war have undermined the government's ability to enforce its edicts in the countryside, leaving the tax burden uncertain for much of the population, and government accounts are extremely opaque and unreliable.

**GOVERNMENT INTERVENTION IN THE ECONOMY**
Score: Not graded

According to the World Bank, the government consumed 39.2 percent of GDP in 2000. (No new data were available at the time this year's *Index* was compiled.) The Economist Intelligence Unit reports that the privatization program launched in 2001 has been started, but key firms like TAAG (Angolan Air Transport) are not included. The government owns a monopoly in the potentially highly profitable oil sector.

 **MONETARY POLICY**
Score: Not graded

Between 1993 and 2003, Angola's weighted average annual rate of inflation was 150.48 percent.

 **CAPITAL FLOWS AND FOREIGN INVESTMENT**
Score: Not graded

During the civil war, only the lucrative oil and diamond industries attracted foreign investors. Coca-Cola's $36 million investment in 2000 was the first significant investment in years outside of the oil and diamond sectors. The government forbids investment in defense, public order and security, and central banking. There are controls on capital and money market transactions, real estate transactions, and personal capital movements. According to the Economist Intelligence Unit, as a result of the end of the war, foreign investment has increased, primarily in the diamond sector.

 **BANKING AND FINANCE**
Score: Not graded

The decades-long conflict and pervasive mismanagement have crippled the banking sector. Banking reforms in 1999 ended the central bank's monopoly on financial services, and two state-owned banks were established: the Banco de Comércio e Indústria (BCI) and the Caixa de Crédito Agroecúaria e Pescas (CAP). The banking sector is highly inefficient and extremely limited. "Because of a lack of security of tenure for collateral, high inflation, and a poor regulatory and legal environment," reports the Economist Intelligence Unit, "domestic banking credits tend to be short term, mostly for import finance.... Most businesses are financed outside the banking system through individuals' savings." The EIU further reports that in February, the government took steps to reduce the dollarization of the economy by altering reserve requirements at the central bank to "make it more attractive for banks to hold kwanza deposits and less attractive to hold foreign-exchange deposits." Amid widespread protests from the banking sector, the government has been quietly repealing these measures.

 **WAGES AND PRICES**
Score: Not graded

Although Angola has made some progress in converting its centrally planned economy to a more open market economy, the government still sets, controls, or manipulates wage rates and prices. The Economist Intelligence Unit reports that the government directly sets the price of fuel and utilities. According to the U.S. Department of State, a minimum wage is adjusted every six months for inflation but is not effectively enforced.

 **PROPERTY RIGHTS**
Score: Not graded

According to the U.S. Department of State, "Angola's legal system is widely regarded as moribund, and the laws and procedures as non-transparent and unlikely to offer real protection to investors in the event of a dispute with politically influential persons." Corruption and bureaucratic inefficiency are pervasive.

 **REGULATION**
Score: Not graded

Government regulations are a severe hindrance to business. Labor regulations are particularly onerous. Corruption and bureaucratic red tape have created an environment in which legal businesses find it nearly impossible to operate. According to the U.S. Department of State, "There are serious and continuing problems with corruption at all levels in Angola. Solicitation of bribes is common and blatant...."

 **INFORMAL MARKET**
Score: Not graded

Transparency International's 2002 score for Angola is 1.7. Therefore, Angola would have an informal market score of 4.5 this year if grading were not suspended.

# ARGENTINA

**Rank: 116**

**Score: 3.48**

**Category: Mostly Unfree**

ARGENTINA

**Present & Past Scores**

(Best) 1
2
3
4 2.85  2.63  2.75  2.53  2.28  2.23  2.29  2.58  3.04
(Worst) 5                                                      3.48
'95  '96  '97  '98  '99  '00  '01  '02  '03  '04

## QUICK STUDY

### SCORES

| | |
|---|---|
| Trade Policy | 4 |
| Fiscal Burden | 3.8 |
| Government Intervention | 2 |
| Monetary Policy | 4 |
| Foreign Investment | 3 |
| Banking and Finance | 4 |
| Wages and Prices | 3 |
| Property Rights | 4 |
| Regulation | 3 |
| Informal Market | 4 |

**Population:** 37,812,817

**Total area:** 2,766,890 sq. km

**GDP:** $249.5 billion

**GDP growth rate:** −10.9%

**GDP per capita:** $6,597

**Major exports:** mineral oils and fuels, cereals, vehicles, vegetable oils, oil seeds and fruits

**Exports of goods and services:** $35.8 billion

**Major export trading partners:** Brazil 28.2%, US 11.1%, Chile 11.0%, Spain 4.1%

**Major imports:** boilers, machines and mechanical equipment, electrical machinery, vehicles, organic chemicals, plastic materials

**Imports of goods and services:** $16 billion

**Major import trading partners:** Brazil 36.5%, US 21.3%, Germany 5.5%, Italy 4.4%

**Foreign direct investment (net):** −$56 million

2002 Data (in constant 1995 US dollars)

The partial economic liberalization of the early 1990s brought a few years of growth to Argentina, but the lack of further reforms drove the economy into a four-year recession and a crisis that left more than 50 percent of the population in poverty. When the crisis struck, Eduardo Duhalde took the presidency for a "transitional period" until new elections were called. The transitional government defaulted on part of its debt and dissolved the convertibility law, which held the peso at par with the dollar; as a result, prices went up, the payment system collapsed, and the economy came to a halt. From Duhalde's perspective, the resulting "import substitution" was an accomplishment because it encouraged domestic production. More realistically, it forced consumption of lower-quality products at higher prices, lowering living standards. In May 2003, new President Nestor Kirchner took office and declared that the state must finance public works to jump-start the economy. He also announced that he would fight tax evasion and strengthen MERCOSUR. Property rights remain threatened. On June 6, 2003, for example, the central bank decided that the tax collection agency could block an individual's access to a safe-deposit box, without a court order, if he or she owed taxes—and regardless of whether the individual shared the box with a person who did not owe taxes. Argentina is reverting to the closed society that characterized the end of the 1980s, with price controls, financial restrictions, inflation, and systematic violation of property rights. Argentina's fiscal burden of government score is 0.1 point better this year; however, its monetary policy score is 3 points worse, its wages and prices score is 1 point worse, and its informal market score is 0.5 point worse. As a result, Argentina's overall score is 0.44 point worse this year.

## TRADE POLICY
### Score: **4–Stable** (high level of protectionism)

As a member of the Southern Cone Common Market (MERCOSUR), Argentina adheres to a common external tariff that ranges from zero to 23 percent. According to the World Bank, Argentina's weighted average tariff rate in 2001 (the most recent year for which World Bank data are available) was 9.2 percent. Non-tariff barriers include sanitary and phytosanitary rules, antidumping, and quotas. The U.S. Department of State reports that "government officials have used phytosanitary rules, safeguard measures involving specific duties, antidumping investigations and other practices to inhibit imports...." Prior government approval is required for specific imports, including "pharmaceuticals, foodstuffs, insecticides, veterinary products, medical services, cosmetics, toiletries and others." A "major nontariff barrier is the automotive industry tariff/quota system." All automobiles must fulfill domestic content requirements. The government also restricts import payments. According to the U.S. Department of State, "Customs procedures are opaque and time-consuming, thus raising the cost for importers."

## FISCAL BURDEN OF GOVERNMENT
### Score—Income Taxation: **3.5–Stable** (high tax rates)
### Score—Corporate Taxation: **4.5–Stable** (very high tax rates)
### Score—Change in Government Expenditures: **2.5–Better** (low decrease)
## Final Score: **3.8–Better** (high cost of government)

Argentina's top income tax rate is 35 percent. The top corporate tax rate is 35 percent. Government expenditures as a share of GDP decreased by 1.2 percentage points to 26.6 percent in 2002, compared to a decline of 0.4 percentage point in 2001. As a result, Argentina's fiscal burden of government score is 0.1 point better this year.

## GOVERNMENT INTERVENTION IN THE ECONOMY
### Score: **2**–Stable (low level)

Based on data from the International Monetary Fund, the government consumed 12.2 percent of GDP in 2002. In the same year, according to the same source, Argentina received 3.94 percent of its total revenues from state-owned enterprises and government ownership of property.

## MONETARY POLICY
### Score: **4**–Worse (high level of inflation)

From 1993 to 2002, Argentina's weighted average annual rate of inflation was 16 percent, up from the –0.95 percent from 1992 to 2001 reported in the 2003 *Index*. As a result, Argentina's monetary policy score is 3 points worse this year.

## CAPITAL FLOWS AND FOREIGN INVESTMENT
### Score: **3**–Stable (moderate barriers)

Argentina's regulations and laws on foreign investment and capital flows have been in flux as the government attempts to restrict capital outflows and resolve its debt default in the wake of the country's financial crisis. Laws are irregularly enforced and frequently changed, and actual rules are unclear. The government has erected significant barriers to capital flows, access to foreign exchange, and investment. "Since late 2002," reports the Economist Intelligence Unit, "some of the most draconian measures have been relaxed. These include the ceiling on the level of banks' foreign exchange holdings, regulations on advance payments for imports, restrictions on interest payments and profit remittances abroad, limits on foreign currency purchases and the obligation to sell export proceeds to the Central Bank…. Despite the relaxation of controls, they remain a severe constraint on operating conditions." Foreign investors and their domestic counterparts receive equal treatment, and most local companies may be wholly owned by foreign investors. Foreign investment is prohibited in a few sectors, including shipbuilding, fishing, border-area real estate, and nuclear power generation.

## BANKING AND FINANCE
### Score: **4**–Stable (high level of restrictions)

Argentina's banking system was devastated by the 2001 economic crisis, government policies freezing bank deposits, frequent judicial rulings limiting access to assets, increasing default on loans, and forced conversion of foreign currency at confiscatory rates. In February 2002, the government converted all dollar deposits at a rate of 1.4 pesos per dollar when the floating exchange rate was around 2 pesos per dollar. Even

then, depositors did not have full access to their funds. Complex withdrawal rules were created, limiting monthly quantities or restricting the form of withdrawal to bonds of the defaulting country. Meanwhile, the peso kept falling, peaking at 3.7 pesos per dollar in November 2002. The government has been printing pesos for subsidized government loans to support insolvent local and provincial banks, and this has led to rapidly accelerating inflation. The national and provincial governments are paying some of their bills with quasi-money: bonds that look like currency and can be used for everyday transactions. In May, the government passed a bill to compensate the Banco Central de la Republica Argentina (the central bank) for issuing pesos required to buy back the quasi-monies, with the eventual goal of withdrawing quasi-monies from circulation. Some foreign banks, such as Canada's Scotiabank and France's Crédit Agricole, have refused to re-capitalize their Argentine branches and, in effect, have closed their doors.

## WAGES AND PRICES
### Score: **3**–Worse (moderate level of intervention)

In response to rising inflation, the government has imposed price controls on certain products. According to the Economist Intelligence Unit, "The Duhalde government imposed price controls on some basic goods (such as fuels and medicines) in early 2002 and is using moral suasion on producers and retailers to curtail abusive pricing. It has also converted utility tariffs into pesos and delinked them from the US consumer price index, which formed the basis for price increases during much of the 1990s…. Companies operating in these fields will be at a significant disadvantage in 2002–03, as price restraints are likely to remain in place for some time as the authorities seek to prevent inflation from becoming institutionalised." The government mandates a minimum wage. Based on the increasing use of price controls, Argentina's wages and prices score is 1 point worse this year.

## PROPERTY RIGHTS
### Score: **4**–Stable (low level of protection)

Private property is not secure, and application of the law is uneven. The "pesification" of 2002, under which dollar deposits were converted into pesos at 1.4 pesos to the dollar—when the market exchange rate was 2 pesos to the dollar, which climbed later in the year to 3.7 to the dollar—represented confiscation of depositors' wealth; it was compounded by the fact that some depositors would have to wait 10 years to recover part of their wealth. Since the crisis began over two years ago, the government has been challenging the terms of contracts signed with most utility providers and has prohibited them from adjusting utility prices as established in those contracts. Corruption in the judiciary is extensive. According to the Economist Intelligence Unit, "the politicized nature of the judiciary has stripped this branch of its legitimacy." For this reason, "Companies should be advised to resort to private arbitration to resolve disputes wherever possible." Another important violation of property rights involves fábricas recuperadas (recovered factories) that have gone bankrupt as a result of the crisis. The term "recovered" refers to the fact that some courts have granted former workers and unions the right to use those factory facilities and the brand name for their own benefit—a quasi-expropriation. According to the Fundación Atlas, Argentina's newly elected president has declared that giving workers the right to use these factories is a "creative alternative" to the current unemployment crisis.

 ## REGULATION
### Score: **3**–Stable (moderate level)

The Economist Intelligence Unit reports that Argentina's "institutional framework is incredibly volatile. Numerous laws, decrees and resolutions have been passed then revised within days of publication." According to the U.S. Department of State, "Businesses in Argentina—foreign and domestic alike—still face problems involving inconsistent application of regulations, fraud and corruption." The labor market remains rigid. The EIU reports that severance costs, pension payments, mandatory contributions to a union-run health plan, mandatory holidays and overtime, and payroll taxes are among the highest barriers to employing workers formally. In addition, reports the U.S. Department of State, "businesses have identified corruption in Argentina as a significant problem for trade and investment. Procurement, regulatory systems, tax collection and health care administration are problem areas.... [T]he government has regulations against bribery of government officials, but enforcement is uneven."

 ## INFORMAL MARKET
### Score: **4**–Worse (high level of activity)

Transparency International's 2002 score for Argentina is 2.8. Therefore, Argentina's informal market score is 4 this year—0.5 point worse than last year.

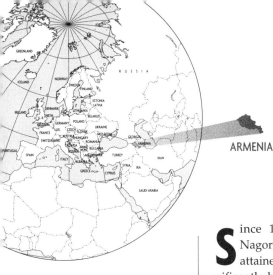

# ARMENIA

Rank: 44

Score: 2.63

Category: Mostly Free

**Present & Past Scores**

(Best) 1
2
3
4
(Worst) 5

3.50  3.50  3.50  3.21  3.03  2.78  2.59  2.63

'96  '97  '98  '99  '00  '01  '02  '03  '04
n/a

Since 1988, Armenia and Azerbaijan have been involved in conflict over the Nagorno–Karabakh region, which further escalated in 1991 after both countries attained independence from the Soviet Union. A cease-fire, in effect since 1994, has significantly helped to strengthen Armenia. Elections were held in March 2003, and President Robert Kocharian was re-elected for another five-year term even though the Organization for Security and Co-operation in Europe claimed that the elections fell short of international standards. The prime minister, appointed by the president, is Andranik Markaryan, who has been in office since May 2000. International aid, foreign direct investment, and domestic restructuring of the economy have helped to stabilize Armenia's severe trade imbalance. Due to the introduction of a liberal trade regime and the mid-1990s successful macroeconomic stabilization, the economy has experienced low inflation and a stable exchange rate. While macroeconomic performance has been impressive, job creation did not occur, and 49.1 percent of the population remains below the poverty line. Armenia's human rights track record is uneven, as police brutality goes largely unreported. The law does not protect religious freedom, and nontraditional denominations have been subjected to harassment and occasional violence. Armenia's banking and finance score is 1 point better this year; however, its trade policy score is 1 point worse, and its fiscal burden of government score is 0.4 point worse. As a result, Armenia's overall score is 0.04 point worse this year.

 **TRADE POLICY**
Score: **2**–Worse (low level of protectionism)

In 2001, according to the World Bank, Armenia's weighted average tariff rate was 2.5 percent, up from the 1.9 percent reported in the 2003 *Index*. The U.S. Department of State reports that most imports are free of prohibitions, quotas, or licensing, but businesses complain about "cumbersome procedures [and] bribes solicited by customs officials." Based on new evidence of customs corruption, Armenia's trade policy score is 1 point worse this year.

 **FISCAL BURDEN OF GOVERNMENT**
Score—Income Taxation: **2**–Stable (low tax rates)
Score—Corporate Taxation: **2**–Stable (low tax rates)
Score—Change in Government Expenditures: **3**–Worse (very low decrease)
Final Score: **2.3**–Worse (low cost of government)

The International Monetary Fund reports that Armenia's top income tax rate is 20 percent. The top corporate tax rate is 20 percent. Government expenditures as a share of GDP decreased 0.6 percentage point to 22.4 percent in 2002, compared to a 3.4 percentage point decrease in 2001. As a result, Armenia's fiscal burden of government score is 0.4 point worse this year.

**GOVERNMENT INTERVENTION IN THE ECONOMY**
Score: **3**–Stable (moderate level)

The World Bank reports that the government consumed 10.7 percent of GDP in 2001. In 2002, based on data from the Ministry of Finance, the government received 0.35 percent of its total revenues from state-owned enterprises and government ownership of property. However, data for revenues from state-owned enterprises may underestimate the level of state involvement in the economy. The government controls some key industries. "The privatisation of the large industrial plants has been difficult, partly because of populist objections to the sale of what are regarded as national institutions," reports the Economist Intelligence Unit. "The government's privatisation programme for 2001–03, which envisages the sale of 932 medium- and large-scale enterprises, therefore appears increasingly unrealistic." Based on the evidence of large state-owned enterprises, 1 point has been added to Armenia's government intervention score.

 **MONETARY POLICY**
Score: **2**–Stable (low level of inflation)

Between 1993 and 2002, Armenia's weighted average annual rate of inflation was 3.07 percent.

 **CAPITAL FLOWS AND FOREIGN INVESTMENT**
Score: **2**–Stable (low barriers)

Armenia offers equal official treatment to foreign investors, who have the same right to establish businesses as native Armenians in most sectors of the economy. Unless specifically authorized, foreign investment is not allowed in consumer co-operatives, collective farms, government enterprises, and enterprises of strategic significance. The government continues to restrict ownership of land by foreigners, although they may lease it. According to the Armenian Embassy, Armenia does not impose any exchange controls or maintain any repatriation limitations that require investors to keep their capital in the country. The International Monetary Fund reports that there are no restrictions or controls on the holding of foreign exchange accounts, invisible transactions, or current transfers.

 **BANKING AND FINANCE**
Score: **1**–Better (very low level of restrictions)

The central bank adopted a reform and consolidation program in 1994 after several banks had collapsed. The banking system is improving as supervision increases, regulation becomes more efficient, and minimum capital requirements are enforced. The Economist Intelligence Unit reports that all banks now adhere to international accounting standards; under the revised standards, several banks were closed, and the number of banks fell from 58 in 1994 to 31 at the end of 2000. Consolidation has left six banks in control of over 65 percent of total banking capital. Foreign banks account for 40 percent of banking capital. The Ministry of Finance and Economy, which regulates the insurance industry, allows the presence of foreign insurance companies. According to the Armenian Embassy, banking regulations allow banks to become involved in a wide array of financial services, including insurance, leasing, and brokerage services, and the government is divesting itself of its ownership in the banking sector. The last state-owned bank, Armsberbank, was sold in September 2001, and the government is selling its share in Armenian Argo Bank (equity is about 10 percent). As a result of the increased evidence of the lack of government involvement, Armenia's banking and finance score is 1 point better this year.

 **WAGES AND PRICES**
Score: **3**–Stable (moderate level of intervention)

According to the U.S. Department of State, "The state continues to control prices for utilities and public transportation…. From time to time, the government conducts rationed sales of basic foods and other consumables (sugar, powdered milk, matches, soap) to the most needy groups at prices much lower than market prices." In January 2002, the Armenian State Repository set new prices (which are used to calculate the tax on exploitation of natural resources) for nonferrous, rare, and precious metals. The government sets a minimum wage by decree.

 **PROPERTY RIGHTS**
Score: **3**–Stable (moderate level of protection)

Private property is guaranteed by law, but neither legal enforcement nor the judicial system provides adequate protection. According to the U.S. Department of State, "The Constitution provides for an independent judiciary; however, in practice, the Constitution's provisions do not insulate the courts fully from political pressure, and in practice, courts [are] subject to pressure from the executive and legislative branches and some judges [are] corrupt. Lengthy public trials sometimes [are] a problem." The same source also notes that Armenian courts "are becoming increasingly independent. The Ministry of Justice is gradually limiting its involvement in civil cases."

 **REGULATION**
Score: **4**–Stable (high level)

A corrupt bureaucracy often applies regulations haphazardly, and political strife hampers the progress of any reforms. According to the U.S. Department of State, "Ambiguous laws and state controlled activities have lead to a situation where certain sectors, though officially open, maintain near monopolies that are difficult to break (e.g., the aviation sector)…. Changes in legislation are only rarely announced or publicly disclosed before implementation." In addition, "bureaucratic procedures can be burdensome and time consuming when an investor negotiates a contract with the Armenian government, as the contract may require approval by several ministries." Corruption continues to affect business. "Despite severe penalties," reports the U.S. Department of State, "bribery is widespread and is the most common form of corruption, especially in the areas of government procurement, all types of transfers and approvals, and such business-related services as company registration, licensing, and land or space allocation."

 **INFORMAL MARKET**
Score: **4**–Stable (high level of activity)

Transparency International's 2000 score for Armenia was 2.5. (2000 was the last year Transparency International reported Armenia's score.) Therefore, Armenia's informal market score is 4 this year.

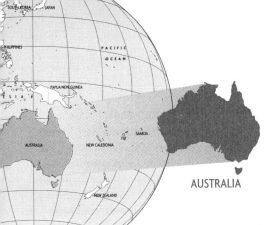

# AUSTRALIA

Rank: 11

Score: 1.88

Category: Free

AUSTRALIA

## QUICK STUDY

### SCORES

| | |
|---|---|
| Trade Policy | 2 |
| Fiscal Burden | 3.8 |
| Government Intervention | 2 |
| Monetary Policy | 2 |
| Foreign Investment | 2 |
| Banking and Finance | 1 |
| Wages and Prices | 2 |
| Property Rights | 1 |
| Regulation | 2 |
| Informal Market | 1 |

**Population:** 19,700,000

**Total area:** 7,713,000 sq. km

**GDP:** $484.6 billion

**GDP growth rate:** 3.5%

**GDP per capita:** $24,598

**Major exports:** coal, crude petroleum, iron ore, aluminum, machinery, financial services, insurance, travel services

**Exports of goods and services:** $104.5 billion

**Major export trading partners:** Japan 18.6%, US 9.7%, South Korea 8.3%, China 7.0%, New Zealand 6.6%

**Major imports:** passenger motor vehicles, aircraft and parts, computers, medicaments, travel services, financial services, insurance

**Imports of goods and services:** $127 billion

**Major import trading partners:** US 18.1%, Japan 12.3%, China 10.1%, Germany 5.7%, UK 4.6%

**Foreign direct investment**

2002 Data (in constant 1995 US dollars)

Tourism plays a significant role in the Australian economy. Settled by the British in 1788, Australia was intended to be a penal colony, yet free settlers came in large numbers, and in 1947 the government embarked on a mass immigration program. What began as a penal colony has become a vibrant member of the British Commonwealth of Nations. Australia is a leader in trade liberalization. According to the U.S. Trade Representative, tariffs have been reduced gradually since the 1970s, and 86 percent of tariffs are below 5 percent. Australia signed a bilateral free trade agreement with Singapore and is negotiating one with the United States. As a leader in the Cairns Group, it has called for agricultural liberalization in the Doha Round of the World Trade Organization. Australia is the world's largest coal exporter, and mining and agriculture comprise the majority of exports. According to the Economist Intelligence Unit, rural and mineral exports, including processed goods, accounted for just under 65 percent of total merchandise exports in 2001–2002. Australia's strict quarantine system has come under fire as being protectionist rather than science-based, and the EIU reports that the foreign investment regime includes restrictions that limit foreign ownership of television stations to 15 percent. Australia's fiscal burden of government score is 0.2 point better this year. As a result, its overall score is 0.02 point better this year.

## TRADE POLICY
### Score: **2**–Stable (low level of protectionism)

According to the World Bank, Australia's weighted average tariff rate in 2001 (the most recent year for which World Bank data are available) was 3.9 percent. The U.S. Department of State reports that non-tariff barriers include "stringent sanitary and phytosanitary restrictions affecting imports of fresh fruit and vegetables and imports of meat and poultry products…. [I]mported agricultural commodities must have an import risk analysis (IRA) [that] can take an average of two years to carry out." In addition, "quotas are in place for five cheese items and for non-manufactured tobacco," as well as for TV broadcasting.

## FISCAL BURDEN OF GOVERNMENT
Score—Income Taxation: **4.5**–Stable (very high tax rates)
Score—Corporate Taxation: **4**–Stable (high tax rates)
Score—Change in Government Expenditures: **2.5**–Better (low decrease)
### Final Score: **3.8**–Better (high cost of government)

Australia's top income tax rate is 47 percent. The top corporate tax rate is 30 percent. Government expenditures as a share of GDP decreased 1 percentage point to 36 percent in 2002, compared to a 1 percentage point increase in 2001. As a result, Australia's fiscal burden of government score is 0.2 point better this year.

## GOVERNMENT INTERVENTION IN THE ECONOMY
### Score: **2**–Stable (low level)

According to the Economist Intelligence Unit, the government consumed 18 percent of GDP in 2002. In the same year, based on data from the Department of Finance and Administration, Australia received 3.14 percent of its total revenues from state-owned enterprises and government ownership of property.

**MONETARY POLICY**
Score: **2**–Stable (low level of inflation)

From 1993 to 2002, Australia's weighted average annual rate of inflation was 3.36 percent.

 **CAPITAL FLOWS AND FOREIGN INVESTMENT**
Score: **2**–Stable (low barriers)

Australia's economy is open to foreign investment, and foreign investors receive national treatment. The Foreign Investment Review Board requires notification of some proposed investment. Foreign investors with investments greater than A$50 million, where the foreign investor would acquire a substantial interest (a shareholding of 15 percent for a single firm or 40 percent for by two or more unrelated foreign interests) in an Australian business, must have prior authorization. The International Monetary Fund reports that proposals to start new businesses with an investment of A$10 million must also receive prior authorization. The government accepts most of these proposals routinely, although they may be rejected if the investment is determined not to be consistent with the country's "national interest," national security, or economic development concerns. According to Australia's Department of the Treasury, 4,520 proposals for investment were evaluated in 2001–2002; only 77 were rejected, all but one of which were in the real estate sector. While no sector is completely closed, foreign investment in television and newspaper media, banking, airlines, airports, shipping, urban real estate, and telecommunications is subject to limitations. Since 1999, foreign airlines have been able to purchase 100 percent equity in a domestic airline and 49 percent in an international Australian airline; the old restrictions remain in effect for the national airline, Qantas.

 **BANKING AND FINANCE**
Score: **1**–Stable (very low level of restrictions)

Australia has a modern, competitive financial system. Banks are relatively free of government control, and foreign banks may be licensed as branches or subsidiaries. As of July 2002, reports the Economist Intelligence Unit, 33 foreign banks were operating in Australia with full banking authority and another 20 were operating as money market corporations. According to the Australian Department of the Treasury, the government has no ownership interest in any bank in Australia. The government has focused on significantly streamlining and reforming financial-sector regulation and does not affect the allocation of credit.

 **WAGES AND PRICES**
Score: **2**–Stable (low level of intervention)

The market determines most wages and almost all prices. According to the Australian Department of the Treasury, the federal minimum wage is roughly 50 percent of the average full-time wage. In addition, Australia's "Award" system, which provides various minimum wages for specific economic sectors, affects approximately 21 percent of Australian workers. There are no national price controls on goods, but Australian states retain the power to impose their own price controls. The Economist Intelligence Unit reports that "several price regulating laws [are] in place.... The Price Surveillance Act gives the Australian Competition and Consumer Commission (ACCC) power to examine the prices of selected goods and services to promote competitive pricing wherever possible and restrain price rises in markets where competition is less than effective."

 **PROPERTY RIGHTS**
Score: **1**–Stable (very high level of protection)

Property is very secure in Australia. According to the Economist Intelligence Unit, "Contractual agreements...are protected by the rule of law and the independence of the judiciary...although backlogs in the court lists can delay cases coming for trial for several years.... [A]buse of political influence is extremely rare." Government expropriation is highly unlikely.

 **REGULATION**
Score: **2**–Stable (low level)

Although the procedure for establishing a company is straightforward, environmental regulations, generated primarily by the states, may not be uniformly applied. Australia's regulatory environment is transparent and for the most part not burdensome. "In areas of the economy dominated by small businesses," reports the Economist Intelligence Unit, "the government favors self-regulation with 'light-handed' intervention by government.... If [the government] is convinced that self regulation is not working, it has the power under the Trade Practices Act to declare the code of conduct mandatory." An Office of Regulation Review monitors new and existing regulations to determine the costs they would impose on business. The EIU reports that "there is no entrenched institutional corruption in the bureaucracy...."

 **INFORMAL MARKET**
Score: **1**–Stable (very low level of activity)

Transparency International's 2002 score for Australia is 8.6. Therefore, Australia's informal market score is 1 this year.

AUSTRIA

# AUSTRIA

Rank: 20
Score: 2.08
Category: Mostly Free

**Present & Past Scores**

(Best) 1
2
3
4
(Worst) 5

2.09 2.06 2.03 2.08 2.08 1.98 2.03 2.08 2.08 2.08

'95 '96 '97 '98 '99 '00 '01 '02 '03 '04

## QUICK STUDY

### SCORES

| | |
|---|---|
| Trade Policy | 2 |
| Fiscal Burden | 4.3 |
| Government Intervention | 2 |
| Monetary Policy | 1 |
| Foreign Investment | 2 |
| Banking and Finance | 2 |
| Wages and Prices | 2 |
| Property Rights | 1 |
| Regulation | 3 |
| Informal Market | 1.5 |

**Population:** 8,141,700

**Total area:** 83,858 sq. km

**GDP:** $273.2 billion

**GDP growth rate:** 0.7%

**GDP per capita:** $33,556

**Major exports:** machinery and transport equipment, consumer goods, chemical products, food, drink and tobacco, paper, travel services, financial services, insurance

**Exports of goods and services:** $145.7 billion

**Major export trading partners:** Germany 32.0%, Italy 8.5%, Switzerland 5.3%, US 5.1%

**Major imports:** machinery and transport equipment, consumer goods, raw materials, financial services, insurance, travel services

**Imports of goods and services:** $138 billion

**Major import trading partners:** Germany 40.3%, Italy 7.1%, US 4.8%, France 3.9%

**Foreign direct investment (net):** −$4.3 billion

2002 Data (in constant 1995 US dollars)

The state's role in Austria's economy has decreased in recent years. The government has relinquished control of the formerly nationalized oil and gas, steel, and engineering companies and has deregulated telecommunications and electricity. Yet Austria remains over-regulated. Foreign investors face rigidities, barriers to market entry, and an elaborate regulatory environment; new laws seeking to prevent the construction of mega stores and forbidding the opening of shops on Sundays; and restrictive environmental standards. As a result, prices are among the highest in the European Union. Under the Proporz system established after World War II, the Social Democrats and the center–right People's Party divided economic power. People's Party Chancellor Wolfgang Schussel has accelerated the pace of market reform and has enacted laws designed to do away with the Proporz system. Parliamentary elections led to reform of the coalition in February 2003. Since then, support for the third-party entrant, the Freedom Party, has fallen while Schussel's People's Party has gained in popularity. Schussel has moved ahead dynamically to confront a pension system that accounts for 15 percent of GDP per annum. The government plans to cut the benefit to future retirees in the private sector by at least 10 percent from present levels. Despite a nationwide strike by indignant unions in May 2003, it appears Schussel will have the political muscle to get this vital reform through parliament.

## TRADE POLICY
### Score: **2**–Stable (low level of protectionism)

Austria's trade policy is the same as the policies of other members of the European Union. In 2001, the common EU weighted average tariff rate was 2.6 percent, up from the 1.8 percent reported in the 2003 *Index*. According to the U.S. Department of State, "The most important tariff quotas for manufactured goods are on chemicals and electronics. Both are administered on a first-come, first-served licensing basis."

## FISCAL BURDEN OF GOVERNMENT
Score—Income Taxation: **5**–Stable (very high tax rates)
Score—Corporate Taxation: **4.5**–Stable (very high tax rates)
Score—Change in Government Expenditures: **3**–Stable (very low decrease)
### Final Score: **4.3**–Stable (high cost of government)

Austria's top income tax rate is 50 percent. The top corporate tax rate is 34 percent. Government expenditures as a share of GDP decreased 0.2 percentage point to 51.9 percent in 2002, as they did in 2001. On net, Austria's fiscal burden of government score is unchanged this year.

## GOVERNMENT INTERVENTION IN THE ECONOMY
### Score: **2**–Stable (low level)

According to the Economist Intelligence Unit, Austria's government consumed 19.4 percent of GDP in 2002. In the same year, based on data from the *Statistical Yearbook*, Austria received 3.24 percent of its total revenues from state-owned enterprises and government ownership of property.

## MONETARY POLICY
Score: **1**–Stable (very low level of inflation)

From 1993 to 2002, Austria's weighted average annual rate of inflation was 2 percent.

## CAPITAL FLOWS AND FOREIGN INVESTMENT
Score: **2**–Stable (low barriers)

Austria welcomes most foreign direct investment, and there is no discrimination against foreign investors. The Economist Intelligence Unit reports that foreign direct investment increased from 5 percent of GDP in 1985 to 18.7 percent in 2001 and that in 1999, 7 percent of the workforce was employed in 2,540 foreign companies that had investments in Austria. The *Financial Times* reports, however, that official bureaucracy discourages foreign companies from investing in Austria. Foreign investment is forbidden in arms and explosives, as well as industries in which the state has a monopoly (casinos, printing of banknotes, and minting coins). The International Monetary Fund reports that restrictions exist for non-residents in the auditing and legal professions, transportation, and electric power generation. There are no controls or requirements on current transfers, access to foreign exchange, or repatriation of profits. Although the national government no longer imposes restrictions on foreign purchase of land, the IMF reports that real estate transactions are subject to approval by local authorities.

## BANKING AND FINANCE
Score: **2**–Stable (low level of restrictions)

Austrian banks offer services ranging from credit to finance, and the government permits savings banks to perform commercial banking functions, including the brokering of securities and mutual funds. According to the Economist Intelligence Unit, there were 907 financial institutions in December 2001, and 27 percent of all assets and 31 percent of all liabilities in 2000 were of foreign origin. Although the banking system is competitive, the government is involved in the banking sector. The EIU reports that "Austrian Investkredit offers long-term financing of up to 20 years. Investkredit, a state controlled bank that specialises in long-term credit and corporate financing for companies based in Austrian [sic], provides a range of services, including bank loans, for mainly small and medium-sized companies. Investkredit has also taken stakes in a number of smaller firms preparing for initial public offerings on the Vienna Stock Exchange." The government maintains reserve and liquid asset requirements for euro deposits and places limits on open foreign exchange positions. In 2002, the European Union fined nine Austrian banks $117 million for fixing banking fees and interest rates.

## WAGES AND PRICES
Score: **2**–Stable (low level of intervention)

Prices are determined primarily by the market. According to the Economist Intelligence Unit, "there are now very few remaining price-controlled goods—primarily rail travel and pharmaceuticals.... Although the law still permits certain price controls, in practice it is rarely implemented." The government affects agricultural prices through its participation in the Common Agricultural Policy, which heavily subsidizes agricultural goods. Austria does not maintain a minimum wage; minimum wages are determined by annual collective bargaining agreements between employers and employee organizations.

## PROPERTY RIGHTS
Score: **1**–Stable (very high level of protection)

Property is very secure in Austria. The Economist Intelligence Unit reports that "contractual agreements are very secure, and the protection of both private property and intellectual property [is] well established."

## REGULATION
Score: **3**–Stable (moderate level)

Austria's regulatory system is characterized in some sectors by complexity and slow, bureaucratic procedures. "The Austrian government has made progress in streamlining its complex and time consuming regulatory environment," reports the U.S. Department of State. "[T]he government has successfully simplified and speeded-up administrative procedures to obtain business permits. In general, the time for obtaining all necessary permits has been reduced to about three months, except for large projects requiring an environmental impact assessment." In 2002, the government proposed a plan to reform the Business Code, providing for "a 'one-stop shop' for the business permit, but not yet including the plant and building permits. The reform also provided for further deregulation and liberalization to facilitate establishment of new businesses, most importantly by simplifying qualification requirements and reducing the number of business categories to only two." The Hayek Institute reports that parts of the proposed reform plan, such as privatization, have been carried out but the proposed plan has not been fully implemented yet. According to the Economist Intelligence Unit, "The Austrian labour market has become more flexible in recent years, with fewer restrictions on hiring and firing than in a number of other EU countries." However, "legislation on industry and its effect on the environment is complex and extensive."

## INFORMAL MARKET
Score: **1.5**–Stable (low level of activity)

Transparency International's 2002 score for Austria is 7.8. Therefore, Austria's informal market score is 1.5 this year.

# AZERBAIJAN

Rank: 106

Score: 3.39

Category: Mostly Unfree

**Present & Past Scores**

(Best) 1
2
3
4
(Worst) 5

4.78 4.58 4.35 4.29 4.33 3.93 3.58 3.50

3.39

'95 '96 '97 '98 '99 '00 '01 '02 '03 '04
n/a

## QUICK STUDY

### SCORES

| | |
|---|---|
| Trade Policy | 3 |
| Fiscal Burden | 3.4 |
| Government Intervention | 3 |
| Monetary Policy | 1 |
| Foreign Investment | 4 |
| Banking and Finance | 4 |
| Wages and Prices | 3 |
| Property Rights | 4 |
| Regulation | 4 |
| Informal Market | 4.5 |

**Population:** 8,116,110

**Total area:** 86,600 sq. km

**GDP:** $3.7 billion

**GDP growth rate:** 9.9%

**GDP per capita:** $460

**Major exports:** oil and gas, machinery, cotton, food-stuffs

**Exports of goods and services:** $912 million

**Major export trading partners:** Italy 57.0%, Israel 7.2%, Georgia 4.5%, Russia 3.4%

**Major imports:** machinery and equipment, foodstuffs, metals, chemicals

**Imports of goods and services:** $2.8 billion

**Major import trading partners:** US 16.1%, Russia 10.7%, Turkey 10.4%, Kazakhstan 7.0%

**Foreign direct investment (net):** $843 million

2001 Data (in constant 1995 US dollars)

**A**zerbaijan gained its independence from the Soviet Union in 1991 and since then has endured political and economic upheaval. Oil is the primary export, and production has increased ever since 1997, but poverty and high levels of unemployment, corruption, and income inequality continue to plague the economy. With the Nagorno–Karabakh regional conflict with Armenia unresolved, 20 percent of Azerbaijan is occupied by Armenia. The authoritarian regime of President Heydar Aliyev, in power since the early 1970s, allows relatively small civic space. A tainted election in 1998 resulted in Aliyev's re-election to another five-year term. As Aliyev has designated his son as his political successor, opposition is likely in the fall 2003 presidential elections. Relations with the U.S. have improved significantly as Aliyev agreed to support the anti-terrorism coalition and a longstanding ban on certain forms of U.S. aid to the country was lifted. Transparency International ranked Azerbaijan as the most corrupt of the former Soviet states and one of the most corrupt countries in the world (84th out of 91). The lack of transparency in the State Oil Fund recently caused the International Monetary Fund to suspend lending. Long-term prospects will depend on management of oil wealth, successful completion of the Baku–Tbilisi–Ceyhan Main Export Pipeline (MEP), and global prices for oil and gas. Azerbaijan's fiscal burden of government score is is 0.1 point better this year, and its government intervention score is 1 point better. As a result, Azerbaijan's overall score is 0.11 point better this year.

## TRADE POLICY
### Score: **3**–Stable (moderate level of protectionism)

According to the International Monetary Fund, Azerbaijan's weighted average tariff rate in 2001 was 7.9 percent, up from the 6.7 percent reported in the 2003 *Index*. The U.S. Department of State reports that "Non-tariff barriers include a weak and unpredictable legal regime, arbitrary tax and customs administration, clear conflicts of interest in regulatory/commercial matters, and corruption. The [government's] inadequate IPR protections amount to a trade barrier. Alcoholic beverages and tobacco products are subject to both quantitative restrictions and import licenses."

## FISCAL BURDEN OF GOVERNMENT
### Score—Income Taxation: **3.5**–Stable (high tax rates)
### Score—Corporate Taxation: **3.5**–Stable (high tax rates)
### Score—Change in Government Expenditures: **3**–Better (very low decrease)
### Final Score: **3.4**–Better (moderate cost of government)

Azerbaijan's top income tax rate is 35 percent. The top corporate tax rate is 27 percent. Government expenditures as a share of GDP decreased by 0.7 percentage point to 19 percent in 2001, compared to an increase of 0.8 percentage point in 2000. As a result, Azerbaijan's fiscal burden of government score is 0.1 point better this year.

## GOVERNMENT INTERVENTION IN THE ECONOMY
### Score: **3**–Better (moderate level)

According to the World Bank, the government consumed 9.8 percent of GDP in 2001, down from the 12.5 percent reported in the 2003 *Index*. As a result, Azerbaijan's government intervention score is 1 point better this year. In 2000, based on data from the Ministry of Finance,

Azerbaijan received 3.22 percent of its total revenues from state-owned enterprises and government ownership of property. According to the Economist Intelligence Unit, however, "Over one-third of revenue comes from SOCAR [State Oil Company of the Azerbaijan Republic]...." The EIU therefore indicates that revenues from state-owned enterprises are at least 33 percent of total government revenues.

## MONETARY POLICY
### Score: **1**–Stable (very low level of inflation)

From 1993 to 2002, Azerbaijan's weighted average annual rate of inflation was 2.72 percent.

## CAPITAL FLOWS AND FOREIGN INVESTMENT
### Score: **4**–Stable (high barriers)

According to the Economist Intelligence Unit, "Outside the oil and gas sectors there has been little FDI activity. This is mainly attributable to the poor investment climate and severe bureaucratic obstacles." Elsewhere, the EIU reports that, although the law protects foreign investors against expropriation, "Apart from the oil sector, foreign companies are unlikely to do well in court against powerful domestic interests. The government has not yet expropriated foreign assets, but there is a risk that it might do so." The government prohibits investments in national security and defense sectors and restricts investment in government-controlled sectors like energy, mobile telephony, and oil and gas. The International Monetary Fund reports that foreign exchange accounts are subject to some restrictions. Payments and transfers are subject to documentation requirements and quantitative limits. The central bank must authorize most capital transactions.

## BANKING AND FINANCE
### Score: **4**–Stable (high level of restrictions)

Azerbaijan's banking system is weak, and most transactions in the economy are conducted in cash. The central bank raised minimum capital requirements in January 2002, leading to the closure of six banks. According to the Economist Intelligence Unit, "The banking sector is dominated by two state-owned banks—United Universal Bank and IBA—which together account for over half of the banking sector's total assets." The sector is very inefficient. "Although many banks offer short-term trade financing, long term loans and mortgages are not available," reports the U.S. Department of State. "Overall, lack of credit is a key constraint to the development of private business in Azerbaijan.... Outside of the donor-backed credit lines, there is essentially no bank credit exceeding 12–18 months." Foreign banks have a minimal presence even though the National Bank of Azerbaijan has increased the limit on foreign bank ownership from 30 percent to 50 percent. HSBC, a bank from the United Kingdom and the only major international bank active in retail banking, withdrew in March 2002.

## WAGES AND PRICES
### Score: **3**–Stable (moderate level of intervention)

In 1993, the government implemented a reform program under which prices were gradually liberalized. According to the U.S. Department of State, "With the exception of goods such as gasoline and certain other products, the government does not set retail prices." However, the Economist Intelligence Unit reports that "Insufficient progress has also been made on liberalising domestic energy prices, a move that would enable domestic gas and electricity companies to operate on a commercial footing. At present, these companies pay very little for their energy supplies, charge even less for their supplies and still are unable to collect payments for energy delivered to consumers. The result is a considerable subsidy that, on paper, is worth as much, if not more, that the government budget." The government sets the nationwide administrative minimum wage by decree. Although subsidies on utilities and price controls on domestic oil prices are significant, price controls do not apply to oil exports and therefore do not affect most oil production.

## PROPERTY RIGHTS
### Score: **4**–Stable (low level of protection)

The legal system does not provide sufficient protection for private property. According to the Economist Intelligence Unit, "As in most post-Soviet republics, the judiciary is the least developed branch of the government. Judicial and police corruption is widespread...." The U.S. Department of State reports that "effective means of protecting and enforcing property and contractual rights are not yet assured. While the [government] does not officially interfere in the court system, in practice courts are weak, judges often inexperienced, and progressive new tax and other economic legislation poorly understood. The Economic Court, which has jurisdiction over commercial disputes, is weak, widely regarded as corruptible, and its decisions are often inconsistent."

## REGULATION
### Score: **4**–Stable (high level)

The procedure for establishing a business is complicated. According to the U.S. Department of State, "Azerbaijan remains a difficult place to do business given arbitrary tax and customs administration, a weak court system, monopolistic regulation of the market, and corruption." In addition, "The lack of transparent policies and effective laws to establish clear rules and foster competition are particularly serious impediments to investment.... Ready access to government rules and regulations is an impediment to doing business.... Corruption is a significant deterrent to investment in Azerbaijan."

## INFORMAL MARKET
### Score: **4.5**–Stable (very high level of activity)

Transparency International's 2002 score for Azerbaijan is 2. Therefore, Azerbaijan's informal market score is 4.5 this year.

*2004 Index of Economic Freedom*

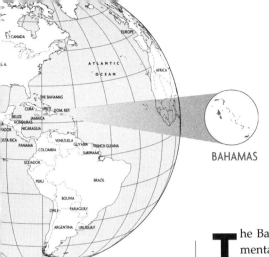

BAHAMAS

# THE BAHAMAS

Rank: 25
Score: 2.25
Category: Mostly Free

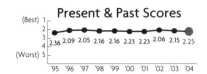

**Present & Past Scores**

(Best) 1
2
3
4
(Worst) 5

2.36 2.09 2.05 2.16 2.16 2.23 2.23 2.06 2.15 2.25

'95 '96 '97 '98 '99 '00 '01 '02 '03 '04

## QUICK STUDY

### SCORES

| | |
|---|---|
| Trade Policy | 5 |
| Fiscal Burden | 1.5 |
| Government Intervention | 2 |
| Monetary Policy | 1 |
| Foreign Investment | 3 |
| Banking and Finance | 2 |
| Wages and Prices | 3 |
| Property Rights | 1 |
| Regulation | 2 |
| Informal Market | 2 |

**Population:** 310,000

**Total area:** 13,940 sq. km

**GDP:** $4.17 billion

**GDP growth rate:** −0.5%

**GDP per capita:** $13,481

**Major exports:** Fish and crawfish, chemicals, rum, fruit and vegetables, pharmaceuticals, travel services, transportation, financial and insurance services

**Exports of goods (fob):** $551 million

**Major export trading partners:** US 34.9%, France 15.1%, Germany 14.0%, Spain 11.7%

**Major imports:** Machinery, manufactured goods, mineral fuels, chemicals, food and live animals, transportation, financial and insurance services

**Imports of goods (fob):** $1.6 billion

**Major import trading partners:** US 34.7%, Korea 17.1%, Italy 7.8%, Singapore 5.6%

2001 Data (in constant 1995 US dollars)

The Bahamas is a member of the British Commonwealth and a constitutional, parliamentary democracy whose economy depends primarily on tourism and offshore banking to generate foreign exchange. According to the U.S. Department of State, tourism accounts for approximately 60 percent of GDP and employs about half of the population. More than 80 percent of all visitors come from the United States. Following the September 11, 2001, terrorist attacks, the U.S. economic slowdown led to a slump in the Bahamian travel industry. Despite the relative prosperity of most citizens, unemployment stands at about 9 percent. Matters would have been worse had the government not reduced public spending at the beginning of the downturn to keep it in line with reduced revenues. The government of Prime Minister Perry Christie, who assumed office in 2002, is thus far committed to keeping public expenditures under control and making the Bahamas more globally competitive to boost revenue. Instead of raising taxes in his May 2003 budget presentation, Christie chose to enforce better collection. The government projects that uncertain economic conditions this year are likely to push public debt to 39 percent of GDP. The Bahamas' regulation score is 1 point worse this year. As a result, its overall score is 0.1 point worse this year.

## TRADE POLICY
### Score: **5**–Stable (very high level of protectionism)

According to the International Monetary Fund, the Bahamas had an average tariff rate of 34 percent in 2001. The U.S. Department of State reports that the government "charges a 7 percent 'stamp tax' on most imports. Higher stamp taxes are charged on some duty free goods, including tourist items such as china, crystal, wristwatches, clocks, jewelry, table linens, leather goods, perfume, wine and liquor." The government also restricts the import of some agricultural goods through import permits.

## FISCAL BURDEN OF GOVERNMENT
Score—Income Taxation: **1**–Stable (very low tax rates)
Score—Corporate Taxation: **1**–Stable (very low tax rates)
Score—Change in Government Expenditures: **3**–Stable (very low decrease)
### Final Score: **1.5**–Stable (low cost of government)

The Bahamas has no income tax, no corporate income tax, no capital gains tax, no inheritance tax, and no value-added tax. Government expenditures as a share of GDP fell more (0.2 percentage point to 19.1 percent) in 2001 than they did in 2000 (0.1 percentage point). On net, the Bahamas' fiscal burden of government score is unchanged this year.

## GOVERNMENT INTERVENTION IN THE ECONOMY
### Score: **2**–Stable (low level)

Based on data from the central bank, the government consumed 11.2 percent of GDP in 2001. In the same year, according to the International Monetary Fund, the Bahamas received 2.3 percent of its revenues from state-owned enterprises and government ownership of property.

## MONETARY POLICY
### Score: **1**–Stable (very low level of inflation)

From 1993 to 2002, the Bahamas' weighted average annual rate of inflation was 2.05 percent.

## CAPITAL FLOWS AND FOREIGN INVESTMENT
### Score: **3**–Stable (moderate barriers)

Foreign investment is restricted in a number of sectors: wholesale and retail operations, commission agencies engaged in import–export trade, real estate and domestic property management agencies, media and advertising, nightclubs and some restaurants, security services building supplies and most construction companies, personal cosmetics and beauty establishments, some fishing operations, auto and appliance service operations, and public transportation. The government imposes controls on capital transactions. All outward capital transfers and inward transfers by non-residents require exchange control approval, and outward transfers by residents are restricted. Sales of bonds and debt securities, shares and other securities, commercial credits, and financial credits are subject to varying approval of the central bank or regulations when involving foreign exchange or non-residents. According to the U.S. Department of State, "Large foreign investors may be held to higher labor, health and safety standards than are local entrepreneurs." Foreigners purchasing real estate for commercial purposes or purchasing more than five acres must obtain a permit from the Investments Board, and non-residents must receive approval to sell real estate locally.

## BANKING AND FINANCE
### Score: **2**–Stable (low level of restrictions)

The Bahamas is one of the financial centers of the Caribbean. The U.S. Department of State reports that as of May 2002, 321 banks and trust companies were licensed, down from 410 in 2000. This is a result of stricter regulation and supervision that has led the government to suspend licenses for a large number of licensed banks that could not show proof of an actual physical presence. The financial sector accounts for 7 percent of GDP and employs about 3 percent of the labor force. The government maintains ownership of the Bahamas Development Bank, which primarily provides financing for commercial, industrial, and agricultural development projects. The financial sector is extremely open to foreigners. In an effort to secure its removal from the Organisation for Economic Co-operation and Development's list of jurisdictions with a non-cooperative record on money laundering, the Bahamas passed a package of legislation to tighten controls on such activity. The new legislation imposes extra regulatory costs on the financial sector but does not significantly reduce the level of economic freedom. The Financial Action Task Force, an intergovernmental body made up of 29 countries designed to combat money laundering, removed the

Bahamas from its list of jurisdictions with a non-cooperative record on money laundering in June 2001.

## WAGES AND PRICES
### Score: **3**–Stable (moderate level of intervention)

The government of the Bahamas maintains price controls on gasoline and diesel oil, motor vehicle parts and accessories, liquefied petroleum, drugs, utility rates, and public transportation. A minimum wage for all non-salaried public-sector workers was established in 1996, and legislation establishing a minimum wage for the private sector was passed in 2001.

## PROPERTY RIGHTS
### Score: **1**–Stable (very high level of protection)

The Bahamas has an advanced and efficient legal system based on English common law. According to the U.S. Department of State, however, "while generally fair, the Bahamian judicial process tends to be much slower than the norm in the United States and the [U.S.] Embassy has received occasional reports of malfeasance on the part of court officials."

## REGULATION
### Score: **2**–Worse (low level)

The Bahamian government generally follows a hands-off approach to business, but the U.S. Department of State reports that "the discretionary issuance of business licenses can result in a lack of transparency in decisions to authorize or to renew the authority of a business. ... Obtaining required permits, especially immigration permits, can take an inordinate length of time." Labor laws can be burdensome, especially for domestic business. According to the U.S. Department of State, "The Fair Labor Standards Act requires at least one 24-hour rest period per week, paid annual vacations, and employer contributions to National Insurance (social security). The Act also requires overtime pay (time and a half) for hours in excess of 48 or on public holidays. A 1988 law provides for maternity leave and the right to re-employment after childbirth.... Local business leaders complain that some of the laws are too restrictive...." In addition, "allegations of improper conduct on the part of Government officials surface regularly...." Based on newly available evidence of the regulatory burden, the Bahamas' regulation score is 1 point worse this year.

## INFORMAL MARKET
### Score: **2**–Stable (low level of activity)

Software, music, and video piracy is a problem. According to *UNIAN News,* the Bahamas is on the U.S. priority watch list for violations of intellectual property rights. The Economist Intelligence Unit reports that illegal drug trafficking and money laundering are also significant.

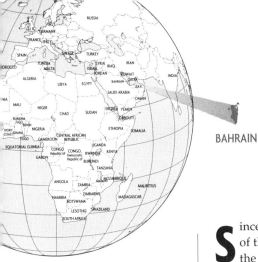

BAHRAIN

# BAHRAIN

Rank: 20
Score: 2.08
Category: Mostly Free

### Present & Past Scores

(Best) 1
2
3  1.78 1.75 1.80 1.90 1.81 1.88 2.01 2.10 2.04 2.08
4
(Worst) 5

'95 '96 '97 '98 '99 '00 '01 '02 '03 '04

## QUICK STUDY

### SCORES

| | |
|---|---|
| Trade Policy | 3 |
| Fiscal Burden | 1.8 |
| Government Intervention | 4 |
| Monetary Policy | 1 |
| Foreign Investment | 2 |
| Banking and Finance | 1 |
| Wages and Prices | 3 |
| Property Rights | 1 |
| Regulation | 2 |
| Informal Market | 2 |

**Population:** 651,000

**Total area:** 620 sq. km

**GDP:** $7.2 billion

**GDP growth rate:** 4.8%

**GDP per capita:** $11,060

**Major exports:** mineral products, base metals, textiles, travel services, transportation

**Exports of goods and services:** $5.7 billion

**Major exports trading partners:** India 9.3%, US 5.1%, Saudi Arabia 3.4%, South Korea 2.5%

**Major imports:** machinery and appliances, mineral products, chemicals, crude oil

**Imports of goods and services:** $4.2 billion

**Major import trading partners:** Saudi Arabia 30.1%, US 12.8%, France 6.7%, UK 5.2%, Germany 4.8%

**Foreign direct investment (net):** −$111.2 million

2001 Data (in constant 1995 US dollars)

Since gaining its independence from Great Britain in 1971, Bahrain has developed one of the most progressive political systems and one of the most advanced economies in the Persian Gulf. Oil replaced pearl fishing as the leading source of income in the 1930s but has been eclipsed by the financial sector in recent years. Because of its relatively cosmopolitan outlook, modern economy, favorable regulatory structure, and excellent communications and transportation infrastructure, Bahrain is home to many multinational firms doing business in the Persian Gulf. Sheikh Hamad bin Isa al-Khalifa, who has adopted a conciliatory policy toward the political opposition and the traditionally disaffected Shi'a community, which makes up roughly two-thirds of the population, won a resounding victory in a February 2001 national referendum that approved his political reform program. He enacted a new constitution in February 2002 and declared himself king, transforming Bahrain from an absolute monarchy into a constitutional monarchy. Bahrain held municipal elections in May 2002; in October 2002, voters (including women) in the country's first parliamentary elections in over 30 years elected 40 members to the Chamber of Deputies. The other half of the National Assembly is composed of 40 members appointed by the king. In June 2002, the Bush Administration signed a Trade and Investment Framework Agreement with Bahrain, in the words of the U.S. Trade Representative, "to deepen our economic relationship" with that country. Because attracting foreign investment is a high priority, Bahrain maintains a hospitable environment for foreign business and seeks to improve its regulatory procedures. Bahrain's fiscal burden of government score is 0.4 point worse this year. As a result, its overall score is 0.04 point worse this year.

## TRADE POLICY

### Score: **3**–Stable (moderate level of protectionism)

According to the World Trade Organization, Bahrain's average applied MFN tariff rate in 2000 (the most recent year for which WTO trade data are available) was 7.7 percent. The government maintains strict labeling requirements on imported products and prohibits imports of irradiated food products, weapons, pornography and materials considered scandalous, wild animals, radio-controlled model airplanes, children's toys containing methyl chloride, and other articles declared injurious by the Ministry of Health, as well as foodstuffs and sweets containing cyclamates. According to the U.S. Department of State, "Import licenses for items to be sold in Bahrain are issued only to locally established companies that are at least 51 percent Bahraini-owned."

## FISCAL BURDEN OF GOVERNMENT

Score—Income Taxation: **1**–Stable (very low tax rates)
Score—Corporate Taxation: **1**–Stable (very low tax rates)
Score—Change in Government Expenditures: **4**–Worse (moderate increase)

### Final Score: **1.8**–Worse (low cost of government)

Bahrain imposes no taxes on income or corporate profits. Government expenditures as a percentage of GDP increased 1.8 percentage points to 27.7 percent in 2001, compared to a decline of 1.8 percentage points in 2000. As a result, Bahrain's fiscal burden of government score is 0.4 point worse this year.

## GOVERNMENT INTERVENTION IN THE ECONOMY
### Score: **4**–Stable (high level)

The World Bank reports that the government consumed 18.5 percent of GDP in 2001. In the same year, according to the International Monetary Fund, Bahrain received 73.9 percent of its total revenues (the largest portion being oil and gas revenues) from state-owned enterprises and government ownership of property.

## MONETARY POLICY
### Score: **1**–Stable (very low level of inflation)

From 1993 to 2002, Bahrain's weighted average annual rate of inflation was –1.0 percent.

## CAPITAL FLOWS AND FOREIGN INVESTMENT
### Score: **2**–Stable (low barriers)

Although attracting foreign investment is one of Bahrain's top priorities, the government still maintains some barriers. In the spring of 2001, Bahrain set up the Economic Development Board to streamline the investment process by creating a "one-stop shop" for potential investors. According to the U.S. Department of State, however, "In general, the Bahraini government does not license companies wishing to compete with existing government-owned or parastatal companies, or which would be a danger to public health or other aspects of the general welfare. As part of its economic diversification program, the government seeks to encourage investment in sectors that are export oriented and which do not compete with established local enterprises…. All significant investments, whether by Bahraini or foreign firms, must go through a lengthy and complicated government approval process." Foreigners may own 100 percent of new industrial businesses, and foreign companies may set up local branch offices without a local sponsor. Except for Gulf Cooperation Council nationals, non-residents are generally prohibited from purchasing land; foreign corporations established in Bahrain and long-term residents may be allowed to purchase property on a case-by case basis. Capital transactions and transfers may not be made to or received from Israel, but there are no other restrictions on capital repatriation or transfers.

## BANKING AND FINANCE
### Score: **1**–Stable (very low level of restrictions)

Over the past 20 years, Bahrain has established itself as a leading financial center for the Persian Gulf region and the Arab world. The country's legal, regulatory, and accounting systems are transparent and meet international standards. It is relatively easy to establish a bank; there are few, if any, restrictions or requirements on new banks; and foreign banks are welcome. "Foreigners and Bahrainis alike have ready access to credit on market terms," reports the U.S. Department of State. "The banking system is sound, and

undergoes examination and supervision by the Bahrain Monetary Agency (BMA), which has an international reputation for excellence." Efforts are being made to increase the liquidity of the Bahrain Stock Exchange, which opened in 1989. According to the Economist Intelligence Unit, "Gulf Co-operation Council (GCC) nationals are now allowed to own up to 100% of a listed firm, rather than 49%, as was previously the case. The ceiling on the stake that other foreigners may own has also been raised from 24% to 49%." The Minister of Commerce has announced that ownership for non-GCC nationals will be increased to 100 percent within three years.

## WAGES AND PRICES
### Score: **3**–Stable (moderate level of intervention)

According to the Economist Intelligence Unit, "In general, the market sets prices. The government imposes no price floors or ceilings, although it enjoys a monopoly in the distribution of certain key goods and services, and as such sets prices. These include power and water provision, telecommunications and petrol retailing." The U.S. Department of State reports that Bahrain has issued guidelines to both the public and private sectors that they should pay employees no less that $397.88 (150 dinars) per month.

## PROPERTY RIGHTS
### Score: **1**–Stable (very high level of protection)

Property is secure, and expropriation is unlikely. The Economist Intelligence Unit reports that "the Bahraini legal system has a good reputation, and foreign firms have been able to resolve disputes satisfactorily through the local courts. There are no prohibitions on the use of international arbitration to safeguard contracts."

## REGULATION
### Score: **2**–Stable (low level)

Bahrain's process for establishing a business is relatively straightforward. According to the U.S. Department of State, Bahrain generally follows a laissez-faire approach, although "its laws and procedures are not always transparent. Bureaucratic procedures can create significant stumbling blocks." In addition, "bureaucracy and poor coordination between ministries on occasion can impede new industrial ventures." Despite the existence of anticorruption laws, there is occasional high-level corruption in contract bidding and the management of successful investments; overall, reports the U.S. Department of State, "petty corruption is rare in Bahrain. The bureaucracy is sometimes inefficient but it is honest."

## INFORMAL MARKET
### Score: **2**–Stable (low level of activity)

With few barriers to imports, smuggling is not a problem. However, the Business Software Alliance reports that the rate of software piracy was 77 percent in 2001.

BANGLADESH

# BANGLADESH

Rank: 131

Score: 3.70

Category: Mostly Unfree

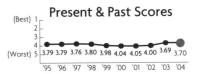

**Present & Past Scores**

(Best) 1
2
3
4
(Worst) 5

3.79 3.79 3.76 3.80 3.98 4.04 4.05 4.00 3.69 3.70

'95 '96 '97 '98 '99 '00 '01 '02 '03 '04

Bangladesh is one of the world's poorest countries, with most of its population living a hand-to-mouth existence. Its economy grew 4.8 percent in 2002, mainly because of a bumper crop and a resurgent garment sector, but Bangladesh is far below the 8 percent growth target many believe is necessary to lift its people from poverty. Export growth has been strong but below its potential because of government bureaucracy, infrastructure bottlenecks, and restrictions on private credit. Bangladesh also faces a looming water crisis as 60 percent of its groundwater shows signs of arsenic contamination. Economic reform continues slowly, with the government loosening foreign direct investment restrictions in some key sectors and regulations on banking and privatizing some state-owned enterprises. Weak law enforcement and pervasive corruption remain major problems. In October 2002, the military was deployed across the country to combat organized crime. However, recent legislation that gives them legal immunity from prosecution during the crackdown could erode human rights and confidence in the rule of law. This, combined with the presence of terrorist groups, undermines domestic security and deters foreign investment. Bangladesh's informal market score is 0.5 point better this year; however, its fiscal burden of government score is 0.1 point worse, and its government intervention score is 0.5 point worse. As a result, Bangladesh's overall score is 0.01 point worse this year.

## TRADE POLICY
### Score: **5–Stable** (very high level of protectionism)

According to the World Bank, Bangladesh's weighted average tariff rate in 2000 (the most recent year for which World Bank data are available) was 21 percent. Corruption is the main non-tariff barrier. According to the U.S. Department of State, "Complaints of higher level corruption in the fair awarding of public and private tenders are frequent…. In this regard, business people consider Customs to be among the worst [government agencies], a thoroughly corrupt organization in which officials routinely exert their power to influence the tariff value of imports and to expedite or delay import and export processing at the ports."

## FISCAL BURDEN OF GOVERNMENT
Score—Income Taxation: **2.5–Stable** (moderate tax rates)
Score—Corporate Taxation: **5–Stable** (very high tax rates)
Score—Change in Government Expenditures: **3.5–Worse** (low increase)
### Final Score: **4–Worse** (high cost of government)

Bangladesh's top income tax rate is 25 percent. The top corporate tax rate is 40 percent, but publicly traded companies with a registered office in Bangladesh are charged a lower corporate tax of 35 percent. Government expenditures as a share of GDP rose 0.4 percentage point to 14.5 percent in 2001, compared to a decline of 0.9 percentage point in 2000. As a result, Bangladesh's fiscal burden of government score is 0.1 point worse this year.

## GOVERNMENT INTERVENTION IN THE ECONOMY
### Score: **3.5–Worse** (high level)

According to the World Bank, the government consumed 4.5 percent of GDP in 2001, down from the 4.6 percent reported in the 2003 *Index*. In the fiscal year 2002–2003, based on data from the Ministry of Finance, Bangladesh received 5.36 percent of its total revenues from state-owned enterprises and government ownership of property. According to the Economist Intelligence Unit, however, "The government employs around one-third of those in formal sector employment, either directly in the civil service or through state owned enterprises (SOEs)." The U.S. Department of State reports that the state owns 40 percent of industrial capacity. According to the World Bank, "in 2000, [state-owned enterprises] accounted for over 25.0% of total fixed capital formation…." Because the state's presence in the economy is so extensive, 2 points have been added to Bangladesh's government intervention score: 1 point for the inaccuracy of the consumption statistic and another point for the inaccuracy of the figure for revenues from state-owned enterprises. Based on the newly available figure for revenues from state-owned enterprises, Bangladesh's government intervention score is 0.5 worse this year.

## MONETARY POLICY
### Score: **1**–Stable (very low level of inflation)

From 1993 to 2002, Bangladesh's weighted average annual rate of inflation was 2.76 percent.

## CAPITAL FLOWS AND FOREIGN INVESTMENT
### Score: **3**–Stable (moderate barriers)

Bangladesh seeks foreign investment and has removed many barriers to such activity. Foreign investors receive national treatment and are allowed full ownership in most sectors. The International Monetary Fund reports that foreign investments, with the exception of investments in the industrial sector, require approval. Most of the barriers that remain are informal or involve inadequate implementation of existing laws. According to the U.S. Department of State, a "major hindrance to increased foreign investment is poor implementation of the new, liberal investment policies. Foreigners often find that the implementing ministries still require unnecessary and slow licenses and permissions. Added to these difficulties are such problems as corruption, labor militancy, an uncertain law and order situation, poor infrastructure, inadequate commercial laws and courts, and policy instability (i.e., policies being altered at the behest of special interests, and decisions taken by previous governments being overturned when new ones come to power)." Payments and transactions for authorized activities are generally not restricted, but approval is required, and some activities are subject to quantitative limits.

## BANKING AND FINANCE
### Score: **4**–Stable (high level of restrictions)

Despite some recent reforms, the banking system remains underdeveloped, inefficient, and dominated by the four state-owned commercial banks. According to the Economist Intelligence Unit, approximately one-third of the loan portfolios of the four state-owned commercial banks and the private domestic banks, which together account for 80 percent of loans and 90 percent of deposits, are classified as non-performing loans. The U.S. Department of State reports that the government encourages the state-owned banks to give loans to money-losing enterprises in both the public and private sectors. Two nationalized companies dominate the insurance sector, although private competition is permitted.

## WAGES AND PRICES
### Score: **3**–Stable (moderate level of intervention)

According to the U.S. Department of State, "Other than a few essential pharmaceutical products and petroleum products, the [government] does not have price controls for the private sector where price levels are determined by the market's price mechanism." However, "The state controls a large portion of the industrial infrastructure through huge, money-losing state-owned enterprises (SOE) that the Government is unable or unwilling to privatize." Bangladesh has no minimum wage, and private-sector employers ignore wages set by the Wage Commission.

## PROPERTY RIGHTS
### Score: **4**–Stable (low level of protection)

The constitution provides for an independent judiciary; however, according to the U.S. Department of State, "a fundamental impediment to investment in Bangladesh is a weak legal system in which the enforceability of contracts is uncertain. Ten years can pass before a court case is heard and a decision delivered…. It is widely acknowledged that in the lower courts, where cases are first brought, corruption is a serious problem."

## REGULATION
### Score: **5**–Stable (very high level)

Corruption is Bangladesh's largest burden on business. Other problems include a bureaucracy characterized by vested interests, lack of transparency, and outdated business laws that do not protect private contracts. According to the U.S. Department of State, "Policy and regulations in Bangladesh are often not clear, consistent, or publicized. Generally, the civil service, businesses, professionals, trade unions and political parties have vested interests in a system in which confidentiality is used as an excuse for lack of transparency…. Businesses must always turn to civil servants to get action, yet may not receive any, even with the support of higher political levels. Unhelpful treatment of businesses by some government officials, coupled with other negatives in the investment climate, raise start-up and operational costs, add to risk, and tend to counteract the [government's] praiseworthy investment incentives."

## INFORMAL MARKET
### Score: **4.5**–Better (very high level of activity)

Transparency International's 2002 score for Bangladesh is 1.2. As a result, Bangladesh's informal market score is 4.5 this year—a 0.5 point improvement.

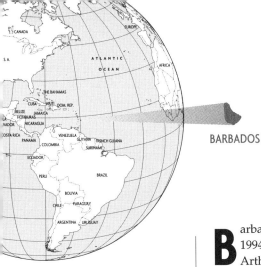

# BARBADOS

Rank: 33

Score: 2.41

Category: Mostly Free

Present & Past Scores

(Best) 1
2
3
4
(Worst) 5

3.15  2.93  2.63  2.86  2.74  2.64  2.53  2.29  2.41

'95  '96  '97  '98  '99  '00  '01  '02  '03  '04
n/a

## QUICK STUDY

### SCORES

| | |
|---|---|
| Trade Policy | 4 |
| Fiscal Burden | 4.6 |
| Government Intervention | 2.5 |
| Monetary Policy | 1 |
| Foreign Investment | 3 |
| Banking and Finance | 2 |
| Wages and Prices | 2 |
| Property Rights | 1 |
| Regulation | 2 |
| Informal Market | 2 |

**Population:** 268,190

**Total area:** 430 sq. km

**GDP:** $2.3 billion

**GDP growth rate:** 1.5%

**GDP per capita:** $8,610

**Major exports:** chemicals, electrical components, food and beverages, sugar, travel services, financial services, insurance services

**Exports of goods and services:** $1.1 billion

**Major export trading partners:** CARICOM 41.1%, US 14.2%, UK 11.7%, Canada 2.8%

**Major imports:** consumer goods, machinery, foodstuffs, construction materials, fuel, insurance services

**Imports of goods and services:** $1.2 billion

**Major import trading partners:** US 41.0%, CARICOM 16.8%, UK 8.0%, Canada 3.8%

**Foreign direct investment (net):** $15.2 million

2001 Data (in constant 1995 US dollars)

**B**arbados, a former British colony, has been governed by the Barbados Labor Party since 1994. The Labor Party's victory in the May 2003 elections gave Prime Minister Owen Arthur a third consecutive term in power, the Labor Party 23 seats in the 30-seat Parliament, and the opposition seven seats. The economy is based on tourism. Although the heavily subsidized sugar industry is diminishing in importance, it remains an important employer and exporter. After the September 11, 2001, terrorist attacks on the United States, reports the Economist Intelligence Unit, the government announced measures "to protect the tourism industry, as well as local manufacturing and agriculture. The fiscal deficit was allowed to widen to 3.2% of GDP, financed mainly by local borrowing...." The offshore financial sector is smaller than others in the Caribbean but makes a significant contribution to the economy and is generally well-regulated. The Organisation for Economic Co-operation and Development has removed Barbados from its list of tax havens, allowing the country to renegotiate important tax treaties, particularly with Canada. The pace of privatization is slow, but the government plans to liberalize the telecommunications industry by mid-2003 (as this year's edition of the *Index* was being compiled), phasing out the monopoly held by Cable and Wireless. Telecommunications competitors are permitted to offer only Internet services. Barbados's trade policy score is 1 point worse this year, and its fiscal burden of government score is 0.2 point worse. As a result, Barbados's overall score is 0.12 point worse this year.

 **TRADE POLICY**

Score: **4**–Worse (high level of protectionism)

As a member of the Caribbean Community and Common Market (CARICOM) trade bloc, Barbados has a common external tariff rate that ranges from 5 percent to 20 percent. The World Trade Organization reports that Barbados's average most favored nation applied tariff rate in 2001 (the most recent year for which reliable data are available) was 16.5 percent, up from the 9.1 percent reported in the 2003 *Index*. As a result, Barbados's trade policy score is 1 point worse this year. Import licenses are required for agricultural products but are granted automatically.

 **FISCAL BURDEN OF GOVERNMENT**

Score—Income Taxation: **4**–Stable (high tax rates)
Score—Corporate Taxation: **5**–Stable (very high tax rates)
Score—Change in Government Expenditures: **4.5**–Worse (high increase)
Final Score: **4.6**–Worse (very high cost of government)

Barbados has a top income tax rate of 40 percent. The top corporate tax rate is 37.5 percent. Government expenditures as a share of GDP increased 2.9 percentage points to 37.2 percent in 2001, compared to a 0.7 percentage point increase in 2000. As a result, Barbados's fiscal burden of government score is 0.2 point worse this year.

 **GOVERNMENT INTERVENTION IN THE ECONOMY**

Score: **2.5**–Stable (moderate level)

According to the World Bank, the government consumed 23.2 percent of GDP in 2001. In 2000, based on data from the International Monetary Fund, the government received 0.9 percent of its total revenues from state-owned enterprises and government ownership of property.

## MONETARY POLICY
### Score: **1**–Stable (very low level of inflation)

From 1993 to 2002, Barbados's weighted average annual rate of inflation was 1.24 percent.

## CAPITAL FLOWS AND FOREIGN INVESTMENT
### Score: **3**–Stable (moderate barriers)

While investment restrictions are relatively minor, capital flows face significant barriers in terms of exchange controls, quantitative limits, and approval requirements from the central bank. Barbados permits 100 percent foreign ownership of enterprises and treats domestic and foreign firms equally. However, according to the U.S. Department of State, "Performance requirements and expectations are central to the administration of certain foreign direct investments. Applications for licenses are more likely to be approved, for example, if local officials believe that the investment will create jobs, increase exports, and foreign exchange earnings, and increase economic activity in Barbados…. Foreign investors are required to finance their investments from external sources or from income generated by the investment." The same source reports that only when a foreign investment creates employment or other benefits to the domestic economy can the investor borrow funds from domestic banks. The International Monetary Fund reports that central bank approval is required for both residents and non-residents to hold foreign exchange accounts. Transactions in foreign currency are restricted: Approval is required for current transfers, transfer of assets, and gifts and inheritance over a certain amount; there are limits on the interest payments that can be paid on investments to a single individual and company; personal payments abroad are subject to limits that vary according to the purpose of the payment; issuance and transfer of securities and money market instruments to non-residents require exchange control approval, as do direct investment and real estate purchases; and the central bank must approve all credit operations.

## BANKING AND FINANCE
### Score: **2**–Stable (low level of restrictions)

The banking system is open to competition. According to the International Monetary Fund, there are seven commercial banks, 14 non-bank financial institutions, 41 credit unions, nine life insurance companies, and 10 general insurance companies. The Economist Intelligence Unit reports that three of the commercial banks are wholly foreign-owned. The government partially privatized its ownership in the Barbados National Bank in 2001 and plans to sell its 57 percent majority share to the Republic Bank of Trinidad and Tobago this year. Legislation passed in 1998 tightened the controls against money laundering and prevented Barbados from being identified in 2000 by the Financial Action Task Force as a "non-cooperative jurisdiction." In January 2002, Barbados was removed from the Organisation for Economic Co-operation

and Development's list of countries with harmful tax policies and thereby avoided sanctions. The central bank imposes minimum interest rates on deposits at commercial banks.

## WAGES AND PRICES
### Score: **2**–Stable (low level of intervention)

The market sets most wages and prices. According to the Department of State, "While the government generally refrains from imposing price controls, certain basic items are controlled." The Embassy of Barbados reports that the prices of gasoline and a few food items remain under government supervision. The government establishes legally enforced minimum wages for specified categories of workers, but only household domestics and shop assistants are subject to a formal minimum wage.

## PROPERTY RIGHTS
### Score: **1**–Stable (very high level of protection)

Private property is well-protected in Barbados. The country's legal tradition is based on British common law, and the courts operate independently and afford citizens a fair public hearing. "By Caribbean standards," reports the U.S. Department of State, "the police and court systems are efficient and unbiased, and the government operates in an essentially transparent manner."

## REGULATION
### Score: **2**–Stable (low level)

The process for establishing a business in Barbados is simple. According to the U.S. Department of State, "Barbados uses transparent policies and effective laws to foster competition and establish clear rules for foreign and domestic investors in the areas of tax, labor, environment, health and safety…. The Ministry of Industry and International Business administers the Companies Act and other statutes dealing with company affairs. The Companies Act is modeled on the Canada Business Corporations Act, and creates flexibility and simplicity for the incorporation and operation of companies in Barbados." In addition, "There are no formal regulation[s] governing monopolies, but legislation was enacted in 2000 to create the Fair Trading Commission (FTC) to provide consumer protection in telecommunications and utilities services." Corruption is not regarded as a major problem.

## INFORMAL MARKET
### Score: **2**–Stable (low level of activity)

Informal market activity is low by global standards, although the U.S. Department of State reports that "black market copies of computer software, designer items, and video tapes are easily accessible." There is some informal labor activity, which the Center for International Private Enterprise says accounts for approximately 6 percent of the labor force.

BELARUS

# BELARUS

Rank: 145

Score: 4.09

Category: Repressed

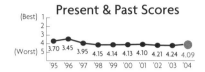

Present & Past Scores

(Best) 1
2
3
4
(Worst) 5

3.70 3.45 3.95 4.15 4.14 4.13 4.10 4.21 4.24 4.09

'95 '96 '97 '98 '99 '00 '01 '02 '03 '04

## QUICK STUDY

### SCORES

| | |
|---|---|
| Trade Policy | 4 |
| Fiscal Burden | 3.4 |
| Government Intervention | 3.5 |
| Monetary Policy | 5 |
| Foreign Investment | 4 |
| Banking and Finance | 4 |
| Wages and Prices | 5 |
| Property Rights | 4 |
| Regulation | 5 |
| Informal Market | 3 |

**Population:** 9,970,260

**Total area:** 207,600 sq. km

**GDP:** $14.9 billion

**GDP growth rate:** 4.1%

**GDP per capita:** $1,494

**Major exports:** mineral products, machinery and equipment, chemicals, textiles

**Exports of goods and services:** $9.3 billion

**Major export trading partners:** Russia 53.2%, Ukraine 5.7%, Poland 3.3%, Germany 3.2%

**Major imports:** foodstuffs, metals, chemicals, machinery and equipment

**Imports of goods and services:** $9.7 billion

**Major import trading partners:** Russia 65.4%, Germany 7.4%, Ukraine 3.4%, Poland 2.5%

**Foreign direct investment (net):** $100 million

2001 Data (in constant 1995 US dollars)

Belarus is both one of the most repressive countries of the former Soviet Union and the one that has retained the closest political and economic ties with Russia. In 1996, President Alexander Lukashenko, whose authoritarian regime has ruled Belarus since 1994, used a non-democratic referendum to replace the constitution with one that broadened his powers and extended his term in office. Serious damage to Belorussian democracy has caused serious harm to relations with the U.S. and the European Union. Arrests and disappearances of opposition leaders and the absence of freedom of expression have isolated Belarus internationally and inhibited foreign investment. Economic mismanagement has caused a dramatic increase in stocks of unsold goods, which by the end of 2001 stood at 60 percent of average monthly output. About 80 percent of all industry remains in state hands. The industrial base has become obsolete, and more than 40 percent of industrial enterprises work at a loss. Existing legislation prevents individual investors from holding more than a 50 percent share of industrial companies. Private land ownership is still absent in the agriculture sector, which remains dominated by Soviet-era collective farms. Belarus relies heavily on Russian economic assistance and remains self-isolated from the West. Lukashenko's policies of economic and political repression foster criticism in Moscow among free-market reformers who oppose maintaining close ties with Belarus's Soviet-style regime. Belarus's government intervention score is 0.5 point worse this year; however, its informal market score is 2 points better. As a result, Belarus's overall score is 0.15 point better this year.

## TRADE POLICY

### Score: **4**–Stable (high level of protectionism)

The World Bank reports that Belarus's weighted average tariff rate in 1997 (the most recent year for which World Bank data are available) was 9.6 percent. According to the European Commission's Market Access Database, Belarus maintains quotas on fertilizers, scrap metals, copper, aluminum, and a number of other goods. The government also has a multiple exchange rate system that acts as a non-tariff barrier.

## FISCAL BURDEN OF GOVERNMENT

Score—Income Taxation: **3**–Stable (moderate tax rates)
Score—Corporate Taxation: **4**–Stable (high tax rates)
Score—Change in Government Expenditures: **2.5**–Stable (low decrease)
Final Score: **3.4**–Stable (moderate cost of government)

The International Monetary Fund reports that Belarus's top income tax rate is 30 percent. The top corporate income tax rate is 30 percent. Government expenditures as a share of GDP decreased 1.6 percentage points to 44.3 percent in 2001, compared to a 1.5 percentage point decline in 2000. Because Belarus's tax rates are unchanged and the decrease in the level of government expenditures as a share of GDP is not significantly different from that of the previous year, Belarus's fiscal burden of government score is unchanged this year.

## GOVERNMENT INTERVENTION IN THE ECONOMY

### Score: **3.5**–Worse (high level)

The World Bank reports that the government consumed 20.7 percent of GDP in 2001. In the same year, according to the International Monetary Fund, Belarus received 1.53 percent of its

101

total revenues from state-owned enterprises and government ownership of property. According to the Economist Intelligence Unit, however, "The Lukashenka administration sees large industrial enterprises as vehicles for the government to provide employment and incomes, rather than simply as economic entities. Privatised control of these enterprises remains the exception, with 95% of the country's industrial output still derived from large state-owned or state-controlled enterprises." Based on the apparent unreliability of reported total revenue figures, 1 point has been added to Belarus's government intervention score. Because of the increase in the level of government consumption, Belarus's government intervention score is 0.5 point worse this year.

## MONETARY POLICY
### Score: **5**–Stable (very high level of inflation)

From 1993 to 2002, Belarus's weighted average annual rate of inflation was 66.95 percent.

## CAPITAL FLOWS AND FOREIGN INVESTMENT
### Score: **4**–Stable (high barriers)

The International Monetary Fund reports that foreign investment must be registered with the Ministry of Foreign Affairs and that financial institutions must register with the National Bank of Belarus. With the exception of insurance organizations and banks, the proportion of a foreign investor's share is not restricted. However, political instability, anti-Western sentiment, an inefficient bureaucracy, corruption, a concerted resistance to the private sector, and the lack of privatization all serve to hinder foreign investment. The government does not permit foreigners to own land. A new investment code that went into effect in 2001 guarantees property rights, the right to remit income, and protection against nationalization without complete and timely compensation. Natural resources, waters, forests, and land are owned exclusively by the state, but 99-year-use agreements are permitted. In 2001, according to the Economist Intelligence Unit, foreign direct investment "accounted for only about 1% of total investment, compared with over 20% in many other CIS countries such as Kazakhstan, the Kyrgyz Republic, Tajikistan and Moldova."

## BANKING AND FINANCE
### Score: **4**–Stable (high level of restrictions)

Although the government has issued licenses to a number of private banks and has divested itself of some of its holdings in state-owned banks, it continues to exert enormous control over the banking sector, which included 27 commercial banks in 2001, and to affect the allocation of credit. According to the Economist Intelligence Unit, the central National Bank of Belarus "has been reduced to a conduit for the government's economic policy." In addition, "commercial banks, although nominally independent, have also frequently been pressured by the government into providing loss-making loans to selected industries and purchasing government-issued securities."

## WAGES AND PRICES
### Score: **5**–Stable (very high level of intervention)

According to the Economist Intelligence Unit, the government subsidizes many basic goods and services, including housing and utilities; intervenes directly in agricultural markets; controls most of the economy through state-owned enterprises; otherwise influences prices through its credit policies and purchasing practices; and "retains tight control over the partly privatised retail sector through price regulation…." The government mandates a monthly minimum wage and determines wages in the private sector; the EIU reports that "private enterprises are not allowed to determine the level of wages and bonuses that they pay employees, but have to follow the elaborate wage scale that governs wages at state-owned enterprises."

## PROPERTY RIGHTS
### Score: **4**–Stable (low level of protection)

The legal system does not fully protect private property, and the inefficient court system does not consistently enforce contracts. According to the U.S. Department of State, "The 1994 Constitution provides for an independent judiciary; however, in practice the judiciary was not independent and was unable to act as a check on the executive branch and its agents. The 1996 Constitution further subordinated the judiciary to the executive branch by giving the President the power to appoint 6 of the 12 members of the Constitutional Court, including the chairman." A law passed in January 2000, reports *The Russia Journal,* enables the government to nationalize the property of any individual or business deemed to be damaging the state.

## REGULATION
### Score: **5**–Stable (very high level)

According to the Economist Intelligence Unit, "The authorities discourage private enterprise through a combination of high taxes, excessive government regulations, and a deliberately anti-business climate. This has led small and medium-sized private enterprises to concentrate in retail and catering, where relatively low sunk costs prevent excessively high losses in the event of official harassment." In addition, "The administration's lack of progress on political and judicial reforms has further dampened investors' interest, while its ideological opposition to the privatisation of large-scale state-held assets has precluded any sizeable privatisation-related inflows."

## INFORMAL MARKET
### Score: **3**–Better (moderate level of activity)

Transparency International's 2002 score for Belarus is 4.8. Therefore, Belarus's informal market score is 3 this year—a 2 point improvement.

BELGIUM

# BELGIUM

Rank: 22
Score: 2.19
Category: Mostly Free

Present & Past Scores

(Best) 1
2
3
4
(Worst) 5

2.06 2.03 2.05 2.06 2.14 2.10 2.10 2.10 2.19

'95 '96 '97 '98 '99 '00 '01 '02 '03 '04
n/a

## QUICK STUDY

### SCORES

| | |
|---|---|
| Trade Policy | 2 |
| Fiscal Burden | 4.4 |
| Government Intervention | 2.5 |
| Monetary Policy | 1 |
| Foreign Investment | 1 |
| Banking and Finance | 2 |
| Wages and Prices | 3 |
| Property Rights | 1 |
| Regulation | 3 |
| Informal Market | 2 |

**Population:** 10,316,000

**Total area:** 30,510 sq. km

**GDP:** $321.4 billion

**GDP growth rate:** 0.7%

**GDP per capita:** $31,155

**Major exports:** chemicals, machinery, transport equipment, transportation, travel services, financial services, computer and information

**Exports of goods and services:** $251.7 billion

**Major export trading partners:** Germany 18.6%, France 16.3%, Netherlands 11.7%, UK 9.6%, US 7.8%

**Major imports:** machinery, chemicals, transport equipment, travel services, financial services, insurance services

**Imports of goods and services:** $236.8 billion

**Major import trading partners:** Germany 17.3%, Netherlands 15.7%, France 12.6%, UK 7.3%, US 6.4%

**Foreign direct investment**

2002 Data (in constant 1995 US dollars)

Belgium has one of Western Europe's most punishing tax systems and one of the world's highest total tax burdens, with government revenue as a share of GDP at 47 percent in 2000. In 1999, economic pressures led to the election of a Liberal-led coalition espousing a "third way." Prime Minister Guy Verhofstadt has made tax reform a priority, spearheading legislation to lower income and corporate tax rates. Corporate tax rates have been lowered from 39 percent to 33 percent, and the top income tax rate has been lowered from 55 percent to 50 percent. The principal objective of the government's fiscal policy agenda is budgetary consolidation, but public debt remains staggeringly high—110 percent of GDP in 2000 despite having declined steadily for years. With 63 percent of Belgium's workers unionized, labor laws remain overly complex, particularly in terms of employment, health, and safety regulations, and lawmakers frequently add to the already onerous European Union labor regulations. Labor rigidities, for example, remain a major bar to hiring and firing. Belgium is still run on a largely corporatist basis; every other year, the business federation and the unions negotiate a national collective bargaining agreement. However, state-owned enterprises constitute a progressively smaller percentage of economic activity. Belgium's fiscal burden of government score is 0.1 point better this year; however, its wages and prices score is 1 point worse. As a result, Belgium's overall score is 0.09 point worse this year.

###  TRADE POLICY
Score: **2**–Stable (low level of protectionism)

As a member of the European Union, Belgium was subject to a common EU weighted average external tariff of 2.6 percent in 2001, according to the World Bank. The Economist Intelligence Unit reports that Belgium comes under the EU's anti-dumping regulation. According to the U.S. Department of State, a number of products are subject to quotas and import licenses.

###  FISCAL BURDEN OF GOVERNMENT
Score—Income Taxation: **5**–Stable (very high tax rates)
Score—Corporate Taxation: **4.5**–Better (very high tax rates)
Score—Change in Government Expenditures: **3.5**–Worse (low increase)
Final Score: **4.4**–Better (high cost of government)

Belgium's top income tax rate is 50 percent, down from 55 percent. The top corporate tax rate is 33 percent, down from 39 percent. Government expenditures as a share of GDP (which had remained unchanged in 2001) rose 0.8 percentage point to 50.2 percent in 2002. On net, Belgium's fiscal burden of government score is 0.1 point better this year.

### GOVERNMENT INTERVENTION IN THE ECONOMY
Score: **2.5**–Stable (moderate level)

Based on data from the Organisation for Economic Co-operation and Development, the government consumed 22.3 percent of GDP in 2002. In 2001, based on data from the National Bank of Belgium, Belgium received 1.26 percent of its total revenues from state-owned enterprises and government ownership of property.

**MONETARY POLICY**
Score: **1**–Stable (very low level of inflation)

From 1993 to 2002, Belgium's weighted average annual rate of inflation was 1.89 percent.

 **CAPITAL FLOWS AND FOREIGN INVESTMENT**
Score: **1**–Stable (very low barriers)

Belgium has an attractive foreign investment climate. Foreign and domestic firms are treated equally, and no approval is required for new investments, with the exception of the banking, insurance, broadcasting, or transport industries. A takeover law requires each owner of 5 percent or more of a corporation's voting stock to notify the Ministry of Economic Affairs and the Banking and Finance Commission. There are few restrictions on foreign investment that do not also apply to domestic investment. Belgium requires majority domestic or European Union ownership in the aviation sector and inland shipping, as well as for Belgian flag vessels operated by shipping companies that do not have their main office in Belgium. There are some restrictions on non-EU investment in public works as required under EU regulations. There are no restrictions on the purchasing of real estate, repatriation of profit, or transfer of capital.

 **BANKING AND FINANCE**
Score: **2**–Stable (low level of restrictions)

Belgium's domestic banking system has undergone privatization in the past few years and is now almost entirely privately owned. There are 68 banks, including 12 branches of foreign banks. There is government oversight, but foreign banks are allowed to operate and are subject to relatively few restrictions. However, according to the Embassy of Belgium, Belgian law makes a distinction between foreign banks coming from a country that is part of the European Economic Area (EEA) and those coming from another country. Credit institutions that are authorized to conduct banking activities in another EEA country do not need to seek authorization from the Banking and Finance Commission to conduct banking services in Belgium. For credit institutions outside the EEA, the Banking and Finance Commission may "refuse to give its authorization…if it feels that a company under Belgian law should be created in order to ensure the protection of savers or a sound and prudent policy of that particular company." Authorization can also be refused to "a credit institution coming from a country which does not offer equivalent market entry conditions for credit institutions under Belgian law." Commercial banks have ventured into new areas of the financial sector, including project financing, securitization of assets, and insurance. However, the government affects the allocation of credit; according to the Economist Intelligence Unit, "An interest-rate subsidy may be available from regional authorities on medium- and long-term borrowing."

 **WAGES AND PRICES**
Score: **3**–Worse (moderate level of intervention)

The market determines most wages and prices in Belgium. According to the Economist Intelligence Unit, "Government price-control powers ended in 1993…. But companies with an annual turnover of 7,436,805.74 [euros] or more must notify the Ministry of Economic Affairs of any price increase or decrease. Moreover, the principle that prices must be 'normal' is still enshrined in legislation and can be enforced in courts." In addition, "Permission is sometimes necessary to put a new product on the market or to increase a price…. The sectors affected [by this requirement] are those where there is a deemed monopoly or an explicit social character (water, electricity and gas distribution; waste handling; homes for the elderly, medicines and implantable medical devices; certain cars; compulsory insurance; fire insurance; petroleum products; taxi transport; cable TV; and certain types of bread)." Belgium also affects agricultural prices through its participation in the Common Agricultural Policy, which heavily subsidizes agricultural goods. According to Timbro, a Swedish think tank, "EU consumers pay roughly 80–100% more for their food than would be the case in a mature free-market regime." Belgium maintains a minimum wage. Based on the government's interference with the market's ability to determine prices over a wide range of goods, as well its mandated minimum wage, Belgium's wages and prices score is 1 point worse this year.

 **PROPERTY RIGHTS**
Score: **1**–Stable (very high level of protection)

Property is well-protected. The Economist Intelligence Unit reports that "contractual agreements are secure in Belgium. The country's laws are codified, and the quality of the Belgian judiciary and civil service is high, though the process is often slow."

 **REGULATION**
Score: **3**–Stable (moderate level)

Regulations are moderately burdensome, especially for small and medium-size enterprises. Problems include high labor costs and social contributions, inflexible labor regulations, high taxation levels, costly work hiring practices, and a perceived lack of consistency in the government's tax policies. According to the Embassy of Belgium, the government has taken steps to simplify the process to open a new business by reducing the number of agencies with which one must deal when starting a business, providing a single company identification number (as opposed to three), and allowing for the filing of taxes via the Internet. Overall, however, much remains to be done, particularly in terms of taxes and labor laws.

 **INFORMAL MARKET**
Score: **2**–Stable (low level of activity)

Transparency International's 2002 score for Belgium is 7.1. Therefore, Belgium's informal market score is 2 this year.

# BELIZE

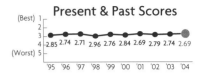

Rank: 46

Score: 2.69

Category: Mostly Free

**Present & Past Scores**

(Best) 1
2
3
4
(Worst) 5

2.85 2.74 2.71 2.96 2.76 2.84 2.69 2.79 2.74 2.69

'95 '96 '97 '98 '99 '00 '01 '02 '03 '04

## QUICK STUDY

### SCORES

| | |
|---|---|
| Trade Policy | 4 |
| Fiscal Burden | 2.9 |
| Government Intervention | 2 |
| Monetary Policy | 1 |
| Foreign Investment | 3 |
| Banking and Finance | 3 |
| Wages and Prices | 2 |
| Property Rights | 3 |
| Regulation | 3 |
| Informal Market | 3 |

**Population:** 247,110

**Total area:** 22,966 sq. km

**GDP:** $788 million

**GDP growth rate:** 5.1%

**GDP per capita:** $3,189

**Major exports:** sugar, marine products, garments

**Exports of goods and services:** $434.3 million

**Major export trading partners:** US 53.8%, UK 23.0%, CARICOM 6.4%, Mexico 1.0%

**Major imports:** manufactured goods, food, beverages and tobaccos, machinery and transportation equipment

**Imports of goods and services:** $584 million

**Major import trading partners:** US 47.2%, Mexico 11.2%, CARICOM 5.0%, UK 2.7%

**Foreign direct investment (net):** $23.3 million

2001 Data (in constant 1995 US dollars)

**B**elize is a constitutional monarchy and member of the British Commonwealth. Prime Minister Said Musa won re-election in March 2003, and his People's United Party continues to enjoy a parliamentary majority. Border disputes with Guatemala dominate Belize's foreign policy agenda, and the date for a solution to the dispute has repeatedly been postponed. According to preliminary estimates, reports the Economist Intelligence Unit, "GDP growth was 4.4% in 2002…. [T]ourism and construction related to post-earthquake reconstruction efforts supported economic activity in 2002." The EIU also reports that the government proposed to reduce the central government deficit to 3 percent of GDP in 2003, but a proposed tax cut and lower public-sector investment will challenge this goal. The U.S. Department of State has expressed concerns about an increase in drug trafficking through Belize and the country's vulnerability to money laundering. Tourism remains one of the most important economic sectors; last year, air arrivals rose by 1.8 percent, and cruise arrivals increased more than sixfold. Belize's fiscal burden of government score is 0.5 point better this year. As a result, its overall score is 0.05 point better this year.

## TRADE POLICY

### Score: **4**–Stable (high level of protectionism)

As a member of the Caribbean Community and Common Market (CARICOM) trade bloc, Belize has a common external tariff rate that ranges from 5 percent to 20 percent. According to the World Bank, Belize's average tariff rate in 2001 (the most recent year for which reliable data are available) was 12.5 percent. The U.S. Department of State reports that a number of products are subject to quotas and import licenses. In addition, "Belizean importers continue to complain that the process for obtaining import licenses is prone to corruption and needless red tape."

## FISCAL BURDEN OF GOVERNMENT

Score—Income Taxation: **2.5**–Stable (moderate tax rates)
Score—Corporate Taxation: **3**–Stable (moderate tax rates)
Score—Change in Government Expenditures: **3**–Better (very low decrease)
### Final Score: **2.9**–Better (moderate cost of government)

Belize's top income tax rate is 25 percent. The top corporate income tax rate is 25 percent. Government expenditures as a share of GDP decreased 0.8 percentage point to 35.3 percent in 2000, compared to an increase of 5 percentage points in 1999. As a result, Belize's fiscal burden of government score is 0.5 point better this year.

## GOVERNMENT INTERVENTION IN THE ECONOMY

### Score: **2**–Stable (low level)

According to the World Bank, the government consumed 13.8 percent of GDP in 2001. In the same year, based on data from the International Monetary Fund, Belize received 1.49 percent of its total revenues from state-owned enterprises and government ownership of property.

## MONETARY POLICY

### Score: **1**–Stable (very low level of inflation)

From 1993 to 2002, Belize's weighted average annual rate of inflation was 0.82 percent.

105

**CAPITAL FLOWS AND FOREIGN INVESTMENT**
Score: **3**–Stable (moderate barriers)

Belize generally is open to foreign investment and allows 100 percent foreign ownership, but a number of sectors—commercial fishing within the barrier reef, merchandising, sugarcane farming, real estate and insurance, internal transportation, some tourism activities, accounting and legal services, entertainment, beauty salons, and restaurants and bars—require special licenses that non-citizens may not acquire. The government encourages foreign investment in tourism, light manufacturing, agriculture, aquaculture and horticulture, deep-sea fishing and processing, and forestry; for profits to be repatriated, foreigners must register all investments with the central bank. According to the International Monetary Fund, both residents and non-residents may hold foreign exchange accounts subject to government approval. The central bank rations its foreign exchange for invisible payments on an ad hoc basis, controls some payments, and requires that repatriation be made through an authorized dealer. All capital transactions must be approved by the central bank.

 **BANKING AND FINANCE**
Score: **3**–Stable (moderate level of restrictions)

Belize has five commercial banks; two state-controlled lending institutions (the Development Finance Corporation and the Small Farmers and Business Bank); and some small credit unions. The U.S. Department of State reports that banking services are open to foreign investors. Belize has agreed to increase its transparency and exchange information on tax matters with Organisation for Economic Co-operation and Development countries to avoid countermeasures and sanctions. The International Financial Services Act, passed in 1999, promotes offshore financial services, and the government offers extensive banking secrecy.

 **WAGES AND PRICES**
Score: **2**–Stable (low level of intervention)

The market sets most wages and prices, but there are controls on the prices of some basic commodities such as rice, flour, beans, sugar, bread, butane gas, and fuel. Belize maintains a two-tiered minimum wage, with workers in agriculture and the export sector having a slightly lower minimum wage than other sectors.

 **PROPERTY RIGHTS**
Score: **3**–Stable (moderate level of protection)

The constitution provides for an independent judiciary, which in practice is subject to political influence. According to the U.S. Department of State, "the judicial system is constrained by a severe lack of trained personnel, and police officers often act as prosecutors in the magistrate's courts." The result is lengthy trial backlogs. In addition, the government has expropriated private land under its right of eminent domain; it claimed that the expropriation was for public purposes, "but several [expropriations] were uncovered as political payoffs."

 **REGULATION**
Score: **3**–Stable (moderate level)

Belize's regulatory regime is not always transparent. According to the U.S. Department of State, "Belize's laws and regulations on tax, labor, customs, and health and safety do not significantly distort or impede the efficient mobilization and allocation of investment capital. However, some investors have found a lack of transparency in the administration of some Belizean laws and procedures, such as compulsory acquisition of land, investment incentive programs and import licenses." Regulations often are applied haphazardly, and obtaining a business license can be complicated. Some labor benefits, such as vacations and sick leave, are required by law. There is a minimum wage. The U.S. Department of State reports that "bribery is officially considered a criminal act in Belize, but laws against bribery are rarely enforced."

 **INFORMAL MARKET**
Score: **3**–Stable (moderate level of activity)

Belize's intellectual property laws are inadequate and insufficiently enforced. Piracy continues to be a problem. According to the U.S. Department of State, there is a thriving parallel market for U.S. dollars. Corruption in awarding contracts is common.

# BENIN

BENIN

Rank: 113

Score: 3.44

Category: Mostly Unfree

### Present & Past Scores

(Best) 1
2
3
4
(Worst) 5

3.53 3.44 3.35 3.29 3.16 3.23 3.46 3.56 **3.44**

'95 '96 '97 '98 '99 '00 '01 '02 '03 '04
n/a

## QUICK STUDY

### SCORES

| | |
|---|---|
| Trade Policy | 4 |
| Fiscal Burden | 4.4 |
| Government Intervention | 4 |
| Monetary Policy | 1 |
| Foreign Investment | 3 |
| Banking and Finance | 3 |
| Wages and Prices | 3 |
| Property Rights | 4 |
| Regulation | 4 |
| Informal Market | 4 |

**Population:** 6,436,660

**Total area:** 112,620 sq. km

**GDP:** $2.7 billion

**GDP growth rate:** 5.0%

**GDP per capita:** $424

**Major exports:** textiles, cotton, petroleum

**Exports of goods and services:** $561.7 million

**Major export trading partners:** Italy 13.7%, India 22.5%, Turkey 5.5%

**Major imports:** foodstuffs, tobacco, petroleum products

**Imports of goods and services:** $848 million

**Major import trading partners:** China 37.5%, France 14.9%, Germany 3.7%, Italy 3.6%

**Foreign direct investment (net):** $43 million

2001 Data (in constant 1995 US dollars)

Benin has had a democratically elected government since 1990. The government is moving ahead slowly with privatization by appointing a foreign bank to manage the divestment of the Sonapra cotton-marketing agency and selling 30 percent of the telecommunications company. From 1980 to 1999, the number of state-owned enterprises fell from 130 to 27. Benin's economy is based on agriculture and is West Africa's second largest producer of cotton. Other exports include cashews, pineapple, and teak timber. The 2003 budget is focused on poverty reduction, infrastructure, and improved governance. However, that bureaucracy, overspending, and corruption continue to hamper the economy is evidenced by Benin's Cotonou port, which the U.S. Department of State says is considered among "the best ports in the region in terms of the speed at which cargo is unloaded and clears customs, but is hampered by corruption." Many of the remaining labor laws from the Marxist period also hinder business. Benin needs to move privatization at a faster pace, address human rights issues, eradicate bureaucracy and corruption, diversify its economic base, and make transparency a priority. Benin's fiscal burden of government score is 0.2 point better this year, and its monetary policy score is 1 point better. As a result, Benin's overall score is 0.12 point better this year.

## TRADE POLICY
### Score: **4–Stable** (high level of protectionism)

Benin is a member of the West African Economic and Monetary Union (WAEMU), which imposes a common external tariff with four rates: 0 percent, 5 percent, 10 percent, and 20 percent. (The other seven members of the WAEMU are Burkina Faso, Guinea–Bissau, Ivory Coast, Mali, Niger, Senegal, and Togo.) According to the World Bank, Benin's weighted average tariff rate in 2001 was 14 percent. The U.S. Department of State reports that non-tariff barriers include specific protective taxes on "strategic" products, such as cigarettes, rice and sugar, and corruption in the customs service.

## FISCAL BURDEN OF GOVERNMENT
### Score—Income Taxation: **5–Stable** (very high tax rates)
### Score—Corporate Taxation: **4.5–Stable** (very high tax rates)
### Score—Change in Government Expenditures: **3.5–Better** (low increase)
### Final Score: **4.4–Better** (high cost of government)

Ernst & Young reports that Benin's top income tax rate is 60 percent. The corporate tax rate is 35 percent. Government expenditures as a share of GDP rose less in 2001 (0.2 percentage point to 20.3 percent) than they did in 2000 (2.5 percentage points). As a result, Benin's fiscal burden of government score is 0.2 point better this year.

## GOVERNMENT INTERVENTION IN THE ECONOMY
### Score: **4–Stable** (high level)

The World Bank reports that in 2001, the government consumed 11.6 percent of GDP. According to the Economist Intelligence Unit, the privatization process has been delayed for years. The government is still working out a plan to divest the Sonapra cotton marketing agency, sell 30 percent of the telecommunications parastatal, and contract out electricity generation. These reforms are "expected to progress very slowly because of bureaucracy, opposition from trade unions, and vested interests."

## MONETARY POLICY
### Score: **1**–Better (very low level of inflation)

From 1993 to 2002, Benin's weighted average annual rate of inflation was 2.98 percent, down from the 3.70 percent from 1992 to 2001 reported in the 2003 *Index*. As a result, Benin's monetary policy score is 1 point better this year. Benin has benefited from a stable currency—a rarity in sub-Saharan Africa—as a member of the CFA franc zone. Fourteen countries use the CFA franc, a common currency with a fixed parity with the euro. (The other countries are Burkina Faso, Cameroon, Central African Republic, Chad, Congo [Brazzaville], Equatorial Guinea, Gabon, Guinea–Bissau, Ivory Coast, Mali, Niger, Senegal, and Togo.)

## CAPITAL FLOWS AND FOREIGN INVESTMENT
### Score: **3**–Stable (moderate barriers)

The investment climate has improved, but the U.S. Department of State reports that foreign investors still must contend with inefficient bureaucracies that are subject to corruption. There are no controls on the purchase of land, except for investments in enterprises, branches, or corporations. Privatization has been open to foreigners but has been marked by a lack of transparency. Privatization efforts have stalled, leaving the government in control of electricity, water, and cotton. The government requires part-Beninese ownership of any privatized company. The International Monetary Fund reports that foreign exchange accounts must be authorized by the government and the Banque Centrale des Etats de l'Afrique de l'Ouest (Central Bank of West African States, or BCEAO). Many capital transactions are subject to reporting requirements and approval by the government and the BCEAO.

## BANKING AND FINANCE
### Score: **3**–Stable (moderate level of restrictions)

The BCEAO, a central bank common to the eight members of the WAEMU, governs Benin's banking system. The eight BCEAO member countries use the CFA franc, pegged to the euro. The Economist Intelligence Unit reports that several bankrupt state-controlled banks have been liquidated. Following restructuring, five privately owned banks now operate in Benin, but their activities are limited to short- and medium-term loans. According to the U.S. Department of State, "Credit is allocated on market terms and foreign investors can get credit on the local market. However, legal, regulatory and accounting systems are often unwieldy. Some observers claim the banking industry is not subject to effective mandatory regulation and most banks are not managed in a transparent fashion." All banks were required to meet a minimum capital adequacy ratio of 8 percent to comply with international accounting standards in 2001, and supervision of the banking system has been strengthened.

## WAGES AND PRICES
### Score: **3**–Stable (moderate level of intervention)

The government sets some prices. The Economist Intelligence Unit reports that Benin pegs energy prices to world prices and updates them on a quarterly basis. The government subsidizes the cotton sector, which accounts for roughly 40 percent of GDP, particularly when the world price for cotton declines, and sets wages for a number of occupations administratively.

## PROPERTY RIGHTS
### Score: **4**–Stable (low level of protection)

Benin's justice system is weak and subject to corruption. According to the U.S. Department of State, there is no separate commercial court system, and "The backlog of civil cases often results in a wait of two or more years before matters proceed to trial…. [C]orruption…remains an impediment to administration of justice."

## REGULATION
### Score: **4**–Stable (high level)

The U.S. Department of State reports that "bureaucratic procedures are insufficiently streamlined and are rarely transparent in practice…. [There is] an excess of paperwork and counter-signings by various ministries. These obstacles work against the 'processing office' (one-stop-shop)," which is aimed at simplifying the investment process, and foster corruption. Many labor laws from the Marxist era still create obstacles to private enterprise.

## INFORMAL MARKET
### Score: **4**–Stable (high level of activity)

There is considerable smuggling between Benin and Nigeria, and Benin is a transit route for illegal narcotics from Nigeria. In 1999, according to the Center for International Private Enterprise, 46 percent of the total labor force worked informally. Music piracy is widespread. The U.S. Department of State reports that "many 'employed' persons work in the informal sector or in exchange for room, board and a pittance."

# BOLIVIA

Rank: 41
Score: 2.59
Category: Mostly Free

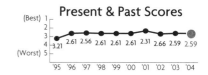

**Present & Past Scores**

(Best) 1
2
3
4
(Worst) 5

3.21 2.61 2.56 2.61 2.61 2.61 2.31 2.66 2.59 2.59

'95 '96 '97 '98 '99 '00 '01 '02 '03 '04

## QUICK STUDY

### SCORES

| | |
|---|---|
| Trade Policy | 3 |
| Fiscal Burden | 2.9 |
| Government Intervention | 2 |
| Monetary Policy | 1 |
| Foreign Investment | 1 |
| Banking and Finance | 2 |
| Wages and Prices | 2 |
| Property Rights | 4 |
| Regulation | 4 |
| Informal Market | 4 |

**Population:** 8,515,220

**Total area:** 1,098,580 sq. km

**GDP:** $8 billion

**GDP growth rate:** 1.2%

**GDP per capita:** $944

**Major exports:** natural gas, processed soya, zinc, gold

**Exports of goods and services:** $1.7 billion

**Major export trading partners:** Brazil 19.7%, Colombia 19.2%, US 14.8%, Argentina 9.1%, Ecuador 8.3%

**Major imports:** raw materials and semi-manufactures, consumer goods, petroleum, foodstuffs

**Imports of goods and services:** $2.2 billion

**Major import trading partners:** Brazil 24.4%, Argentina 17.9%, US 13.9%, Chile 9.3%, Peru 6.7%

**Foreign direct investment (net):** $590.9 million

2001 Data (in constant 1995 US dollars)

Over the past year, Bolivia teetered on the brink of instability. In 2002, a close vote threw the election of President Gonzalo Sánchez de Lozada into the Bolivian Congress, where he won by a slim margin over Evo Morales, an indigenous activist and opponent of coca eradication. In 2003, protests co-opted by Morales and fellow activist Felipe Quispé forced Sánchez Lozada out of office. As a congressman, Morales has threatened to end what he calls "blind obedience" to the United States on coca eradication and to the International Monetary Fund on paying back international loans and keeping austere budgets. During the administrations of Presidents Hugo Banzer and Jorge Quiroga, Bolivia sharply reduced its drug crop production and adopted some free-market reforms; but lack of road infrastructure and technical assistance limited the success of a U.S.-imposed alternate crop development plan to wean farmers away from lucrative coca crops. Now Bolivia is caught in a regional economic downturn and a sputtering development scheme. In February 2003, President Sánchez de Lozada's proposal to impose a first-ever tax on the middle class inspired 7,000 police to walk off the job, his cabinet to resign, and riots that claimed the lives of 27 people. In May, 50 congressmen staged a hunger strike to protest inaction on farm subsidies. Meanwhile, plans to tap Bolivia's rich natural gas reserves and build a pipeline to the Pacific Ocean stalled, and local lawmakers seem unwilling to consider market reforms that would liberate the country's productive potential as opposed to backsliding toward a welfare state.

### TRADE POLICY
Score: **3**–Stable (moderate level of protectionism)

According to the World Bank, Bolivia's weighted average tariff rate in 1999 (the most recent year for which World Bank data are available) was 9 percent. There are no significant non-tariff barriers.

### FISCAL BURDEN OF GOVERNMENT
Score—Income Taxation: **1.5**–Stable (low tax rates)
Score—Corporate Taxation: **3**–Stable (moderate tax rates)
Score—Change in Government Expenditures: **4**–Worse (moderate increase)
Final Score: **2.9**–Worse (moderate cost of government)

Bolivia has a flat income tax of 13 percent. The corporate tax rate is 25 percent. Government expenditures as a share of GDP increased 1.9 percentage points to 31.9 percent in 2001, compared to a decline of 2.5 percentage points in 2000. As a result, Bolivia's fiscal burden of government score is 0.5 point worse this year.

### GOVERNMENT INTERVENTION IN THE ECONOMY
Score: **2**–Stable (low level)

The World Bank reports that the government consumed 14.8 percent of GDP in 2001. In the same year, according to the International Monetary Fund, Bolivia received 2.17 percent of its total revenues from state-owned enterprises and government ownership of property.

## MONETARY POLICY
### Score: **1**–Stable (very low level of inflation)

From 1993 to 2002, Bolivia's weighted average annual rate of inflation was 1.55 percent.

## CAPITAL FLOWS AND FOREIGN INVESTMENT
### Score: **1**–Stable (very low barriers)

Bolivia encourages foreign investment. Foreign investors face the same laws as domestic investors, and there is no screening process. Few restrictions remain in effect, and those that apply to the petroleum and mining industries are minimal. The mining law permits foreign firms to operate within 50 kilometers of international borders through joint ventures and service contracts with domestic firms, amending the previous ban on foreign investment in that region. The International Monetary Fund reports that both residents and non-residents may hold foreign exchange accounts; there are no restrictions or controls on payments, transactions, transfers, purchase of real estate, access to foreign exchange, or repatriation of profits. According to the same source, "All foreign credits…and credits to the private sector with official guarantees are subject to prior authorization by the [Ministry of Finance] and to control by the [Central Bank of Bolivia]."

## BANKING AND FINANCE
### Score: **2**–Stable (low level of restrictions)

New laws reformed Bolivia's banking system in 1993 and 1995, clarifying the legality of factoring, leasing, foreign currency hedging, permitting banks to hold foreign currency accounts, increasing reserve requirements, and prohibiting insider lending. Government-owned banks no longer exist, and the Economist Intelligence Unit reports that reform has led to consolidation, with the number of local retail banks shrinking to nine from 14 in 1995. Over 95 percent of total deposits are U.S. dollar denominated. Bolivia's banking sector is open to foreign investment. According to the EIU, "Most local banks now have some level of foreign participation…. Three wholly foreign banking operations have a presence in some larger cities; they mainly engage in corporate lending."

## WAGES AND PRICES
### Score: **2**–Stable (low level of intervention)

There are few price controls. According to the U.S. Department of State, "Bolivia enjoys an open market, with the Government of Bolivia imposing price controls only on petroleum products, the price of which is set by the Superintendent of Hydrocarbons. Prices of some basic consumer goods are set by the respective municipal governments, such as bread, meat, and vegetables." The minimum wage is subject to annual renegotiation.

## PROPERTY RIGHTS
### Score: **4**–Stable (low level of protection)

Legal protection of private property in Bolivia is weak. While the judiciary is independent, according to the U.S. Department of State, "investors should be aware…that there is a severe lack of transparency in the country's judicial system…. Corruption is a problem throughout Bolivia's political structure, including various levels of the executive, legislative and judiciary branches…. [T]he threat of corruption complicates activities for…firms that have invested in Bolivia. The most egregious cases have involved individuals employing the legal system to harass firms to extract exorbitant payments."

## REGULATION
### Score: **4**–Stable (high level)

"Although some bureaucratic procedures have been reduced," reports the U.S. Department of State, "plenty of red tape and archaic policies remain at all levels of the Bolivian Government. The last two administrations worked to 'de-bureaucratize' the government, with modest success at best. Public sector corruption also remains a major challenge." According to the Economist Intelligence Unit, "Repeated cases of corruption and influence peddling by top officials continue to emerge."

## INFORMAL MARKET
### Score: **4**–Better (high level of activity)

Transparency International's 2002 score for Bolivia is 2.2, up from the 2 reported in the 2003 *Index.* Therefore, Bolivia's informal market score is 4 this year—a 0.5 point improvement.

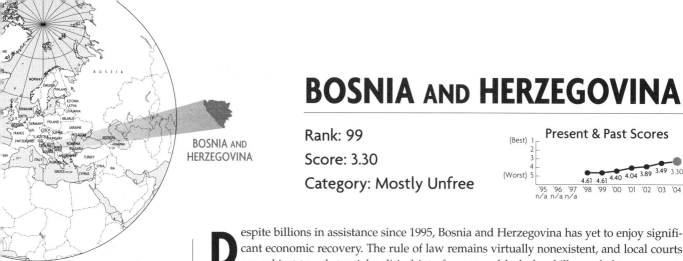

# BOSNIA AND HERZEGOVINA

BOSNIA AND HERZEGOVINA

Rank: 99

Score: 3.30

Category: Mostly Unfree

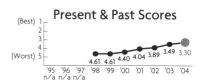

Present & Past Scores

(Best) 1
2
3
4
(Worst) 5

4.61  4.61  4.40  4.04  3.89  3.49  3.30

'95  '96  '97  '98  '99  '00  '01  '02  '03  '04
n/a  n/a  n/a

## QUICK STUDY

### SCORES

| | |
|---|---|
| Trade Policy | 3 |
| Fiscal Burden | 2.5 |
| Government Intervention | 2.5 |
| Monetary Policy | 1 |
| Foreign Investment | 4 |
| Banking and Finance | 2 |
| Wages and Prices | 3 |
| Property Rights | 5 |
| Regulation | 5 |
| Informal Market | 5 |

**Population:** 4,059,999

**Total area:** 51,129 sq. km

**GDP:** $6.4 billion

**GDP growth rate:** 6.0%

**GDP per capita:** $1,584

**Major exports:** clothing, wood products, base metal

**Exports of goods and services:** $1.7 billion

**Major export trading partners:** Italy 29.4%, Germany 15.2%, Croatia 15.1%, Austria 10%

**Major imports:** machinery and equipment, fuel, chemicals, foodstuffs

**Imports of goods and services:** $3.47 billion

**Major import trading partners:** Croatia 21.2%, Slovenia 15.2%, Germany 13.9%, Italy 13.3%

**Foreign direct investment (net):** $147.1 million

2001 Data (in constant 1995 US dollars)

Despite billions in assistance since 1995, Bosnia and Herzegovina has yet to enjoy significant economic recovery. The rule of law remains virtually nonexistent, and local courts are subject to substantial political interference and lack the skills needed to prosecute any but the simplest crimes fairly and effectively. Corruption occurs at the highest levels. Elections in 2002 brought governments to power at the state and entity level dominated by the three nationalist parties; there is little likelihood of political stability. Most of the older political parties in all three ethnic communities (Serbian, Croatian, and Muslim) are linked to organized crime. Such problems as intrusive bureaucracy, long and costly registration procedures, and restrictive labor laws, along with obvious political fragility, remain unaddressed. Much of the economy is centered on the informal market, and the economy overall remains controlled by a political elite at odds with reforms that would lead to greater openness. On the other hand, there are signs of marginal revival. The government has improved its revenue collection through the stricter enforcement of existing legislation, there has been an increase in trade across inter-entity boundaries, and GDP grew at a rate of 3.8 percent in 2002. Bosnia and Herzegovina's trade policy score is 1 point worse this year; however, its fiscal burden of government score is 0.4 point better, its government intervention score is 0.5 point better, and its monetary policy and banking and finance scores are 1 point better. As a result, Bosnia and Herzegovina's overall score is 0.19 point better this year.

## TRADE POLICY
### Score: **3–Worse** (moderate level of protectionism)

The World Bank reports that Bosnia and Herzegovina's weighted average tariff rate in 2001 was 6.6 percent, up from the 3.4 percent reported in the 2003 *Index*. As a result, Bosnia and Herzegovina's trade policy score is 1 point worse this year. According to the Economist Intelligence Unit and other sources, non-tariff barriers take the form of corruption and inefficiencies in the customs clearance process.

## FISCAL BURDEN OF GOVERNMENT
### Score—Income Taxation: **1–Better** (very low tax rates)
### Score—Corporate Taxation: **4–Stable** (high tax rates)
### Score—Change in Government Expenditures: **1–Stable** (very high decrease)
### Final Score: **2.5–Better** (moderate cost of government)

According to the International Monetary Fund, Bosnia and Herzegovina's top income tax rate is 5 percent, down from the 25 percent reported in the 2003 *Index*. As a result, Bosnia and Herzegovina's fiscal burden of government score is 0.4 point better this year. The top corporate tax rate is 30 percent. The IMF notes that government expenditures as a share of GDP decreased more in 2001 (9.8 percentage points to 56.1 percent) than they did in 2000 (4.5 percentage points).

## GOVERNMENT INTERVENTION IN THE ECONOMY
### Score: **2.5–Better** (moderate level)

Based on data from the International Monetary Fund, the government consumed 21.6 percent of GDP in 2001, down from the 65.9 percent reported in the 2003 *Index*. As a result, Bosnia and Herzegovina's government intervention score is 0.5 point better this year. In

2002, based on data from the Central Bank of Herzegovina, Bosnia and Herzegovina received 4.1 percent of its total revenues from state-owned enterprises and government ownership of property.

### MONETARY POLICY
Score: **1–Better** (very low level of inflation)

Between 1995 and 2002, Bosnia and Herzegovina's weighted average annual rate of inflation was 1.46 percent, down from the 3.19 percent between 1994 and 2001 reported in the 2003 *Index*. As a result, Bosnia and Herzegovina's monetary policy score is 1 point better this year.

### CAPITAL FLOWS AND FOREIGN INVESTMENT
Score: **4–Stable** (high barriers)

Bosnia and Herzegovina grants national treatment to foreign investors, protects investors from changes in laws pertaining to foreign investment, and protects investments against expropriation and nationalization of assets. There are no restrictions on the types of business activities open to foreign investment, with the exception of armaments and public information, in which foreign control is limited to 49 percent. However, the U.S. Department of State reports that "foreign investors continue to face a number of serious obstacles including a complex legal and regulatory framework, non-transparent business procedures, and weak judicial structures." A November 12, 2002, *Financial Times* article reports that Bosnia and Herzegovina's foreign direct investment per capita was Southeast Europe's lowest at the end of 2001, because of the country's excessive bureaucracy. According to the International Monetary Fund, foreign exchange accounts are permitted for both residents and non-residents and there are no controls on real estate transactions, personal capital transactions, or capital and money market instruments.

### BANKING AND FINANCE
Score: **2–Better** (low level of restrictions)

Bosnia and Herzegovina's banking sector has been improving. According to the U.S. Department of State, "Increased capital requirements, independent bank regulatory agencies, consolidation of smaller banks, deposit insurance agencies and the entry of several foreign banks have all bolstered confidence in the banking system." Most banks, reports the Economist Intelligence Unit, "are privately owned and undercapitalised, many of them having only the statutory minimum level of capital.... The state-owned banks have also been in no position to lend, because a large proportion of their loan portfolios are non-performing and they have acute liquidity problems." Foreign banks have steadily increased their presence and now control about 60 percent to 70 percent of the banking system, according to the *Financial Times*. Based on evidence that the state plays a smaller role in the banking system and that foreign banks do not face significant obstacles, Bosnia and Herzegovina's banking and finance score is 1 point better this year.

### WAGES AND PRICES
Score: **3–Stable** (moderate level of intervention)

The government sets some prices. "Although the markets generally determine prices," reports the U.S. Department of State, "certain goods and services are still subject to government control (electricity, gas, telecom services). The government has the ability to influence pricing policy at companies under its direct or indirect control." The government mandates a minimum wage.

### PROPERTY RIGHTS
Score: **5–Stable** (very low level of protection)

According to the U.S. Department of State, "Bosnia's laws remain an unwieldly combination of communist-era statutes and internationally imposed reforms. Enforcement is tenuous at best...." In addition, the "judicial system, which is still evolving, does not yet adequately cover commercial activities. There are no commercial/economic courts in Bosnia and Herzegovina and no efficient way to resolve commercial disputes. Contract law, in practice, is almost unenforceable.... [B]usiness people report that judges typically seek bribes or are subject to influence by public officials. Even when there is a positive decision from the court, there may be no way to enforce a judgment."

### REGULATION
Score: **5–Stable** (very high level)

Bosnia and Herzegovina's business environment is characterized by lack of transparency, and its investment process is both plodding and burdensome. The *Financial Times* reports that the country "keeps out foreign investment because of the ridiculous nature of its bureaucracy." In addition, according to the U.S. Department of State, "Establishing a business in Bosnia can be an extremely burdensome and time-consuming process for investors. In the Federation, there are 14 different administrative approvals needed for registration. The average time to complete the process in the Federation is 95 days.... [H]owever, the entire process can often take a year or more.... The myriad of state, entity and municipal administrations creates a heavily bureaucratic system lacking transparency. This is particularly problematic for investors." The current government recently signed an agreement with the International Monetary Fund that commits it to reduce bureaucratic and legislative obstacles for business, but nothing has been done.

### INFORMAL MARKET
Score: **5–Stable** (very high level of activity)

Bosnia and Herzegovina's informal market is extensive. "Within Bosnia," reports *The Economist*, "about half of the Serb Republic and two fifths of the Muslim Croat Federation have no formal jobs." According to the Economist Intelligence Unit, "It is believed that a significant part of trade still goes unrecorded."

# BOTSWANA

Rank: 39

Score: 2.55

Category: Mostly Free

**Present & Past Scores**

(Best) 1
2
3
4  3.38  3.09  2.75  2.90  2.91  2.93  2.95  2.99  2.49  2.55
(Worst) 5

'95 '96 '97 '98 '99 '00 '01 '02 '03 '04

## QUICK STUDY

### SCORES

| | |
|---|---|
| Trade Policy | 3 |
| Fiscal Burden | 3 |
| Government Intervention | 4.5 |
| Monetary Policy | 3 |
| Foreign Investment | 2 |
| Banking and Finance | 2 |
| Wages and Prices | 2 |
| Property Rights | 2 |
| Regulation | 2 |
| Informal Market | 2 |

**Population:** 1,695,000

**Total area:** 600,370 sq. km

**GDP:** $7.1 billion

**GDP growth rate:** 6.3%

**GDP per capita:** $4,130

**Major exports:** copper and nickel, diamonds, textiles, meat products

**Exports of goods and services:** $3.5 billion

**Major export trading partners:** UK 85.9%, SACU 6.5%, Zimbabwe 2.6%, US 0.2%

**Major imports:** machinery and transport equipment, textiles, petroleum products

**Imports of goods and services:** $3.1 billion

**Major import trading partners:** SACU 77.6%, UK 4.4%, Zimbabwe 3.2%, US 1.8%

**Foreign direct investment (net):** $29.6 million

2001 Data (in constant 1995 US dollars)

Botswana should remain stable throughout 2003, with the ruling Botswana Democratic Party (BDP) firmly in control for the foreseeable future. Despite recent talk of the opposition uniting to challenge the BDP, consolidation of the Botswana National Front (BNF) and the Botswana Congress Party (BCP) will do little to offset the power of the BDP. Botswana continues to prosper; with growth averaging just over 7 percent for the past two decades, its economy has grown more than that of any other country in the developing world. According to the World Bank, its gross national income achieved a rate of US$3,713, making Botswana one of the few lower-middle-income countries on the continent. With diamond exports set to increase by 11 percent to 30 million carats, *The Economist* estimates a surge in GDP growth to 7.4 percent in 2003 from 3.5 percent. In addition to its robust diamond market, Botswana maintains a healthy service economy, including the government, at 44 percent of GDP. HIV/AIDS continues to be a problem; estimates place 39 percent of those aged 15–49 as infected with the disease, and despite vigorous programs to combat it, these numbers are likely to remain high for some time. Botswana's informal market score is 0.5 point better this year; however, its trade policy score is 1 point worse, and its fiscal burden of government score is 0.1 point worse. As a result, Botswana's overall score is 0.06 point worse this year.

###  TRADE POLICY
#### Score: **3–Worse** (moderate level of protectionism)

Botswana is part of the Southern African Customs Union (SACU) with South Africa, Lesotho, Swaziland, and Namibia. According to the World Trade Organization, in 2002 (the most recent year for which WTO data are available), the SACU had an average common external tariff rate of 11.4 percent, up from the 8.5 percent reported in the 2003 *Index*. As a result, Botswana's trade policy score is 1 point worse this year. There are few if any non-tariff barriers.

###  FISCAL BURDEN OF GOVERNMENT
Score—Income Taxation: **2.5–Stable** (moderate tax rates)
Score—Corporate Taxation: **3–Stable** (moderate tax rates)
Score—Change in Government Expenditures: **3.5–Worse** (low increase)
#### Final Score: **3–Worse** (moderate cost of government)

Botswana has one of Southern Africa's lower tax burdens. The top income tax rate is 25 percent. The top corporate tax rate is 25 percent. Government expenditures as a share of GDP rose 0.5 percentage point to 42.6 percent in 2001, compared to a 0.5 percentage point decrease in 2000. As a result, Botswana's fiscal burden of government score is 0.1 point worse this year.

###  GOVERNMENT INTERVENTION IN THE ECONOMY
#### Score: **4.5–Stable** (very high level)

According to the World Bank, the government consumed 27.2 percent of GDP in 2001. During the period from June 2001–May 2002, based on data from the Bank of Botswana, Botswana received 65.3 percent of its total revenues from state-owned enterprises and government ownership of property.

113

## MONETARY POLICY
### Score: **3**–Stable (moderate level of inflation)

From 1993 to 2002, Botswana's weighted average annual rate of inflation was 7.79 percent.

 ## CAPITAL FLOWS AND FOREIGN INVESTMENT
### Score: **2**–Stable (low barriers)

Botswana is encouraging foreign investment, particularly in the non-mining sector. The Economist Intelligence Unit reports, however, that "the plethora of agencies—such as the Botswana Development Corporation, the National Development Bank, the Botswana Export Development and Investment Authority, and the Botswana Export Credit Insurance and Guarantee Company—need to be consolidated to offer a more efficient service." The government restricts foreign investment in a number of areas, including manufacture of school furniture, welding and bricklaying, hawkers and vendors, butchery and produce, petrol filling stations, bars and liquor stores, supermarkets, and retail, but these restrictions are easily circumvented in most cases. Most utilities, telecommunications, postal services, water, railways, and agriculture are closed to private investment, but the U.S. Department of State reports that "these restrictions are not a meaningful impediment to serious foreign investment." Botswana permits 100 percent foreign ownership of other businesses, although there is a screening process. Exchange controls were eliminated in 1999. The evidence indicates that, while barriers to foreign investment exist, they do not represent a serious impediment.

 ## BANKING AND FINANCE
### Score: **2**–Stable (low level of restrictions)

Botswana's banking system is competitive and advanced, compared to those of most other African states. According to the U.S. Department of State, "The country's policies facilitate the free flow of financial resources in support of the flow of resources in the produce and factor markets. Credit is available on market terms, and foreign investors have access to credit on the local market." The government is involved in the banking sector through two parastatals—Botswana Development Corporation and the National Development Bank—whose primary purpose is to provide long-term financing. The insurance sector and the stock market have been growing strongly in recent years. Although the government owns some development banks, there are no barriers to foreign banks and no restrictions on credit or interest rates, and there is no evidence of government influence on private banks.

 ## WAGES AND PRICES
### Score: **2**–Stable (low level of intervention)

Price controls have been eliminated, but the government exerts some influence over the price of agricultural goods through subsidies. Local farmers receive extensive government relief in drought years—in some cases, to such an extent that profits increase during drought, according to the Economist Intelligence Unit, which also reports that "Cattle farmers receive significant financial support and generous tax treatment." The minimum daily wage, determined by the Cabinet with advice from government, labor, and private-sector representatives, was extended to domestic workers in 2002.

 ## PROPERTY RIGHTS
### Score: **2**–Stable (high level of protection)

The constitution provides for an independent judiciary, and the government respects this provision in practice. According to the U.S. Department of State, "The Botswana constitution provides for a judiciary, which is independent of both the executive and legislative authorities.... The legal system is sufficient to conduct secure commercial dealings." However, "the judicial system did not [always] provide timely fair trials due to a serious and increasing backlog of cases."

 ## REGULATION
### Score: **2**–Stable (low level)

Regulation is transparent and evenly applied. The U.S. Department of State reports that "the Botswana government adheres to transparent policies and maintains effective laws to foster competition and establishes clear rules for operation. Bureaucratic procedures are streamlined and open, although somewhat slow, and not excessively overbearing compared to other African countries." The government has made some efforts to make it easier for small businesses to open and operate, creating a one-stop shop for investors to avoid unnecessary bureaucratic steps to start a new business. According to the U.S. Department of State, "Investors with experience in other developing nations describe the lack of obstruction or interference by government as among the country's most important assets."

 ## INFORMAL MARKET
### Score: **2**–Better (low level of activity)

Transparency International's 2002 score for Botswana is 6.4, up from the 6 reported in the 2003 *Index*. Therefore, Botswana's informal market score is 2 this year—a 0.5 point improvement.

# BRAZIL

Rank: 80
Score: 3.10
Category: Mostly Unfree

Present & Past Scores

(Best) 1
2
3
4
(Worst) 5

3.46 3.56 3.28 3.36 3.19 3.46 3.21 3.06 3.01 3.10
'95 '96 '97 '98 '99 '00 '01 '02 '03 '04

## QUICK STUDY

### SCORES

| | |
|---|---|
| Trade Policy | 4 |
| Fiscal Burden | 2.5 |
| Government Intervention | 4 |
| Monetary Policy | 3 |
| Foreign Investment | 3 |
| Banking and Finance | 3 |
| Wages and Prices | 2 |
| Property Rights | 3 |
| Regulation | 3 |
| Informal Market | 3.5 |

**Population:** 174,630,000

**Total area:** 8,511,965 sq. km

**GDP:** $811.8 billion

**GDP growth rate:** 1.5%

**GDP per capita:** $5,549

**Major exports:** transport equipment and parts, soybean, meal and oils

**Exports of goods and services:** $68.5 billion

**Major export trading partners:** US 24.2%, Argentina 11.6%, Germany 5.4%, Netherlands 4.4%

**Major imports:** machinery and electrical equipment, chemical products, oil

**Imports of goods and services:** $74.6 billion

**Major import trading partners:** US 27.4%, Argentina 13.5%, Germany 8.9%, Japan 5.0%

**Foreign direct investment (net):** $12.6 billion

2002 Data (in constant 1995 US dollars)

**B**razil's economy is the largest in Latin America. From 1994 to 2002, former President Fernando Henrique Cardoso advanced reform on many fronts, but the economy is still burdened with structural problems that undermine the prospects for long-term growth, including a convoluted tax system, barriers to foreign investment in some sectors, government management of most of the oil and electricity sector as well as a significant part of the banking system, a weak judiciary, and an overabundance of red tape. In October 2002, Luiz Inacio "Lula" da Silva became president on a predominantly leftist platform. However, once in office, da Silva's message became more practical, and he has sent signals that his policies will preserve and advance needed reforms. As of this writing, he enjoyed high public approval and, against what many had predicted, was on very good terms with the financial markets. In late April 2003, President da Silva took his boldest step by introducing a bill to reform the pensions and the tax system. These reforms are critical to improve economic performance. Brazil remains very closed to trade. Tariffs outside MERCOSUR are very high by international standards, and quotas and other regulations prevent Brazil from trading freely. The volume of Brazil's exports is only about 50 percent of Mexico's, even though Mexico's economy is half the size of Brazil's. Brazil's fiscal burden of government score is 0.9 point worse this year. As a result, its overall score is 0.09 point worse this year.

## TRADE POLICY
### Score: **4**–Stable (high level of protectionism)

As a member of the Southern Cone Common Market (MERCOSUR), Brazil adheres to a common external tariff that ranges from zero to 23 percent. According to the World Bank, Brazil's weighted average tariff rate in 2001 (the most recent year for which World Bank data are available) was 11.1 percent. According to the U.S. Department of State, "All importers must register with SECEX [Secretariat of Foreign Trade] to access SISCOMEX [a computerized trade documentation system]; registrations requirements are onerous, including a minimum capital requirement." Some items are subject to a non-automatic import license, but since they can be identified only through SISCOMEX, many foreign suppliers cannot know in advance which products need a license.

## FISCAL BURDEN OF GOVERNMENT
Score—Income Taxation: **2.5**–Stable (moderate tax rates)
Score—Corporate Taxation: **1.5**–Stable (low tax rates)
Score—Change in Government Expenditures: **4.5**–Worse (high increase)
### Final Score: **2.5**–Worse (moderate cost of government)

Brazil's top income tax rate is 27.5 percent. The top corporate tax rate is 15 percent. Government expenditures as a share of GDP increased 2.5 percentage points to 26.5 percent in 2002, compared to a 6.6 percentage point decrease in 2001. As a result, Brazil's fiscal burden of government score is 0.9 point worse this year.

## GOVERNMENT INTERVENTION IN THE ECONOMY
### Score: **4**–Stable (high level)

Based on data from the International Monetary Fund, the government consumed 19.3 percent of GDP in 2002. Despite privatization efforts, the government remains a significant presence in the economy. The Economist Intelligence Unit reports that the government owns Petrobras, the oil giant, and Eletrobras, the state energy company that controls a number of generation companies. According to the U.S. Department of State, "The government is also considering a privatization of Infraero, which runs the country's sixty-seven airports."

## MONETARY POLICY
### Score: 3–Stable (moderate level of inflation)

From 1993 to 2002, Brazil's weighted average annual rate of inflation was 8.40 percent.

## CAPITAL FLOWS AND FOREIGN INVESTMENT
### Score: 3–Stable (moderate barriers)

Constitutional amendments in 1995 dissolved legal distinctions between foreign and domestically owned companies; foreign capital may enter Brazil freely and receives national treatment. Constitutional reform adopted in 2002 allows foreign investment of up to 30 percent in Brazilian media. Restrictions on foreign investment in certain sectors, including nuclear energy, health services, rural property, fishing, mail and telegraph, aviation, and aerospace, remain in effect. Most foreign investment in the banking sector is approved, but new investments are reviewed on a case-by-case basis. Foreigners are allowed to take part in the ongoing privatization process. The International Monetary Fund reports that only authorized foreign exchange dealers, Brazilians living abroad, credit card companies, insurance and reinsurance companies, embassies, international organizations, foreign citizens in transit, foreign transportation companies, and energy companies may hold foreign exchange accounts.

## BANKING AND FINANCE
### Score: 3–Stable (moderate level of restrictions)

Brazil's highly developed and efficient banking system is the largest in South America and offers a wide range of financial services. The Office of the U.S. Trade Representative reports that as of September 2002, foreign-owned or foreign-controlled banks accounted for 28 percent of total bank assets. The government still maintains ownership of some banks. According to the U.S. Department of State, however, "The number of such state-level banking institutions has fallen in recent years due to the central government's financial and banking reform efforts. Four of Brazil's states still have state-owned or state-controlled banks offering public and private banking services." The government affects the allocation of credit. "Bank finance at a reasonable cost to industry and commerce is scarce," reports the Economist Intelligence Unit. "This failing can be viewed in part as a direct consequence of crowding out by the public sector and base interest rates that are high by international standards.... BNDES [the National Bank for Economic and Social Development] continues to play a central role of long-term, low-interest credit to industry."

## WAGES AND PRICES
### Score: 2–Stable (low level of intervention)

The market determines most prices in Brazil, with some exceptions. According to the Economist Intelligence Unit, "Some public goods and services supplied by state-owned enterprises or by local governments remain under government control. Although many public services and infrastructure investments ... were either privatized or transferred to private management through public concessions, the federal government still oversees tariffs and prices, especially in telecoms and energy, through regulatory agencies for these sectors." The government removed all controls on gasoline and diesel fuel in January 2002. A mandated minimum wage is adjusted by the government each year.

## PROPERTY RIGHTS
### Score: 3–Stable (moderate level of protection)

Expropriation of property is unlikely. "Contracts in Brazil are generally considered secured," reports the Economist Intelligence Unit, "although it is important to specify the jurisdiction for any disputes. Each state has its own judicial system, and a national court system exists for matters outside state jurisdiction.... The judiciary and civil service are considered fair, but their decision-making is hampered by time consuming procedures." According to the U.S. Department of State, "The judiciary...is inefficient, subject to political and economic influence, and plagued by problems relating to lack of resources and training of officials." Judicial decisions can take years, and "decisions of the Supreme Federal Tribunal are not automatically binding on lower courts, leading to more appeals than would otherwise occur."

## REGULATION
### Score: 3–Stable (moderate level)

Brazil's regulatory structure is not entirely transparent. Many regulations continue to restrain business activity and frequently are not applied evenly or consistently. "Although some improvements have been made," reports the U.S. Department of State, "the Brazilian legal and procedural system is complex and often far from transparent.... The central government has historically exercised considerable control over private business through extensive and frequently changing regulations. The bureaucracy has broad discretionary authority." According to the Economist Intelligence Unit, "The management of the civil service remains bureaucratic and inefficient...." The labor market is highly rigid. The U.S. Department of State reports that corruption is "a persistent problem in Brazil." Lax enforcement of existing laws against corruption is part of the problem.

## INFORMAL MARKET
### Score: 3.5–Stable (high level of activity)

Transparency International's 2002 score for Brazil is 4. Therefore, Brazil's informal market score is 3.5 this year.

# BULGARIA

Rank: 78

Score: 3.08

Category: Mostly Unfree

BULGARIA

### Present & Past Scores

(Best) 1
2
3
4
(Worst) 5

3.56  3.50  3.53  3.60  3.49  3.35  3.28  3.28  3.23  3.08

'95 '96 '97 '98 '99 '00 '01 '02 '03 '04

## QUICK STUDY

### SCORES

| | |
|---|---|
| Trade Policy | 4 |
| Fiscal Burden | 1.8 |
| Government Intervention | 2.5 |
| Monetary Policy | 4 |
| Foreign Investment | 3 |
| Banking and Finance | 2 |
| Wages and Prices | 2 |
| Property Rights | 4 |
| Regulation | 4 |
| Informal Market | 3.5 |

**Population:** 8,020,000

**Total area:** 110,910 sq. km

**GDP:** $13.1 billion

**GDP growth rate:** 4.0%

**GDP per capita:** $1,630

**Major exports:** textiles, clothing and footwear, base metals, mineral fuels, machinery and transport equipment

**Exports of goods and services:** $8.5 billion

**Major export trading partners:** Italy 15.0%, Germany 9.5%, Greece 8.8%, Turkey 8.15%

**Major imports:** machinery and transport equipment, mineral fuels, chemicals, plastics

**Imports of goods and services:** $10.8 billion

**Major import trading partners:** Russia 19.9%, Germany 15.2%, Italy 9.6%, France 6.0%

**Foreign direct investment (net):** $608.9 million

2001 Data (in constant 1995 US dollars)

Twelve years after economic reforms started under the first non-communist government, led by Philip Dimitrov, Bulgaria's government is finding it difficult to build political support for a far-reaching economic stabilization policy. A majority coalition is led by Prime Minister Simeon Saxe-Coburg, the former king, who was elected in July 2001. Former socialist leader Georgi Purvanov won the presidential elections in November 2001, and center–right parties are in opposition. From 1994 to 1997, the economy deteriorated under a socialist government. Between 1997 and 2001, the center–right government led by the Union of Democratic Forces implemented vital economic reforms and effective privatization in all major sectors. Privatization of the electricity and telecommunications industries occurred in 2002, and the economy has grown more competitive. Since pegging the national currency to the euro in 1997, the Currency Board Arrangement has continued to promote increases in foreign investment. Account deficits have narrowed. Despite rising oil prices, inflation continues to decline along with the external debt-to-GDP ratio. The labor market has also seen moderate gains as wages have increased and labor productivity has grown. Bulgaria received a formal invitation to join NATO in December 2002 and is expected to finalize its ascension by the spring of 2004; it may benefit economically if the U.S. moves some of its NATO bases to Bulgarian ports and air bases. Bulgaria's active lobbying for accession to the European Union seems to be succeeding. Bulgaria retains free trade agreements with the European Free Trade Area and continues to participate in the Central European Free Trade Agreement. Bulgaria's government intervention score is 0.5 point worse this year, and its property rights score is 1 point worse; however, its fiscal burden of government, monetary policy, and banking and finance scores are 1 point better. As a result, Bulgaria's overall score is 0.15 point better this year.

### TRADE POLICY
### Score: **4–Stable** (high level of protectionism)

According to the World Bank, Bulgaria's weighted average tariff rate in 2001 (the most recent year for which World Bank trade data are available) was 10.9 percent. The main non-tariff barrier is customs regulations, which the U.S. Department of State describes as "cumbersome, arbitrary and inconsistent." The most common problems cited are excessive documentation requirements, slow processing of shipments, and corruption.

### FISCAL BURDEN OF GOVERNMENT
Score—Income Taxation: **2.5–Better** (moderate tax rates)
Score—Corporate Taxation: **1.5–Better** (low tax rates)
Score—Change in Government Expenditures: **1.5–Better** (high decrease)
Final Score: **1.8–Better** (low cost of government)

Bulgaria's top income tax rate is 29 percent, down from the 38 percent reported in the 2003 *Index*. The top corporate tax rate is 15 percent, down from the 20 percent reported in the 2003 *Index*. Government expenditures as a share of GDP, after having remained unchanged in 2000, declined 3.5 percentage points to 34.5 percent in 2001. Based on lower income and corporate tax rates, as well as a lower level of government expenditures as a share of GDP, Bulgaria's fiscal burden of government score is 1 point better this year.

## GOVERNMENT INTERVENTION IN THE ECONOMY
### Score: **2.5**–Worse (moderate level)

The World Bank reports that the government consumed 16.1 percent of GDP in 2001. In the same year, according to the International Monetary Fund, Bulgaria received 9.85 percent of its total revenues from state-owned enterprises and government ownership of property, up from the 4.4 percent reported in the 2003 *Index*. As a result, Bulgaria's government intervention score is 0.5 point worse this year.

## MONETARY POLICY
### Score: **4**–Better (high level of inflation)

From 1993 to 2002, Bulgaria's weighted average annual rate of inflation was 11.33 percent, down from the 20.83 percent from 1992 to 2001 reported in the 2003 *Index*. As a result, Bulgaria's monetary policy score is 1 point better this year.

## CAPITAL FLOWS AND FOREIGN INVESTMENT
### Score: **3**–Stable (moderate barriers)

The law mandates equal treatment for foreign investors, and investors may repatriate 100 percent of profits. Non-residents may not purchase or own land, and non-residents inheriting land must dispose of it within three years, but ownership of buildings and lease of land are permitted. Bulgaria maintains some restrictions on foreign investment in armament companies, banking and insurance, development and exploration of natural resources, and real estate purchases in certain geographical areas. Foreigners are also treated equally in public procurement, but the Economist Intelligence Unit reports that "this area remains problematic, as implementation is poor and further progress is required. There have been many complaints from foreign companies, for example, that tender processes are subject to irregularities." A well-entrenched bureaucracy remains an obstacle to foreign investment. The International Monetary Fund reports that residents may hold foreign exchange accounts subject to some restrictions; non-residents may hold foreign exchange accounts without restriction on transactions less than lev 20,000. Prior registration with the central bank is required for most capital transactions.

## BANKING AND FINANCE
### Score: **2**–Better (low level of restrictions)

Bulgaria's banking system has undergone major reform since 1997. With the possibility of bailouts eliminated under the currency board, banks have had to focus instead on sound banking practices. There are no restrictions on foreign banks, and *The Wall Street Journal* reports that foreign banks hold approximately 90 percent of total banking assets. Bulgaria has given up all ownership in the banking sector. As a result, Bulgaria's banking and finance score is 1 point better this year. According to the Economist Intelligence Unit, "The sale of Biochim Bank—the last state-owned commercial bank…proved to be a

success, despite the failure of past attempts to privatise it." *The Wall Street Journal* reports that DSK (the former State Savings Bank) was sold in June 2003. The insurance sector has been open to foreign firms since 1997; however, majority foreign ownership joint ventures in Bulgarian banks and insurance companies are subject to government approval.

## WAGES AND PRICES
### Score: **2**–Stable (low level of intervention)

The market determines most wages and prices. According to the Economist Intelligence Unit, "There is very little threat of price controls being imposed. Price controls have been steadily dismantled, and the government will resist calls for their reinstatement unless there is an extremely severe economic crisis. Following the deregulation of the price of bread and other staple foods in early 1999, the only state-regulated prices left are those set by public monopolies, which are gradually being adjusted to reflect the true cost of their provision." Bulgaria maintains a minimum wage.

## PROPERTY RIGHTS
### Score: **4**–Worse (high level of protection)

Bulgaria's constitution provides for an independent judiciary. However, reports the U.S. Department of State, "ineffective rule of law, especially in the judicial system, limits investor confidence in the ability of the courts to enforce contracts, ownership and shareholders rights, and intellectual property rights. There is also a perception that it is difficult to have judicial decisions enforced." According to a Coalition 2000 report, the judiciary is one of the places where corruption is most pervasive. Based on new evidence with respect to the level of corruption in the judiciary, Bulgaria's property rights score is 1 point worse this year.

## REGULATION
### Score: **4**–Stable (high level)

The U.S. Department of State reports that "an abundance of licensing and regulatory regimes, their sometimes arbitrary interpretation and enforcement by the bureaucracy, and the incentives thus created for corruption, have long been seen as an impediment to investment." In addition, according to the Economist Intelligence Unit, labor laws are rigid. Corruption in the bureaucracy is a serious problem. "Although the Bulgarian government has achieved some successes in the fight against organized crime and corruption," reports the U.S. Department of State, "many observers believe that corruption and political influence in business decision-making continue to be significant problems in Bulgaria's investment climate."

## INFORMAL MARKET
### Score: **3.5**–Stable (high level of activity)

Transparency International's 2002 score for Bulgaria is 4. Therefore, Bulgaria's informal market score is 3.5 this year.

# BURKINA FASO

Rank: 95

Score: 3.28

Category: Mostly Unfree

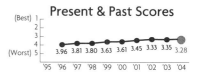

**Present & Past Scores**

(Best) 1
2
3
4
(Worst) 5

3.96 3.81 3.80 3.63 3.61 3.45 3.33 3.35 3.28

'95 '96 '97 '98 '99 '00 '01 '02 '03 '04

Since gaining its independence from France in 1960, Burkina Faso has endured much economic hardship. Violence in the Ivory Coast has greatly disrupted trade and has closed some industries in the western part of this landlocked nation; the Economist Intelligence Unit reports that "turmoil in Burkina Faso's most economically important neighbor continues to send shockwaves throughout the economy." Burkina Faso receives significant amounts of foreign aid. In 2003, under the heavily indebted poor countries (HIPC) initiative, it will receive $47 million, most of which is designated for education, health care, and poverty reduction according to the EIU, which reports that "Burkina Faso is expected to negotiate a new poverty reduction and growth facility (PRGF) with the International Monetary Fund (IMF) in 2003." The country has a poor human rights record, according to the U.S. Department of State. While the constitution approved by referendum in 1991 provided separate legal, executive, and judicial branches, the Department notes that in the last election, "the judiciary was subject to executive influence." Burkina Faso's fiscal burden of government score is 0.3 point worse this year, and its capital flows and foreign investment score is 1 point worse; however, its government intervention and monetary policy scores are 1 point better. As a result, Burkina Faso's overall score is 0.07 point better this year.

## QUICK STUDY

### SCORES

| | |
|---|---|
| Trade Policy | 4 |
| Fiscal Burden | 3.8 |
| Government Intervention | 3 |
| Monetary Policy | 1 |
| Foreign Investment | 3 |
| Banking and Finance | 3 |
| Wages and Prices | 3 |
| Property Rights | 4 |
| Regulation | 4 |
| Informal Market | 4 |

**Population:** 11,552,570

**Total area:** 274,200 sq. km

**GDP:** $3 billion

**GDP growth rate:** 5.6%

**GDP per capita:** $250

**Major exports:** cotton, livestock, gold

**Exports of goods and services:** $350.5 million

**Major export trading partners:** Singapore 14.9%, Italy 13.8%, France 7.3%, Ghana 6.1%

**Major imports:** petroleum goods, foodstuffs, capital goods

**Imports of goods and services:** $748.9 million

**Major import trading partners:** Ivory Coast 29.6%, France 24.3%, Nigeria 3.7%, Italy 3.4%

**Foreign direct investment (net):** $8.9 million

2001 Data (in constant 1995 US dollars)

## TRADE POLICY
### Score: **4**–Stable (high level of protectionism)

Burkina Faso is a member of the West African Economic and Monetary Union (WAEMU), which imposes a common external tariff with four rates: 0 percent, 5 percent, 10 percent, and 20 percent. (The other seven members of the WAEMU are Benin, Guinea–Bissau, Ivory Coast, Mali, Niger, Senegal, and Togo.) According to the World Bank, Burkina Faso's weighted average tariff rate in 2001 was 10.1 percent. The U.S. Department of State reports that non-tariff barriers take the form of licenses, extraneous fees, and corruption in the customs offices.

## FISCAL BURDEN OF GOVERNMENT
Score—Income Taxation: **3**–Stable (moderate tax rates)
Score—Corporate Taxation: **4.5**–Stable (very high tax rates)
Score—Change in Government Expenditures: **3**–Worse (very low decrease)
### Final Score: **3.8**–Worse (high cost of government)

The Embassy of Burkina Faso reports that Burkina Faso's top income tax rate is 30 percent. The top corporate tax rate is 35 percent. Government expenditures as a percentage of GDP decreased less in 2001 (0.6 percentage point to 26.4 percent) than they did in 2000 (2.4 percentage points). As a result, Burkina Faso's fiscal burden of government score is 0.3 point worse this year.

## GOVERNMENT INTERVENTION IN THE ECONOMY
### Score: **3**–Better (moderate level)

The World Bank reports that the government consumed 13.8 percent of GDP in 2001 and received 1.9 percent of its total revenues from state-owned enterprises and government ownership of property in 2002. Despite its privatization program, the government remains active in the economy. "As of May 2000," reports the Economist Intelligence Unit, "22 state enterprises have been successfully privatized.... The main enterprises awaiting privatization

119

include: Office national de télécommunications (Onatel), Poura gold mine, Office national de l'eau (ONEA), Société nationale de cinéma du Burkina (Sonacib), Centre national d'équipement agricole (CNEA), Ouagadougou and Bobo-Dioulasso airports." The same source reports that the government also owns Sofitex, the country's public-sector cotton enterprise. This has significant implications, since more than 80 percent of the population depends on subsistence agriculture and cotton exports. Based on the apparent unreliability of the figure for revenues from state-owned enterprises, 1 point has been added to Burkino Faso's government intervention score, which is nevertheless 1 point better this year.

## MONETARY POLICY
### Score: **1–Better** (very low level of inflation)

From 1993 to 2002, Burkina Faso's weighted average annual rate of inflation was 2.57 percent, down from the 3.16 percent from 1992 to 2001 reported in the 2003 *Index.* Burkina Faso has benefited from a stable currency—a rarity in sub-Saharan Africa—as a member of the CFA franc zone. Fourteen countries use the CFA franc, a common currency with a fixed parity with the euro. (The other 13 countries are Benin, Cameroon, Central African Republic, Chad, Congo [Brazzaville], Equatorial Guinea, Gabon, Guinea–Bissau, Ivory Coast, Mali, Niger, Senegal, and Togo.) Based on its lower weighted average rate of inflation, Burkina Faso's monetary policy score is 1 point better this year.

## CAPITAL FLOWS AND FOREIGN INVESTMENT
### Score: **3–Worse** (moderate barriers)

There are few restrictions on investment; however, a poorly developed infrastructure and growing corruption hinder foreign investment. According to the U.S. Department of State, "Investment and mining codes permit full repatriation of profits, 100 percent ownership of companies, and many tax exemptions." However, unofficial barriers such as a weak legal system and increasing corruption are problems for foreign investors. The International Monetary Fund reports that residents may hold foreign exchange accounts with permission of the government and the Central Bank of West African States, or BCEAO. Payments and transfers over a specified amount require supporting documents, and proceeds from non-WEAMU countries must be surrendered to an authorized dealer. All capital investments abroad by residents require government approval, as do most commercial and financial credits. Based on the evidence of corruption and restrictions on capital flows, Burkina Faso's capital flows and foreign investment score is 1 point worse this year.

## BANKING AND FINANCE
### Score: **3–Stable** (moderate level of restrictions)

The BCEAO, a central bank common to the eight members of the WEAMU, governs Burkina Faso's banking system. The eight member countries use the CFA franc that is issued by the BCEAO and pegged to the euro. In the past, the government has been known for heavily regulating and controlling the banking system through its direct ownership of many of the country's banks. According to the Economist Intelligence Unit, "Since the early 1990s, Burkina Faso's banking system has undergone restructuring, and the government has adopted the principle of limiting state participation to a maximum 25% in the banking sector." The Organisation for Economic Co-operation and Development reports that most bank credit goes to Sofitex, the state-owned cotton firm. Overall, government involvement remains substantial.

## WAGES AND PRICES
### Score: **3–Stable** (moderate level of intervention)

By 1998, as part of a World Bank program, the government had eliminated many price controls. According to the U.S. Department of State, "Prices have been freed up, and the public sector has been restructured." The government works in conjunction with representatives from the cotton producers' associations along with representatives from Sofitex, the cotton parastatal, to determine the price of cotton, which is Burkina Faso's largest export crop. The large public sector continues to influence some prices. Burkina Faso's labor code establishes a monthly minimum wage, which was last set in 1996.

## PROPERTY RIGHTS
### Score: **4–Stable** (low level of protection)

Burkina Faso's judicial system is weak. Villagers have their own customary or traditional courts. According to the U.S. Department of State, "The Constitution provides for an independent judiciary; however…the President has extensive appointment and other judicial powers. The Constitution stipulates that the Head of State is also the President of the Superior Council of the Magistrature, which can nominate and remove some high-ranked magistrates and can examine the performance of individual magistrates."

## REGULATION
### Score: **4–Stable** (high level)

Establishing a business in Burkina Faso can be difficult. The rule of law is lacking, and regulations can be applied unevenly and inconsistently. According to the African Development Bank, "some foreign investors…object to legal abuses and the growth of corruption." The government is trying to reform the regulatory structure; the Economist Intelligence Unit reports that Burkina Faso's principal donor countries are "increasingly vocal in expressing concern about…signs of growing corruption within the public administration."

## INFORMAL MARKET
### Score: **4–Stable** (high level of activity)

Transparency International's 2000 score for Burkina Faso was 3. Therefore, Burkina Faso's informal market score is 4 this year.

# BURMA (MYANMAR)

Rank: 151

Score: 4.45

Category: Repressed

Present & Past Scores

(Best) 1 2 3 4 (Worst) 5

4.45 4.38 4.31 4.15 4.28 4.45 4.33 4.35 **4.45**

'95 '96 '97 '98 '99 '00 '01 '02 '03 '04
n/a

BURMA

## QUICK STUDY

### SCORES

| | |
|---|---|
| Trade Policy | 5 |
| Fiscal Burden | 3 |
| Government Intervention | 3.5 |
| Monetary Policy | 5 |
| Foreign Investment | 5 |
| Banking and Finance | 4 |
| Wages and Prices | 4 |
| Property Rights | 5 |
| Regulation | 5 |
| Informal Market | 5 |

**Population:** 48,320,440

**Total area:** 678,500 sq. km

**GDP:** $7.3 billion

**GDP growth rate:** 9.7%

**GDP per capita:** $152

**Major exports:** gas, pulses and beans, teak and other hardwoods, fish products, apparel

**Exports of goods (fob):** $2 billion

**Major export trading partners:** Thailand 29.3%, India 13.6%, US 12.8%, Singapore 6.3%

**Major imports:** machinery and transport equipment, base metals, crude oil, electrical machinery

**Imports of goods (fob):** $2.3 billion

**Major import trading partners:** Singapore 22.5%, Japan 13.1%, South Korea 12.2%, Malaysia 11.9%, China 10.5%

**Foreign direct investment (net):** $110.2 million

2001 Data (in constant 1995 US dollars)

In May 2002, Burma's ruling junta, the State Peace and Development Council (SPDC), released the country's domestically and internationally revered opposition figure, Aung San Suu Kyi, from house arrest and opened negotiations with her party, the National League for Democracy (NLD), purportedly to implement a democratic transition. Internationally, the SPDC hired a public relations firm in Washington, and high-level delegations were sent to and from neighboring China, Thailand, and India. In June 2003, with no reported progress in political and economic reform, the SPDC re-detained Aung San Suu Kyi amid massive rioting and a run on Burma's private banks. Coherent economic policy is difficult to detect, and economic data are either nonexistent or of questionable value; however, the negative effects of economic decisions made by the junta are easy to see. Inflation in 2002 was at 50 percent. Growth forecasts of 3.2 percent for 2004 are based largely on expected garment sales in the U.S., but strong opponents in the U.S. Congress are calling for a ban on Burmese imports. Burma's monetary policy score is 1 point worse this year. As a result, its overall score is 0.1 point worse this year.

## TRADE POLICY
### Score: **5**–Stable (very high level of protectionism)

The World Bank reports that Burma's weighted average tariff rate in 2001 was 4.8 percent. However, based on data from the Economist Intelligence Unit and the Asian Development Bank, its average tariff rate in 2001 was 29 percent (based on import duties as a percent of total imports). Based on the range of tariffs and Burma's protection of domestic parastatals, the 29 percent average seems to be a more accurate measure of the country's trade barriers than the 4.8 percent reported by the World Bank. The U.S. Department of State reports that "permits [are] required for imports, exports and most other business activities…. Importers and exporters say it is extremely difficult to obtain the necessary business permits without paying for them 'unofficially.'"

## FISCAL BURDEN OF GOVERNMENT
### Score—Income Taxation: **3**–Stable (moderate tax rates)
### Score—Corporate Taxation: **4**–Stable (high tax rates)
### Score—Change in Government Expenditures: **1**–Stable (very high decrease)
## Final Score: **3**–Stable (moderate cost of government)

Burma's top income tax rate is 30 percent. The top corporate tax rate is 30 percent. Government expenditures as a share of GDP declined 5.2 percentage points to 6.6 percent in 2000. Government expenditure data for 2001 are not available; therefore, the change in Burma's government expenditure score is based on data from the 2003 *Index.*

## GOVERNMENT INTERVENTION IN THE ECONOMY
### Score: **3.5**–Stable (high level)

Based on data from the Economist Intelligence Unit, the government consumed 2 percent of GDP in 2000. In the same year, according to the International Monetary Fund, Burma received 30.63 percent of its total revenues from state-owned enterprises and government ownership of property. However, the Economist Intelligence Unit reports that the official figures "use methods of compilation and estimation that are not transparent and are not supported by available anecdotal evidence." According to the U.S. Department of State, the government owns a "large number of money-losing state economic enterprises" in several sectors, including mining and power, transport, domestic trade and manufacturing, and "the military holding companies—Myanmar Economic Corporation (MEC) and Union of Myanmar Economic Holdings Ltd. (UMEHL)—are extensively engaged in the manufacturing sector and exert increasing influence over business activities. The leadership has tried unsuccessfully to adopt a policy of import substitution and self-reliance." Based on the apparent unreliability of reported government consumption figures, 1 point has been added to Burma's government intervention score.

 ## MONETARY POLICY
### Score: **5**–Worse (very high level of inflation)

Between 1993 and 2002, Burma's weighted average annual rate of inflation was 42.33 percent, up from the 14.94 percent from 1992 to 2001 reported in the 2003 *Index*. As a result, Burma's monetary policy score is 1 point worse this year.

 ## CAPITAL FLOWS AND FOREIGN INVESTMENT
### Score: **5**–Stable (very high barriers)

According to the Economist Intelligence Unit, "Little effort is made to encourage private or foreign investment, even in priority sectors. Instead the business climate remains extremely difficult, hampered by parlous infrastructure and distribution networks, widespread corruption, shortages of capital, restrictions on access to and repatriation of foreign exchange, and erratic policymaking. These problems have…contributed to the recent slump in foreign investment approvals." The International Monetary Fund reports that both residents and non-residents may hold foreign exchange accounts with government approval (except for diplomatic missions and international organizations and their employees, who are permitted to hold such accounts at the Myanmar Foreign Trade Bank). Foreign firms are prohibited from owning land, which deprives them of access to local credit markets as credit institutions require real estate as collateral for making loans.

 ## BANKING AND FINANCE
### Score: **4**–Stable (high level of restrictions)

Burma's financial sector consists of the central bank, state banks, private banks, and foreign representative bank offices. Although private banks accounted for 64 percent of all savings in 1999–2000, government influence over the banking sector remains extensive. "The central bank of Myanmar still provides 60% of all credit," reports the Economist Intelligence Unit, and "private banks have also been hampered by government policy. For example, in March 1998, as foreign exchange reserves dwindled, the junta revoked nine banks' licenses to conduct foreign-exchange trading, leaving only two state-owned banks…to conduct foreign-exchange transactions." The government also caps interest rates that private banks can pay on deposits.

 ## WAGES AND PRICES
### Score: **4**–Stable (high level of intervention)

The government lifted some price controls in the early 1990s; according to the U.S. Department of State, however, "State economic enterprises and the military holding companies…benefit from official favoritism." The Economist Intelligence Unit reports that Burma may end its paddy procurement policy, whereby the government purchases 10 percent of all paddy output at officially fixed rates, and that if it should do so "(an outcome that is by no means guaranteed), farmers will soon be permitted to trade all of their output at market prices and thereby increase their incomes." A minimum wage applies to government employees and the employees of a few traditional industries.

 ## PROPERTY RIGHTS
### Score: **5**–Stable (very low level of protection)

Private property is not protected in Burma. "Lawyers cannot defend their clients independently," reports the U.S. Department of State, "especially in cases where the State has a special interest…. [J]udges do not allow a free defense in 'policy cases' and decisions are predetermined by the SPDC." In addition, "Pervasive corruption further serves to undermine the impartiality of the justice system."

 ## REGULATION
### Score: **5**–Stable (very high level)

Regulations lack transparency and are applied unevenly. According to the U.S. Department of State, "The resulting socialist-style policies, including state monopolization of major exports, a large number of money-losing state economic enterprises, a bloated bureaucracy slow to make decisions, and a tendency to rely on administrative controls rather than market forces to steer the economy, have dimmed prospects for development. Policy shifts also tend to be ad hoc, capricious and inconsistent, while regulatory changes are often arbitrary and unpublished."

 ## INFORMAL MARKET
### Score: **5**–Stable (very high level of activity)

The U.S. Department of State reports that the informal market "is quite large. Since the import of most consumer goods is officially prohibited…these goods are smuggled into Burma and sold on the black market. However, because of cronyism and corruption the black market here includes some of the swankiest shops in Rangoon selling expensive consumer products to wealthy Burmese and expatriates. The black market is larger than regular border trade, but has a significantly smaller value than normal overseas trade (which includes imports of expensive fuel and machinery)."

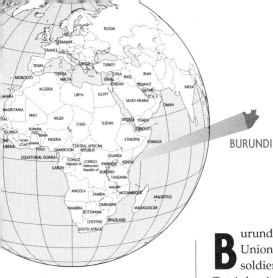

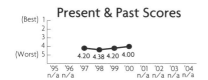

# BURUNDI

**Rank: Suspended**

**Score: n/a**

**Category: n/a**

**Present & Past Scores**

(Best) 1
2
3
4
(Worst) 5

4.20 4.38 4.20 4.00

'95 '96 '97 '98 '99 '00 '01 '02 '03 '04
n/a n/a                    n/a n/a n/a n/a

## QUICK STUDY

### SCORES

| | |
|---|---|
| Trade Policy | n/a |
| Fiscal Burden | n/a |
| Government Intervention | n/a |
| Monetary Policy | n/a |
| Foreign Investment | n/a |
| Banking and Finance | n/a |
| Wages and Prices | n/a |
| Property Rights | n/a |
| Regulation | n/a |
| Informal Market | n/a |

**Population:** 6,938,011

**Total area:** 27,830 sq. km

**GDP:** $976.5

**GDP growth rate:** 3.2%

**GDP per capita:** $141

**Major exports:** coffee and tea, manufactures, hides

**Exports of goods and services:** $328 million

**Major export trading partners:** Switzerland 32.6%, Germany 19.2%. Kenya 17.4%, US 7.3%

**Major imports:** capital goods, food, consumer goods

**Imports of goods and services:** $411 million

**Major import trading partners:** Belgium 12.0%, France 10.6%, Tanzania 9.5%, Kenya 6.2%

**Foreign direct investment (net):** n/a

2001 Data (in constant 1995 US dollars)

**B**urundi continues to deal with instability due to a long-running civil war. An African Union peacekeeping force composed of South African, Ethiopian, and Mozambican soldiers was sent to Burundi to monitor the cease-fire between Hutu rebels and the Tutsi-dominated army. According to the Associated Press, "Tutsi and Hutu political parties signed a power-sharing accord in August 2000 which led to the inauguration of the transitional government in November 2001." Despite the peace process, rebels continued to fight. Domitien Ndayizeye, who became president on April 30, is from the country's Hutu majority. His term will be the second half of the three-year transition period that is scheduled to end with general elections. International donors are awaiting a successful transition before disbursing their funds. The Economist Intelligence Unit reports that privatization is a condition for World Bank assistance; "[state-owned] companies have tended to serve a political function as a source of patronage with which to reward supporters, and the World Bank's privatization process would serve to dismantle this." Poor rains in recent years have harmed agricultural production among subsistence farmers, which is a major concern since the majority of the population depends on subsistence agriculture.

## TRADE POLICY
### Score: Not graded

Based on data from the World Trade Organization, Burundi's average tariff rate as of January 1, 2003, was 23.5 percent. The WTO reports that Burundi's "tariff structure remained unchanged between 1993 and January 1st, 2003, when maximum rates were lowered from 100 to 40 percent." Non-tariff barriers include difficult border crossings, an inefficient customs service, and border thieves and bandits.

## FISCAL BURDEN OF GOVERNMENT
### Score—Income Taxation: Not graded
### Score—Corporate Taxation: Not graded
### Score—Change in Government Expenditures: Not graded
## Final Score: Not graded

According to the International Monetary Fund, Burundi's top income tax rate is 60 percent. The top corporate tax rate is 40 percent. Government expenditures as a share of GDP increased 2.5 percentage points to 27.3 percent in 2001, compared to a 4.3 percentage point decrease the previous year.

## GOVERNMENT INTERVENTION IN THE ECONOMY
### Score: Not graded

The World Bank reports that the government consumed 13.5 percent of GDP in 2001. In the same year, according to the International Monetary Fund, Burundi received 4.63 percent of its total revenues from state-owned enterprises and government ownership of property.

## MONETARY POLICY
### Score: Not graded

From 1993 to 2002, Burundi's weighted average annual rate of inflation was 3.8 percent.

## CAPITAL FLOWS AND FOREIGN INVESTMENT
Score: Not graded

The government treats domestic and foreign firms equally and actively seeks investment, but continued fighting has made Burundi a dangerous place in which to invest. According to the Economist Intelligence Unit, "Burundi has never been a significant destination for foreign direct investment (FDI) and its already low levels of FDI have declined even further because of war and sanction, being officially recorded as nil in 1996–97. There was some evidence of improvement in 2000, although there will not be a significant pick up in FDI until the privatisation programme is activated." The International Monetary Fund reports that residents may hold foreign exchange accounts, but documentation must be submitted to the central bank, withdrawals over set limits require supporting documentation, and central bank approval is required to hold them abroad. Non-residents may hold foreign exchange accounts and withdraw funds up to a set limit upon presentation of documentation. Of the few capital transactions for which the IMF has information, most—including credit operations, direct investment, and personal capital movements—are subject to restrictions or authorization requirements.

## BANKING AND FINANCE
Score: Not graded

The banking system is severely underdeveloped and subject to government influence. "War since 1993, sanctions and an aid freeze in 1993–99 forced the Banque de la Republique du Burundi (BRB, the central bank), to abandon its previous monetary prudence and to lend heavily to the government," reports the Economist Intelligence Unit. "The BRB also relaxed its regulation of the commercial banking sector, taking a permissive approach to minimum reserve requirements…. There are seven commercial banks in Burundi, all of which have been heavily involved in lending to the government…. Credit to the private sector rose by 10%…although in general banks are hindered by weak balance sheets owing to a large number of bad loans."

## WAGES AND PRICES
Score: Not graded

Wages and prices in Burundi are affected by a large public sector, import substitution policies, and government subsidies, particularly for agriculture. The International Monetary Fund reports that the government directly influences the price of coffee. The government mandates a number of minimum wages based on location and skill.

## PROPERTY RIGHTS
Score: Not graded

Private property is subject to government expropriation and armed banditry. According to the U.S. Department of State, "in practice, the judiciary is not independent of the executive and is dominated by ethnic Tutsis…. [M]ost citizens assume that the courts promote the interests of the dominant Tutsi minority."

## REGULATION
Score: Not graded

Burundi's continuing instability and massive, corrupt bureaucracy make it difficult to establish a business. According to the Economist Intelligence Unit, "Civil conflict and the international sanctions from 1996 to 1999, including a cut-off in non-humanitarian assistance, resulted in a siege approach to economic management. This included rationing foreign exchange, imposing an overvalued exchange rate for official imports and financing the fiscal deficit through monetary growth and borrowings from the Banque de la Republique du Burundi (the central bank). Economic distortions have provided fertile ground for corruption." The large number of state-owned enterprises is another impediment to the establishment of businesses.

## INFORMAL MARKET
Score: Not graded

Burundi's informal market is larger than its formal market and still growing. The Economist Intelligence Unit reports that "the importing of fuel by informal economic routes has become profitable and increasingly common." In addition, "War, instability, and the imposition of sanctions have resulted in an increasing portion of external trade being unrecorded, and total crossborder trade is larger than indicated by official statistics."

CAMBODIA

# CAMBODIA

Rank: 63

Score: 2.90

Category: Mostly Free

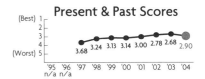

Present & Past Scores

(Best) 1
2
3
4
(Worst) 5

3.68  3.24  3.13  3.14  3.00  2.78  2.68  2.90

'95  '96  '97  '98  '99  '00  '01  '02  '03  '04
n/a  n/a

## QUICK STUDY

### SCORES

Trade Policy                        4
Fiscal Burden                     2.5
Government Intervention 2.5
Monetary Policy                   1
Foreign Investment             3
Banking and Finance           2
Wages and Prices               3
Property Rights                   4
Regulation                         4
Informal Market                  3

**Population:** 12,265,220

**Total area:** 181,040 sq. km

**GDP:** $3.8 billion

**GDP growth rate:** 5.3%

**GDP per capita:** $317

**Major exports:** fisheries products, garments, rubber

**Exports of goods and services:** $2.25 billion

**Major export trading partners:** US 57.9%, Germany 7.8%, UK 6.8%, China (including Hong Kong) 6.5%, Japan 3.6%

**Major imports:** petroleum products, construction materials, vehicles and motorcycles, clothing

**Imports of goods and services:** $2.3 billion

**Major import trading partners:** Thailand 23.5%, China (including Hong Kong) 20.8%, Singapore 18.6%, South Korea 5.1%, Vietnam 4.6%

**Foreign direct investment (net):** $101.3 million

2001 Data (in constant 1995 US dollars)

Cambodia's July 27, 2003, general elections were marred by violence, irregularities in voter registration, and some suppression of the press. As expected, the Cambodian People's Party (CPP) handily retained its dominant position. The Sam Rainsy Party (SRP) remains the only viable opposition party, gaining ground as the fortunes of the royalist FUNCINPEC party continued to decline. Following the general elections, political violence declined and internal stability returned to Cambodia. Relations with Thailand have fully recovered from the anti-Thai riots of January 2003, and Phnom Penh's relations with Laos, Vietnam, and other members of the Association of Southeast Asian Nations (ASEAN) remain strong. Cambodia successfully hosted the ASEAN Regional Forum in June 2003, and the Kingdom's external security remains stable. Economic reform often appears illusional in Cambodia, but Cambodia met its tariff reduction obligations to ASEAN and joined the World Trade Organization as scheduled in September 2003. Cambodia's fiscal burden of government score is 0.3 point better this year; however, its trade policy score is 2 points worse, and its government intervention score is 0.5 point worse. As a result, Cambodia's overall score is 0.22 point worse this year.

## TRADE POLICY
### Score: **4–Worse** (high level of protectionism)

According to the World Bank, Cambodia's average tariff was 16.5 percent in 2001, up from the 8.5 percent reported in the 2003 *Index*. As a result, Cambodia's trade policy score is 2 points worse this year. Import licenses have been abolished for most items but remain in effect for pharmaceuticals.

## FISCAL BURDEN OF GOVERNMENT
### Score—Income Taxation: **2–Stable** (low tax rates)
### Score—Corporate Taxation: **2–Stable** (low tax rates)
### Score—Change in Government Expenditures: **4–Better** (moderate increase)
### Final Score: **2.5–Better** (moderate cost of government)

According to the International Monetary Fund, Cambodia's top income tax rate is 20 percent. The top corporate income tax rate also is 20 percent. Government expenditures as a share of GDP rose 1.9 percentage points to 17.7 percent in 2001, compared to an increase of 3.2 percentage points in 2000. As a result, Cambodia's fiscal burden of government score is 0.3 point better this year.

## GOVERNMENT INTERVENTION IN THE ECONOMY
### Score: **2.5–Worse** (moderate level)

The World Bank reports that the government consumed 6 percent of GDP in 2001. In the same year, based on data from the International Monetary Fund, Cambodia received 19.31 percent of its total revenues from state-owned enterprises and government ownership of property. Based on newly available data on the level of revenues from state-owned enterprises, Cambodia's government intervention score is 0.5 point worse this year.

## MONETARY POLICY
### Score: **1**–Stable (very low level of inflation)

Between 1993 and 2002, Cambodia's weighted average annual rate of inflation was 2.42 percent.

## CAPITAL FLOWS AND FOREIGN INVESTMENT
### Score: **3**–Stable (moderate barriers)

According to the U.S. Department of State, "All sectors of the economy are open to foreign investment, there are no performance requirements, and no sectors in which foreign investors are denied national treatment." Sectors in which restrictions on foreign investment still apply include publishing, printing, radio and television broadcasting, gemstone exploitation, brick making, rice mills, wood and stone carving, and silk weaving. The government still must approve most foreign investments, and foreigners are not permitted to own investment companies. A bureaucratic approval process and corruption act as unofficial impediments to foreign investment. The International Monetary Fund reports that there are no restrictions or controls on the holding of foreign exchange accounts by either residents or non-residents. Non-residents may not own land in Cambodia.

## BANKING AND FINANCE
### Score: **2**–Stable (low level of restrictions)

Cambodia's banking system remains underdeveloped. According to the Economist Intelligence Unit, 16 banks were active in 2002: nine private banks, three foreign bank branches, two joint-venture banks, and two state-owned banks. After the 1999 Financial Institutions Law took effect, 12 were closed after they were declared non-viable. The EIU reports that the government plans to privatize the state-owned Foreign Trade Bank but that it is taking longer than expected. The government has liberalized interest rates, established reserve requirements, capped total exposure allowed to any one individual or client, and capped bank positions in foreign currency as a percent of the bank's net worth.

## WAGES AND PRICES
### Score: **3**–Stable (moderate level of intervention)

The market determines some prices. "Beginning in 1989," according to the Asia Society, "the pace of reform accelerated…. A number of important new laws were approved by the legislative body. They included the lifting of price controls with the exception of some key commodities, such as petroleum, electricity, cement, iron and fertilizer…." The government also influences prices through state-owned utilities. The Labor Law establishes a minimum wage based on recommendations from the Labor Advisory Committee. The minimum wage can vary regionally but applies only to the garment and footwear industries.

## PROPERTY RIGHTS
### Score: **4**–Stable (low level of protection)

Cambodia's legal system does not protect private property effectively. According to the Economist Intelligence Unit, "There is a lack of real separation in government, with the executive branch commonly dominating the legislature and the judiciary. The National Assembly's agenda, for example, is largely driven and controlled by the executive, which is dominated by the [Cambodia's People Party]. Judges are highly vulnerable to political pressure. King Sihanouk used to exert some control over the executive, but his powers have diminished and it is doubtful that that his successor will have the same authority." In addition, reports the U.S. Department of State, "The local and foreign business communities have reported frequent problems with inconsistent judicial rulings as well as outright corruption…. Corruption is a far greater problem in Cambodian courts than government interference in judicial decisions." The Land Titling system is not fully functional; most property owners do not have documentation to prove their ownership.

## REGULATION
### Score: **4**–Stable (high level)

Both potential and existing businesses continue to be burdened by Cambodia's politicized, cumbersome, and inefficient bureaucracy, as well as its non-transparent regulation and lack of infrastructure. The U.S. Department of State reports that "significant gaps in the legal system, the weakness of key financial institutions such as the banking sector, and problems of non-transparency and corruption continue to deter investment." In addition, "Investors often complain that decisions of Cambodian regulatory agencies are inconsistent, irrational, or corrupt…. The Cambodian government is still in the process of drafting laws and regulations that establish a framework for the market economy." According to the Economist Intelligence Unit, "Investors have also been put off by red tape, high utility costs and corruption, all of which detract from the advantages of low labor costs."

## INFORMAL MARKET
### Score: **3**–Stable (moderate level of activity)

Much informal market activity occurs in labor and pirated intellectual property, but illegal logging is also widespread despite some attempt to crack down on the problem; according to the Economist Intelligence Unit, "officially, the contribution of forestry to GDP was 2.7% in 1998, but this is almost certainly an underestimate because of widespread illegal logging." Smuggling, particularly over the Thai border, continues to be extensive.

*2004 Index of Economic Freedom*

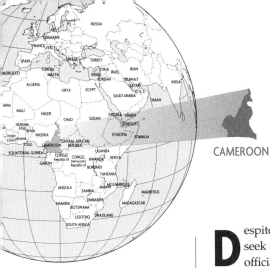

# CAMEROON

CAMEROON

Rank: 127

Score: 3.63

Category: Mostly Unfree

**Present & Past Scores**

(Best) 1
2
3
4
(Worst) 5

3.51  4.08  3.95  3.96  3.70  3.73  3.50  3.45  3.54  3.63

'95  '96  '97  '98  '99  '00  '01  '02  '03  '04

## QUICK STUDY

### SCORES

| | |
|---|---|
| Trade Policy | 5 |
| Fiscal Burden | 4.8 |
| Government Intervention | 3.5 |
| Monetary Policy | 2 |
| Foreign Investment | 3 |
| Banking and Finance | 3 |
| Wages and Prices | 3 |
| Property Rights | 4 |
| Regulation | 4 |
| Informal Market | 4 |

**Population:** 15,197,470

**Total area:** 475,440 sq. km

**GDP:** $10.6 billion

**GDP growth rate:** 5.3%

**GDP per capita:** $696

**Major exports:** coffee, cocoa, timber and cork, oil

**Exports of goods and services:** $3.1 billion

**Major export trading partners:** Italy 21.7%, Spain 12.2%, France 10.6%

**Major imports:** fuel, manufactures, machines and electrical equipment, transport equipment

**Imports of goods and services:** $3.3 billion

**Major import trading partners:** France 28.8%, Nigeria 11.9%, Italy 2.7%

**Foreign direct investment (net):** $194 million

2001 Data (in constant 1995 US dollars)

Despite speculation that the era of President Paul Biya will come to end with his refusal to seek an additional term, officials say such reports are premature. Urged by senior party officials, Mr. Biya will likely spend much of 2003 campaigning for his re-election. Mr. Biya has recently renewed his focus on the border dispute between his country and neighboring Nigeria. In a congratulatory message, he called on newly re-elected Nigerian President Olusegun Obaasanjo to pursue normalization of relations between the two countries. *The Economist* estimates that economic growth in 2003 is likely to reach 4.3 percent, down from an initial target of 5 percent. Recent shortages of electricity coupled with lowered oil production (nearly 6 percent of GDP in FY 2001–2002) are to blame for this readjustment. In addressing its national debt, the government is expected to continue its reforms in line with the International Monetary Fund's 2000–2003 poverty reduction and growth facility (PRGF). Successful implementation of the PRGF, which requires heavy investment in education, health, infrastructure, improved governance, and private-sector development, will allow Cameroon to receive full debt relief from the heavily indebted poor countries (HIPC) initiative. Completion of the PRGF is slated for first quarter 2004, although Cameroon is expected to receive some type of assistance to keep the process on course. Cameroon's informal market score is 0.5 point better this year; however, its fiscal burden of government score is 0.4 point worse, and its monetary policy score is 1 point worse. As a result, Cameroon's overall score is 0.09 point worse this year.

## TRADE POLICY

### Score: **5**–Stable (very high level of protectionism)

Cameroon is a member of the Central African Economic and Monetary Community (CEMAC), which also includes the Central African Republic, Chad, the Republic of Congo, Equatorial Guinea, and Gabon. The U.S. Trade Representative reports that in 2001, CEMAC applied a common average external tariff of 18.4 percent. In addition, "there are other surtaxes assessed on imports that vary according to the nature of the item, the quantity of the item in the shipment, and even the mode of transport." According to the U.S. Department of State, some imports are prohibited, "including specific sanitary products, chemicals, toxic waste, some cosmetics and some food items."

## FISCAL BURDEN OF GOVERNMENT

Score—Income Taxation: **5**–Stable (very high tax rates)
Score—Corporate Taxation: **5**–Stable (very high tax rates)
Score—Change in Government Expenditures: **4**–Worse (moderate increase)
### Final Score: **4.8**–Worse (very high cost of government)

Cameroon's top income tax rate is 60 percent. The top corporate tax rate is 38.5 percent. Government expenditures as a share of GDP increased by 1.2 percentage points to 18.6 percent in 2001, compared to a decline of 1.5 percentage points in 2000. As a result, Cameroon's fiscal burden of government score is 0.4 point worse this year.

## GOVERNMENT INTERVENTION IN THE ECONOMY

### Score: **3.5**–Stable (high level)

The World Bank reports that the government consumed 11.2 percent of GDP in 2001. In 2001–2002, based on data from the Economist Intelligence Unit, Cameroon received 21.61 percent of its revenue just from its state-owned oil companies.

127

## MONETARY POLICY
### Score: **2**–Worse ( low level of inflation)

Between 1993 and 2002, Cameroon's weighted average annual rate of inflation was 3.71 percent, up from 2.34 percent between 1992 and 2001. As a result, Cameroon's monetary policy score is 1 point worse this year. Cameroon has benefited from a stable currency—a rarity in sub-Saharan Africa—as a member of the CFA franc zone. Fourteen countries use the CFA franc, a common currency with a fixed parity with the euro. (The other 13 countries are Benin, Burkina Faso, Central African Republic, Chad, Congo [Brazzaville], Equatorial Guinea, Gabon, Guinea–Bissau, Ivory Coast, Mali, Niger, Senegal, and Togo.)

## CAPITAL FLOWS AND FOREIGN INVESTMENT
### Score: **3**–Stable (moderate barriers)

According to the U.S. Department of State, Cameroon's new Investment Charter "provides support to investors and guarantees fair and prompt settlement of investment-related, commercial and industrial disputes…. The new Charter guarantees: the freedom to undertake any production, service provision or commercial activity, irrespective of their nationality; equal treatment in the conduct of any activity in conformity with the law on competition; property rights; and dispatch in concession and land acquisition procedures." It is expected that laws to implement the new Investment Charter will be passed by June 2004. In the meantime, foreign investment will be regulated by the 1990 investment code, which the U.S. Department of State describes as "attractive on paper…. Arbitrary application of the code by the administration and courts, however, made it much less appealing." The International Monetary Fund reports that transfers are subject to numerous requirements, controls, and authorization depending on the transaction. Both residents and non-residents may hold accounts in freely convertible foreign exchange. Most capital transactions require approval of or declaration to the government.

## BANKING AND FINANCE
### Score: **3**–Stable (moderate level of restrictions)

The banking sector has been in crisis for much of the past decade, but the government has made some effort to restructure and reform the system. In January 2000, the state sold the last majority government-owned bank to Banques Populaires Group of France. Three new private banks have been established since 2000, and the sector now includes 10 commercial banks. However, costs remain high because of limited competition and judicial weakness. In the insurance sector, reports the Economist Intelligence Unit, the government has privatized its holdings of the state-owned Société camerounaise d'assurances-réassurances. According to the U.S. Department of State, "After more than a decade of bank restructuring, Cameroon's banking system is more solid but is still plagued by the unwillingness of many bankers to take

risks, a lack of modern banking products and a generally low quality of service."

## WAGES AND PRICES
### Score: **3**–Stable (moderate level of intervention)

According to the U.S. Department of State, "Some price controls were lifted in 1994 (however those on water, electricity, collective passenger surface transport, pharmaceuticals, petroleum products, and schoolbooks remain)." The government controls prices for cotton—a major agricultural product and export—through its monopoly on marketing, collection, and supply of inputs and fertilizer. By law, the Ministry of Labor sets a single minimum wage that applies to all sectors of the economy.

## PROPERTY RIGHTS
### Score: **4**–Stable (low level of protection)

A reportedly corrupt government and an uncertain legal environment can result in the confiscation of private property. "Under the current judicial system," reports the U.S. Department of State, "local and foreign investors…have found it complicated and costly to enforce contract rights, protect property rights, obtain a fair and expeditious hearing before the courts or defend themselves against frivolous lawsuits." Implementation of the Organisation pour l'Harmonisation du Droit des Affaires en Afrique (OHADA) treaty has not delivered strong results in curbing corruption in the judiciary.

## REGULATION
### Score: **4**–Stable (high level)

Existing regulations are applied unevenly and impose a substantial burden on businesses. According to the U.S. Department of State, "Potential investors should be aware that…obtaining government approvals after incorporation in Cameroon can be a lengthy process involving a series of government ministries." The African Development Bank reports that "despite the establishment of anti-corruption committees within ministries and some arrests and prosecutions, government services still suffer from widespread corruption."

## INFORMAL MARKET
### Score: **4**–Better (high level of activity)

Transparency International's 2002 score for Cameroon is 2.2. Therefore, Cameroon's informal market score is 4 this year—a 0.5 point improvement.

# CANADA

Rank: 16

Score: 1.98

Category: Free

Present & Past Scores

(Best) 1
2
3
4
(Worst) 5

2.10 2.08 2.08 2.09 2.04 2.06 2.01 1.90 2.00 1.98

'95 '96 '97 '98 '99 '00 '01 '02 '03 '04

## QUICK STUDY

### SCORES

| | |
|---|---|
| Trade Policy | 2 |
| Fiscal Burden | 2.8 |
| Government Intervention | 3 |
| Monetary Policy | 1 |
| Foreign Investment | 3 |
| Banking and Finance | 2 |
| Wages and Prices | 2 |
| Property Rights | 1 |
| Regulation | 2 |
| Informal Market | 1 |

**Population:** 31,499,560

**Total area:** 9,976,140 sq. km

**GDP:** $741.4 billion

**GDP growth rate:** 3.3%

**GDP per capita:** $23,537

**Major exports:** automobile products, machinery and equipment, energy products, forest products, agricultural products, travel services, insurance services, computer and information, transportation

**Exports of goods and services:** $316.3 billion

**Major export trading partners:** US 84.8%, Japan 2.4%, UK 1.4%

**Major imports:** machinery and equipment, automobile products, travel services, financial services, insurance services

**Imports of goods and services:** $291.8 billion

**Major import trading partners:** US 71.5%, Japan 3.3%, UK 2.9%

**Foreign direct investment**

2002 Data (in constant 1995 US dollars)

Canada is the world's seventh largest market economy and has experienced solid economic growth under the Liberal government of Jean Chrétien, who won his third national parliamentary majority in November 2000. The federal government's corporate tax rate, under proposed scheduled decreases, should fall to 21 percent by 2004. The U.S. economic boom significantly encouraged Canada's rapid growth during the 1990s; the United States is Canada's largest trading partner, accounting for 85 percent of all Canadian exports and amounting to almost $400 billion a year. In recent years, since the establishment of the North American Free Trade Area (NAFTA), there have been record numbers of cross-border mergers and acquisitions. With two-way trade accounting for an astounding $1.5 billion per day, the U.S.–Canadian economic relationship is the largest that has ever existed between two countries. Chrétien intends to use healthy federal finances to allow the government to honor its tax cutting program while increasing government spending to bolster Canada's health care system. In the long run, further liberalization will be critical. For example, while NAFTA has been an impetus behind Canadian trade liberalization, federal regulatory regimes still affect foreign investment in telecommunications, publishing, broadcasting, aviation, mining, and fishing. Canada's fiscal burden of government score is 0.2 point better this year. As a result, its overall score is 0.02 point better this year, causing Canada to be classified as a "free" economy.

 ## TRADE POLICY
### Score: **2**–Stable (low level of protectionism)

According to the World Bank, Canada's weighted average tariff rate in 2001 (the most recent year for which World Bank data are available) was 0.9 percent. According to the *Financial Post*, non-tariff barriers include "ownership requirements, including textiles and clothing, telecommunications, TV and film, aviation and marine transportation, insurance, steel and agriculture." In some cases, the government also resorts to anti-dumping measures. The U.S. Department of State reports that "Canada closely restricts imports of certain "supply managed" agricultural products…[including] dairy products, eggs and poultry."

 ## FISCAL BURDEN OF GOVERNMENT
Score—Income Taxation: **2.5**–Stable (moderate tax rates)
Score—Corporate Taxation: **3**–Stable (moderate tax rates)
Score—Change in Government Expenditures: **2.5**–Better (low decrease)
### Final Score: **2.8**–Better (moderate cost of government)

Canada's base federal income tax rate is 29 percent. The base federal corporate tax rate is 23 percent. There is also a 4 percent surtax on corporate profits, which yields a 24.12 percent overall top federal corporate tax rate. The base federal corporate tax rate is scheduled to fall to 21 percent by 2006. Government expenditures as a share of GDP decreased 1.1 percentage points to 40.6 percent in 2002, compared to a 0.5 percentage point increase in 2001. As a result, Canada's fiscal burden of government score is 0.2 point better this year.

 ## GOVERNMENT INTERVENTION IN THE ECONOMY
### Score: **3**–Stable (moderate level)

The Canadian Embassy reports that the government consumed 21.3 percent of GDP in 2002. In 2001, according to the International Monetary Fund, Canada received 6.27 percent of its

total revenues from state-owned enterprises and government ownership of property.

## MONETARY POLICY
### Score: **1**–Stable (very low level of inflation)

From 1993 to 2002, Canada's weighted average annual rate of inflation was 2.32 percent.

## CAPITAL FLOWS AND FOREIGN INVESTMENT
### Score: **3**–Stable (moderate barriers)

The government of Canada regulates foreign investment through the 1985 Investment Canada Act. "The purpose of the act," reports the Economist Intelligence Unit, "is to encourage investment in Canada…that contributes to economic growth and employment opportunities. Special investment and ownership rules govern some sectors, including financial services, communications, transport and those related to cultural heritage or national identity. These include businesses such as publishing, broadcasting, and film-making." The government must be notified about any foreign investments in a new business or foreign investments that acquire direct control of a Canadian firm that has assets of C$5 million or more or is culturally sensitive. In 2002, the C$5 million threshold was increased to C$218 million for foreign companies from countries that belong to the World Trade Organization. There are no restrictions on current transfers, repatriation of profits, purchase of real estate, or access to foreign exchange.

## BANKING AND FINANCE
### Score: **2**–Stable (low level of restrictions)

Canada has a private financial system with some restrictions. The Economist Intelligence Unit reports that the banking system "is well developed and dominated by six, large domestic banks. Ownership of the banks is restricted, and their activities are highly regulated…. Canadian banks continue to be restricted in some activities—measures that protect other enterprises. Mergers are prohibited between big banks and big insurance companies. Banks may not provide leases for vehicles, which has been legislated to protect car retailers, and they may not sell insurance products through their branch networks." According to the Department of Finance, the only government-owned bank is the Business Development Bank of Canada, which typically has been "'the lender of last resort' for companies unable to source financing through private markets."

## WAGES AND PRICES
### Score: **2**–Stable (low level of intervention)

The market sets most prices. According to the Economist Intelligence Unit, "There are no broad controls on prices for goods and services in Canada, although private companies that operate monopoly services, such as telephones and cable television, are subject to price regulation…. State-owned monopolies, such as the provincial power utilities, submit rates for government approval by the government." Additional price controls cover poultry, eggs, dairy, wheat, rail revenues for grain traffic, seaway pricing, and telecommunications. The government also provides substantial subsidies for agriculture. Provinces have jurisdiction over price controls on energy, and provinces or territories set minimum wages.

## PROPERTY RIGHTS
### Score: **1**–Stable (very high level of protection)

Private property is well-protected in Canada. The judiciary is independent; the Economist Intelligence Unit reports that "judges and civil servants are generally honest, and bribery and other forms of corruption are rare."

## REGULATION
### Score: **2**–Stable (low level)

It is relatively easy to establish a business in Canada. According to the U.S. Department of State, "incorporation is a straightforward and inexpensive procedure, accomplished federally under the Canada Business Corporations Act, or provincially under provincial corporate statutes. An average of three–four weeks is required to process an application." To reduce the level of bureaucracy, both information on the administrative procedure to open a business and the necessary forms are available on-line. The regulatory system is thorough but essentially transparent. Regulations differ from province to province, as well as from one municipality to the next, as in other countries that have a federal system. The government has deregulated the telecommunications services sector to a considerable degree, allowing growth in the domestic market. It also allows e-commerce to operate with a minimal regulatory burden.

## INFORMAL MARKET
### Score: **1**–Stable (very low level of activity)

Transparency International's 2001 score for Canada is 9. Therefore, Canada's informal market score is 1 this year.

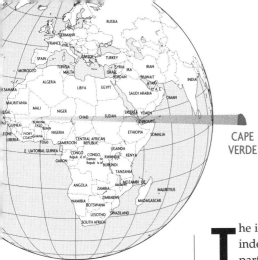

# CAPE VERDE

CAPE VERDE

**Rank: 60**

**Score: 2.86**

**Category: Mostly Free**

### Present & Past Scores

(Best) 1
2
3
4
(Worst) 5

3.60 3.80 3.74 3.91 3.76 3.56 3.30 3.25 **2.86**

'95 '96 '97 '98 '99 '00 '01 '02 '03 '04
n/a

## QUICK STUDY

### SCORES

| | |
|---|---|
| Trade Policy | 5 |
| Fiscal Burden | 3.6 |
| Government Intervention | 2 |
| Monetary Policy | 1 |
| Foreign Investment | 3 |
| Banking and Finance | 3 |
| Wages and Prices | 2 |
| Property Rights | 3 |
| Regulation | 2 |
| Informal Market | 4 |

**Population:** 446,400

**Total area:** 4,033 sq. km

**GDP:** $692 million

**GDP growth rate:** 3.3%

**GDP per capita:** $1,550

**Major exports:** fish products, fuel, clothing and footwear

**Exports of goods and services:** $178.6 million

**Major export trading partners:** Portugal 53.3%, UK 26.6%, US 13.3%

**Major imports:** fuels, food, and industrial products

**Imports of goods and services:** $395.1 million

**Major import trading partners:** Portugal 54.0%, Netherlands 10.5%, Italy 6.5%

**Foreign direct investment (net):** n/a

2001 Data (in constant 1995 US dollars)

The island nation of Cape Verde was a one-party Marxist state from the time it became independent from Portugal until 1991, when constitutional changes allowed multi-party elections. Cape Verde was the first sub-Saharan African state to hold free elections. It has close economic and political ties to Portugal and the European Union, and its currency is pegged to the euro. Cape Verde has few natural resources, frequent droughts, and serious water shortages. The Economist Intelligence Unit reports that "the economy is dominated by the services sector—essentially transport, commerce and government spending, funded by remittances and grants from abroad—which accounted for 72% of GDP in 2000." Agriculture and fishing employ much of the population but contribute only about 11 percent of GDP. The government's economic priorities include controlling public spending, reducing domestic debt, and privatizing the remaining state-owned companies. The government also plans to reduce the corporate income tax rate from 35 percent to 30 percent and introduce a value added tax. Cape Verde's trade policy score is 1 point worse this year; however, its fiscal burden of government score is 0.9 point better, its government intervention score is 3 points better, and its wages and prices score is 1 point better. As a result, Cape Verde's overall score is 0.39 point better this year, causing Cape Verde to be classified as a "mostly free" economy.

### TRADE POLICY
#### Score: 5–Worse (very high level of protectionism)

Cape Verde's tariff rates range from 5 percent to 50 percent. According to the International Monetary Fund and the Embassy of Cape Verde, the average tariff rate in 2002 was 23.5 percent, up from the 13.3 percent reported in the 2003 *Index*. As a result, Cape Verde's trade policy score is 1 point worse this year. The U.S. Department of State reports that "imports…are subject to a general customs service tax of 7 percent and a consumption tax on non-priority goods, ranging from 5 percent to up to 60 percent for hard liquor." In addition, "Pharmaceuticals may only be imported by public institutions."

### FISCAL BURDEN OF GOVERNMENT
#### Score—Income Taxation: 4.5–Stable (very high tax rates)
#### Score—Corporate Taxation: 4.5–Stable (very high tax rates)
#### Score—Change in Government Expenditures: 1–Better (very high decrease)
### Final Score: 3.6–Better (high cost of government)

The International Monetary Fund reports that Cape Verde's top income tax rate is 45 percent. The top corporate tax rate is 35 percent. According to the African Development Bank, government expenditures as a share of GDP declined 18.6 percentage points to 26.4 percent in 2001, compared to a 2.6 percentage point increase in 2000. As a result, Cape Verde's fiscal burden of government score is 0.9 point better this year.

### GOVERNMENT INTERVENTION IN THE ECONOMY
#### Score: 2–Better (low level)

The World Bank reports that the government consumed 12.9 percent of GDP in 2001, down from the 25.3 percent reported in the 2003 *Index*. In the same year, based on data from the International Monetary Fund, Cape Verde received 5 percent of its total revenues from state-owned enterprises and government ownership of property. Based on the lower percentage of government consumption and newly available data on revenues from state-owned enterprises, Cape Verde's government intervention score is 3 points better this year.

## MONETARY POLICY
### Score: **1**–Stable (very low level of inflation)

From 1993 to 2002, Cape Verde's weighted average annual rate of inflation was 2.03 percent.

## CAPITAL FLOWS AND FOREIGN INVESTMENT
### Score: **3**–Stable (moderate barriers)

Recognizing that Cape Verde, with its limited resources, must be integrated into the global economy, the government encourages foreign investment—particularly in tourism, fishing, light manufacturing, communications, and transportation. All sectors of the economy are now open to investment, for which a permit and registration with the central bank are required. The International Monetary Fund reports that both residents and non-residents may hold foreign exchange accounts, subject to government approval and regulations. Most payments and transfers are subject to controls. Real estate transactions require central bank approval. While most capital transactions are permitted, most of them also are subject to advance approval by the central bank.

## BANKING AND FINANCE
### Score: **3**–Stable (moderate level of restrictions)

Cape Verde's underdeveloped banking system is overseen by the central bank, which gained greater autonomy following July 1999 constitutional reforms and a new banking law passed in May 2002. Cape Verde also had four commercial banks in 2002. Legislation implemented in 1993 removed restrictions on establishing private banks and barriers to foreign banks, but new banks must be authorized by the central bank, and 50 percent of bank employees must be Cape Verdean.

## WAGES AND PRICES
### Score: **2**–Better (low level of intervention)

The market determines most prices, but the government still maintains price controls on certain products. The Economist Intelligence Unit reports that the government establishes fuel prices, and the Embassy of Cape Verde reports that the government controls the price of water and electricity. Cape Verde has privatized many of its state-owned operations, precluding the government from affecting prices through subsidies to the state-owned firms. There is no private-sector minimum wage, but most private wages are linked to those of equivalent civil servants. Based on the evidence that the government influences only a minimal number of prices, Cape Verde's wages and prices score is 1 point better this year.

## PROPERTY RIGHTS
### Score: **3**–Stable (moderate level of protection)

Private property is only moderately protected in Cape Verde. According to the U.S. Department of State, "The Constitution provides for a judiciary independent of the executive branch…. [H]owever, there continued to be accusations of politicized and biased judicial decisions." In addition, "The judiciary generally provides due process rights. However the right to an expeditious trial is constrained by a seriously overburdened and understaffed judicial system. A backlog of cases routinely leads to trial delays of 6 months."

## REGULATION
### Score: **2**–Stable (low level)

Government efforts to streamline the cumbersome bureaucracy and increase transparency have made it easier to establish a business. According to the U.S. Department of State, "Bureaucratic procedures have been simplified in a number of cases…. The Center for Tourism, Investment and Export Promotion, PROMEX, has become a one-stop shop for external investors. In general, external investment operations are subject to prior authorization from the minister in charge of economic affairs. An application is submitted to PROMEX, and within thirty days the investor should get a reply. If government action is not forthcoming, within 30 days, approval is automatic." Mass privatizations have eased the burden of competing with state-owned enterprises, although the process has been criticized for a lack of transparency. Regulations are applied evenly in most cases.

## INFORMAL MARKET
### Score: **4**–Stable (high level of activity)

Cape Verde has a widespread informal market, mainly in consumer goods, luxury items, and Western books, video and audiocassettes, and movies.

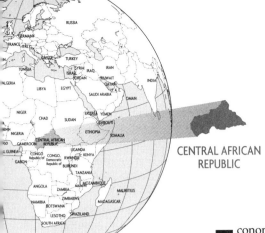

# CENTRAL AFRICAN REPUBLIC

Rank: 105

Score: 3.38

Category: Mostly Unfree

## QUICK STUDY

### SCORES

| | |
|---|---|
| Trade Policy | 5 |
| Fiscal Burden | 3.8 |
| Government Intervention | 4 |
| Monetary Policy | 1 |
| Foreign Investment | 2 |
| Banking and Finance | 3 |
| Wages and Prices | 3 |
| Property Rights | 4 |
| Regulation | 4 |
| Informal Market | 4 |

**Population:** 3,770,820

**Total area:** 622,984 sq. km

**GDP:** $1.3 billion

**GDP growth rate:** 1.5%

**GDP per capita:** $344

**Major exports:** cotton, coffee, timber, diamonds

**Exports of goods and services:** $105.1 billion

**Major export trading partners:** Belgium 53%, Kazakhstan 9%, Spain 9%

**Major imports:** food, textiles, petroleum products, machinery, electrical equipment

**Imports of goods and services:** $129.4 billion

**Major import trading partners:** France 26%, Cameroon 13%, Spain 5%

**Foreign direct investment (net):** $7.2 million

2001 Data (in constant 1995 US dollars)

Economic growth in the Central African Republic has been hindered by political instability. The country endured successive military governments from 1960, when it gained its independence from France, until the establishment of civilian government in 1993. Three military mutinies in 1996 and 1997 were suppressed with the aid of a French-funded African peacekeeping force, which was succeeded by a United Nations peacekeeping mission that left in 2000 after overseeing the 1998 legislative elections and 1999 presidential elections. An attempted coup in May–June 2001 was quelled only with the support of Libyan armed forces. General François Bozize, who seized the presidency by force on May 15, 2003, is supported by nearly all of the political parties including the main opposition party. According to the Economist Intelligence Unit, he "has declared the coup to be a temporary break with democracy and has promised to hold free and fair multiparty elections, following a transitional period which will last between 18 and 30 months." The main exports are diamonds and timber, and the previous government promised to clamp down on the illegal diamond trade by introducing a certification of origin system; it is uncertain whether the new government will honor this commitment. *The Economist* reports that diamond smugglers love the Central African Republic for "its long unpatrolled borders." Overall, the country has a poorly educated population and a long history of poor economic policies. The Central African Republic's property rights score is 1 point worse this year. As a result, its overall score is 0.1 point worse this year.

###  TRADE POLICY
Score: **5**–Stable (very high level of protectionism)

The Central African Republic is a member of the Central African Economic and Monetary Community (CEMAC), which also includes Cameroon, Chad, the Republic of Congo, Equatorial Guinea, and Gabon. In 2002, according to the U.S. Trade Representative, CEMAC applied an average common external tariff of 18.4 percent; however, "there are other surtaxes assessed on imports which can vary according to the nature of the item, the quantity of the particular item in the shipment, and even the mode of transport."

###  FISCAL BURDEN OF GOVERNMENT
Score–Income Taxation: **5**–Stable (very high tax rates)
Score–Corporate Taxation: **4**–Stable (high tax rates)
Score–Change in Government Expenditures: **2**–Stable (moderate decrease)
Final Score: **3.8**–Stable (high cost of government)

The International Monetary Fund reports that the Central African Republic's top income tax rate is 50 percent. The top corporate tax rate is 30 percent. Government expenditures as a share of GDP fell less in 2001 (2.4 percentage points to 13.2 percent) than they did in 2000 (2.5 percentage points). Based on its stable tax rates and relatively stable level of government expenditures as a share of GDP, the Central African Republic's fiscal burden of government score is unchanged this year.

###  GOVERNMENT INTERVENTION IN THE ECONOMY
Score: **4**–Stable (high level)

The World Bank reports that the government consumed 11.4 percent of GDP in 2001. According to the U.S. Department of State, "The role of the…government in the economy is diminishing in the commercial and industrial sectors, as it is currently privatizing certain companies. After privatizing its water company, parastatal banks and oil company, the C.A.R. government plans to privatize 60% of its share in Socatel, the telecommunication company, with 40% being controlled by France Cable, a French company."

## MONETARY POLICY
### Score: **1**–Stable (very low level of inflation)

From 1993 to 2002, the Central African Republic's weighted average annual rate of inflation was 1.60 percent. The Central African Republic has benefited from a stable currency—a rarity in sub-Saharan Africa—as a member of the CFA franc zone. Fourteen countries use the CFA franc, a common currency with a fixed parity with the euro. (The other 13 countries are Benin, Burkina Faso, Cameroon, Chad, Congo [Brazzaville], Equatorial Guinea, Gabon, Guinea–Bissau, Ivory Coast, Mali, Niger, Senegal, and Togo.)

## CAPITAL FLOWS AND FOREIGN INVESTMENT
### Score: **2**–Stable (low barriers)

According to the U.S. Department of State, the Central African Republic "is in the process of adopting a more attractive investment code. This new code…is designed to open up the country to foreign investors while complying with the treaty creating the Central African states economic and monetary community…. There is no single sector/matter in which foreign investors are denied national treatment in the C.A.R." Although state-owned enterprises hinder foreign investment, foreigners have won a significant presence in some formerly state-dominated sectors, such as telecommunications, and full ownership of businesses by foreigners is permitted. The International Monetary Fund reports that residents may hold foreign exchange accounts. Transfers and payments to countries other than France, Monaco, members of the West African Economic and Monetary Union, members of the CEMAC, and Comoros are subject to government approval and some reporting requirements. Sale or issue of capital market securities and commercial credits requires government approval.

## BANKING AND FINANCE
### Score: **3**–Stable (moderate level of restrictions)

The banking and finance sector is underdeveloped. There are only four commercial banks, and the Economist Intelligence Unit reports that the banking sector's "performance…has been undermined by the accumulation of dubious debts, in particular by the state, and the non-realisation of promised credits." The government has privatized the two largest banks, Banque internationale pour le Centrafrique and Commercial Bank Centrafrique. Credit is allocated on market terms, and foreigners have access to credit on the local market, although it is limited by the banking sector's small size.

## WAGES AND PRICES
### Score: **3**–Stable (moderate level of intervention)

The government still influences prices through its state-owned companies and subsidies and directly controls some prices. The Economist Intelligence Unit reports that "cotton production [one of the principal economic outputs] recovered slightly… partly as a result of the government's strategy to maintain farm gate prices despite falling international prices." The Minister of Labor has the authority to set the minimum wage by decree. The minimum wage varies by sector and type of work.

## PROPERTY RIGHTS
### Score: **4**–Worse (low level of protection)

According to the U.S. Department of State, "[E]xecutive interference has been reported [and] courts are not functioning due to inefficient administration, shortage of trained personnel, growing salary arrears, and a lack of material resources." Property rights have weakened in the wake of the March 2003 coup d'état. The Economist Intelligence Unit reports that the country's economy and institutions have been affected by "the instability of the recent months of insurgency as well as by the coup itself, in which many businesses were looted, leaving them severely decapitalized…. [R]esidents are still being deterred from returning to their homes because of the absence of civil authority." Based on increasing instability with respect to the protection of property, the Central African Republic's property rights score is 1 point worse this year.

## REGULATION
### Score: **4**–Stable (high level)

The state maintains a considerable presence, in part through parastatals, in such important sectors as telecommunications and cotton, the main cash crop. Corruption is a problem, as the Economist Intelligence Unit reports, partly because payment of civil servants' salaries is at best sporadic. According to the U.S. Department of State, "Setting up a business…requires voluminous paperwork and approvals from the ministries of commerce, finance and justice. The government is trying to simplify this process." The government also is trying to reform the labor code and improve transparency in the regulatory system, but much remains to be done.

## INFORMAL MARKET
### Score: **4**–Stable (high level of activity)

Informal market activity, especially diamond smuggling, is extensive. According to the Economist Intelligence Unit, "Officially only 500,000 carats of jewel-quality diamonds were exported from the country in 2000, however Antwerp's diamond trade alone records imports into Belgium of 900,000 carats from the CAR." Smuggling of arms also takes place. In addition, a significant part of the population is employed in the informal economy.

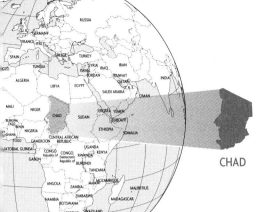

# CHAD

Rank: 124

Score: 3.54

Category: Mostly Unfree

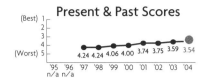

Present & Past Scores

(Best) 1
2
3
4
(Worst) 5

'95 '96 '97 '98 '99 '00 '01 '02 '03 '04
n/a n/a 4.24 4.24 4.06 4.00 3.74 3.75 3.59 3.54

CHAD

### SCORES

| | |
|---|---|
| Trade Policy | 5 |
| Fiscal Burden | 4.4 |
| Government Intervention | 3 |
| Monetary Policy | 3 |
| Foreign Investment | 3 |
| Banking and Finance | 2 |
| Wages and Prices | 2 |
| Property Rights | 4 |
| Regulation | 4 |
| Informal Market | 5 |

**Population:** 7,916,010

**Total area:** 1,284,200 sq. km

**GDP:** $1.8 billion

**GDP growth rate:** 8.5%

**GDP per capita:** $230

**Major exports:** cotton, livestock, meat

**Exports of goods and services:** $247.5 million

**Major export trading partners:** Portugal 28%, Germany 15%, France 7%, Poland 6%

**Major imports:** petroleum products, foodstuffs, textiles, machinery

**Imports of goods and services:** $1.2 billion

**Major import trading partners:** US 38%, France 26%, Cameroon 8%, Nigeria 5%

**Foreign direct investment (net):** $67.3 million

2001 Data (in constant 1995 US dollars)

Chad remains mired in conflict both inside and outside of its borders. Internally, President Idriss Deby faces pressure from a variety of groups for his reluctance to open up the democratic process. Externally, relations between Chad and the Central African Republic remain strained. Libya's recent withdrawal from the CAR could improve this relationship, but the CAR's insistence that Chad was involved in a 2002 coup against the Republic also could offset any gains. With 80 percent of the workforce employed in subsistence agriculture, herding, and fishing, the government will press ahead with its internal reforms to meet the International Monetary Fund–World Bank heavily indebted poor countries initiative. The Economist Intelligence Unit predicts that strong growth of 10.9 percent in 2002 will be followed by 15 percent growth in GDP for 2003. While cattle production had been the main foreign-exchange earner in 2001, the production of oil in July from the much-criticized Doba oil project will be the catalyst for future economic growth. It is estimated that 50,000 barrels per day will be produced during the remainder of 2003 and that production will rise to 219,000 barrels per day in 2004, substantially increasing revenue. In addition to encouraging further economic growth, this will allow President Deby to reinforce his military infrastructure and confront rebel activity in the northern and eastern regions of the country. Chad's fiscal burden of government score is 0.5 point better this year. As a result, its overall score is 0.05 point better this year.

## TRADE POLICY
### Score: **5**–Stable (very high level of protectionism)

Chad is a member of the Central African Customs and Economic Union (CEMAC), which also includes Cameroon, Central African Republic, Republic of Congo, Equatorial Guinea, and Gabon. In 2002, according to the U.S. Trade Representative, CEMAC applied an average common external tariff of 18.4 percent. Customs corruption acts as a non-tariff barrier. The U.S. Department of State reports that "corruption exists in all levels of government and in many different ministries. It may be most pervasive in the customs and tax enforcement services as well as the judiciary and the government procurement office."

## FISCAL BURDEN OF GOVERNMENT
### Score—Income Taxation: **5**–Stable (very high tax rates)
### Score—Corporate Taxation: **5**–Stable (very high tax rates)
### Score—Change in Government Expenditures: **2.5**–Better (low decrease)
### Final Score: **4.4**–Better (high cost of government)

The International Monetary Fund reports that Chad's top income tax rate is 65 percent. The top corporate tax is 45 percent. Government expenditures as a share of GDP decreased 1.5 percentage points to 18.8 percent in 2001, compared to a 2.3 percentage point increase in 2000. As a result, Chad's fiscal burden of government score is 0.5 point better this year.

## GOVERNMENT INTERVENTION IN THE ECONOMY
### Score: **3**–Stable (moderate level)

The World Bank reports that the government consumed 7.8 percent of GDP in 2001. Although the majority of state-owned enterprises have been privatized, the Economist Intelligence Unit reports that the government still owns a large share of CotonTchad, a cotton monopoly that provides seeds and inputs for farmers and has a monopoly over sales, processing, and marketing of cotton. Cotton is Chad's top export and a source of cash for 12 percent of the population.

## MONETARY POLICY
### Score: **3**–Stable (moderate level of inflation)

From 1993 to 2002, Chad's weighted average annual rate of inflation was 6.48 percent. Chad has benefited from a stable currency—a rarity in sub-Saharan Africa—as a member of the CFA franc zone. Fourteen countries use the CFA franc, a common currency with a fixed parity with the euro. (The other 13 countries are Benin, Burkina Faso, Cameroon, Central African Republic, Congo [Brazzaville], Equatorial Guinea, Gabon, Guinea–Bissau, Ivory Coast, Mali, Niger, Senegal, and Togo.)

## CAPITAL FLOWS AND FOREIGN INVESTMENT
### Score: **3**–Stable (moderate barriers)

Chad welcomes foreign investment, places no limits on foreign ownership, and provides equal treatment to foreign investors. Foreign investments in the cotton, electricity, and telecommunications sectors are restricted to protect state-owned enterprises; these sectors, however, are being privatized. The U.S. Department of State reports that "constraints [on investment] include: limited infrastructure, chronic energy shortages, high energy costs, a scarcity of skilled labor, a high tax burden and corruption." All investments must be reviewed and approved by the government. The International Monetary Fund reports that both residents and non-residents may hold foreign exchange accounts with government approval. Capital transactions, payments, and transfers to France, Monaco, members of the CEMAC, members of the West African Economic and Monetary Union, and Comoros are permitted freely. Capital transactions, payments, and transfers to other countries are subject to exchange control approval, quantitative limits, and government approval in most cases. Overall, the government's investment policy is bureaucratic but does not discriminate against foreign investment.

## BANKING AND FINANCE
### Score: **2**–Stable (low level of restrictions)

Chad's banking system is small, offers few services, and is regulated by the regional Commission de Banque de l'Afrique Centrale. According to the U.S. Department of State, "The banking sector has improved in recent years after the three largest banks…were privatized and all major banks underwent internal reforms in 1990 to improve lending practices and reduce the volume of bad debt. Credit is available from commercial banks on market terms…. Regulations and financial policies generally do not impede competition in the financial sector."

## WAGES AND PRICES
### Score: **2**–Stable (low level of intervention)

"Over the past decade," reports the U.S. Department of State, "the government…has made progress in privatizing state enterprises, eliminating price controls and liberalizing the economy." Over the past eight years, the government has privatized 16 state-owned companies and liquidated 14 companies. The sugar company has been sold, and privatization of state-owned cotton enterprises is proceeding. Chad's labor code requires the government to set minimum wages.

## PROPERTY RIGHTS
### Score: **4**–Stable (low level of protection)

Protection of private property is weak. The U.S. Department of State describes Chad's judiciary as "ineffective, underfunded, overburdened, and subject to executive interference. In practice government officials and other influential persons often enjoyed immunity from judicial sanction." In addition, "There is a widespread perception that the courts should be avoided at all costs, so most disputes are settled out of court. There have been so few commercial disputes taken to court that it is difficult to judge the effectiveness of the courts in this area."

## REGULATION
### Score: **4**–Stable (high level)

Chad's massive and corrupt government bureaucracy makes it hard to establish a business. "While government policies themselves do not hinder approval," reports the U.S. Department of State, "bureaucratic procedures are often cumbersome or slow. Clear rules exist on paper but they are not always followed…. Restrictive labor laws also discourage investment." In addition, "Corruption exists in all levels of government and in many different ministries."

## INFORMAL MARKET
### Score: **5**–Stable (very high level of activity)

According to the U.S. Department of State, "Like many other developing countries, Chad has a small formal sector and a large, thriving informal sector." In addition, "Most goods sold in Chad are from wholesale import/export houses. Examples include clothing, grains, flour, pharmaceuticals, personal care products, foodstuffs, hardware, household goods, appliances, televisions, and radios. Many of these products enter Chad through informal channels, as collusion between smugglers and customs agents is common. Unofficial imports include petroleum products, consumer goods, sugar, soap and cigarettes."

# CHILE

Rank: 13

Score: 1.91

Category: Free

CHILE

## Present & Past Scores

(Best) 1
2
3
4
(Worst) 5

2.60 2.61 2.26 2.10 2.13 2.04 2.03 1.88 2.01 1.91

'95 '96 '97 '98 '99 '00 '01 '02 '03 '04

## QUICK STUDY

### SCORES

| | |
|---|---|
| Trade Policy | 2 |
| Fiscal Burden | 2.6 |
| Government Intervention | 2 |
| Monetary Policy | 1 |
| Foreign Investment | 2 |
| Banking and Finance | 2 |
| Wages and Prices | 2 |
| Property Rights | 1 |
| Regulation | 3 |
| Informal Market | 1.5 |

**Population:** 15,100,000

**Total area:** 756,950 sq. km

**GDP:** $85.5 billion

**GDP growth rate:** 2.1%

**GDP per capita:** $5,659

**Major exports:** copper, fresh fruit, paper and printing

**Exports of goods and services:** $31.2 billion

**Major export trading partners:** US 19.0%, Japan 10.5%, UK 4.3%, Brazil 3.8%

**Major imports:** consumer goods, chemicals, motor vehicles, fuels, heavy industrial machinery

**Imports of goods and services:** $22.3 billion

**Major import trading partners:** Argentina 18.1%, US 17.0%, Brazil 8.5%, China 5.9%

**Foreign direct investment (net):** $1.02 billion

2002 Data (in constant 1995 US dollars)

**C**hile has been a model of economic reform for Latin America since the beginning of the 1980s; yet President Ricardo Lagos, who took office in March 2000, has promoted reversal of some reforms, such as labor deregulation, tax cuts, and spending restraint. These measures raised the cost of investment and cast doubt on whether Chile will remain a model of reform for the rest of Latin America. Several corruption scandals resulting in the resignation of the central bank's president have tarnished the image of the ruling Concertación party and have upset President Lagos, the opposition, and business. According to the Economist Intelligence Unit, "the government and the opposition…have together agreed to a plan to modernize state institutions and improve transparency." The macroeconomy and governability, however, remain unaffected. Two years ago, the government proposed a pro-growth agenda. The bills to advance this agenda, as described by the EIU, "seek to liberalise the country's regulatory regimes, increase transparency and efficiency in state institutions, reduce the scope for…judicial arbitrariness, and increase [labor and capital] market flexibility." The only goal to be carried out, however, is the one related to tradable fishing quotas. On February 2003, a free trade agreement with Europe came into effect. On June 6, 2003, Chile signed a free trade agreement with the United States that could be ratified before the end of the year. Chile's monetary policy score is 1 point better this year. As a result, its overall score is 0.1 point better this year, causing Chile to be classified as a "free" economy.

## TRADE POLICY
### Score: **2**–Stable (low level of protectionism)

On January 1, 2003, according to the U.S. Trade Representative, the government reduced the flat tariff rate of 7 percent on most products to 6 percent. Chile has by far the best tariff regime in its region; however, its tariffs are still high by global standards. On some agricultural goods, such as wheat, vegetable oils, and sugar, Chile applies a complex price band system that will be phased out with implementation of the Chile–U.S. free trade agreement.

## FISCAL BURDEN OF GOVERNMENT
Score—Income Taxation: **4**–Stable (high tax rates)
Score—Corporate Taxation: **1.5**–Stable (low tax rates)
Score—Change in Government Expenditures: **3.5**–Stable (low increase)
### Final Score: **2.6**–Stable (moderate cost of government)

Chile's top income tax rate is 40 percent, down from 43 percent. The top corporate income tax rate is 16.5 percent, up from 16 percent, and is slated to increase to 17 percent in 2004. Government expenditures as a share of GDP increased 0.2 percentage point to 23.7 percent in 2002, compared to a 0.6 percentage point increase in 2001. Based on its stable tax rates and relatively stable level of government expenditures as a share of GDP, Chile's fiscal burden of government score is unchanged this year.

## GOVERNMENT INTERVENTION IN THE ECONOMY
### Score: **2**–Stable (low level)

The Economist Intelligence Unit reports that the government consumed 12.6 percent of GDP in 2002. In 2001, according to the International Monetary Fund, Chile received 3.47 percent of its total revenues from state-owned enterprises and government ownership of property.

137

## MONETARY POLICY
### Score: **1**–Better (very low level of inflation)

From 1993 to 2002, Chile's weighted average annual rate of inflation was 2.94 percent, down from the 3.72 percent from 1992 to 2001 reported in the 2003 *Index*. As a result, Chile's monetary policy score is 1 point better this year.

## CAPITAL FLOWS AND FOREIGN INVESTMENT
### Score: **2**–Stable (low barriers)

Chile's investment regime is transparent and easy to navigate, and most sectors are open to foreigners without restriction. According to the Economist Intelligence Unit, "Foreign companies are allowed to conduct business in Chile on the same basis as local companies and they enjoy guaranteed access to foreign exchange for repatriation of capital and profits. There are no local-content requirements." The U.S. Department of State reports that a major exception to Chile's open foreign investment regime is the requirement that fishing vessels within Chile's Exclusive Economic Zone must have majority Chilean ownership. The government also requires that senior management of radio and television stations must be Chilean. The International Monetary Fund reports that on April 19, 2001, all controls on real estate transactions by non-residents were abolished. In the same year, the central bank eliminated all exchange restrictions on trade and capital flows.

## BANKING AND FINANCE
### Score: **2**–Stable (low level of restrictions)

According to the Economist Intelligence Unit, Chile's banking sector is "well capitalised and prudently managed, and is ranked among the most solid in the world." At the end of 2002, there were 25 banks. The state-owned Banco del Estado is also the fourth largest commercial bank. The 1997 banking law continued the gradual liberalization of the mid-1990s by allowing banks to open branches abroad and to enter the insurance and foreign investment funds businesses domestically. The EIU reports that the central bank "modified its Compendium of Financial Norms in October 2000, substantially widening the range of foreign-currency operations banks may offer by including domestic savings accounts and overdrafts, domestic credits and trading in foreign-currency instruments issued by local residents."

## WAGES AND PRICES
### Score: **2**–Stable (low level of intervention)

The market determines pricing policy to a significant extent. According to the Economist Intelligence Unit, "Price controls exist only in sectors dominated by natural monopolies, including postal services, water, electricity and telephone service…. Major agricultural products such as cooking oils, sugar and wheat are covered by a system of price bands to encourage local production." Chile maintains a minimum wage.

## PROPERTY RIGHTS
### Score: **1**–Stable (very high level of protection)

Private property is well-protected. The Economist Intelligence Unit reports that "contractual agreements in Chile are probably the most secure in Latin America, and the local public administration is generally honest."

## REGULATION
### Score: **3**–Stable (moderate level)

The U.S. Department of State reports that "approval procedures [to start a business] are expeditious, and applications are typically approved within a matter of days and almost always within one month." Government regulation, however, can be burdensome. According to the Office of the U.S. Trade Representative, "the most heavily regulated areas of the Chilean economy are utilities, the banking sector, securities markets and pension funds. Other regulations tend to be focused on labor, environment and health standards." Labor laws are somewhat rigid and, according to the Economist Intelligence Unit, provide "several statutory fringe benefits" such as mandatory vacations, leaves of absence for union leaders to conduct union work, working hours, and compensation for termination of employment. The labor laws are especially harmful to small and medium-size businesses, which tend to be labor-intensive and employ 75 percent of the population. Corruption in the bureaucracy exists, but only on a small scale.

## INFORMAL MARKET
### Score: **1.5**–Stable (low level of activity)

Transparency International's 2002 score for Chile is 7.5. Therefore, Chile's informal market score is 1.5 this year.

CHINA

# CHINA, PEOPLE'S REPUBLIC OF

Rank: 128
Score: 3.64
Category: Mostly Unfree

Present & Past Scores

(Best) 1
2
3
4
(Worst) 5

3.78 3.78 3.73 3.69 3.56 3.49 3.55 3.56 3.54 3.64

'95 '96 '97 '98 '99 '00 '01 '02 '03 '04

## QUICK STUDY

### SCORES

| | |
|---|---|
| Trade Policy | 5 |
| Fiscal Burden | 4.4 |
| Government Intervention | 3.5 |
| Monetary Policy | 1 |
| Foreign Investment | 4 |
| Banking and Finance | 4 |
| Wages and Prices | 3 |
| Property Rights | 4 |
| Regulation | 4 |
| Informal Market | 3.5 |

**Population:** 1,284,303,705

**Total area:** 9,596,960 sq. km

**GDP:** $1.2 trillion

**GDP growth rate:** 8.0%

**GDP per capita:** $925

**Major exports:** machinery and equipment; textiles and clothing, footwear, toys and sporting goods, mineral fuels

**Exports of goods and services:** $328.9 billion

**Major export trading partners:** US 21.5%, Hong Kong 18.0%, Japan 14.9%, EU 14.8%

**Major imports:** machinery and equipment, mineral fuels, plastics, iron and steel, chemicals

**Imports of goods and services:** $292.6 billion

**Major import trading partners:** Japan 18.1%, EU 13.1%, Taiwan 12.9%, US 9.2%

**Foreign direct investment (net):** $47.3 billion

2002 Data (in constant 1995 US dollars)

China's highly publicized "political transition" during the November 2002 16th Party Congress and the March 2003 Tenth National People's Congress left retiring President Jiang Zemin with control of military and foreign affairs, leaving issues of economics and domestic stability to new President Hu Jintao and new Premier Wen Jiabao. With their political futures threatened by frequent crises in the labor, agriculture, and heavy industries sectors, among others, China's new leaders seem inclined to slow down or even halt massive economic reforms undertaken previously. President Hu and Premier Wen have already ordered the government to bail out state-owned banks burdened with cumbersome nonperforming loans. Beijing has abandoned its privatization program, levied new rules to hamper foreign investment in the retail sector, added new restrictions on the importation of farm goods, and replaced tariffs with tax rebates to protect the semiconductor industry. The Communist Party has neglected ballooning social welfare programs rather than improve efficiency by opening the system to free-market reforms. In short, China's leaders continue to seek short-term fixes for major economic dislocations by returning to heavily centralized, and often protectionist, macroeconomic policies. Meanwhile, independent financial organizations have cast serious doubts on the veracity of China's economic statistics. The Hong Kong Shanghai Banking Corporation has noted that "data for growth in fixed asset investment and industrial production may have been exaggerated by 50 percent and 20 percent respectively." Morgan Stanley has calculated China's total actual government debt at 160 percent of GDP, and the debt burden of China's banking system ranges from $450 billion to $500 billion. Beijing is also believed to have understated the economic impact of the severe acute respiratory syndrome (SARS) epidemic, lowering growth projections from 9 percent to 7.5 percent despite a standstill in foreign orders for new products and countrywide sales disruptions due to quarantines. China's government intervention score is 1 point worse this year. As a result, its overall score is 0.1 point worse this year.

 ## TRADE POLICY
### Score: **5**–Stable (very high level of protectionism)

According to the World Bank, China's weighted average tariff rate in 2001 (the most recent year for which World Bank data are available) was 14.3 percent. The Economist Intelligence Unit reports that the government sets quotas for general commodities, machinery, and electronic products. The government also controls trade flows with import and export licenses. In June 2003, for example, according to the *Financial Times*, it decided to delay the issuance of licenses to import soyabeans, in order to support local soyabean farmers. The EIU reports that, in addition to quotas and licenses, "China retains regulatory control over imports via commodity inspection, registration requirements and quarantine rules."

 ## FISCAL BURDEN OF GOVERNMENT
### Score—Income Taxation: **4.5**–Stable (very high tax rates)
### Score—Corporate Taxation: **4.5**–Stable (very high tax rates)
### Score—Change in Government Expenditures: **4**–Stable (moderate increase)
### Final Score: **4.4**–Stable (high cost of government)

China's top income tax rate is 45 percent. The top corporate tax rate is 33 percent. Government expenditures as a share of GDP increased about the same in 2001 (1.9 percentage points to 20 percent) as in 2000 (1.8 percentage points). Based on its stable tax rates and relatively stable level of government expenditures as a share of GDP, China's fiscal burden of government score is unchanged this year.

## GOVERNMENT INTERVENTION IN THE ECONOMY
### Score: 3.5–Worse (high level)

The World Bank reports that the government consumed 13.7 percent of GDP in 2001. In the same year, according to the Economist Intelligence Unit, China reported receiving 6.62 percent of its total revenues from state-owned enterprises and government ownership of property, up from the 4.52 percent reported in the 2003 *Index*. According to the American Enterprise Institute, however, "China's system…[has] a large state sector, party committees even in private enterprises, [and] corporate boards that are unable to fire managers…." In addition, reports the *Financial Times*, "China's 150,000 state-owned enterprises…still employ more than 50m workers." The Chinese government actively intervenes in the stock market. Based on the apparent unreliability of reported total revenue figures, 1 point has been added to China's government intervention score. Based on the increase in the level of revenues from state-owned enterprises, China's government intervention score is 1 point worse this year.

## MONETARY POLICY
### Score: 1–Stable (very low level of inflation)

From 1993 to 2002, China's weighted average annual rate of inflation was –0.32 percent. However, the government influences prices through direct price controls and through subsidies administered by state-owned enterprises; therefore, it is likely that official inflation figures underestimate the true rate.

## CAPITAL FLOWS AND FOREIGN INVESTMENT
### Score: 4–Stable (high barriers)

Although China was the largest recipient of foreign direct investment in 2002 (due more to lower foreign investment to the United States than to higher investment to China), substantial barriers continue to impede foreign investment. China's foreign investment policy is designed to prevent foreign companies from competing with some state-owned industries while directing them toward desired sectors, such as new or high-technology sectors and investment to develop Central and Western China. According to the U.S. Trade Representative, "Barriers to investment include opaque and inconsistently enforced laws and regulations and a lack of a rules-based legal infrastructure." New foreign investment regulations that took effect on April 1, 2002, require that various Chinese bureaucracies must regularly update a Foreign Investment Catalogue for the government to use as a guide for approving foreign investment projects. "Among other things," reports the U.S. Department of State, "the new catalogue aims to implement sectoral openings that China committed to in its WTO accession agreement, including banking,

insurance, petroleum extraction, and distribution." The government regulates the flow of foreign exchange in and out of the country. According to the U.S. Department of State, "To better control this flow, almost all Chinese enterprises and agencies are required to turn over their foreign currency earnings to the banks in exchange for renminbi…." The International Monetary Fund reports that the government imposes restrictions, prohibitions, and requirements for government approval on nearly all transactions involving capital and money market instruments, derivatives, credit operations, real estate, and direct investment.

## BANKING AND FINANCE
### Score: 4–Stable (high level of restrictions)

The U.S. Department of State reports that "China's banking system has undergone significant changes in the last two decades: banks are now functioning more like banks than before. Nevertheless, China's banking industry has remained in the government's hands even though banks have gained more autonomy. China's accession to WTO will lead to a significant opening of this industry to foreign competition." The level of China's adherence to WTO rules and the impact of membership on the financial sector have yet to be determined. The government remains firmly in control of the banking sector and directs lending to state-favored projects, businesses, and individuals. According to *The Economist*, "The four big state-owned banks that dominate the system direct four-fifths of their lending to state-owned enterprises which destroy value more often than they create it. The vibrant private and export sectors—which have created perhaps 40m new jobs in the past five years…are left largely to fend for themselves. They rely on retained earnings and foreign direct investment, or else on informal sources of credit." Although the government is relaxing controls on interest rates, the central bank affects the allocation of credit by setting interest rates on deposits and loans.

## WAGES AND PRICES
### Score: 3–Stable (moderate level of intervention)

According to the Economist Intelligence Unit, "The State Development Planning commission imposes price controls on only 13 categories of products, compared with 141 categories a decade ago; as a result, prices of more than 90% of products traded in China are now determined by market forces. In general, prices remain controlled only for goods and services deemed essential, such as foodstuffs and tobacco. Price maintenance is rarely an issue for commodities (except for perhaps silk) since most food, transport, and energy prices are kept far below their free-market levels." The government also influences prices through subsidies to its extensive state-owned enterprises. A Price Law passed in 1998 makes it illegal for individual companies to engage in price collusion and price slashing to eliminate competition. China does not have a national mandatory minimum wage, but the Labor Law allows local governments to determine their own minimum wage.

## PROPERTY RIGHTS
### Score: **4**–Stable (low level of protection)

China's judicial system is weak. The Economist Intelligence Unit reports that "many [foreign firms] prefer arbitration because of concerns about the speed and impartiality of the courts. A related concern for foreign companies is the weak tradition of consistent implementation of court rulings...." In addition, "The spread of corruption in post-reform China has also affected the courts.... [T]he security of contracts remains problematic.... [F]oreign investors often complain of the maze of regulatory difficulties they encounter in pressing their local partners to adhere to previously agreed understandings." According to the U.S. Department of State, "in practice, the judiciary receives policy guidance from both the Government and the Communist Party, whose leaders use a variety of means to direct courts on verdicts and sentences in sensitive cases.... Corruption and conflicts of interest also affect judicial decision making.... Police and prosecutorial officials often ignore the due process provisions of the law and of the Constitution."

## REGULATION
### Score: **4**–Stable (high level)

China's regulatory regime is not transparent, and enforcement of existing laws is not consistent, although some improvements may be seen in the future now that China has become a member of the World Trade Organization. The U.S. Department of State reports that "China's legal and regulatory system lacks transparency and consistent enforcement despite the promulgation of thousands of regulations, opinions, and notices affecting...investment. Although the Chinese government has simplified the legal and regulatory environment for...investors in recent years, China's laws and regulations are still often ambiguous." Corruption is widespread. According to the Economist Intelligence Unit, "Foreign companies investing in China tend to encounter rather different forms of organized dishonesty.... [M]unicipal officials have often given their approval to foreign-invested projects after their children have been granted places in schools abroad...."

## INFORMAL MARKET
### Score: **3.5**–Stable (high level of activity)

Transparency International's 2002 score for China is 3.5. Therefore, China's informal market score is 3.5 this year.

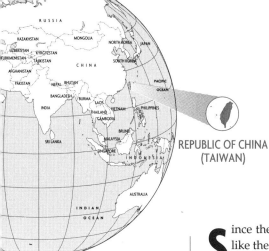

# CHINA, REPUBLIC OF (TAIWAN)

Rank: 34

Score: 2.43

Category: Mostly Free

Present & Past Scores

(Best) 1 2 3 4 (Worst) 5

2.26 2.23 2.21 2.24 2.09 1.98 2.18 2.38 2.29 2.43

'95 '96 '97 '98 '99 '00 '01 '02 '03 '04

## QUICK STUDY

### SCORES

| | |
|---|---|
| Trade Policy | 2 |
| Fiscal Burden | 3.3 |
| Government Intervention | 2.5 |
| Monetary Policy | 1 |
| Foreign Investment | 3 |
| Banking and Finance | 3 |
| Wages and Prices | 2 |
| Property Rights | 2 |
| Regulation | 3 |
| Informal Market | 2.5 |

**Population:** 22,521,000

**Total area:** 35,980 sq. km

**GDP:** $291.9 billion

**GDP growth rate:** 3.5%

**GDP per capita:** $12,960

**Major exports:** electrical equipment and machinery, textiles, metals, plastics, chemicals

**Exports of goods and services:** $155.3 billion

**Major export trading partners:** Hong Kong 23.6%, US 20.5%, Japan 9.2%, China 7.6%

**Major imports:** machinery and electrical equipment, precision instruments, minerals

**Imports of goods and services:** $129.9 billion

**Major import trading partners:** Japan 24.2%, US 16.1%, China 7.1%, South Korea 6.8%

**Foreign direct investment (net):** −$3.1billion

2002 Data (in constant 1995 US dollars)

Since the late 1960s, Taiwan has been one of the world's fastest-growing economies, but like the other "Asian Tigers," it has experienced slower GDP growth as the economy has matured. A weak financial sector, the 2000–2001 global economic downturn, and rivalry between President Chen Shui-bian's party and the Kuomintang (KMT), which dominated the legislature, contributed to negative growth in 2001; however, the legislative elections of December 2001 gave renewed consensus to economic reforms, and by mid-2003, financial reforms were succeeding. Relaxed rules on foreign investment in the transportation, power supply, financial, and telecommunications sectors attracted capital, and the banking system also strengthened. During 2002 and 2003, the Chen Shui-bian administration eliminated state monopolies in petroleum, tobacco, and alcoholic beverages. Privatization of the state corporations slowed as a result of legal challenges from labor and a sagging stock market, but these reforms still helped push GDP growth in 2002 to 3.5 percent. The Chen Shui-bian administration has indicted legislators, city and county officials, and former and current bank officials, and these anti-corruption efforts have improved the business environment. The government has responded to calls from foreign businesses for tough anti-piracy laws. It also continues to ease restrictions on Taiwan businesses that trade and invest in China. Taiwan direct investment in China in the first four months of 2003 was 74 percent above the same period in 2002. Taiwan's fiscal burden of government score is 0.1 point better this year; however, its government intervention score is 0.5 point worse, and its banking and finance score is 1 point worse. As a result, Taiwan's overall score is 0.14 point worse this year.

### TRADE POLICY

Score: **2**–Stable (low level of protectionism)

The World Bank reports that Taiwan's weighted average tariff rate in 2001 (the most recent year for which World Bank data are available) was 3.5 percent. According to the Economist Intelligence Unit, of the "159 items subject to import bans...91 were made restricted based on tariff-based conversion...rates and tariff-rate quotas...." Labeling laws require Chinese labeling in most imported products.

### FISCAL BURDEN OF GOVERNMENT

Score—Income Taxation: **4**–Stable (high tax rates)

Score—Corporate Taxation: **3**–Stable (moderate tax rates)

Score—Change in Government Expenditures: **3**–Better (very low decrease)

Final Score: **3.3**–Better (moderate cost of government)

Taiwan's top income tax rate is 40 percent. The top corporate tax rate is 25 percent. Government expenditures as a share of GDP decreased 0.8 percentage point to 24.2 percent in 2002, compared to a 0.7 percentage point increase in 2001. As a result, Taiwan's fiscal burden of government score is 0.1 point better this year.

### GOVERNMENT INTERVENTION IN THE ECONOMY

Score: **2.5**–Worse (moderate level)

Based on data from the Economist Intelligence Unit, the government consumed 12.6 percent of GDP in 2002. In the same year, based on data from Taiwan's Ministry of Finance, Taiwan received 7.56 percent of its total revenues from state-owned enterprises and government ownership of property, up from the 4.91 percent reported in the 2003 *Index*. As a result, Taiwan's government intervention score is 0.5 point worse this year.

## MONETARY POLICY
### Score: **1**–Stable (very low level of inflation)

From 1993 to 2002, Taiwan's weighted average annual rate of inflation was 0.02 percent.

## CAPITAL FLOWS AND FOREIGN INVESTMENT
### Score: **3**–Stable (moderate barriers)

Taiwan continues to relax investment restrictions but maintains some formal barriers to foreign investment. The government's Negative List for Investment by Overseas Chinese and Foreign Nationals forbids foreign investment in 28 categories of domestic business and restricts foreign investment in 46 other categories. Outside of the sectors included on the Negative List, foreign investors are accorded national treatment. In February 2003, Taiwan removed the restrictions on foreign investment in liquor production, but approval is still required. Foreigners are limited to 60 percent ownership of telecommunications, including a 49 percent limit on foreign direct investment, and foreign ownership of airlines is limited to 33 percent. The Securities and Exchange Commission raised the portfolio investment limit to $3 billion for qualified foreign institutional investors (QFII) and relaxed qualifications for QFIIs in May 2001 to make all portfolio investors eligible to trade securities in Taiwan. In November 2001, the government lifted its 50-year ban on direct trade and investment in China, but it also established limitations on such investment in certain cases. According to the U.S. Department of State, "There are relatively few restrictions [on] converting or transferring funds associated with direct investment…. For purposes other than trade, no prior approval is required if the cumulative amount of inward or outward remittances is less than U.S. $5 million for a person or U.S. $40 million for a corporation."

## BANKING AND FINANCE
### Score: **3**–Worse (moderate level of restrictions)

The U.S. Department of State reports that there were 47 domestic commercial banks and 36 foreign banks in 2002, but the Economist Intelligence Unit reports that foreign banks accounted for only 5.79 percent of total bank assets. The government is privatizing its state-owned banks but continues to maintain a substantial presence. According to the Economist Intelligence Unit, "although some banks have been privatised, the state has remained an important player in the financial sector. In 2002 the government still held stakes in 17 banks, and since the 1990s officials have frequently pressured state-linked banks to continue lending to companies suffering from short-term financial difficulties but with otherwise 'normal' operations. A further weakness with the financial system has been the division of responsibility for regulation

and supervision between three separate bodies…." The EIU reports that the government accounted for a market share of almost 60 percent of banking assets in 2001. The sector continues to be hindered by non-performing loans, estimated at 15.4 percent of bank loans in 2002. According to a February 8, 2003, *Economist* article, "Instead of letting the many weaker commercial banks fail, the government expensively props them up. So the banks lose even more money as they write off bad loans, without much prospect that this will reduce their bad-loan ratio." Based on evidence that the government plays a large role in the banking sector, inadequately supervises the sector, and props up weak banks, Taiwan's banking and finance score is 1 point worse this year.

## WAGES AND PRICES
### Score: **2**–Stable (low level of intervention)

Most wages and prices are set by the market. According to the Economist Intelligence Unit, "Domestic price controls apply primarily to public utilities or to implement specific government policies." The few price controls in effect apply to electricity, salt, telecommunications, postage, and oil. The government mandates a minimum wage.

## PROPERTY RIGHTS
### Score: **2**–Stable (high level of protection)

The judiciary may be subject to corruption and political influence, although these problems do not represent a serious impediment to business activity. "The judiciary's biggest problems," reports the Economist Intelligence Unit, "are corruption associated with 'black gold' (that is, organized crime), slow decision making and lack of training to handle complex commercial or technological cases."

## REGULATION
### Score: **3**–Stable (moderate level)

Taiwan's business regulations can be burdensome. Comprehensive laws and regulations govern taxes, labor, health, and safety. Many investors complain of unrealistic wording in regulations and inconsistent enforcement. According to the U.S. Department of State, "Although corruption has been a source of complaints by…businesspeople with operations in Taiwan, its impact on foreign direct investment decisions has been relatively less serious than in [other] areas…." In addition, "corruption has been reported as most pervasive in the area of government procurement, particularly in local-level construction tenders. The authorities generally investigate allegations of corruption and take action to penalize corrupt officials."

## INFORMAL MARKET
### Score: **2.5**–Stable (moderate level of activity)

Transparency International's 2002 score for Taiwan is 5.6. Therefore, Taiwan's informal market score is 2.5 this year.

# COLOMBIA

COLOMBIA

Rank: 83

Score: 3.13

Category: Mostly Unfree

**Present & Past Scores**

(Best) 1
2
3
4
(Worst) 5

3.10  3.15  3.23  3.19  2.99  3.14  3.00  2.94  3.10  3.13

'95  '96  '97  '98  '99  '00  '01  '02  '03  '04

## QUICK STUDY

### SCORES

| | |
|---|---|
| Trade Policy | 4 |
| Fiscal Burden | 4.3 |
| Government Intervention | 3.5 |
| Monetary Policy | 3 |
| Foreign Investment | 2 |
| Banking and Finance | 2 |
| Wages and Prices | 2 |
| Property Rights | 4 |
| Regulation | 3 |
| Informal Market | 3.5 |

**Population:** 43,035,168

**Total area:** 1,138,910 sq. km

**GDP:** $98 billion

**GDP growth rate:** 1.4%

**GDP per capita:** $2,277

**Major exports:** oil, coal, coffee

**Exports of goods and services:** $18.8 billion

**Major export trading partners:** US 44.9%, Venezuela 10.5%, Ecuador 3.7%, Germany 3.6%

**Major imports:** consumer goods, transportation equipment, chemicals

**Imports of goods and services:** $18.4 billion

**Major import trading partners:** US 30.9%, Venezuela 8.0%, Japan 5.3%, Brazil 4.8%

**Foreign direct investment (net):** $2.1 billion

2001 Data (in constant 1995 US dollars)

U nder President Alvaro Uribe, Colombia has begun to deal with needed reforms, drug trafficking, and the country's three terrorist armies. In addition to assessing a one-time tax on assets of middle- and upper-class Colombians to raise $780 million to help train two new elite army battalions and establish a network of paid civilian informants, Uribe initiated plans to double Colombia's army combat and police forces from 100,000 to 200,000 troops to extend a security presence to the countryside. In one year, eradication of coca and opium poppy is roughly double that achieved in the same amount of time by previous President Andrés Pastrana. Judicial reforms have separated judge and prosecutor functions and provide for more transparent oral trials. But other reforms are still needed. Inadequate road infrastructure hinders mobility of government security forces and subjects commercial traffic to roadblocks and guerrilla ambushes on main arteries. Less than 10 percent of the population contributes to Colombia's convoluted and poorly enforced tax system. And outside of major cities, some 1,000 municipalities throughout the country lack any official government presence. In this climate, rebel and paramilitary forces still pursue each other and innocent bystanders with impunity. Violence financed by drug trafficking contributes to a loss of about $24 billion from Colombia's $100 billion annual GDP. Nonetheless, the unemployment rate has declined slightly over the past year from 20 percent to 19 percent, and foreign investment is beginning to return because of the government's willingness to crack down on criminal elements. Colombia's fiscal burden of government score is 0.3 point worse this year. As a result, its overall score is 0.03 point worse this year.

## TRADE POLICY
### Score: **4–Stable** (high level of protectionism)

According to the World Bank, Colombia's weighted average tariff rate in 2001 (the most recent year for which World Bank data are available) was 11 percent. The U.S. Trade Representative reports that "thirteen basic agricultural commodities…and an additional 146 commodities considered substitute or related products are subject to tariffs calculated under the price band system. [This] system lacks transparency and can be manipulated to provide arbitrary levels of import protection, often resulting in artificially high, prohibitive tariff rates." The government controls imports of certain agricultural products, such as chicken and turkey, through licensing requirements. Customs procedures can be complex and burdensome.

## FISCAL BURDEN OF GOVERNMENT
### Score—Income Taxation: **3.5–Stable** (high tax rates)
### Score—Corporate Taxation: **5–Worse** (very high tax rates)
### Score—Change in Government Expenditures: **3.5–Stable** (low increase)
### Final Score: **4.3–Worse** (high cost of government)

Colombia's top income tax rate is 38.5 percent, up from 35 percent. The top corporate tax rate is 38.5 percent, up from 35 percent. However, government expenditures as a share of GDP increased less in 2001 (0.1 percentage point to 20.4 percent) in 2001 than they did in 2000 (1 percentage point). On net, Colombia's fiscal burden of government score is 0.3 point worse this year.

145

## GOVERNMENT INTERVENTION IN THE ECONOMY
### Score: **3.5**–Stable (high level)

The Economist Intelligence Unit estimates that the government consumed 20.8 percent of GDP in 2002. In the same year, based on data from the International Monetary Fund, Colombia received 19.8 percent of its total revenues from state-owned enterprises and government ownership of property.

## MONETARY POLICY
### Score: **3**–Stable (moderate level of inflation)

From 1993 to 2002, Colombia's weighted average annual rate of inflation was 7.34 percent.

## CAPITAL FLOWS AND FOREIGN INVESTMENT
### Score: **2**–Stable (low barriers)

Colombia permits 100 percent foreign ownership in all sectors of its economy, with the exception of defense and waste disposal. Investments are subject to a simple registration and licensing process, and the law mandates equal treatment for foreign and domestic investors. The International Monetary Fund reports that residents who work in certain international-related companies may hold foreign exchange accounts. Non-residents may hold foreign exchange accounts subject to reporting requirements. Other than registration requirements and temporary restrictions, there are no controls on payments and transfers. Non-residents may purchase real estate. Some capital transactions are subject to registration and reporting requirements. Although foreign ownership up to 100 percent is permitted, the Banking Superintendent must approve foreign investment above 10 percent in any Colombian financial entity. Foreign exploration and development of petroleum resources must be carried out under an association contract with Ecopetrol, the state oil company. According to the Economist Intelligence Unit, "Government policies towards foreign investors continue to be highly favourable. However, frequent changes in tax and other legislation are often cited by potential investors as an important deterrent."

## BANKING AND FINANCE
### Score: **2**–Stable (low level of restrictions)

Foreign banks have complete access to credit and the entire financial system, and the private sector directs almost all credit. Domestic banks may sell securities, insurance policies, and investment services, and domestic and foreign banks are treated as equals. The Economist Intelligence Unit reports that there are 27 commercial banks (five of which are mortgage banks); six financial corporations; and 30 commercial financing companies. During the 1998–1999 recession, the government took over several banks and advised others to close. It has since liquidated or privatized most of

these banks. According to the EIU, "The role of the public banking subsector has been limited to selected activities such as agriculture and to a lesser degree small and medium-sized manufacturing firms." Colombia allows foreign firms to own 100 percent of insurance firm subsidiaries but does not allow foreign insurance companies to establish local branch offices.

## WAGES AND PRICES
### Score: **2**–Stable (low level of intervention)

"The government allows market forces to determine price levels for most goods and services," reports the Economist Intelligence Unit. "Price controls apply to only a few pharmaceutical products, petroleum derivatives, natural gas, some petrochemicals, school books, school tuition, residential rents, public utility services, and ground-and-air transportation fares.... [T]he agricultural ministry may also intervene temporarily to freeze the prices of basic foodstuffs through agreements with regional wholesalers." The government sets a uniform minimum wage every January that serves as a benchmark for collective bargaining in tripartite negotiations among representatives of government, employers, and organized labor.

## PROPERTY RIGHTS
### Score: **4**–Stable (low level of protection)

Protection of property is weak in Colombia. According to the Economist Intelligence Unit, "Although the Supreme Court is held in high regard, the lower levels of the Judiciary and civil service are susceptible to corruption and intimidation." Law enforcement in commercial cases is weak and slow. The U.S. Department of State reports that "the high number of civilian kidnappings, terrorism and corruption [generates] a negative general security situation [that] distorts everyday life and...seriously undermines business and investor confidence."

## REGULATION
### Score: **3**–Stable (moderate level)

According to the U.S. Department of State, "the Colombian government bureaucracy still constitutes a barrier...for both local and foreign companies." Labor laws are somewhat rigid. Statutory fringe benefits include vacation days, end-of-the-year bonuses, paid holidays, social security, and health insurance. Corruption in the bureaucracy remains a problem, reports the U.S. Department of State, despite the anti-corruption efforts of different administrations.

## INFORMAL MARKET
### Score: **3.5**–Stable (high level of activity)

Transparency International's 2002 score for Colombia is 3.6. Therefore, Colombia's informal market score is 3.5 this year.

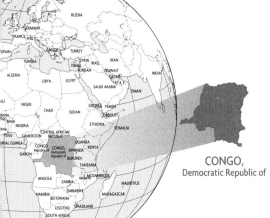

CONGO,
Democratic Republic of

# CONGO, DEMOCRATIC REPUBLIC OF (FORMERLY ZAIRE)

Rank: Suspended

Score: n/a

Category: n/a

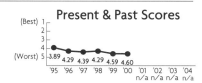

Present & Past Scores

(Best) 1
2
3
4
(Worst) 5

3.89  4.29  4.39  4.29  4.59  4.60

'95 '96 '97 '98 '99 '00 '01 '02 '03 '04
n/a n/a n/a n/a

**V**iolence, both past and present, has seriously damaged the Democratic Republic of Congo. Estimates of the number killed in the war are as high as 2.5 million. President Joseph Kabila, the son of assassinated President Laurent Kabila, maintains his control of the government despite a rocky transition characterized by political posturing and frequent public disputes. In spite of continued domestic friction, however, a positive future is possible. With one of the world's largest populations and an abundance of economic resources, the Democratic Republic of Congo still has the potential for significant economic growth and development. Inflation, a serious problem for many years, has fallen dramatically from 358 percent in 2001 to 16 percent–17 percent in 2002. Diamonds, the country's principal export, account for $400 million, significantly greater than the second greatest export: crude oil, which accounts for $141 million. The Economist Intelligence Unit forecasts a 5.5 percent gain in real GDP in 2003 followed by 6.5 percent in 2004. Though the Republic of Congo remains highly dependent on its agriculture sector, which accounted for nearly 55 percent of GDP in 2000, the government has shown a willingness to deal with past problems and seek a constructive economic plan for the future.

## QUICK STUDY

### SCORES

| | |
|---|---|
| Trade Policy | n/a |
| Fiscal Burden | n/a |
| Government Intervention | n/a |
| Monetary Policy | n/a |
| Foreign Investment | n/a |
| Banking and Finance | n/a |
| Wages and Prices | n/a |
| Property Rights | n/a |
| Regulation | n/a |
| Informal Market | n/a |

**Population:** 52,354,100

**Total area:** 2,345,410 sq. km

**GDP:** $4.45 billion

**GDP growth rate:** −4.5%

**GDP per capita:** $85

**Major exports:** diamond, crude oil, copper

**Exports of goods and services:** $2.6 billion

**Major export trading partners:** Belgium 59.7%, US 12.9%, Zimbabwe 7.4%, France 6.9%

**Major imports:** fuels, machinery and mining equipment, foodstuffs

**Imports of goods and services:** $3.3 billion

**Major import trading partners:** South Africa 18.2%, Belgium 16.4%, Nigeria 11.8%, France 5.9%

**Foreign direct investment (net):** n/a

2001 Data (in constant 1995 US dollars)

## TRADE POLICY
### Score: Not graded

According to the U.S. Department of State, "Congo adopted the harmonized system of tariff classification in 1988. The majority of the tariffs are ad valorem and are calculated on a CIF [cost, insurance, and freight] basis. Congo's tariff rates (droit d'entrée) as set by decrees in January 1997 are: 5% heavy equipment, industrial raw materials, agricultural and veterinary inputs and kits for assembly (ckd)[;] 15% light equipment, spare parts, items of social use, mkd assembly kits[;] 20% products competing with local goods in short supply[;] 30% products competing with local goods in adequate supply, luxury goods." There is no new information about trade tariffs. The U.S. Department of State also reports that "most of the country's trade barriers result from complex regulations, a multiplicity of administrative agencies, and a frequent lack of professionalism and control by officials responsible for their enforcement."

## FISCAL BURDEN OF GOVERNMENT
### Score—Income Taxation: Not graded
### Score—Corporate Taxation: Not graded
### Score—Change in Government Expenditures: Not graded
### Final Score: Not graded

According to the International Monetary Fund, the Democratic Republic of Congo's official top income tax rate is 60 percent. The top corporate tax rate is 40 percent. Government expenditures as a share of GDP decreased 1.1 percentage points to 8.7 percent in 2001, compared to a 0.7 percentage point increase in 2000.

## GOVERNMENT INTERVENTION IN THE ECONOMY
### Score: Not graded

The Economist Intelligence Unit reports that in 2001 (the most recent year for which data are available), the government consumed 1.4 percent of GDP. The government dominates the economy. According to the U.S. Department of State, "Much of the government's revenue is kept 'off-book,' and not included in published statistics on revenue and expenditure. Further, published budget figures do not include credit purchases by the government, which were extensive and out of control."

## MONETARY POLICY
### Score: Not graded

From 1993 to 2002, the Democratic Republic of Congo's weighted average inflation rate was 164.02 percent.

## CAPITAL FLOWS AND FOREIGN INVESTMENT
### Score: Not graded

According to the U.S. Department of State, "The current investment climate in the Democratic Republic of Congo is dismal. The economy has been in decline since a policy of rampant nationalization was instituted in the mid-1970's, and the two wars fought in the country during the last four years have caused a sharp drop in economic activity…. Pervasive corruption, the lack of a functioning legal mechanism for conversion and repatriation of funds, macroeconomic mismanagement…are among the burdens companies operate under in the DRC." The Economist Intelligence Unit adds that foreign direct investment has been minimal over the past five years but that the government is working on new investment codes to attract foreign investment in the mining and forestry sectors. The International Monetary Fund reports that there are no restrictions on foreign exchange accounts for the credit or debit of international transactions for either residents or non-residents.

## BANKING AND FINANCE
### Score: Not graded

The banking system has collapsed in most of the country, and the banks that remain are hampered by an unpredictable monetary policy and unrecoverable loans. "In such risky conditions," reports the Economist Intelligence Unit, "loan credit has entirely ceased except for short-term trade finance. Consequently, most businesses finance their operations from their own revenue or from the informal financial sector." In 2001, the Democratic Republic of Congo liberalized foreign currency transactions. The government maintains a 40 percent share in Societe financiere de developpement, which lends primarily to the manufacturing and agricultural sectors.

## WAGES AND PRICES
### Score: Not graded

According to the U.S. Department of State, "After a surge in inflation during 1999 the government began enforcing price control laws, creating a Commission on Economic Crimes…. Prices are nominally under the control of the Ministry of Economy and an interministerial consultative price commission. But enforcement is inconsistent." The Economist Intelligence Unit reports that the government liberalized fuel prices. Although most citizens are engaged in subsistence agriculture or otherwise outside of the formal economy, the government has a minimum wage policy.

## PROPERTY RIGHTS
### Score: Not graded

Private property is not secure, both because of corruption and because of government expropriation. According to the U.S. Department of State, "The law provides for an independent judiciary; however, in practice the judiciary was not independent of the executive branch…." In addition, "courts are marked by a high degree of corruption, public administration is not yet reliable, and both expatriates and nationals are subject to selective application of a complex legal code." Property rights are severely threatened in some war-torn regions. The government, according to BBC News, has no control over large parts of the country.

## REGULATION
### Score: Not graded

The regulatory environment significantly undermines economic activity. The U.S. Department of State reports that "Congo has never been able to provide a well-defined, stable, and transparent legal or regulatory framework for the orderly conduct of business and protection of investment. The country's laws and regulations have never been codified…. Combined with the micro-interventionism of the overmanned and underpaid Congolese administration, this has long been a major impediment to both foreign and domestic investment…. Existing tax, labor, and safety regulations are not onerous in themselves, but impose major burdens because they can be capriciously applied and there are no rapid and impartial adjudication mechanisms for relief."

## INFORMAL MARKET
### Score: Not graded

According to the U.S. Department of State, "The institutionalized corruption of the Mobutu regime evolved a dual economy. Individuals and businesses in the 'formal' sector—both private and state-owned—operated with high costs under extensive and unpredictably enforced laws, kept double books, and frequently colluded with corrupt officials to secure commercial advantage or simply to remain in business. In the 'second' ('informal' or 'parallel') economy, operators sought to evade taxes and regulation altogether."

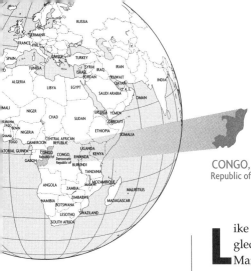

# CONGO, REPUBLIC OF

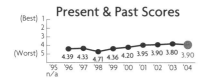

CONGO,
Republic of

Rank: 139

Score: 3.90

Category: Mostly Unfree

**Present & Past Scores**

(Best) 1
2
3
4
(Worst) 5

'95  '96  '97  '98  '99  '00  '01  '02  '03  '04
n/a

4.39  4.33  4.71  4.36  4.20  3.95  3.90  3.80  3.90

Like the neighboring Democratic Republic of Congo, the Republic of Congo has struggled with persistent violence. After a round of secret negotiations that concluded in March, both government and rebels appear to be committed to bringing peace to the Pool region, an area southwest of Brazzaville in which fighting between the two groups has gone on for some time. The step toward peace comes at an opportune time as nearly 150,000 people have been internally displaced and 65,000 have been without aid since the army limited access to the Pool region. Congo's failure to meet the macroeconomic performance indicators set out by the International Monetary Fund and the World Bank has damaged its ability to secure a formal lending agreement by June of 2003. At the same time, President Denis Sassou-Nguesso has promised to promote recovery in the nation's health care, education, and agriculture. According to the Economist Intelligence Unit, Congo faces a 1 percent economic contraction in 2003 followed by a 0.5 percent contraction in 2004. Structural reforms and a visible commitment to change may improve these projections at some point, but given the loss of economic output as a result of the war, problems are expected in the short term. Congo's fiscal burden of government score is 1 point worse this year. As a result, its overall score is 0.1 point worse this year.

## TRADE POLICY
### Score: **5**–Stable (very high level of protectionism)

Congo is a member of the Central African Economic and Monetary Community(CEMAC), which also includes Cameroon, the Central African Republic, Chad, Equatorial Guinea, and Gabon. In 2002, according to the U.S. Trade Representative, CEMAC applied a common external tariff of 18.4 percent. The most significant non-tariff barriers include import licenses, red tape, an inefficient customs service, and theft of imported goods by government officials.

## FISCAL BURDEN OF GOVERNMENT
Score—Income Taxation: **5**–Stable (very high tax rates)
Score—Corporate Taxation: **5**–Stable (very high tax rates)
Score—Change in Government Expenditures: **5**–Worse (very high increase)
### Final Score: **5**–Worse (very high cost of government)

Congo's top income tax rate is 50 percent. The top corporate tax rate is 39 percent, down from the 40 percent reported in the 2003 *Index*. According to the African Development Bank, government expenditures as a share of GDP increased 6.5 percentage points to 32 percent in 2001, compared to a 7.3 percentage point decrease the previous year. As a result, Congo's fiscal burden of government score is 1 point worse this year.

## GOVERNMENT INTERVENTION IN THE ECONOMY
### Score: **4**–Stable (high level)

The World Bank reports that the government consumed 10.7 percent of GDP in 2001. In the same year, according to the International Monetary Fund, Congo received 66.21 percent of its total revenues from state-owned enterprises and government ownership of property.

149

## MONETARY POLICY
Score: **1**–Stable (very low level of inflation)

From 1993 to 2002, Congo's weighted average annual rate of inflation was 2.51 percent. Congo has benefited from a stable currency—a rarity in sub-Saharan Africa—as a member of the CFA franc zone. Fourteen countries use the CFA franc, a common currency with a fixed parity with the euro. (Other members are Benin, Burkina Faso, Cameroon, Central African Republic, Chad, Equatorial Guinea, Gabon, Guinea–Bissau, Ivory Coast, Mali, Niger, Senegal, and Togo.)

 ## CAPITAL FLOWS AND FOREIGN INVESTMENT
Score: **4**–Stable (high barriers)

Ongoing conflict between the government and militia groups has undermined the foreign investment environment. Foreign investment is virtually nonexistent beyond the oil sector and forestry, although privatization has attracted some interest. According to the International Monetary Fund "Investments of over CFAF 100 million…require the approval of the [Ministry of Economy, Finance, and Budget] within 30 days, unless they involve the creation of a mixed public/private-ownership enterprise." The IMF also reports that residents are permitted to hold foreign exchange accounts. Most non-residents are not permitted to hold foreign exchange accounts. Payments and transfers to countries other than France, Monaco, members of the CEMAC, members of the West African Economic and Monetary Union, and Comoros are subject to documentation requirements. Payments for travel outside of the franc zone face quantitative limits. Residents must receive government approval to borrow from abroad or to lend abroad.

 ## BANKING AND FINANCE
Score: **4**–Stable (high level of restrictions)

Congo's central bank, as it is for five other countries of the Central African region of the franc zone, is the Banque des Etats de l'Afrique Centrale. Banks remain under the control or influence of corrupt government officials. According to the Economist Intelligence Unit, "Poor management, political interference and the accumulation of non-performing loans, many of which have involved prominent individuals as well as public enterprises, have crippled the local banking sector…. Because of civil war, and the fact that loan recovery cannot be guaranteed through the justice system, many banks have ceased providing loan credit, except on short-term basis, and now generate their revenue mostly through transaction fees."

 ## WAGES AND PRICES
Score: **3**–Stable (moderate level of intervention)

The government continues to influence prices through state-owned companies in transport, telecommunications, electricity, and water utilities. The Economist Intelligence Unit reports that "Public service and parastatal companies have traditionally been the foundation of formal-sector activity in Brazzaville." The labor code stipulates a monthly minimum wage.

 ## PROPERTY RIGHTS
Score: **4**–Stable (low level of protection)

According to the U.S. Department of State, "The Constitution provides for an independent judiciary; however, in practice the judiciary continues to be corrupt, overburdened, under financed, and subject both to political influence and bribery. Lack of resources continues to be a severe problem; almost nothing remains of judicial records, case decisions, and law books following the looting during the civil wars of the late 1990s."

 ## REGULATION
Score: **4**–Stable (high level)

The Economist Intelligence Unit reports that corruption remains a considerable problem. Regulations are burdensome and enforced haphazardly, and labor laws favor militant unions at the expense of employers. In addition, "The…main security risks to business in Congo are the lack of clarity in regulation and slow and poorly functioning government institutions on which investors may depend for routine matters." According to *Global Edge,* high costs of labor, energy, raw materials, and transportation and a restrictive labor law are among the factors discouraging investment. The EIU reports that in October 2002, the government set a new license system for timber companies, which, in exchange for a 15-year permit, must increase their cooperation with communities living near the concessions.

 ## INFORMAL MARKET
Score: **5**–Stable (very high level of activity)

Congo's informal market is huge. The Economist Intelligence Unit reports that "about 60% of the population earns a livelihood from, or has links to, the informal agricultural sector." Smuggling of ivory and diamonds is extensive.

COSTA RICA

# COSTA RICA

COSTA RICA

Rank: 50

Score: 2.71

Category: Mostly Free

**Present & Past Scores**

(Best) 1
2
3
4
(Worst) 5

3.04 3.00 3.03 3.00 3.00 2.88 2.84 2.73 2.71 2.71

'95 '96 '97 '98 '99 '00 '01 '02 '03 '04

## QUICK STUDY

### SCORES

| | |
|---|---|
| Trade Policy | 3 |
| Fiscal Burden | 3.1 |
| Government Intervention | 2 |
| Monetary Policy | 3 |
| Foreign Investment | 2 |
| Banking and Finance | 3 |
| Wages and Prices | 2 |
| Property Rights | 3 |
| Regulation | 3 |
| Informal Market | 3 |

**Population:** 3,873,000

**Total area:** 51,100 sq. km

**GDP:** $15 billion

**GDP growth rate:** 0.9%

**GDP per capita:** $3,900

**Major exports:** coffee, bananas textiles, industrial and manufactured goods

**Exports of goods and services:** $7.1 billion

**Major export trading partners:** US 49.7%, Netherlands 5.5%, Guatemala 4.2%, Nicaragua 3.2%

**Major imports:** raw materials, consumer goods, capital goods

**Imports of goods and services:** $6.8 billion

**Major import trading partners:** US 53.5%, Mexico 5.8%, Venezuela 4.6%, Japan 3.5%

**Foreign direct investment (net):** $397 million

2001 Data (in constant 1995 US dollars)

Despite investor friendliness and a relatively stable political atmosphere, Costa Rica is burdened with debt from an unsustainably large public sector and popular expectations that a welfare state can be maintained on a low tax base. According to the International Monetary Fund, public-sector deficit is up to 6 percent of GDP and public debt equals nearly 50 percent of GDP. Real GDP growth has slowed to a fraction of a digit; unemployment is close to 7 percent, its highest level in 17 years; and the U.S. Department of State reports that 21 percent of the population lives below the poverty line. While social indicators are much higher than they are for other countries in the region, recent increases in unemployment and poverty are alarming to most Costa Ricans. Since assuming the presidency in 2002, Abel Pacheco has faced continuing resistance to the implementation of more fiscally responsible policies and to the privatization of inefficient state monopolies in the energy and telecommunications sectors. This year, strikes by workers in those sectors have produced demands for wage increases that his administration has been unable to resist. Costa Rica's fiscal burden of government and government intervention scores are 0.5 point better this year; however, its trade policy score is 1 point worse. As a result, Costa Rica's overall score is unchanged this year.

## TRADE POLICY
### Score: **3**–Worse (moderate level of protectionism)

According to the World Bank, Costa Rica's weighted average tariff rate in 2001 (the most recent year for which World Bank data are available) was 4.3 percent, up from the 3.7 percent reported in the 2003 *Index*. As a result, Costa Rica's trade policy score is 1 point worse this year. The U.S. Trade Representative reports that "Costa Rican customs procedures remain complex and bureaucratic despite recent laws and improvements, such as the establishment of an electronic 'one-stop' import and export window...." In addition, "the process of obtaining standard sanitary and phitosanitary documentation can often be cumbersome and lengthy."

## FISCAL BURDEN OF GOVERNMENT
### Score—Income Taxation: **2.5**–Stable (moderate tax rates)
### Score—Corporate Taxation: **4**–Stable (high tax rates)
### Score—Change in Government Expenditures: **2**–Better (moderate decrease)
### Final Score: **3.1**–Better (moderate cost of government)

Costa Rica's top income tax rate is 25 percent. The top corporate income tax rate is 30 percent. Government expenditures as a share of GDP decreased 2.3 percentage points to 21.1 percent in 2001, compared to a 1.2 percentage point increase in 2000. As a result, Costa Rica's fiscal burden of government score is 0.5 point better this year.

## GOVERNMENT INTERVENTION IN THE ECONOMY
### Score: **2**–Better (low level)

The World Bank reports that in 2001 the government consumed 14.4 percent of GDP. As a result, Costa Rica's government intervention score is 0.5 point better this year. In the same year, according to the International Monetary Fund, Costa Rica received 4.28 percent of its total revenues from state-owned enterprises and government ownership of property.

151

## MONETARY POLICY
### Score: 3–Stable (moderate level of inflation)

From 1993 to 2002, Costa Rica's weighted average annual rate of inflation was 9.9 percent.

## CAPITAL FLOWS AND FOREIGN INVESTMENT
### Score: 2–Stable (low barriers)

Costa Rica offers one of Central America's best investment climates, and foreign investors are treated the same as domestic investors. State monopolies constrain some investment opportunities, particularly in the electricity, telecommunications, and insurance sectors. The government requires that a certain percentage of Costa Ricans participate in the operation of electrical power, broadcasting, professional services, and wholesale distribution sectors. There are no controls on capital flows, but reporting requirements are mandatory for some transactions. According to the International Monetary Fund, Costa Rica has no restrictions or controls on the holding of foreign exchange accounts by either residents or non-residents. The Economist Intelligence Unit reports that foreigners can easily acquire real estate.

## BANKING AND FINANCE
### Score: 3–Stable (moderate level of restrictions)

Costa Rica's banking system consists of the central bank; three state-owned banks, which account for nearly half of total banking assets; a state-owned mortgage bank; 18 commercial banks; four mutual house-building companies; 12 private finance companies; and 27 savings and loans cooperatives. According to the Economist Intelligence Unit, "The state continues to play a dominant role in the banking sector and bank credit policy often reflects the political aims of the government, resulting in subsidised loans to unprofitable sectors, thereby diverting scarce resources from more productive activities." The EIU also reports that foreign investors account for nearly half of the private banks.

## WAGES AND PRICES
### Score: 2–Stable (low level of intervention)

The market determines most prices. However, the Public Services Regulatory Authority applies price controls on goods on the basic consumption list, which includes foods, school uniforms, shoes, agricultural chemicals, tools, and medicines. According to the Economist Intelligence Unit, "These prices are monitored to ensure that price increases are reasonable." The government also controls fuel prices. Costa Rica's constitution provides for a minimum wage, which is set by a tripartite council representing government, business, and labor.

## PROPERTY RIGHTS
### Score: 3–Stable (moderate level of protection)

Private property is not entirely safe. The U.S. Department of State reports that investors "face an error-prone land titling system and sluggish judicial system vis-à-vis civil cases. Past government expropriation policies have created problems for some [foreign] investors. In addition, land invasions by squatters also remain problematic. While the Costa Rican government has made progress in resolving expropriation cases and has made improvements in the legal framework, some cases, as well as land invasions by squatters, remain unresolved." According to the Economist Intelligence Unit, the judiciary is considered generally honest, but court procedures are cumbersome and slow. "In Costa Rica, a civil law suit will typically last up to six years.... At the core of the Judiciary's problems lie an outdated set of administrative procedures and lack of resources."

## REGULATION
### Score: 3–Stable (moderate level)

According to the U.S. Department of State, "Costa Rican laws, regulations and practices are generally transparent and foster competition, except in monopoly sectors where competition is explicitly excluded.... Bureaucratic procedures are frequently long, involved and discouraging to newcomers." The government has created an on-line investor manual and one-stop windows to ease the regulatory burden. Some regulations (for example, those requiring environmental impact studies) are moderately burdensome, and the government requires private companies to grant vacations, a substantial holiday bonus, overtime, and social insurance. The U.S. Department of State also reports that some businesses complained of corruption in the administration of public tenders. High fees charged in the cargo port of Limon, for example, are often attributed to corruption, and developers of tourism facilities cite municipal level corruption as a problem.

## INFORMAL MARKET
### Score: 3–Stable (moderate level of activity)

Transparency International's 2002 score for Costa Rica is 4.5. Therefore, Costa Rica's informal market score is 3 this year.

# CROATIA

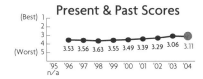

CROATIA

Rank: 82
Score: 3.11
Category: Mostly Unfree

### Present & Past Scores

(Best) 1
2
3
4
(Worst) 5

3.53 3.56 3.63 3.55 3.49 3.39 3.29 3.06 3.11

'95 '96 '97 '98 '99 '00 '01 '02 '03 '04
n/a

In Croatia, elections in January 2000 brought to power a fractious coalition led by the Social Democrats and Social Liberals, leaving the longtime ruling Croatian Democratic Union in the unaccustomed role of opposition. Former Communist Ivica Racan became premier and inherited an economy in shambles. Former President Franjo Tudjman and his allies had plundered the national treasury, partly by manipulating privatization of state-owned companies. Croatia's unemployment rate in 1999 was 20.8 percent; at the end of 2001, it had risen to 22.3 percent. The new government inherited a foreign debt burden of $9 billion, equal to approximately 45 percent of GDP. Even though the government recognizes that it needs to pursue privatization, the reform process has stalled. For example, a row within the government led Racan to dismiss the entire board of the privatization agency. An early 2003 agreement with the International Monetary Fund commits the government to limiting the 2003 deficit to 5 percent of GDP, but the likelihood that parliamentary elections will be held late in the year makes planned expenditure cuts more difficult to achieve. A rare bright spot for Racan is that unions, after threatening to launch a general strike, have agreed to join the government in negotiations to reform the rigid labor laws. Croatia's banking and finance score is 1 point better this year; however, its trade policy score is 1 point worse, and its fiscal burden of government score is 0.5 point worse. As a result, Croatia's overall score is 0.05 point worse this year.

## TRADE POLICY
### Score: **4**–Worse (high level of protectionism)

According to the World Bank, Croatia's weighted average tariff rate in 2001 was 9.8 percent, up from the 6.11 percent reported in the 2003 *Index*. As a result, Croatia's trade policy score is 1 point worse this year. Non-tariff barriers include strict testing and certification requirements for some foods, pharmaceuticals, and electronics. The U.S. Department of State reports that last year, "the government adopted a decree designed to curb imports. The legislation…sets up procedures for introducing temporary measures such as increased duties or limitations on allowed quantities (quotas) of goods whose import damages domestic industries."

## FISCAL BURDEN OF GOVERNMENT
Score—Income Taxation: **3.5**–Stable (high tax rates)
Score—Corporate Taxation: **2**–Stable (low tax rates)
Score—Change in Government Expenditures: **5**–Worse (very high increase)
### Final Score: **3.1**–Worse (moderate cost of government)

Croatia's top income tax rate is 35 percent. The top corporate tax rate is 20 percent. Government expenditures as a share of GDP increased 8.5 percentage points in 2002, compared to a 0.9 percentage point decrease in 2001. As a result, Croatia's fiscal burden of government score is 0.5 point worse this year.

## GOVERNMENT INTERVENTION IN THE ECONOMY
### Score: **2.5**–Stable (moderate level)

Based on data from the Economist Intelligence Unit, the government consumed 21.7 percent of GDP in 2002. In 2001, according to the International Monetary Fund, Croatia received 1.19 percent of its total revenues from state-owned enterprises and government ownership of property.

153

## MONETARY POLICY
### Score: **2**–Stable (low level of inflation)

From 1993 to 2002, Croatia's weighted average annual rate of inflation was 3.16 percent.

## CAPITAL FLOWS AND FOREIGN INVESTMENT
### Score: **3**–Stable (moderate barriers)

The U.S. Department of State reports that the government is attempting to undo the harm done to foreign investment under the previous regime by "[taking] active measures to welcome foreign investors, privatize state monopolies, and improve the Croatian business environment." Foreign investors have the same rights and status as domestic investors and may invest in nearly every sector of the economy. According to the Economist Intelligence Unit, however, "There have been many instances of foreign-owned companies suffering as a result of powerful local firms abusing their competitive position. This is partly a by-product of...the lack of development of the competition authorities. The political and business establishments are closely intertwined, with long-standing relationships." All foreign direct investments must be registered with the commercial courts, and foreigners may purchase real estate only with permission from the government, according to the International Monetary Fund. The IMF also reports that both residents and non-residents are technically allowed to hold foreign exchange accounts, but numerous limitations are enforced, and government approval is required in certain instances. Payments and transfers face few restrictions.

## BANKING AND FINANCE
### Score: **2**–Better (low level of restrictions)

The Economist Intelligence Unit reports that 46 banks were operating in Croatia as of December 2002, with foreign banks owning over 90 percent of total bank assets. A law passed by the parliament in 2001 brought banking regulations more closely into harmonization with European Union standards—for example, by raising capital adequacy requirements. In the first quarter of 2002, the government privatized its holdings in Dubrovacka banka and Splitska banka. In August 2002, however, according to the EIU, it announced that "the Croatian Postal Bank will merge with Croatia Banka and that the state will retain majority ownership." Because foreign banks have a strong presence in the banking sector and the government is reducing its share in the sector through privatization, Croatia's banking and finance score is 1 point better this year.

## WAGES AND PRICES
### Score: **3**–Stable (moderate level of intervention)

The government has the authority to determine prices on a wide range of goods and services. The Economist Intelligence Unit reports that the government controls the price of natural and liquefied gas, rail and boat passenger transport, electricity, television license fees, unprocessed wood, and standardized envelopes. In addition, "the prices of some goods are governed by formulas laid by the government. These include the retail price of petrol (gasoline)...." In January 2001, the government abolished price controls on milk, bread, and telephone subscriptions. In 1999, the government signed a collective bargaining agreement establishing a monthly minimum wage.

## PROPERTY RIGHTS
### Score: **4**–Stable (low level of protection)

The court system is cumbersome and inefficient. According to the U.S. Department of State, "Huge case backlogs mean that business disputes can go unresolved for years; some investors have chosen to insist that contract arbitration take place outside of Croatia. The Government of Croatia has made a commitment to reinvigorate its efforts to reform the judiciary, but much remains to be done." The same source reports that the government's "anti-corruption plan also involves reform of the judiciary, one of the areas most in need of reform, according to the prime minister."

## REGULATION
### Score: **4**–Stable (high level)

Croatia's bureaucracy, like the bureaucracies of other post-communist regimes, remains entrenched, and red tape abounds. The Economist Intelligence Unit cites high wage costs and "restrictive labour laws" as considerable impediments to business. It also reports that "corruption (inspired by impenetrable thickets of bureaucracy) seems to be a [great] source of worry for foreign businesses. Often, gratuities are requested to speed up the process...." The government recognizes that the bureaucracy and administrative barriers remain problems and has pledged to trim the overgrown civil service.

## INFORMAL MARKET
### Score: **3.5**–Stable (high level of activity)

Transparency International's 2002 score for Croatia is 3.8. Therefore, Croatia's informal market score is 3.5 this year.

# CUBA

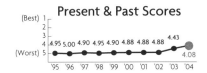

**Rank:** 144

**Score:** 4.08

**Category:** Repressed

CUBA

**Present & Past Scores**

(Best) 1
2
3
4  4.95  5.00  4.90  4.95  4.90  4.88  4.88  4.88  4.43
(Worst) 5  ●  ●  ●  ●  ●  ●  ●  ●  ●  ●  4.08
'95  '96  '97  '98  '99  '00  '01  '02  '03  '04

**N**ew worries about international terrorism and a hemispheric economic downturn have affected Cuba's principal sources of income: tourism and sugar. A number of decrepit mills were closed last year, and fewer visitors are flocking to the Caribbean's political Jurassic Park—the 44-year dictatorship of self-styled "Maximum Leader" Fidel Castro. Thanks to oil supplied under extremely generous credit terms by Venezuelan President Hugo Chávez, Cuba does not have to worry much about energy needs; but food imports are harder to come by because the regime is chronically in debt, behind in payments to creditors, and already has spent about $200 million in hard currency buying grain and food products from U.S. producers on a cash basis—hoping the purchase would be a stepping stone to a line of credit in the United States. In April, President Castro jailed some 80 dissidents and independent journalists on the island while world attention was focused on the war in Iraq. As a result, Cuba is unlikely to receive any aid from the European Union this year, and the Italian Parliament has voted to eliminate its modest charity to the island. Cuba's fiscal burden of government score is 0.5 point worse this year, but its monetary policy score is 4 points better. As a result, Cuba's overall score is 0.35 point better this year.

 **TRADE POLICY**
**Score: 3–Stable** (moderate level of protectionism)

According to the World Bank, Cuba's weighted average tariff rate in 1997 (the most recent year for which World Bank data are available) was 8.2 percent. The Lexington Institute reports that "foreign trade was decentralized as 350 enterprises were permitted to import and export on their own authority." Cuba maintains significant non-tariff barriers. The government inspects and approves most imports. In many cases, customs officials also confiscate imports (especially scarce goods like electronics) for their own use, and such corruption enjoys official sanction.

 **FISCAL BURDEN OF GOVERNMENT**
       Score—Income Taxation: **5**–Stable (very high tax rates)
       Score—Corporate Taxation: **4**–Stable (high tax rates)
       Score—Change in Government Expenditures: **4**–Worse (moderate increase)
  **Final Score: 4.3**–Worse (high cost of government)

According to information from the Pi Management Association, Cuba's top income tax rate is 50 percent and its corporate tax rate is 30 percent. Wholly owned foreign businesses are assessed a 35 percent rate, but the standard 30 percent rate is used to score this factor, with the 35 percent tax viewed as a foreign investment barrier. Government expenditures as a share of GDP increased by 2 percentage points to 54.2 percent in 2001, compared to a 2 percentage point decline the previous year. As a result, Cuba's fiscal burden of government score is 0.5 point worse this year.

**GOVERNMENT INTERVENTION IN THE ECONOMY**
**Score: 4.5**–Stable (very high level)

The World Bank reports that the government consumed 23 percent of GDP in 2001. In the same year, as indicated by data from the Economist Intelligence Unit, Cuba received 11.05 percent of its total revenues from state-owned enterprises and government ownership of property. The state, however, produces most economic output and employs most of the labor force. According

155

to the United Nations, "The industrial sector in Cuba is dominated by large state-owned enterprises. About 90% of productive institutions are managed directly by ministries, and the rest by the local government." The Economist Intelligence Unit reports that the state employs more than 75 percent of the labor force. Based on the apparent unreliability of the figure for government revenues, 1 point has been added to this factor.

 **MONETARY POLICY**
Score: **1**–Better (very low level of inflation)

Data from the Economist Intelligence Unit indicate that from 1995 to 2002, Cuba's weighted average rate of inflation was 1.84 percent. Cuba artificially keeps inflation low through its extensive use of wage and price controls, which is picked up under the wages and prices factor. Based on the availability of data on the rate of inflation, however, Cuba's monetary policy score is 4 points better this year.

 **CAPITAL FLOWS AND FOREIGN INVESTMENT**
Score: **4**–Stable (high barriers)

Foreign investment is permitted on a case-by-case basis. All investments must go through the state, and licensing is required for all businesses. Cuba's constitution still outlaws all foreign ownership of property and real estate. Officially, all sectors of the economy except defense, education, and health care are open to foreign investment. The nickel mining, oil, tourism, and telecommunications sectors have attracted the most foreign investment. According to the Economist Intelligence Unit, "The authorities are firmly committed to maintaining the apparatus for extensive economic planning....The opening of the economy to foreign investment will remain tightly controlled, but investors will continue to trickle in." The foreign investment law provides additional protection against expropriation, but all arbitration must take place in government ministries that afford the investor little protection.

 **BANKING AND FINANCE**
Score: **5**–Stable (very high level of restrictions)

Reform of the banking system, initiated in 1994, has involved restructuring existing banks, modernizing banking regulations, and expanding the system. Most notably, central bank functions were stripped from the Banco Nacional de Cuba, and a new central bank, the Banco Central de Cuba, was created in 1997. Although the government has established a new set of state-owned banks over the past several years and has opened a series of state-run bureaux de change, which convert Cuban pesos for U.S. dollars at the "unofficial" exchange rate, it still controls all banking activity. In 1999, Cuba created a monetary policy committee that meets weekly to determine domestic interest rates. It has permitted over a dozen foreign banks to open representative offices but does not allow them to operate freely. Some changes also have been introduced in the insurance sector. According to the Economist Intelligence Unit, "Products not known for 35

years, such as travel and medical insurance, and personal pensions, are being promoted. The first insurance joint ventures with foreign capital were announced in early 1997." The government, however, fully controls this sector as well.

 **WAGES AND PRICES**
Score: **5**–Stable (very high level of intervention)

The government sets virtually all wages and prices. It also sets numerous minimum wages that vary according to occupation. According to the U.S. Department of State, "The Government supplemented the minimum wage with free education, subsidized medical care (daily pay is reduced by 40 percent after the third day of being admitted to a hospital), housing, and some food (this subsidized food is enough for about 1 week per month)...[and] rationed most basic necessities such as food, medicine, clothing, and cooking gas...."

 **PROPERTY RIGHTS**
Score: **5**–Stable (very low level of protection)

Private ownership of land and productive capital by Cuban citizens is limited to farming and self-employment. According to the U.S. Department of State, "The Constitution...explicitly subordinates the courts to the ANPP [National Assembly of People's Power] and the Council of State, which is headed by Fidel Castro. The ANPP and its lower level counterparts choose all judges.... The law and trial practices do not meet international standards for fair public trials."

 **REGULATION**
Score: **4**–Stable (high level)

Cuba's government regulates the entire economy by owning and controlling the means of production. However, private entrepreneurship is heavily regulated. According to *The Economist*, "Cuba, out of necessity, has allowed capitalism into its socialist system. But it then keeps capitalism down...with a mass of complex and sometimes contradictory rules and regulations. Just when [investors] find out how things work, the rules change again." In addition, "except for food service operations...assistants and employees are not permitted.... [P]rivate taxis are barred from picking up passengers at tourist hotels or airports.... [T]eachers may not work as private tutors." The same source, however, reports that "In some cases, the legal framework eventually changes to accommodate the gray-market private sector."

 **INFORMAL MARKET**
Score: **5**–Stable (very high level of activity)

Cuba's informal market is huge. Even basic economic activities—including the sale of milk and bread, transportation services, and housing—are performed in the informal market. According to *The Washington Times*, "the black market... accounts for 50 percent of all retail transactions." The informal market in currency is likewise substantial.

CYPRUS

# CYPRUS

Rank: 14

Score: 1.95

Category: Free

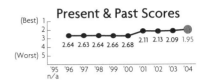

Present & Past Scores

(Best) 1
2
3
4
(Worst) 5

2.64  2.63  2.64  2.66  2.68   2.11  2.13  2.09  1.95

'95  '96  '97  '98  '99  '00  '01  '02  '03  '04
n/a

## QUICK STUDY

### SCORES

| | |
|---|---|
| Trade Policy | 2 |
| Fiscal Burden | 2.5 |
| Government Intervention | 2 |
| Monetary Policy | 1 |
| Foreign Investment | 3 |
| Banking and Finance | 2 |
| Wages and Prices | 2 |
| Property Rights | 1 |
| Regulation | 2 |
| Informal Market | 2 |

**Population:** 760,653

**Total area:** 9,250 sq. km

**GDP:** $11.1 billion

**GDP growth rate:** 4.0%

**GDP per capita:** $14,592

**Major exports:** pharmaceuticals, clothing, potatoes, citrus, cigarettes, travel services, transportation

**Exports of goods and services:** $5.1 billion

**Major export trading partners:** UK 20.5%, Russia 9.5%, Greece 9.2%, United Arab Emirates 8.6%, Syria 6.6%

**Major imports:** consumer goods, fuels and lubricants, chemicals, transport equipment, insurance services

**Imports of goods and services:** $5.7 billion

**Major import trading partners:** US 9.8%, Greece 9.3%, Italy 9.2%, UK 9.1%, Germany 7.1%

**Foreign direct investment (net):** −$49.3 million

2001 Data (in constant 1995 US dollars)

The Greek portion of Cyprus is set to join the European Union in May 2004, with euro entry probably occurring by around 2007. The desire to meet EU requirements has helped liberalize the Cypriot economy. For example, the central bank has been able to speed up the full liberalization of capital flows, long an impediment to foreigners doing business on the island. However, sluggish economic growth—the Cypriot economy grew by around 1.7 percent in 2002—helped lead to the victory of the left-leaning coalition government of President Tassos Papadopoulos, whose allies include the nominally communist party. The new government is even less likely to privatize remaining state-owned companies, such as airports or the Cyprus Telecoms Authority. On March 11, 2003, the U.N.-sponsored talks on uniting Cyprus collapsed as President Rauf Denktash, the Turkish Cypriot leader, refused to put the U.N. draft for a settlement to a referendum. With the Cyprus question dominating life on the island, economic policy is less of a priority. Cyprus's fiscal burden of government score is 0.9 point better this year, and its government intervention score is 0.5 point better. As a result, Cyprus's overall score is 0.14 point better this year, causing Cyprus to be classified as a "free" economy.

###  TRADE POLICY
**Score: 2–Stable** (low level of protectionism)

Based on data from the Economist Intelligence Unit and Cyprus's Central Bank, Cyprus's average tariff rate in 2002 was 2.83 percent (based on import duties as a percentage of total imports). The government maintains some non-tariff barriers. According to the U.S. Department of State, "the 20 percent price preference granted to locally produced goods and services for public tenders is clearly discriminatory against foreign bidders. It is also contrary to EU practice and the WTO's Government Procurement Agreement." Other non-tariff barriers include strict labeling requirements.

### FISCAL BURDEN OF GOVERNMENT
Score—Income Taxation: **3–Better** (moderate tax rates)
Score—Corporate Taxation: **1.5–Better** (low tax rates)
Score—Change in Government Expenditures: **4–Worse** (moderate increase)
**Final Score: 2.5–Better** (moderate cost of government)

Cyprus's top income tax rate is 30 percent, down from the 40 percent reported in the 2003 *Index*. The top corporate tax rate is 15 percent, down from the 25 percent reported in the 2003 *Index*. However, government expenditures as a share of GDP increased more (1.6 percentage points to 38.2 percent) in 2001 than they did in 2000 (0.1 percentage point). On net, Cyprus's fiscal burden of government score is therefore 0.9 point better this year.

###  GOVERNMENT INTERVENTION IN THE ECONOMY
Score: **2–Better** (low level)

The Economist Intelligence Unit reports that the government consumed 17.7 percent of GDP in 2001. In the same year, based on data from the Ministry of Finance, Cyprus received 2.59 percent of its total revenues from state-owned enterprises and government ownership of property, down from the 8.2 percent reported in the 2003 *Index*. As a result, Cyprus's government intervention score is 0.5 point better this year.

157

## MONETARY POLICY
### Score: **1**–Stable (very low level of inflation)

From 1993 to 2002, Cyprus's weighted average annual rate of inflation was 2.69 percent.

 ## CAPITAL FLOWS AND FOREIGN INVESTMENT
### Score: **3**–Stable (moderate barriers)

In January 2000, Cyprus liberalized all foreign direct investment controls on local businesses for residents of the European Union, who may now own 100 percent of local companies and any company listed on the Cyprus Stock Exchange. All applications for direct investment by a foreigner must go through official review, but the government generally grants investment permits in a timely and nondiscriminatory fashion. Foreign ownership in agriculture, manufacturing, services, wholesale and retail, tourism, banking, insurance, newspaper and magazine publishing houses, and new airlines is subject to various minimum investment amounts, maximum ownership restrictions, or approval processes. The U.S. Department of State reports that investments in "saturated" sectors, which include real estate development, higher education, and public utilities, is discouraged. The International Monetary Fund reports that real estate purchases of land abroad by residents and in Cyprus by non-residents are subject to restrictions and approval. Transfers of assets, gifts, and loans between residents and non-residents require central bank approval or are subject to restrictions.

 ## BANKING AND FINANCE
### Score: **2**–Stable (low level of restrictions)

Cyprus's six domestic banks provide a full range of services and have solid international ratings. According to the Embassy of Cyprus, there are only two state-owned banks, which control 4.5 percent of total bank assets. The January 2000 liberalization of foreign investment permits non-residents to own up to 50 percent of a Cypriot bank, up from 15 percent, but acquisition of more than 10 percent requires central bank approval. Interest rates were liberalized as of January 1, 2001, and are now set by the market. Effective January 2001, the government lifted restrictions on foreign-currency–denominated lending for more than two years to residents. There have been allegations of money laundering through Cypriot banks.

 ## WAGES AND PRICES
### Score: **2**–Stable (low level of intervention)

The market sets most prices. The U.S. Department of State reports that "the Government has abolished price controls on all products, with the exception of gasoline and cement. Price controls on these two products will be removed upon accession to the EU." The government mandates a minimum wage.

 ## PROPERTY RIGHTS
### Score: **1**–Stable (very high level of protection)

Private property in Cyprus is well-protected. "Effective means are available for enforcing property and contractual rights," reports the U.S. Department of State. "The Constitution…provides for an independent judiciary, provisions which generally are respected in practice…. Cyprus inherited many elements of its legal system from the United Kingdom, including the presumption of innocence, the right to due process, and the right of appeal. Throughout Cyprus, a fair public trial is provided for in law and accorded in practice."

 ## REGULATION
### Score: **2**–Stable (low level)

It is relatively easy to establish a business in Cyprus. According to the U.S. Department of State, "Existing procedures and regulations affecting business…are sufficiently transparent and applied in practice without bias…." The Cypriot Embassy reports that opening a new business "usually takes a month on average but through the acceleration procedure introduced the last few years…the time is reduced to 4-7 days." In addition, the U.S. Embassy in Cyprus "is not aware of any U.S. firms identifying corruption as an obstacle to foreign direct investment in Cyprus."

 ## INFORMAL MARKET
### Score: **2**–Stable (low level of activity)

The protection of intellectual property rights has improved since passage of modern copyright and patent laws in 1994 and 1998, respectively, but there are still concerns about violations. The U.S. Department of State reports that "the U.S. Embassy in Nicosia has received an increasing number of complaints about a rising level of IPR piracy from representatives of the business community, which attributes the increase to ineffective implementation of these laws" There is some informal labor activity, particularly among illegal immigrants.

CZECH
REPUBLIC

# CZECH REPUBLIC

Rank: 32

Score: 2.39

Category: Mostly Free

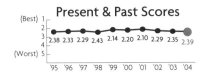

Present & Past Scores

(Best) 1
2
3
4
(Worst) 5

2.38 2.33 2.29 2.43 2.14 2.20 2.10 2.29 2.35 2.39

'95 '96 '97 '98 '99 '00 '01 '02 '03 '04

## QUICK STUDY

### SCORES

| | |
|---|---|
| Trade Policy | 3 |
| Fiscal Burden | 3.9 |
| Government Intervention | 2.5 |
| Monetary Policy | 1 |
| Foreign Investment | 2 |
| Banking and Finance | 1 |
| Wages and Prices | 2 |
| Property Rights | 2 |
| Regulation | 3 |
| Informal Market | 3.5 |

**Population:** 10,200,774

**Total area:** 78,866 sq. km

**GDP:** $58.1 billion

**GDP growth rate:** 2.0%

**GDP per capita:** $5,696

**Major exports:** machinery and equipment, intermediate manufactured goods, chemicals, raw materials and fuels

**Exports of goods and services:** $52.3 billion

**Major export trading partners:** Germany 38.1%, Slovakia 8.0%, Austria 5.8%, Poland 5.2%, France 3.9%

**Major imports:** machinery and transport equipment, raw materials and fuels, chemicals

**Imports of goods and services:** $58.4 billion

**Major import trading partners:** Germany 32.9%, Slovakia 5.4%, Russia 5.5%, Italy 5.3%

**Foreign direct investment (net):** $8.1 billion

2002 Data (in constant 1995 US dollars)

The Czech Republic has one of Central Europe's most developed and industrialized economies. Exports to the European Union, especially Germany, and foreign investment led economic growth in 2000–2002. The private sector accounts for nearly 80 percent of GDP, but the government continues to retain ownership in many key industries. Challenges to economic transformation include completing industrial restructuring, increasing transparency in capital market transactions, covering the losses accumulated by formerly state-owned banks, and reforming the health care and pension systems. In addition, the state-funded welfare programs are excessively expensive and inefficient. A member of the NATO alliance since 1999, the Czech Republic has made a significant contribution to the war on terrorism by deploying units with the International Security Assistance Force in Afghanistan. The Czech Republic has finalized its accession to the EU in 2003 and will assume membership as early as May 2004. The EU has contributed significant amounts of assistance to the Czech Republic, preparing it for that accession. Weak minority governments since 1996 have led to the lack of political consensus and decisive structural reform, but Prime Minister Vladimir Spidla, of the center–left Czech Social Democratic Party, is committed to a stabilization strategy within a policy guided by EU standards that has hastened reforms in the administrative, regulatory, and judicial systems. Former center–right Prime Minister Vaclav Klaus was elected President of the Czech Republic by the Parliament on February 28, 2003, and will serve a five-year term. The Czech Republic's monetary policy score is 1 point better this year; however, its fiscal burden of government score is 0.9 point worse, and its government intervention score is 0.5 point worse. As a result, the Czech Republic's overall score is 0.04 point worse this year.

## TRADE POLICY

### Score: **3–Stable** (moderate level of protectionism)

According to the World Bank, the Czech Republic's weighted average tariff rate in 1999 (the most recent year for which World Bank data are available) was 5.8 percent. The U.S. Department of State reports that "technical barriers continue to hamper imports of certain agricultural and food products.... A lack of consistency in the application of customs norms can also act as a non-tariff barrier."

## FISCAL BURDEN OF GOVERNMENT

### Score—Income Taxation: **3–Stable** (moderate tax rates)
### Score—Corporate Taxation: **4–Stable** (high tax rates)
### Score—Change in Government Expenditures: **4.5–Worse** (high increase)
### Final Score: **3.9–Worse** (high cost of government)

The Czech Republic's top income tax rate is 32 percent. The top corporate income tax rate is 31 percent. Government expenditures as a share of GDP increased 2.7 percentage points to 45.3 percent in 2002, compared to a decline of 4.3 percentage points in 2001. As a result, the Czech Republic's fiscal burden of government score is 0.9 point worse this year.

## GOVERNMENT INTERVENTION IN THE ECONOMY

### Score: **2.5–Worse** (moderate level)

The Economist Intelligence Unit reports that the government consumed 21.4 percent of GDP in 2002, up from the 19.1 percent reported in the 2003 *Index.* As a result, the Czech Republic's government intervention score is 0.5 point worse this year. In 2001, according to the International Monetary Fund, the Czech Republic received 2.08 percent of its total revenues from state-owned enterprises and government ownership of property.

## MONETARY POLICY
### Score: **1**–Better (very low level of inflation)

Between 1993 and 2002, the Czech Republic's weighted average annual rate of inflation was 2.81 percent, down from 4.56 percent between 1992 and 2001. As a result, the Czech Republic's monetary policy score is 1 point better this year.

## CAPITAL FLOWS AND FOREIGN INVESTMENT
### Score: **2**–Stable (low barriers)

The Czech Republic is open to foreign investment. Foreign investors receive national treatment and may invest in nearly all sectors, with the exception of transport and industries related to defense or national security. As of January 1, 2002, non-Czech entities can acquire non-agricultural, non-forest land. There are no restrictions on payments or proceeds transactions or on current transfers, and both residents and non-residents may hold foreign exchange accounts. Prior authorization is required for issuance of debt securities and money market securities. There are limits on open foreign exchange positions. The U.S. Department of State reports that a lack of transparency and a 10 percent preference for Czech bidders impedes foreign tenders for government contracts.

## BANKING AND FINANCE
### Score: **1**–Stable (very low level of restrictions)

According to the U.S. Department of State, "The government privatized the last state-owned bank in 2001 and…foreign-controlled banks now manage 90% of total banking assets." Subject to approval by the central bank, a foreign bank may establish a wholly owned bank, buy into an existing bank, or open a branch. The Economist Intelligence Unit reports that, as of March 2001, there were 63 banks, of which 26 were partially or wholly foreign-owned. Czech banks are allowed to sell securities and make some investments. The sector remains burdened by a backlog of bankruptcy claims, although reform of the bankruptcy code should help resolve this situation.

## WAGES AND PRICES
### Score: **2**–Stable (low level of intervention)

The market sets most wages and prices. According to the Economist Intelligence Unit, "The Price Law (Law 526/1990), effective since January 1991, provides the government with broad powers to regulate prices. In theory, the Ministry of Finance can fix prices directly, set minimum or maximum prices for any commercial transaction and establish periods when prices may not change…. Despite its broad powers, the government generally favours a laissez-faire pricing policy on most products. Goods and services still subject to controls include energy, some raw materials, domestic rents, and rail and bus transport. Maximum prices also apply on mail and telecommunications tariffs." The government mandates a minimum wage.

## PROPERTY RIGHTS
### Score: **2**–Stable (high level of protection)

Private property is well-protected. The Economist Intelligence Unit reports that "contractual agreements are generally secure in the Czech Republic." According to the U.S. Department of State, however, "Due to the newness and inexperience of the Czech post-communist court system, judicial decisions may vary from court to court. Commercial disputes, particularly those related to bankruptcy proceedings, can drag on for years."

## REGULATION
### Score: **3**–Stable (moderate level)

Red tape and bureaucratic corruption are still a big problem. According to the *Financial Times*, "Business leaders argue that job creation would be easier if the government cut red tape and corruption in the bureaucracy…. [F]oreign executives say that the Czech Republic can still often be an opaque business environment, particularly for smaller companies that cannot take complaints to the prime minister." The Economist Intelligence Unit reports that "firms must meet myriad local standards on health, hygiene, ventilation, and utilities use, among others." In addition, "to establish a company or change a registration, bundles of documents stamped by notaries have to be submitted to a special judge at a regional court." This problem is further complicated by the absence of office equipment, staff, and skills to handle the workload. As a result, companies are almost forced to hire lawyers and bribe officials to complete the process. Reform of the civil service has been pushed back to 2005.

## INFORMAL MARKET
### Score: **3.5**–Stable (high level of activity)

Transparency International's 2002 score for the Czech Republic is 3.7. Therefore, the Czech Republic's informal market score is 3.5 this year.

# DENMARK

Rank: 8

Score: 1.80

Category: Free

Present & Past Scores

(Best) 1
2
3   2.13  1.98  2.11  2.13  2.29  2.10  1.79  1.71  1.80
4
(Worst) 5

'95  '96  '97  '98  '99  '00  '01  '02  '03  '04
n/a

## QUICK STUDY

### SCORES

| | |
|---|---|
| Trade Policy | 2 |
| Fiscal Burden | 4 |
| Government Intervention | 3 |
| Monetary Policy | 1 |
| Foreign Investment | 2 |
| Banking and Finance | 1 |
| Wages and Prices | 2 |
| Property Rights | 1 |
| Regulation | 1 |
| Informal Market | 1 |

**Population:** 5,368,354

**Total area:** 43,094 sq. km

**GDP:** $211.7 billion

**GDP growth rate:** 1.6%

**GDP per capita:** $39,435

**Major exports:** manufactured goods, agricultural products, fuels, ships, transportation, travel services

**Exports of goods and services:** $91.6 billion

**Major export trading partners:** Germany 19.6%, Sweden 11.8%, UK 9.5%, US 6.9%, Norway 5.5% (2001)

**Major imports:** transport equipment, capital goods, intermediate goods

**Imports of goods and services:** $81.7 billion

**Major import trading partners:** Germany 21.9%, Sweden 12.1%, UK 7.5%, Netherlands 7.1%, France 5.7% (2001)

**Foreign direct investment (net):** $1 billion

2002 Data (in constant 1995 US dollars)

With a population over 5 million, the Kingdom of Denmark consists of the Jutland peninsula and over 400 islands, including Greenland and the Faroe Islands. It also consists of a large welfare state with high taxes. The Danish system includes free public education, health care coverage from cradle to grave, and subsidized care for children and the elderly. According to the Economist Intelligence Unit, "One feature that Denmark shares with most of the other Nordic economies is its high level of state expenditure to total economic activity, which is now among the highest in the world." To fund such expenditures, Danes shoulder a high tax burden. The business sector, notes the U.S. Department of State, "believes that the high income taxes and the series of environmental taxes imposed on business, can jeopardize Danish competitiveness and incentives to work." The government plans to implement tax cuts for personal income in stages from 2004–2007 while maintaining the current level of publicly provided services. Yet, as the EIU observes, it "has yet to show how it intends to finance the cuts." The road to greater growth in Denmark must include drastic reductions in taxes and the welfare state. Denmark's fiscal burden of government score is 0.1 point better this year, but its wages and prices score is 1 point worse. As a result, Denmark's overall score is 0.09 point worse this year.

###  TRADE POLICY
#### Score: **2**–Stable (low level of protectionism)

Because Denmark is a member of the European Union, its trade policy is the same as the policies of other EU members. The World Bank reports that the EU's common external weighted average tariff rate in 2001 was 2.6 percent. According to the Economist Intelligence Unit, "Labeling, health and safety regulations are not particularly onerous," and the government, with very few exceptions, requires no import licenses. As part of the EU, Denmark applies quantitative restrictions to certain imports.

###  FISCAL BURDEN OF GOVERNMENT
Score—Income Taxation: **5**–Stable (very high tax rates)
Score—Corporate Taxation: **4**–Stable (high tax rates)
Score—Change in Government Expenditures: **3**–Better (very low decrease)
#### Final Score: **4**–Better (high cost of government)

Denmark's top income tax rate is 59 percent. The top corporate tax rate is 30 percent. Government expenditures as a share of GDP remained unchanged at 55.3 percent in 2002, compared to an increase of 0.5 percentage point in 2001. On net, Denmark's fiscal burden of government score is 0.1 point better this year.

### GOVERNMENT INTERVENTION IN THE ECONOMY
#### Score: **3**–Stable (moderate level)

According to the Economist Intelligence Unit and the Embassy of Denmark, the government consumed 26.1 percent of GDP in 2002. In 2001, based on data from Statistics Denmark, Denmark received 5.36 percent of its revenues from state-owned enterprises and government ownership of property.

**MONETARY POLICY**
Score: **1**–Stable (very low level of inflation)

From 1993 to 2002, Denmark's weighted average annual rate of inflation was 2.44 percent.

 **CAPITAL FLOWS AND FOREIGN INVESTMENT**
Score: **2**–Stable (low barriers)

Foreign investors, including those from outside the European Union, are subject to the same laws as domestic investors. The International Monetary Fund reports that non-residents are prohibited from purchasing real estate except in cases in which the person formerly resided in Denmark for at least five years, is an EU national working in Denmark, or is a non-EU national with a valid residence or business permit. In general, there are few restrictions on investment and no screening process. Notable exceptions are limitations on foreign ownership in hydrocarbon exploration, arms production, aircraft, and ships registered in the Danish International Ships Register. The country's liberal investment regime has attracted increasingly high levels of foreign investment in the past several years.

 **BANKING AND FINANCE**
Score: **1**–Stable (very low level of restrictions)

Denmark's banking system is open to foreign competition and largely independent of government. The same rules apply to commercial and savings banks, and banks may provide services in a wide variety of areas including mortgage financing, stock trading, leasing, factoring, investment, real estate, and insurance. There are 650 financial institutions, including 169 banks, with the largest bank (Danske Bank) accounting for a 52.4 percent market share. The Economist Intelligence Unit reports that "non-performing loans among the large Nordic players are the lowest in Europe, with Danske Bank leading the way in terms of asset quality." in 2000, there were at least 30 Danish venture capital companies.

 **WAGES AND PRICES**
Score: **2**–Worse (low level of intervention)

The market sets wages and most prices. According to the Economist Intelligence Unit, "The government retains the power to intervene with price controls in an emergency—such as during a period of accelerating inflation.... Otherwise, none apply." Denmark affects agricultural prices through its participation in the Common Agricultural Policy, a program that heavily subsidizes agricultural goods. As a result, Denmark's wages and prices score is 1 point worse this year. According to Timbro, a Swedish think tank, "EU consumers pay roughly 80–100% more for their food than would be the case in a mature free-market regime." There is no mandated minimum wage, but various negotiated labor agreements effectively set a minimum wage for their respective economic sectors.

 **PROPERTY RIGHTS**
Score: **1**–Stable (very high level of protection)

The judiciary is independent and, in general, both fair and efficient. The Economist Intelligence Unit reports that "the country provides a high level of professionalism in the judiciary and civil service. Given the slow pace of Denmark's legal system, however, out-of-court settlements are common."

 **REGULATION**
Score: **1**–Stable (very low level)

Establishing a business is a simple process. Regulations are applied evenly and efficiently in most cases, and the government takes a laissez-faire approach to the free market. The Economist Intelligence Unit reports that "Denmark has been introducing a string of regulatory changes to increase the flexibility of the local workforce.... [L]abor laws...are flexible and efficient in practice." The Danish Embassy reports that Denmark's labor market is "very liberal, in marked contrast to a number of EU countries." According to a report on the labor market issued by the Confederation of Danish Industries, one indicator of labor flexibility is the "high proportion of smaller and medium sized firms—firms that are quickly able to adapt to changing demands and conditions." The U.S. Department of State reports that "Denmark applies high standards with regard to environment, health and safety, and labor. Bureaucratic procedures appear streamlined and transparent, and corruption is generally unknown."

 **INFORMAL MARKET**
Score: **1**–Stable (very low level of activity)

Transparency International's 2002 score for Denmark is 9.5. Therefore, Denmark's informal market score is 1 this year.

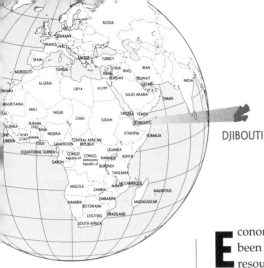

DJIBOUTI

# DJIBOUTI

Rank: 92
Score: 3.23
Category: Mostly Unfree

Present & Past Scores

(Best) 1
2
3
4
(Worst) 5

3.18 3.29 3.28 3.48 3.48 3.26 3.30 3.23

'95 '96 '97 '98 '99 '00 '01 '02 '03 '04
n/a n/a

Economic growth in Djibouti, which has been independent from France since 1977, has been hindered by a bloated civil service, lack of transparency, corruption, and a lack of resources. Economist Intelligence Unit reports indicate that the January 2003 election, in which all deputies loyal to President Ismael Omar Guelleh held their seats in parliament, was rigged. In addition, according to the U.S. Department of State, there have been "credible reports that security forces beat, physically abused, and raped prisoners and detainees." A service-based economy centered on the port, the railway, and French, German, and U.S. bases accounted for an estimated 81 percent of GDP in 2001 (at factor cost). In November 2002, the International Monetary Fund reported that "economic growth remains too slow to reduce widespread poverty and high unemployment, and a comprehensive strategy to promote private investment and job creation is therefore urgently needed." Meanwhile, nomadic subsistence is the primary occupation for those living outside the capital city. Djibouti Telecom and Electricite de Djibouti are targeted for privatization. To achieve growth, the government will have to move forward with these privatizations, reduce the size of the civil service, and work on eliminating pervasive corruption. Djibouti's trade policy score is 1 point worse this year; however, its fiscal burden of government score is 0.2 point better, and its government intervention score is 1.5 points better. As a result, Djibouti's overall score is 0.07 point better this year.

## TRADE POLICY
### Score: **5**–Worse (very high level of protectionism)

The International Monetary Fund reports that Djibouti's average tariff rate in 2002 was 21 percent. As a result, Djibouti's trade policy score is 1 point worse this year. Importers need a license to import goods. In addition, according to the Economist Intelligence Unit, trade is constrained by "strict and cumbersome 'rules of origin' criteria."

## FISCAL BURDEN OF GOVERNMENT
Score—Income Taxation: **3**–Stable (moderate tax rates)
Score—Corporate Taxation: **3**–Stable (moderate tax rates)
Score—Change in Government Expenditures: **2**–Better (moderate decrease)
### Final Score: **2.8**–Better (moderate cost of government)

The International Monetary Fund reports that Djibouti's top income tax rate is 30 percent. The top corporate tax rate is 25 percent. Government expenditures as a share of GDP decreased 2.2 percentage points to 30.9 percent in 2001, compared to a 0.3 percentage point decrease in 2000. As a result, Djibouti's fiscal burden of government score is 0.2 point better this year.

## GOVERNMENT INTERVENTION IN THE ECONOMY
### Score: **3.5**–Better (high level)

The World Bank reports that the government consumed 24.4 percent of GDP in 2001. In 2002, according to the International Monetary Fund, Djibouti received 1.88 percent of its total revenues from state-owned enterprises and government ownership of property. However, much of Djibouti's GDP is produced by the state. The Economist Intelligence Unit reports that the government owns "all the principal public utilities: water; electricity; postal services

163

and telecommunications; and the railway (owned jointly with Ethiopia) and port." The government also owns two pharmaceutical factories and dairy products plants and, according to the EIU, employs 56 percent of the labor force. The government agreed with the International Monetary Fund on the need to privatize many state-owned enterprises, but little has been done. Based on the level of state-owned enterprise, 1 point has been added to Djibouti's government intervention score. As a result of a change in the *Index* methodology, Djibouti's government intervention score is 1.5 points better this year.

### MONETARY POLICY
#### Score: **1**–Stable (very low level of inflation)

From 1993 to 2002, based on data from the International Monetary Fund's 2003 *World Economic Outlook,* Djibouti's weighted average annual rate of inflation was 1.68 percent.

### CAPITAL FLOWS AND FOREIGN INVESTMENT
#### Score: **3**–Stable (moderate barriers)

According to the U.S. Department of State, "The government of Djibouti welcomes all foreign direct investment…. In principle there is no screening of investment or other discriminatory mechanisms. That said, certain sectors, most notably public utilities, are state owned and some parts are not currently open to investors." Investment is inhibited also by numerous administrative difficulties, including what the U.S. Department of State calls "a 'circular dependency' [by which] the Finance Ministry will issue a license only if an investor possesses an approved investor visa, while the Interior Ministry will only issue an investor visa to a licensed business." The International Monetary Fund reports that both residents and non-residents may hold foreign exchange accounts, and there are no restrictions on payments or transfers. Credit transactions, direct investment, and international lending are subject to controls.

### BANKING AND FINANCE
#### Score: **3**–Stable (moderate level of restrictions)

"Djibouti is essentially a city-state," reports the Economist Intelligence Unit, "so there is little banking activity outside the capital." The EIU reports that only three commercial banks operate in the country. The government has a stake in the Banque pour le commerce et l'industrie. Commercial banks provide only short-term financing and lending, which is allocated at market rates.

### WAGES AND PRICES
#### Score: **2**–Stable (low level of intervention)

The market sets wages and prices for most products. The *Addis Tribune* reports that Djibouti maintains fixed prices for chat, fruit, and vegetables imported from Ethiopia. According to the U.S. Department of State, "only the basic commodities such as rice, sugar, and oil have controlled prices." Djibouti maintains a minimum wage.

### PROPERTY RIGHTS
#### Score: **4**–Stable (low level of protection)

Private property rights are weakly protected; the courts are frequently overburdened, and the enforcement of contracts can be time-consuming and cumbersome. "For settlement of disputes," reports the U.S. Department of State, "Djibouti's legal system is based on French law. It is complex and far from transparent. Government interference in the court system is common. Djibouti does have written commercial and bankruptcy laws, but they are not applied consistently." In addition, "While there are laws against corruption, they are rarely enforced, in part because most people prefer to deal with corruption issues on their own rather than involve complicated legal mechanisms."

### REGULATION
#### Score: **4**–Stable (high level)

Djibouti's regulations are both cumbersome and significantly burdensome. The U.S. Agency for International Development reports that "the most recurrent problem mentioned by investors in almost every stage of the investment start-up process is the lack of procedural transparency. There are few formal, written guidelines. The success of many applications and requests hinges on the approval of the Minister responsible for the particular portfolio…. [T]he company registration process is dispersed across several agencies with little or no coordination among them; moreover, there are numerous duplicative requirements among these agencies."

### INFORMAL MARKET
#### Score: **4**–Stable (high level of activity)

Much of Djibouti's economic activity, especially trade in pirated trademarks and computer software, occurs in the informal market. According to the Economist Intelligence Unit, about 25 percent of the labor force works informally. A large share of trade with other countries is also done informally. Laws protecting intellectual property are not adequately enforced.

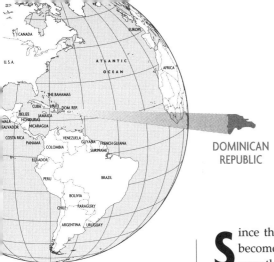

# DOMINICAN REPUBLIC

Rank: 120
Score: 3.51
Category: Mostly Unfree

### Present & Past Scores

(Best) 1
2
3
4
(Worst) 5

3.63  3.39  3.24  3.26  3.20  3.03  3.04  3.19  3.29  3.51

'95  '96  '97  '98  '99  '00  '01  '02  '03  '04

## QUICK STUDY

### SCORES

| | |
|---|---|
| Trade Policy | 5 |
| Fiscal Burden | 3.1 |
| Government Intervention | 1.5 |
| Monetary Policy | 3 |
| Foreign Investment | 3 |
| Banking and Finance | 4 |
| Wages and Prices | 4 |
| Property Rights | 4 |
| Regulation | 4 |
| Informal Market | 3.5 |

**Population:** 8,505,200

**Total area:** 48,730 sq. km

**GDP:** $17.6 billion

**GDP growth rate:** 2.7%

**GDP per capita:** $2,077

**Major exports:** coffee, sugar, tobacco

**Exports of goods and services:** $4.8 billion

**Major export trading partners:** US 86.5%, Netherlands 1.8%, Belgium 1.7%, France 1.2%, Haiti 1.0%

**Major imports:** cotton and fabrics, chemicals, foodstuffs, petroleum

**Imports of goods and services:** $6.2 billion

**Major import trading partners:** US 58.6%, Venezuela 8.5%, Mexico 4.5%, Spain 2.7%

**Foreign direct investment (net):** $1 billion

2001 Data (in constant 1995 US dollars)

Since the allegedly fraudulent elections of 1994, the Dominican Republic has steadily become a more transparent and stable democracy. Its economy has experienced steady growth by relying on tourism, industrial free trade zones, and telecommunications. Protectionism still plagues local businesses and the agricultural sector, although high growth rates have masked these problems over the past decade, and lagging tourism and a major banking scandal are hurting the economy. Without reforms to increase investor confidence, improve competitiveness, and diversify exports, the Dominican Republic will have to wait for a rebound in travel to see new growth. Other problems include a steady influx of Haitian migrants and refugees who must compete with numerous unskilled Dominicans for jobs. Venezuela, which had been the country's chief petroleum supplier, halted deliveries shortly after the Dominican government supported the U.S. decision to send troops to disarm Saddam Hussein in Iraq. Meanwhile, President Hipólito Mejía has been lobbying U.S. officials to have his country included in the U.S.–Central American Free Trade Agreement now under negotiation. The Dominican Republic's fiscal burden of government score is 0.2 point worse this year; in addition, and its banking and finance score and wages and prices score are 1 point worse. As a result, the Dominican Republic's overall score is 0.22 point worse this year.

## TRADE POLICY
### Score: **5**–Stable (very high level of protectionism)

According to the World Bank, the Dominican Republic's weighted average tariff rate in 2000 (the most recent year for which World Bank data are available) was 20.3 percent, up from the 15.8 percent reported in the 2003 *Index*. The U.S. Trade Representative reports that "Import permits are required for most agricultural products.... [T]he current process for granting import licenses appears to be arbitrary." In addition, "Customs Department interpretations often provoke complaints by business persons...." Many appeal to a "negotiated fee" to gain faster customs clearance.

## FISCAL BURDEN OF GOVERNMENT
Score—Income Taxation: **2.5**–Stable (moderate tax rates)
Score—Corporate Taxation: **3**–Stable (moderate tax rates)
Score—Change in Government Expenditures: **4**–Worse (moderate increase)
Final Score: **3.1**–Worse (moderate cost of government)

The Dominican Republic's top income tax rate is 25 percent. The top corporate tax rate is 25 percent. Government expenditures as a share of GDP increased 1.6 percentage points to 16.3 percent in 2001, compared to a decline of 0.1 percentage point in 2000. As a result, the Dominican Republic's fiscal burden of government score is 0.2 point worse this year.

## GOVERNMENT INTERVENTION IN THE ECONOMY
### Score: **1.5**–Stable (low level)

The World Bank reports that the government consumed about 9 percent of GDP in 2001. In 2000, according to the International Monetary Fund, the Dominican Republic received 2.89 percent of its total revenues from state-owned enterprises and government ownership of property.

## MONETARY POLICY
### Score: **3**–Stable (moderate level of inflation)

From 1993 to 2002, the Dominican Republic's weighted average annual rate of inflation was 6.33 percent.

## CAPITAL FLOWS AND FOREIGN INVESTMENT
### Score: **3**–Stable (moderate barriers)

The Dominican Republic has liberalized a portion of its foreign investment policy. There are no limits on foreign control of businesses or screening of foreign investment, but investments must be registered with the Central Bank of the Dominican Republic. The U.S. Department of State reports that foreign investment is permitted in all sectors except the disposal and storage of toxic, hazardous, or radioactive waste; activities affecting public health; activities affecting the country's environmental equilibrium; and activities related to defense and security. According to the U.S. Trade Representative, "Dominican legislation does not contain effective procedures for settling disputes arising from Dominican government actions…. [S]everal investors have outstanding disputes related to expropriated property." The International Monetary Fund reports that both residents and non-residents may hold foreign exchange accounts. Payments and transfers are subject to documentation requirements. Some capital transactions are subject to approval, documentation, or reporting requirements.

## BANKING AND FINANCE
### Score: **4**–Worse (high level of restrictions)

The Economist Intelligence Unit reports that the Dominican Republic's banking system consists of 12 multiple service banks (of which two are foreign-owned), five public banks, and 18 development banks. The government owns the largest bank, Banco de Reservas, and this year nationalized the third largest bank, Baninter. There is evidence that government officials have been receiving illegal payments from Baninter. According to the EIU, "The collapse of Baninter…has provoked public outrage following revelations that many leading politicians have been receiving illicit payments and gifts from the bank during the past three administrations." Based on the government's growing involvement in the banking sector, the Dominican Republic's banking and finance score is 1 point worse this year.

## WAGES AND PRICES
### Score: **4**–Worse (high level of intervention)

The government increasingly interferes with the market's ability to determine prices. Price controls on sugar, petroleum derivatives, cement for construction, staples, and agricultural products remain in effect. Since agriculture and sugar refining are among the most dynamic sectors of the economy, price controls in these areas significantly affect the economy. The government also subsidizes the liquefied natural gas, public transportation, electricity, and retail food sectors to keep these prices artificially low. According to the Economist Intelligence Unit, "the government faces pressures on the spending side as it tries to cushion the impact of price rises on the poor. A number of direct subsidies have been maintained, strengthened or introduced to assist the poorest…." The government also maintains a minimum wage. Based on the increasing evidence of government influence on prices, the Dominican Republic's wages and prices score is 1 point worse this year.

## PROPERTY RIGHTS
### Score: **4**–Stable (low level of protection)

The judiciary is not completely independent. The court system is inefficient, corruption and bureaucratic red tape run high, and the government can expropriate property. Despite recent judicial reforms, according to the U.S. Department of State, "Dominican and foreign business leaders have complained of judicial and administrative corruption, and have charged that corruption affects the settlement of business disputes…. Several foreign firms and individuals have outstanding disputes with the Dominican Government concerning expropriated property or non fulfillment of contractual obligations."

## REGULATION
### Score: **4**–Stable (high level)

Business regulations are still burdensome. The U.S. Department of State reports that "red tape and differences between law and actual practice remain significant problems…. A highly centralized regulatory and administrative system adversely affects the business climate. The interpretation of laws and regulations is often arbitrary. This has contributed to an unstable and capricious regulatory environment. Businesses, domestic as well as foreign, complain that the rules of the game are constantly changing." In addition, "Corruption continues to be a concern among inventors…. [F]irms, bound by the Foreign Corrupt Practices Act, face difficulty in accessing justice within the local system."

## INFORMAL MARKET
### Score: **3.5**–Stable (high level of activity)

Transparency International's 2002 score for the Dominican Republic is 3.5. Therefore, the Dominican Republic's informal market score is 3.5 this year.

# ECUADOR

Rank: 126

Score: 3.60

Category: Mostly Unfree

**Present & Past Scores**

(Best) 1
2
3
4
(Worst) 5

3.39  3.33  3.21  3.10  3.09  3.14  3.51  3.60  3.58  3.60

'95  '96  '97  '98  '99  '00  '01  '02  '03  '04

## QUICK STUDY

### SCORES

| | |
|---|---|
| Trade Policy | 4 |
| Fiscal Burden | 3 |
| Government Intervention | 3 |
| Monetary Policy | 5 |
| Foreign Investment | 3 |
| Banking and Finance | 3 |
| Wages and Prices | 3 |
| Property Rights | 4 |
| Regulation | 4 |
| Informal Market | 4 |

**Population:** 12,879,520

**Total area:** 283,560 sq. km

**GDP:** $19 billion

**GDP growth rate:** 5.6%

**GDP per capita:** $1,478

**Major exports:** bananas, oil, shrimp

**Exports of goods and services:** $5.8 billion

**Major export trading partners:** US 38.3%, Peru 7.3%, Colombia 7.0%, Italy 4.3%, Venezuela 3.6%

**Major imports:** raw materials, machinery and equipment, fuel, consumer goods

**Imports of goods and services:** $5.4 billion

**Major import trading partners:** US 24.7%, Colombia 14.4%, Japan 6.6%, Venezuela 5.5%, Chile 5.0%

**Foreign direct investment (net):** $1.2 billion

2001 Data (in constant 1995 US dollars)

Lucio Gutierrez, the former army colonel who led a brief coup against the government of President Jamil Mahuad in January 2000, was elected president of Ecuador on November 24, 2002. Backed mainly by indigenous groups, Gutierrez embraced populist policies and vowed to fight poverty and corruption. Although he had no previous political or economic experience, he set to work calming international financial institutions by maintaining the successful dollarization and market reforms of his immediate predecessor, President Gustavo Noboa, in paying off debts and avoiding reckless spending. Initially ambivalent about helping in the U.S.-backed Andean counternarcotics effort, President Gutierrez agreed to allow continued U.S. military use of the Manta airbase for counternarcotics operations. He is, however, skating on thin ice. Needed market reforms to spur growth and make Ecuador more competitive run counter to the politics of his narrow support base, which continues to believe in subsidies and price controls to provide a small measure of support for the nation's majority poor. Ecuador's fiscal burden of government score is 0.2 point worse this year. As a result, its overall score is 0.02 point worse this year.

## TRADE POLICY

### Score: **4**–Stable (high level of protectionism)

According to the World Bank, Ecuador's weighted average tariff rate in 1999 (the most recent year for which World Bank data are available) was 11.3 percent. The U.S. Trade Representative reports that "prior authorization for certain goods is required before the Central Bank can issue an import license. Importers must also obtain authorization from Ecuador's Internal Revenue Service for tax and tariff purposes.... Agriculture often denies the issuance of import permits in order to protect local producers."

## FISCAL BURDEN OF GOVERNMENT

Score—Income Taxation: **2.5**–Stable (moderate tax rates)
Score—Corporate Taxation: **3**–Stable (moderate tax rates)
Score—Change in Government Expenditures: **3.5**–Worse (low increase)
### Final Score: **3**–Worse (moderate cost of government)

Ecuador's top income tax rate is 25 percent. The top corporate tax rate is 25 percent. Government expenditures as a share of GDP increased 0.3 percentage point to 22.1 percent in 2001, compared to a decline of 1.2 percentage points in 2000. As a result, Ecuador's fiscal burden of government score is 0.2 point worse this year.

## GOVERNMENT INTERVENTION IN THE ECONOMY

### Score: **3**–Stable (moderate level)

The World Bank reports that the government consumed 10 percent of GDP in 2001. According to the Economist Intelligence Unit, "the state participates in about 190 companies in agriculture, communications, energy, finance, industry, mining, storage, transport and tourism." Among these companies are Andinatel and Pacifitel (telecommunications); Electroguayas, Hidroagoyan, Hidropucara, Termoesmeraldas and Termopichincha (electricity generating); Transelectric (electricity transmission); and Petroecuador (oil).

## MONETARY POLICY
### Score: **5**–Stable (very high level of inflation)

From 1993 to 2002, Ecuador's weighted average annual rate of inflation was 27.13 percent.

## CAPITAL FLOWS AND FOREIGN INVESTMENT
### Score: **3**–Stable (moderate barriers)

Ecuador grants foreign firms national treatment; however, according to the Economist Intelligence Unit, foreign investors have been deterred by "shifting legal regimes, especially frequent changes to tax law, the idiosyncratic nature of Ecuador's market and, until recently, the lack of access to majority stakes in state companies." In March 2002, Ecuador increased the maximum stake that foreign investors could acquire in the privatization of state-owned enterprises from 35 percent to 51 percent. Prior authorization is required for investment in fishing and industries considered vital to national security, and investment in radio and television broadcasting is restricted. The U.S. Department of State reports that investments in the oil sector must be conducted with the state-owned oil company. The International Monetary Fund reports that both residents and non-residents may hold foreign exchange accounts. Payments and transfers are largely unrestricted. Capital and money market transactions are subject to controls, and all foreign loans to or guaranteed by the government must be approved by the central bank.

## BANKING AND FINANCE
### Score: **3**–Stable (moderate level of restrictions)

The financial crisis in late 1998 and 1999 led to a government takeover of most commercial banks and a freeze on bank deposits. As of October 2002, according to the Economist Intelligence Unit, the government controlled 8.87 percent of total bank assets. Only one bank taken over by the government (Pacifico) still operates; the others have been closed, and the government is in the process of paying off account holders. The EIU reports that although the government has reimbursed 90 percent of deposits, US$137 million in deposits were still frozen as of mid-2002. All new banks are required to meet higher capital standards. The state retains significant influence over the financial sector, but it appears that the financial crisis has been largely resolved.

## WAGES AND PRICES
### Score: **3**–Stable (moderate level of intervention)

The government sets some prices. According to the Economist Intelligence Unit, this includes a freeze on electricity, cooking gas, and telephone rates in 2002 and subsidies for public transportation. "In general," reports the EIU, "the government does not have a policy of fixing prices. However, bananas, coffee, cocoa, pharmaceuticals and fuels are exceptions to the rule." Since coffee, bananas, and cocoa comprise a large portion of the country's output, controls on these products have a significant effect on the economy. The gov-

ernment periodically sets the minimum wage after consulting with the Commission on Salaries, but the Congress also has the authority to amend the minimum wage.

## PROPERTY RIGHTS
### Score: **4**–Stable (low level of protection)

The rule of law in Ecuador is weak and does not adequately protect private property rights. The Economist Intelligence Unit reports that Ecuador's "judiciary is highly politicized and bribery is a major problem. The court system is opaque and legal procedures are slow. Property rights are protected by legislation but enforcement is weak." In addition, "the legal system is severely under-funded, and inefficient and corrupt at every level. At the lower levels, judges are widely perceived to be susceptible to bribery. The higher courts are politicized and sometimes biased against foreign investors."

## REGULATION
### Score: **4**–Stable (high level)

According to the Economist Intelligence Unit, "The civil service is renowned for slowing investment decisions with needless bureaucracy. Though efforts have been made to reduce size, cost and corruption at higher levels, the bureaucracy is still complex, much larger than necessary and often inefficient." The U.S. Department of State reports that "Ecuador has laws and regulations to combat official corruption, but they are rarely enforced. Illicit payments for official favors and theft of public funds take place frequently." In addition, reports the EIU, "the labor market remains relatively rigid."

## INFORMAL MARKET
### Score: **4**–Stable (high level of activity)

Transparency International's 2001 score for Ecuador is 2.2. Therefore, Ecuador's informal market score is 4 this year.

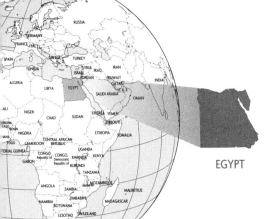

EGYPT

# EGYPT

Rank: 95

Score: 3.28

Category: Mostly Unfree

Present & Past Scores

(Best) 1
2
3
4
(Worst) 5

3.69 3.40 3.49 3.31 3.35 3.58 3.53 3.53 3.39 3.28

'95 '96 '97 '98 '99 '00 '01 '02 '03 '04

With a population of 65 million, Egypt is the largest Arab country and has long played a leading role in Middle Eastern affairs. Under the cautious leadership of President Hosni Mubarak, the government has implemented incremental economic reforms to renovate the inefficient socialist economic system built up by the regime of Gamal Abdel Nasser in the 1950s and 1960s without at the same time jeopardizing future political stability. Overall, economic reform has taken a back seat to social concerns such as stemming unemployment and maintaining subsidies on food, energy, and other key commodities to maintain a social safety net for Egypt's large mass of poor people. In recent years, the pace of economic reform has slowed and little progress has been made in privatizing or streamlining the swollen public sector. Political stability has been enhanced by the government's success in containing the radical Islamic movements that threatened the country with persistent terrorism in the early 1990s. Egypt's economy, the second largest in the Arab world after Saudi Arabia's, has been hurt by the post–September 11 downturn in foreign tourism, Suez Canal tolls, and exports, but the development of a natural gas export market and the beginning of gas exports to Jordan should encourage future growth. In January 2003, the Mubarak government dropped the pegged exchange rate and floated the Egyptian pound. Egypt's fiscal burden of government score is 0.1 point better this year, and its government intervention score is 1 point better. As a result, Egypt's overall score is 0.11 point better this year.

## TRADE POLICY
### Score: **4**–Stable (high level of protectionism)

According to the World Bank, Egypt's weighted average tariff rate in 1998 (the most recent year for which World Bank data are available) was 13.8 percent. The U.S. Trade Representative reports that the main non-tariff barriers include mandatory quality control standards, burdensome import license requirements, and non-transparent sanitary and phytosanitary measures. According to the U.S. Department of State, "Customs procedures are subjective when it comes to identifying whether a commodity fits in one tariff category or another."

## FISCAL BURDEN OF GOVERNMENT
Score—Income Taxation: **4**–Stable (high tax rates)
Score—Corporate Taxation: **5**–Stable (very high tax rates)
Score—Change in Government Expenditures: **3**–Better (very low decrease)
### Final Score: **4.3**–Better (high cost of government)

Egypt's top income tax rate is 40 percent. The corporate tax rate is 40 percent. Government expenditures as a share of GDP decreased 0.1 percentage point to 30 percent in 2001, compared to a 0.3 percentage point increase in 2000. As a result, Egypt's fiscal burden of government score is 0.1 point better this year.

## GOVERNMENT INTERVENTION IN THE ECONOMY
### Score: **3**–Better (moderate level)

The World Bank reports that the government consumed 11.9 percent of GDP in 2001. In the 2002–2003 fiscal year, based on data from the Economist Intelligence Unit, Egypt received

12.02 percent of its total revenues from state-owned enterprises and government ownership of property. Based on a new methodology used to analyze this factor, Egypt's government intervention score is 1 point better this year.

## MONETARY POLICY
### Score: **1**–Stable (very low level of inflation)

From 1993 to 2002, Egypt's weighted average annual rate of inflation was 2.68 percent.

## CAPITAL FLOWS AND FOREIGN INVESTMENT
### Score: **3**–Stable (moderate barriers)

A revised investment law has eliminated pre-incorporation approval and replaced it with a notification requirement for statistical purposes. The U.S. Department of State reports that the investment law "is designed to allocate investment to targeted economic sectors and to promote decentralization of industry from the crowded geographical area of the Nile Valley…. [The law] allows 100% foreign ownership and guarantees the right to remit income earned in Egypt and to repatriate capital. Other key provisions include: guarantees against confiscation, sequestration and nationalization; the right to own land; the right to maintain foreign currency bank accounts; freedom from administrative attachment; the right to repatriate capital and profits; and equal treatment regardless of nationality." Approval is nearly automatic for specified sectors. According to the Economist Intelligence Unit, however, "FDI fell from more than US$1bn in 1998–2000, to about US$500m in 2001 owing to…underlying constraints of stifling bureaucracy." Foreigners may not own agricultural land, and prior approval from the cabinet is required for investment in military production and in the Sinai region. The International Monetary Fund reports that both residents and non-residents may hold foreign exchange accounts. There are no restrictions on payments and transfers. The Capital Market Authority must approve bond issues.

## BANKING AND FINANCE
### Score: **4**–Stable (high level of restrictions)

Although the private sector is increasing its market share, four state-owned banks still dominate Egypt's banking sector, accounting for approximately 57 percent of total bank assets, 70 percent of deposits, and 59 percent of loans. According to the Economist Intelligence Unit, "State banks generally suffer from low capitalization, a high percentage of poorly performing loans (extended not just to public enterprises but also to well-connected individuals), massive overstaffing and stifling bureaucracy." Four majority foreign-owned insurance companies now operate in Egypt, according to the U.S. Department of State. The Egyptian Parliament has approved a new law permitting 100 percent ownership for foreign insurance companies and authorizing privatization of state-owned insurance companies.

## WAGES AND PRICES
### Score: **3**–Stable (moderate level of intervention)

Price controls on most goods have been removed. According to the Economist Intelligence Unit, the elimination of price controls and subsidies "has been achieved in many sectors, with the notable exceptions of energy (including fuel), transport, medicine, and some basic foods. Energy prices are about 20% below international levels, though the government has committed itself to eliminating the implicit energy subsidy on petroleum products and raising natural gas and electricity tariffs to their long-run marginal cost." The government sets a national minimum wage.

## PROPERTY RIGHTS
### Score: **3**–Stable (moderate level of protection)

Although private property is protected by the constitution, the legal code is complex and can create delays. The Economist Intelligence Unit reports that "a commercial case takes, on average, six years to be decided, and appeal procedures can extend the court cases beyond 15 years…. Nevertheless, local contractual arrangements are generally secure." According to the U.S. Department of State, "The Egyptian legal system provides protection for real and personal property, but laws on real estate ownership are complex and titles to real property may be difficult to establish and trace. The government is moving slowly to modernize the laws on real estate ownership and tenancy."

## REGULATION
### Score: **4**–Stable (high level)

According to the U.S. Department of State, "Red tape remains a business impediment in Egypt, including a multiplicity of regulations and regulatory agencies, delays in clearing goods through customs, arbitrary decision-making, high market entry transaction costs, and a generally unresponsive commercial court system." Businesses report corruption among lower-level government officials. In April 2003, reports the Economist Intelligence Unit, the Parliament approved a new labor law under which "employers can more easily terminate workers' contracts within a notice period that depends on the employee's length of service…. The new law also provides more generous holiday, sickness and pilgrimage provisions…."

## INFORMAL MARKET
### Score: **3.5**–Stable (high level of activity)

Transparency International's 2002 score for Egypt is 3.4. Therefore, Egypt's informal market score is 3.5 this year.

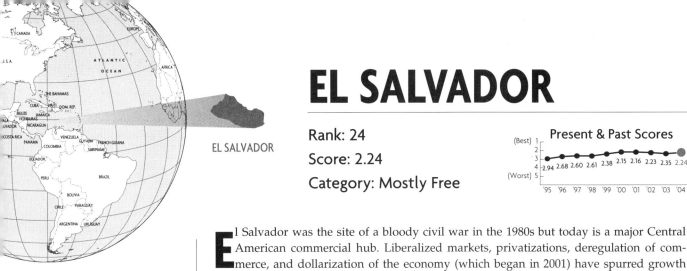

# EL SALVADOR

EL SALVADOR

Rank: 24
Score: 2.24
Category: Mostly Free

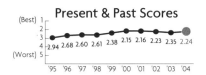

Present & Past Scores

(Best) 1
2
3
4
(Worst) 5

-2.94  2.68  2.60  2.61  2.38  2.15  2.16  2.23  2.35  2.24

'95  '96  '97  '98  '99  '00  '01  '02  '03  '04

## QUICK STUDY

### SCORES

| | |
|---|---|
| Trade Policy | 2 |
| Fiscal Burden | 3.4 |
| Government Intervention | 1.5 |
| Monetary Policy | 1 |
| Foreign Investment | 2 |
| Banking and Finance | 2 |
| Wages and Prices | 2 |
| Property Rights | 3 |
| Regulation | 2 |
| Informal Market | 3.5 |

**Population:** 6,399,470

**Total area:** 21,040 sq. km

**GDP:** $11.2 billion

**GDP growth rate:** 2.0%

**GDP per capita:** $1,757

**Major exports:** coffee, sugar, shrimp

**Exports of goods and services:** $4.3 billion

**Major export trading partners:** US 65.4%, Guatemala 11.5%, Costa Rica 3.3%, Germany 1.7%

**Major imports:** raw materials, consumer goods, capital goods, petroleum, foodstuffs

**Imports of goods and services:** $5.2 billion

**Major import trading partners:** US 49.0%, Guatemala 8.7%, Mexico 6.2%, Japan 2.5%

**Foreign direct investment (net):** $249.3 million

2001 Data (in constant 1995 US dollars)

El Salvador was the site of a bloody civil war in the 1980s but today is a major Central American commercial hub. Liberalized markets, privatizations, deregulation of commerce, and dollarization of the economy (which began in 2001) have spurred growth and kept inflation low despite devastating earthquakes and harsh cycles of rain and drought. Official unemployment hovers about 6.5 percent, and 37 percent of the population lives below the poverty level compared to 80 percent in Venezuela. The availability of credit for consumers was already growing before 2001, but dollarization and the availability of cheaper international financing have helped to lower interest rates. Monthly remittances from Salvadorans living in the United States continue to pour into the central bank at about $150 million a month, according to the U.S. Department of State. Along with maquila exports, it is the largest source of foreign exchange. Problems remain, however. Although there are no more politically motivated killings and disappearances, Colombian drug mafias have invaded Central America, overwhelming El Salvador's still numerically inadequate police force. The justice system functions slowly, and money from powerful oligarchs still corrupts judges. The coffee industry, which accounts for most of the country's agricultural exports, has been battered by low prices generated by an oversupply of lower-quality beans flooding the market from other parts of the world. The industry lost an estimated 40,000 jobs in 2002. Construction to remedy earthquake damage and expand needed infrastructure will require additional international financing. El Salvador's fiscal burden of government score is 0.4 point worse this year; however, its government intervention score is 0.5 point better, and its monetary policy score is 1 point better. As a result, El Salvador's overall score is 0.11 point better this year.

###  TRADE POLICY
#### Score: **2**–Stable (low level of protectionism)

According to the World Bank, El Salvador's weighted average tariff rate in 2001 (the most recent year for which World Bank data are available) was 6.4 percent. Non-tariff barriers are almost nonexistent.

###  FISCAL BURDEN OF GOVERNMENT
#### Score—Income Taxation: **3**–Stable (moderate tax rates)
#### Score—Corporate Taxation: **3**–Stable (moderate tax rates)
#### Score—Change in Government Expenditures: **4.5**–Worse (high increase)
### Final Score: **3.4**–Worse (moderate cost of government)

According to the Embassy of El Salvador, the top income tax rate is 30 percent. The top corporate income tax rate is 25 percent. Government expenditures as a share of GDP increased 2.4 percentage points to 17.6 percent in 2002, compared to a 0.1 percentage point decrease in 2001. As a result, El Salvador's fiscal burden of government score is 0.4 point worse this year.

###  GOVERNMENT INTERVENTION IN THE ECONOMY
#### Score: **1.5**–Better (low level)

The World Bank reports that the government consumed 10 percent of GDP in 2001, down from the 10.2 percent reported in the 2003 *Index*. As a result, El Salvador's government intervention score is 0.5 point better this year. In the same year, according to the International

Monetary Fund, El Salvador received 1.78 percent of its total revenues from state-owned enterprises and government ownership of property.

## MONETARY POLICY
### Score: **1–Better** (very low level of inflation)

From 1993 to 2002, El Salvador's weighted average annual rate of inflation was 2.34 percent., down from the 3.14 percent from 1992 to 2001 reported in the 2003 *Index*. As a result, El Salvador's monetary policy score is 1 point better this year.

## CAPITAL FLOWS AND FOREIGN INVESTMENT
### Score: **2–Stable** (low barriers)

El Salvador maintains a very open foreign investment climate. Under the 1999 Investment Law, foreign investors receive equal treatment. The International Monetary Fund reports that the government limits foreign direct investment in commerce, industry, certain services, and fishing; investments in railroads, piers, and canals require government approval. Foreign investors may own no more than 49 percent equity stakes in television and radio broadcasting. According to the Economist Intelligence Unit, "The main constraints on growth in foreign investment are high crime levels, an inefficient judiciary, and declining wage and export competitiveness." There are no controls or requirements on current transfers, purchase of real estate, or access to foreign exchange.

## BANKING AND FINANCE
### Score: **2–Stable** (low level of restrictions)

Foreign banks can operate on the same basis as domestic banks under a modern banking law passed in 1999. Most local and foreign banks are allowed to offer a wide range of financial services. Regulations on opening branches of foreign banks are open and transparent. There are 13 banks and one non-bank financial institution, two of which are state-owned. Market forces determine interest rates. The Monetary Integration Law converted all financial system assets, liabilities, and operations to U.S. dollars on January 1, 2001.

## WAGES AND PRICES
### Score: **2–Stable** (low level of intervention)

Most prices are determined by the market. The government maintains price controls on liquid propane gas, public transportation, electricity, and telephone services. The Economist Intelligence Unit reports that the government liberalized the price of gasoline in 2001. El Salvador has a minimum wage.

## PROPERTY RIGHTS
### Score: **3–Stable** (moderate level of protection)

Property rights are not well-protected in El Salvador. According to the U.S. Department of State, "the Constitution provides for an independent judiciary and the Government respects this provision in practice. However, the judiciary suffers from inefficiency and corruption." In addition, "A purge of the judicial system is getting underway and some corrupt judges and administrators have been removed from their posts. However, investors must be aware that the legal and regulatory system can act arbitrarily, and should take all due precautions to protect their property and investments." According to the Economist Intelligence Unit, two of the "main constraints on growth in foreign investment are high crime levels [and] an inefficient judiciary…."

## REGULATION
### Score: **2–Stable** (low level)

El Salvador has made significant progress in reducing onerous regulations. According to the U.S. Department of State, "the laws and policies of El Salvador are relatively transparent and generally foster competition." The labor law requires that 90 percent of the labor force at plants and in clerical jobs be composed of Salvadorans, but foreigners may hold professional and technical positions. New business projects need to submit environmental impact studies to obtain a license. The U.S. Department of State reports that "bureaucratic procedures have improved in recent years and are relatively streamlined for foreign investors."

## INFORMAL MARKET
### Score: **3.5–Stable** (high level of activity)

Transparency International's 2002 score for El Salvador is 3.4. Therefore, El Salvador's informal market score is 3.5 this year.

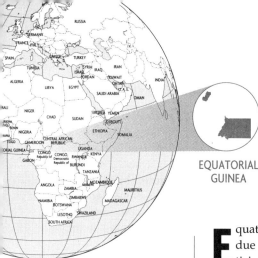

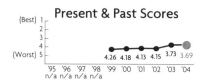

# EQUATORIAL GUINEA

EQUATORIAL GUINEA

Rank: 130
Score: 3.69
Category: Mostly Unfree

**Present & Past Scores**

(Best) 1
2
3
4
(Worst) 5

4.26  4.18  4.13  4.15  3.73  3.69
'95  '96  '97  '98  '99  '00  '01  '02  '03  '04
n/a n/a n/a n/a

## QUICK STUDY

### SCORES

| | |
|---|---|
| Trade Policy | 5 |
| Fiscal Burden | 2.9 |
| Government Intervention | 2 |
| Monetary Policy | 3 |
| Foreign Investment | 3 |
| Banking and Finance | 4 |
| Wages and Prices | 4 |
| Property Rights | 4 |
| Regulation | 4 |
| Informal Market | 5 |

**Population:** 469,088

**Total area:** 28,051 sq. km

**GDP:** $740 million

**GDP growth rate:** 1.3%

**GDP per capita:** $1,578

**Major exports:** petroleum, timber, cocoa

**Exports of goods and services:** $723.3 million

**Major export trading partners:** Spain 31.9%, China 27.5%, US 25.8%, France 2.1%

**Major imports:** manufactured goods and equipment

**Imports of goods and services:** $373.4 million

**Major import trading partners:** US 27.7%, Spain 15.4%, UK 12.3%, France 8.8%

**Foreign direct investment (net):** $78 million

2001 Data (in constant 1995 US dollars)

Equatorial Guinea's economy is dominated by corruption and oil. Recent GDP growth is due to investment in the oil sector, and the government's priority is to expand its participation. "As the government will be focused on the oil sector," reports the Economist Intelligence Unit, "there will be little urgency in other policy areas, such as the modernization of agriculture, the reform of the budgetary process and improved governance, demands made by the IMF in 2002 as a condition for the resumption of a formal lending agreement." The U.S. Department of State notes that "investment and other use of oil revenues lacked transparency despite repeated calls from international financial institutions and citizens for greater financial openness." Some countries have halted foreign aid because of the lack of transparency and lack of economic reform. Corruption pervades the country. According to an EIU report, the United Nations continues to criticize the judicial system as nepotistic, corrupt, and incompetent. Equatorial Guinea desperately needs transparency in its political process as well. The fairness of the December 2002 presidential election, in which Teodoro Obiang Nguema Mbasago won 97 percent of the votes, has been questioned. Obiang has been in office since 1979, when he seized power in a coup, and two of his sons are government ministers. Equatorial Guinea's fiscal burden of government score is 0.6 point worse this year, but its government intervention score is 1 point better. As a result, Equatorial Guinea's overall score is 0.04 point better this year.

###  TRADE POLICY
### Score: **5**–Stable (very high level of protectionism)

Equatorial Guinea is a member of the Central African Economic and Monetary Community (CEMAC), which also includes Cameroon, the Central African Republic, Chad, the Republic of Congo, and Gabon. In 2001, reports the U.S. Trade Representative, CEMAC applied a common average external tariff of 18.4 percent. According to the U.S. Department of State, "Customs fraud is endemic in Equatorial Guinea and protracted negotiations with customs officers over the value of imported goods are common."

###  FISCAL BURDEN OF GOVERNMENT
Score—Income Taxation: **2**–Stable (low tax rates)
Score—Corporate Taxation: **3**–Stable (moderate tax rates)
Score—Change in Government Expenditures: **3.5**–Worse (low increase)
### Final Score: **2.9**–Worse (moderate cost of government)

Equatorial Guinea's top income tax rate is 20 percent. The top corporate tax rate is 25 percent. Government expenditures as a share of GDP increased 0.3 percentage point to 10.8 percent in 2001, compared to a 7 percentage point decrease in 2000. As a result, Equatorial Guinea's fiscal burden of government score is 0.6 point worse this year.

###  GOVERNMENT INTERVENTION IN THE ECONOMY
### Score: **2**–Better (low level)

The Economist Intelligence Unit reports that the government consumed 3 percent of GDP in 2001, down from the 6.7 percent reported in the 2003 *Index.* As a result, Equatorial Guinea's government intervention score is 1 point better this year. According to the U.S. Department of State, the government plays an active role in the oil sector, awards licenses for exploration and extraction of oil to the private sector, and created a state-owned oil company in 2001 to take advantage of the country's large oil resources.

## MONETARY POLICY
### Score: **3**–Stable (moderate level of inflation)

Data from the International Monetary Fund's *2003 World Economic Outlook* indicate that from 1993 to 2002, Equatorial Guinea's weighted average annual rate of inflation was 9.81 percent. Equatorial Guinea has benefited from a stable currency—a rarity in sub-Saharan Africa—as a member of the CFA franc zone. Fourteen countries use the CFA franc, a common currency with a fixed parity with the euro. (The other 13 countries are Benin, Burkina Faso, Cameroon, Central African Republic, Chad, Congo [Brazzaville], Gabon, Guinea–Bissau, Ivory Coast, Mali, Niger, Senegal, and Togo.)

## CAPITAL FLOWS AND FOREIGN INVESTMENT
### Score: **3**–Stable (moderate barriers)

According to the U.S. Department of State, the law governing investments imposes "minimal eligibility and performance requirements and no time limitations…. Foreign investment is not screened, and foreign equity ownership is not subject to limitation, although additional advantages can be gained by having a national majority partner." Lack of transparency, bureaucratic red tape, and corruption impede investment. Foreign investment is not permitted in the manufacture of arms, explosives, or other weapons; collection, treatment, and storing of toxic or dangerous materials and waste; or production of alcoholic beverages aside from beer. The International Monetary Fund reports that both residents and non-residents may hold foreign exchange accounts, but approval is required, except for accounts in euros. Capital transactions, payments, and transfers to countries other than France, Monaco, members of the CEMAC, members of the West African Economic and Monetary Union, and Comoros are subject to exchange control approval, government approval, and quantitative limits in some cases.

## BANKING AND FINANCE
### Score: **4**–Stable (high level of restrictions)

The Banque Centrale des Etats de l'Afrique Centrale has acted as Equatorial Guinea's central bank since the country joined the franc zone in 1985, and the Economist Intelligence Unit reports that the banking sector "is adequately supervised by the Commission bancaire de l'Afrique centrale (Cobac, the regional banking commission)." According to the U.S. Department of State, "Of the thirty banks operating in Central Africa, two work in Equatorial Guinea. Both operate only two branches in the country…." These two banks are the only commercial banks, and the government has a minority ownership stake in one of them.

## WAGES AND PRICES
### Score: **4**–Stable (high level of intervention)

The Economist Intelligence Unit reports that in January 2002, the commerce minister announced "a new regime of fixed prices. Items covered include tinned sardines, meat, powdered milk, sugar, cooking oil, rice, matches, medicines, construction materials, agricultural products and school books." In 2001, the government created a three-tiered system that sets minimum wages for foreign energy companies, private-sector companies outside the energy sector, and the government and all other firms.

## PROPERTY RIGHTS
### Score: **4**–Stable (low level of protection)

Government corruption, an inefficient judiciary, and poor law enforcement prevent legal protection of private property. According to the U.S. Department of State, "Judges serve at the pleasure of the President, and they are appointed, transferred, and dismissed for political reasons. Corruption is widespread." Equatorial Guinea recently became a member of OHADA (Organisation pour l'Harmonisation du Droit des Affaires en Afrique), a regional organization that focuses primarily on training judges and lawyers in commercial law to help reform the protection of property and enforcement of contracts in member countries.

## REGULATION
### Score: **4**–Stable (high level)

The regulatory structure in Equatorial Guinea imposes a great burden on business. According to the U.S. Department of State, "the lack of respect for the rule of law and corruption on the part of GREG [Equato-Guinean government] officials have retarded the development of open commercial activities and impeded the conduct of normal business relations." In addition, "While business laws promote a liberalized economy, the business climate remains very difficult. Application of the laws remains selective. Corruption among officials is widespread, and many business deals are concluded under non-transparent circumstances."

## INFORMAL MARKET
### Score: **5**–Stable (very high level of activity)

Recent reports indicate that the informal market, especially in labor, is huge. According to Inter Press Services, Equatorial Guinea is a transit point for the smuggling of children into Ivory Coast, Gabon, and Nigeria, where they are employed in farming and street vending. The government offers no protection for intellectual property rights.

ESTONIA

# ESTONIA

Rank: 6

Score: 1.76

Category: Free

**Present & Past Scores**

(Best) 1
2
3
4
(Worst) 5

2.40 2.44 2.46 2.43 2.29 2.19 1.89 1.73 1.68 1.76

'95 '96 '97 '98 '99 '00 '01 '02 '03 '04

## QUICK STUDY

### SCORES

| | |
|---|---|
| Trade Policy | 1 |
| Fiscal Burden | 2.1 |
| Government Intervention | 2 |
| Monetary Policy | 2 |
| Foreign Investment | 1 |
| Banking and Finance | 1 |
| Wages and Prices | 2 |
| Property Rights | 2 |
| Regulation | 2 |
| Informal Market | 2.5 |

**Population:** 1,358,500

**Total area:** 45,227 sq. km

**GDP:** $6.8 billion

**GDP growth rate:** 5.8%

**GDP per capita:** $4,984

**Major exports:** machinery and equipment, wood and paper, clothing and footwear, transportation, travel services, computer and information

**Exports of goods and services:** $5.4 billion

**Major export trading partners:** Finland 24.8%, Sweden 15.3%, Germany 9.9%, Latvia 7.4%

**Major imports:** machinery and equipment, chemicals, transport equipment, financial services

**Imports of goods and services:** $6.5 billion

**Major import trading partners:** Finland 17.1%, Germany 11.2%, Sweden 9.5%, Russia 7.4%

**Foreign direct investment (net):** $168.4 million

2002 Data (in constant 1995 US dollars)

The rapid and decisive reform begun after the dissolution of the Soviet Union and the regaining of independence in 1991 has allowed Estonia to achieve one of Eastern Europe's most free-market–oriented economies. Tight budgetary policies, foreign trade liberalization, and extensive privatization are the core of structural reform. The government also lifted import tariffs, introduced a flat tax on corporate profits and personal income, and exempted the undistributed profits of companies from income tax as of the end of 1999. Since 1992, Estonia has followed a Currency Board Arrangement (CBA), with the kroon now pegged to the euro. The monetary base is fully backed by foreign exchange reserves. Estonia's three largest banks, which account for 90 percent of total assets, are fully owned by foreigners. Economic development is closely tied to the European Union, especially Sweden and Finland, which together account for more than 50 percent of Estonia's exports. Estonia has closed negotiations on 27 out of 31 chapters of EU law and hopes to join the EU in 2004. The economy continues to grow: GDP increased by 6.4 percent in 2000 and 5.4 percent in 2001. Today, Estonia has the most advanced information infrastructure among the formerly communist Eastern European states. Arnold Ruutel was elected President on September 21, 2001, for a five-year term. On January 28, 2002, the Reform Party and the Center Party formed a new coalition government; and in April 2003, Juhan Parts was elected the new prime minister. Estonia's government intervention score is 0.5 point better this year; however, its fiscal burden of government score is 0.3 point worse, and its wages and prices score is 1 point worse. As a result, Estonia's overall score is 0.08 point worse this year.

 **TRADE POLICY**
Score: **1**–Stable (very low level of protectionism)

According to the World Bank, Estonia's weighted average tariff rate in 1995 (the most recent year for which World Bank data are available) was 0.4 percent. The Embassy of Estonia reports that the weighted average tariff rate in 2002 was 0.053 percent. Non-tariff barriers are virtually nonexistent.

 **FISCAL BURDEN OF GOVERNMENT**
Score—Income Taxation: **2.5**–Stable (moderate tax rates)
Score—Corporate Taxation: **1**–Stable (very low tax rates)
Score—Change in Government Expenditures: **4**–Worse (moderate increase)
Final Score: **2.1**–Worse (low cost of government)

Estonia has a flat income tax rate of 26 percent, which the government intends to reduce to 20 percent by 2006. The corporate tax on reinvested profits is 0 percent. Based on data from the Ministry of Finance and Estonia's Statistical Office, government expenditures as a share of GDP increased 1.2 percentage points to 38.5 percent in 2002, compared to a 1.2 percentage point decrease the previous year. As a result, Estonia's fiscal burden of government score is 0.3 point worse this year.

 **GOVERNMENT INTERVENTION IN THE ECONOMY**
Score: **2**–Better (low level)

Based on data from the International Monetary Fund, the government consumed 20 percent of GDP in 2002, down from the 20.7 percent reported in the 2003 Index. As a result, Estonia's

175

government intervention score is 0.5 point better this year. The IMF reports that in 2001, Estonia received 3.07 percent of its total revenues from state-owned enterprises and government ownership of property.

## MONETARY POLICY
### Score: **2**–Stable (low level of inflation)

From 1993 to 2002, Estonia's weighted average annual rate of inflation was 4.25 percent. Estonia's success in bringing inflation down from the high rates experienced in the early 1990s is a direct result of the country's currency board, which restricts the government's ability to print money.

## CAPITAL FLOWS AND FOREIGN INVESTMENT
### Score: **1**–Stable (very low barriers)

Estonia is open to foreign investment, and foreign investors receive national treatment. The government allows foreigners to invest in all sectors, with requirements restricted to nondiscriminatory regulation and documentation to establish clear ownership. The International Monetary Fund reports that Estonia limits foreign capital in the aviation and maritime sectors to 49 percent but that this restriction will be eliminated upon Estonia's accession to the EU, currently scheduled for May 1, 2004. There are no exchange controls and no repatriation limitations that force investors to keep their capital in the country. Foreigners may own real estate. The government requires licenses for investment in banking, mining, gas and water supply or related structures, railroads and transport, energy, and communications networks, but this requirement does not restrict investment and is applied in a routine, evenhanded manner.

## BANKING AND FINANCE
### Score: **1**–Stable (very low level of restrictions)

Estonia has a sound, prudently regulated banking sector that is considered the strongest and most developed in the Baltic States. Its universal banking system allows banks to engage in a wide range of financial activities, including insurance, leasing, and brokerage services. The government welcomes foreign participation in the banking sector, which is currently dominated by foreign banks. The U.S. Department of State reports that "Estonia's financial sector is modern and efficient. Credit is allocated on market terms and foreign investors are able to obtain credit on the local market…."

## WAGES AND PRICES
### Score: **2**–Worse (low level of intervention)

The market determines most wages and prices. However, the Economist Intelligence Unit reports that "the prices of power (electricity and gas), heating, water, public transport, postage, tobacco, and some housing rents are administered. Most administered prices have been raised in recent years to ensure that costs are recovered." According to the Embassy of Estonia, prices representing 24.9 percent of the goods and services in the consumer price index are administratively controlled. In preparation for membership in the European Union, Estonia signed an agreement in 2001 to boost the minimum wage from the current 32 percent of average gross wages to 41 percent of gross wages by 2008. Only 5 percent to 6 percent of the workforce is affected by the minimum wage. Based on the evidence that the government controls some prices, Estonia's wages and prices score is 1 point worse this year.

## PROPERTY RIGHTS
### Score: **2**–Stable (high level of protection)

Estonia has made significant progress toward establishing an independent judiciary and protecting private property rights. The U.S. Department of State reports that "Estonia's efforts to create a modern, western legal system from the remnants of the Soviet system is a work in progress.… Estonia's judiciary is independent and insulated from government influence. Property rights and contracts are enforced by the courts. In increasingly infrequent instances, judicial decisions in these and other matters can be arbitrary and indifferent to the law…." In October 2002, reports the Economist Intelligence Unit, "the European Commission commended Estonia's improvements in training the judiciary and reorganizing the courts."

## REGULATION
### Score: **2**–Stable (low level)

Regulations in Estonia are transparent and evenly applied. Businesses face some bureaucratic hurdles, but overall, procedures are far simpler than in other countries in the region. According to the U.S. Department of State, "The Government has set out transparent policies and effective laws to foster competition and establish clear 'rules of the game.' However, due to the small size of Estonia's commercial community, instances of favoritism are not uncommon despite the regulations and procedures that are designed to limit it." The Estonian Embassy reports that it takes about 30 days to obtain a permit to start a business and that some specific activities, such as mining, public utilities, production of alcohol and tobacco, gambling, and banking, require a license. The U.S. Department of State reports that "surveys of American and other non-Estonian businesses have shown the issues of corruption and/or protection rackets are not an important concern for these companies."

## INFORMAL MARKET
### Score: **2.5**–Stable (moderate level of activity)

Transparency International's 2002 score for Estonia is 5.6. Therefore, Estonia's informal market score is 2.5 this year.

ETHIOPIA

# ETHIOPIA

Rank: 101

Score: 3.33

Category: Mostly Unfree

**Present & Past Scores**

(Best) 1
2
3
4
(Worst) 5

'95 '96 '97 '98 '99 '00 '01 '02 '03 '04

3.90 3.80 3.80 3.70 3.68 3.70 3.88 3.70 3.79 3.33

## QUICK STUDY

### SCORES

| | |
|---|---|
| Trade Policy | 4 |
| Fiscal Burden | 3.8 |
| Government Intervention | 3 |
| Monetary Policy | 1 |
| Foreign Investment | 3 |
| Banking and Finance | 4 |
| Wages and Prices | 3 |
| Property Rights | 4 |
| Regulation | 4 |
| Informal Market | 3.5 |

**Population:** 65,816,060

**Total area:** 1,127,127 sq. km

**GDP:** $8 billion

**GDP growth rate:** 7.7%

**GDP per capita:** $121

**Major exports:** coffee, oilseeds, leather products

**Exports of goods and services:** $1.3 billion

**Major export trading partners:** Djibouti 13.2%, Italy 9.4%, Japan 9.2%, Saudi Arabia 9.0%

**Major imports:** consumer goods, petroleum and petroleum products, food, motor vehicles

**Imports of goods and services:** $2.1 billion

**Major import trading partners:** Saudi Arabia 29.3%, Italy 7.2%, India 6.7%, US 4.2%

**Foreign direct investment (net):** $46.6 million

2001 Data (in constant 1995 US dollars)

Ethiopia's past may be repeating itself as the country once again struggles to feed its people. A disappointing harvest brought about by widespread crop failure has put more than 12 million Ethiopians in danger of starvation. The country's mixed farming economy, which makes up 50 percent of GDP, remains susceptible to adverse weather conditions and fluctuating commodity prices. In an effort to gain some degree of control over future economic performance, the government has begun the transition process to a market-based system. However, with a looming famine, this shift will face significant disruption in the short term. The Economist Intelligence Unit estimates that the crop failure will contribute heavily to a 2 percent decline in GDP growth for fiscal 2003. As soon as the crisis subsides, a robust economic rebound and renewed focus on fiscal and banking reform are expected. Externally, increased tensions with neighboring Eritrea are likely to continue for some time. This follows a pattern of poor relations that has existed since 1962. Currently, some 4,200 troops from the United Nations patrol the Temporary Security Zone. There is little doubt that the ability of the government to keep these strains in check will have a profound effect on Ethiopia's economic future. Ethiopia's trade policy score and capital flows and foreign investment score are 1 point better this year; in addition, its fiscal burden of government score is 0.6 point better, and its government intervention score is 2 points better. As a result, Ethiopia's overall score is 0.46 point better this year.

###  TRADE POLICY
**Score: 4–Better** (high level of protectionism)

According to the World Bank, Ethiopia's weighted average tariff rate in 2001 (the most recent year for which World Bank data are available) was 11 percent, down from the 18.1 percent reported in the 2003 *Index*. As a result, Ethiopia's trade policy score is 1 point better this year. With respect to non-tariff barriers, the U.S. Trade Representative reports that "strict foreign exchange control regime [is] administered by the national bank.... [Also,] an importer must apply for an import permit and obtain a letter of credit for 100 percent of the value of imports before an order can be placed. Delays in customs clearance also remain a barrier to trade."

###  FISCAL BURDEN OF GOVERNMENT
Score—Income Taxation: **4–Stable** (high tax rates)
Score—Corporate Taxation: **4.5–Stable** (very high tax rates)
Score—Change in Government Expenditures: **2–Better** (moderate decrease)
**Final Score: 3.8–Better** (high cost of government)

Ethiopia's top income tax rate is 40 percent. The top corporate tax rate is 35 percent. Government expenditures as a share of GDP decreased 2.7 percentage points to 30.4 percent in 2001, compared to a 2.5 percentage point increase the previous year. As a result, Ethiopia's fiscal burden of government score is 0.6 point better this year.

###  GOVERNMENT INTERVENTION IN THE ECONOMY
**Score: 3–Better** (moderate level)

The World Bank reports that the government consumed 17.5 percent of GDP in 2001, down from the 23.3 percent reported in the 2003 *Index*. In 1999, according to the International Monetary Fund, Ethiopia received 17.49 percent of its total revenues from state-owned enterprises and government ownership of property. Based on a lower level of government consumption and newly available data on revenues from state-owned enterprises, Ethiopia's government intervention score is 2 points better this year.

## MONETARY POLICY
### Score: **1**–Stable (very low level of inflation)

From 1993 to 2002, Ethiopia's weighted average annual rate of inflation was –0.56 percent.

## CAPITAL FLOWS AND FOREIGN INVESTMENT
### Score: **3**–Better (moderate barriers)

Foreign investment is extremely low as fewer than 35 foreign firms are currently active, according to the Economist Intelligence Unit; however, the government is taking steps to liberalize its investment code. In 1998, the telecommunications, hydroelectric, and defense sectors were opened to foreign investment, although investments in telecommunications and defense must be in partnership with the government. The EIU reports that "foreign investors may now freely undertake certain activities that were previously the preserve of state bodies, including air freight and the import of propane and butane gas. The travel and tour operator business have also been opened to foreigners in an effort to boost tourism. Other changes include a reduction in the minimum level of investment required by foreign firms…. Minimum capital requirements have been lifted entirely for investors exporting at least 75% of their output." According to the U.S. Trade Representative, Ethiopia does not maintain local content requirements, and there are no restrictions on repatriation of earnings, capital, fees, or royalties. However, Ethiopia still prohibits foreign investments in the electricity, postal service, airline, and financial sectors. The International Monetary Fund reports that only Ethiopian passport holders can purchase real estate. Based on the government's liberalization of the foreign investment laws, Ethiopia's capital flows and foreign investment score is 1 point better this year.

## BANKING AND FINANCE
### Score: **4**–Stable (high level of restrictions)

It is only since 1994 that the government has permitted private banks and insurance companies. These services are limited to domestic concerns; foreign firms are prohibited from investing in the banking and insurance sectors. The presence of private banks and insurance firms in the financial sector has grown. According to the Economist Intelligence Unit, "By 2002 six private banks and eight private insurance companies were operating alongside the CBE [Commercial Bank of Ethiopia] and two far smaller state-owned banks." The U.S. Department of State reports that the state-owned CBE, which dominates the retail-banking sector, "has approximately 80 percent of the assets of the entire banking system and an official non-performing assets ratio of 42 percent." The government affects the allocation of credit by controlling interest rates.

## WAGES AND PRICES
### Score: **3**–Stable (moderate level of intervention)

Many price controls have been removed. In the agricultural sector, the government has abolished most marketing boards, allowing farmers to sell their agricultural products at prices determined by the market. According to the U.S. Department of State, "All retail prices except petroleum, fertilizers and pharmaceuticals have been decontrolled." However, the government influences prices through state-owned utilities and the large number of state-owned enterprises. The government mandates a minimum wage for both private and public employees, and individual industries and services have established their own minimum wages.

## PROPERTY RIGHTS
### Score: **4**–Stable (low level of protection)

Ethiopia's judicial system does not offer a high level of protection of personal property. According to the U.S. Department of State, "the Constitution provides for an independent judiciary; however, the judiciary remains weak and overburdened…." In addition, "The commercial code is antiquated and the overworked judicial system unpracticed in adjudicating business disputes."

## REGULATION
### Score: **4**–Stable (high level)

Ethiopia's cumbersome bureaucracy deters investment. Much of the economy remains under state control, and the evidence suggests that businesses also must contend with political favoritism. According to the Economist Intelligence Unit, "Corruption in Ethiopia poses various problems for its business environment, as patronage networks are firmly entrenched and political clout is often used to gain economic prowess." The U.S. Department of State reports that "state-owned enterprises have considerable de facto advantages over private firms, particularly in the realm of Ethiopia's regulatory and bureaucratic environment, and including ease of access to credit and speedier customs clearance."

## INFORMAL MARKET
### Score: **3.5**–Stable (high level of activity)

Transparency International's 2002 score for Ethiopia is 3.5. Therefore, Ethiopia's informal market score is 3.5 this year.

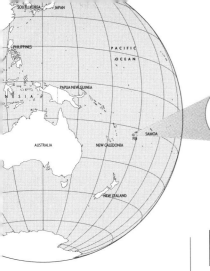

FIJI

FIJI

Rank: 76

Score: 3.06

Category: Mostly Unfree

Present & Past Scores

(Best) 1
2
3
4
(Worst) 5

3.49 3.24 3.23 3.23 3.29 3.29 3.50 3.54 3.48 3.06

'95 '96 '97 '98 '99 '00 '01 '02 '03 '04

F iji has a population of around 845,000 and a parliamentary government. It is a beautiful yet struggling country, rife with racial tension, and many reforms are needed to get it on the right path. The next major reform will be a restructuring of the sugar industry (sugar is one of Fiji's primary exports). According to the Economist Intelligence Unit, "the restructuring programme, which is scheduled to take five years, is expected to see a substantial reduction in the government's stake in the state-run company, Fiji Sugar, and a diversification of its assets." An increase in the value-added tax (VAT) from 10% to 12.5% was implemented at the beginning of 2003. The economy has been deeply affected by the racial tensions between the indigenous Fijians and Indo-Fijians. These tensions are complicated by the fact that the Fiji Labor Party was not given the number of seats it should have received after the 2001 general election. The EIU notes that the "government's political priorities in this racially charged environment include the resolution of the land-lease issue and the fate of Indian tenant farmers who have been or are about to be removed from indigenous Fijian-held property." Such issues need to be resolved for the economy to continue to grow. Fiji's trade policy and monetary policy scores are 1 point better this year; in addition, its fiscal burden of government score is 0.2 point better, and its government intervention score is 2 points better. As a result, Fiji's overall score is 0.42 point better this year.

## QUICK STUDY

### SCORES

| | |
|---|---|
| Trade Policy | 4 |
| Fiscal Burden | 3.6 |
| Government Intervention | 2 |
| Monetary Policy | 1 |
| Foreign Investment | 4 |
| Banking and Finance | 2 |
| Wages and Prices | 3 |
| Property Rights | 4 |
| Regulation | 3 |
| Informal Market | 4 |

**Population:** 817,000

**Total area:** 18,270 sq. km

**GDP:** $2.3 billion

**GDP growth rate:** 2.6%

**GDP per capita:** $2,763

**Major exports:** garments, sugar, fish, gold

**Exports of goods and services:** $1.2 billion (2000)

**Major export trading partners:** Australia 25.6%, US 22.5%, UK 15.1%, New Zealand 4.2%

**Major imports:** machinery and transport equipment, manufactured goods, food, mineral fuels

**Imports of goods and services:** $1.2 billion (2000)

**Major import trading partners:** Australia 39.8%, New Zealand 18.7%, Singapore 5.5%, US 5.0%, Japan 4.7%

**Foreign direct investment (net):** −$39 million

2001 Data (in constant 1995 US dollars)

### TRADE POLICY
#### Score: **4**–Better (high level of protectionism)

According to the World Trade Organization, Fiji's average tariff rate in 1996 (the most recent year for which WTO trade data are available) was 12.4 percent, down from the 25.6 percent reported in the 2003 *Index*. As a result, Fiji's trade policy score is 1 point better this year. The U.S. Department of State reports that "some goods are absolutely restricted and some subject to quotas." In addition, "Products subject to specific import licensing are powdered milk, bulk butter, seed potatoes, rice, coffee, canned fish, lubricants, transformer and circuit breaker oils, cleansing oils and hydraulic brake oils."

### FISCAL BURDEN OF GOVERNMENT
Score—Income Taxation: **3**–Stable (moderate tax rates)
Score—Corporate Taxation: **4**–Stable (high tax rates)
Score—Change in Government Expenditures: **3.5**–Better (low increase)
#### Final Score: **3.6**–Better (high cost of government)

Fiji's top individual and corporate tax rates are both 30 percent, down from 32 percent in 2002. Government expenditures as a share of GDP increased less in 2001 (0.8 percentage point to 30 percent) than they did in 2000 (1.5 percentage points). As a result, Fiji's fiscal burden of government score is 0.2 point better this year.

### GOVERNMENT INTERVENTION IN THE ECONOMY
#### Score: **2**–Better (low level)

The International Monetary Fund reports that the government consumed 16.4 percent of GDP in 2001. In 2000, based on data from the same source, Fiji received 4.59 percent of its total revenues from state-owned enterprises and government ownership of property. Based on newly available data on revenues from state-owned enterprises and a new methodology used to grade this factor, Fiji's government intervention score is 2 points better this year.

## MONETARY POLICY
### Score: 1–Better (very low level of inflation)

From 1993 to 2002, Fiji's weighted average annual rate of inflation was 2.45 percent, down from the 3.38 percent from 1992 to 2001 reported in the 2003 *Index.* As a result, Fiji's monetary policy score is 1 point better this year.

## CAPITAL FLOWS AND FOREIGN INVESTMENT
### Score: 4–Stable (high barriers)

Fiji places a number of restrictions on foreign investment but also offers a number of tax incentives to would-be investors in preferred activities. The government must approve all potential foreign investments and requires potential investors to undergo a series of bureaucratic registration and regulatory processes. According to the U.S. Department of State, "Investments that are export oriented, offer import substitution and/or self sufficiency will receive the strongest support from government." Fiji discourages foreign acquisition of a controlling interest in established Fijian businesses unless such acquisition is in the "national interest." According to the International Monetary Fund, residents are permitted to hold foreign exchange accounts. Non-residents may hold foreign exchange accounts subject to certain regulations. Most payments and transfers are subject to government approval and limitations on amounts. The IMF reports that all capital transfers require approval by the Reserve Bank of Fiji.

## BANKING AND FINANCE
### Score: 2–Stable (low level of restrictions)

Fiji's banking system includes two merchant banks and five foreign-owned commercial banks. The commercial banks are permitted a wide range of services, although the sector has been shaken by a recent banking crisis. According to the Economist Intelligence Unit, "The government effectively withdrew from the commercial banking sector after bailing out the state-owned National Bank of Fiji in 1998. An Australian financial services group, Colonial Ltd, acquired 51% of the bank in 1999." Since the sale of the National Bank of Fiji, foreign banks have dominated the banking sector, and the government's influence is limited.

## WAGES AND PRICES
### Score: 3–Stable (moderate level of intervention)

In 1973, Fiji established a Prices and Incomes Board with the authority to impose wage freezes and price controls on a number of commodities. The PIB imposes controls when there are significant price changes to protect the interests of consumers or suppliers. According to the U.S. Department of State, "There are a number of basic food items under price control. The Minister responsible is empowered under the Counter-Inflation Act to alter, remove or add any item from price control." In May 2002, Fiji increased the price of certain types of gasoline. There is no national minimum wage, but the Ministry for Labor sets and enforces minimum wages for certain sectors of the economy.

## PROPERTY RIGHTS
### Score: 4–Stable (low level of protection)

Protection of property is highly uncertain in Fiji. According to the U.S. Department of State, "Prior to the May [2000] takeover of Parliament, the judiciary was independent; however, with the purported abrogation of the Constitution and other events, including abolition of the Supreme Court, the status of the Judiciary is uncertain."

## REGULATION
### Score: 3–Stable (moderate level)

The U.S. Department of State reports that "enactment of the Foreign Investment Act of 1999 establishes transparent and simple procedures for the registration of foreign investors and is expected to streamline and reduce the time required for foreign investment approvals…. [T]he transparency of implementation is yet to be seen." In addition, "there is room for greater transparency, both in the government procurement and in the investigative processes." Continuing political instability makes regulatory reform difficult.

## INFORMAL MARKET
### Score: 4–Stable (high level of activity)

Piracy of such intellectual property as video and sound recordings and motion pictures is rampant. The Economist Intelligence Unit reports that smuggling—especially the smuggling of drugs, arms, and people—is significant.

# FINLAND

Rank: 14

Score: 1.95

Category: Free

**Present & Past Scores**

(Best) 1
2
3  2.34  2.18  2.09  2.19  2.06  2.04  1.89  1.85  1.95
4
(Worst) 5

'95 '96 '97 '98 '99 '00 '01 '02 '03 '04
n/a

FINLAND

C overed with forests and known as the home of Nokia, Finland houses a population of more than 5 million. Finland has a strong trading background, with forest products remaining its most crucial raw material resource, but has recently become a leader in telecommunications and technology as well. According to the *Financial Times*, "the Finnish population is ageing more rapidly than in any other industrialized land and the prospect of labour shortages is looming." Early retirement is a problem, and the government is in the process of introducing measures to resolve this issue. The Economist Intelligence Unit reports that the unemployment rate in 2002 was 9.1 percent—the same as the rate for 2001. Youth unemployment (unemployment in the labor force between the ages of 15 and 24) was 15.7 percent as of December 2002. Adding to Finland's other problems are high taxes. According to Maija Torkko of Nokia, Finland has lost its relative competitiveness as a result of its recent decision to raise the corporation tax rate while it has been lowered in competing countries. The EIU notes that the 2003 budget "reduced all income tax rates by 0.3 percentage points, with the rate on the lowest income band declining to 12.7% and the highest to 35.7%." The government needs to do more, however, both by further reducing income tax rates and by addressing the problematic corporate rates. Finland's government intervention score is 1 point worse this year. As a result, its overall score is 0.1 point worse this year.

## QUICK STUDY

### SCORES

| | |
|---|---|
| Trade Policy | 2 |
| Fiscal Burden | 3.5 |
| Government Intervention | 3 |
| Monetary Policy | 1 |
| Foreign Investment | 2 |
| Banking and Finance | 2 |
| Wages and Prices | 2 |
| Property Rights | 1 |
| Regulation | 2 |
| Informal Market | 1 |

**Population:** 5,206,295

**Total area:** 337,030 sq. km

**GDP:** $167.8 billion

**GDP growth rate:** 1.6%

**GDP per capita:** $32,230

**Major exports:** metal, machinery and transport equipment, electrical and optical equipment, chemicals, rubber, plastics, travel services, insurance

**Exports of goods and services:** $83.1 billion

**Major export trading partners:** Germany 12.4%, US 9.7%, UK 9.6%, Sweden 8.4%, Russia 5.9% (2001)

**Major imports:** raw materials, consumer goods, foodstuffs, chemicals, petroleum products, insurance, travel services

**Imports of goods and services:** $57.4 billion

**Major import trading partners:** Germany 14.5%, Sweden 10.2%, Russia 9.6%, US 6.9%, UK 6.4% (2001)

**Foreign direct investment (net):** –$642 million

2002 Data (in constant 1995 US dollars)

## TRADE POLICY
### Score: **2**–Stable (low level of protectionism)

As a member of the European Union, Finland had a common weighted average external tariff of 2.6 percent in 2001. The Economist Intelligence Unit reports that "regulations on food and consumer goods and health regulations for imports are strict and comprehensive in Finland."

## FISCAL BURDEN OF GOVERNMENT

Score—Income Taxation: **3.5**–Stable (high tax rates)
Score—Corporate Taxation: **3.5**–Stable (high tax rates)
Score—Change in Government Expenditures: **3.5**–Stable (low increase)
Final Score: **3.5**–Stable (high cost of government)

Finland's top income tax rate is 36 percent, down from the 37 percent reported in the 2003 *Index*, and is scheduled to be lowered to 35.5 percent effective July 1, 2003. (This rate will be reflected in next year's edition of the *Index*, as the cut-off date for policy changes is June 30, 2003.) The top corporate tax rate is 29 percent. Government expenditures as a share of GDP rose more in 2002 (0.2 percentage point to 49.2 percent) than they did in 2001 (0.1 percentage point). Because the reduction in the top income tax rate was not large enough to affect Finland's income taxation score and the increase in government expenditures as a share of GDP is not significantly different from that for the previous year, Finland's fiscal burden of government score is unchanged this year.

## GOVERNMENT INTERVENTION IN THE ECONOMY
### Score: **3**–Worse (moderate level)

According to Finland's Statistics Bureau, the government consumed 21.6 percent of GDP in 2002, up from the 19.9 percent reported in the 2003 *Index*. In 2001, according to the same source, Finland received 6.7 percent of its total revenues from state-owned enterprises and government ownership of property. Based on the higher level of government consumption and the increase in revenues from state-owned enterprises, Finland's government intervention score is 1 point worse this year.

 **MONETARY POLICY**
Score: **1**–Stable (very low level of inflation)

From 1993 to 2002, Finland's weighted average annual rate of inflation was 1.93 percent.

 **CAPITAL FLOWS AND FOREIGN INVESTMENT**
Score: **2**–Stable (low barriers)

Finland welcomes foreign investment, and few restrictions remain in effect. Foreign investments do not require prior approval, although the International Monetary Fund reports that "Acquisition of shares giving at least one-third of the voting rights in a Finnish defense enterprise to a single foreign owner requires prior confirmation by the Ministry of Defense." Non–European Economic Area investors must apply for a license to invest in a number of monitored industries, including national security–related sectors, banking and insurance, mining, travel agencies, and restaurants. Restrictions on the purchase of land apply only to non-residents purchasing land in the Aaland Islands for recreational purposes or secondary residences. There are no exchange controls and no restrictions on current transfers or repatriation of profits.

 **BANKING AND FINANCE**
Score: **2**–Stable (low level of restrictions)

Finland's banking system generally is in line with the rest of the European Union. The state-owned Leonia Bank has merged with Sampo, Finland's largest insurance company, with government ownership of 40.3 percent. Even though the government has ownership stake in a bank that competes with private banks, the industry is open to foreign competition; six foreign banks have branches in Finland, and seven foreign credit institutions have offices. A foreign bid for more than a one-third share of a credit institution or commercial bank must be approved by the Ministry of Finance. Banks may engage in some related financial services, such as the buying and selling of securities. Recently passed legislation defines the rules by which mortgage banks may issue mortgage bonds. Legislation passed in July 2000 allows credit institutions to use their own methods to calculate market risk.

 **WAGES AND PRICES**
Score: **2**–Stable (low level of intervention)

The market determines most wages and prices. The Embassy of Finland reports that the government influences prices in public health care services, taxis, and long-distance bus travel. The government also affects agricultural prices through its participation in the Common Agricultural Policy, a program that heavily subsidizes agricultural goods. According to Timbro, a Swedish think tank, "EU consumers pay roughly 80–100% more for their food than would be the case in a mature free-market regime." Finland does not have a legislated minimum wage, but it does require all employers to meet minimum wages established through collective bargaining agreements in each industrial sector.

 **PROPERTY RIGHTS**
Score: **1**–Stable (very high level of protection)

Private property is safe in Finland. The Economist Intelligence Unit reports that "contractual obligations, for both government and business, are strictly honored in Finland. The quality of the judiciary and the civil service is generally high." There is no history of government expropriation.

 **REGULATION**
Score: **2**–Stable (low level)

Finland maintains an open and transparent regulatory structure. There are some legal requirements to conduct business, especially for non–European Economic Area residents or companies. The U.S. Department of State reports that "Finnish tax, labor, health and safety, and related laws and policies are largely neutral towards the efficient mobilization and allocation of investment." The government has streamlined investment approval procedures and has lifted restrictions on buying real estate. According to the Embassy of Finland, the government has "adopted the one-stop-shop concept to reduce information search costs in relation to regulatory requirements." Construction and environmental permits are required to protect the environment, and many activities that are deemed to have a detrimental effect on the environment are prohibited. The Economist Intelligence Unit reports that "high costs and restrictive laws characterize the Finnish labor market." Corruption in the bureaucracy is almost nonexistent.

 **INFORMAL MARKET**
Score: **1**–Stable (very low level of activity)

Transparency International's 2002 score for Finland is 9.7. Therefore, Finland's informal market score is 1 this year.

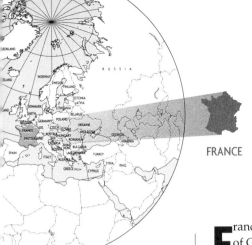

# FRANCE

FRANCE

Rank: 44

Score: 2.63

Category: Mostly Free

**Present & Past Scores**

(Best) 1
2
3
4
(Worst) 5

2.30  2.31  2.33  2.34  2.34  2.44  2.49  2.85  2.74  2.63

'95  '96  '97  '98  '99  '00  '01  '02  '03  '04

**Population:** 62,230,800

**Total area:** 547,030 sq. km

**GDP:** $1.8 trillion

**GDP growth rate:** 1.2%

**GDP per capita:** $29,782

**Major exports:** intermediate goods, capital goods, motor vehicles and transport equipment, processed foods and drinks

**Exports of goods and services:** $523 billion

**Major export trading partners:** Germany 14.5%, UK 10.3%, Spain 9.7%, Italy 9.1%, US 8.1%

**Major imports:** intermediate goods, motor vehicles and transport equipment, energy

**Imports of goods and services:** $479.6 billion

**Major import trading partners:** Germany 17.2%, Italy 9.0%, US 8.0%, UK 7.3%, Spain 7.2%

**Foreign direct investment (net):** –$17.4 billion

2002 Data (in constant 1995 US dollars)

France remains a relatively statist country. Public expenditure amounted to 52.6 percent of GDP in 2001, and the state employs 25 percent of the workforce—double the percentage in both Germany and the United Kingdom. France also remains awash in regulation. Most notoriously, since February 2000, the legal workweek has been a miniscule 35 hours for firms of 20 or more workers, and it takes twice as long to register a business in France as it does in any other country. France has striven mightily to preserve its overregulated politico-economic culture by adopting protectionist stances in global trading forums. The need for microeconomic reforms in the pensions system is becoming urgent given France's demographic profile: At present, 10 workers support four pensioners; by 2040, those some 10 workers will be forced to support seven pensioners. Such realities are reflected in France's persistently high unemployment rate (around 9.3 percent in March 2003) and the fact that France violated the European Union Stability Pact guideline of limiting its deficit to 3 percent of GDP in 2002, with similar violations likely in 2003 and 2004. However, since the overwhelming re-election victory of President Jacques Chirac in May 2002, the government he appointed, led by Prime Minister Jean-Pierre Raffarin, has made pension reform the centerpiece of its economic program. Hundreds of thousands of Frenchmen have protested the proposed changes in a series of union-led general strikes, but the plan will be debated in parliament in June 2003. The pension controversy could well prove to be the make-or-break moment for the Raffarin government. France's fiscal burden of government score is 0.1 point better this year, and its capital flows and foreign investment score is 1 point better. As a result, its overall score is 0.11 point better this year.

## TRADE POLICY

### Score: **2**–Stable (low level of protectionism)

As a member of the European Union, France had a weighted average tariff rate of 2.6 percent in 2001. According to the Economist Intelligence Unit, "An import license may be required for certain products subject to quotas (textiles are a particularly sensitive category). The quotas applied correspond to EU levels, though trade policy has yet to be completely harmonized throughout the European Union." Some products require import licenses, approval of which takes from six to 12 months.

## FISCAL BURDEN OF GOVERNMENT

Score—Income Taxation: **4.5**–Better (very high tax rates)
Score—Corporate Taxation: **4.5**–Stable (very high tax rates)
Score—Change in Government Expenditures: **3.5**–Stable (low increase)
### Final Score: **4.3**–Better (high cost of government)

France's top income tax rate is 49.58 percent, down from the 52.75 percent reported in the 2003 *Index*. The top corporate tax is 34.33 percent (a 33.33 percent corporate tax rate plus a 3 percent surcharge). Government expenditures as a share of GDP increased more in 2002 (1 percentage point to 54 percent) than they did in 2001 (0.3 percentage point). Because the increase in government expenditures as a share of GDP is not significantly different from that of the previous year, France's change in government expenditures score is unchanged this year. Based on the lower top income tax rate, France's overall fiscal burden of government score is 0.1 point better this year.

## GOVERNMENT INTERVENTION IN THE ECONOMY
### Score: **5**–Stable (very high level)

Based on data from the Economist Intelligence Unit, the government consumed 23.8 percent of GDP in 2002. The EIU reports that the government "still owns all of Electricité de France, Gaz de France, EMC chemicals, the post office, SNCF (trains) and RATP (metro)" and has "golden shares in Air France, Areva, France Telecom, Renault and Snecma (Aeroplane engines)." The French Embassy reports that both Air France and France Telecom have been partially privatized, with the government holding over 50 percent of their shares.

## MONETARY POLICY
### Score: **1**–Stable (very low level of inflation)

From 1993 to 2002, France's weighted average annual rate of inflation was 1.77 percent.

## CAPITAL FLOWS AND FOREIGN INVESTMENT
### Score: **2**–Better (low barriers)

There is no investment screening process for most sectors, and rules for investors are straightforward. The U.S. Department of State reports that some restrictions in the agriculture, aircraft production, energy, financial services, defense, maritime, publishing, telecommunications, and tourism sectors tend to favor investors from other European Union countries. According to the International Monetary Fund, "An authorization is required for investments pertaining to public order, public health, and defense." The government maintains strict quotas for European and French programming on television and radio, and for legal and accounting services, that limit foreign investment in these areas. Both residents and non-residents may hold foreign exchange accounts. There are no restrictions or controls on payments, transactions, transfers, or repatriation of profits, and non-residents may purchase real estate. Based on the evidence that foreign investment remains restricted in a relatively few sectors, France's capital flows and foreign investment score is 1 point better this year.

## BANKING AND FINANCE
### Score: **3**–Stable (moderate level of restrictions)

The government has enacted reforms to return all large banks to private ownership, increase competition in the banking industry, and open some financial services to foreign banks. The U.S. Department of State reports that there are 184 foreign banks operating in France. The government retains a 10 percent stake in Crédit Lyonnais, which was kept afloat in the 1990s only through massive amounts of state assistance that represented the largest banking bailout ever undertaken in any country. Foreign banks may now belong to the French stock exchange and purchase shares in French brokerage firms. According to the U.S. Department of State, the government "retains ownership of the Caisse des Depots et

Consignations and minority stakes in several major financial institutions, including Credit Lyonnais. The French postal service, La Poste, an independent public entity, holds 10% of the French financial services market."

## WAGES AND PRICES
### Score: **2**–Stable (low level of intervention)

The market freely determines prices of most goods and services. The government, reports the Economist Intelligence Unit, "has powers under the Commerce Code to impose price controls, but it uses them lightly. Most pharmaceuticals are one exception; books are another." The government also controls prices in state monopolies, such as gas and electricity, rail transportation, and telephone services. France affects agricultural prices through its participation in the Common Agricultural Policy, a program that heavily subsidizes agricultural goods. According to Timbro, a Swedish think tank, "EU consumers pay roughly 80–100% more for their food than would be the case in a mature free-market regime." France has a minimum wage that is revised whenever the cost of living index increases by 2 percent.

## PROPERTY RIGHTS
### Score: **2**–Stable (high level of protection)

According to the Economist Intelligence Unit, "Contractual agreements are secure in France, and both the judiciary and the civil service are highly professional. The bureaucracy is competent , though entanglements in the apparatus are common and can be time consuming." There are some impediments to acquiring property. The constitution states that any company defined as a national public service or natural monopoly must pass into state ownership.

## REGULATION
### Score: **3**–Stable (moderate level)

Unlike the other members of the European Union, France has resisted pressure to deregulate its economy. According to the U.S. Department of State, "Although some reforms have been implemented to address structural rigidities in the labor market, experts question whether unemployment will drop below the presumed structural rate of unemployment, estimated at 8.5 percent, absent further significant liberalization." Companies are concerned with local standards, including rigorous testing and approval procedures that must be undertaken before goods—particularly those that entail risk—can be sold in France. The U.S. Department of State reports that "deregulation is far from complete and the state remains very involved in economic life."

## INFORMAL MARKET
### Score: **2**–Stable (low level of activity)

Transparency International's 2002 score for France is 6.3. Therefore, France's informal market score is 2 this year.

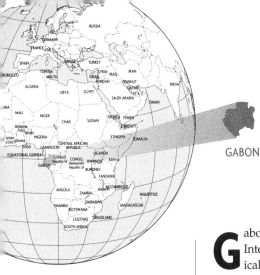

# GABON

Rank: 111

Score: 3.43

Category: Mostly Unfree

**Present & Past Scores**

(Best) 1
2
3
4
(Worst) 5

3.19 3.40 3.31 3.18 3.09 3.26 3.38 3.33 3.18 3.43

'95 '96 '97 '98 '99 '00 '01 '02 '03 '04

## QUICK STUDY

### SCORES

| | |
|---|---|
| Trade Policy | 5 |
| Fiscal Burden | 4.8 |
| Government Intervention | 3.5 |
| Monetary Policy | 1 |
| Foreign Investment | 3 |
| Banking and Finance | 3 |
| Wages and Prices | 3 |
| Property Rights | 3 |
| Regulation | 4 |
| Informal Market | 4 |

**Population:** 1,260,794

**Total area:** 267,667 sq. km

**GDP:** $5.5 billion

**GDP growth rate:** 2.5%

**GDP per capita:** $4,378

**Major exports:** petroleum, timber, manganese

**Exports of goods and services:** $2.6 billion

**Major export trading partners:** US 42.8%, France 20.9%, China 6.4%, South Korea 3.3%

**Major imports:** machinery and mechanical appliances, prepared foodstuffs

**Imports of goods and services:** $2 billion

**Major import trading partners:** France 62.7%, US 5.7%, UK 3.8%, Belgium 2.6%

**Foreign direct investment (net):** $134.5 million

2001 Data (in constant 1995 US dollars)

Gabon's economy continues to need reform across the board. According to the Economist Intelligence Unit, "high oil prices have given [President El Hadj Omar] Bongo some political breathing space by masking the looming economic and financial crisis caused by declining oil production, but Gabon's economic problems remain severe." Gabon is rich in natural resources, notably oil, minerals, and timber. The Organisation for Economic Co-operation and Development reports that "oil provides 76 percent of all export earnings, 66 percent of government revenue and about 42 percent of current GDP in 2001." Gabon is highly dependent on oil trade and needs to expand into other sectors. Timber is the second largest resource, but the industry is hampered by an increased timber export tax and illegal logging. The new International Monetary Fund program for Gabon includes the privatization of state-owned industries such as Air Gabon and Gabon Telecom. Gabon's human rights record continues to be dismal. According to the U.S. Department of State, security forces often abuse prisoners and detainees, and arbitrary arrest and detention continue. Corruption also remains a problem. The local elections in December 2002 are viewed with suspicion because of low voter turnout and allegations of electoral fraud. The government needs to tackle corruption, cut the timber export tax, and privatize more state industries. Gabon's fiscal burden of government score is 1 point worse this year; in addition, its government intervention score is 0.5 point worse, and its informal market score is 1 point worse. As a result, Gabon's overall score is 0.25 point worse this year.

###  TRADE POLICY
#### Score: **5**–Stable (very high level of protectionism)

Gabon is a member of the Central African Economic and Monetary Community (CEMAC), which also includes Cameroon, Central African Republic, Chad, Republic of Congo, and Equatorial Guinea. The U.S. Trade Representative reports that in 2001, CEMAC applied an average common external tariff of 18.4 percent. According to the U.S. Department of State, "There are few barriers in the crude oil sector [Gabon's largest economic sector]...." The government prohibits the importation of sugar in order to protect the sugar monopoly.

###  FISCAL BURDEN OF GOVERNMENT
#### Score—Income Taxation: **5**–Stable (very high tax rates)
#### Score—Corporate Taxation: **4.5**–Stable (very high tax rates)
#### Score—Change in Government Expenditures: **5**–Worse (very high increase)
#### Final Score: **4.8**–Worse (very high cost of government)

According to the International Monetary Fund, Gabon's top income tax rate is 50 percent, down from the 55.5 percent reported in the 2003 *Index*. The corporate tax rate is 35 percent. Government expenditures as a share of GDP increased 7 percentage points to 28.8 percent in 2001, compared to a 5.5 percentage point decline in 2000. As a result, Gabon's fiscal burden of government score is 1 point worse this year.

### GOVERNMENT INTERVENTION IN THE ECONOMY
#### Score: **3.5**–Worse (high level)

The Economist Intelligence Unit reports that the government consumed 15.9 percent of GDP in 2001, up from the 10 percent reported in the 2003 *Index*. As a result, Gabon's government intervention score is 0.5 point worse this year. In the same year, according to the

International Monetary Fund, Gabon received 20.23 percent of its total revenues just from the state-owned oil company.

## MONETARY POLICY
### Score: **1**–Stable (very low level of inflation)

From 1993 to 2002, Gabon's weighted average annual rate of inflation was 0.69 percent. Gabon's economy has benefited from a stable currency—a rarity in sub-Saharan Africa—as a member of the CFA franc zone. Fourteen countries use the CFA franc, a common currency with a fixed parity with the euro. (The other 13 countries are Benin, Burkina Faso, Cameroon, Central African Republic, Chad, Equatorial Guinea, Guinea–Bissau, Ivory Coast, Mali, Niger, Republic of Congo, Senegal, and Togo.)

## CAPITAL FLOWS AND FOREIGN INVESTMENT
### Score: **3**–Stable (moderate barriers)

Foreign investors face minimal restrictions in most areas, and foreign businesses may compete with local businesses. According to the U.S. Department of State, "Gabon seeks to encourage and increase its openness to foreign investment, but lack of transparency and bureaucracy pose practical obstacles." A new investment charter should streamline and liberalize the foreign investment climate; for example, it would grant foreign companies with head offices in Gabon the same rights as Gabonese companies. However, this code has not been fully enacted, and foreign companies still do not enjoy national treatment. The government still dominates the most lucrative economic sectors, most notably oil. The International Monetary Fund reports that residents may hold foreign exchange accounts and that non-residents may hold them if they receive prior approval from the government. Transfers and payments, including repatriation of profits, to countries other than France, Monaco, members of the West African Economic and Monetary Union, members of the CEMAC, and Comoros must be approved by the government. Capital transactions are subject to various requirements, controls, and official authorization.

## BANKING AND FINANCE
### Score: **3**–Stable (moderate level of restrictions)

Gabon's banking system is open to both foreign and domestic competition, but the state maintains a significant role through majority ownership in two banks and stakes in three others. Banks with some government involvement account for more that 85 percent of banking assets. According to the International Monetary Fund, there are six commercial banks, six finance companies, six insurance companies, two savings banks, and two securities firms. The three largest banks— Banque Internationale pour le Commerce et l'Industrie du Gabon, BGFIBANK, and Union Gabonaise de Banque—hold more than 80 percent of deposits and loans. The IMF reports that banking supervision lacks rigor and transparency, that the banking sector is heavily dependent on the government, and that "the continued exposure of banks to public enterprises

and to Government suppliers indicates that declines in fiscal revenues—for example due to oil price declines and/or shrinking output level—can have a negative impact on banks."

## WAGES AND PRICES
### Score: **3**–Stable (moderate level of intervention)

Some prices are set by the market and some by the government. According to the International Monetary Fund, "Price setting is in principle free. Restrictions do exist, however, for the following items: petroleum, school books, water and electricity, certain kinds of bread, cement, certain kinds of cooking oil, drinking water, medical glasses, surgical equipment, local beer, sugar and public transportation." The minimum wage—originally negotiated by representatives from labor, employers, and the government and then set by government decree—has not changed since 1994.

## PROPERTY RIGHTS
### Score: **3**–Stable (moderate level of protection)

Private property is moderately well-protected in Gabon. According to the Economist Intelligence Unit, "The president…effectively controls the judiciary (including the Constitutional Court) [and] both chambers of parliament (where the PDG [Gabonese Democratic Party] has large majorities)…." The U.S. Department of State reports that "Gabon has laws and regulations to combat corruption and to seek greater transparence, [but] they are not effectively enforced. Gabon and other countries doing business in Gabon do not always treat giving or accepting a bribe as a criminal act."

## REGULATION
### Score: **4**–Stable (high level)

Both the U.S. Department of State and the Economist Intelligence Unit report that corruption is pervasive and that complex regulations impede business. According to the U.S. Department of State, "Corruption is prevalent and is an obstacle for…business in Gabon." Although the government has made efforts to reduce bureaucracy and regulation— parastatals employ 20 percent of formal-sector workers—success has been limited, in large part because of entrenched political interests.

## INFORMAL MARKET
### Score: **4**–Worse (high level of activity)

According to the Energy Information Association, "Gabon's informal sector has grown dramatically due to higher domestic prices, relatively lower salaries, and a scarcity of official, or formal—particularly public sector—employment opportunities." Informal logging and software piracy are prevalent. Corruption in the bureaucracy forces most Gabonese entrepreneurs out of the formal economy. Based on increasing evidence of informal market activity, Gabon's informal market score is 1 point worse this year.

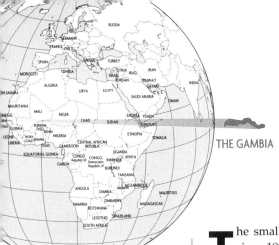

THE GAMBIA

# THE GAMBIA

Rank: 124
Score: 3.54
Category: Mostly Unfree

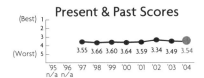

Present & Past Scores

(Best) 1
2
3
4
(Worst) 5

3.55 3.66 3.60 3.64 3.59 3.34 3.49 3.54

'95 '96 '97 '98 '99 '00 '01 '02 '03 '04
n/a n/a

## QUICK STUDY

### SCORES

| | |
|---|---|
| Trade Policy | 4 |
| Fiscal Burden | 4.4 |
| Government Intervention | 4 |
| Monetary Policy | 2 |
| Foreign Investment | 3 |
| Banking and Finance | 3 |
| Wages and Prices | 3 |
| Property Rights | 3 |
| Regulation | 4 |
| Informal Market | 5 |

**Population:** 1,340,770

**Total area:** 11,300 sq. km

**GDP:** $511.7 million

**GDP growth rate:** 6.0%

**GDP per capita:** $382

**Major exports:** groundnut products, fish

**Exports of goods and services:** $278.5 million

**Major export trading partners:** Belgium–Luxembourg 14.8%, Brazil 8.1%, Netherlands 6.5%, UK 5.3%, Japan 4.2%

**Major imports:** food and beverages, machinery and transport equipment, minerals and fuels

**Imports of goods and services:** $365.7 million

**Major import trading partners:** China (including Hong Kong) 59.2%, UK 19.6%, Netherlands 15.1%, Brazil 14.1%, France 13.6%

**Foreign direct investment (net):** $26.9 million

2001 Data (in constant 1995 US dollars)

The smallest of all African countries, The Gambia has maintained consistent growth since 1998. President Yahya Jammeh and his Alliance for Patriotic Reorientation and Construction (APRC) are expected to remain in power for the foreseeable future due to the opposition's weakness and lack of unity. Externally, The Gambia will continue to pursue the favor of the United States by maintaining its commitment to the war on terrorism. In the past, such cooperation was responsible for its admission to the Africa Growth and Opportunity Act (AGOA). Domestically, the government will concentrate on meeting the requirements set forth by the International Monetary Fund in its poverty reduction and growth facility (PRGF). Structural reforms, privatization, an improved environment for business, and budget transparency are all stated priorities for the government; however whether success will be achieved in these areas is an entirely different matter. Recent slowdowns in economic growth have continued into 2003, with the Economist Intelligence Unit estimating growth at 4 percent of GDP. The Gambia's economy, greatly supported by its agriculture market, is to blame for the slowdown with another failed crop year. A bright spot has been the increase in tourism over the past year. From October of 2002 to May of 2003, a projected 100,000 tourists were to have visited the country, contributing millions of dollars in new revenue. The Gambia's fiscal burden of government score is 0.5 point worse this year. As a result, its overall score is 0.05 point worse this year.

### TRADE POLICY
#### Score: 4–Stable (high level of protectionism)

Based on data from the International Monetary Fund, The Gambia's average tariff rate in 2001 was 14.4 percent (based on import duties as a percentage of total imports). There are no reports of non-tariff barriers.

### FISCAL BURDEN OF GOVERNMENT
#### Score—Income Taxation: 3.5–Stable (high tax rates)
#### Score—Corporate Taxation: 4.5–Stable (very high tax rates)
#### Score—Change in Government Expenditures: 5–Worse (very high increase)
### Final Score: 4.4–Worse (high cost of government)

According to the Embassy of The Gambia, the top income tax rate is 35 percent. The top corporate tax rate is 35 percent. The African Development Bank reports that government expenditures as a share of GDP increased 16.4 percentage points to 38.5 percent. This contrasts with a decline of 0.6 percentage point in the previous year. As a result, The Gambia's fiscal burden of government score is 0.5 point worse this year.

### GOVERNMENT INTERVENTION IN THE ECONOMY
#### Score: 4–Stable (high level)

In 2001, according to the World Bank, the government consumed 15.4 percent of GDP. The public sector is large. The Economist Intelligence Unit reports that some of the major parastatals include "the Gambia Ports Authority, Nawec, the Gambia Civil Aviation Authority, the Social Security and Housing Finance Corporation, the Gambia Public Transport Corporation…Gambia Telecommunications (Gamtel)…National Printing and Stationery Corporation (NPSC)…and the Maintenance Services Agency (MSA)."

187

**MONETARY POLICY**
Score: **2**–Stable (low level of inflation)

From 1993 to 2002, The Gambia's weighted average annual rate of inflation was 5.77 percent.

 **CAPITAL FLOWS AND FOREIGN INVESTMENT**
Score: **3**–Stable (moderate barriers)

The government grants equal treatment to domestic and foreign firms and actively seeks foreign investment. There is repatriation of profits, and foreign investors are allowed to invest without a local partner. Other factors, such as political instability, serve as practical impediments to foreign investment. The Gambian constitution provides guarantees against expropriation, but in February 1999, the government took control of the assets of a Swiss-based groundnut-producing company (Alimenta), now known as the Gambia Groundnut Council. In October 2000, Alimenta and The Gambia settled out of court with The Gambia agreeing to pay Alimenta (with assistance from European Union grants) $11.4 million for lost earnings and investment. The International Monetary Fund reports that residents and non-residents may hold foreign exchange accounts. There are no restrictions on payments and transfers. Some capital transactions are controlled.

 **BANKING AND FINANCE**
Score: **3**–Stable (moderate level of restrictions)

Although the government has privatized some of its holdings in the banking sector, it continues to exercise a heavy influence. According to the Economist Intelligence Unit, "Gambia Commercial and Development Bank was wholly owned by the government but has now been sold to private interests, and the other commercial bank, the International Bank for Commerce and Industry, is also privately owned. A new development bank, the Arab Gambian Islamic Bank, opened in Banjul in January 1998." The government sold a majority of its share in the Trust Bank to private investors between 1997 and 1999. The government, however, does affect the allocation of credit. According to the U.S. Department of State, "Significant government borrowing has created high real interest rates, effectively limiting local capital access to a small and well-established cadre of import-export traders and a few other businesses."

 **WAGES AND PRICES**
Score: **3**–Stable (moderate level of intervention)

The market sets some prices. However, the government still influences prices through state-owned companies that are active in the agriculture, maritime, water and electricity, aviation, public transport, and telecommunications sectors. The government also directly controls the price of fuel. Minimum wages are set through six industrial councils (with participation from the government, labor, and employers on each council) that govern commerce, artisans, transport, port operations, agriculture, and fisheries.

 **PROPERTY RIGHTS**
Score: **3**–Stable (moderate level of protection)

According to the U.S. Department of State, "The Constitution provides for an independent judiciary; however, the judiciary reportedly at times was subject to executive branch pressure, especially at lower levels. Nevertheless, the courts have demonstrated independence on several occasions, at times in significant cases."

 **REGULATION**
Score: **4**–Stable (high level)

Establishing a business in The Gambia can be difficult because of bureaucratic inefficiency, lack of transparency, and what the Economist Intelligence Unit characterizes as "institutional corruption." The U.S. Department of State reports that corruption "is becoming increasingly institutionalized. Business people occasionally encounter extortion, bribery, or fraud." Political uncertainty adds to the problem.

 **INFORMAL MARKET**
Score: **5**–Stable (very high level of activity)

The Gambia's informal market is large. Most of this activity occurs in smuggled consumer goods, labor, and pirated intellectual property. Smuggling of gasoline is reportedly pervasive. According to the Economist Intelligence Unit, "Most regional trading activity takes place in the informal economy, which raises doubt as to the validity of any official figures on The Gambia's trade patterns."

# GEORGIA

GEORGIA

Rank: 91
Score: 3.19
Category: Mostly Unfree

Present & Past Scores

(Best) 1
2
3
4
(Worst) 5

3.94 3.88 3.78 3.85 3.80 3.68 3.48 3.40 3.19

'95 '96 '97 '98 '99 '00 '01 '02 '03 '04
n/a

## QUICK STUDY

### SCORES

| | |
|---|---|
| Trade Policy | 4 |
| Fiscal Burden | 2.4 |
| Government Intervention | 1.5 |
| Monetary Policy | 3 |
| Foreign Investment | 3 |
| Banking and Finance | 3 |
| Wages and Prices | 3 |
| Property Rights | 4 |
| Regulation | 4 |
| Informal Market | 4 |

**Population:** 5,279,250

**Total area:** 69,700 sq. km

**GDP:** $2.6 billion

**GDP growth rate:** 4.5%

**GDP per capita:** $526

**Major exports:** scrap metals and aluminum, ferro alloys

**Exports of goods and services:** $1 billion

**Major export trading partners:** Russia 23.0%, Turkey 21.5%, Azerbaijan 3.3%, US 3.0%, Germany 2.5%

**Major imports:** machinery and machines, oil products

**Imports of goods and services:** $1.5 billion

**Major import trading partners:** Turkey 15.3%, Russia 13.3%, Azerbaijan 10.7%, Germany 10.1%, US 4.1%

**Foreign direct investment (net):** $143 million

2001 Data (in constant 1995 US dollars)

Georgia regained its independence in 1992. Viewed as the gateway between Europe and Asia, it could benefit significantly if East–West trade, including trade in energy resources, expands. Soviet-era leader Eduard Shevardnadze was elected president in 1995 and reelected for another five-year term in April 2000. Georgian sovereignty and territorial integrity suffer from secession in Abkhazia and South Ossetia, separatism in Adjara, and the ongoing conflict between Russia and the Chechen insurgents, which spills over into Georgian territory. These conflicts make parts of Georgia ungovernable. The economic situation remains dire because of a chronic failure to collect taxes, a large informal economy, and high levels of corruption. The outlook may improve with the start of construction on the Baku–Tbilisi–Ceyhan oil pipeline and the Baku–Tbilisi–Erzerum gas pipeline in 2003. Approximately 80 percent of Georgia's large and medium-sized enterprises have been privatized, although the state-run energy sector remains unreformed. The government has adopted a modern commercial code and several other market-oriented laws. Georgia joined the World Trade Organization in June 2000 and was granted permanent normal trade relations (PNTR) status by the United States in December 2000; it also aspires to join NATO. Georgia's fiscal burden of government score is 0.4 point worse this year; however, its government intervention score is 0.5 point better, and its monetary policy and informal market scores are 1 point better. As a result, Georgia's overall score is 0.21 point better this year.

## TRADE POLICY
### Score: **4**–Stable (high level of protectionism)

According to the World Bank, Georgia's weighted average tariff rate in 1999 (the most recent year for which World Bank data are available) was 9.9 percent. The U.S. Department of State reports that imported goods are subject to excise taxes. Some goods require an import license. The U.S. Department of State also reports that "a report commissioned by the World Bank in 2001 named customs as the largest single administrative barrier to foreign direct investment."

## FISCAL BURDEN OF GOVERNMENT
Score—Income Taxation: **2**–Stable (low tax rates)
Score—Corporate Taxation: **2**–Stable (low tax rates)
Score—Change in Government Expenditures: **3.5**–Worse (low increase)
### Final Score: **2.4**–Worse (low cost of government)

Georgia's top income tax rate is 20 percent. The top corporate tax rate is 20 percent. Government expenditures as a share of GDP rose 0.3 percentage point to 14.3 percent in 2001, compared to a 2.7 percentage point decline in 2000. As a result, Georgia's fiscal burden of government score is 0.4 point worse this year.

## GOVERNMENT INTERVENTION IN THE ECONOMY
Score: **1.5**–Better (low level)

The World Bank reports that the government consumed 8.6 percent of GDP in 2001, down from the 12.5 percent reported in the 2003 *Index*. As a result, Georgia's government intervention score is 0.5 point better this year. In the same year, according to the International Monetary Fund, Georgia received 0.12 percent of its total revenues from state-owned enterprises and government ownership of property.

189

**MONETARY POLICY**
Score: **3**–Better (moderate level of inflation)

Data from the International Monetary Fund's 2003 *World Economic Outlook* indicate that from 1993 to 2002, Georgia's weighted average annual rate of inflation was 9.36 percent, down from the 15.88 percent from 1992 to 2001 reported in the 2003 *Index*. As a result, Georgia's monetary policy score is 1 point better this year.

 **CAPITAL FLOWS AND FOREIGN INVESTMENT**
Score: **3**–Stable (moderate barriers)

Georgia places few official restrictions on investment, and foreigners receive equal treatment under the law. According to the U.S. Department of State, "The formal legislative framework…conforms to internationally accepted norms and principles…and aims to establish favorable conditions— but not preferential treatment—for foreign investors." Most sectors of the economy are open to foreign investment, although exceptions exist for some infrastructure projects and agricultural land. The Economist Intelligence Unit reports that "foreign investment in other sectors is likely to remain marginal, owing to the poor business environment and lack of reform. Foreign investors have been deterred by predatory tax enforcement, a lack of adequate legal protection, pervasive corruption and the arbitrary application of regulations." The International Monetary Fund reports that residents may hold foreign exchange accounts but that non-residents may not. There are limits and bona fide tests for all payments and current transfers. Capital transactions are not restricted but must be registered with the government.

 **BANKING AND FINANCE**
Score: **3**–Stable (moderate level of restrictions)

The state has largely divested itself of banks, and two formerly state-owned banks are among the largest banks in the country, according to the International Monetary Fund. "Reform of the banking sector began in mid-1995," reports the Economist Intelligence Unit, "with the National Bank of Georgia (NBG, the central bank) assuming a supervisory role. The NBG instituted bank consolidation and reform, imposing increasingly stringent reporting requirements." Foreign banks are increasing their presence. The U.S. Department of State reports that 22 banks have been created with foreign capital and that foreign investment accounts for approximately one-third of bank capital. Despite these reforms, the banking sector remains weak and focused on short-term lending rather than on long-term finance. According to the U.S. Department of State, "only 3 percent of Georgians have bank accounts, reflecting the widespread mistrust in financial stability of the institutions."

 **WAGES AND PRICES**
Score: **3**–Stable (moderate level of intervention)

According to the U.S. Department of State, "State price controls are being phased out. Georgia already has liberated most prices and is gradually raising regulated prices, such as utility tariffs, to market levels." The government continues to influence prices through subsidies to the energy and health care sectors. Georgia has a minimum wage for state workers but not for the private sector.

 **PROPERTY RIGHTS**
Score: **4**–Stable (low level of protection)

According to *The Washington Times*, "In Georgia, when one engages in a discussion about politics and economics, conversation quickly turns to one word: corruption." Corruption in the judiciary is still a problem despite the government's substantial improvement in trying to raise the level of efficiency and fairness in the courts. According to the same source, "In adjudicating [business] disputes, the performance of the Georgian court system has been mixed. Both foreign and Georgian investors have expressed a lack of confidence in the competence, independence, and impartiality of lower court decisions, in addition to the ever present concerns about their ability to be corrupted."

 **REGULATION**
Score: **4**–Stable (high level)

Establishing a business can be difficult despite government efforts to foster a market economy. According to the U.S. Department of State, "Streamlining procedures within a bureaucracy…is a major challenge for Georgia's reformers…. Investors face innumerable petty obstacles and near constant frustration at the day-to-day difficulties of doing business in Georgia." Corruption, according to several sources, is a major impediment to doing business.

 **INFORMAL MARKET**
Score: **4**–Better (high level of activity)

Transparency International's 2002 score for Georgia is 2.4. Therefore, Georgia's informal market score is 4 this year—1 point better than last year.

GERMANY

# GERMANY

Rank: 18

Score: 2.03

Category: Mostly Free

**Present & Past Scores**

(Best) 1
2
3  2.15 2.26 2.25 2.36 2.26 2.24 2.04 2.00 2.03 2.03
4
(Worst) 5

'95  '96  '97  '98  '99  '00  '01  '02  '03  '04

Germany has both the largest and weakest economy in the European Union. In the 10 years ending in 2001, annual GDP growth averaged just 1.5 percent; in February 2003, unemployment stood at 11 percent. In 2002, the economy grew at a rate of only 0.2 percent and the DAX (Germany's leading stock exchange) lost 44 percent of its value. Germany's economic problems cannot be explained primarily by the global economic slowdown, as Germany has been affected far more than its Western European peers; rather, the answer lies in the country's structural problems. Non-wage labor costs are equal to a staggeringly high 42 percent of gross wages. Fundamental economic reform of Germany's welfare and labor market systems has become imperative. The heavy burden of reunification remains an enduring drag on the country as a whole. Since 1997, despite subsidies from Western Germany to the East amounting to 4.5 percent of Western GDP per annum, Eastern Germany has been slipping ever further behind the West. In the spring of 2003, following his paper-thin re-election, Chancellor Gerhard Schroeder proposed a series of reforms that would limit to 12 months instead of 32 the amount of time those under 55 can claim full unemployment benefits, initiate a big cut in health care spending, and allow for limited flexibility to hire and fire workers. Despite continued strikes and opposition from the left wing of his Social Democratic Party, Schroeder has yet to water down his proposals significantly. His historical legacy depends on seeing the reform process through to fruition.

## TRADE POLICY
### Score: **2**–Stable (low level of protectionism)

As a member of the European Union, according to the World Bank, Germany had a weighted average tariff of 2.6 percent in 2001. Germany maintains the EU's import quotas and antidumping provision. According to the Economist Intelligence Unit, it also "has the usual array of local buying preferences, as well as packaging and food-and-drug trademark laws, all of which sometimes constitute import barriers."

## FISCAL BURDEN OF GOVERNMENT
Score—Income Taxation: **4.5**–Stable (very high tax rates)
Score—Corporate Taxation: **3.5**–Worse (high tax rates)
Score—Change in Government Expenditures: **3.5**–Better (low increase)
### Final Score: **3.8**–Stable (high cost of government)

Germany's top income tax rate is 48.5 percent and is scheduled to be reduced to 42 percent by 2005. The top corporate tax rate is 26.5 percent, but an additional 5.5 percent solidarity tax raises this rate to 27.96 percent, up from the 26.37 percent reported in the 2003 *Index.* Ernst and Young reports that the top corporate tax rate will decrease to 25 percent in 2004. In addition, government expenditures as a share of GDP increased less in 2002 (0.3 percentage point to 48.6 percent) than they did in 2001 (2.4 percentage points). On net, Germany's fiscal burden of government score is unchanged this year.

## GOVERNMENT INTERVENTION IN THE ECONOMY
### Score: **2**–Stable (low level)

Data from the Economist Intelligence Unit indicate that the government consumed 19.1 percent of GDP in 2002. In 2001, based on data from Germany's Federal Statistical Office,

191

Germany received 2 percent of its total revenues from state-owned enterprises and government ownership of property.

## MONETARY POLICY
### Score: 1–Stable (very low level of inflation)

From 1993 to 2002, Germany's weighted average annual rate of inflation was 1.61 percent.

## CAPITAL FLOWS AND FOREIGN INVESTMENT
### Score: 1–Stable (very low barriers)

Germany welcomes foreign investment and imposes no permanent currency or administrative controls on foreign investments. Some businesses, including certain financial institutions and passenger transport businesses, require licenses. Otherwise, foreign and domestic investors receive equal treatment and face the same regulatory hurdles in establishing a business. There are no restrictions or barriers with respect to capital transactions or current transfers, real estate purchases, repatriation of profits, or access to foreign exchange.

## BANKING AND FINANCE
### Score: 3–Stable (moderate level of restrictions)

Germany's banking system is well-regulated, but it also is dominated by public-sector financial institutions. According to a February 20, 2003, *Economist* article, "Germany's big private banks have only a small retail franchise. Between them, they have less than 4% of the money in Germans' savings accounts and make only 14% of all loans to companies and households. The country's 520 mainly municipally owned *Sparkassen,* or savings banks have more than half of all savings deposits and make 20% of loans; the 12 *Landesbanken,* regional banks owned by a mixture of federal states and associations of *Sparkassen,* have about 16% of the lending market…." The combination of increased competition resulting from the opening of European Union markets and unwise speculative financing has put some banks at risk. For example, the Economist Intelligence Unit reports the "disclosure in May 2001 that Bankgesellschaft Berlin, the country's 11th largest bank, had incurred massive losses and was only surviving through aid from the Berlin state, which owns 57% of the bank." *The Economist* reports that one reason why Germany's banks are experiencing rising bad loans is that, because they are "in public ownership, the *Sparkassen* are less bothered than the big banks about profitability. Supporting local businesses matters at least as much to them." Banks may engage in a wide array of services, including securities trading.

## WAGES AND PRICES
### Score: 2–Stable (low level of intervention)

The market sets most prices. According to the Economist Intelligence Unit, "Price controls are limited to maximum prices (for example, on rent), minimum prices (mainly for agricultural products, under EU regulations [i.e., Common Agricultural Policy]) and price-calculation ordinances (for example, for public utilities and insurance premiums). The Federal Cartel Office (Bundeskartellamt) moves against companies that abuse their dominant market position through 'excessive' price increases." Germany does not maintain an official minimum wage; the U.S. Department of State reports that "wages and salaries were set either by collective bargaining agreements between unions and employer federations or by individual contracts. Covering approximately 90 percent of all wage and salary earners, the collective bargaining agreements set minimum pay rates and were enforceable by law."

## PROPERTY RIGHTS
### Score: 1–Stable (very high level of protection)

Property is well-protected in Germany. The judiciary is both independent and efficient. The Economist Intelligence Unit reports that "contractual agreements are secure in Germany, and both the judiciary and the civil service are highly professional. The courts are decentralized, reflecting the country's federal system; there are separate supreme courts to deal with cases on commercial, tax, labour and constitutional issues."

## REGULATION
### Score: 3–Stable (moderate level)

Businesses must contend with a vast and confusing web of regulations that hinder free enterprise. According to the U.S. Department of State, "Many new investors consider bureaucracy excessive…. The German government recognizes that certain aspects of German tax, labor, health, environmental and safety regulations are overly burdensome and impede new investment." Germany's wages and fringe benefits are among the highest in the world, and labor market rigidities have raised unemployment and slowed growth during the past year. The Economist Intelligence Unit reports that in March 2003, in an effort to increase flexibility in the labor market, the government outlined a major reform initiative, including "substantial tightening of benefits for the unemployed, measures to reduce health insurance contributions, further pension reform, liberalization of the crafts sector, and a minor easing of unemployment protection legislation." The legislation still has not been enacted. Corruption is minimal, although Transparency International reports that "the construction sector, the privatization of former East German enterprises, and the awarding of public contracts represent areas of some continued concern."

## INFORMAL MARKET
### Score: 1.5–Stable (low level of activity)

Transparency International's 2002 score for Germany is 7.3. Therefore, Germany's informal market score is 1.5 this year.

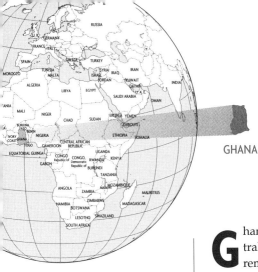

# GHANA

Rank: 109
Score: 3.40
Category: Mostly Unfree

Present & Past Scores

| (Best) 1 | | | | | | | | | |
|---|---|---|---|---|---|---|---|---|---|
| 2 | | | | | | | | | |
| 3 | | | | | | | | | |
| 4 | | | | | | | | | |
| (Worst) 5 | 3.54 | 3.54 | 3.53 | 3.29 | 3.29 | 3.24 | 3.29 | 3.59 | 3.54 | 3.40 |
| | '95 | '96 | '97 | '98 | '99 | '00 | '01 | '02 | '03 | '04 |

## QUICK STUDY

### SCORES

| | |
|---|---|
| Trade Policy | 4 |
| Fiscal Burden | 4 |
| Government Intervention | 3.5 |
| Monetary Policy | 4 |
| Foreign Investment | 3 |
| Banking and Finance | 3 |
| Wages and Prices | 3 |
| Property Rights | 3 |
| Regulation | 3 |
| Informal Market | 3.5 |

**Population:** 19,707,870

**Total area:** 238,540 sq. km

**GDP:** $8.3 billion

**GDP growth rate:** 4.0%

**GDP per capita:** $421

**Major exports:** gold, cocoa beans, timber

**Exports of goods and services:** $2.9 billion

**Major export trading partners:** Netherlands 11.5%, US 10.0%, UK 9.4%, Germany 6.0%, Nigeria 4.2%

**Major imports:** petroleum, foodstuffs

**Imports of goods and services:** $3.9 billion

**Major import trading partners:** Nigeria 20.2%, UK 7.1%, US 6.9%, China 5.6%

**Foreign direct investment (net):** $32.3 million

2001 Data (in constant 1995 US dollars)

Ghana's stability is in doubt as former President Jerry Rawlings continues to be the central figure in a rumored coup. Africa's first country to gain its independence, Ghana remains one of the poorest in the world, even though its per capita output is double those of its neighbors in the region. This is partly the result of Ghana's reliance on a mostly rural economy and the fact that gold and cocoa account for much of its foreign exchange. Like many African countries, its dependence on commodities has made it vulnerable to extreme price fluctuations in the market. Such was the case in 1999 when falling prices led to massive economic fallout that affected multiple sectors of the economy. Despite these setbacks, efforts to combat poverty have generally been positive: The poverty rate has declined to 39 percent in 2001 from 51.7 percent in 1992. According to the World Bank, the government will continue to focus on reducing borrowing, cutting public enterprises' deficits, and restructuring the domestic debt. It has succeeded in privatizing over 200 enterprises, and inflation continues to fall. Ghana's economy is projected to grow 5.2 percent in 2003, although domestic instability may cause that target to be reduced dramatically. Ghana's fiscal burden of government score is 0.1 point worse this year; however, its government intervention score is 0.5 point better, and its monetary policy score is 1 point better. As a result, Ghana's overall score is 0.14 point better this year.

## TRADE POLICY

### Score: **4**–Stable (high level of protectionism)

According to the World Bank, Ghana's weighted average tariff rate in 2000 (the most recent year for which World Bank data are available) was 9.7 percent. The U.S. Trade Representative reports that non-tariff barriers include import licenses and strict testing, labeling, and certification standards for certain products.

## FISCAL BURDEN OF GOVERNMENT

Score—Income Taxation: **3**–Better (moderate tax rates)
Score—Corporate Taxation: **4**–Stable (high tax rates)
Score—Change in Government Expenditures: **5**–Worse (very high increase)
### Final Score: **4**–Worse (high cost of government)

Ghana's top income tax rate is 30 percent, down from the 35 percent reported in the 2003 *Index*. The top corporate tax rate is 32.5 percent. Government expenditures as a share of GDP increased more in 2001 (3.7 percentage points to 31.4 percent) than they did in 2000 (1.5 percentage points). On net, Ghana's fiscal burden of government score is 0.1 point worse this year.

## GOVERNMENT INTERVENTION IN THE ECONOMY

### Score: **3.5**–Better (high level)

The World Bank reports that the government consumed 15.6 percent of GDP in 2001. In the same year, based on data from the International Monetary Fund, Ghana received 37.05 percent of its total revenues from state-owned enterprises and government ownership of property. Based on newly available data on revenues from state-owned enterprises, Ghana's government intervention score is 0.5 point better this year.

## MONETARY POLICY
### Score: **4**–Better (high level of inflation)

From 1993 to 2002, Ghana's weighted average annual rate of inflation was 19.97 percent, down from the 28.82 percent from 1992 to 2001 reported in the 2003 *Index*. As a result, Ghana's monetary policy score is 1 point better this year.

## CAPITAL FLOWS AND FOREIGN INVESTMENT
### Score: **3**–Stable (moderate barriers)

Ghana encourages foreign investment. The foreign investment code eliminates screening of foreign investment, guarantees capital repatriation, and provides equal treatment with respect to taxes, imports, and access to foreign exchange. According to the U.S. Department of State, however, foreign investors are denied national treatment (i.e., face the same laws as domestic investors) in the real estate, banking, securities, and fishing sectors. The only remaining precondition for foreign investment is a minimum capital requirement. The areas restricted to native Ghanaians are petty trading, taxi services, gambling and lotteries, beauty salons, and barbershops. While largely open to foreigners, privatization has been slow, and the process has been cited for lack of transparency. The International Monetary Fund reports that residents may hold foreign exchange accounts but must receive permission to hold them abroad. Non-residents may hold foreign exchange accounts but must get permission from the government. Payments and transfers face few restrictions. Most capital transactions must be approved by the Bank of Ghana.

## BANKING AND FINANCE
### Score: **3**–Stable (moderate level of restrictions)

The financial sector, though small, has become increasingly competitive since the initiation of liberalization in 1992. The sector consists of 17 banks: nine commercial banks, five merchant banks, and three development banks. The Economist Intelligence Unit reports that four foreign banks are operating in Ghana. The government remains active through two development banks: the National Investment Bank and the Agricultural Development Bank. Two state-owned companies dominate the insurance sector, but the number of companies in competition has risen to 19, and the state-owned State Insurance Company is slated for privatization. Private insurance companies must be at least 40 percent Ghanaian-owned.

## WAGES AND PRICES
### Score: **3**–Stable (moderate level of intervention)

The market sets most wages and prices, but the government influences the prices of utilities, maintains some food subsidies, manipulates prices through its remaining government enterprises, and influences the prices of cocoa (Ghana's major export). The Economist Intelligence Unit reports that after the government ended its subsidy to the fuel sector, fuel prices increased 90.4 percent. The government, however, also has created an independent body to fix the price of fuel. A tripartite commission composed of representatives of government, labor, and employers sets the minimum wage, which this year was raised by 28 percent to compensate labor for the rise in fuel prices.

## PROPERTY RIGHTS
### Score: **3**–Stable (moderate level of protection)

Land ownership is complex in Ghana. According to the U.S. Department of State, "the issue of clear title over land has been a thorny one. A thorough search at the Lands Commission to ascertain the identity of the true owner of any land being offered for sale is extremely important. Investors should be aware that, in some cases, land records are incomplete or non-existent and therefore clear title may be impossible to establish." Protection of intellectual property rights is weak. Ghana's judicial system suffers from political influence and inadequate resources. According to the Economist Intelligence Unit, "there have been some accusations from the [National Democratic Congress] that the judiciary is biased towards the government…. The courts are used extensively for civil, business and criminal cases…. Overall, Ghana's judiciary is relatively well respected and independent, but its reputation continues to suffer from the political interference of previous decades." The U.S. Department of State reports that corruption is present in the judiciary, but on a much lower scale than in other African countries.

## REGULATION
### Score: **3**–Stable (moderate level)

Regulations in Ghana are moderately burdensome. According to the U.S. Department of State, "The GIPC [Ghana Investment Promotion Center] was established …[in] 1994 as a one-stop shop for economic, commercial and investment information for entrepreneurs interested in starting a business or investing in Ghana. The GIPC utilizes databases, documentation, formal presentations, investment missions, country-specific investment fora and basic counseling services to carry out its activities. Under the GIPC Act of 1994, investment projects in all sectors of the economy, other than the mining and petroleum sectors, are free to establish without prior approval of the GIPC." However, reports the U.S. Trade Representative, "Bureaucratic inertia is sometimes a problem…and administrative approvals often take longer than they should." The U.S. Department of State notes that "while corruption exists in Ghana, it is somewhat less prevalent than in many other countries in the region."

## INFORMAL MARKET
### Score: **3.5**–Stable (high level of activity)

Transparency International's 2002 score for Ghana is 3.9. Therefore, Ghana's informal market score is 3.5 this year.

# GREECE

GREECE

Rank: 54

Score: 2.80

Category: Mostly Free

Present & Past Scores

(Best) 1
2
3
4  3.15  2.95  2.81  2.89  2.88  2.69  2.69  2.84  2.79  2.80
(Worst) 5

'95  '96  '97  '98  '99  '00  '01  '02  '03  '04

## QUICK STUDY

### SCORES

| | |
|---|---|
| Trade Policy | 2 |
| Fiscal Burden | 4 |
| Government Intervention | 2 |
| Monetary Policy | 2 |
| Foreign Investment | 3 |
| Banking and Finance | 3 |
| Wages and Prices | 3 |
| Property Rights | 3 |
| Regulation | 3 |
| Informal Market | 3 |

**Population:** 10,988,000

**Total area:** 131,940 sq. km

**GDP:** $150.6 billion

**GDP growth rate:** 4.0%

**GDP per capita:** $13,706

**Major exports:** food and beverages, manufactured goods, petroleum products

**Exports of goods and services:** $28.4 billion

**Major export trading partners:** Germany 11.7%, Italy 8.8%, UK 8.5%, US 5.7%

**Major imports:** foodstuffs, manufactured goods, chemicals

**Imports of goods and services:** $40.7 billion

**Major import trading partners:** Germany 12.9%, Italy 11.3%, France 5.9%, Netherlands 5.3%

**Foreign direct investment (net):** −$607 million

2002 Data (in constant 1995 US dollars)

Since joining the European Union in 1981, Greece has worked to bring its economy into line with the economies of other members, and the momentum for free-market reform increased with Costas Simitis's rise to the premiership as leader of the Panhellenic Socialist Movement (PASOK). Simitis comes from PASOK's economic reform wing and was able to steer Greece into the EU's single currency as of January 1, 2001. In doing so, the Simitis government reorganized the tax collection system, which led to a surge in government revenue and enabled Greece to adopt the euro, a major goal of the present government. During 2002, GDP grew by a healthy 3.8 percent, driven by high levels of investment in the run-up to the 2004 Olympic Games, which will be hosted by Athens. However, unemployment also remained high, at around 10 percent in 2002, as did inflation, which, at an annualized rate of around 4 percent in March 2003, is the highest in the euro zone. Greece's fiscal burden of government score is 0.1 point worse this year. As a result, its overall score is 0.01 point worse this year.

### TRADE POLICY
#### Score: **2**–Stable (low level of protectionism)

As a member of the European Union, Greece had a common weighted average tariff rate of 2.6 percent in 2001, according to the World Bank. The Economist Intelligence Unit reports that "Greece complies with EU regulations referring to the special-import regime on certain products, including textiles, steel and some industrial goods originating in China."

### FISCAL BURDEN OF GOVERNMENT
#### Score—Income Taxation: **4**–Stable (high tax rates)
#### Score—Corporate Taxation: **4.5**–Stable (very high tax rates)
#### Score—Change in Government Expenditures: **3**–Worse (very low decrease)
### Final Score: **4**–Worse (high cost of government)

Greece's top income tax rate is 40 percent. The top corporate tax rate is 35 percent. Government expenditures as a share of GDP declined less in 2002 (0.7 percentage point to 46.3 percent) than they did in 2001 (1.9 percentage points). As a result, Greece's fiscal burden of government score is 0.1 point worse this year.

### GOVERNMENT INTERVENTION IN THE ECONOMY
#### Score: **2**–Stable (low level)

The World Bank reports that the government consumed 15 percent of GDP in 2001. In 2000, based on data from the International Monetary Fund, Greece received 2.32 percent of its total revenues from state-owned enterprises and government ownership of property.

### MONETARY POLICY
#### Score: **2**–Stable (low level of inflation)

From 1993 to 2002, Greece's weighted average annual rate of inflation was 3.52 percent.

195

## CAPITAL FLOWS AND FOREIGN INVESTMENT
### Score: **3**–Stable (moderate barriers)

Although Greece officially welcomes foreign investment, it also maintains a number of restrictions. The government restricts both foreign and domestic investment in utilities but has recently begun to liberalize the telecommunications and energy sectors. The U.S. Department of State reports that "U.S. and other non-EU investors receive less advantageous treatment than domestic or EU investors in the banking, mining, broadcasting, maritime, and air transport sectors (these sectors were opened to EU citizens due to EU single market rules)." According to the Economist Intelligence Unit, "Prospective foreign investors find the Greek bureaucracy obstructive…. Moreover, many decisions are delayed because individuals in the bureaucracy are wary of accountability and unnecessarily refer decisions to higher authorities. The government recognizes this and has created the Hellenic Centre for Investments…to help overcome the problem…." The International Monetary Fund reports that both residents and non-residents may hold foreign exchange accounts. There are no restrictions or controls on payments, transactions, transfers, or repatriation of profits.

## BANKING AND FINANCE
### Score: **3**–Stable (moderate level of restrictions)

As a condition of membership in the European Union, the government has liberalized the banking system in ways that facilitate foreign competition and have led to the sale of six public-sector banks. The sector is undergoing a consolidation through a number of mergers and acquisitions. The Economist Intelligence Unit reports that there were 15 commercial banks at the end of 2002, of which the five largest accounted for 80 percent to 85 percent of total assets, deposits, and loans in the banking sector. The government indirectly controls the largest commercial bank, the National Bank of Greece, and the fourth largest commercial bank, Commercial Bank of Greece. According to the EIU, legislation has been passed to privatize these banks but has not been implemented. The U.S. Department of State reports that state-controlled financial institutions account for 51 percent of deposits and 44 percent of loans; foreign banks account for 11 percent of deposits and 13 percent of loans; and private banks account for 38 percent of deposits and 43 percent of loans.

## WAGES AND PRICES
### Score: **3**–Stable (moderate level of intervention)

According to the U.S. Department of State, "The only remaining price controls are on pharmaceuticals. The government can also set maximum prices for fuel and private school tuition fees, and has done so several times in the last several years. About one quarter of the goods and services included in the Consumer Price Index (CPI) are produced by state-controlled companies. As a result, the government retains con-siderable indirect control over pricing." Greece also affects agricultural prices through its participation in the Common Agricultural Policy, a program that heavily subsidizes agricultural goods. According to Timbro, a Swedish think tank, "EU consumers pay roughly 80–100% more for their food than would be the case in a mature free-market regime." Collective bargaining between the General Confederation of Greek Workers and the Employers Association sets a nationwide minimum wage that is ratified by the Ministry of Labor and enforced under the law.

## PROPERTY RIGHTS
### Score: **3**–Stable (moderate level of protection)

The U.S. Department of State reports that enforcing property and contractual rights through the court system is very time-consuming. According to the Economist Intelligence Unit, "Contractual agreements can be problematic…. The judiciary is supposed to be non-partisan but tends to reflect the political sensibilities of the government of the day…. In Greece it is wise to seek legal assistance from the outset [instead of when encountering legal difficulties] to avoid pitfalls." Expropriation of property is unlikely.

## REGULATION
### Score: **3**–Stable (moderate level)

The government is very bureaucratic, and regulations, because of their complexity and uneven application by civil servants, are not transparent. The Economist Intelligence Unit reports that "doing business in Greece is fraught with bureaucratic pitfalls." According to the U.S. Department of State, companies cite "cases where there are multiple laws covering the same issue, resulting in confusion over which law applies in which situation…. [T]he complexity of government regulations and procedures—and the perceived inconsistent implementation by the Greek civil administration—[are considered] to be the greatest impediment to investing and operating in Greece." The government has created the Hellenic Centre for Investments to answer investors' concerns, but investors still find the bureaucracy burdensome. The EIU reports that the labor reforms approved in 2001 "will do little to reduce the rigidities of the Greek labour market."

## INFORMAL MARKET
### Score: **3**–Stable (moderate level of activity)

Transparency International's 2002 score for Greece is 4.2. Therefore, Greece's informal market score is 3 this year.

# GUATEMALA

GUATEMALA

Rank: 87
Score: 3.16
Category: Mostly Unfree

**Present & Past Scores**

(Best) 1
2
3
4
(Worst) 5

3.36 3.15 2.89 2.91 2.89 2.91 2.88 3.00 3.01 3.16

'95 '96 '97 '98 '99 '00 '01 '02 '03 '04

G uatemala's $20 billion GDP and 12 million citizens make it the largest economy in Central America. Yet a high crime rate, weak rule of law, and manipulation of the judicial system by politicians and powerful oligarchs continue to foster an uncertain investment climate. In January 2003, the U.S. government decertified Guatemala on counternarcotics cooperation for failing to contain the expanding operations of four local drug cartels. According to the U.S. Department of State, about 40 percent of the cocaine that arrives in the United States each year passes through Guatemala. The country is suffering one of its worst political crises since democratic reforms took hold nearly 20 years ago. As an example, Efraín Ríos Montt, an army general who became president during the 1980s through a coup, asked the Constitutional Court to overturn an article that prevents ex-coup leaders from being elected president. Even before a decision was rendered, Ríos Montt announced his intention to run for president in the November 9, 2003, contest. Guatemala is not ready for an open trade environment. Amnesty International has described the existence of a "corporate mafia state" in which certain economic actors collude with public officials and common criminals to pursue economic gain. Before Guatemala can be integrated into the proposed U.S.–Central America Free Trade Agreement, it must demonstrate that it can comply with international standards of transparency and fulfill transnational accords. Guatemala's government intervention score is 0.5 point worse this year, and its capital flows and foreign investment score is 1 point worse. As a result, Guatemala's overall score is 0.15 point worse this year.

## QUICK STUDY

### SCORES

| | |
|---|---|
| Trade Policy | 3 |
| Fiscal Burden | 3.6 |
| Government Intervention | 2 |
| Monetary Policy | 3 |
| Foreign Investment | 4 |
| Banking and Finance | 2 |
| Wages and Prices | 2 |
| Property Rights | 4 |
| Regulation | 4 |
| Informal Market | 4 |

**Population:** 11,683,000

**Total area:** 108,890 sq. km

**GDP:** $18.2 billion

**GDP growth rate:** 2.1%

**GDP per capita:** $1,554

**Major exports:** coffee, sugar, bananas, apparel, petroleum

**Exports of goods and services:** $3.7 billion

**Major export trading partners:** US 55.3%, El Salvador 9.4%, Costa Rica 3.9%, Nicaragua 3.1%, Germany 3.0%

**Major imports:** fuels, construction materials, machinery and transport equipment

**Imports of goods and services:** $5.5 billion

**Major import trading partners:** US 32.8%, Mexico 9.3%, South Korea 8.2%, El Salvador 6.6%, Venezuela 4.1%

**Foreign direct investment (net):** $396 million

2001 Data (in constant 1995 US dollars)

### TRADE POLICY
Score: **3**–Stable (moderate level of protectionism)

According to the World Bank, Guatemala's weighted average tariff rate in 2001 (the most recent year for which World Bank data are available) was 5.6 percent. Red tape and customs corruption hinder trade. The U.S. Department of State reports that Guatemala "imposes tariff rates quotas (TRQ) for corn, rice, wheat and wheat flour, apples, poultry meat and poultry by-products (fresh, frozen, or refrigerated, with some exceptions), and fresh and frozen red meat."

### FISCAL BURDEN OF GOVERNMENT
Score—Income Taxation: **3**–Stable (moderate tax rates)
Score—Corporate Taxation: **4**–Stable (high tax rates)
Score—Change in Government Expenditures: **3.5**–Stable (low increase)
Final Score: **3.6**–Stable (high cost of government)

Guatemala's top income tax rate is 31 percent. The top corporate income tax rate is 31 percent. Government expenditures as a share of GDP rose slightly more in 2001 (0.6 percentage point to 12.9 percent) than they did in 2000 (0.2 percentage point). On net, Guatemala's fiscal burden of government score is unchanged this year.

### GOVERNMENT INTERVENTION IN THE ECONOMY
Score: **2**–Worse (low level)

The World Bank reports that the government consumed 7.7 percent of GDP in 2001. In the same year, according to the International Monetary Fund, Guatemala received 5.08 percent of its total revenues from state-owned enterprises and government ownership of property, up from the 2.07 percent reported in the 2003 Index. As a result, Guatemala's government intervention score is 0.5 point worse this year.

## MONETARY POLICY
### Score: **3**–Stable (moderate level of inflation)

From 1993 to 2002, Guatemala's weighted average annual rate of inflation was 7.66 percent.

## CAPITAL FLOWS AND FOREIGN INVESTMENT
### Score: **4**–Worse (high barriers)

Although Guatemala grants foreign investors national treatment and allows the full repatriation of profits, substantial barriers remain in effect. The government restricts investment in surface transportation, insurance, mining, fishing, forestry, airlines, and professional services (including legal and accounting services). Minerals, petroleum, and natural resources are considered the property of the state. The International Monetary Fund reports that residents and non-residents may hold foreign exchange accounts. There are few restrictions or controls on payments, transactions, and transfers. Foreign companies may purchase real estate. According to the U.S. Department of State, "Though Guatemala passed a foreign investment law in 1998 to streamline and facilitate foreign investment, time-consuming administrative procedures, arbitrary bureaucratic impediments, corruption, and a sometimes anti-business attitude of the current administration are a reality." Based on the evidence of both official and unofficial barriers to foreign investment, Guatemala's capital flows and foreign investment score is 1 point worse this year.

## BANKING AND FINANCE
### Score: **2**–Stable (low level of restrictions)

The government has liberalized the banking sector to allow for more foreign participation and domestic competition. There are 28 domestic banks, two foreign banks, and one state-owned bank. The U.S. Department of State reports that state intervention in the financial sector is largely restricted to a regulatory role and the implementation of monetary policy. A series of banking laws passed in 2002, reports the Economist Intelligence Unit, "make intervening in troubled banks much easier, since the Banking Superintendency now supervises all banks. Consumer confidence has also increased because of the measures, which require more transparency and increased supervision." The government minimally affects the allocation of credit. According to the U.S. Department of State, "Credit is not…directed by the government with the exception of a small amount of lending subsidized by the government—principally for small businesses, small farms or low-income housing." The Organisation for Economic Co-operation and Development lists Guatemala as a noncompliant state in the fight against money laundering and has advised banks headquartered in its member nations to be cautious about doing business in Guatemala.

## WAGES AND PRICES
### Score: **2**–Stable (low level of intervention)

According to the Economist Intelligence Unit, "Guatemala has no price controls and is gradually eliminating subsidies on various economic activities and products (such as fuel)…. [T]he government maintains some 24,000 direct subsidies, among them a Q12,000-per-house subsidy on construction costs." Guatemala has a minimum wage law, but the U.S. Department of State reports that noncompliance is common in the agriculture sector and the extensive informal sector. The Economist Intelligence Unit reports that a recent government-decreed increase in gasoline prices was later overturned by the Constitutional Court.

## PROPERTY RIGHTS
### Score: **4**–Stable (low level of protection)

The Economist Intelligence Unit reports that the Guatemalan "judicial system continues to show signs of weakness and lack of independence." According to the U.S. Department of State, "Resolution of business disputes through Guatemala's judicial system is time consuming and often unreliable. Corruption in the judiciary is not uncommon." In addition, "Land invasions by squatters are increasingly common in rural areas. It can be difficult to obtain and enforce eviction notices, as land title is often clouded and the police tend to avoid actions against squatters that could provoke violence."

## REGULATION
### Score: **4**–Stable (high level)

Regulations are both patchy and vague, causing significant bureaucratic obstacles to establishing a business. According to the U.S. Department of State, problems for business include "time-consuming administrative procedures, arbitrary bureaucratic impediments, corruption, and a sometimes anti-business attitude of the current administration." In addition, "regulations often contain few explicit criteria for government administrators, resulting in ambiguous requirements that are applied inconsistently or retroactively by different government agencies." The Economist Intelligence Unit and other sources report that the government of current President Alfonso Portillo has been plagued by allegations of corruption.

## INFORMAL MARKET
### Score: **4**–Stable (high level of activity)

Transparency International's 2002 score for Guatemala is 2.5. Therefore, Guatemala's informal market score is 4 this year.

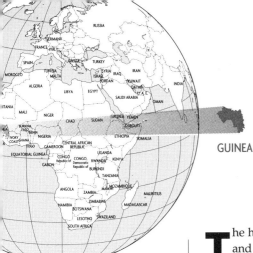

# GUINEA

Rank: 93

Score: 3.24

Category: Mostly Unfree

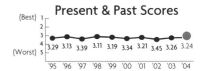

**Present & Past Scores**

(Best) 1
2
3
4
(Worst) 5

3.29  3.13  3.39  3.11  3.19  3.34  3.21  3.45  3.26  3.24

'95  '96  '97  '98  '99  '00  '01  '02  '03  '04

## QUICK STUDY

### SCORES

| | |
|---|---|
| Trade Policy | 5 |
| Fiscal Burden | 4.4 |
| Government Intervention | 1 |
| Monetary Policy | 2 |
| Foreign Investment | 4 |
| Banking and Finance | 2 |
| Wages and Prices | 2 |
| Property Rights | 4 |
| Regulation | 4 |
| Informal Market | 4 |

**Population:** 7,579,660

**Total area:** 245,857 sq. km

**GDP:** $4.6 billion

**GDP growth rate:** 2.1%

**GDP per capita:** $613

**Major exports:** bauxite, gold, aluminum, diamonds

**Exports of goods and services:** $1 billion

**Major export trading partners:** Belgium 16.4%, US 10.9%, Spain 10.4%, France 8.8%

**Major imports:** petroleum products, metals, transport equipment, machinery

**Imports of goods and services:** $1.1 billion

**Major import trading partners:** France 15.9%, US 11.5%, Ivory Coast 8.6%, Belgium 7.7%

**Foreign direct investment (net):** $32.3 million

2001 Data (in constant 1995 US dollars)

The health of President Lansana Conte will factor heavily into Guinea's outlook for 2003 and beyond. Unless a viable successor emerges before his inevitable passing, the military can be expected to assume control of the government under the guise of maintaining law and order. The continued conflict with Liberia will keep the border between the two countries tense, driving away foreign investment and distracting the country from its internal obligations. Growth will depend almost entirely on Guinea's performance in its more traditional markets. Guinea is a major producer of bauxite (25 percent of the world's market), a mineral important to both Russian and U.S. firms, and exports gold, diamonds, and aluminum. Whether emerging markets can buttress the mining industry has always been a question of investor confidence. Given Guinea's supply of bauxite and its relative stability compared to neighboring Sierra Leone, Liberia, and Ivory Coast, outside aid will probably continue, albeit conservatively because of the government's struggle to meet basic provisions of the poverty reduction and growth facility (PRGF)—traditionally an area in which other African countries have been penalized. The Economist Intelligence Unit projects that real GDP will grow by 5 percent in 2003 and 2004 despite myriad political difficulties. Guinea's fiscal burden of government score is 0.3 point worse this year, and its capital flows and foreign investment score is 1 point worse; however, its government intervention is 0.5 point better, and its monetary policy score is 1 point better. As a result, Guinea's overall score is 0.02 point better this year.

## TRADE POLICY
### Score: **5–Stable** (very high level of protectionism)

The World Bank reports that Guinea's average tariff rate in 1998 (the most recent year for which World Bank data are available) was 16.4 percent. According to the U.S. Department of State, importers need a formal import authorization from the central bank to import quantities that exceed US$5,000 in value. In addition, "Corruption remains a significant factor in clearing products through customs."

## FISCAL BURDEN OF GOVERNMENT
Score—Income Taxation: **4–Stable** (high tax rates)
Score—Corporate Taxation: **4.5–Stable** (very high tax rates)
Score—Change in Government Expenditures: **4.5–Worse** (high increase)
### Final Score: **4.4–Worse** (high cost of government)

Guinea's top income tax rate is 40 percent. The top corporate tax rate is 35 percent. Government expenditures as a share of GDP increased more in 2001 (2.4 percentage points to 19.1 percent) than they did in 2000 (0.5 percentage point). As a result, Guinea's fiscal burden of government score is 0.3 point worse this year.

## GOVERNMENT INTERVENTION IN THE ECONOMY
### Score: **1–Better** (very low level)

The World Bank reports that the government consumed 4.8 percent of GDP in 2001, down from the 6 percent reported in the 2003 *Index*. As a result, Guinea's government intervention score is 0.5 point better this year. In 1999 (the most recent year for which these data were available), according to the International Monetary Fund, Guinea received 2.29 percent of its total revenues from state-owned enterprises and government ownership of property.

199

## MONETARY POLICY
### Score: **2**–Better (low level of inflation)

Data from the International Monetary Fund's *2003 World Economic Outlook* indicate that from 1993 to 2002, Guinea's weighted average annual rate of inflation was 3.70 percent, down from the 6.48 percent from 1992 to 2001 reported in the 2003 *Index.* As a result, Guinea's monetary policy score is 1 point better this year.

## CAPITAL FLOWS AND FOREIGN INVESTMENT
### Score: **4**–Worse (high barriers)

Although Guinea's investment code officially welcomes foreign investment and provides national treatment to foreign investors, investment is still hampered by corruption and bureaucratic inefficiency. "Until June of 2001," reports the U.S. Department of State, "private operators managed the production, distribution and fee-collection operations of water and electricity under performance based contracts with the [government]. However, both sectors have continued to battle inefficiency, corruption and nepotism over the past year, and foreign private investors in these operations have recently departed the country in frustration." Foreign investors are restricted from majority ownership in radio, television, and newspapers, and the central bank must authorize all real estate transactions. According to the International Monetary Fund, both residents and non-residents may hold foreign exchange accounts, but residents may hold foreign exchange accounts abroad only with approval of the Central Bank of the Republic of Guinea. Payments and transfers are subject to government approval in some cases, and repatriation is controlled. The IMF reports that all capital transfers through the official exchange market and most capital transactions must be authorized by the central bank. Based on the evidence of capital controls and higher levels of corruption, Guinea's capital flows and foreign investment score is 1 point worse this year.

## BANKING AND FINANCE
### Score: **2**–Stable (low level of restrictions)

There are few restrictions on banks, and foreign banks are welcome. Most banks are in private hands pursuant to a massive privatization of the banking industry in the late 1980s and early 1990s. In 2002, there were six commercial banks, most of which were foreign-owned. According to the Economist Intelligence Unit, "The banking system is progressively gaining public confidence, as demonstrated by the steady rise in demand deposits.... [G]rowing confidence in the banking system has encouraged an increase in medium-term lending." Nevertheless, Guinea's banking system remains fragile and is unable to meet the private sector's development needs. "Since banks are conservative and risk averse," reports the U.S. Department of State, "there is not a significant amount of capital available to finance large investments. Banks prefer to finance trade. Commercial banks favor short term lending at high interest rates (25–30%), as there is an astronomically high potential for default." Reform of the banking system, including reduced government borrowing and improved authority by the central bank to supervise banks and impose Basle committee principles, was scheduled to be completed in 2000 but has stalled.

## WAGES AND PRICES
### Score: **2**–Stable (low level of intervention)

Price controls have been removed, but the Ministry of Trade reserves the right to introduce emergency price control measures. The government has made some significant progress in privatization but still sets prices for fuel and for state-run utility companies. The Labor Code allows the government to set a minimum wage by decree, but the government has not yet done so.

## PROPERTY RIGHTS
### Score: **4**–Stable (low level of protection)

Property is not completely secure in Guinea. According to the U.S. Department of State, "The Constitution provides for the judiciary's independence; however, judicial authorities routinely defer to executive authorities in politically sensitive cases.... Because of corruption and nepotism in the judiciary, relatives of influential members of the Government often are, in effect, above the law.... Many citizens are wary of judicial corruption and instead prefer to rely on traditional systems of justice at the village or urban neighborhood level."

## REGULATION
### Score: **4**–Stable (high level)

Red tape and a large bureaucracy in Guinea deter investment. The U.S. Department of State reports that "corruption is rampant and has a negative impact on even the most straightforward business transactions." In addition, "Business is routinely conducted through the payment of bribes rather than by the rule of law. Though it is illegal to pay bribes in Guinea, there is no enforcement, and it is, in practice, difficult and time consuming to conduct business without paying bribes."

## INFORMAL MARKET
### Score: **4**–Stable (high level of activity)

Guinea has an active informal market. According to the U.S. Department of State, "Both formal and informal money transfer services have expanded greatly in Guinea in recent years." In addition, "The Informal sector continues to be a major contributor to the economy." The government is revising its laws on intellectual property rights to meet international standards but has no administrative or regulatory structure with which to enforce any such legislation.

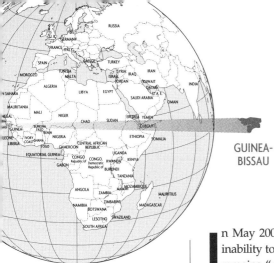

# GUINEA–BISSAU

GUINEA-
BISSAU

Rank: 139

Score: 3.90

Category: Mostly Unfree

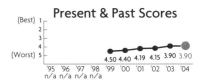

Present & Past Scores

(Best) 1
2
3
4
(Worst) 5

'95  '96  '97  '98  '99  '00  '01  '02  '03  '04
n/a n/a n/a n/a n/a    4.50 4.40 4.19 4.15 3.90 3.90

## QUICK STUDY

### SCORES
| | |
|---|---|
| Trade Policy | 5 |
| Fiscal Burden | 3.5 |
| Government Intervention | 2.5 |
| Monetary Policy | 2 |
| Foreign Investment | 3 |
| Banking and Finance | 5 |
| Wages and Prices | 3 |
| Property Rights | 5 |
| Regulation | 5 |
| Informal Market | 5 |

**Population:** 1,225,624

**Total area:** 36,120 sq. km

**GDP:** $252 million

**GDP growth rate:** 0.2%

**GDP per capita:** $206

**Major exports:** cashew nuts, fish and shrimp

**Exports of goods and services:** $99 million

**Major export trading partners:** Uruguay 40.7%, Thailand 27.9%, India 25.7%

**Major imports:** foodstuffs, petroleum products

**Imports of goods and services:** $125.5 million

**Major import trading partners:** Portugal 22.9%, Senegal 15.6%, China 10.4%, Taiwan 5.2%

**Foreign direct investment (net):** $26.9 million

2001 Data (in constant 1995 US dollars)

I n May 2003, Guinea–Bissau's elections were postponed due to inadequate funding and an inability to update voter registries. Guinea–Bissau is one of the world's poorest countries and remains "dangerously unstable," according to the Economist Intelligence Unit. Recent economic failures can be traced directly to President Kumba Yala and the collapse of the nation's infrastructure after armed conflict in 1998–1999. Since that time, a flood of investment has left the country. Because any rapid reduction in political instability and corruption is unlikely, the government will continue to experience difficulty in attracting major sources of foreign investment. The International Monetary Fund has required that, to qualify for future support, the government of Guinea–Bissau must reduce its fiscal deficit and improve its fiscal management; as of April 2003, these requirements had not been met. Despite the obvious effects that the lack of aid will have on its people, the government persists in its patronage appointments and overall ineptitude in meeting the nation's needs. It is therefore little wonder that the EIU has projected that the economy of Guinea–Bissau will contract by 1 percent in 2003 and 1.5 percent in 2004. Guinea–Bissau's fiscal burden of government score is 0.5 point better this year, but its government intervention score is 0.5 point worse; in addition, its monetary policy score is 1 point better this year, but its trade policy score is 1 point worse. As a result, Guinea–Bissau's overall score is unchanged this year.

## TRADE POLICY
### Score: **5**–Worse (very high level of protectionism)

Guinea–Bissau is a member of the West African Economic and Monetary Union (WAEMU), which imposes a common external tariff with four rates: 0 percent, 5 percent, 10 percent, and 20 percent. (The other seven members of the WAEMU are Benin, Burkina Faso, Ivory Coast, Mali, Niger, Senegal, and Togo.) The World Bank reports that in 2001 (the most recent year for which World Bank data are available), Guinea–Bissau's weighted average tariff rate was 14.3 percent, up from the 12 percent reported in the 2003 *Index.* As a result, Guinea–Bissau's trade policy score is 1 point worse this year. Non-transparent customs procedures are a major non-tariff barrier.

## FISCAL BURDEN OF GOVERNMENT
### Score—Income Taxation: **2**–Stable (low tax rates)
### Score—Corporate Taxation: **4.5**–Stable (very high tax rates)
### Score—Change in Government Expenditures: **3**–Better (very low decrease)
### Final Score: **3.5**–Better (high cost of government)

Data from the International Monetary Fund indicate that Guinea–Bissau's top income tax rate is 20 percent. The top corporate tax rate is 35 percent, but a 50 percent rate applies to profits earned from oil products. (The standard 35 percent rate was used to score this factor.) Government expenditures as a share of GDP decreased 0.8 percentage point to 43.3 percent in 2001, compared to a 3.8 percentage point increase in 2000. As a result, Guinea–Bissau's fiscal burden of government score is 0.5 point better this year.

## GOVERNMENT INTERVENTION IN THE ECONOMY
### Score: **2.5**–Worse (moderate level)

The World Bank reports that the government consumed 12.3 percent of GDP in 2001. In the same year, based on data from the International Monetary Fund, Guinea–Bissau received

201

6.83 percent of its total revenues from state-owned enterprises and government ownership of property, up from the 1.41 percent reported in the 2003 Index. As a result, Guinea–Bissau's government intervention score is 0.5 point worse this year.

## MONETARY POLICY
### Score: **2–Better** (low level of inflation)

Data from the International Monetary Fund's 2003 *World Economic Outlook* indicate that from 1993 to 2002, Guinea–Bissau's weighted average annual rate of inflation was 4.27 percent, down from the 6.11 percent from 1992 to 2001 reported in the 2003 *Index.* Guinea–Bissau has benefited from a stable currency—a rarity in sub-Saharan Africa—as a member of the CFA franc zone. Fourteen countries use the CFA franc, a common currency with a fixed parity with the euro. (The other 13 countries are Benin, Burkina Faso, Cameroon, Central African Republic, Chad, Congo [Brazzaville], Equatorial Guinea, Gabon, Ivory Coast, Mali, Niger, Senegal, and Togo.) Based on its lower weighted average annual rate of inflation, Guinea–Bissau's monetary policy score is 1 point better this year.

## CAPITAL FLOWS AND FOREIGN INVESTMENT
### Score: **3–Stable** (moderate barriers)

Political and economic instability, a weak infrastructure, an unskilled workforce, and a small local market have all discouraged foreign investment in Guinea–Bissau. However, there is some foreign investment in the fishing industry and oil exploration. The government has entered into agreements with foreign oil companies, allowing them to fund all exploration costs, and if commercial operations are approved, the state-owned PetroGuin oil company will bear 30 percent of the costs. The investment code provides for incentives for investment and guarantees against nationalization and expropriation. The International Monetary Fund reports that both residents and non-residents may hold foreign exchange accounts with permission of the Banque Centrale des Etats de l'Afrique de l'Ouest (Central Bank of West African States, or BCEAO). The government must authorize outward capital transactions. Capital transfers to members of the WAEMU are unrestricted, aside from direct investments. The government must approve most personal capital movements between residents and non-residents, such as personal loans, gifts or inheritances, or transfer of assets. Overall, barriers are moderate by global standards.

## BANKING AND FINANCE
### Score: **5–Stable** (very high level of restrictions)

The BCEAO, a central bank common to the eight members of the WAEMU, governs Guinea–Bissau's banking system, which is beginning to recover after having been shut down during the war. According to the Economist Intelligence Unit, "There is one commercial bank, Banco Africano Ocidentale (BAO), which was established in 2001 with local and Portuguese capital…. All

banks were closed during the civil war and only reopened in July 1999. Banking has been severely weakened, as local businesses were decapitalised during the war and many loans are now unrecoverable." Of the other two banks that were active briefly after the conflict, the Banco Totta e Acores withdrew from the country in March 2002 and the Banco Internationales da Guiné–Bissau has been liquidated.

## WAGES AND PRICES
### Score: **3–Stable** (moderate level of intervention)

"Since 1987," reports the Economist Intelligence Unit, "government policy, with the support of the IMF and World Bank, has aimed at macroeconomic stabilization and structural reforms, including reducing the fiscal deficit, removing price controls, reforming the public sector and strengthening the role of private enterprise." The government reports that "only five basic products are subject by law to price controls: fuels, electricity, water, telecommunications and rice." Since rice is the most important crop in this mostly agricultural economy, price controls on rice are significant. The Council of Ministers sets a minimum wage annually for various categories of work.

## PROPERTY RIGHTS
### Score: **5–Stable** (very low level of protection)

Protection of property in Guinea–Bissau is extremely weak. According to the U.S. Department of State, "The Constitution provides for an independent judiciary; however judges were poorly trained and paid and sometimes were subject to political pressures and corruption. The Supreme Court was especially vulnerable to political pressure because its members are appointed by the President and often were replaced."

## REGULATION
### Score: **5–Stable** (very high level)

According to the Economist Intelligence Unit, "the greatest risk [for investors] arises from the country's political instability, depressed business environment, periodic inability of the government to honour its financial and commercial obligations, and slow, weakly functioning local institutions on which investors or other foreign parties may depend. Enforcement of contracts cannot be assured through the local justice system." The same source reports that corruption is a substantial problem in the public sector.

## INFORMAL MARKET
### Score: **5–Stable** (very high level of activity)

Guinea–Bissau's informal market is so large that it eclipses the legal market. According to the Economist Intelligence Unit, "there is an active trade in smuggled diamonds from Guinea–Conakry and Liberia." In addition, "There is a thriving regional trade in food products, which is unrecorded. Large amounts of exports of fishing products also appear to be unrecorded."

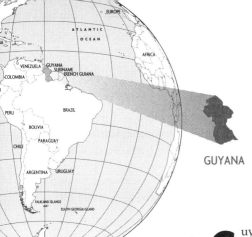

# GUYANA

Rank: 83

Score: 3.13

Category: Mostly Unfree

**Present & Past Scores**

(Best) 1
2
3
4
(Worst) 5

3.70 3.38 3.35 3.55 3.30 3.35 3.35 3.28 3.20 3.13

'95 '96 '97 '98 '99 '00 '01 '02 '03 '04

---

## QUICK STUDY

### SCORES

| | |
|---|---|
| Trade Policy | 4 |
| Fiscal Burden | 3.8 |
| Government Intervention | 3.5 |
| Monetary Policy | 2 |
| Foreign Investment | 3 |
| Banking and Finance | 2 |
| Wages and Prices | 2 |
| Property Rights | 3 |
| Regulation | 4 |
| Informal Market | 4 |

**Population:** 766,256

**Total area:** 214,970 sq. km

**GDP:** $721.5 million

**GDP growth rate:** 1.5%

**GDP per capita:** $942

**Major exports:** sugar, gold, aluminum, bauxite

**Exports of goods and services:** $684.8 million

**Major export trading partners:** US 21.6%, Canada 19.9%, UK 11.8%

**Major imports:** machinery, food, manufactures, petroleum

**Imports of goods and services:** $802.7 million

**Major import trading partners:** US 23.7%, Chile 16.2%, Trinidad and Tobago 12.9%, UK 5.5%

**Foreign direct investment (net):** $50.2 million

2001 Data (in constant 1995 US dollars)

---

**G**uyana gained its independence from the United Kingdom in 1966 and throughout the 1970s and 1980s pursued an inward-looking development strategy that transformed it into one of the poorest countries in the Americas. In the 1990s, however, former President Desmond Hoyte advanced a recovery plan to open the economy. Relations between the two main political parties were tense early this year when the opposition People's National Congress–Reform (PNC–R) party boycotted Parliament and blocked the appointment of parliamentary commissions. In May, reports the Economist Intelligence Unit, the new leader of the opposition, Robert Cobin, and President Bharrat Jagdeo announced a "process of 'constructive engagement' between government and opposition." In September 2002, the International Monetary Fund approved an initial disbursement for Guyana under the poverty reduction and growth facility (PRGF) for US$7 million in aid. More disbursements are attached to fiscal targets and some structural reforms. The money will be invested in capital projects that, according to the EIU, will likely spur construction and distribution. The government is negotiating the liberalization of the telecommunications sector, which could help develop such subsectors as call centers and Internet connections. Guyana's government intervention score is 1 point worse this year; however, its fiscal burden of government score is 0.7 point better, and its banking and finance score is 1 point better. As a result, Guyana's overall score is 0.07 point better this year.

## TRADE POLICY
### Score: **4**–Stable (high level of protectionism)

As a member of the Caribbean Community and Common Market (CARICOM), Guyana has a common external tariff rate that ranges from 5 percent to 20 percent. According to the World Bank, Guyana's weighted average tariff rate in 2001 (the most recent year for which World Bank data are available) was 9.9 percent. According to the U.S. Department of State, "[C]ustoms procedures present problems relating to inconsistent valuations of imports by customs officials and delays in customs clearance. Some businesses have alleged that customs officers may delay processing in hopes of attaining inducements to expedite clearances."

## FISCAL BURDEN OF GOVERNMENT
### Score—Income Taxation: 3–Stable (moderate tax rates)
### Score—Corporate Taxation: 5–Stable (very high tax rates)
### Score—Change in Government Expenditures: 2–Better (moderate decrease)
### Final Score: **3.8**–Better (high cost of government)

Guyana's top income tax rate is 33.3 percent. The top corporate tax rate is 45 percent. Data from the Economist Intelligence Unit indicate that government expenditures as a share of GDP decreased 2 percentage points to 53.4 percent in 2001, compared to a 13.4 percentage point increase in 2000. As a result, Guyana's fiscal burden of government score is 0.7 point better this year.

## GOVERNMENT INTERVENTION IN THE ECONOMY
### Score: **3.5**–Worse (high level)

The World Bank reports that the government consumed 25.4 percent of GDP in 2001, up from the 17.4 percent reported in the 2003 *Index*. In the June 1999–June 2000 fiscal year, based on data from the International Monetary Fund, Guyana received 17.29 percent of its total revenues from state-owned enterprises and government ownership of property, up from the 9.42 percent reported in the 2003 *Index*. As a result, Guyana's government intervention score is 1 point worse this year.

## MONETARY POLICY
### Score: **2**–Stable (low level of inflation)

From 1993 to 2002, Guyana's weighted average annual rate of inflation was 4.19 percent.

## CAPITAL FLOWS AND FOREIGN INVESTMENT
### Score: **3**–Stable (moderate barriers)

Licenses are required for some activities and the process for securing them can be time-consuming. The investment regime is still undeveloped, and the government tends toward caution in approving new investments. According to the U.S. Department of State, "After years of a state-dominated economy…the mechanisms for private investment, both domestic and foreign, are still evolving. Much crucial legislation is outdated and is currently being revised, including laws pertaining to resource use, mining, and the formation of private companies and capital markets…. While there is no 'screening' of investment, the centralized process of decision-making and lack of transparency can result in delays and frustration for foreign investors." The International Monetary Fund reports that both residents involved in exporting activities and non-residents may hold foreign exchange accounts. Payments and transfers are not restricted, but the IMF reports that capital transactions and all credit operations are controlled. Banks must receive government approval before lending to foreign enterprises. Guyana's constitution guarantees the right of foreigners to own property or land.

## BANKING AND FINANCE
### Score: **2**–Better (low level of restrictions)

Guyana's banking system is becoming more competitive but remains underdeveloped. According to the Economist Intelligence Unit, "Financial services will…continue to underperform, as the profitability of domestic financial institutions is constrained by the sizeable bad-loan portfolio and the lack of attractive lending opportunities." The lack of an efficient inter-bank trading system can make it difficult to obtain foreign exchange; however, both banks and private operations are permitted to offer foreign exchange services. There are seven commercial banks, the two largest of which—the Bank of Nova Scotia and National Bank of Industry and Commerce (NBIC)—are foreign-owned. In March 2003, the last state-owned bank, the Guyana National Co-Operative Bank (GNCB), was sold to the NBIC. The International Monetary Fund reports that banks must obtain approval from the Ministry of Finance before lending to non-resident enterprises. Based on the privatization of the last state-owned bank, Guyana's banking and finance score is 1 point better this year.

## WAGES AND PRICES
### Score: **2**–Stable (low level of intervention)

The market sets most prices. The U.S. Department of State reports, however, that the government sets electricity prices, and the World Bank notes that the government subsidizes water for poor households. The Labor Act and the Wages Council Act give the Labor Minister the authority to set minimum wages, but Guyana does not have a legislated private-sector minimum wage.

## PROPERTY RIGHTS
### Score: **3**–Stable (moderate level of protection)

Guyana's judicial system is often slow and inefficient. According to the U.S. Department of State, "The Constitution provides for an independent judiciary, but law enforcement officials and prominent lawyers questioned the independence of the judiciary and accused the Government of intervening in certain cases." In addition, "Delays in judicial proceedings are caused by shortages of trained court personnel and magistrates, inadequate resources…occasional alleged acts of bribery, poor tracking of cases, and slowness of police preparing cases for trial."

## REGULATION
### Score: **4**–Stable (high level)

Some sectors of the economy, such as utilities and other state-owned industries, are highly regulated, and the bureaucracy is extensive. According to the U.S. Department of State, "Bureaucratic procedures are cumbersome and time-consuming. Decision-making is centralized and businesspersons, both Guyanese and foreign, say it is often difficult to know who the decision-makers are on a given issue or what the rationale was for decisions made. One of the biggest obstacles in establishing a business is navigating land deeds and title registries. Getting clear title to land is one of the most frequent administrative difficulties for prospective businesses." Lack of transparency is also an impediment, as is corruption. Businessmen, reports the U.S. Department of State, complain that "government officials have solicited bribes as a prerequisite for the granting of licenses and permits needed to operate their businesses."

## INFORMAL MARKET
### Score: **4**–Stable (high level of activity)

Guyana has a rather large informal market. According to the Economist Intelligence Unit, "The gold and diamond industries have been prey in recent years to extensive smuggling, which has distorted the official production figures." In addition, "There are also several hundred Brazilian garimpeiros (informal gold miners) operating in Guyana." According to the U.S. Department of State, "Patent and trademark infringement are also common. Pirating of TV satellite signals is widespread and takes place with impunity."

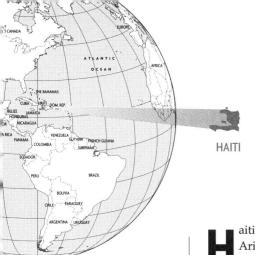

# HAITI

**Rank:** 137

**Score:** 3.78

**Category:** Mostly Unfree

### Present & Past Scores

(Best) 1
2
3
4
(Worst) 5

4.79  4.64  4.35  4.43  4.26  4.33  4.13  4.08  3.86
3.78

'95  '96  '97  '98  '99  '00  '01  '02  '03  '04

Haiti is three years into a political standoff that began when President Jean-Bertrand Aristide's ruling Lavalas Party reportedly manipulated the May 2000 parliamentary elections to ensure that a majority of its candidates got into office. An armed intervention to restore President Aristide to office after a coup was followed by a premature pullout of forces that left this Caribbean nation in the hands of a party supported essentially by mob rule. In September 2002, the Permanent Council of the Organization of American States (OAS) passed a resolution urging the investigation of political assassinations by gangs allied with Aristide's party, the formation of a credible electoral council, and the establishment of a secure climate in which new elections could be held in return for OAS support for renewal of international assistance. Aristide's government, however, has refused to impose public order or rein in partisan mobs, and political opponents have not been able to agree on a new electoral council. In 2003, Aristide named an adviser allegedly involved in the violent murder of a one-time presidential candidate to lead Haiti's police force. As disorder and chaos increase, the economy continues to shrink. Haiti now imports twice what it exports. For a population of 8 million people, there are only about 30,000 jobs in manufacturing or assembly industries. Electricity is available only for a few hours each day, and most citizens survive through subsistence agriculture in one of the world's most environmentally degraded places. Haiti's trade policy score is 1 point worse this year, and its fiscal burden of government score is 0.2 point worse; however, its monetary policy and informal market scores are 1 point better. As a result, Haiti's overall score is 0.08 point better this year.

### TRADE POLICY
#### Score: **4**–Worse (high level of protectionism)

As a member of the Caribbean Community and Common Market (CARICOM), Haiti has a common external tariff rate that ranges from 5 percent to 20 percent. According to the World Bank, Haiti's average tariff rate in 1995 (the most recent year for which World Bank tariff data are available) was 10 percent, up from the 5.9 percent reported in the 2003 *Index*. As a result, Haiti's trade policy score is 1 point worse this year. The U.S. Department of State reports that the government has removed most non-tariff barriers, but the inefficiency of the state-owned international seaport remains a significant barrier. The government requires a license to import agricultural products.

### FISCAL BURDEN OF GOVERNMENT
#### Score—Income Taxation: **3**–Stable (moderate tax rates)
#### Score—Corporate Taxation: **4.5**–Stable (very high tax rates)
#### Score—Change in Government Expenditures: **3**–Worse (very low decrease)
#### Final Score: **3.8**–Worse (high cost of government)

According to the Embassy of Haiti, Haiti's top income tax rate is 30 percent. The top corporate income tax rate is 35 percent. An additional levy of 30 percent on deemed distributions to foreign shareholders in addition to the normal tax—domestic firms pay only a 15 percent additional withholding tax—serves as a barrier to foreign investment. (The standard corporate tax rate was used to grade this factor.) Government expenditures as a share of GDP decreased less in 2001 (0.4 percentage point to 10.1 percent) than they did in 2000 (1.5 percentage points). As a result, Haiti's fiscal burden of government score is 0.2 point worse this year.

## GOVERNMENT INTERVENTION IN THE ECONOMY
### Score: **3**–Stable (moderate level)

The World Bank reports that the government consumed 7 percent of GDP in 2001. According to the U.S. Department of State, "The original list of government owned companies that were slated for privatization under the terms of the law on the modernization of public enterprises included: the flour mill, cement factory, telephone company (TELECO), electric company (EDH), port authority, airport authority, edible oil plant and two commercial banks. The flourmill [*sic*] and cement plant were the first privatization transactions to be completed, in 1998 and 1999 respectively. Despite indications from the government to the contrary, no further progress on privatization has been made to date."

## MONETARY POLICY
### Score: **3**–Better (moderate level of inflation)

From 1993 to 2002, Haiti's weighted average annual rate of inflation was 11.24 percent, down from the 13.63 percent from 1992 to 2001 reported in the 2003 *Index*. As a result, Haiti's monetary policy score is 1 point better this year.

## CAPITAL FLOWS AND FOREIGN INVESTMENT
### Score: **4**–Stable (high barriers)

Haiti has made efforts to attract foreign investment, but the U.S. Department of State reports that judicial inadequacies, lack of transparency, corruption, inefficient government, poor financial services, and a paucity of clear and enforceable laws and regulations discourage investment. The government has taken up legislation to remove the discrimination that foreigners face from the tax code but has yet to enact it. The International Monetary Fund reports that residents may hold foreign exchange accounts for specific purposes—for example, for export proceeds or receipts from non-governmental organizations—and non-residents may hold foreign exchange accounts without restriction. There are no restrictions on payments and transfers. All inward direct investments require government approval.

## BANKING AND FINANCE
### Score: **3**–Stable (moderate level of restrictions)

Although Haiti now welcomes foreign banks and recent changes allow foreign banks to engage in a variety of financial services, the banking system remains underdeveloped. The Economist Intelligence Unit reports that "Haiti has a rudimentary banking sector, reflecting the country's low levels of income and savings and the small number of people involved in the formal economy." The U.S. Department of State reports that there are seven locally incorporated banks, two foreign banks, a private development financial institution, two mortgage banks, and two state owned banks. The government reportedly plans to privatize the two state-owned banks but,

according to the U.S. Department of State, is unlikely to do so in the near future.

## WAGES AND PRICES
### Score: **3**–Stable (moderate level of intervention)

According to the U.S. Department of State, "There are few government subsidies or price controls, and goods are traded at market prices…. The government does, however, regulate prices of petroleum products such as gasoline." It also influences prices through the extensive state-owned sector, which includes (but is not limited to) enterprises in the telecommunications, energy, port, airport, agriculture, and banking sectors. A tripartite commission composed of six members appointed by the president sets Haiti's minimum daily wage.

## PROPERTY RIGHTS
### Score: **5**–Stable (very low level of protection)

Property is not secure in Haiti. The U.S. Department of State reports that "commercial operations of investors and other entrepreneurs may be severely compromised by weak enforcement mechanisms, limited resources in the judiciary, as well as limited experience by most members of the judiciary with commercial issues, and by an antiquated, overly cumbersome legal system. Working through the Haitian courts is a lengthy process and cases often go on for years. For this reason, many disputes are settled out of court." According to the Economist Intelligence Unit, "Political structures are prey to personal ambition and factionalism among politicians, while the judicial system suffers from inadequate resources, inefficiency and corruption. Persistent fear makes juries and witnesses unreliable, leading to both impunity and wrongful convictions."

## REGULATION
### Score: **5**–Stable (very high level)

It is virtually impossible to open a business legally under Haitian law, which the U.S. Department of State reports is "deficient in a number of areas, including operation of the judicial system; organization and operation of the executive branch; publication of laws, regulations and official notices; establishment of companies; land tenure and real property law and procedures; bank and credit operations; insurance and pension regulation; accounting standards; civil status documentation; customs law and administration; international trade and investment promotion; foreign investment regime; and regulation of market concentration and competition." According to the same source, businesses cite corruption as an impediment to investing in Haiti.

## INFORMAL MARKET
### Score: **4**–Better (high level of activity)

Transparency International's 2002 score for Haiti is 2.2. Therefore, Haiti's informal market score is 4 this year—1 point better than last year.

HONDURAS

# HONDURAS

Rank: 121

Score: 3.53

Category: Mostly Unfree

**Present & Past Scores**

(Best) 1
2
3
4
(Worst) 5

3.58 3.58 3.58 3.51 3.71 3.51 3.50 3.33 3.19 3.53

'95 '96 '97 '98 '99 '00 '01 '02 '03 '04

## QUICK STUDY

### SCORES

| | |
|---|---|
| Trade Policy | 3 |
| Fiscal Burden | 3.3 |
| Government Intervention | 4 |
| Monetary Policy | 3 |
| Foreign Investment | 4 |
| Banking and Finance | 3 |
| Wages and Prices | 3 |
| Property Rights | 4 |
| Regulation | 4 |
| Informal Market | 4 |

**Population:** 6,584,730

**Total area:** 112,090 sq. km

**GDP:** $4.7 billion

**GDP growth rate:** 2.6%

**GDP per capita:** $712

**Major exports:** coffee, bananas, shrimp, lobster, tobacco

**Exports of goods and services:** $1.9 billion

**Major export trading partners:** US 45.7%, El Salvador 10.2%, Guatemala 9.7%, Belgium 4.7%, Germany 4.3%

**Major imports:** manufactures and industrial raw materials, machinery and transport equipment, food and animal products

**Imports of goods and services:** $2.3 billion

**Major import trading partners:** US 46.2%, Guatemala 9.9%, El Salvador 6.2%, Mexico 4.7%, Costa Rica 3.5%

**Foreign direct investment (net):** $174.9 million

2001 Data (in constant 1995 US dollars)

With regular elections since 1982, Honduras has developed a stable, democratic, and market-oriented economy. Despite susceptibility to hurricanes shared by other Central American and Caribbean nations, it has an agreeable climate and underdeveloped potential as a tourist destination. Nonetheless, progress is stymied by a narrow economic base—agriculture and clothing assembly—and by concentrated ownership of assets, endemic corruption, a weak judiciary despite recent reforms in the administration of justice, and a growing crime rate resulting in part from an influx of Colombian drug traffickers. A third of the workforce labors in agriculture, where coffee and bananas are top exports. However, low world coffee prices have weakened sales. Low demand for manufactured products on the world economy has had a similarly negative impact on maquiladora operations. The central bank estimates this year's growth at only 2 percent—0.6 percent less than the 2.6 percent annual population growth rate. Two-thirds of the population now lives in poverty, and a third of all Honduran children suffer from malnutrition. Investment in education is low: The average Honduran student finishes only four years of primary schooling. Better public security, a more educated workforce, and a diversified export sector are needed for Honduras to take full advantage of the U.S.–Central American Free Trade Agreement (CAFTA). Honduras's fiscal burden of government score is 0.4 point worse this year, and its capital flows and foreign investment, wages and prices, and property rights scores are 1 point worse. As a result, Honduras's overall score is 0.34 point worse this year.

###  TRADE POLICY

Score: **3**–Stable (moderate level of protectionism)

According to the World Bank, Honduras's weighted average tariff rate in 2001 (the most recent year for which World Bank data are available) was 7.5 percent. The U.S. Trade Representative reports that "Honduras implements a price band mechanism for imports of yellow corn, sorghum, and corn meal…. [T]he government also maintains a seasonal restriction on the price band…to provide additional protection to local grain farmers during the main harvest season."

###  FISCAL BURDEN OF GOVERNMENT

Score—Income Taxation: **2.5**–Stable (moderate tax rates)
Score—Corporate Taxation: **3**–Stable (moderate tax rates)
Score—Change in Government Expenditures: **4.5**–Worse (high increase)
Final Score: **3.3**–Worse (moderate cost of government)

According to Ernst and Young, Honduras's top income tax rate is 25 percent. The top corporate tax rate is 25 percent. Government expenditures as a share of GDP increased 2.6 percentage points to 26 percent in 2001, compared to a 0.4 percentage point decrease in 2000. As a result, Honduras's fiscal burden of government score is 0.4 point worse this year.

###  GOVERNMENT INTERVENTION IN THE ECONOMY

Score: **4**–Stable (high level)

The World Bank reports that the government consumed 13.9 percent of GDP in 2001. According to the U.S. Department of State, "Since the mid-1990s three governments have pledged to accelerate the privatisation programme, with the partial-privatisation of the state-owned telecoms company, the Empresa Hondureña de Telecomunicaciones (Hondutel), a priority, but the sale has repeatedly stalled…. The part-privatisation of the generation and billing arms of the state-owned electricity company, the Empresa Nacional de Energía (ENEE), went ahead in 2000."

## MONETARY POLICY
### Score: **3**–Stable (moderate level of inflation)

From 1993 to 2002, Honduras's weighted average annual rate of inflation was 8.73 percent.

## CAPITAL FLOWS AND FOREIGN INVESTMENT
### Score: **4**–Worse (high barriers)

Although the government seeks foreign investment, the U.S. Department of State reports that the "investment climate is hampered by high levels of crime, judicial insecurity, high levels of corruption, low education levels among the population, inadequate financial supervision and a poorly developed infrastructure." According to the U.S. Trade Representative, "Corruption appears to be most pervasive in the following areas: government procurement, performance requirements, the regulatory system, and the buying and selling of real estate, particularly land title transfers." The same source notes that the constitution "requires that all foreign investment complement, but not substitute for, national investment." Government authorization is required for foreign investment in private health care services, telecommunications, electricity, air transport, tourism, fishing and hunting, exploration and exploitation of minerals, forestry, agriculture, insurance and financial services, and private education. Foreign ownership of land near the coast or along borders is generally prohibited, but such land may be purchased with permission from the government for tourism purposes. The International Monetary Fund reports that both residents and non-residents may hold foreign exchange accounts. Payments and transfers are not restricted, and few capital transactions require official approval. Based on the evidence of corruption and restrictions on foreign investment, Honduras's capital flows and foreign investment score is 1 point worse this year.

## BANKING AND FINANCE
### Score: **3**–Stable (moderate level of restrictions)

The banking sector is inefficient and underdeveloped. The Economist Intelligence Unit reports that four banks have collapsed or faced government intervention since 1999. According to the U.S. Department of State, "The Honduran banking system, currently comprised of 20 private banks, is considered weak and in need of further consolidation." The EIU also reports that there are six foreign banks operating in Honduras, but that they serve only a limited base. The government operates two state-owned banks and must approve any foreign investment in financial services and insurance.

## WAGES AND PRICES
### Score: **3**–Worse (moderate level of intervention)

According to the U.S. Department of State, "The Honduran government controls the prices for coffee and medicines, and regulates the prices of gasoline, diesel, and liquid propane gas. In addition, it keeps an informal control over prices of certain staple products such as milk and sugar, by pressuring producers and retailers to keep prices as low as possible." The Economist Intelligence Unit reports that, after Hurricane Mitch in 1998, "severe price controls were placed on basic products. These were lifted at end-1999, but the government reserves the rights to impose price controls as needed." The government also influences prices through the country's extensive state-owned sector, which includes (but is not limited to) enterprises in the telecommunications, port, electricity, highways, and postal sectors. A minimum wage system established in 2000 applies to all sectors of the economy but varies according to work and geographic area. Based on the level of government interference with prices, either directly or through state-owned enterprises, Honduras's wages and prices score is 1 point worse this year.

## PROPERTY RIGHTS
### Score: **4**–Worse (low level of protection)

Protection of property is somewhat weak. According to the Economist Intelligence Unit, "the judicial system in Honduras has long been criticized for its biases, inefficiency and lack of independence. It can take years to prosecute and pass judgment on a case, and the number of cases pending resolution has increased considerably over the past few years." The U.S. Department of State reports that the commercial code "is antiquated and needs to be updated…. Most investment and property disputes are long lasting and arduous…. [C]laimants frequently complain about the lack of transparency and the slow administration of justice in the courts. There are also complaints that the Honduran judicial system caters to favoritism, external pressure and bribes." Expropriation of property is possible. According to the U.S. Department of State, "The Honduran government generally expropriates property for purposes of land reform (usually related to a land invasion by farmer groups) or for public use such as construction of an airport. Land disputes related to actions by the Honduran National Agrarian Institute (INA) are common for both Honduran and foreign landowners. According to the National Agrarian Reform Law, idle land fit for farming can be expropriated and awarded to landless poor. Generally, an INA expropriation case begins after squatters target and invade unprotected property…. In most cases, claimants have found that pursuing the subsequent legal avenues is costly and time consuming, and rarely lead[s] to positive results. Compensation for land expropriated under the Agrarian Reform Law, when awarded, is paid in 20-year government bonds." Based on newly available evidence of significant expropriation, Honduras's property rights score is 1 point worse this year.

## REGULATION
### Score: **4**–Stable (high level)

Businesses are subject to significant red tape, lack of transparency, and the absence of an established rule of law. According to the U.S. Department of State, "Honduran labor laws and the civil procedures code are outdated. The Honduran government often lacks the resources or political will to implement or enforce existing laws. Property registration often is not up to date, nor can the results of title searches be relied upon. There is no title insurance in Honduras. Procedural red tape to obtain government approval for investment activities is still very common." The U.S. Trade Representative reports that corruption remains endemic.

## INFORMAL MARKET
### Score: **4**–Stable (high level of activity)

Transparency International's 2002 score for Honduras is 2.7. Therefore, Honduras's informal market score is 4 this year.

# HONG KONG

HONG KONG

Rank: 1

Score: 1.34

Category: Free

**Present & Past Scores**

(Best) 1
2
3 1.51 1.50 1.54 1.40 1.51 1.40 1.29 1.39 1.44 1.34
4
(Worst) 5
'95 '96 '97 '98 '99 '00 '01 '02 '03 '04

H ong Kong remains one of the world's freest economies, as well as its 10th largest trading entity and 11th largest banking center. Ever since the People's Republic of China regained control in July 1997, the fear has been that Hong Kong's promised autonomy would slowly erode. The Chinese government's treatment of severe acute respiratory syndrome (SARS) in 2003 as a "state secret" hampered Hong Kong's ability to stem the contagion. Over 1,700 people were infected, and 300 died in Hong Kong alone. Expected 2003 GDP growth of 1.6 percent reflects a boom in tourism from Mainland China. In early July, in the face of strong public protest, the Hong Kong government withdrew planned anti-subversion legislation (Article 23 of its Basic Law) that threatened to hamper full and accurate journalistic coverage of developments inside China and their effects on Hong Kong. The eventual fate of this legislation is unclear. Hong Kong's budget deficit approaches $9 billion (5.4 percent of GDP). The government plans to raise income and corporate tax rates and cut spending on civil service pay and social welfare payments. Future revenue is anticipated through privatization of public assets, mainly in the transportation sector. The Hong Kong government has announced plans to provide real estate assistance to the telecommunications and logistics sectors, build low-rent public housing, and create more tourist attractions. In June 2003, according to the *Financial Times,* "the government made US$92 million available to create 32,000 temporary jobs" in response to the high unemployment rate. These are indications that the Hong Kong government may venture into the marketplace more obtrusively than in the past which could adversely affect its future scores. However, because Hong Kong's government intervention score is 1 point better this year, as a result, its overall score is 0.1 point better this year.

## QUICK STUDY

### SCORES

| | |
|---|---|
| Trade Policy | 1 |
| Fiscal Burden | 1.9 |
| Government Intervention | 2 |
| Monetary Policy | 1 |
| Foreign Investment | 1 |
| Banking and Finance | 1 |
| Wages and Prices | 2 |
| Property Rights | 1 |
| Regulation | 1 |
| Informal Market | 1.5 |

**Population:** 6,773,200

**Total area:** 1,092 sq. km

**GDP:** $168.6 billion

**GDP growth rate:** 2.3%

**GDP per capita:** $24,891

**Major exports:** clothing, electrical machinery and apparatus, textiles, jewelry, insurance services, financial services, transportation, travel services

**Exports of goods and services:** $287.9 billion

**Major export trading partners:** China 39.3%, US 21.3%, Japan 5.4%, UK 3.5%

**Major imports:** electrical machinery and appliances, telecommunications and sound equipment, travel services, transportation (a large share of which is re-exported)

**Imports of goods and services:** $272.9 billion

**Major import trading partners:** China 44.2%, Japan 11.3%, Taiwan 7.2%, US 5.6%

**Foreign direct investment (net):** −$3.6 billion

2002 Data (in constant 1995 US dollars)

### TRADE POLICY

**Score: 1–Stable** (very low level of protectionism)

Hong Kong is basically duty-free. There are no quotas and no antidumping or countervailing duties. Licenses are required for few products, but issuance is very fast. According to the Hong Kong Economic and Trade Office, "Hong Kong only maintains those non-tariff measures which are required to protect public health, safety, security and the environment to fulfill [Hong Kong's] obligations undertaken to [its] trading partners and under international agreements."

### FISCAL BURDEN OF GOVERNMENT

Score—Income Taxation: **1.5**–Stable (low tax rates)
Score—Corporate Taxation: **1.5**–Stable (low tax rates)
Score—Change in Government Expenditures: **3**–Stable (very low decrease)
**Final Score: 1.9**–Stable (low cost of government)

Hong Kong has increased its top income and corporate tax rates effective April 1, 2003. According to the Economic and Trade Office, Hong Kong maintains a dual income tax system under which individuals are taxed progressively between 2 percent and 18.5 percent (up from 17 percent) on income adjusted for deductions and allowances or at a flat rate of 15.5 percent (up from 15 percent) on their gross income. In 2004, the top progressive tax rate will increase to 20 percent, and the flat tax rate will increase to 16 percent. Individuals are taxed at whatever tax liability is lowest. For purposes of grading the *Index,* the top income tax rate is based on the flat rate of 15.5 percent. The top corporate tax rate has increased to 17.5 percent, up from 16 percent reported in the 2003 *Index.* However, government expenditures as a share of GDP decreased less in 2002 (0.1 percentage point to 21.5 percent) than they did in

2001 (0.3 percentage point). On net, Hong Kong's fiscal burden of government score is unchanged this year.

## GOVERNMENT INTERVENTION IN THE ECONOMY
### Score: **2**–Better (low level)

Based on data from Hong Kong's Census and Statistics Bureau, the government consumed 10.3 percent of GDP in 2002. In the April 2002–March 2003 fiscal year, according to the Economic and Trade Office, Hong Kong received 1.6 percent of its revenues from state-owned enterprises and government ownership of property. Based on the use of a new methodology to grade this factor, Hong Kong's government intervention score is 1 point better this year. Hong Kong intervened in its stock market in August 1998, purchasing some $15.2 billion in private stocks. Soon afterward, the government established a tracker fund (TrackHK) on the stock market as a vehicle to dispose of the shares acquired. "The government disposed of the final batch of TrackHK shares on October 15th [2002]," reports the Economist Intelligence Unit. "The final disposal brought relief to investors who had been complaining that the sale of TrackHK shares was putting downward pressure on share prices at a time of bearish sentiment in the market." According to the U.S. Department of State, however, "The government decided to retain a portion of the [TrackHK] stocks (worth about US$410 million) as a long-term investment. The HKMA [Hong Kong Monetary Authority] is responsible for the management of these stocks. [TrackHK] is traded on the stock exchange." According to the Hong Kong Economic and Trade Office, the retained portion of the investment will be managed by external managers to avoid any conflict of interest. The EIU reports that the government also intervenes by holding off the auction of land. It has done so in June 1998 (for the first time in 20 years) and again from November 2002 through the end of 2003 in an attempt to stabilize property prices. Ever since Finance Minister Antony Leung indicated during his 2002 budget speech that the government could be a "proactive market enabler," investors have been increasingly concerned that the government will become more interventionist. In his 2003 budget speech, Leung emphasized that "the government must continue to support the market in policy-making instead of participating in it directly," but the possibility of government intervention is still a concern.

## MONETARY POLICY
### Score: **1**–Stable (very low level of inflation)

From 1993 to 2002, Hong Kong's weighted average annual rate of inflation was –2.67 percent.

## CAPITAL FLOWS AND FOREIGN INVESTMENT
### Score: **1**–Stable (very low barriers)

Among all the world's governments, Hong Kong's is one of the most receptive to investment and does not discriminate between foreign and domestic investors. According to the Economist Intelligence Unit, "The simplicity of procedures for investing, expanding and establishing a local company is a major attraction for foreign investment in Hong Kong." There are virtually no restrictions on foreign capital, ownership of property or companies, or investment except in the media sector. The EIU reports that foreign entities may own no more than 49 percent of local broadcast stations or cable operations. There are no controls or requirements on current transfers, purchase of real estate, access to foreign exchange, or repatriation of profits. The Securities and Futures Bill, which came into effect on April 1, 2003, consolidates 10 existing ordinances and introduces some new elements to simplify the regulatory environment, increase transparency, and strengthen the securities regulator.

## BANKING AND FINANCE
### Score: **1**–Stable (very low level of restrictions)

Hong Kong is a global banking center and 11th in the world in volume of external transactions. Banks are classified as licensed banks, restricted licensed banks (RLBs), and deposit taking companies (DTCs). There were 147 licensed banks, 49 RLBs, and 54 DTCs in Hong Kong at the end of 2001. Banks are independent of the government, and foreign banks are free to operate with only limited restrictions. In November 2001, the Hong Kong Monetary Authority (HKMA) removed all remaining restrictions on the number of branches foreign banks are allowed to maintain in Hong Kong. In May 2002, the HKMA reduced market entry requirements for foreign banks by lowering the asset and deposit criteria for new foreign bank branches. Hong Kong does not have deposit insurance, but in April 2003, a Deposit Protection Scheme Bill was introduced in the Legislative Council. The Economic and Trade Office expects the deposit insurance scheme to be operational in 2005 if legislation is passed this year. Regulations governing financial activities in Hong Kong are light compared to world standards, although the International Monetary Fund lists caps on the aggregate holding of share capital and land as a percent of an institution's capital base. In January 2002, Hong Kong's Securities and Futures Commission enacted new disclosure and selection criteria for index funds to improve transparency and investor protection.

## WAGES AND PRICES
### Score: **2**–Stable (low level of intervention)

Hong Kong's market largely sets wages and prices, although price controls are imposed on rent for some residential properties, public transport, and electricity. There is no minimum wage for local employees; however, Hong Kong does impose a minimum wage on imported workers, including foreign domestic helpers. According to the U. S. Department of State, Hong Kong's labor laws incorporate the principle of "fair wages" and require compliance with wage agreements; at the same time, Hong Kong has no mandatory minimum wage and no specific statutory protection for collective bargaining, although the government does not impede or discourage such arrangements.

## PROPERTY RIGHTS
### Score: **1**–Stable (very high level of protection)

The government of Hong Kong fully protects private property rights. The legal system to protect these rights is both efficient and effective. According to the U.S. Department of State, "The local court system provides effective enforcement of contracts, dispute settlements and protection of rights, including intellectual property. Secured interests in property are recognized and enforced." There is a growing concern, however, that the legal protection of the business environment may be fading. According to the Hong Kong Policy Research Institute, "the issue of legislating to fulfill [Hong Kong's] responsibility under Article 23 of the Basic Law has aroused much public concern, especially among the publishers and media...." (Article 23 of the Basic Law establishes that Hong Kong will enact laws on its own to prohibit any act of treason, secession, sedition, or subversion against the Central People's Government of China.) So far, Hong Kong's record on protecting property rights remains one of the world's best; but given China's record on suppressing individual freedom, there is growing concern on the part of businesses that the Hong Kong government may be increasingly inclined to legislate to prevent individual freedom, which would affect, for example, investors in the media business. According to the Economist Intelligence Unit, "the government controls all land in Hong Kong...and renewable land leases are granted or sold via public auction, tender or...private treaty. The leases can be traded."

## REGULATION
### Score: **1**–Stable (very low level)

The regulations imposed on business are few, not burdensome, and applied uniformly. The procedure for starting a business is relatively simple. According to the Economist Intelligence Unit, "the government runs a Business License Information Service with a one-stop service to provide information on the licensing requirements for all business operations.... It normally takes the registrar six working days to process documents and issue a certificate of incorporation." Hong Kong's labor code is strictly enforced, but the regulations are not significantly burdensome. The Economist Intelligence Unit reports that "companies considering a major new industrial project in Hong Kong should provide an outline to the Environmental Protection Department (EPD) early in the planning stage for advice on any requirements for environmental assessment."

## INFORMAL MARKET
### Score: **1.5**–Stable (low level of activity)

Transparency International's 2002 score for Hong Kong is 8.2. Therefore, Hong Kong's informal market score is 1.5 this year.

# HUNGARY

HUNGARY

Rank: 42
Score: 2.60
Category: Mostly Free

**Present & Past Scores**

(Best) 1
2
3
4
(Worst) 5

2.93 2.98 3.04 2.94 2.89 2.43 2.38 2.23 2.55 2.60

'95 '96 '97 '98 '99 '00 '01 '02 '03 '04

## QUICK STUDY

### SCORES

| | |
|---|---|
| Trade Policy | 3 |
| Fiscal Burden | 3 |
| Government Intervention | 2 |
| Monetary Policy | 3 |
| Foreign Investment | 2 |
| Banking and Finance | 2 |
| Wages and Prices | 3 |
| Property Rights | 2 |
| Regulation | 3 |
| Informal Market | 3 |

**Population:** 10,152,000

**Total area:** 93,030 sq. km

**GDP:** $58.2 billion

**GDP growth rate:** 3.3%

**GDP per capita:** $5,733

**Major exports:** machinery and equipment, food, beverages and tobacco, raw materials, fuels and electricity

**Exports of goods and services:** $41.4 billion

**Major export trading partners:** Germany 34.9%, Austria 8.7%, Italy 5.9%, US 5.6%

**Major imports:** machinery and equipment, food products, manufactures

**Imports of goods and services:** $43.1 billion

**Major import trading partners:** Germany 26.3%, Italy 8.3%, Austria 7.9%, Russia 6.8%

**Foreign direct investment (net):** $597.6 million

2002 Data (in constant 1995 US dollars)

Hungary, a multiparty democracy, is one of the success stories of post-communist transformation. Power shifts between center–left and center–right are common. In the April 2002 elections, the Socialists, led by Peter Medgyessy, and their liberal partners, the Free Democrats, defeated the ruling center–right FIDESZ party after the latter had become increasingly nationalist. Successive governments have implemented economic liberalization and privatization that have led to majority foreign ownership in major industries. The private sector accounts for over 80 percent of GDP, and 90 percent of the banking sector is privately held. Thanks to consistent liberalization and a predictable exchange rate policy, Hungary now attracts one-third of Central and Eastern Europe's total foreign direct investment. FDI has greatly improved the Hungarian economy: Foreign companies are responsible for increased numbers of jobs and account for 70 percent of exports, approximately three-quarters of which are to European Union countries. Among the major unresolved economic problems are the unreformed public sector, which is draining finances, and large industrial subsidies. Hungary's economic achievements, combined with the advanced harmonization of its legal system, have made it a viable candidate for EU accession in 2004; it also has been a member of NATO since 1999 and is a founding member of the World Trade Organization and the Central European Free Trade Agreement. Hungary's informal market score is 0.5 point worse this year. As a result, its overall score is 0.05 point worse this year.

###  TRADE POLICY
**Score: 3–Stable** (moderate level of protectionism)

According to the World Bank, Hungary's weighted average tariff rate in 1997 (the most recent year for which World Bank data are available) was 4.5 percent. The Economist Intelligence Unit reports that "import licenses are required for…food, medicines, textiles, energy carriers, floor covering, clothing, footwear, cars, precious stones and metals, hazardous chemicals and explosives, tires, paper and wood…. [A] global quota [applies] to textiles, jewelry and precious metals, motor vehicles, domestic cleaning products, shoes and clothes, among other products."

###  FISCAL BURDEN OF GOVERNMENT
**Score—Income Taxation: 4–Stable** (high tax rates)
**Score—Corporate Taxation: 2–Stable** (low tax rates)
**Score—Change in Government Expenditures: 4–Stable** (moderate increase)
**Final Score: 3–Stable** (moderate cost of government)

Hungary's top income tax rate is 40 percent. The top corporate income tax rate is 18 percent. Government expenditures as a share of GDP rose less in 2002 (1.3 percentage points to 52.2 percent) than they did in 2001 (1.8 percentage points). On net, Hungary's fiscal burden of government score is unchanged this year.

### GOVERNMENT INTERVENTION IN THE ECONOMY
**Score: 2–Stable** (low level)

Based on data from the World Bank, the government consumed 11 percent of GDP in 2001. In 2000, according to the International Monetary Fund, Hungary received 3.43 percent of its total revenues from state-owned enterprises and government ownership of property.

**MONETARY POLICY**
Score: **3**–Stable (moderate level of inflation)

From 1993 to 2002, Hungary's weighted average annual rate of inflation was 7.21 percent.

 **CAPITAL FLOWS AND FOREIGN INVESTMENT**
Score: **2**–Stable (low barriers)

Hungary is very open to foreign investment and is a leader in foreign investment reform. The U.S. Department of State reports that Hungarian companies with foreign ownership account for 70 percent of total exports and 33 percent of GDP. With few exceptions, the government allows 100 percent foreign ownership in almost all firms. The law does not discriminate against foreign investors, and government approval is not required in most cases. Foreigners may not purchase agricultural land. Licenses for air transport and shipping and asset management services are subject to approval. The government restricts ownership of broadcasting and newspapers and continues to hold a "golden share" with power to veto sales in many privatized "strategic" enterprises. The National Bank of Hungary permits foreign exchange accounts held by residents, subject to approval, and non-residents are free to hold foreign exchange accounts. Hungary places no restrictions or controls on payments for or proceeds from invisible transactions, current transfers, real estate transactions, or repatriation of profits. Some issues or sales of capital market securities, bonds, debt securities, derivatives, credits, and some outward direct investments require authorization.

 **BANKING AND FINANCE**
Score: **2**–Stable (low level of restrictions)

The banking industry is increasingly competitive. Banks are relatively free from burdensome government oversight, and the Economist Intelligence Unit reports that "The state's role in commercial banking is minimal." Foreign banks face no barriers to entry into the Hungarian market. According to the EIU, "The trend of declining state shareholdings has been accompanied by a corresponding increase in foreign ownership, from 14.9% in 1994 to 67.6% by 2000." The government continues to hold equity in four credit institutions but has indicated that it plans to sell Postabank, a state-owned retail bank.

 **WAGES AND PRICES**
Score: **3**–Stable (moderate level of intervention)

Hungary controls some prices. The central government maintains price controls on pharmaceuticals, long-distance public transport, basic telephone service, basic postal service, electricity, natural gas, and water supply and sewage. Local governments control prices on steam and hot water supply, local public transport, local water supply and sewage disposal, rent, and certain public services. The central government offers a wholesale price floor for many agricultural products and price ceilings for housing. According to the Hungarian Embassy, central government price controls cover 10 percent of total consumption, and local government price controls cover 6 percent of total consumption. Hungary has a minimum wage.

 **PROPERTY RIGHTS**
Score: **2**–Stable (high level of protection)

The constitution provides for an independent judiciary, and the government respects this provision in practice. The threat of expropriation is low. However, the Economist Intelligence Unit reports that the court system is slow and severely over-burdened, and it may take more than a year to obtain a final ruling on a contract dispute.

 **REGULATION**
Score: **3**–Stable (moderate level)

Much of Hungary's regulatory regime corresponds with European Union standards. A business license is required only for a few activities, and the government has streamlined the process for obtaining a license. However, regulations are not always transparent or evenly applied. There is some corruption in the bureaucracy. According to the Economist Intelligence Unit, "personal connections can considerably accelerate and improve the changes of success in bureaucratic and many other processes. A study by Gallup…has shown that 32% of small and medium-sized enterprises had encountered corruption in the course of business."

 **INFORMAL MARKET**
Score: **3**–Worse (moderate level of activity)

Transparency International's 2002 score for Hungary is 4.9. Therefore, Hungary's informal market score is 3 this year— 0.5 point worse than the 2.5 reported in the 2003 *Index*.

ICELAND

# ICELAND

**Rank:** 17
**Score:** 2.00
**Category:** Mostly Free

Present & Past Scores

(Best) 1
2
3
4
(Worst) 5

2.30 2.20 2.20 2.11 2.16 2.18 1.93 2.00

'95 '96 '97 '98 '99 '00 '01 '02 '03 '04
n/a n/a

Hosting the smallest population of any country in the Organisation for Economic Co-operation and Development, and with unemployment around 3 percent, Iceland has, according to *The Economist*, "managed to make itself the sixth richest country per capita in the world, measured in purchasing-power terms." Exports, particularly of marine products, drive the economy, accounting for 25 percent of GDP. Despite benefiting from trade, reports the Economist Intelligence Unit, "Iceland's agricultural sector is nevertheless one of the most heavily subsidized and protected in the world." Iceland is a member of the European Free Trade Agreement and part of the European Economic Area. It is not a member of the European Union, but polls conducted over the past year reveal that the majority of voters favor EU membership. David Oddsson has served as prime minister since 1991 and is Europe's longest-serving prime minister. Though he won the May 10 election, Oddson will step down in September 2004. No party won a working majority, and the two present governing parties (Oddsson's conservative Independence Party and the Progressive Party) have agreed to continue in coalition. Foreign Affairs Minister Halldor Asgrimsson will become the new prime minister. Iceland's fiscal burden of government score is 0.2 point worse this year, and its government intervention score is 0.5 point worse. As a result, Iceland's overall score is 0.07 point worse this year, causing Iceland to be classified as a "mostly free" economy.

## QUICK STUDY

### SCORES

| | |
|---|---|
| Trade Policy | 2 |
| Fiscal Burden | 3 |
| Government Intervention | 3 |
| Monetary Policy | 2 |
| Foreign Investment | 2 |
| Banking and Finance | 3 |
| Wages and Prices | 1 |
| Property Rights | 1 |
| Regulation | 2 |
| Informal Market | 1 |

**Population:** 288,201

**Total area:** 103,000 sq. km

**GDP:** $9 billion

**GDP growth rate:** −0.5%

**GDP per capita:** $31,417

**Major exports:** marine products, aluminum, ferrosilicon, agricultural products

**Exports of goods and services:** $3.1 billion

**Major export trading partners:** UK 18.2%, Germany 14.9%, Netherlands 10.9%, US 10.3%, Portugal 5.5%

**Major imports:** industrial supplies and capital goods, transport equipment, fuel and lubricants, consumer goods

**Imports of goods and services:** $3.5 billion

**Major import trading partners:** Germany 12.2%, US 11.1%, Denmark 8.6%, Norway 7.8%, UK 7.5%

**Foreign direct investment (net):** −$118 million

2002 Data (in constant 1995 US dollars)

## TRADE POLICY
### Score: **2**–Stable (low level of protectionism)

The World Bank reports that Iceland's weighted average tariff rate in 2001 (the most recent year for which World Bank data are available) was 3.4 percent. According to the U.S. Department of State, "Most agricultural products are subject to high tariffs and import of some, such as uncooked meat, is prohibited for phyto-sanitary reasons…. Imported meat must be hormone-free. Iceland maintains strict phyto-sanitary regulations, since many animal diseases common elsewhere are not present in the country."

## FISCAL BURDEN OF GOVERNMENT
Score—Income Taxation: **4.5**–Worse (very high tax rates)
Score—Corporate Taxation: **2**–Stable (low tax rates)
Score—Change in Government Expenditures: **3.5**–Stable (low increase)
### Final Score: **3**–Worse (moderate cost of government)

According to Ernst and Young, Iceland's top income tax rate is 48.76 percent, up from the 35 percent reported in the 2003 *Index*. The top corporate tax rate is 18 percent. Government expenditures as a share of GDP increased more in 2002 (1 percentage point to 44.6 percent) than they did in 2001 (0.5 percentage point). This increase is not substantial enough to alter Iceland's change in government expenditures score. Based on the increase in its income tax rate, Iceland's fiscal burden of government score is 0.2 point worse this year.

## GOVERNMENT INTERVENTION IN THE ECONOMY
### Score: **3**–Worse (moderate level)

Based on data from Statistics Iceland, the government consumed 25.1 percent of GDP in 2002. In 2001, based on data from the Ministry of Finance, Iceland received 6.91 percent of its total revenues from state-owned enterprises and government ownership of property, up from the 1.1 percent reported in the 2003 Index. As a result, Iceland's government intervention score is 0.5 point worse this year.

## MONETARY POLICY
### Score: **2**–Stable (low level of inflation)

From 1993 to 2002, Iceland's weighted average annual rate of inflation was 5.33 percent.

## CAPITAL FLOWS AND FOREIGN INVESTMENT
### Score: **2**–Stable (low barriers)

Iceland generally welcomes foreign investment, and foreign investors receive domestic treatment, although the government still maintains some restrictions in such key areas as fishing, aviation, and energy. In the fishing industry, for example, foreign ownership is limited to 25 percent. There are no controls or requirements on current transfers, access to foreign exchange, or repatriation of profits. Iceland does not have many barriers, but those that exist—particularly in the fishing industry—affect a major portion of the economy.

## BANKING AND FINANCE
### Score: **3**–Stable (moderate level of restrictions)

Since joining the European Economic Area, Iceland has complied with European Union directives by liberalizing and deregulating financial markets and allowing Icelandic financial institutions to operate on a cross-border basis in the EEA and EEA financial institutions to operate similarly in Iceland. According to the Central Bank of Iceland, 172 foreign insurance companies have licenses to provide services in Iceland, and as of June 2002, foreign banks provided 27 percent of total credit. The Icelandic Investment Bank has been completely privatized, and the government is working to privatize its two remaining commercial banks, the National Bank of Iceland and the Agricultural Bank of Iceland. According to a July 6, 2003, *Finanews* article, the divestment is due to be completed in December 2003. (The cut-off date for including any policy changes in the *Index* was June 30, 2003). If privatization of the two remaining state-owned banks is successful, Iceland's banking and finance score is likely to improve in future editions of the *Index*.

## WAGES AND PRICES
### Score: **1**–Stable (very low level of intervention)

The market sets most prices in Iceland, although agriculture remains subsidized. According to the Economist Intelligence Unit, "The agricultural sector is one of the most heavily subsidized and protected in the world." However, the very low portion of economic output resulting from the agricultural sector minimizes the impact of agricultural subsidies. Collective bargaining agreements set workers' pay, hours, and working conditions; government plays a minor role, pri-

marily as a mediator, in this process. Iceland does not have a minimum wage.

## PROPERTY RIGHTS
### Score: **1**–Stable (very high level of protection)

Private property is well-protected in Iceland. The U.S. Department of State reports that "the Constitution and law provide for an independent judiciary, and the Government generally respected this provision in practice…. With limited exceptions, trials were public and conducted fairly, with no official intimidation."

## REGULATION
### Score: **2**–Stable (low level)

Over the past several years, significant deregulation and some privatization have opened the economy to greater competition and efficiency. The U.S. Department of State reports that "Icelandic laws regulating business practices are consistent with those of most [Organisation for Economic Cooperation and Development] member states, and are increasingly based on European Union directives as a result of Iceland's EEA membership. Much of Iceland's financial regulatory system was put in place only in the 1990s, thus it is not yet clear where the boundaries of regulatory authority lie in some areas." Some of the economy—especially fishing and agriculture—remains heavily regulated. For example, reports the Economist Intelligence Unit, "Iceland has traditionally stood aloof from membership of the EU, largely in order to maintain exclusive control of its vital fisheries resource." Opponents of EU membership find the EU's common fisheries policy unacceptable for an economy that relies so heavily on fishing.

## INFORMAL MARKET
### Score: **1**–Stable (very low level of activity)

Transparency International's 2002 score for Iceland is 9.4. Therefore, Iceland's informal market score is 1 this year.

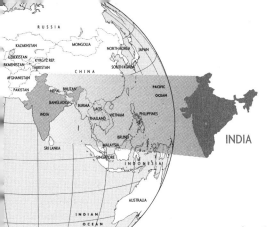

# INDIA

Rank: 121

Score: 3.53

Category: Mostly Unfree

Present & Past Scores

(Best) 1
2
3
4
(Worst) 5

3.93 3.93 3.88 3.83 3.93 3.93 3.91 3.61 3.58 3.53

'95 '96 '97 '98 '99 '00 '01 '02 '03 '04

After instituting a bold economic reform program in 1991, India experienced robust growth throughout most of the 1990s before losing momentum at the end of the decade. It has since posted steady, if not spectacular, growth, but many are rightly disappointed at the failure to exploit the economy's untapped potential. In 2002, the economy grew slightly more than 4 percent, largely because of robust industrial growth and higher spending on capital goods. Interest rates are at historic lows, and India's current account is in surplus after 24 years of deficit. Nevertheless, many believe that India cannot become the regional economic powerhouse it aspires to be without a "second generation" of reforms. New Delhi has taken some positive steps by lowering agricultural subsidies, enacting new laws that make it faster and easier to convict loan defaulters, relaxing some restrictions on foreign investment, and privatizing major state-owned enterprises like its largest car manufacturer and international telephone company. Numerous structural problems, however, continue to be a drag on the economy. The government continues to restrict 700 sectors to small-scale industries, preventing larger companies from taking advantage of economies of scale. A convoluted regulatory system, including draconian laws that ensure labor market rigidity, discourages private sector investment, and an underdeveloped securities market and a public deficit that is 5.6 percent of GDP have driven up the price of capital. India's fiscal burden of government score is 0.5 point better this year. As a result, its overall score is 0.05 point better this year.

## TRADE POLICY
### Score: **5**–Stable (very high level of protectionism)

According to the World Bank, India's weighted average tariff rate in 2001 (the most recent year for which World Bank data are available) was 28.2 percent. India requires onerous licenses for many products. According to the Economist Intelligence Unit, the government "has directed that 133 imported products must comply with the mandatory quality standards applicable to domestic products and be registered with the Bureau of Indian Standards for this purpose."

## FISCAL BURDEN OF GOVERNMENT
Score—Income Taxation: **3**–Stable (moderate tax rates)
Score—Corporate Taxation: **5**–Worse (very high tax rates)
Score—Change in Government Expenditures: **2**–Better (moderate decrease)
### Final Score: **3.8**–Better (high cost of government)

India's top income tax rate is 31.5 percent, up from the 30 percent reported in the 2003 *Index*. The top corporate tax rate is 36.75 percent (a top rate of 35 percent plus a 5 percent surcharge), up from the 35 percent reported in the 2003 *Index*. However, government expenditures as a share of GDP decreased 2.4 percentage points to 28.2 percent in 2001, compared to a 3.8 percentage point increase in 2000. On net, India's fiscal burden of government score is 0.5 point better this year.

## GOVERNMENT INTERVENTION IN THE ECONOMY
### Score: **3.5**–Stable (high level)

The World Bank reports that the government consumed 13.1 percent of GDP in 2001. In the same year, according to the International Monetary Fund, India received 21.13 percent of its total revenues from state-owned enterprises and government ownership of property.

## MONETARY POLICY
Score: **2**–Stable (low level of inflation)

From 1993 to 2002, India's weighted average annual rate of inflation was 4.33 percent.

## CAPITAL FLOWS AND FOREIGN INVESTMENT
Score: **3**–Stable (moderate barriers)

India is taking some gradual steps to attract more foreign investment. A May 1, 2003, *Wall Street Journal* article reports that India is setting up special economic zones, where investment restrictions are less stringent, but that "progress has been slow...." The government recently relaxed foreign investment restrictions in the defense equipment, print media, and airport ground handling sectors. Nevertheless, substantial barriers remain. According to the International Monetary Fund, some foreign investment "requires the approval of the Foreign Investment Promotion Board (FIPB) and for another seven items where less than 100% is allowed. There are other exclusions, such as industrial licensing and locational policies." The IMF reports that central bank approval is required for residents to open foreign currency accounts, either domestically or abroad, and that such accounts are subject to significant restrictions. Non-residents may hold foreign exchange and domestic currency accounts, subject to approval and conditions. Some payments and transfers face quantitative limits. The IMF reports that capital transactions and some credit operations are subject to certain restrictions and requirements.

## BANKING AND FINANCE
Score: **4**–Stable (high level of restrictions)

Although the government has adopted a more tolerant policy toward foreign banks in recent years, it still dominates the banking sector. According to the U.S. Department of State, "In terms of business, the state-owned banks account for more than 70 percent of deposits and loans." There are 50 foreign banks operating 200 branches, but they account for only 13 percent of total deposits. The government also affects the allocation of credit. "All commercial banks face stiff restrictions on the use of both their assets and liabilities," reports the U.S. Department of State. "The RBI [Reserve Bank of India, the central bank] requires that domestic Indian banks make 40 percent of their loans at concessional rates to priority sectors selected by the government.... Since July 1993, foreign banks have been required to make 32 percent of their loans to these priority sector[s]."

## WAGES AND PRICES
Score: **3**–Stable (moderate level of intervention)

Although India is removing price controls on some goods, the government continues to influence prices on a number of goods and services. In April 2002, the government eliminated price controls in the petroleum sector. It continues to subsidize liquefied petroleum gas and kerosene but plans to phase out these subsidies over the next three to five years. The Economist Intelligence Unit reports that the government plans to remove price controls on fertilizer by 2006 and is taking steps to remove price controls on sugar. According to the same source, "The Essential Commodities Act of 1955 applies price controls at the factory, wholesale and retail levels on 'essential' commodities. Some agricultural commodities—such as sugar and certain cereals—are subject to domestic price and marketing arrangements." The government mandates numerous minimum wages that vary according to state and industry.

## PROPERTY RIGHTS
Score: **3**–Stable (moderate level of protection)

Protection of property rights is applied unevenly in India. The Economist Intelligence Unit reports that "large backlogs create delays—sometimes years long—in reaching decisions. Consequently, foreign corporations often include clauses for international arbitration in their contracts." According to the U.S. Department of State, "Critics say that liquidating a bankrupt company may take as long as 20 years." Protection of property for local investors, particularly the smallest ones, is weak.

## REGULATION
Score: **4**–Stable (high level)

Businesses must contend with an extensive web of federal and state regulations that tend to punish successful small businesses and impede the full realization of the labor market's potential. According to the *Financial Times*, "India's manufacturing sector continues to be held back by a web of archaic regulations. These include reservations for small-scale industries, covering 800 products in a self-defeating policy that prevents small businesses from growing. They also include punitive industrial disputes rules that inhibit companies from hiring labour owing to the near impossibility of shedding it later. Similar laws deter companies from outsourcing work to contract labourers. Cumulatively, such restrictions have skewed domestic and foreign investment towards capital—as opposed to labor—intensive operations. Thus, India's greatest resource, its cheap plentiful labour, is effectively locked out of large-scale manufacturing." The regulatory web fosters corruption in the bureaucracy. *The Economist* reports that "Delhi's 200,000–250,000 bicycle-rickshaw pullers collectively pay bribes of 20m–25m rupees a month for the privilege of being allowed to pursue their lucrative profession."

## INFORMAL MARKET
Score: **4**–Stable (high level of activity)

Transparency International's 2002 score for India is 2.7. Therefore, India's informal market score is 4 this year.

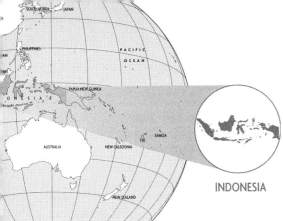

# INDONESIA

INDONESIA

Rank: 136

Score: 3.76

Category: Mostly Unfree

**Present & Past Scores**

(Best) 1
2
3
4
(Worst) 5

3.58  3.00  3.05  3.00  3.14  3.60  3.60  3.49  3.43  3.76

'95 '96 '97 '98 '99 '00 '01 '02 '03 '04

After five years of political and economic turmoil, Indonesia's economy has stabilized and is growing slowly. The successful execution of an International Monetary Fund macro-economic program by President Megawatti Sukarnoputri's administration has led to mild economic growth and relative political stability. Indonesia's stock market has performed among the best in Asia, and its sovereign debt has been upgraded from CCC+ to B– by Standard & Poor's. However, economic growth is expected to be only about 3 percent in 2003, compared to more than 7 percent during the 1990–1996 period. A national election is scheduled for June 2004, but the result may or may not be positive in terms of fiscal responsibility and political stability. The police and military are fighting insurgencies and communal violence across the archipelago, and although the government is not threatened, political fallout from human rights abuses by the security force could influence donor countries. The economy is also burdened with the effects on tourism of the October 2002 Bali bombing and the severe acute respiratory syndrome (SARS) epidemic. SARS has not yet infected Indonesia, but the overall slowdown in tourism in Asia has affected the economy. Indonesia's fiscal burden of government score is 0.8 point worse this year, and its government intervention score is 0.5 point worse; in addition, its capital flows and foreign investment score and wages and prices score are 1 point worse. As a result, Indonesia's overall score is 0.33 point worse this year.

## TRADE POLICY
### Score: **3**–Stable (moderate level of protectionism)

The World Bank reports that Indonesia's weighted average tariff rate in 2000 (the most recent year for which World Bank data are available) was 5.4 percent. According to the U.S. Department of State, "the following goods are still subject to import restrictions, licensing and/or prohibition: narcotics, psychotropics, explosive materials, fire-arms and ammunition, fireworks, certain books and printed materials, audio and /or visual recording media, telecommunications equipment, color photocopying equipment…, endangered wild fauna and flora…, certain species of fish, medicines, unregistered food and beverages at the Department of Health, dangerous materials, pesticides, ozone-depleting substances and goods containing ozone depleting substances, wastes, culturally valuable goods, and other items."

## FISCAL BURDEN OF GOVERNMENT
### Score—Income Taxation: **3.5**–Stable (high tax rates)
### Score—Corporate Taxation: **4**–Stable (high tax rates)
### Score—Change in Government Expenditures: **5**–Worse (very high increase)
### Final Score: **4.1**–Worse (high cost of government)

Indonesia's top income tax rate is 35 percent. The top corporate income tax rate is 30 percent. Government expenditures as a share of GDP increased 6.6 percentage points to 23.8 percent in 2001, compared to a 3.9 percentage point decline in 2000. As a result, Indonesia's fiscal burden of government score is 0.8 point worse this year.

## GOVERNMENT INTERVENTION IN THE ECONOMY
### Score: **4**–Worse (high level)

The World Bank reports that the government consumed 7.4 percent of GDP in 2001. In the same year, according to the International Monetary Fund, Indonesia received 5.14 percent of

221

its total revenues from state-owned enterprises and government ownership of property. Indonesia's Statistics Office, however, reports that the government employs over 20 percent of the labor force. According to the Economist Intelligence Unit, the following companies are on the privatization list: "Semen Gresik and Indocement Tunggal Prakasa (cement); Indosat (telecommunications); Indo Farma and Kimia Farma (pharmaceuticals); Angkasa Pura I (airport operations); Tambang Bukit Asam (coal mining); Wisma Nusantara Internasional (property); and Bank Mandiri." Based on the apparent unreliability of figures for government consumption and revenues, 2 points have been added to Indonesia's government intervention score (1 point per unreliable figure). As a result, Indonesia's government intervention score is 0.5 point worse this year.

 ## MONETARY POLICY
### Score: **3**–Stable (moderate level of inflation)

From 1993 to 2002, Indonesia's weighted average annual rate of inflation was 11.86 percent.

 ## CAPITAL FLOWS AND FOREIGN INVESTMENT
### Score: **4**–Worse (high barriers)

Although the government opened many sectors to foreign investment in 1998 and continues to seek foreign investment, substantial barriers remain. According to the government's 2000 "negative list," 11 business sectors are closed to both foreign and domestic investment. Eight are open to domestic investment but closed to foreign investment. Foreign investors establishing a joint venture with a local partner may own up to 45 percent in the following sectors: port construction, electricity, shipping, processing and distribution of public drinking water, public rail transportation, and medical services. With respect to unofficial impediments, according to the Economist Intelligence Unit, "Corruption among civil servants remains a disincentive for foreign investors. Facilitation fees, personal relationships and a subjective legal system limit the abilities of foreign firms to obtain permits, licenses, and government contracts and concessions." The International Monetary Fund reports that by the eleventh year of production, foreign ownership of direct investments must be divested and that for investments greater than $50 million, at least 50 percent of foreign ownership must be divested by the twentieth year. Both residents and non-residents may hold foreign exchange checking and time deposit accounts. There are no restrictions on payments and transfers. Beginning in January 2001, Indonesia prohibited lending and overdraft to non-residents, placing funds with non-residents, purchase of rupiah-denominated securities issued by non-residents, interoffice transactions in rupiah, and equity participation in rupiah with non-residents. Based on the growing evidence of corruption and substantial official barriers to foreign investment, Indonesia's capital flows and foreign investment score is 1 point worse this year.

 ## BANKING AND FINANCE
### Score: **4**–Stable (high level of restrictions)

According to the U.S. Department of State, the government of Indonesia "launched a massive bank recapitalization program in 1999 that has stabilized the banking sector. While the banking sector is no longer in immediate threat of collapse, lending activity is far from pre-crisis levels, and several large state-owned banks continue to lose money." State-owned banks traditionally have dominated the sector, and a February 6, 2003, *Economist* article notes that "the Indonesian Bank Restructuring Agency (IBRA) controls almost all the biggest banks, formerly private ones as well as seven state banks." The Economist Intelligence Unit reports that the government is undertaking an extensive program of banking-sector privatization. In May 2003, a 51 percent stake of Bank Danamon (Indonesia's fifth largest bank) was sold to Asia Finance Indonesia, and the IBRA plans to sell another 20 percent on the stock market. The government plans to sell a 30 percent stake of Bank Mandiri (the country's largest bank), a 52.05 percent stake of Bank Lippo, and a 30 percent stake of Bank Rakyat Indonesia in the third quarter of 2003. The IBRA plans to sell a 71 percent stake in Bank International Indonesia in November 2003. Based on the fact that, despite the privatization that is taking place, the government still dominates the banking sector, Indonesia's banking and finance score is unchanged this year. If Indonesia should succeed in reducing its holdings, its score could improve in future editions of the *Index*.

 ## WAGES AND PRICES
### Score: **3**–Worse (moderate level of intervention)

According to the Economist Intelligence Unit, "A handful of commodities and services remained classified as under 'administered prices.' These include petrol, electricity, liquefied petroleum gas, rice, cigarettes, cement, hospital services, potable/piped water, city transport, air transport, telephone charges, trains, salt, toll-road tariffs and postage." The government influences prices through the extensive state-owned sector, which includes (but is not limited to) enterprises in the banking, textile, cement, pharmacy, telecommunications, paper, hotel, and coal sectors. In 2002, the government raised the price of fuel by 22 percent, local telephone rates by 17 percent, and long distance rates by 13 percent. Regional wage councils consisting of workers, employers, and the government establish minimum wages for their areas. Based on the extent of government-imposed price controls and the government's ability to influence prices through state-owned enterprises, Indonesia's wages and prices score is 1 point worse this year.

 ## PROPERTY RIGHTS
### Score: **4**–Stable (low level of protection)

Court rulings can be arbitrary and inconsistent, and the judicial system suffers from corruption. The Economist

Intelligence Unit reports that "Indonesia's judiciary has an erratic record of arbitration with foreign businesses, and the legislature is only now implementing laws on investment and banking. Protection of property rights is even worse. Despite pressure from the international community for Indonesia to honour internationally binding contracts, the government has suspended many private infrastructure projects for economic and political reasons. Moreover, the court system does not provide adequate legal recourse for settling property disputes." The same source reports that judicial corruption is rampant.

## REGULATION
### Score: **4**–Stable (high level)

Indonesia's regulatory environment is plagued by corruption and red tape. According to the Economist Intelligence Unit, "Facilitation fees, personal relationships and a subjective legal system limit the abilities of foreign firms to obtain per-mits, licenses, and government contracts and concessions." The U.S. Department of State reports that "Indonesia has a tangled regulatory and legal environment where most firms, both foreign and domestic, attempt to avoid the justice system. Laws and regulations are often vague and require substantial interpretation by implementing offices, leading to business uncertainty and rent seeking opportunities. Deregulation has been somewhat successful in removing barriers, creating more transparent trade and investment regimes, and has alleviated, but not eliminated, red tape. U.S. businesses routinely cite transparency problems and red tape as factors hindering operations."

## INFORMAL MARKET
### Score: **4.5**–Stable (very high level of activity)

Transparency International's 2002 score for Indonesia is 1.9. Therefore, Indonesia's informal market score is 4.5 this year.

# IRAN

Rank: 148

Score: 4.26

Category: Repressed

**Present & Past Scores**

(Best) 1
2
3
4
(Worst) 5

4.79 4.80 4.76 4.56 4.69 4.84 4.63 4.30
4.26

'95 '96 '97 '98 '99 '00 '01 '02 '03 '04
n/a

IRAN

Iran had one of the Middle East's most advanced economies before it was crippled by the 1979 Islamic revolution, the 1980–1988 Iran–Iraq war, and widespread economic mismanagement. Hopes for systematic political and economic reform were raised under President Mohammed Khatami, who was re-elected in June 2001, but Khatami remains hamstrung by opposition from entrenched bureaucrats who permeate the state agencies and by Islamic hard-liners in the judiciary and other state institutions who value ideological purity over economic progress. President Khatami, in an effort to gain important concessions from hard-line clerics embedded in the government and to mitigate a growing rift among coalition reformers disillusioned by the slow pace of economic reform, has threatened to resign unless legislation extending the president's judicial authority is approved. Khatami has made little progress in reforming Iran's economy. In 2002, however, his government was able to establish a new unified currency regime, and the central bank has authorized the establishment of the first private banks since the 1979 revolution. The Economist Intelligence Unit has forecasted economic growth in 2003 at 5.7 percent, an estimate that reflects an increase in non-oil industrial and manufacturing output spurred by reduced import restrictions and a subsequent rise in domestic demand. Iran's fiscal burden of government score is 0.6 point worse this year; however, its trade policy score is 1 point better. As a result, Iran's overall score is 0.04 point better this year.

## TRADE POLICY
### Score: **2**–Better (low level of protectionism)

According to a World Bank study, Iran's weighted average tariff rate in 2000 was 3.1 percent, down from the 6.1 percent reported in the 2003 *Index*. As a result, Iran's trade policy score is 1 point better this year. According to the Economist Intelligence Unit, "Prohibited imports…include some luxury items, alcohol, pork, narcotics, guns and ammunition, aerial cameras, radio transmitters and 'indecent' media…. In addition, videos or music CDs brought into Iran may be held by customs authorities for vetting or may be confiscated." The World Bank reports that "the main instruments of commercial policy have been non-tariff barriers and the system of multiple exchange rates rather than explicit import tariffs."

## FISCAL BURDEN OF GOVERNMENT
### Score—Income Taxation: **5**–Stable (very high tax rates)
### Score—Corporate Taxation: **3**–Stable (moderate tax rates)
### Score—Change in Government Expenditures: **3.5**–Worse (low increase)
### Final Score: **3.6**–Worse (high cost of government)

Iran's top income tax rate is 54 percent. The top corporate tax rate was recently reduced to 25 percent. Government expenditures as a share of GDP increased 0.8 percentage point to 19.4 percent in 2001, compared to a 7.1 percentage point decrease in 2000. As a result, Iran's fiscal burden of government score is 0.6 point worse this year.

## GOVERNMENT INTERVENTION IN THE ECONOMY
### Score: **5**–Stable (very high level)

The World Bank reports that the government consumed 13.2 percent of GDP in 2001. However, this figure underestimates the level of state involvement in the economy. The

225

Economist Intelligence Unit reports that "inefficient state owned enterprises (SOEs), and politically powerful individuals and institutions such as the bonyad (Islamic 'charities' that control large business conglomerates) have established a tight grip on much of the nonoil economy, utilising their preferential access to domestic credit, foreign-exchange, licences, and public contracts to protect their positions. These advantages have made it difficult for the private sector to compete, and as a result it remains small…." Based on the apparent unreliability of reported government consumption figures, 1 point has been added to Iran's government intervention score. Another point has been added based on the significant presence of state-owned enterprises.

## MONETARY POLICY
### Score: **4**–Stable (high level of inflation)

From 1993 to 2002, Iran's weighted average annual rate of inflation was 13.92 percent.

## CAPITAL FLOWS AND FOREIGN INVESTMENT
### Score: **4**–Stable (high barriers)

The government updated its foreign investment code for the first time in over 50 years when the Law on the Attraction and Protection of Foreign Investment was enacted in May 2002. According to the Economist Intelligence Unit, "The bill contains certain limitations to foreign investment, not permitting a market share of greater than 25% in one sector, or 35% in individual industries. The law does, however, include a guarantee on the repatriation in hard currency of profits earned in the domestic economy, rather than only export earnings, and also guarantees market-rate compensation for assets that are nationalised. Crucially, it allows for international arbitration in legal disputes, a key demand for foreign investors unwilling to be exposed to the vagaries of the Iranian judicial system." Although the new law provides some liberalization of foreign investment, the EIU reports that "a range of problems must still be addressed before foreign investment flows begin to strengthen, not least the latent political hostility towards foreign business apparent in the post-revolution constitution. Even investment flows into the oil sector have been affected by political pressures, and many deals with foreign energy companies have fallen behind schedule." The International Monetary Fund reports that most payments and transfers are subject to limitations, quantitative limits, or approval requirements. All credit operations are subject to government controls, as are most personal capital movements.

## BANKING AND FINANCE
### Score: **5**–Stable (very high level of restrictions)

The ability of banks to charge interest is restricted under Iran's interpretation of Islamic law. Much of Iran's commercial bank loan portfolio is tied up in low-return loans to state-owned enterprises and politically connected individuals or businesses. In 1998, foreign banks were allowed to establish limited ventures in the free-trade zones. In April 2000, the government announced that it would permit private banks for the first time since the 1979 revolution, when private banks were nationalized. The central bank approved the first three private banks in mid-2001, and one bank, Karafarinan, began operations in 2002. The impact of the introduction of private banks on Iran's banking sector is expected to be minimal, however. According to the Economist Intelligence Unit, "Even by local standards, the banks are extremely small, and are likely to post slow growth in their first years of operation as the central bank sets cautious limits on their activities. Their freedom to set market-determined 'interest' rates will also be circumscribed by Bank Markazi's insistence that they remain within 2 percentage points of those offered by the state-owned commercial banks."

## WAGES AND PRICES
### Score: **4**–Stable (high level of intervention)

According to the Economist Intelligence Unit, "Most domestic prices have now been deregulated and 'price enforcement courts' abolished, but political considerations have prevented the removal of subsidies and price controls on 'essential' items, such as fuel, power and core foodstuffs." The government provides massive subsidies that affect prices for various commodities. "The total spent annually on state subsidies," reports the EIU, "has been estimated at some US$8bn–10bn…. Gasoline, for example, is sold at just 10% of its international price." The government sets minimum wages for each sector and region.

## PROPERTY RIGHTS
### Score: **5**–Stable (very low level of protection)

Property rights are not protected in Iran. According to the Economist Intelligence Unit, "The rule of law in Iran is inconsistent and unsatisfactory. Recourse to the courts is unwieldy and often counter-productive and rarely leads to the swift resolution of outstanding disputes…. Few foreign firms have had satisfactory experiences when seeking to bring a contract dispute before a court. The judicial system is opaque and very slow moving, and Iranian parties—both public and private—are adept at employing effective delaying tactics, substantially increasing the time and financial cost of legal action." The U.S. Department of State reports that "the court system is not independent and is subject to government and religious influence. It serves as the principal vehicle of the State to restrict freedom and reform in the Society." The EIU reports that the government permits private investment in state land but not land ownership.

## REGULATION
### Score: **5**–Stable (very high level)

The government effectively discourages the establishment of new businesses. According to the Economist Intelligence

Unit, "Contract negotiations are often lengthy, prolonged by the exhaustive details demanded by state agencies, and the slow functioning bureaucracy, which often requires approval from an extensive number of higher officials before legal agreement can be concluded." President Khatami's attempts at reform have been largely unsuccessful. The EIU reports that corruption is a continuing problem.

 ## INFORMAL MARKET
### Score: **5**–Stable (very high level of activity)

Smuggling is rampant. "In 2000," reports a study from the University of Linz, Austria, "the informal economy was estimated to be 17.48% of GDP." In addition, according to the Economist Intelligence Unit, "The highly fluid nature of Iran's labour market and the large size of the informal services sector make accurate estimates of employment levels difficult." There is an active informal market in currency.

# IRAQ

Rank: Suspended

Score: n/a

Category: n/a

**Present & Past Scores**

(Best) 1
2
3
4
(Worst) 5

4.85  4.85  4.85  4.85  4.90  4.90  5.00

'95  '96  '97  '98  '99  '00  '01  '02  '03  '04
n/a                                    n/a  n/a

## QUICK STUDY

### SCORES

| | |
|---|---|
| Trade Policy | n/a |
| Fiscal Burden | n/a |
| Government Intervention | n/a |
| Monetary Policy | n/a |
| Foreign Investment | n/a |
| Banking and Finance | n/a |
| Wages and Prices | n/a |
| Property Rights | n/a |
| Regulation | n/a |
| Informal Market | n/a |

**Population:** 23,750,180

**Total area:** 437,072 sq. km

**GDP:** n/a

**GDP growth rate:** n/a

**GDP per capita:** n/a

**Major exports:** crude oil

**Exports of goods and services:** n/a

**Major export trading partners:** n/a

**Major import:** food, medicine, manufactures

**Imports of goods and services:** n/a

**Major import trading partners:** n/a

**Foreign direct investment (net):** n/a

2001 Data (in constant 1995 US dollars)

The defeat and overthrow of Iraqi dictator Saddam Hussein by the allied coalition led by the United States is bound to have far-reaching implications for the Iraqi economy. The war and its chaotic aftermath initially undermined the economy, but the lifting of United Nations economic sanctions, the anticipated revival of Iraqi oil exports, and impending economic reforms should give Iraq a brighter economic future. Under Saddam Hussein's leadership, Iraq's economy was devastated by the 1980–1988 war against Iran, the 1991 Gulf War, and the resulting U.N. economic sanctions. Saddam's Ba'athist socialist policies imposed extensive central planning on the industrial economy and foreign trade while leaving most agriculture, some small-scale industry, and some services to private entrepreneurs. The economy is dominated by the oil sector, which provides more than 90 percent of hard currency earnings. Although reliable economic data remain scarce, the Economist Intelligence Unit forecast in March 2003 that real GDP would contract by approximately 7.5 percent in 2003 as a result of the war but would rebound to grow by around 15 percent in 2004. Iraq has refused to provide basic economic data to the United Nations—a requirement of membership for any other international organization. The lack of data is so complete that international financial institutions, foreign government agencies, and private businesses that provide economic analysis and data refuse to publish any official data or estimates on Iraq's economy. This situation makes it impossible to score several factors and raises questions about the reliability of data in the others. As a result, Iraq has been suspended from grading since compilation of the 2003 *Index*.

## TRADE POLICY
### Score: Not graded

Iraq is trying to reconstruct its economy. Trade sanctions were lifted after the war, and according to *Taipei Times*, "The US-led Administration in Iraq is to establish a major credit facility…to lubricate overseas trade." There is no clear trade policy at this point.

## FISCAL BURDEN OF GOVERNMENT
### Score—Income Taxation: Not graded
### Score—Corporate Taxation: Not graded
### Score—Change in Government Expenditures: Not graded
## Final Score: Not graded

According to the Economist Intelligence Unit, "There is no tradition of direct taxation in Iraq. The political necessity of relieving the economic hardship of ordinary Iraqis, in order to maximise support for interim governing bodies, and of seeking international financial assistance in this process is likely to prevent the introduction of taxation [in the near future]." Data on taxation and government expenditure are not available.

## GOVERNMENT INTERVENTION IN THE ECONOMY
### Score: Not graded

There are no data on government consumption and revenues from state-owned enterprises. "With American blessings," reports *The New York Times*, "the Iraqi government is still paying full salaries to at least 200,000 employees at government ministries and the country's huge moribund government-owned companies…. American officials estimate that as many as

250,000 people work for government-owned companies and civilian government ministries, and most of those jobs currently involve little or no work."

## MONETARY POLICY
Score: Not graded

Data from the Economist Intelligence Unit indicate that from 1993 to 2002, Iraq's weighted average annual rate of inflation was 69.18 percent.

## CAPITAL FLOWS AND FOREIGN INVESTMENT
Score: Not graded

Foreign investment is expected to play a key role in the rebuilding of Iraq. According to a June 10, 2003, *Financial Times* article, "coalition officials have announced plans to speed up privatisation of Iraqi state enterprises, starting within a year, and have made it clear that foreign companies will be welcome to participate." The interim chief executive of Iraq's Ministry of Oil announced in May 2003 that Iraq would be seeking foreign investors to help it produce and explore crude oil.

## BANKING AND FINANCE
Score: Not graded

In a February 2003 report, the United States Institute of Peace states that "the banking system in Iraq is virtually non-existent." According to an April 22, 2003, *International Herald Tribune* article, "Rejuvenating the lifeblood of Iraq's commerce is a priority. Near the top of the list is rebuilding a central bank that can back a new national currency, issue loans, set interest rates and manage the country's billions of dollars of debt."

## WAGES AND PRICES
Score: Not graded

The May 28, 2003, edition of the *Taipei Times* reported that a rationing system that existed under Saddam Hussein's regime—and on which an estimated 60 percent of Iraqis depend for basic goods—would be preserved but that, according to Paul Bremer, head of the Coalition Provisional Authority, "In the long term we would like to see market prices brought into the economy…."

## PROPERTY RIGHTS
Score: Not graded

There is no protection of property in Iraq. The aftermath of the war resulted in high insecurity, rioting, and looting, discouraging any kind of investment. U.S. forces are trying to help Iraqis feel safer, but that remains a daunting task.

## REGULATION
Score: Not graded

All Iraqi business regulations were abolished after the regime lost the war. At the moment, there is no legal framework for the conduct of business in Iraq.

## INFORMAL MARKET
Score: Not graded

Smuggling of all kinds of products is rampant. The informal economy will grow until a clear set of rules for formal business is established.

# IRELAND

Rank: 5

Score: 1.74

Category: Free

Ireland is a modern, highly industrialized economy that has grown by 80 percent in real terms over the past decade. GDP per capita is now 122 percent of the European Union's average. Newly re-elected Prime Minister Bertie Ahern, whose Fianna Fail party governs in coalition with the Progressive Democrats, seems certain to maintain Ireland's markedly pro-business stance. Ireland has one of the world's most pro-business environments, especially for foreign businesses and foreign investment. The Ahern government lowered the Irish corporate tax rate from 16 percent to 12.5 percent in January 2003, far below the EU average of 30 percent. Not surprisingly, Ireland has become a major center for U.S. investment in Europe, especially for the computer, software, and engineering industries. Although accounting for 1 percent of the euro-zone market, it receives nearly one-third of U.S. investment in the EU. GDP growth totaled 6.3 percent in 2002. However, inflation has begun to rise; by the end of 2002, the rate had reached 4.7 percent, well above the EU average. Given Ireland's extensive social welfare system, U.S. employers find that the marginal cost of employing workers is high, though less expensive than in the major Western European states. There also have been pressures to harmonize the Irish economy with the more statist economic ethos found in Continental Europe. A relatively weaker budgetary position requires that previously unsustainable levels of growth in government expenditure be curtailed. Ireland's fiscal burden of government score is 0.4 point better this year; however, its informal market score is 0.5 point worse. As a result, Ireland's overall score is 0.01 point worse this year.

## QUICK STUDY

### SCORES

| | |
|---|---|
| Trade Policy | 2 |
| Fiscal Burden | 2.4 |
| Government Intervention | 2 |
| Monetary Policy | 2 |
| Foreign Investment | 1 |
| Banking and Finance | 1 |
| Wages and Prices | 2 |
| Property Rights | 1 |
| Regulation | 2 |
| Informal Market | 2 |

**Population:** 3,897,000

**Total area:** 70,280 sq. km

**GDP:** $116.1 billion

**GDP growth rate:** 6.3%

**GDP per capita:** $29,792

**Major exports:** machinery and transport equipment, manufactured materials, computer and information, travel services, financial services

**Exports of goods and services:** $121.1 billion

**Major export trading partners:** UK 23.9%, US 18.1%, Germany 7.2%, France 5.0%, Japan 3.6%

**Major imports:** chemicals, manufactured materials, food and live animals, insurance services, financial services

**Imports of goods and services:** $96.3 billion

**Major import trading partners:** UK 35.9%, US 15.8%, Belgium 14.4%, Germany 6.4%, France 4.1%

**Foreign direct investment (net):** $16.4 billion

2002 Data (in constant 1995 US dollars)

## TRADE POLICY

### Score: **2**–Stable (low level of protectionism)

As a member of the European Union, Ireland had a weighted average tariff rate of 2.6 percent in 2001. The Economist Intelligence Unit reports that "approval is required for non-European Union imports of clothing, textiles and footwear. There are a few specific quotas, mainly on imports (such as textiles and yarn) that compete with locally produced goods, but these do not apply to products originating in EU member states."

## FISCAL BURDEN OF GOVERNMENT

Score—Income Taxation: **4**–Stable (high tax rates)
Score—Corporate Taxation: **1**–Better (very low tax rates)
Score—Change in Government Expenditures: **3.5**–Better (low increase)
### Final Score: **2.4**–Better (low cost of government)

Ireland's top income tax rate is 42 percent. The top corporate tax rate is 12.5 percent, down from the 16 percent reported in the 2003 *Index*. Government expenditures as a share of GDP increased less in 2002 (0.9 percentage point to 34.4 percent) than they did in 2001 (1.6 percentage points). Based on the lower top corporate tax rate and the smaller rate of increase in government expenditures as a share of GDP, Ireland's fiscal burden of government score is 0.4 point better this year.

## GOVERNMENT INTERVENTION IN THE ECONOMY

### Score: **2**–Stable (low level)

Data from Ireland's Central Statistics Office indicate that the government consumed 13.3 percent of GDP in 2002. In the same year, based on data from the Ministry of Finance, Ireland received 3.8 percent of its revenues from state-owned enterprises and government ownership of property.

 **MONETARY POLICY**
Score: **2**–Stable (low level of inflation)

From 1993 to 2002, Ireland's weighted average annual rate of inflation was 4.65 percent.

 **CAPITAL FLOWS AND FOREIGN INVESTMENT**
Score: **1**–Stable (very low barriers)

Ireland welcomes foreign investment, and barriers are minimal. The Economist Intelligence Unit reports that in terms of foreign investment per capita, Ireland was the European Union's largest recipient with almost three times as much foreign investment per capita as the Netherlands, which was the second highest. There is no approval process for foreign investment or capital inflows unless the company is applying for incentives. Restrictions apply to Irish airlines and agricultural land. There are no restrictions or barriers with respect to current transfers, repatriation of profits, or access to foreign exchange. Although permission is rarely withheld, individuals and businesses whose primary residence or office is not located in the EU or the European Economic Area must obtain permission from the Ministry of Agriculture, Food, and Rural Development to purchase land.

 **BANKING AND FINANCE**
Score: **1**–Stable (very low level of restrictions)

Ireland's banking and financial system is both advanced and generally competitive. According to the U.S. Department of State, "Credit is allocated on market terms. There is no discrimination between Irish and foreign firms…. The Irish banking system is sound." The Ministry of Finance reports that the government completed the sale of ACC bank in March 2002, ending government involvement in the banking sector. Dublin has attracted a number of foreign banks through its International Financial Services Center (IFSC), which offers banks a corporate tax rate of 10 percent; the European Commission, however, viewed the 10 percent corporate tax rate as an aid to industry, which is prohibited under European Union regulations. Ireland is now phasing out the corporate tax break for financial institutions.

 **WAGES AND PRICES**
Score: **2**–Stable (low level of intervention)

The market determines most prices. Ireland affects agricultural prices through its participation in the Common Agricultural Policy, a program that heavily subsidizes agricultural goods. Timbro, a Swedish think tank, reports that "EU consumers pay roughly 80–100% more for their food than would be the case in a mature free-market regime." The government intervenes in wage-setting through the National Wage Partnership Program. The latest deal, called Sustaining

Progress, increased nominal wages by 7 percent over a period of 18 months. According to the Economist Intelligence Unit, "A significant difficulty with Ireland's wage agreements is the rigidity they introduce to the labour market." These agreements influence both public-sector and private-sector wages. Ireland implemented a new national minimum wage in 2001.

 **PROPERTY RIGHTS**
Score: **1**–Stable (very high level of protection)

Expropriation of property is highly unlikely. Property receives good protection from the court system. The Economist Intelligence Unit reports that "contractual agreements are secure in Ireland, and both the judiciary and the civil service are of high quality."

 **REGULATION**
Score: **2**–Stable (low level)

Overall, Ireland's policy framework promotes an open and competitive business environment. Regulations are applied uniformly and are not particularly onerous. The U.S. Department of State reports that "Ireland has an open and transparent business climate. Surveys by private sector consultants and others, such as the [Organisation for Economic Co-operation and Development], consistently find Ireland has one of the most supportive environments for business in Europe. This is due, in part, to the country's broad, bipartisan political support for pro-business policies." Environmental protection has become increasingly important as a result of Ireland's membership in the European Union. According to the Economist Intelligence Unit, "the government has put increasing emphasis on 'precautionary' and 'polluter pays' principles." Mining investments need authorization from the Department of Public Enterprise. The EIU reports that "[labor] legislation has been enacted over the years [and] should not present special difficulties to employers, but it is strictly enforced." Corruption is not a serious problem for investors.

 **INFORMAL MARKET**
Score: **2**–Worse (low level of activity)

Transparency International's 2002 score for Ireland is 6.9, down from the 7.5 reported in the 2003 *Index*. As a result, Ireland's informal market score is 2 this year—0.5 point worse than the 1.5 reported in the 2003 *Index*.

# ISRAEL

ISRAEL

Rank: 29
Score: 2.36
Category: Mostly Free

**Present & Past Scores**

(Best) 1
2
3
4
(Worst) 5

2.90 2.81 2.64 2.65 2.68 2.70 2.60 2.55 2.40 2.36

'95 '96 '97 '98 '99 '00 '01 '02 '03 '04

## QUICK STUDY

### SCORES

| | |
|---|---|
| Trade Policy | 2 |
| Fiscal Burden | 4.6 |
| Government Intervention | 2.5 |
| Monetary Policy | 1 |
| Foreign Investment | 2 |
| Banking and Finance | 3 |
| Wages and Prices | 2 |
| Property Rights | 2 |
| Regulation | 3 |
| Informal Market | 1.5 |

**Population:** 6,640,000

**Total area:** 20,770 sq. km

**GDP:** $104.6 billion

**GDP growth rate:** −1.0%

**GDP per capita:** $15,759

**Major exports:** electronic communication, medical and scientific equipment, chemicals, chemical products and cut diamonds

**Exports of goods and services:** $38.6 billion

**Major export trading partners:** US 48.2%, Belgium 7.4%, Germany 6.0%, UK 4.8%, Hong Kong 3.6%

**Major imports:** machinery and equipment, fuel, chemicals

**Imports of goods and services:** $54.7 billion

**Major import trading partners:** US 23.5%, Belgium 10.2%, Germany 7.9%, UK 6.7%

**Foreign direct investment (net):** $524.6 million

2002 Data (in constant 1995 US dollars)

Israel has carried a heavy defense burden since gaining independence in 1948, fighting a series of wars against neighboring Arab states before signing peace treaties with Egypt in 1979 and Jordan in 1994. The Israeli economy boomed in the early 1990s, fueled by the influx of Jewish immigrants from the former Soviet Union and a strong high-technology sector; but the collapse of the 1993 Oslo peace agreement with the Palestinians and the onset of the intifada in September 2000 have depressed the tourism industry, discouraged foreign investment, and contributed to an economic recession in 2001–2002. Prime Minister Ariel Sharon, who won a landslide re-election victory in January 2003, has focused on security policies to reduce the threat of Palestinian terrorism, leaving economic reform plans to Finance Minister (and former Prime Minister) Benjamin Netanyahu. Netanyahu has proposed an emergency economic recovery program to rein in the growth of the public sector, reinvigorate the stalled privatization program, and set realistic fiscal targets, but his austerity plans face stiff political resistance. Recent data suggest that Israel's economy may have bottomed out, led by export growth and a rise in public consumption; the Economist Intelligence Unit predicts economic growth of 0.8 percent in 2003. Israel's fiscal burden of government score is 0.4 point better this year. As a result, its overall score is 0.04 point better this year.

 **TRADE POLICY**
### Score: 2–Stable (low level of protectionism)

According to the World Bank, Israel's weighted average tariff rate in 1993 (the most recent year for which World Bank data are available) was 4 percent. The Economist Intelligence Unit reports that "certain classes of goods may be prohibited from entry on grounds of health, environmental or obscenity regulations. Local Hebrew labeling is required for some products."

 **FISCAL BURDEN OF GOVERNMENT**
Score—Income Taxation: **5**–Stable (very high tax rates)
Score—Corporate Taxation: **5**–Stable (very high tax rates)
Score—Change in Government Expenditures: **3.5**–Better (low increase)
### Final Score: **4.6**–Better (very high cost of government)

Israel's top income tax rate is 50 percent. The top corporate tax rate is 36 percent. Government expenditures as a share of GDP increased less in 2002 (1 percentage point to 55.5 percent) than they did in 2001 (7.3 percentage points). As a result, Israel's fiscal burden of government score is 0.4 point better this year.

 **GOVERNMENT INTERVENTION IN THE ECONOMY**
### Score: 2.5–Stable (moderate level)

The International Monetary Fund reports that the government consumed 31 percent of GDP in 2002. In 2001, according to the IMF, Israel received 3.52 percent of its total revenues from state-owned enterprises and government ownership of property.

 **MONETARY POLICY**
### Score: 1–Stable (very low level of inflation)

From 1993 to 2002, Israel's weighted average annual rate of inflation was 2.83 percent.

## CAPITAL FLOWS AND FOREIGN INVESTMENT
### Score: **2**–Stable (low barriers)

There are no significant barriers to foreign investment except for those that apply to regulated sectors like banking, insurance, defense industries, and such state-owned interests as the national airline and the power monopoly. Israel otherwise permits 100 percent foreign ownership of businesses, although a foreign-owned entity must register with the government. Government procurement gives a 15 percent price preference to Israeli suppliers; in addition, when it signed the World Trade Organization's Government Procurement Agreement, Israel retained the right to set aside at least 20 percent of subcontracts for Israeli firms through 2004. According to the International Monetary Fund, both residents and non-residents may hold foreign exchange accounts, and there are no controls or restrictions on current transfers, repatriation of profits, and invisible transactions. Direct investment, money market instruments, securities, debt securities, and other capital transactions by residents are limited to a portion of their assets. Political instability is a far greater disincentive to foreign investment than is the level of government restrictions.

## BANKING AND FINANCE
### Score: **3**–Stable (moderate level of restrictions)

The commercial banking system is highly concentrated, with the five largest banks accounting for over 90 percent of banking assets. Israel's four largest banks came under government control after the 1983 banking crisis, and the government still owns a significant portion of the banking sector. The government fully privatized Mizrahi in 1998 and privatized Bank Hapoalim, Israel's largest bank, in two stages in 1997 and 2000. It has yet to sell its shares in the second and third largest banking groups—Bank Leumi (in which it holds a 40 percent share) and Israel Discount Bank (56 percent)—and owns a controlling stake in the Industrial Development Bank. The government must approve any foreign investment in the highly regulated banking and insurance sectors, but foreign banks are expanding their presence According to the Economist Intelligence Unit, "owing to liberalisation in the capital markets, foreign banks have become more interested in Israel…. Three foreign banks…provide wholesale and retail banking services in Israel." Banks are prohibited from selling insurance and are allowed to manage pension funds only on a very limited basis.

## WAGES AND PRICES
### Score: **2**–Stable (low level of intervention)

Although most price controls have been lifted, they remain in effect in a few areas. According to the Economist Intelligence Unit, "The Law for the Supervision of Prices of Goods and Services authorises the Treasury and the Ministry of Industry and Trade to impose price controls on goods and services supplied by a monopoly, or in the framework of restricted trade. Controls may also be imposed if there is a large concentration in the supply of a good, or if the goods and services are subsidised, or if their producers receive support from the state budget. The government is entitled to impose price controls on goods and services deemed vital." Israel has a minimum wage.

## PROPERTY RIGHTS
### Score: **2**–Stable (high level of protection)

"In spite of the fractious political environment," reports the Economist Intelligence Unit, "contractual arrangements in Israel are generally secure. The country's legal system (largely based on the UK's but increasingly influenced by US attitudes and trends) is highly regarded as independent, fair and honest." Expropriation is possible, particularly for Palestinians, although it reportedly occurs only if the property is linked to a terrorist threat and expropriation is deemed to be in the interest of national security. Because expropriation is not the norm and occurs only in the context of national security, it is not considered a generalized threat to the protection of property.

## REGULATION
### Score: **3**–Stable (moderate level)

Israel has identified deregulation and encouragement of competition as official policies. However, the U.S. Department of State reports that "tax, labor, health, and safety laws can be impediments to…investors. Although the current trend is towards deregulation, Israel's bureaucracy can still be difficult to navigate…. It is important that potential investors get approvals or other commitments made by regulatory officials in writing before proceeding, rather than relying on unofficial oral promises." Bribery and corruption are not regarded as serious impediments.

## INFORMAL MARKET
### Score: **1.5**–Stable (low level of activity)

Transparency International's 2002 score for Israel is 7.3. Therefore, Israel's informal market score is 1.5 this year.

ITALY

# ITALY

Rank: 26
Score: 2.26
Category: Mostly Free

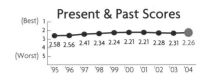

**Present & Past Scores**

(Best) 1
2
3
4
(Worst) 5

2.58 2.56 2.41 2.34 2.24 2.21 2.21 2.28 2.31 2.26

'95 '96 '97 '98 '99 '00 '01 '02 '03 '04

Italy is divided economically and culturally into two distinctive zones. Southern Italy is poor and heavily subsidized, while the northern part of the country remains one of Europe's most affluent regions. After more than 50 governments since World War II, the May 2001 election of Prime Minister Silvio Berlusconi seemed to give Italy a chance to enact the structural reforms that could reverse its low-growth, high-unemployment cycle. However, little has happened, and a string of promised reforms has been postponed or forgotten. Serious structural problems relating to the state's huge pension liabilities (amounting to 15 percent of Italy's yearly GDP—the highest figure in Europe), labor market rigidities, and bureaucratic burdens remain unaddressed. Italy's labor market is among the most rigid in Western Europe, with Italian law forcing large firms in effect to take on workers for life as the difficulties involved in dismissing them remain excessively high. It is therefore not surprising that the Italian economy has underperformed the rest of the euro zone throughout the past half-decade: In 2002, it grew by only 0.4 percent. The Berlusconi government has attempted a partial reform of the labor laws; in early February 2003, parliament approved reforms that somewhat increased the flexibility of Italy's rigid labor market through the introduction of employment contracts such as those relating to jobs on call and job sharing. Italy's fiscal burden of government score is 0.5 point better this year. As a result, its overall score is 0.05 point better this year.

## TRADE POLICY
### Score: **2**–Stable (low level of protectionism)

As a member of the European Union, Italy had a weighted average tariff rate of 2.6 percent in 2001. The Economist Intelligence Unit reports that imports outside the European Economic Area are restricted for sensitive products, such as steel, textiles, clothing, furs, and ivory, and that "for some products under quota, importers may apply to the Foreign Trade Institute...for a clearance, valid for three months." Italy has adopted the EU's common antidumping code for industrial goods.

## FISCAL BURDEN OF GOVERNMENT
Score—Income Taxation: **4.5**–Stable (very high tax rates)
Score—Corporate Taxation: **4.5**–Better (very high tax rates)
Score—Change in Government Expenditures: **3**–Better (very low decrease)
### Final Score: **4.1**–Better (high cost of government)

Italy's top income tax rate is 45 percent. The top corporate income tax rate is 34 percent, down from the 36 percent reported in the 2003 *Index.* Government expenditures as a percent of GDP decreased 0.8 percentage point to 47.7 percent in 2002, compared to a 1.6 percentage point increase in 2001. Based on its lower corporate tax rates and decrease in government expenditures as a share of GDP, Italy's fiscal burden of government score is 0.5 point better this year.

## GOVERNMENT INTERVENTION IN THE ECONOMY
### Score: **2**–Stable (low level)

The Economist Intelligence Unit reports that the government consumed 19.2 percent of GDP in 2002. In the same year, according to the Italian Embassy, Italy received 1.13 percent of its total revenues from state-owned enterprises and government ownership of property.

## MONETARY POLICY
Score: **1**–Stable (very low level of inflation)

From 1993 to 2002, Italy's weighted average annual rate of inflation was 2.52 percent.

## CAPITAL FLOWS AND FOREIGN INVESTMENT
Score: **2**–Stable (low barriers)

Italy generally welcomes foreign investment, although the government has the authority to veto mergers and acquisitions involving foreign investors for "reasons essential to the national economy." The government does not screen foreign investment, and the tax code does not discriminate against foreign investments. Foreigners may invest in any of the state-owned firms undergoing privatization except those relating to defense. According to the U.S. Department of State, "Foreign investors generally find no major impediments to investing in Italy, although bureaucratic requirements can be burdensome." Foreign citizens may not buy land along the Italian border, which falls under the jurisdiction of the Ministry of Defense. There are no barriers to repatriation of profits, capital transfers, payments, or current transfers.

## BANKING AND FINANCE
Score: **2**–Stable (low level of restrictions)

Italy's banking sector was dominated by the state until a recent spate of privatizations. With the sale of its remaining stake in Banco di Napoli in 2000, the government now has only a minimal presence in the banking sector. According to the Italian Embassy, government ownership of banks at both the central and local levels is 10 percent of total bank assets. The result has been greater banking concentration as private banks have merged with or bought stakes in former state banks; in 2002, the five largest bank groups had a market share of 56 percent, compared to 36 percent in 1995. Foreign banks are increasing their presence. The Economist Intelligence Unit reports that there were 74 foreign banks in 2001, up from 41 in 1990. Banks face some government restrictions and regulations; for example, in order to sell life and property insurance, firms must receive permission from the government. In February 2001, the government fixed the maximum rate on long-term mortgage rates at 9.96 percent. The Banking Law requires approval from the Bank of Italy if a foreign entity wants to raise its level of ownership in a bank above 5 percent.

## WAGES AND PRICES
Score: **2**–Stable (low level of intervention)

The market determines most wages and prices. The government, however, has the power to introduce price controls through the Interministerial Committee on Economic Programming and does impose price controls on a few goods. According to the Economist Intelligence Unit, "Goods and services now subject to rate setting at the national level include electricity, gas, telephone rates, prescription drugs...radio and television licenses, highway tolls, postal tariffs, certain fares for domestic travel (air, lake ferry, bus and railway) and drinking water." Italy also affects agricultural prices through its participation in the Common Agricultural Policy, a program that heavily subsidizes agricultural goods. According to Timbro, a Swedish think tank, "EU consumers pay roughly 80–100% more for their food than would be the case in a mature free-market regime." Minimum wages are set through collective bargaining agreements on a sector-by-sector basis that traditionally applies to all workers regardless of union affiliation. If labor and employers cannot reach an agreement, the courts can step in to set a "fair" wage, though this rarely happens.

## PROPERTY RIGHTS
Score: **2**–Stable (high level of protection)

Italy's constitution provides for an independent judiciary. The Economist Intelligence Unit reports that "contractual agreements in Italy are generally secure. The Judiciary and the bureaucracy are usually fair in their dealings with foreigners. Nevertheless, the prospect of long delays in the overburdened judicial system often leads companies to settle disputes out of court.... [C]orruption and improper business practices are more common than in Northern Europe. Extortion rackets by organized crime are a problem particularly in construction and retailing and specially...in the southern half of the country."

## REGULATION
Score: **3**–Stable (moderate level)

Red tape, slow deregulation, and regulations that vary from region to region and are inefficiently implemented all contribute to a non-transparent system. According to a European Commission report, it is now easier to establish a company in Italy, but many procedures are still complicated. The Economist Intelligence Unit reports that "there are now more than 40,000 laws that make up Italian environmental legislation; they are highly fragmented, and regional authorities interpret them inconsistently." The government is trying to get legislature approval for a reform package that will add flexibility to a very rigid labor market. Corruption in the bureaucracy remains a problem. The level of corruption in Italy is the highest among the G–7 countries, and the U.S. Department of State reports that "surveys of the business community in Italy routinely identify such domestic corruption as a disincentive to investing or doing business in the south and some other less-developed areas of Italy."

## INFORMAL MARKET
Score: **2.5**–Stable (moderate level of activity)

Transparency International's 2002 score for Italy is 5.2. Therefore, Italy's informal market score is 2.5 this year.

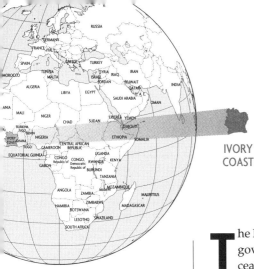

# IVORY COAST

IVORY
COAST

Rank: 89

Score: 3.18

Category: Mostly Unfree

Present & Past Scores

(Best) 1
2
3
4
(Worst) 5

3.43  3.83  3.80  3.74  3.73  3.68  3.08  3.00  3.16  3.18

'95  '96  '97  '98  '99  '00  '01  '02  '03  '04

## QUICK STUDY

### SCORES

| | |
|---|---|
| Trade Policy | 4 |
| Fiscal Burden | 4.3 |
| Government Intervention | 1.5 |
| Monetary Policy | 2 |
| Foreign Investment | 3 |
| Banking and Finance | 2 |
| Wages and Prices | 3 |
| Property Rights | 4 |
| Regulation | 4 |
| Informal Market | 4 |

**Population:** 16,410,080

**Total area:** 322,460 sq. km

**GDP:** $11.7 billion

**GDP growth rate:** −0.9%

**GDP per capita:** $715

**Major exports:** cocoa, coffee, petroleum, timber

**Exports of goods and services:** $4.3 billion

**Major export trading partners:** France 13.3%, Netherlands 9.4%, US 8.3%, Mali 5.8%, Germany 5.4%

**Major imports:** petroleum, food, transport equipment

**Imports of goods and services:** $3.7 billion

**Major import trading partners:** Nigeria 23.0%, France 22.6%, China 5.5%, Italy 3.8%, US 3.4%

**Foreign direct investment (net):** $197.3 million

2001 Data (in constant 1995 US dollars)

The Ivory Coast remained troubled into the early part of 2003. Highlighted by the French government's continued military presence in the central region, tensions relating to the cease-fire are expected to remain for some time. While the country has been able to hold on to its fragile government of national unity, the humanitarian fallout persists, with thousands of West Africans displaced as a result of the eight-month crisis. Factored with the HIV epidemic that continues to plague the sub-Saharan region, this situation makes the country's short-term financial prospects appear risky at best. Economically, the Ivory Coast continues to be hurt by domestic instability. It is still the world's largest supplier of cocoa at 40 percent of market share, but *The Economist* estimates that production is likely to fall in 2004 as a result of continued conflict that threatens to interrupt trade through the country's ports. With this trade contributing about 40 percent GDP to the Union Economique et Monetaire Ouest Africaine, such interruptions will negatively affect neighboring countries that rely heavily on Ivory Coast transport facilities for imports and exports. The Ivory Coast is also the continent's largest supplier of robusta coffee, ranking fourth or fifth in the world, and maintains healthy reserves of oil, natural gas, gold, iron, and nickel, which could provide for a positive economic future. GDP during 2003 will likely shrink by 4.3 percent. The Ivory Coast's fiscal burden of government score is 0.2 point worse this year. As a result, its overall score is 0.02 point worse this year.

## TRADE POLICY
### Score: **4**–Stable (high level of protectionism)

The Ivory Coast is a member of the West African Economic and Monetary Union (WAEMU), which imposes a common external tariff with four rates: 0 percent, 5 percent, 10 percent, and 20 percent. (The other seven members of the WAEMU are Benin, Burkina Faso, Guinea–Bissau, Mali, Niger, Senegal, and Togo.) According to the World Bank, Ivory Coast's weighted average tariff rate in 2001 (the most recent year for which World Bank data are available) was 9.6 percent. Imports of certain animal products, livestock, and petroleum require a license. The U.S. Department of State reports that "Corruption has the greatest impact with regard to the judiciary, contract awards, customs, and tax enforcement."

## FISCAL BURDEN OF GOVERNMENT
### Score—Income Taxation: **5**–Stable (very high tax rates)
### Score—Corporate Taxation: **4.5**–Stable (very high tax rates)
### Score—Change in Government Expenditures: **3**–Worse (very low decrease)
### Final Score: **4.3**–Worse (high cost of government)

The Ivory Coast's top income tax rate is 60 percent. The top corporate income tax rate is 35 percent. Government expenditures as a share of GDP decreased less in 2001 (0.1 percentage point to 18 percent) than they did in 2000 (1.5 percentage points). As a result, the Ivory Coast's fiscal burden of government score is 0.2 point worse this year.

## GOVERNMENT INTERVENTION IN THE ECONOMY
### Score: **1.5**–Stable (low level)

The World Bank reports that the government consumed 9.1 percent of GDP in 2001. In 2001, according to the International Monetary Fund, the Ivory Coast received 0.84 percent of its

total revenues from state-owned enterprises and government ownership of property.

## MONETARY POLICY
### Score: **2**–Stable (low level of inflation)

From 1993 to 2002, the Ivory Coast's weighted average annual rate of inflation was 3.28 percent. The Ivory Coast has benefited from a stable currency—a rarity in sub-Saharan Africa—as a member of the CFA franc zone. Fourteen countries use the CFA franc, a common currency with a fixed parity with the euro. (The other 13 countries are Benin, Burkina Faso, Cameroon, Central African Republic, Chad, Congo [Brazzaville], Equatorial Guinea, Gabon, Guinea–Bissau, Mali, Niger, Senegal, and Togo.)

## CAPITAL FLOWS AND FOREIGN INVESTMENT
### Score: **3**–Stable (moderate barriers)

According to the U.S. Department of State, "There are no significant limits on foreign investment, nor are there generally differences in treatment of foreign and national investors, either in terms of the level of foreign ownership or sector of investment." Investments from outside the franc zone require government approval. Purchases of real estate are permitted, but they must be reported to the government if they involve investment in an enterprise, branch, or corporation. The International Monetary Fund reports that foreign exchange accounts by both residents and non-residents are permitted but must be approved. Transfers to countries other than France, Monaco, members of the WAEMU, members of the Central African Economic and Monetary Community (CEMAC), and Comoros must also be approved by the government. Other transfers are subject to numerous requirements, controls, and authorization depending on the transaction. Foreign investors remain wary because of political instability, corruption, an inefficient bureaucracy, and unstable legal protections.

## BANKING AND FINANCE
### Score: **2**–Stable (low level of restrictions)

The Banque Centrale des Etats de l'Afrique de l'Ouest (Central Bank of West African States, or BCEAO), a central bank common to the eight members of the WAEMU, governs the Ivory Coast's banking system. Member countries use the CFA franc that is issued by the BCEAO and pegged to the euro. The government has largely divested its holdings in the banking sector but still owns two specialized financial institutions for making loans to the agriculture and housing sectors. The four largest banks are majority-owned by the private sector—three by foreign banks.

## WAGES AND PRICES
### Score: **3**–Stable (moderate level of intervention)

Following wide price swings in 2000 and 2001, the government has backtracked on its 1999 decision to liberalize prices for cocoa and has approved a new Bourse du café et cacao, which is 66 percent owned by the growers and 33 percent owned by the exporters, to monitor and set minimum producer prices every three months; the Autorité to manage a system of purchasing quotas, which are revised every three months; and the Fond de régulation et de contrôle to finance price stabilization through taxation on cocoa exports and forward selling. "Although most parties in [Ivory Coast] acknowledge that the current system of cocoa marketing needs reform," reports the Economist Intelligence Unit, "vested interests and political unrest have delayed any real progress. This is unlikely to change until 2004." The government last set monthly minimum wage rates, which vary by occupation, in 1996. Most people work informally in the agriculture sector, where the minimum wage is ineffective.

## PROPERTY RIGHTS
### Score: **4**–Stable (low level of protection)

According to the U.S. Department of State, "Enforcement of contract rights can be a time consuming and expensive process. Court cases move slowly and some do not appear to be judged on their legal or contractual merits. This has led to a widely-held view in the business community that there are corrupt magistrates." In practice, the court system "is subject to executive branch, military, and other outside influences" and "follows the lead of the executive in national security and politically sensitive issues."

## REGULATION
### Score: **4**–Stable (high level)

The Ivory Coast's bureaucracy obstructs business activity. The Economist Intelligence Unit reports that "heavy red tape pervades public administration, making it sometimes slow and inefficient." The government has made some efforts to increase regulatory transparency and overall competitiveness. Some of the steps taken, according to the U.S. Department of State, include "the creation of a centralized Office of Public Bids in the Ministry of Finance in an effort to ensure compliance with international bidding practices…the establishment of an Inspector General's office for the Government; the dissolution of the nontransparent cocoa and coffee marketing board; and the creation of regulatory bodies for the increasingly-liberalized telecommunications and electricity sectors." The same source reports that companies see corruption as an impediment to doing business.

## INFORMAL MARKET
### Score: **4**–Stable (high level of activity)

Transparency International's 2002 score for the Ivory Coast is 2.7. Therefore, the Ivory Coast's informal market score is 4 this year.

# JAMAICA

JAMAICA

Rank: 56

Score: 2.81

Category: Mostly Free

**Present & Past Scores**

(Best) 1
2
3
4
(Worst) 5

3.16  2.99  2.86  2.89  2.91  2.61  3.01  3.01  2.73  2.81

'95  '96  '97  '98  '99  '00  '01  '02  '03  '04

## QUICK STUDY

### SCORES

| | |
|---|---|
| Trade Policy | 4 |
| Fiscal Burden | 4.1 |
| Government Intervention | 2.5 |
| Monetary Policy | 3 |
| Foreign Investment | 1 |
| Banking and Finance | 2 |
| Wages and Prices | 2 |
| Property Rights | 3 |
| Regulation | 3 |
| Informal Market | 3.5 |

**Population:** 2,668,230

**Total area:** 10,990 sq. km

**GDP:** $5.6 billion

**GDP growth rate:** 1.7%

**GDP per capita:** $2,171

**Major exports:** alumina, bauxite, sugar, bananas

**Exports of goods and services:** $2.7 billion

**Major export trading partners:** US 31.0%, Canada 15.6%, UK 12.8%

**Major imports:** raw materials, machinery and transport equipment, fuels

**Imports of goods and services:** $2.97 billion

**Major import trading partners:** US 44.4%, CARICOM 12.8%, EU 9.4%

**Foreign direct investment (net):** $580 million

2001 Data (in constant 1995 US dollars)

An independent member of the British Commonwealth, Jamaica is a popular tourist destination in the Caribbean. But like other tourist havens, its economy is susceptible to external variables that affect travel. Tourism declined in 2001 following the terrorist attacks on the United States and remained in a slump as a result of the subsequent U.S. economic slowdown. Attempting to pay off external debt accumulated in excessive public spending during the 1990s, Jamaica could hardly afford a downturn. With the budget deficit at about 8.4 percent of GDP and public debt at 141 percent of GDP, 64 percent of Jamaica's budget goes to debt service. Unemployment hovers at 15 percent, and with 1,000 murders in 2002, Jamaica now has the world's third highest homicide rate. Prime Minister P. J. Patterson, elected in October 2002, has established plans to develop new tourist facilities, promote investment, and identify new tourism markets by 2010. Jamaica's government intervention score is 0.5 point better this year; however, its fiscal burden of government score is 0.8 point worse, and its informal market score is 0.5 point worse. As a result, Jamaica's overall score is 0.08 point worse this year.

###  TRADE POLICY
#### Score: **4**–Stable (high level of protectionism)

As a member of the Caribbean Community and Common Market (CARICOM), Jamaica has a common external tariff rate that ranges from 5 percent to 20 percent. According to the World Bank, Jamaica's weighted average tariff rate in 2001 (the most recent year for which World Bank data are available) was 10.3 percent. Jamaica restricts some imports to protect local industry. The U.S. Department of State reports that "there are still several items that require an import license. These items include milk powder, refined sugar, plants and parts of plants for perfume or pharmaceutical purposes, gum-resins, vegetable saps and extracts, certain chemicals, motor vehicles and parts, arms and ammunition, and certain toys, such as water pistols and gaming machines." Jamaica can depart from its common external tariff through the Minimum Rate Approach, a mechanism that is used to exceed the agreed minimum rates on several key goods.

###  FISCAL BURDEN OF GOVERNMENT
#### Score—Income Taxation: **2.5**–Stable (moderate tax rates)
#### Score—Corporate Taxation: **4.5**–Stable (very high tax rates)
#### Score—Change in Government Expenditures: **5**–Worse (very high increase)
#### Final Score: **4.1**–Worse (high cost of government)

Jamaica's top income tax rate is 25 percent. The top corporate tax rate is 33.3 percent. Government expenditures as a share of GDP increased 5.2 percentage points to 39.2 percent in 2001, compared to a 3.5 percentage point decrease in 2000. As a result, Jamaica's fiscal burden of government score is 0.8 point worse this year.

###  GOVERNMENT INTERVENTION IN THE ECONOMY
#### Score: **2.5**–Better (moderate level)

The World Bank reports that the government consumed 15.6 percent of GDP in 2001. In the same year, according to the International Monetary Fund, Jamaica received 8.09 percent of its total revenues from state-owned enterprises and government ownership of property, down from the 17.11 percent reported in the 2003 *Index*. As a result, Jamaica's government intervention score is 0.5 point better this year.

## MONETARY POLICY
### Score: **3**–Stable (moderate level of inflation)

From 1993 to 2002, Jamaica's weighted average annual rate of inflation was 7.19 percent.

## CAPITAL FLOWS AND FOREIGN INVESTMENT
### Score: **1**–Stable (very low barriers)

Jamaica encourages foreign investment in all sectors. Foreign investors and domestic interests receive equal treatment, and foreign investors are not excluded from acquiring privatized state-owned enterprises. The U.S. Department of State reports that non-CARICOM foreign companies may now have 100 percent foreign ownership in broadcasting services. The government is allowing competition, including competition from foreign investors, in the telecommunications sector. There is no screening of foreign investments, but an environmental impact assessment is required for new investments. The International Monetary Fund reports that there are no restrictions on foreign exchange accounts, which may be held by both residents and non-residents. There are no restrictions on transactions, transfers, or repatriation of funds, and non-residents may purchase real estate. Sale or issue of money market instruments by non-residents, sale or issue of those instruments abroad by residents, or purchase abroad of similar instruments by residents requires government approval.

## BANKING AND FINANCE
### Score: **2**–Stable (low level of restrictions)

A 1996 financial crisis prompted a government bailout of the banking and insurance sectors as well as strengthened supervision and regulation. The Financial Sector Adjustment Company (FINSAC) was created to provide funding, to reorganize illiquid and close insolvent financial institutions, and then to divest their assets. Since assuming control of over 12 financial institutions and intervening in 10 others during the financial crisis of the 1990s, FINSAC has divested itself of the banks and insurance companies that it acquired. "According to the Ministry of Finance," reports the U.S. Department of State, "FINSAC met significant targets over the last five years and has largely completed its mission to restructure and rehabilitate the Jamaican financial sector.... [FINSAC] will also complete its exit from the financial sector by [February 2003]." The rescue of the financial sector, completed with the March 2002 sale of the National Commercial Bank, entailed a cost estimated at 30 percent of GDP. Foreign banks hold over 80 percent of deposits in the banking sector. The rapid divestiture of banks taken over after the 1996 crisis has left the government with a minimal presence.

## WAGES AND PRICES
### Score: **2**–Stable (low level of intervention)

According to the U.S. Department of State, "Most prices are freely determined by the market. Notable exceptions are services, such as telecommunications, electricity, water and bus fares.... While there are no official or government policies on price regulation or control, the Fair Trading Commission (FTC) and the Consumer Affairs Commission (CAC) do monitor pricing of consumer items." Jamaica has a minimum wage law, but most workers are paid more than the minimum.

## PROPERTY RIGHTS
### Score: **3**–Stable (moderate level of protection)

The likelihood of expropriation is remote, and private property is protected. The U.S. Department of State reports that "Jamaica's legal system is based on English common law principles and the rules in relation to the enforceability of contracts are therefore based on the English common law. The Jamaican judicial system therefore recognizes and upholds the sanctity of contracts." However, the judiciary lacks adequate resources, and this creates delays. In some cases, according to the U.S. Department of State, "trials...are delayed for years, and other cases are dismissed because files cannot be located." An inadequate police force further weakens the security of property rights; the same source reports that "crime poses a greater threat to foreign investment than do politically motivated activities."

## REGULATION
### Score: **3**–Stable (moderate level)

Most regulations are moderately burdensome, and red tape can be a problem. According to the U.S. Department of State, "A cumbersome bureaucracy has been identified as a major disincentive to investment in Jamaica." In addition, "Although there has been improvement in the approval process for most investment projects, the time can take anywhere from three months for Free Zone projects to over a year for large mining and greenfield projects." New developments require environmental impact assessments prior to approval. The U.S. Department of State and other sources identify corruption as a problem, although the government has proposed anti-corruption legislation that would penalize bribery.

## INFORMAL MARKET
### Score: **3.5**–Worse (high level of activity)

Transparency International's 2002 score for Jamaica is 4. Therefore, Jamaica's informal market score is 3.5 this year—0.5 point worse than the 3 reported in the 2003 *Index*.

JAPAN

# JAPAN

Rank: 38

Score: 2.53

Category: Mostly Free

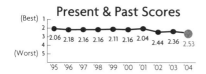

Present & Past Scores

(Best)

2.06 2.18 2.16 2.16 2.11 2.16 2.04 2.44 2.36 2.53

(Worst)

'95 '96 '97 '98 '99 '00 '01 '02 '03 '04

## QUICK STUDY

### SCORES

| | |
|---|---|
| Trade Policy | 2 |
| Fiscal Burden | 4.3 |
| Government Intervention | 2 |
| Monetary Policy | 1 |
| Foreign Investment | 3 |
| Banking and Finance | 4 |
| Wages and Prices | 2 |
| Property Rights | 2 |
| Regulation | 3 |
| Informal Market | 2 |

**Population:** 127,435,000

**Total area:** 377, 835 sq. km

**GDP:** $5.5 trillion

**GDP growth rate:** 0.2%

**GDP per capita:** $43,088

**Major exports:** transport equipment, electrical machinery, chemicals, metals

**Exports of goods and services:** $595.9 billion

**Major export trading partners:** US 28.5%, China 9.6%, South Korea 6.9%, Taiwan 6.3%, Hong Kong 6.1%

**Major imports:** machinery and equipment, mineral fuels, food, chemicals, raw materials

**Imports of goods and services:** $515.6 billion

**Major import trading partners:** China 18.3%, US 17.1%, South Korea 4.6%, Indonesia 4.2%, Australia 4.1%

**Foreign direct investment (net):** −$20.6 billion

2002 Data (in constant 1995 US dollars)

apan may still be the world's second largest economy after the United States, but for more than a decade, it has experienced little sustained growth, experiencing a less than 1 percent increase in GDP in 2001 and 2002. Despite the promises of sweeping reforms made two years ago by Prime Minister Junichiro Koizumi when he entered office, the prospects for a strong economic turnaround remain uncertain because of the lack of political will to enact real structural reforms. Unemployment is at an historic high, averaging 5.5 percent in 2002. The problem of non-performing loans (NPLs), in particular among the banks, remains serious despite the 1999 creation of the Revitalization and Collection Corporation, which was supposed to allow for their disposal. The banks are struggling to deal with $433 billion in NPLs as new bad loans are accumulating faster than the old ones can be written off. The government's policy priorities seem to be focused on preventing an economic crisis rather than pursuing implementation of structural reforms. Areas of immediate concern include the declining value of the stock market and deflation. Adding to the drag on growth is the poor performance of Japanese exports. Imports grew by a mere 1.4 percent during the first quarter of 2003. The total value of the country's two-way foreign trade was only 17.1 percent of GDP. This is due to unofficial restrictions on merchandise imports to protect the less efficient sectors of Japanese industry. Without significant and dramatic changes in the economy, Japan could be headed for a devastating collapse. Japan's fiscal burden of government score is 0.7 point worse this year, and its banking and finance score is 1 point worse. As a result, Japan's overall score is 0.17 point worse this year.

## TRADE POLICY

### Score: **2**–Stable (low level of protectionism)

According to the World Bank, Japan's weighted average tariff rate in 2001 (the most recent year for which World Bank data are available) was 2.1 percent. The Economist Intelligence Unit reports that the government has established minimum-access quantities for rice, wheat, barley, starch, and peanuts; "imports exceeding these [minimum] quantities are allowed, though still with high tariffs." Japan also maintains import restrictions for endangered species and products such as ivory, animal parts, and certain furs; swords and firearms; and more-than-two-month supplies of medicines and cosmetics for personal use.

## FISCAL BURDEN OF GOVERNMENT

### Score—Income Taxation: **3.5**–Stable (high tax rates)
### Score—Corporate Taxation: **5**–Worse (very high tax rates)
### Score—Change in Government Expenditures: **3.5**–Worse (low increase)
### Final Score: **4.3**–Worse (high cost of government)

Japan's top income tax rate is 37 percent. The top corporate tax rate is 40.9 percent, up from the 30 percent reported in the 2003 *Index*. Government expenditures as a share of GDP increased 0.6 percentage point to 38.6 percent in 2002, compared to a 0.6 percentage point decrease in 2001. Based on the increase in the top corporate tax rate and the shift from a falling to a rising level of government expenditures as a share of GDP, Japan's fiscal burden of government score is 0.7 point worse this year.

## GOVERNMENT INTERVENTION IN THE ECONOMY
### Score: **2**–Stable (low level)

According to the Economist Intelligence Unit, the government consumed 17.9 percent of GDP in 2002. In the same year, based on data from Japan's Statistics Bureau, Japan received 1.28 percent of its total revenues from state-owned enterprises and government ownership of property. The government intervenes in the stock market. In October 2002, according to CNN.com, the Bank of Japan announced that it would buy $2 trillion yen in shares of ailing banks throughout the year, until September 2003.

## MONETARY POLICY
### Score: **1**–Stable (very low level of inflation)

From 1993 to 2002, Japan's weighted average annual rate of inflation was –0.80 percent.

## CAPITAL FLOWS AND FOREIGN INVESTMENT
### Score: **3**–Stable (moderate barriers)

While most direct legal restrictions on foreign investment have been removed, many bureaucratic and informal barriers remain in effect, as evidenced by Japan's last-place standing among Organisation for Economic Co-operation and Development nations in foreign direct investment as a percentage of output. According to the Economist Intelligence Unit, "The attitude of the Japanese government towards foreign investment is ambivalent. Although officially the government welcomes foreign investors, in practice there remain a complex array of informal restrictions maintained by government and business alike designed to protect existing players." Foreign investors need to notify and obtain approval from the government for investments in the following restricted areas: agriculture, forestry, petroleum, electricity, gas, water, aerospace, telecommunications, and leather manufacturing. There are no restrictions or controls on the holding of foreign exchange accounts, or on invisible transactions, current transfers, repatriation of profits, or real estate transactions, by residents or non-residents.

## BANKING AND FINANCE
### Score: **4**–Worse (high level of restrictions)

Japan's banking system, although competitive, suffers from a large number of non-performing loans. According to the U.S. Department of State, the government estimates the value of non-performing loans at 8 percent of GDP; private analysts estimate that it could be as high as 25 percent of GDP. The relationship between banks and large corporations is part of the problem in resolving the banking crisis because a lack of transparency and impartiality impedes the banks' ability to deal with failing companies. The fifth largest bank, Resona Holdings, collapsed in May 2003 and was bailed out by the government at a cost of $17 billion. Resona has effectively been nationalized, as the government now controls over 50 percent of the bank's equity. According to an article in the May 20, 2003, edition of *The New York Times,* "By repeatedly supporting the weakest players in the economy…the government has created a moral hazard: Managers are free to go on making mistakes because they know the government will ultimately come to the rescue. Consumers, too, are spared the need to judge which institutions are strong or to avoid weak banks because their deposits are protected in any case." The government does not hinder the formation of foreign banks; the U.S. Department of State reports that there are nearly 100 foreign banks operating in Japan. The government does, however, affect the supply of credit through its state-run postal savings system, which has been renamed Japan Post and converted into an independent public corporation (as opposed to being controlled by various government bureaucracies). Japan Post is the world's largest single pool of savings, valued at $2 trillion or 50 percent of GDP. According to the Economist Intelligence Unit, "Private-sector banks have long complained that the existence of such a large state-run savings system distorts the country's credit market by encouraging the disintermediation of funds from the private sector, and they have lobbied vociferously for the system to be privatised." Based on the evidence that the government is increasing its presence in the banking sector, Japan's banking and finance score is 1 point worse this year.

## WAGES AND PRICES
### Score: **2**–Stable (low level of intervention)

The market sets most wages and prices. According to the Economist Intelligence Unit, "There are no formal price controls except on rice (for which there are also import quotas). But indirect regulation continues to influence prices on a wide range of products…. Although prices for many imported consumer goods have fallen sharply in recent years, they are still substantially higher than international prices." The government also maintains a price support program for agricultural goods. The U.S. Department of State reports that minimum wages are set on a regional or industry basis with input advisory councils composed of three groups: business, workers, and "public interest" organizations.

## PROPERTY RIGHTS
### Score: **2**–Stable (high level of protection)

In general, property rights are secure in Japan, although the judicial system at times becomes an obstacle to business. According to the Economist Intelligence Unit, "Japan has civil courts for enforcing property and contractual rights. The courts do not discriminate against foreign investors, but these courts are ill suited for litigation of investment and business disputes. Moreover, Japanese courts are slow; there are virtually no discovery procedures to compel disclosure of evidence from the opposing party, the courts lack contempt powers to compel a witness to testify or a party to comply with an injunction and preliminary injunctions are almost impossible to obtain."

## REGULATION
### Score: **3**–Stable (moderate level)

Japan has taken steps toward deregulation in recent years, but remaining regulations impose a substantial burden on businesses. According to the U.S. Department of State, "Japan's reputation for protectionism and red tape…is well deserved…. [T]he Japanese economy remains over-regulated and those regulations can be used to hinder foreign firms' attempts to gain access to the market." Bureaucrats and regulators are much more powerful in Japan than in other countries, having wide discretion to act as they see fit. The U.S. Department of State reports that the "Prime Minister launched an initiative, called the Special Zones for Structural Reform, that empowers local governments in Japan to take the lead on deregulation by establishing zones where businesses can be unfettered by onerous regulations. To date, the Prime Minister has approved 117 of these zones."

## INFORMAL MARKET
### Score: **2**–Stable (low level of activity)

Transparency International's 2002 score for Japan is 7.1. Therefore, Japan's informal market score is 2 this year.

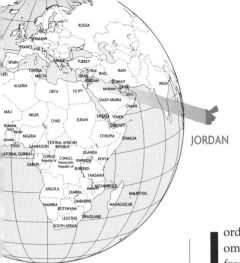

# JORDAN

JORDAN

Rank: 51

Score: 2.73

Category: Mostly Free

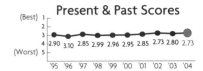
## QUICK STUDY

### SCORES

| | |
|---|---|
| Trade Policy | 4 |
| Fiscal Burden | 3.8 |
| Government Intervention | 3.5 |
| Monetary Policy | 1 |
| Foreign Investment | 2 |
| Banking and Finance | 2 |
| Wages and Prices | 2 |
| Property Rights | 3 |
| Regulation | 3 |
| Informal Market | 3 |

**Population:** 5,030,925

**Total area:** 92,300 sq. km

**GDP:** $8.2 billion

**GDP growth rate:** 4.2%

**GDP per capita:** $1,639

**Major exports:** manufactured goods, pharmaceuticals, machinery and transport equipment

**Exports of goods and services:** $4.1 billion

**Major export trading partners:** India 11.7%, US 9.6%, Saudi Arabia 5.6%, Israel 3.7%

**Major imports:** machinery and transport equipment, manufactured goods, food and live animals

**Imports of goods and services:** $6.3 billion

**Major import trading partners:** Germany 8.8%, US 7.8%, Italy 5.6%, France 5.5%

**Foreign direct investment (net):** $82.5 million

2001 Data (in constant 1995 US dollars)

Jordan is a small, poor constitutional monarchy with few economic resources and an economy that historically has been supported by foreign loans, foreign aid, and remittances from a large expatriate population. However, it also has made substantial, albeit slow, progress in liberalizing its economy. King Abdullah II, who succeeded his father, the late King Hussein, has undertaken a bold program of economic reform since coming to power in 1999. In 2000, Jordan acceded to the World Trade Organization after successfully implementing extensive legislative and regulatory reforms, as well as improving security measures for foreign-owned intellectual property. The following year, Jordan and the U.S. signed a Free Trade Agreement. In 2001, King Abdullah launched a five-year plan for Social and Economic Transformation (PSET) to further accelerate privatization and stimulate economic growth. Tourism, an important source of foreign exchange, has been hurt by political violence and terrorism in Israel and the disputed Palestinian territories. Jordan also suffers from high unemployment, the end of Iraqi-provided subsidized oil, and a heavy debt burden. Its fiscal deficit, according to the Economist Intelligence Unit, will reach nearly 10 percent in 2003 and 2004. A calmer regional environment, however, should encourage foreign and domestic investment, stimulate the service sector, and increase employment opportunities. Jordan's fiscal burden of government score is 0.3 point worse this year; however, its trade policy is 1 point better. As a result, Jordan's overall score is 0.07 point better this year.

## TRADE POLICY
### Score: **4**–Better (high level of protectionism)

According to the World Bank, Jordan's weighted average tariff rate in 2001 (the most recent year for which World Bank data are available) was 13.5 percent, down from the 18.9 percent reported in the 2003 *Index*. As a result, Jordan's trade policy score is 1 point better this year. The government maintains non-tariff barriers through an inefficient customs clearance process. According to the U.S. Department of State, "Actual appraisal and tariff assessment practices are frequently arbitrary and may even differ from written regulations…. Delays in clearing customs are common." In addition, "Imports of raw leather are restricted to the Jordan Tanning Company; crude oil and its derivatives (except metallic oils) and household gas cylinders are restricted to the Jordan Petroleum Refinery Company; cement is restricted to the Jordan Cement Factories Company; explosives and gun powder are restricted to the Jordan Phosphate Mines Company; and used tires are restricted to tire…factories."

## FISCAL BURDEN OF GOVERNMENT
### Score–Income Taxation: **2.5**–Stable (moderate tax rates)
### Score–Corporate Taxation: **4.5**–Stable (very high tax rates)
### Score–Change in Government Expenditures: **3.5**–Worse (low increase)
### Final Score: **3.8**–Worse (high cost of government)

Jordan's top income tax rate is 25 percent. The top corporate tax rate is 35 percent. Government expenditures as a share of GDP increased 0.8 percentage point to 35 percent in 2001, compared to a 1.2 percentage point decrease in 2000. As a result, Jordan's fiscal burden of government score is 0.3 point worse this year.

## GOVERNMENT INTERVENTION IN THE ECONOMY
### Score: **3.5**–Stable (high level)

The World Bank reports that the government consumed 23 percent of GDP in 2001. In the same year, according to the International Monetary Fund, Jordan received 14.34 percent of its total revenues from state-owned enterprises and government ownership of property.

## MONETARY POLICY
### Score: **1**–Stable (very low level of inflation)

From 1993 to 2002, Jordan's weighted annual rate of inflation averaged 1.71 percent.

## CAPITAL FLOWS AND FOREIGN INVESTMENT
### Score: **2**–Stable (low barriers)

The government—most notably King Abdullah—actively promotes foreign investment. There is no formal screening process, but foreign investors face a minimum capital requirement of $70,000. The International Monetary Fund reports that residents and non-residents are permitted to hold foreign exchange accounts. There are no restrictions or controls on payments, transactions, transfers, purchase of real estate (provided Jordan and the country of residence for the individual or business have a reciprocal relationship and Cabinet approval is obtained), or repatriation of profits. According to the IMF, "Nonresident investments are limited to a maximum of 49% ownership or 50% subscription in shares in the following major sectors: commerce and trade services, construction, contracting, and transportation.... Investments in the following sectors are not permitted for nonresidents: investigation and security, quarrying and mining, waste removal, sport clubs, and transportation of goods and passengers."

## BANKING AND FINANCE
### Score: **2**–Stable (low level of restrictions)

Jordan's banking system is open to foreign investment. Supervision has been strengthened, and regulations have been clarified and updated, through banking reform. The U.S. Department of State reports that the banking law passed in 2000 "protects depositors' interests, diminishes money market risk, guards against the concentration of lending, and includes articles on new banking practices (e-commerce and e-banking) and money laundering." Jordan has 14 commercial banks (of which five are foreign), two Islamic banks, and five investment banks; the Economist Intelligence Unit reports that the Arab Bank dominates the sector, accounting for 60 percent of assets. The banking system remains burdened by non-performing loans, which the U.S. Department of State estimates at 30 percent of all loans.

## WAGES AND PRICES
### Score: **2**–Stable (low level of intervention)

The government has removed most price controls, but it determines the price of fuel through subsidies. There is a minimum wage for all workers except domestic servants, those working in small family businesses, and agricultural workers.

## PROPERTY RIGHTS
### Score: **3**–Stable (moderate level of protection)

The judiciary is independent but subject to political influence. According to the U.S. Department of State, "the judiciary is subject to influence from the executive branch.... The Ministry of Justice has great influence over a judge's career and subverts the judicial system in favor of the executive branch." The U.S. Department of State reports that the purpose of a law passed in June 2001 was "to limit the Ministry of Justice's influence over a judge's career and prevent it from subverting the judicial system in favor of the executive branch.... [However], judges complain of telephone surveillance by the government." Expropriation is unlikely.

## REGULATION
### Score: **3**–Stable (moderate level)

Jordan's regulatory environment is moderately bureaucratic and burdensome, although the government is attempting to reform the system and reduce red tape. According to the U.S. Department of State, "The government is slowly implementing policies to improve competition and foster transparency. These reforms aim to change an existing system that can be influenced greatly by family affiliations and business ties. Although in many instances bureaucratic procedures have been streamlined, red tape and opaque procedures still present problems for foreign and domestic investors. The arbitrary applications of customs, tax, labor, health and other laws or regulations, particularly at the level of local government, have impeded investment."

## INFORMAL MARKET
### Score: **3**–Stable (moderate level of activity)

Transparency International's 2002 score for Jordan is 4.5. Therefore, Jordan's informal market score is 3 this year.

# KAZAKHSTAN

**Rank: 131**

**Score: 3.70**

**Category: Mostly Unfree**

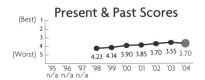

Present & Past Scores

(Best) 1
2
3
4
(Worst) 5

'95 '96 '97 '98 '99 '00 '01 '02 '03 '04
n/a n/a n/a  4.23 4.14 3.90 3.85 3.70 3.55 3.70

KAZAKHSTAN

## QUICK STUDY

### SCORES
Trade Policy                    4
Fiscal Burden                   3.5
Government Intervention 2.5
Monetary Policy                 3
Foreign Investment              5
Banking and Finance             4
Wages and Prices                3
Property Rights                 4
Regulation                      4
Informal Market                 4

**Population:** 14,825,530

**Total area:** 2,717,300 sq. km

**GDP:** $25.5 billion

**GDP growth rate:** 13.2%

**GDP per capita:** $1,720

**Major exports:** mineral products, ferrous metals, food products, chemicals

**Exports of goods and services:** $10.8 billion

**Major export trading partners:** Russia 20.2%, Italy 11.2%

**Major imports:** machinery and equipment, mineral products, ferrous metals, chemicals

**Imports of goods and services:** $8.4 billion

**Major import trading partners:** Russia 45.4%, Germany 7.4%, US 5.4%

**Foreign direct investment (net):** $2.5 billion

2001 Data (in constant 1995 US dollars)

Kazakhstan enjoys large oil and gas reserves and high per capita foreign investment in the energy sector while its population remains relatively small at 14 million people. Energy exports are constrained by the inadequate capacity of pipelines that run through Russia. The opening of the U.S.-owned Caspian Pipeline Consortium in 2001 has substantially raised crude exports. Kazakhstan has not joined the Baku–Tbilisi–Ceyhan Main Export Pipeline construction consortium but may do so in the future. A pipeline to China has also been proposed. President Nursultan Nazarbayev, a Soviet-era leader, has further concentrated political power, violated civil rights, and tightened control of the media. Clan networks and centralized control affect politics and economics, while the tax code is plagued by a lack of transparency. U.S. courts and Swiss magistrates have indicted U.S. intermediaries for alleged Foreign Corrupt Practices Act violations and other offenses in dealings with Kazakhstani leaders at the highest level. After a government reshuffle in 2001, the new prime minister stated that the interests of foreign and domestic investors needed to be "reconciled," signifying a more restrictive investment climate. Russia remains a key source of imports and a major market for exports. In March 2002, the U.S. Department of Commerce recognized Kazakhstan for its significant progress toward developing a market economy and granted it "market economy" status. Kazakhstan is a member of the United Nations, the Organization for Security and Co-operation in Europe, the North Atlantic Cooperation Council, and the Commonwealth of Independent States. Kazakhstan's government intervention score is 0.5 point worse this year, and its capital flows and foreign investment score is 1 point worse. As a result, Kazakhstan's overall score is 0.15 point worse this year.

## TRADE POLICY
### Score: **4–Stable** (high level of protectionism)

According to the U.S. Trade Representative, Kazakhstan's weighted average tariff rate in 2002 was 10 percent. Non-tariff barriers take the form of customs corruption.

## FISCAL BURDEN OF GOVERNMENT
### Score—Income Taxation: **3–Stable** (moderate tax rates)
### Score—Corporate Taxation: **4–Stable** (high tax rates)
### Score—Change in Government Expenditures: **3–Stable** (very low decrease)
### Final Score: **3.5–Stable** (high cost of government)

Kazakhstan's top income tax rate is 30 percent. The top corporate tax rate is 30 percent. Government expenditures as a share of GDP fell more in 2001 (0.4 percentage point to 21.8 percent) than they did in 2000 (0.2 percentage point). On net, Kazakhstan's fiscal burden of government score is unchanged this year.

## GOVERNMENT INTERVENTION IN THE ECONOMY
### Score: **2.5–Worse** (moderate level)

The World Bank reports that the government consumed 16.5 percent of GDP in 2001. In the same year, according to the International Monetary Fund, Kazakhstan received 8.62 percent of its total revenues from state-owned enterprises and government ownership of property, up from the 2.81 percent reported in the 2003 *Index*. As a result, Kazakhstan's government intervention score is 0.5 point worse this year.

## MONETARY POLICY
### Score: **3**–Stable (moderate level of inflation)

Data from the International Monetary Fund's *2003 World Economic Outlook* indicate that from 1993 to 2002, Kazakhstan's weighted average annual rate of inflation was 7.91 percent.

## CAPITAL FLOWS AND FOREIGN INVESTMENT
### Score: **5**–Worse (very high barriers)

Although Kazakhstan opened its economy to foreign investment during the 1990s and became one of the largest recipients of foreign direct investment among the former communist countries, the government has recently undertaken a series of measures that are undermining foreign investment. A foreign investment law passed in January 2003, reports the Economist Intelligence Unit, "denies new investors contractual immunity against possible future changes in the republic's legislation…. Of particular concern is the abrogation of foreign companies' automatic right of appeal to international arbitration courts. The new law implies that, from now on, government approval could be needed before such an appeal." The government also is seeking to build up domestic capital at the expense of foreign capital. According to the EIU, "The government's stated long-term objective is to return control of the Kazakh economy to Kazakh nationals, which in effect means ousting foreign owners and building up local firms. One of the measures used to achieve this is the local content requirement content, whereby foreign firms are asked to source at least 25% of goods and services from Kazakh providers." No sectors of the economy are closed to investors, but the government does impose a 25 percent cap on foreign capital in the banking system and a 20 percent ceiling on foreign ownership in companies in the media and telecommunications sectors. It also screens foreign investment proposals in a process that is often non-transparent and slow. Based on the number of government measures designed to undermine foreign investment, Kazakhstan's capital flows and foreign investment score is 1 point worse this year.

## BANKING AND FINANCE
### Score: **4**–Stable (high level of restrictions)

According to the U.S. Department of State, "The banking system of Kazakhstan is the most developed in Central Asia, and rapidly moving towards adoption of international banking standards under the strong supervision of the National Bank of Kazakhstan." The number of banks has fallen from 55 in 2000 to 35 in June 2003 because of mergers, increased capital requirements by the central bank, and the re-licensing of smaller banks as credit unions or partnerships. Three banks dominate the sector: Kazkommertsbanks; Turan-Alem Bank (a merger of failed state-owned banks); and Halyk Bank (a state-owned savings bank). These three banks are closely connected with the government. According to the Economist

Intelligence Unit, "There are a few major banks that dominate the sector, and these are increasingly identified with government factions—it is difficult to control a substantial local enterprise in Kazakhstan and not have government connections." There are 15 banks with at least one-third foreign ownership. The government is a dominant force in the banking industry and maintains 100 percent ownership of the Development Bank of Kazakhstan and the Export–Import Bank of Kazakhstan. Foreign insurance companies may not operate in Kazakhstan except through joint ventures with domestic firms.

## WAGES AND PRICES
### Score: **3**–Stable (moderate level of intervention)

Most price controls were liberalized in 1991, when Kazakhstan began a series of broad-based reforms in an effort to move from a planned economy to a market economy. The government still controls prices when considered necessary. It also sets a monthly minimum wage.

## PROPERTY RIGHTS
### Score: **4**–Stable (low level of protection)

Kazakhstan's legal system does not provide sufficient protection for private property. The U.S. Department of State reports that "Kazakhstan is still in the process of building the institutional capabilities of its court system. Until this is complete, the performance of courts in the country will be less than optimal." According to the Economist Intelligence Unit, "Observance of contracts in Kazakhstan is poor and getting worse…. Little progress has been made in Kazakhstan on developing an independent and competent Judiciary…. [C]orruption remains widespread, and the judiciary views itself more as an arm of the executive than as an enforcer of contracts or guardian of fundamental rights." In addition, "Current legislation severely curtails private land ownership."

## REGULATION
### Score: **4**–Stable (high level)

According to the U.S. Department of State, "Transparency in the application of laws remains…an obstacle to expanded trade and investment…. [I]nvestors complain of moving goalposts and corruption…. Although the State Agency for Investments was established to facilitate foreign investment, it had limited success in addressing the concerns of foreign investors…. Often, contradictory norms hinder the functioning of the legal system." The Economist Intelligence Unit reports that "the bureaucracy is inefficient, and by the government's own admission corruption is widespread."

## INFORMAL MARKET
### Score: **4**–Stable (high level of activity)

Transparency International's 2002 score for Kazakhstan is 2.3. Therefore, Kazakhstan's informal market score is 4 this year.

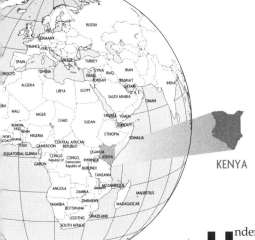

# KENYA

KENYA

Rank: 94

Score: 3.26

Category: Mostly Unfree

**Present & Past Scores**

(Best) 1
2
3
4
(Worst) 5

| 3.45 | 3.54 | 3.26 | 3.06 | 3.09 | 3.05 | 3.26 | 3.28 | 3.21 | 3.26 |
'95 '96 '97 '98 '99 '00 '01 '02 '03 '04

U nder newly elected President Mwai Kibaki and his National Rainbow Coalition, Kenya's government must demonstrate its ability to tackle institutional reform: Rampant corruption, neglected infrastructure, and a struggling economy are all challenges that must be faced. At the end of April 2003, the government passed two of three anti-corruption bills; the third one was under discussion at the time of this writing. In the short term, Finance Minister David Mwiraria will attempt to revive donor support from the International Monetary Fund and World Bank. IMF support remains contingent on the satisfaction of three conditions: commitment to privatization, anti-corruption legislation, and the prosecution of high-profile offenders. Long-term strategies such as debt rescheduling and poverty reduction will depend on Kenya's ability to meet these short-term objectives. Despite these hurdles, the economy continues to grow. Real GDP grew by 0.8 percent in 2002, but *The Economist* projects a 2.5 percent increase in 2003 followed by 3.3 percent in 2004. These numbers, however, represent a heavy dependence on the agriculture sector, which accounts for 24 percent of GDP and traditionally has been subject to variable rainfall patterns. In Kenya, as in many other African countries, Islamic fundamentalism remains an unpredictable factor. Recent attempts by al-Qaeda to conduct terrorist operations have brought about disruptions in tourism and other associated industries. Given Kenya's unfortunate proximity to Somalia, this threat is likely to continue for the foreseeable future. Kenya's government intervention score is 1.5 point better this year; however, its trade policy and monetary policy scores are 1 point worse. As a result, Kenya's overall score is 0.05 point worse this year.

## QUICK STUDY

### SCORES

| | |
|---|---|
| Trade Policy | 5 |
| Fiscal Burden | 3.6 |
| Government Intervention | 2.5 |
| Monetary Policy | 2 |
| Foreign Investment | 3 |
| Banking and Finance | 3 |
| Wages and Prices | 2 |
| Property Rights | 3 |
| Regulation | 4 |
| Informal Market | 4.5 |

**Population:** 30,735,760

**Total area:** 582,650 sq. km

**GDP:** $9.9 billion

**GDP growth rate:** 1.1%

**GDP per capita:** $325

**Major exports:** tea, coffee, fish products, petroleum products

**Exports of goods and services:** $3.3 billion

**Major export trading partners:** UK 13.5%, Tanzania 12.5%, Uganda 12.0%, Germany 5.5%

**Major imports:** petroleum products, iron and steel, motor vehicles

**Imports of goods and services:** $3.8 billion

**Major import trading partners:** UK 12.0%, United Arab Emirates 9.8%, Japan 6.5%, India 4.4%

**Foreign direct investment (net):** –$24.2 million

2001 Data (in constant 1995 US dollars)

## TRADE POLICY

Score: **5**–Worse (very high level of protectionism)

The World Bank reports that Kenya's weighted average tariff rate in 2001 (the most recent year for which World Bank data are available) was 15.5 percent, up from the 12.4 percent reported in the 2003 *Index*. As a result, Kenya's trade policy score is 1 point worse this year. According to the U.S. Department of State, "Non tariff barriers include the requirement to use a GOK [government of Kenya] appointed inspection firm for imports. Some U.S. firms may find packaging and labeling requirements difficult to meet." Licensing requirements are similarly burdensome.

## FISCAL BURDEN OF GOVERNMENT

Score—Income Taxation: **3**–Stable (moderate tax rates)
Score—Corporate Taxation: **4**–Stable (high tax rates)
Score—Change in Government Expenditures: **3.5**–Stable (low increase)
Final Score: **3.6**–Stable (high cost of government)

Kenya's top income tax rate is 30 percent. The top corporate income tax rate is 30 percent. Government expenditures as a share of GDP increased by the same amount (0.6 percentage point to 26.3 percent) in 2001 as they did in 2000. As a result, Kenya's fiscal burden of government score is unchanged this year.

## GOVERNMENT INTERVENTION IN THE ECONOMY

Score: **2.5**–Better (moderate level)

The World Bank reports that the government consumed 16.8 percent of GDP in 2001, down from the 18 percent reported in the 2003 *Index*. In the July 2001–June 2002 fiscal year, based on data from the World Bank, Kenya received 7.4 percent of its total revenues from state-owned enterprises and government ownership of property. Based on the lower level of government consumption and newly available data on revenues from state-owned enterprises, Kenya's government intervention score is 1.5 point better this year.

 ## MONETARY POLICY
### Score: 2–Worse (low level of inflation)

From 1993 to 2002, Kenya's weighted average annual rate of inflation was 3.80 percent, up from the 2.49 percent from 1992 to 2001 reported in the 2003 *Index*. As a result, Kenya's monetary policy score is 1 point worse this year.

 ## CAPITAL FLOWS AND FOREIGN INVESTMENT
### Score: 3–Stable (moderate barriers)

Kenya's government has relaxed its screening standards and is developing a one-stop shop for investment approval. According to the U.S. Department of State, foreign and domestic investment is restricted in those sectors in which the state has a monopoly. These sectors include the power, telecommunications, and ports sectors. The government often discriminates in favor of domestic bids. Foreign branches are assessed higher tax rates than domestic companies or locally incorporated foreign subsidiaries. Work permits, which are becoming increasingly hard to obtain (even for expatriates), are required for all foreign nationals wishing to work in the country. The International Monetary Fund reports that both residents and non-residents may hold foreign exchange accounts. There are no controls or requirements for payments and transfers. Most capital transactions are permitted, but government approval is required for the sale or issue of capital and money market instruments, derivatives, and purchase of real estate by non-residents.

 ## BANKING AND FINANCE
### Score: 3–Stable (moderate level of restrictions)

Kenya's banking system is troubled. As of mid-2002, an estimated 41percent of loans were non-performing, with most of these loans held by state-controlled banks. Two state-controlled banks (Kenya Commercial Bank and National Bank of Kenya) dominate the sector along with two international banks (Barclays and Standard Chartered). The Economist Intelligence Unit reports that plans to privatize Kenya Commercial Bank have been suspended and that it is unclear when privatization might resume. According to the U.S. Department of State, "The banking problems in Kenya are the result of poor bank management, inadequate government supervision, political pressure to make loans that are rarely paid, and current economic conditions." In August 2001, the government passed a law that capped interest rates; on January 24, 2002, the courts ruled the law unconstitutional. "Nevertheless," reports the Economist Intelligence Unit, "some banks have already reimbursed some depositors for

overcharged interest, and there is considerable confusion whether the court ruling overrides parliament."

 ## WAGES AND PRICES
### Score: 2–Stable (low level of intervention)

According to the Economist Intelligence Unit, "Price controls were abolished some years ago, but the legal mechanism to control prices exists in part IV of the Restrictive Trade Practices, Monopolies and Price Controls Act." The government intervenes in agriculture markets to various degrees to support farmers. It also protects the sugar industry for political reasons, as sugar accounts for a large portion of formal employment. Kenya has a minimum wage for blue-collar workers.

 ## PROPERTY RIGHTS
### Score: 3–Stable (moderate level of protection)

Expropriation of property is unlikely in Kenya. However, reports the Economist Intelligence Unit, "Although... arrangements [are] more secure than in many other African countries, abuses and disputes are common. The country's judicial system is widely regarded as overloaded, inefficient and often corrupt. There is little confidence in the lower courts." According to the U.S. Department of State, "Property and contractual rights are enforceable, but long delays in resolving commercial cases are common. The system is subject to political influence, which erodes the confidence of the judicial system." Newly elected President Kibaki recently launched an anti-graft investigation against the country's top judge, who resigned soon thereafter.

 ## REGULATION
### Score: 4–Stable (high level)

Kenya's bureaucracy remains significantly burdensome. The Economist Intelligence Unit reports that "investors should be aware that the official register is in a deplorable state; it has never been computerized or properly updated." In 1999, the government updated the Local Government Act in an effort to streamline the bureaucracy, creating what the EIU calls a "single business permit in place of a multitude of different licenses." The government gives local authorities "discretion to choose the appropriate schedule of fees to charge, depending on the size and level of development of the local authority concerned"; but businesses complain that, because of this discretion, they sometimes have to "pay more for a single business permit than they have paid before for many trading licenses." The EIU further reports that "Employees at the Ministry of Public Works demand the biggest bribes.... Local government officials take the smallest bribes, at only KSh110 on average."

 ## INFORMAL MARKET
### Score: 4.5–Stable (very high level of activity)

Transparency International's 2002 score for Kenya is 1.9. Therefore, Kenya's informal market score is 4.5 this year.

NORTH
KOREA

# KOREA, DEMOCRATIC REPUBLIC OF (NORTH KOREA)

Rank: 155

Score: 5.00

Category: Repressed

Present & Past Scores

(Best) 1
2
3
4 5.00 5.00 5.00 5.00 5.00 5.00 5.00 5.00 5.00
(Worst) 5

'95 '96 '97 '98 '99 '00 '01 '02 '03 '04

The Democratic People's Republic of Korea (DPRK) remains the world's most closed economy. Kim Jong-Il maintains full authoritarian control of the country's political system, society, and economy. The economy has been on the verge of collapse for the past decade, registering negative growth for nine consecutive years through 1998 and modest positive growth since 1999. In 2001, GDP grew by 3.7 percent, largely because of government construction projects. Since 1995, North Korea has depended on outside aid to feed its 22 million people, and it is estimated that as many as 3 million people have starved to death. In July 2002, the regime made some efforts to implement radical but limited reforms. Prices and wages were raised tenfold or more for producers and consumers, presumably to meet market dynamics and create incentives; the result, predictably, was rampant inflation. Without a viable and functioning economy, the regime has chosen to dedicate its international trade to such illegal activities as arms sales, counterfeiting, and the traffic in drugs and human beings. In 2001, official exports from legitimate businesses totaled just $650 million, while exports from illegal drugs totaled between $500 million and $1 billion. More than $100 million came from counterfeit U.S. currency. Casting a shadow over all of North Korea's domestic problems are unresolved security issues, which were raised to heightened levels in 2003. The pursuit of clandestine nuclear weapons programs in violation of several international agreements, including the Nuclear Non-Proliferation Treaty, is the greatest challenge to North Korea's future economic stability.

## QUICK STUDY

### SCORES

Trade Policy                     5
Fiscal Burden                    5
Government Intervention          5
Monetary Policy                  5
Foreign Investment               5
Banking and Finance              5
Wages and Prices                 5
Property Rights                  5
Regulation                       5
Informal Market                  5

**Population:** 22,384,230

**Total area:** 120,540 sq. km

**GDP:** n/a

**GDP growth rate:** 3.7%

**GDP per capita:** n/a

**Major exports:** minerals, metallurgical products, manufactures (including armaments), textiles and fishery products

**Exports of goods and services:** n/a

**Major export trading partners:** Japan 36.3%, South Korea 21.5%, China 5.2% (2000)

**Major imports:** petroleum, coking coal, machinery and equipment; textiles, grain

**Imports of goods and services:** n/a

**Major import trading partners:** China 26.7%, South Korea 16.2%, Japan 12.3% (2000)

**Foreign direct investment (net):** n/a

2001 Data (in constant 1995 US dollars)

## TRADE POLICY

Score: **5**–Stable (very high level of protectionism)

The government controls all imports and exports. According to the Economist Intelligence Unit, "Trade with the outside world is mainly handled by the Foreign Trade Bank." Essentially, North Korea is closed to trade except for some imports manufactured in South Korea, China, and Japan.

## FISCAL BURDEN OF GOVERNMENT

Score—Income Taxation: n/a
Score—Corporate Taxation: n/a
Score—Change in Government Expenditures: n/a

Final Score: **5**–Stable (very high cost of government)

No data on income or corporate tax rates are available. According to the Economist Intelligence Unit, "The picture is changing, as *de facto* private enterprise emerges to complement or supplant the failing formal economy…. Peasants' markets, never abolished, have expanded, as has private crossborder trade with China. The authorities are trying to check, control, or at least tax all this, with mixed success." Data from the EIU indicate that government expenditures as a share of GDP increased 12.6 percentage points to 62.8 percent in 2001, compared to a 7.3 percentage point decrease in 2000. These data, however, are highly suspect and should be treated with caution.

## GOVERNMENT INTERVENTION IN THE ECONOMY

Score: **5**–Stable (very high level)

The government owns all property and sets production levels for most products, and state-owned industries account for nearly all GDP. According to the U.S. Department of State, "The State directs all significant economic activity, and only government-controlled labor unions are permitted." However, reports the Economist Intelligence Unit, "although heavy industry

251

is centrally owned and planned, the production of consumer goods is left to provinces and localities to manage as best they can." In addition, "de facto private enterprise [is emerging] to complement or supplant the failing formal economy. Constitutional revisions in 1998 gave more scope both to co-operatives and private property. Peasants' markets…have expanded." In May 2003, the government was accused of trafficking in drugs to obtain hard foreign currency.

## MONETARY POLICY
### Score: **5**–Stable (very high level of inflation)

In July 2002, North Korea introduced price and wage reforms that consisted of a reduction in government subsidies and the government's telling producers to charge prices that more closely reflect costs. The reforms did not address the supply side. Farmers are not free to increase their production to respond to higher prices. "The result," reports a May 1, 2003, *Economist* article, "has been rampant inflation that has made life even more miserable for most North Koreans, except the Pyongyang elite." As a consequence, in July the official exchange rate of the North Korean won was revised from 2.15 to the dollar to 150. The black-market rate is now rumored to be closer to 800.

## CAPITAL FLOWS AND FOREIGN INVESTMENT
### Score: **5**–Stable (very high barriers)

According to the Economist Intelligence Unit, "North Korea has the dubious distinction of being first in and last out of the debt crisis of the developing world, initially defaulting in the 1970s and remaining mired in debt today…. Few creditors have been paid since the 1980s…. Not even legal action by a consortium of over 100 banks from 17 countries and judgments by the International Court of Arbitration have prompted North Korea to pay up. Unsurprisingly, this has affected its ability to attract foreign investment…." In 1991, North Korea attempted to attract foreign investment by creating a special economic zone at Rajin-Sonbong, but the EIU reports that "Rajin-Sonbong is remote and still lacks basic infrastructure. Wage rates are uncompetitively high, as the state controls labour supply and insists on its cut…. So far, ABB, a Swiss-Swedish power engineering group, is the only major multinational committed, although it has financial problems of its own."

## BANKING AND FINANCE
### Score: **5**–Stable (very high level of restrictions)

"As a communist command economy," reports the Economist Intelligence Unit, "North Korea largely lacks a financial sector in the capitalist sense. Most funding for industry comes from the state, which also earns revenue by taking a percentage on transactions among enterprises…. Most foreign banks will not touch North Korea because of debts dating back to the 1970s…. Since the June 2000 inter-Korean summit South Korean banks have been considering

possible investment in the North, but so far there is no system for the direct settlement of payments despite an agreement to create one." The central bank also serves as a commercial bank with a network of 227 local branches. The state-owned Changgwang Credit Bank, founded in 1983, has 172 branches. The state holds a monopoly on insurance through the State Insurance Bureau and the Korea Foreign Insurance Company. Foreigners may not use banking services, and Western tourists are charged in U.S. dollars rather than won.

## WAGE AND PRICES
### Score: **5**–Stable (very high level of intervention)

The government controls and determines all wages and prices. According to the Economist Intelligence Unit, "Economic decline has been a classic malfunctioning of a centrally planned economy, in which price signals still play little part in official resource allocation, the result being inefficiency and shortages." In 2002, the government told businesses that they could no longer expect government subsidies and that they should charge prices that reflect their costs. "This was done without official promulgation," reports the EIU, "so the exact scope remains uncertain…." As a July 25, 2002, *Economist* article notes, "it would surely be premature to say that the world's last Stalinist state has embraced Adam Smith. There is more to a market system than merely adjusting prices to more sensible levels." According to the U.S. Department of State, "Government ministries set wages. The State assigned all jobs."

## PROPERTY RIGHTS
### Score: **5**–Stable (very low level of protection)

Property rights are not guaranteed in North Korea. Almost all property belongs to the state, and the U.S. Department of State reports that "the judiciary is not independent."

## REGULATION
### Score: **5**–Stable (very high level)

The government regulates the economy heavily. According to the *Financial Times*, Kim Jong-Il refuses to follow China's example of opening to foreign investment and relaxing borders; this refusal has serious implications because "the country's economy, stripped of its industries and starved of energy, is unsustainable." The Economist Intelligence Unit reports indications that local government officials have stepped up extortion-like tactics to help raise revenue.

## INFORMAL MARKET
### Score: **5**–Stable (very high level of activity)

North Korea's informal market is immense even though the government imprisons many who engage in such activity. Informal market activity in agricultural goods flourishes as a result of famines and oppressive government policies. There is also an active informal market in currency and in trade with China.

SOUTH
KOREA

# KOREA, REPUBLIC OF (SOUTH KOREA)

Rank: 46

Score: 2.69

Category: Mostly Free

**Present & Past Scores**

(Best) 1
2
3
4
(Worst) 5

2.41 2.49 2.31 2.30 2.38 2.50 2.35 2.49 2.75 2.69

'95 '96 '97 '98 '99 '00 '01 '02 '03 '04

South Korea's economy posted strong growth of 6.3 percent in 2002 despite global growth of only 2.2 percent. Much of this growth was fueled by high domestic consumer spending and heavy dependence on international trade. In 2001, total foreign trade represented over 70 percent of GDP. Nevertheless, despite poor economic conditions in the important U.S. and Japanese export markets, the economy remains remarkably resilient because of supportive macroeconomic policies and deregulation, especially in the services sector, that have allowed domestic demand to act as an important driver of growth. The election of President Roh Moo Hyun was initally regarded as a positive sign for the economy, as he had pledged to continue his predecessor's reform policies. However, his first month in office saw inconsistent policies being applied to reforms of both radical labor union activities and the excessive market domination of the major "chaebols" or business groups. The greatest challenge to South Korea's continued economic success may be security concerns over North Korea's nuclear programs. Uncertainty over the stability of the Korean peninsula has drawn the international market's attention away from economic fundamentals in South Korea to geopolitics and the uncertain future of U.S.–South Korea relations. In the first quarter of 2003, foreign direct investment was down 48 percent from the same period a year earlier. High oil prices led to three consecutive months of trade deficits, a rarity for the export-driven economy. Thus, while domestic policies geared toward restructuring and reforming the economy are important, external geopolitical factors may have greater impact on the performance of the South Korean economy in the long run. South Korea's trade policy score is 1 point worse this year; however, its fiscal burden of government score is 0.1 point better, and its government intervention score is 1.5 point better. As a result, South Korea's overall score is 0.06 point better this year.

## QUICK STUDY

### SCORES

| | |
|---|---|
| Trade Policy | 4 |
| Fiscal Burden | 3.4 |
| Government Intervention | 2.5 |
| Monetary Policy | 2 |
| Foreign Investment | 2 |
| Banking and Finance | 3 |
| Wages and Prices | 2 |
| Property Rights | 2 |
| Regulation | 3 |
| Informal Market | 3 |

**Population:** 47,640,000

**Total area:** 98,480 sq. km

**GDP:** $677.9 billion

**GDP growth rate:** 6.3%

**GDP per capita:** $14,230

**Major exports:** electronic products, passenger cars, machinery and equipment, chemical and chemical products, steel, ship, textiles

**Exports of goods and services:** $371.8 billion

**Major export trading partners:** US 20.2%, China 14.6%, Japan 9.3%, Hong Kong 6.2%

**Major imports:** crude petroleum, machinery and equipment, chemical and chemical products

**Imports of goods and services:** $248.9 billion

**Major import trading partners:** Japan 19.6%, US 15.1%, China 11.4%, Saudi Arabia 5.0%

**Foreign direct investment (net):** −$630 million

2002 Data (in constant 1995 US dollars)

## TRADE POLICY

### Score: **4**–Worse (high level of protectionism)

The Embassy of South Korea reports that South Korea's weighted average tariff rate in 2002 (the most recent year for which reliable data are available) was 9.2 percent, up from the 5.9 percent reported in the 2003 *Index*. As a result, South Korea's trade policy score is 1 point worse this year. According to the Economist Intelligence Unit, a "negative list" includes over 800 commodities that are restricted or prohibited. In addition, "pharmaceuticals…medical devices, cosmetics and food products are particularly vulnerable to cumbersome and costly testing requirements."

## FISCAL BURDEN OF GOVERNMENT

### Score—Income Taxation: **3.5**–Stable (high tax rates)
### Score—Corporate Taxation: **3.5**–Stable (high tax rates)
### Score—Change in Government Expenditures: **3**–Better (very low decrease)
### Final Score: **3.4**–Better (high cost of government)

South Korea's top income tax rate is 36 percent. The top corporate tax rate is 27 percent. Government expenditures as a share of GDP remained unchanged at 24.6 percent in 2002, compared to a 0.2 percentage point increase in 2001. As a result, South Korea's fiscal burden of government score is 0.1 point better this year.

## GOVERNMENT INTERVENTION IN THE ECONOMY

### Score: **2.5**–Better (moderate level)

Based on data from the International Monetary Fund, the government consumed 10.6 percent of GDP in 2002. In the same year, according to the Ministry of Finance, South Korea received 6.8 percent of its total revenues from state-owned enterprises and government ownership of property. Based on newly available data on revenues from state-owned enterprises and the use of a new methodology to grade this factor, South Korea's government intervention score is 1.5 point better this year.

## MONETARY POLICY
### Score: 2–Stable (low level of inflation)

From 1993 to 2002, South Korea's weighted average annual rate of inflation was 3.03 percent.

## CAPITAL FLOWS AND FOREIGN INVESTMENT
### Score: 2–Stable (low barriers)

The Foreign Investment Promotion Act of November 1998 and other reforms substantially opened the South Korean economy to foreign investment. According to the U.S. Trade Representative, 27 sectors (primarily media and communications, electric power–related sectors, and certain agricultural sectors) are partially closed to foreign investment, and only two sectors (radio and television broadcasting) are completely closed. The government has also removed the restrictions on foreign investments that acquire companies through mergers and acquisitions. The Korea Investment Service Center, a one-stop-shop, has simplified investment procedures, and foreign investment zones and industrial complexes offer foreign investors special incentives. According to the International Monetary Fund, residents and non-residents are permitted to hold foreign exchange accounts. Payments, transactions, transfers, or repatriation of profits are subject to reporting requirements or restrictions on amounts permitted for specified periods.

## BANKING AND FINANCE
### Score: 3–Stable (moderate level of restrictions)

The government is taking up a number of measures to reform Korea's financial system. The U.S. Department of State reports that the government "set up the Korean Asset Management Corporation (KAMCO) to dispose of non-performing assets; required banks to raise their capital adequacy ratios…introduced strengthened asset classification standards for banks; and imposed 'forward-looking' criteria (FLC) to force the banks to provision adequately for non-performing loans…." The government maintains majority ownership of several large commercial banks and has a significant stake in several others, but it also is working to privatize its state-owned holdings. According to the Korean Embassy, the government issued an initial public offering of 11.8 percent of its holdings of Woori Financial Holding Company in June 2002 but has not yet found an investor; the government is currently negotiating with Shinhan Financial Holding Co. over the sale of Chohung bank; and the state-owned Seoul Bank was merged with Hana Bank in August 2002. Korea has also opened itself to foreign banking. An amendment to the Banking Act raised the ceiling on foreign ownership of a nationwide domestic bank from 4 percent to 10 percent, although the Korean Embassy reports that this limit can be exceeded with permission from the Financial Supervisory Commission.

## WAGES AND PRICES
### Score: 2–Stable (low level of intervention)

The market sets most prices, although the government has the power to control prices on some products. According to the Korean Embassy, the government controls the price of electricity, water, telephone services, postal services, public transportation services, and coal briquettes but liberalized prices on cigarettes and liquefied petroleum gas in 2001. The government also maintains stockpiles of foodstuffs that it releases into the market to offset seasonal price fluctuations. South Korea maintains a minimum wage that is reviewed annually.

## PROPERTY RIGHTS
### Score: 2–Stable (high level of protection)

Private property is secure, and expropriation is highly unlikely. However, the justice system can be inefficient and slow. The Economist Intelligence Unit reports that "a contract is often considered a broadly defined consensus statement that allows for flexibility and adjustment…. [L]egal procedures in South Korea can be cumbersome and expensive." According to the U.S. Department of State, "Legal proceedings are expensive and time-consuming. Lawsuits often are contemplated only as a last resort, signaling the end of a business relationship."

## REGULATION
### Score: 3–Stable (moderate level)

Despite government efforts to deregulate, the regulatory environment remains difficult for both domestic and foreign firms. Labor regulations are highly burdensome. The Korea Economic Institute reports that "procedural restrictions are still imposed on layoffs initiated by management. To discharge redundant employees, for example, a firm must obtain advance consent from labor unions and show that its business conditions approach bankruptcy." According to the U.S. Department of State, "Laws and regulations are framed in general terms and are subject to differing interpretations by government officials, who rotate frequently…. Mid-level bureaucrats rely on unpublished ministerial guidelines and unwritten administrative advice for direction.… [T]he rule-making process continues to be opaque and non-transparent." Deregulation has taken a back seat, despite government promises to improve the regulatory environment. The U.S. Department of State reports that there is corruption in the bureaucracy.

## INFORMAL MARKET
### Score: 3–Stable (moderate level of activity)

Transparency International's 2002 score for South Korea is 4.5. Therefore, South Korea's informal market score is 3 this year.

# KUWAIT

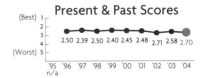

**Present & Past Scores**

Rank: 48

Score: 2.70

Category: Mostly Free

(Best) 1
2
3
4
(Worst) 5

2.50 2.39 2.50 2.40 2.45 2.48 2.71 2.58 2.70

'95 '96 '97 '98 '99 '00 '01 '02 '03 '04
n/a

KUWAIT

## QUICK STUDY

### SCORES

| | |
|---|---|
| Trade Policy | 2 |
| Fiscal Burden | 1.5 |
| Government Intervention | 4.5 |
| Monetary Policy | 1 |
| Foreign Investment | 4 |
| Banking and Finance | 3 |
| Wages and Prices | 3 |
| Property Rights | 3 |
| Regulation | 3 |
| Informal Market | 2 |

**Population:** 2,044,273

**Total area:** 17,820 sq. km

**GDP:** $27.3 billion

**GDP growth rate:** −1.0%

**GDP per capita:** $13,345

**Major exports:** oil, fertilizers and refined products

**Exports of goods and services:** $16.1 billion

**Major export trading partners:** Japan 21.2%, South Korea 12.7%, US 12.4%, Singapore 7.7%

**Major imports:** food, construction materials, clothing, vehicles and parts

**Imports of goods and services:** $11 billion

**Major import trading partners:** US 12.9%, Germany 9.5%, Japan 8.3%, UK 7.3%

**Foreign direct investment (net):** −$254 million

2001 Data (in constant 1995 US dollars)

K uwait, a small constitutional emirate ruled by the Al-Sabah family since 1756, controls roughly 10 percent of the world's oil supply, which accounts for nearly 50 percent of GDP and 90 percent of export revenues. The government committed to a five-year reform program designed to reduce the state's role in the economy through privatization, encourage employment in the private sector, reduce entitlements, roll back high levels of protection against foreign competition, and trim the extensive welfare system. However, efforts to transform Kuwait from a welfare state into a market economy and ease its reliance on a bloated public sector, which employs around 94 percent of the workforce, have progressed slowly as the Kuwaiti people cling to generous government subsidies. Furthermore, the strength of the government's commitment to economic reform is undermined by its erratic policy implementation, closely tied to the rise and fall of prices on the international oil market. Political pressure from Islamist and populist forces in the parliament, who share a vested interest in the current system of government handouts, has stalled additional measures to liberalize the economy. A large number of legislators continue to oppose Project Kuwait, a $7 billion investment plan to develop oilfields in northern Kuwait, because it would allow foreign investment in the Kuwaiti oil industry. The removal of Saddam Hussein's hostile regime in neighboring Iraq will reduce the political uncertainties associated with this project and help boost the economy by giving Kuwait an opportunity to participate in Iraq's postwar reconstruction and serve as a transshipment port for goods bound for Iraq. Kuwait's fiscal burden of government score is 0.2 point worse this year, and its property rights score is 1 point worse. As a result, Kuwait's overall score is 0.12 point worse this year.

 **TRADE POLICY**

Score: **2**–Stable (low level of protectionism)

According to the World Bank, Kuwait has an average tariff rate of 4 percent since 1997. The U.S. Department of State reports that Kuwait prohibits imports of "pork, pork products, alcoholic beverages, products containing alcoholic beverages, gambling machines and materials that could be considered pornographic. Kuwait also prohibits imports from Israel and imports of Israeli made products." The same source reports that government procurement policies cater generally to Kuwaiti firms.

 **FISCAL BURDEN OF GOVERNMENT**

Score—Income Taxation: **1**–Stable (very low tax rates)
Score—Corporate Taxation: **1**–Stable (very low tax rates)
Score—Change in Government Expenditures: **3**–Worse (very low decrease)
Final Score: **1.5**–Worse (low cost of government)

The U.S. Department of State reports that Kuwait has no income tax. No corporate taxes are assessed on companies that are wholly owned by Kuwaitis or citizens of Gulf Cooperation Council (GCC) countries. Foreign corporations are subject to a 55 percent corporate income tax rate, but this is considered a foreign investment barrier; therefore, the domestic taxation rate has been used to score this factor. Government expenditures as a share of GDP decreased less in 2001 (0.6 percentage point to 40.7 percent) than they did in 2000 (2.2 percentage points). As a result, Kuwait's fiscal burden of government score is 0.2 point worse this year.

255

## GOVERNMENT INTERVENTION IN THE ECONOMY
### Score: **4.5**–Stable (very high level)

The World Bank reports that the government consumed 26.3 percent of GDP in 2001. Most GDP comes from oil production, nearly all of which is owned by the government. In the April 2001–March 2002 fiscal year, based on data from the Economist Intelligence Unit, Kuwait received 66.95 percent of its total revenues from state-owned enterprises and government ownership of property. According to the U.S. Department of State, the government intervenes in the stock market.

## MONETARY POLICY
### Score: **1**–Stable (very low level of inflation)

From 1993 to 2002, Kuwait's weighted average annual rate of inflation was 1.53 percent.

## CAPITAL FLOWS AND FOREIGN INVESTMENT
### Score: **4**–Stable (high barriers)

Kuwait is open to some types of foreign investment, but there are significant restrictions. Recently passed (but not yet implemented) legislation allows foreign companies 100 percent foreign ownership of Kuwaiti companies in certain industries, which the U.S. Department of State reports have not yet been identified. The government continues to charge foreign corporations a 55 percent corporate income tax rate, while companies wholly owned by Kuwaitis or GCC citizens are not charged a corporate tax. Except for GCC citizens, foreigners may not own real estate. Kuwait still restricts foreign investment in the oil sector. The International Monetary Fund reports that residents and non-residents may hold foreign exchange accounts, and there are no restrictions or controls on payments, transactions, transfers, or repatriation of profits.

## BANKING AND FINANCE
### Score: **3**–Stable (moderate level of restrictions)

Banking in Kuwait is competitive and meets international standards. The banking sector has been opened to foreign competition, and the government sold a stake in the Bank of Kuwait and the Middle East to a Bahrain-based (but partly Kuwaiti-owned) bank in March 2001. There are seven commercial banks, including one Islamic bank, which have 140 branches and offer the usual bank services. Foreigners are restricted to a maximum of 49 percent ownership in a Kuwaiti bank and may not issue insurance. There are three government-owned banks, which provide financing for industrial and agricultural projects, real estate, and housing. Banks are relatively free of government control, but there are ties between the state and the banking sector.

## WAGES AND PRICES
### Score: **3**–Stable (moderate level of intervention)

The government sets some prices. According to the Economist Intelligence Unit, "Kuwait applies price controls to key products and services…. Many key services, including health, housing, education, telecommunications, water and electricity, are subsidised by the government and are therefore subject to price controls. The Ministry of Health sets prices for medicinal drugs and healthcare products." The government does not mandate a minimum wage in the private sector, but it does set wages in the public sector, in which over 93 percent of Kuwaitis are employed.

## PROPERTY RIGHTS
### Score: **3**–Worse (moderate level of protection)

Private property is protected in Kuwait, but the U.S. Department of State reports that claimants in both commercial and investment disputes are frustrated by the slow pace of the legal system and that "the Kuwaiti judicial system recognizes and enforces foreign judgments only when reciprocal arrangements are in place." According to the Economist Intelligence Unit, the constitution and law provide for an independent judiciary; in practice, however, the Amir appoints all judges. In addition, the majority of the judges are non-citizens, and renewal of their appointments is subject to government approval. According to the U.S. Department of State, "non-citizen judges work under 1 to 3 year renewable contracts, which undermine their independence. Also, the Amir has the constitutional power to pardon or commute all sentences." Based on the evidence of government influence on the judiciary, Kuwait's property rights score is 1 point worse this year.

## REGULATION
### Score: **3**–Stable (moderate level)

State involvement in the economy is considerable, and competition with state-owned or private Kuwaiti concerns is difficult. Regulations are applied evenly in most cases, but bureaucratic procedures and red tape can cause considerable delay. According to the U.S. Department of State, "the government of Kuwait has not developed effective antitrust laws to foster competition, and its bureaucracy often resembles that of a developing country." In addition, "the often lengthy procurement process in Kuwait occasionally results in accusations of attempted bribery or the offering of other inducements by foreign bidders."

## INFORMAL MARKET
### Score: **2**–Stable (low level of activity)

Kuwait's informal market is confined mainly to pirated computer software, video and cassette recordings, and other similar products. The Business Software Alliance reports that "Kuwait had the 15th worst piracy rate" in 2002.

KYRGYZ
REPUBLIC

# KYRGYZ REPUBLIC

Rank: 103

Score: 3.36

Category: Mostly Unfree

### Present & Past Scores

(Best) 1
2
3
4
(Worst) 5

4.00 3.73 3.78 3.80 3.65 3.41 3.36
'95 '96 '97 '98 '99 '00 '01 '02 '03 '04
n/a n/a n/a

## QUICK STUDY

### SCORES

| | |
|---|---|
| Trade Policy | 4 |
| Fiscal Burden | 3.1 |
| Government Intervention | 2.5 |
| Monetary Policy | 3 |
| Foreign Investment | 3 |
| Banking and Finance | 3 |
| Wages and Prices | 3 |
| Property Rights | 4 |
| Regulation | 4 |
| Informal Market | 4 |

**Population:** 4,955,000

**Total area:** 198,500 sq. km

**GDP:** $2.1 billion

**GDP growth rate:** 5.3%

**GDP per capita:** $417

**Major exports:** electricity, machinery, foodstuffs

**Exports of goods and services:** $502.1 million

**Major export trading partners:** Germany 28.7%, Uzbekistan 17.7%, Russia 12.9%, China 8.7%

**Major imports:** machinery, oil and gas, chemicals, foodstuffs

**Imports of goods and services:** $460.5 million

**Major import trading partners:** Russia 23.9%, Uzbekistan 13.5%, Kazakhstan 10.3%, US 9.7%

**Foreign direct investment (net):** $26 million

2001 Data (in constant 1995 US dollars)

In 1998, the Kyrgyz Republic became the first member of the Commonwealth of Independent States to join the World Trade Organization. It was granted membership because it was one of the first CIS countries to accept an International Monetary Fund economic program. According to the World Bank, however, "Investment has been limited, and infrastructure and social services have slowly been deteriorating...." GDP grew by 5.3 percent in 2001 (largely because of the gold mining industry) and –0.5 percent in 2002. A proposed World Bank Country Assistance Strategy for 2003–2006 is designed to help the government implement its National Poverty Reduction Strategy with operations of US$171 million, a significant portion of which will be extended as grants. The World Bank also approved two credits: the US$20 million Governance Structural Adjustment Credit and US$7.78 million Governance Technical Assistance Credit. Ratification of the 1999 Sino–Kyrgyz border treaty, under which the Kyrgyz Parliament ceded some 95,000 hectares of disputed territory to China, led to two weeks of protests, as a result of which President Askar Akaev—who has been elected four times even though the constitution allows only two terms—forced Prime Minister Kurmanbek Bakiev and his cabinet to step down on May 22, 2002. The increased threat of terrorism has prompted antiterrorist cooperation with Russia and the U.S. during and after the war in Afghanistan, including the opening of Western and Russian military bases. On August 2, 2003, heads of the law enforcement and security agencies of Kazakhstan, Kyrgyzstan, Tajikistan, and Uzbekistan agreed to conduct future joint operations against international terrorists, religious extremists, and drug traffickers. The Kyrgyz Republic's government intervention score is 0.5 point worse this year; however, its monetary policy score is 1 point better. As a result, the Kyrgyz Republic's overall score is 0.05 point better this year.

## TRADE POLICY

### Score: **4**–Stable (high level of protectionism)

The Ministry of External Trade and Industry reports that the Kyrgyz Republic has a "scheme of tariffs ranges…(0, 5%, 6.5%, 10%, 17.5%, and 20%)." No current information on the average tariff rate is available. According to the U.S. Department of State, the government "has a uniform import tariff of ten percent on most goods." According to the International Monetary Fund, "Non-tariff barriers for imports consist of fees for services rendered, quantitative restrictions, and import licenses."

## FISCAL BURDEN OF GOVERNMENT

### Score—Income Taxation: **2**–Better (low tax rates)
### Score—Corporate Taxation: **4**–Stable (high tax rates)
### Score—Change in Government Expenditures: **2.5**–Worse (low decrease)
## Final Score: **3.1**–Stable (moderate cost of government)

According to the International Monetary Fund, the Kyrgyz Republic's top income tax rate is 20 percent, down from the 35 percent reported in the 2003 *Index*. The top corporate tax rate is 30 percent. Government expenditures as a share of GDP decreased less in 2001 (1.8 percentage points to 16.2 percent) than they did in 2000 (5.9 percentage points). On net, the Kyrgyz Republic's fiscal burden of government score is unchanged this year.

## GOVERNMENT INTERVENTION IN THE ECONOMY
### Score: **2.5**–Worse (moderate level)

The World Bank reports that the government consumed 17.3 percent of GDP in 2001. In 2002, according to the International Monetary Fund, the Kyrgyz Republic received 7.4 percent of its total revenues from state-owned enterprises and government ownership of property, up from the 3.44 percent reported in the 2003 *Index*. As a result, the Kyrgyz Republic's government intervention score is 0.5 point worse this year.

## MONETARY POLICY
### Score: **3**–Better (moderate level of inflation)

From 1993 to 2002, the Kyrgyz Republic's weighted average annual rate of inflation was 6.07 percent, down from the 13.49 percent from 1992 to 2001 reported in the 2003 Index. As a result, the Kyrgyz Republic's monetary policy score is 1 point better this year.

## CAPITAL FLOWS AND FOREIGN INVESTMENT
### Score: **3**–Stable (moderate barriers)

The Kyrgyz Republic has opened most of its economy to foreign investment, adopted guarantees against expropriation or nationalization, allowed investors to bid on privatized firms, and established a State Committee on Foreign Investments to serve as a one-stop shop for investors. Foreign investors receive national treatment. The U.S. Department of State reports that "sanctity of contracts and other such concepts are developing and not uniformly implemented. Individual investors can become involved in disputes over licensing, registration, enforcement of contracts, and the like, particularly at the middle and lower levels of officialdom. Corruption is a serious problem." Bureaucratic delays, lack of transparency, imprecise laws governing investment, and unfair implementation of the laws also impede investment. The International Monetary Fund reports that non-residents must obtain approval from the Ministry of Justice to purchase real estate. Foreign exchange accounts are permitted for both residents and non-residents. There are no restrictions on payments and transfers, but most capital transactions must be registered with or reported to the relevant government authority regulating that activity.

## BANKING AND FINANCE
### Score: **3**–Stable (moderate level of restrictions)

The Kyrgyz Republic's underdeveloped banking system is being reorganized through a number of liquidations and consolidations. There are 20 commercial banks, all but two of which are private, and four foreign-owned banks. According to the Economist Intelligence Unit, "Even after the closure of several insolvent banks in 2001, the banking sector is far from being able to play any sort of central role in investment financing. Substantial improvements are required to increase the capitalisation of the sector, mobilise savings, improve bank

supervision and strengthen the legislative framework governing the sector." The central bank established a minimum capital requirement in July 2000. There are 29 small insurance companies, and the small stock exchange lists 70 to 80 companies.

## WAGES AND PRICES
### Score: **3**–Stable (moderate level of intervention)

The government lifted most price controls and removed most subsidies in 1994 but continues to influence prices through its state-owned enterprises, which include (but are not limited to) enterprises in agriculture, mining, telecommunications, energy, aviation, printing, and recreation. According to the U.S. Department of State, "The Government mandated the national minimum wage…. The Federation of Trade Unions was responsible for enforcing all labor laws, including the law on minimum wages; minimum wage regulations largely were observed."

## PROPERTY RIGHTS
### Score: **4**–Stable (low level of protection)

The legal system does not protect private property sufficiently. "The judiciary is nominally independent," reports the Economist Intelligence Unit, "but suffers from a lack of reform, low salaries and corruption. The president recommends appointments to the Constitutional Court, the Supreme Court and the Supreme Court of Arbitration. Criminal trials involving opposition members and journalists in recent years have revealed the administration's strong political influence over the system…."

## REGULATION
### Score: **4**–Stable (high level)

According to the U.S. Department of State, "the legal and regulatory system…is still developing. Although the body of new commercial law promises to be an effective basis for commerce, implementing regulations and court procedures, in many cases, remain to be worked out and the law is not always implemented fully. In an effort to assist foreign investors on a variety of issues, the state committee for foreign investments and economic development established an agency based on the 'one-stop-shop' model. However, businesses report that registration with this new agency does not prevent bureaucratic holdups in other parts of the Kyrgyz government." The European Bank for Reconstruction and Development reports that "corruption is widespread."

## INFORMAL MARKET
### Score: **4**–Stable (high level of activity)

Piracy of such products as computer software and CDs remains significant. The Business Software Alliance estimates that the rate of software piracy in 2000 was 90 percent. The University of Linz, Austria, reports that the informal economy was about 36 percent of GDP in 2000, and the Center for International Private Enterprise reports that about 24 percent of the population works informally.

# LAOS

Rank: 151

Score: 4.45

Category: Repressed

**Present & Past Scores**

(Best) 1
2
3
4
(Worst) 5

4.51  4.70  4.63  4.75  4.80  4.75  4.81  4.73

4.45

'95  '96  '97  '98  '99  '00  '01  '02  '03  '04
n/a

Laos remains a politically stable one-party communist state. It is also Southeast Asia's poorest country and one of the world's most repressed economies. The Lao People's Revolutionary Party began a market-oriented reform program in 1986 and negotiated a bilateral trade agreement with the United States in 1997. However, Laos is one of only four countries in the world that does not yet have normal trade relations with the United States, and the bilateral agreement will not take effect until the U.S. Congress approves normal trade relations. Laos is a member of the Association of Southeast Asian Nations and is lowering tariff barriers consistent with its obligations as part of the ASEAN Free Trade Area. The communist government recognizes the growing problem of corruption among party members but has not instituted the necessary political reforms to make public officials accountable or strengthen the rule of law. Laos's fiscal burden of government score is 0.3 point better this year; in addition, its government intervention score is 1.5 points better, and its monetary policy score is 1 point better. As a result, Laos's overall score is 0.28 point better this year.

## TRADE POLICY
### Score: **5**–Stable (very high level of protectionism)

According to the World Bank, Laos's weighted average tariff rate in 2000 (the most recent year for which World Bank data are available) was 14.2 percent. The U.S. Department of State reports that "non-tariff barriers, such as a quota on the import of automobiles, still exist…. Importing from and exporting to Laos still requires authorization from several national and local authorities, which can be a time-consuming and less-than-transparent process."

## FISCAL BURDEN OF GOVERNMENT
Score—Income Taxation: **4**–Stable (high tax rates)
Score—Corporate Taxation: **4.5**–Stable (very high tax rates)
Score—Change in Government Expenditures: **3**–Better (very low decrease)
### Final Score: **4**–Better (high cost of government)

The International Monetary Fund reports that Laos's top income tax rate is 40 percent. The top corporate tax rate is 35 percent. Government expenditures as a share of GDP decreased 0.1 percentage point to 20 percent in 2001, compared to a 1.9 percentage point increase in 2000. As a result, Laos's fiscal burden of government score is 0.3 point better this year.

## GOVERNMENT INTERVENTION IN THE ECONOMY
### Score: **3.5**–Better (high level)

Based on data from the International Monetary Fund, the government consumed 19.7 percent of GDP in 2001. In the 2000–2001 fiscal year, based on data from the IMF, Laos received 20.75 percent of its total revenues from state-owned enterprises and government ownership of property. Based on newly available data on revenues from state-owned enterprises, Laos's government intervention score is 1.5 points better this year.

## MONETARY POLICY
Score: **4**–Better (high level of inflation)

Between 1993 and 2002, Laos's weighted average annual rate of inflation was 15.93 percent, down from the 25.03 percent between 1992 and 2001 reported in the 2003 *Index*. As a result, Laos's monetary policy score is 1 point better this year.

## CAPITAL FLOWS AND FOREIGN INVESTMENT
Score: **4**–Stable (high barriers)

In 2000, the U.S. Department of State reported that Laos's "foreign investment law guarantees foreign investors protection on their investments and property from government confiscation, seizure or nationalization without compensation; operations free from government interference; the right to lease [but not own] land, transfer leasehold interests, and make improvements on land or buildings; and repatriate earnings. Foreign investors may invest in either joint ventures with Lao partners or in wholly foreign-owned entities." However, the same source reports that the country is not open to foreign investment in practice, and a lack of transparency and bureaucratic red tape represent significant barriers. The International Monetary Fund reports that both residents and non-residents may hold foreign exchange accounts subject to certain restrictions and that there are no restrictions on payments and transfers. All capital transactions require central bank approval. The evidence indicates that the government does not actively discourage foreign investment, but the process is bureaucratic, opaque, and subject to corruption.

## BANKING AND FINANCE
Score: **5**–Stable (very high level of restrictions)

Banking reform began in 1988 when the state bank devolved its commercial lending activities and assumed a central bank supervisory role. Domestic banks collapsed during the Asian financial crisis. The state merged three government-owned banks in the North as Lanexang Bank and the three government-owned banks in the South as Lao May Bank. The Economist Intelligence Unit reports that "nearly 50% of total [banking] assets are owned by the state-owned Banque pour le Commerce Exterieur Lao (BCEL), which handles foreign trade and other overseas transactions. Foreign banks have been permitted to open full branches since 1992, but they are limited to the Vientiane municipality." In addition, "There are still major problems in the banking sector, where politically directed lending remains the norm." The insurance sector is dominated by Assurance Générales du Laos, in which the government currently has a 49 percent stake.

## WAGES AND PRICES
Score: **4**–Stable (high level of intervention)

In 2000, the U.S. Department of State reported that "The government still sets production targets for the agricultural sector, as well as for some industries, and controls the price on a few essential goods, such as cement and gasoline." Since the agricultural sector is the economy's main sector, constituting 50.9 percent of total output in 2001, these controls are a major constraint. The government also controls the price of electricity and influences prices through its extensive state-owned sector. Laos maintains a daily minimum wage.

## PROPERTY RIGHTS
Score: **5**–Stable (very low level of protection)

The U.S. Department of State reports that "foreign investors are not permitted to own land. The government grants long-term leases, and allows the ownership of property on leased land and the right to transfer and improve leasehold interests." In addition, "foreign investors are generally advised to seek arbitration outside of Laos, since Laos' domestic arbitration authority lacks the ability to enforce its decisions." The same source reports that "senior government and party officials influence the courts…. [I]mpunity is a problem as is corruption. Many observers believe that judges can be bribed."

## REGULATION
Score: **5**–Stable (very high level)

According to the Economist Intelligence Unit, "The environment for both domestic firms and foreign investors is still far from easy, owing to persistent red tape and corruption." According to the U.S. Department of State, "Foreign investors most frequently cite inconsistencies in the interpretation and application of existing laws as among the greatest impediments to investment. The lack of transparency in an increasingly centralized decision-making process, as well as the difficulty encountered in obtaining general information, augments the perception of the regulatory framework as arbitrary and inscrutable."

## INFORMAL MARKET
Score: **5**–Stable (very high level of activity)

The informal market in Laos is larger than the formal economy. There are no copyright or patent laws, piracy is rampant, and the informal market in currency is thriving. The Economist Intelligence Unit reports that there is extensive informal market activity in the logging industry and slash-and-burn cultivation. In addition, "Laos is still the largest producer of opium in the world and a major transit route and destination for amphetamines."

LATVIA

# LATVIA

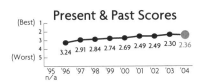

**Present & Past Scores**

(Best) 1
2
3
4
(Worst) 5

3.24 2.91 2.84 2.74 2.69 2.49 2.49 2.30 2.36

'95 '96 '97 '98 '99 '00 '01 '02 '03 '04
n/a

Rank: 29
Score: 2.36
Category: Mostly Free

## QUICK STUDY

### SCORES

| | |
|---|---|
| Trade Policy | 2 |
| Fiscal Burden | 2.6 |
| Government Intervention | 2.5 |
| Monetary Policy | 1 |
| Foreign Investment | 2 |
| Banking and Finance | 2 |
| Wages and Prices | 2 |
| Property Rights | 3 |
| Regulation | 3 |
| Informal Market | 3.5 |

**Population:** 2,345,800 (2002)

**Total area:** 64,589 sq. km

**GDP:** $7 billion (2002)

**GDP growth rate:** 6.1% (2002)

**GDP per capita:** $2,985 (2002)

**Major exports:** wood and wood products, textiles, metals, machinery and equipment

**Exports of goods and services:** $3.7 billion

**Major export trading partners:** Germany 16.7%, UK 15.7%, Lithuania 8.1%, Russia 5.9%

**Major imports:** machinery and equipment, chemicals, fuels

**Imports of goods and services:** $4.2 billion

**Major import trading partners:** Germany 17.0%, Russia 9.2%, Lithuania 8.5%, Finland 8.0%

**Foreign direct investment (net):** $174 million

2001 Data (in constant 1995 US dollars)

Since regaining its independence in 1991, Latvia has transformed its economy. The privatization program is 97 percent complete, the currency is strong, and both the financial system and the overall economy have been liberalized. Virtually all small and medium-size companies have been privatized. A flourishing private sector accounted for 68 percent of GDP in 2000. Banks and real estate have also been privatized. Most prices have been freed, and the trade regime has been liberalized in all sectors in accordance with Latvia's 1999 accession to the World Trade Organization. Vaira Vike-Freiberga, elected in 1999, is Latvia's first woman president and one of its most popular political figures. The government has adopted a number of laws over the past three years, including a new commercial code harmonized with that of the European Union. In 2002, Latvia was invited to join both the EU and NATO; its accession to NATO, as well as the accession of six other former communist states, was ratified unanimously by the U.S. Senate in May 2003. Future economic development is closely tied to the EU, which accounts for 60 percent of Latvia's exports. The national currency has been pegged to the special drawing right (SDR, International Monetary Fund currency basket) since 1994, and this has prevented excessive government spending. Both foreign and domestic investments have been growing. GDP grew by 6.1 percent in 2002. Privatization of the remaining state shares in major industries such as telecommunications, power, and shipping remains one of the government's major objectives. Latvia's fiscal burden of government score is 0.1 point worse this year, and its government intervention score is 0.5 point worse. As a result, Latvia's overall score is 0.06 point worse this year.

## TRADE POLICY
### Score: **2**–Stable (low level of protectionism)

According to the World Bank, Latvia's weighted average tariff rate in 2001 (the most recent year for which World Bank data are available) was 2.6 percent. The U.S. Department of State reports that "Latvia requires licenses for the imports of grains, sugar, fuel, tobacco, alcohol and arms, and for the export of ferrous and non-ferrous metal scrap, ethyl alcohol, and spirits."

## FISCAL BURDEN OF GOVERNMENT
Score—Income Taxation: **2.5**–Stable (moderate tax rates)
Score—Corporate Taxation: **2**–Better (low tax rates)
Score—Government Expenditures: **4**–Worse (moderate increase)
### Final Score: **2.6**–Worse (moderate cost of government)

Latvia has a flat income tax rate of 25 percent. The corporate tax rate is 19 percent, down from the 25 percent reported in the 2003 *Index*. However, government expenditures as a share of GDP increased 1.9 percentage points to 39.3 percent in 2002, compared to a 3.1 percentage point decrease in 2001. On net, Latvia's fiscal burden of government score is 0.1 point worse this year.

## GOVERNMENT INTERVENTION IN THE ECONOMY
### Score: **2.5**–Worse (moderate level)

Based on data from the Economist Intelligence Unit, the government consumed 20.5 percent of GDP in 2002, up from the 17.7 percent reported in the 2003 *Index*. As a result, Latvia's government intervention score is 0.5 point worse this year. In 2001, according to the

International Monetary Fund, Latvia received 2.12 percent of its total revenues from state-owned enterprises and government ownership of property.

## MONETARY POLICY
### Score: **1**–Stable (very low level of inflation)

From 1993 to 2002, Latvia's weighted average annual rate of inflation was 1.88 percent.

## CAPITAL FLOWS AND FOREIGN INVESTMENT
### Score: **2**–Stable (low barriers)

Latvia welcomes foreign investment, and foreigners receive national treatment. The government has no screening process, and foreigners may bid on companies undergoing privatization. Foreign investors are permitted to invest in most industries but are not allowed to hold controlling shares in companies involved in security services, air transport, or gaming interests. Foreign investors may own land for agricultural or forestry purposes if there is an existing investment protection agreement between Latvia and the country in which the investor is based, or if more than 50 percent of the fixed capital is owned by a Latvian citizen or the government. According to the International Monetary Fund, both residents and non-residents may hold foreign exchange accounts; there are no restrictions or controls on payments, transactions, transfers, or repatriation of profits; and non-residents may purchase buildings and land unless the land is near the border or in an environmentally sensitive area.

## BANKING AND FINANCE
### Score: **2**–Stable (low level of restrictions)

Latvia suffered a banking crisis in 1995 and 1998 that led to the liquidation and consolidation of a number of banks. The banking system has largely recovered, and regulations now require minimum accounting and financial standards, minimum capital requirements, restrictions on exposure, and open foreign exchange positions. Latvia has implemented a universal banking system that is competitive and mostly free of onerous government regulation, although the central bank vigorously enforces all banking regulations. According to the Embassy of Latvia, the government wholly owns one bank, the Mortgage and Land Bank. The government sold a 25 percent stake in the Savings Bank in May and plans to sell its remaining shares to employees and former employees by the end of 2003. According to the U.S. Department of State, "Foreign banks have the right to open subsidiaries and branch offices in Latvia and the licenses are granted using the same procedure as with domestic banks. Currently there are four foreign banks operating in Latvia, two German banks, one Estonian bank and Finnish Bank Merita branch." Private pension funds must invest at least 85 percent of their assets domestically, and insurance companies must seek permission from the Financial and Capital Markets Commission to invest more than 10 percent of their technical reserves abroad.

## WAGES AND PRICES
### Score: **2**–Stable (low level of intervention)

The market determines most wages and prices. According to the Embassy of Latvia, the government regulates the price of such goods and services as rent, water, waste disposal, sewerage services, electricity, gas, heat supply, medical services, transportation, postal services, and telephone services. In all, the government regulates the prices of approximately 16 percent of the goods and services in the consumer price index. It also mandates a minimum wage.

## PROPERTY RIGHTS
### Score: **3**–Stable (moderate level of protection)

Latvia's constitution provides for an independent judiciary, which in practice is inefficient and subject to corruption. The Economist Intelligence Unit reports that "judicial institutions enjoy independence from political influence, but are regarded as inefficient, with long delays in court hearings and enforcement of decisions." According to the U.S. Department of State, "The courts must rely on the Ministry of Justice for support, and the judiciary is not well trained, efficient, or free from corruption." Overall, "improvements in the judicial system are needed to accelerate the adjudication of cases, to strengthen the enforcement of court decisions, and to upgrade professional standards."

## REGULATION
### Score: **3**–Stable (moderate level)

Establishing a business is relatively easy, but some regulations are confusing and contradictory, leading to a lack of transparency. According to the U.S. Department of State, "Government bureaucracy, corruption and organized crime, typical of the old Soviet Bloc countries, have been the main impediments to…trade and investment also in Latvia. While these obstacles have sometimes made it more complicated to do business in Latvia than in the west, very few…companies have abandoned the Latvian market because of them." In addition, "it is often alleged that bribe-taking—ranging from low-level bureaucrats in a position to delay or speed up bureaucratic procedures, to high-level officials involved in awarding government contracts—is not uncommon."

## INFORMAL MARKET
### Score: **3.5**–Stable (high level of activity)

Transparency International's 2002 score for Latvia is 3.7. Therefore, Latvia's informal market score is 3.5 this year.

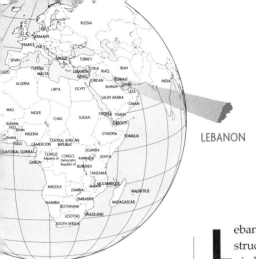

LEBANON

# LEBANON

Rank: 83

Score: 3.13

Category: Mostly Unfree

Present & Past Scores

(Best) 1 2 3 4 (Worst) 5

2.96 2.78 3.06 3.03 3.06 2.65 3.01 3.09 3.13

'95 '96 '97 '98 '99 '00 '01 '02 '03 '04
n/a

**Population:** 4,384,680

**Total area:** 10,400 sq. km

**GDP:** $12.7 billion

**GDP growth rate:** 1.3%

**GDP per capita:** $2,890

**Major exports:** food products, jewelry, chemical products, metal products

**Exports of goods and services:** $1.5 billion

**Major export trading partners:** France 11.8%, US 10.2%, Saudi Arabia 9.4%, United Arab Emirates 9.1%

**Major imports:** food products, vehicles, material and other mineral products, chemical products

**Imports of goods and services:** $5.3 billion

**Major import trading partners:** Italy 10.2%, France 8.8%, Germany 7.7%, Switzerland 6.7%

**Foreign direct investment (net):** $225 million

2001 Data (in constant 1995 US dollars)

Lebanon has made substantial progress toward rebuilding its physical and political infrastructure after a devastating 16-year civil war, although much of the country remains occupied by neighboring Syria. Over the past decade, the cost of rebuilding highways, schools, airports, housing, power stations, and government buildings has pushed public debt to 160 percent of GDP. Lebanon's fiscal debt continues to hold at a crisis level of 17 percent, and unemployment remains high at 25 percent. In response to its heavy debt burden, the government has adopted a fiscal adjustment program focusing on tax reforms and modernization, privatization, expenditure rationalization, and improved debt management. However, the pace of privatization has been slow. An important test of the government's commitment to economic reform will be its divestment of two mobile phone licenses; the sale was scheduled for the late summer of 2002 but has been delayed yet again by protracted negotiations and political infighting. The government has proven its commitment to foreign investment and transparency. Lebanon maintains the most liberal banking regime in the Middle East. There are no restrictions on foreign exchange and investment, and banking secrecy is strictly enforced. In 2001, the Syrian government, bowing to growing resentment of its military occupation, redeployed nearly all of its 25,000 troops away from Lebanon's densely populated coastal plain. Nonetheless, Syria continues to influence all major government decisions, and its presence serves as a daily reminder of the limits on Lebanon's sovereignty. Lebanon's trade policy score is 1 point better this year; however, its fiscal burden of government score is 0.4 point worse, and its wages and prices score is 1 point worse. As a result, Lebanon's overall score is 0.04 point worse this year.

## TRADE POLICY

### Score: **4**–Better (high level of protectionism)

According to the World Bank, Lebanon's weighted average tariff rate in 2001 (the most recent year for which World Bank data are available) was 12 percent, down from the 19.1 percent reported in the 2003 *Index*. As a result, Lebanon's trade policy score is 1 point better this year. The U.S. Department of State reports that non-tariff barriers include "30 types of import controls…administered…by various ministries, which may issue and administer a range of prohibitions, restrictions, licenses and certificates."

## FISCAL BURDEN OF GOVERNMENT

Score—Income Taxation: **2**–Stable (low tax rates)

Score—Corporate Taxation: **1.5**–Stable (low tax rates)

Score—Change in Government Expenditures: **4**–Worse (moderate increase)

### Final Score: **2.3**–Worse (low cost of government)

Lebanon's top income tax rate is 20 percent. The top corporate tax rate is 15 percent. Government expenditures as a share of GDP increased 1.2 percentage points to 35.2 percent in 2001, compared to a 1.6 percentage point decrease in 2000. As a result, Lebanon's fiscal burden of government score is 0.4 point worse this year.

## GOVERNMENT INTERVENTION IN THE ECONOMY

### Score: **3**–Stable (moderate level)

The World Bank reports that the government consumed 18.3 percent of GDP in 2001. In the same year, based on data from the Ministry of Finance, Lebanon received 17.22 percent of its

total revenues from state-owned enterprises and government ownership of property.

### MONETARY POLICY
Score: **1**–Stable (very low level of inflation)

Data from the International Monetary Fund's *2003 World Economic Outlook* indicate that from 1993 to 2002, Lebanon's weighted average annual rate of inflation was 1.25 percent.

### CAPITAL FLOWS AND FOREIGN INVESTMENT
Score: **3**–Stable (moderate barriers)

Lebanon does not discriminate between national and foreign investments in most sectors. An April 2001 amendment to the 1969 law governing purchases of real estate eased legal limits on foreign investment in real estate, removed legal distinctions between Arab and other foreign investment, and reduced registration fees. The U.S. Department of State reports that "in some cases, government red tape and corruption constitute major obstacles to investment and entrepreneurial activity." According to the International Monetary Fund, both residents and non-residents may hold foreign exchange accounts, but central bank approval is required to purchase treasury securities, money market instruments, and derivatives, and some credit operations are prohibited. There are no restrictions on payments and transfers.

### BANKING AND FINANCE
Score: **2**–Stable (low level of restrictions)

Lebanon's banking regime is the most liberal in the region, with few restrictions on domestic bank formation and few barriers to foreign banks. According to the U.S. Department of State, the Banking Control Commission, which regulates Lebanon's banking system, "is compliant with most of the CORE principles of the Basel Committee on banking control and ensures that all banks comply with Basel regulations on capital adequacy ratio." However, the Economist Intelligence Unit reports that many private-sector borrowers are crowded out of the market because more than 60 percent of bank credit goes to the government. In June 2002, Lebanon was removed from the list of countries judged not to be cooperating with international efforts to fight money laundering.

### WAGES AND PRICES
Score: **3**–Worse (moderate level of intervention)

According to the U.S. Department of State, "The Consumer Protection Department at the Ministry of Economy and Trade controls prices and monitors the quality of bread and petroleum derivatives, and the expiration dates of consumables. The Technical Center for Price Control at the Ministry of Economy and Trade surveys supermarket prices of consumer goods every two months. The Ministry of Health also controls the price of pharmaceuticals." The government subsidizes the production of certain arable crops, such as tobacco,

and indirectly affects prices of some utilities such as electricity through its state-owned enterprises. It also mandates a monthly minimum wage. Based on the evidence that the government influences a broad range of prices, either directly or through its state-owned enterprises, Lebanon's wages and prices score is 1 point worse this year.

### PROPERTY RIGHTS
Score: **4**–Stable (low level of protection)

The Economist Intelligence Unit reports that the government significantly influences the judiciary. According to the U.S. Department of State, a survey of foreign investors revealed "that contract enforcement and the unpredictable judiciary system were considered the most important risk factors. The government does not consider that contract annulment has a negative impact on foreign investments in Lebanon, arguing Lebanon always honored all its obligations."

### REGULATION
Score: **4**–Stable (high level)

According to the U.S. Department of State, "Transparency has never been strong in Lebanon. The government does not always establish clear rules of the game." A United Nations Economic and Social Council for West Asia 2001 survey quoted by the U.S. Department of State reflects that "the main obstacles [to business] are: bureaucratic and administrative red tape, lack of transparency, corruption, slow customs procedures and the level of customs duties, work ethics, unexpected changes in economic policies, infrastructure and tax regulations. Major problems faced by start-ups include complex administrative procedures for obtaining approvals and permits and difficulty accessing information."

### INFORMAL MARKET
Score: **5**–Stable (very high level of activity)

Lebanon's informal market includes extensive trade in pirated intellectual property such as trademarks, patents, and copyrights. According to the U.S. Department of State, "Unauthorized copying of imported books, videotapes, cassettes, and computer software is common…." Informal market trade, especially with Syria, is extensive and includes such goods as pharmaceuticals, illicit drugs, weapons, and cigarettes. In 2000, according to the University of Linz, Austria, the informal economy was estimated to be about 36 percent of GDP.

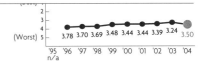

# LESOTHO

**Rank: 118**

**Score: 3.50**

**Category: Mostly Unfree**

| | '95 n/a | '96 | '97 | '98 | '99 | '00 | '01 | '02 | '03 | '04 |
|---|---|---|---|---|---|---|---|---|---|---|
| | | 3.78 | 3.70 | 3.69 | 3.48 | 3.44 | 3.44 | 3.39 | 3.24 | 3.50 |

(Worst) 5

## QUICK STUDY

### SCORES

| | |
|---|---|
| Trade Policy | 4 |
| Fiscal Burden | 3.5 |
| Government Intervention | 3.5 |
| Monetary Policy | 3 |
| Foreign Investment | 4 |
| Banking and Finance | 3 |
| Wages and Prices | 3 |
| Property Rights | 3 |
| Regulation | 4 |
| Informal Market | 4 |

**Population:** 2,061,728

**Total area:** 30,355 sq. km

**GDP:** $1.2 billion

**GDP growth rate:** 4.0%

**GDP per capita:** $563

**Major exports:** food and live animals, clothing, footwear, wool

**Exports of goods and services:** $393.9 million

**Major export trading partners:** North America 73.3%, SACU 26.2%, EU 0.5%

**Major imports:** food, vehicles, machinery, medicine, petroleum products

**Imports of goods and services:** $992.9 million

**Major import trading partners:** SACU 82.8%, Asia 14.9%, North America 0.7%

**Foreign direct investment (net):** $105.8 million

2001 Data (in constant 1995 US dollars)

**A** constitutional monarchy, Lesotho has maintained an unstable democracy since 1993. The Lesotho Congress for Democracy (LCD), led by Prime Minister Pakalitha Mosisili, continues to be the country's dominant political party; there is some dissension, but it is not expected to affect the LCD's position significantly, at least in the short term. Lesotho is situated in the southern part of the continent and is completely surrounded by South Africa, to which it remains very closely linked. Recent numbers indicate that 26 percent of Lesotho's exports went to South Africa in 2001, compared to the 73 percent that went to all of North America in the same year. With few natural resources, Lesotho's agricultural sector is small as a percentage of GDP. According to the Economist Intelligence Unit, industry continues to be the largest economic sector, contributing nearly 45 percent of GDP. The EIU estimates that from 1995–1997, GDP grew by roughly 10 percent a year. While not quite as robust, projections for 2003 and 2004 are nonetheless respectable at 4 percent of GDP. Lesotho will continue to seek assistance in dealing with its growing HIV/AIDS epidemic, which threatens the kingdom's future stability. In February 2003, a program to supply anti-retroviral medication to pregnant HIV-infected women was instituted to stem the tide of HIV-infected childbirths. Lesotho's trade policy score and capital flows and foreign investment score are 1 point worse this year; in addition, its fiscal burden of government score is 0.1 point worse, and its government intervention score is 0.5 point worse. As a result, Lesotho's overall score is 0.26 point worse this year.

### TRADE POLICY
**Score: 4–Worse** (high level of protectionism)

Lesotho belongs to the Southern African Customs Union (SACU), a regional trade arrangement with South Africa, Botswana, Namibia, and Swaziland. According to the World Trade Organization, in 2002 (the most recent year for which WTO data are available), the SACU had an average common external tariff rate of 11.4 percent, up from the 8.5 percent reported in the 2003 *Index*. As a result, Lesotho's trade policy score is 1 point worse this year. Non-tariff barriers include import controls on a number of agricultural products.

### FISCAL BURDEN OF GOVERNMENT
Score—Income Taxation: **3.5–Stable** (high tax rates)
Score—Corporate Taxation: **4.5–Stable** (very high tax rates)
Score—Change in Government Expenditures: **1.5–Worse** (high decrease)
Final Score: **3.5–Worse** (high cost of government)

Lesotho's top income tax rate is 35 percent. The top corporate tax rate is 35 percent. According to the African Development Bank, government expenditures as a share of GDP fell less in 2001 (3 percentage points) than they did in 2000 (13.2 percentage points). As a result, Lesotho's fiscal burden of government score is 0.1 point worse this year.

### GOVERNMENT INTERVENTION IN THE ECONOMY
Score: **3.5–Worse** (high level)

The World Bank reports that the government consumed 24.3 percent of GDP in 2001, up from the 18.3 percent reported in the 2003 *Index*. As a result, Lesotho's government intervention score is 0.5 point worse this year. In the April 2000–March 2001 fiscal year, based on data

265

from the International Monetary Fund, Lesotho received 14.76 percent of its total revenues from state-owned enterprises and government ownership of property.

## MONETARY POLICY
### Score: 3–Stable (moderate level of inflation)

From 1993 to 2002, Lesotho's weighted average annual rate of inflation was 10.32 percent.

## CAPITAL FLOWS AND FOREIGN INVESTMENT
### Score: 4–Worse (high barriers)

Despite government policy, political instability and corruption discourage foreign investment. According to the Economist Intelligence Unit, "The government's medium-term strategy aims to attract significant private-sector foreign direct investment. Achieving this will be a major challenge.... Private investment is...sensitive to the economic climate, and investor confidence was shaken badly by the unrest in 1998.... [I]nvestor confidence will remain fragile until an atmosphere of political stability is firmly re-established." *Lex Africa* reports that foreign investors are limited to a 49 percent equity share in investments where specific trading licenses are required or where the purpose of the investment is to acquire land from the state. The International Monetary Fund reports that both residents and non-residents may hold foreign exchange accounts with government approval. Some payments and transfers are subject to prior government approval and some limitations. Most capital restrictions apply to residents, outward direct investment is prohibited, and real estate purchases abroad require government approval. Based on the evidence of capital controls, official investment restrictions, and unofficial barriers such as corruption and political instability, Lesotho's capital flows and foreign investment score is 1 point worse this year.

## BANKING AND FINANCE
### Score: 3–Stable (moderate level of restrictions)

The government privatized the state-owned Lesotho Bank in 1999 and completed the liquidation of the Lesotho Agricultural Development Bank in 2000. The Central Bank of Lesotho has sought to encourage greater competition, particularly by increasing the participation of foreign banks. Despite an overhaul of the regulatory environment through the 1999 Financial Institutions Act and the 2000 Central Bank Act, the banking system remains small, underdeveloped, and hindered by non-performing loans. According to the Economist Intelligence Unit, "This is owing to a culture of non-repayment, which stems from historical reasons—politicians exploited Lesotho Bank and parastatals crowded out the private sector. Potential new entrants are also concerned about problems with commercial courts, which are under-resourced and have a huge case backlog." The state remains active in the financial system through two state-owned development banks that provide industrial credits and other ser-

vices. The government has been reducing its activities in the insurance sector.

## WAGES AND PRICES
### Score: 3–Stable (moderate level of intervention)

Many prices have been liberalized in Lesotho, but the government still influences prices through large state-owned utilities and direct intervention in the agricultural sector, which employs over 50 percent of the labor force. According to the Economist Intelligence Unit, "A history of direct government involvement has limited private-sector involvement in the commercial development of the [agriculture] sector.... The programme for privatising agricultural parastatals has not made much headway either, with little interest being shown by the private sector." The Wage Advisory Board (a tripartite group of unions, government, and employers) sets a national minimum wage annually.

## PROPERTY RIGHTS
### Score: 3–Stable (moderate level of protection)

Private property is guaranteed, and expropriation is unlikely. According to the U.S. Department of State, "The Constitution provides for an independent judiciary; however, in the past, magistrates appeared to be subject at times to government and chieftainship influence." Lesotho's legal system also is inefficient and subject to police abuse.

## REGULATION
### Score: 4–Stable (high level)

The bureaucracy is large, and corruption is prevalent. According to the Economist Intelligence Unit, "In June the High Court found Lahmeyer International, a German engineering consulting firm, guilty of paying bribes of approximately US$600,000 to Masupha Sole, formerly chief executive of the Lesotho Highlands Development Authority (LHAD), in return for favorable decisions in awarding contracts for the Lesotho Highlands Project (LHWP).... In June 2002 Mr Sole was found guilty on 13 counts of bribery and was sentenced to 18 years imprisonment." The government has pledged to address labor market inflexibility and the inefficient public sector as part of its International Monetary Fund agreement, but specific results have yet to be seen.

## INFORMAL MARKET
### Score: 4–Stable (high level of activity)

Lesotho has a substantial informal market, primarily in consumer goods. Smuggling of firearms, automobiles, and dagga (a narcotic) between South Africa and Lesotho is a concern. According to the World Bank, "more than 85% of the population of 2 million lives in rural areas, engaged mainly in agricultural and informal activities."

LIBYA

# LIBYA

Rank: 154

Score: 4.55

Category: Repressed

**Present & Past Scores**

(Best) 1
2
3
4
(Worst) 5

4.95  4.95  4.95  4.95  4.85  4.90  4.60  4.48  4.55

'95 '96 '97 '98 '99 '00 '01 '02 '03 '04
n/a

Libya's state-dominated economy depends primarily on oil revenues, which provide all export earnings and approximately 25 percent of GDP. Climatic conditions and poor soils severely limit agricultural output within this barren desert country, which imports nearly 75 percent of its food. The government continues to pursue its goal of international acceptance and seems eager to portray Libya as a moderate Islamic country, intolerant of Muslim extremists. After protracted negotiations, for example, Libya has accepted "civil liability" for its role in the Lockerbie bombing, and negotiations continue over a compensation settlement for the victims. Libyan leader Muammar Qadhafi continues to tout an economic liberalization program, focused on structural modernization and privatization, in the belief that global economic integration will attract much-needed foreign direct investment and expand economic growth. However, the regime's continued commitment to quasi-Marxist economic theories and hostility to capitalism, as evidenced by bureaucratic red tape, inefficient resource allocation, poor infrastructure, and frequent policy reversals, have slowed reform and resulted in poor economic performance. Despite growing international pressure to lift its sanctions permanently (the U.N. lifted its sanctions in 1999), the United States continues to maintain economic sanctions against Libya for its support of terrorism. Libya's fiscal burden of government score is 0.7 point worse this year. As a result, its overall score is 0.07 point worse this year.

## QUICK STUDY

### SCORES

| | |
|---|---|
| Trade Policy | 5 |
| Fiscal Burden | 4.5 |
| Government Intervention | 5 |
| Monetary Policy | 1 |
| Foreign Investment | 5 |
| Banking and Finance | 5 |
| Wages and Prices | 5 |
| Property Rights | 5 |
| Regulation | 5 |
| Informal Market | 5 |

**Population:** 5,410,297

**Total area:** 1,759,540 sq. km

**GDP:** $25 billion

**GDP growth rate:** 1.1%

**GDP per capita:** $4,625

**Major exports:** refined petroleum products, crude oil

**Exports of goods (fob):** $10.7 billion

**Major export trading partners:** Italy 39.6%, Germany 15.5%, Spain 14%, Turkey 6.9%

**Major imports:** manufactured goods, food, machinery and transport equipment

**Imports of goods (fob):** $3.6 billion

**Major import trading partners:** Italy 29.1%, Germany 12.4%, UK 6.7%, Tunisia 6.3%

**Foreign direct investment (net):** n/a

2001 Data (in constant 1995 US dollars)

## TRADE POLICY
### Score: 5–Stable (very high level of protectionism)

The World Bank reports that Libya's weighted average tariff rate in 1996 (the most recent year for which World Bank data are available) was 21.3 percent. According to the Economist Intelligence Unit, "Import controls, despite being eased since the suspension of UN sanctions, remain tight even by regional standards."

## FISCAL BURDEN OF GOVERNMENT
Score—Income Taxation: **5**–Stable (very high tax rates)
Score—Corporate Taxation: **5**–Worse (very high tax rates)
Score—Change in Government Expenditures: **3**–Worse (very low decrease)
### Final Score: **4.5**–Worse (very high cost of government)

Libya's government remains dedicated to the redistribution of wealth. According to PricewaterhouseCoopers, the top income tax rate is 90 percent. The top corporate tax rate is 64 percent (60 percent plus a 4 percent jihad tax), up from the 35 percent reported in the 2003 *Index*. Government expenditures as a share of GDP decreased less in 2000 (0.7 percentage point to 29.8 percent) than they did in 1999 (4.7 percentage points). On net, Libya's fiscal burden of government score is 0.7 point worse this year.

## GOVERNMENT INTERVENTION IN THE ECONOMY
### Score: **5**–Stable (very high level)

The World Bank reports that the government consumed 21 percent of GDP in 2001. According to the Economist Intelligence Unit, "It was only in 1988 that the government made its first concessions towards private ownership. In mid-1996 the liberalisation of private-sector retail activities came to an abrupt halt when the government instituted 'purification committees', which were charged with rooting out corruption and enforcing trade and currency regulations. Since 1999, private-sector growth has resumed and been given extra impetus by changes in laws on trading and import activities and on the formation of private companies or partnerships. In 2002 the economy and finance ministers, and Sayf al-Islam Qadhafi, a son of Colonel Qadhafi, indicated that the objective now is to transform the economy into a market economy, through liberalisation and privatisation. Little, however, has been instigated thus far…."

## MONETARY POLICY
### Score: **1**–Stable (very low level of inflation)

Data from the International Monetary Fund's *2003 World Economic Outlook* indicate that from 1993 to 2002, Libya's weighted average annual rate of inflation was –0.87 percent. These data must still be viewed with caution because of the government's role in setting prices and wages.

## CAPITAL FLOWS AND FOREIGN INVESTMENT
### Score: **5**–Stable (very high barriers)

"Foreign participation in industrial ventures set up after March 20, 1970, is permitted on a minority basis," reports the International Monetary Fund, "but only if it leads to increased production in excess of local requirements, introduction of the latest technology, and cooperation with foreign firms in exporting the surplus production." According to the Economist Intelligence Unit, "Despite efforts by Libyan authorities, it would appear that foreign investment inflows have been slow…. Procedures for obtaining visitor visas…vary from the straightforward and reliable to the near impossible…. The import of materials and equipment for investment projects is consistently subject to long and unexplained delays at the ports and customs…. The Libyan Foreign Investment Board (LFIB), which is meant to facilitate inflows of foreign capital, is unable by itself to remove the entrenched bureaucratic practices and other obstacles that deter foreign investment." The IMF reports that both residents and (with prior approval) non-residents may hold foreign currency accounts. Payments for authorized imports are not restricted; all other payments require government approval. Repatriation and most capital transactions, including approval requirements for transactions involving capital and money market instruments, credit operations, direct investment, and real estate, are controlled.

## BANKING AND FINANCE
### Score: **5**–Stable (very high level of restrictions)

Libya's banking system has been under state control since the 1970s and remains highly centralized. "In 2002," reports the Economist Intelligence Unit, "Libyan finance and banking officials indicated that they are considering privatising some of the country's banks. However, no clear privatisation plan or prospectus has been published and foreign investor interest remains low…. Transparency in the financial sector is very poor, in addition to which some state banks apparently have heavy debt burdens. In these circumstances, there is no

capital market to speak of." A 1993 law permits both foreign and private banking. The first private bank since 1969 opened in December 1996; the only foreign banks with representative offices in Libya include Bahrain's Arab Banking Corporation, Malta's Bank of Valletta, and Egypt's Suez Bank.

## WAGES AND PRICES
### Score: **5**–Stable (very high level of intervention)

Aside from limited small farming, small business, and the one private bank, the government controls the economy and sets most wages and prices. It influences wages in both the public and private sectors, and the labor law establishes levels of compensation, pensions, minimum rest, and working hours. According to the Economist Intelligence Unit, "Public-sector salaries have been fixed for more than 20 years, by law Number 15 of 1981."

## PROPERTY RIGHTS
### Score: **5**–Stable (very low level of protection)

The U.S. Department of State reports that Libya's judiciary "is not independent." According to the Economist Intelligence Unit, there is little land ownership, and the government may re-nationalize the little private property that is granted, especially to foreign companies.

## REGULATION
### Score: **5**–Stable (very high level)

It is nearly impossible to establish a business in Libya. "In the 1990s," according to the most recent U.S. Department of State report, "government efforts to allow the private sector to emerge again were undermined by periodic crackdowns by 'purification committees', which had been set up to combat corruption. Since 2000 some restrictions on private sector activity have been removed allowing private business to grow, especially in commerce but also in areas such as oil services. However, many restrictions remain in place and entrepreneurs and businessmen still lack confidence in the government's commitment to the development of the private sector." The same source reports that corruption is a considerable problem. There are no current reports on business regulations in Libya.

## INFORMAL MARKET
### Score: **5**–Stable (very high level of activity)

Most consumer items must be smuggled into the country, and there is a large informal market in currency. According to the Economist Intelligence Unit, "Many public-sector workers…make up for their poor salaries through unofficial perks or corrupt practices, or by moonlighting in Libya's large informal sector."

# LITHUANIA

**Rank: 22**

**Score: 2.19**

**Category: Mostly Free**

**Present & Past Scores**

(Best) 1
2
3
4
(Worst) 5

3.50  3.05  2.98  2.90  2.84  2.53  2.35  2.21  2.19

'95  '96  '97  '98  '99  '00  '01  '02  '03  '04
n/a

## QUICK STUDY

### SCORES
Trade Policy                           2
Fiscal Burden                        2.4
Government Intervention 2.5
Monetary Policy                    1
Foreign Investment              2
Banking and Finance            1
Wages and Prices                 2
Property Rights                    3
Regulation                           3
Informal Market                   3

**Population:** 3,462,600

**Total area:** 65,200 sq. km

**GDP:** $8.5 billion

**GDP growth rate:** 6.2%

**GDP per capita:** $2,464

**Major exports:** mineral products, transport equipment, textiles, machinery and equipment, chemicals

**Exports of goods and services:** $6.5 billion

**Major export trading partners:** UK 13.5%, Russia 12.1%, Germany 10.3%, Latvia 9.6%, Denmark 5.0%

**Major imports:** machinery and equipment, mineral products, transport equipment, chemicals, clothing

**Imports of goods and services:** $8.6 billion

**Major import trading partners:** Russia 21.4%, Germany 17.2%, Italy 4.9%, Poland 4.8%, UK 3.3%

**Foreign direct investment (net):** $640.8 million

2002 Data (in constant 1995 US dollars)

Lithuania is one of the economic leaders among the post-Soviet countries. President Rolandas Paksas was elected in January 2003. Despite 12 percent unemployment, according to Lithuania's Department of Statistics, the GDP growth rate for 2002 was 6.2 percent. Nearly all small businesses and some 60 percent of industrial enterprises have been privatized. The private sector produces approximately 80 percent of GDP. A currency board arrangement has been in place since 1994; in February 2002, the government substituted the euro for the U.S. dollar as the peg currency. At the end of 2001, the Seimas (Lithuania's parliament) amended tax legislation, simplifying the tax base while reducing fiscal exemptions on corporate profits. Lithuania's economic policies are driven by the government's principal foreign policy goal of entering European institutions. Lithuania has been offered membership in both NATO and the European Union as part of the 2003–2004 wave of enlargement. Following EU negotiations, the government agreed to shut down Ignalina, its nuclear power station that supplies most of the country's energy. Lithuania's fiscal burden of government score is 0.3 point worse this year, and its government intervention score is 0.5 point worse; however, its banking and finance score is 1 point better. As a result, Lithuania's overall score is 0.02 point better this year.

## TRADE POLICY
### Score: **2**–Stable (low level of protectionism)

According to the World Bank, Lithuania's weighted average tariff rate in 1997 (the most recent year for which World Bank data are available) was 2.4 percent. The Embassy of Lithuania reports that the government also imposes quotas, sanitary and phytosanitary measures, and quality requirements on about 62 products. Quality requirements for dairy products, cereals, flour, fresh fruits, and vegetables must be approved by the Ministry of Agriculture. According to the International Monetary Fund, the government requires import licenses for health and national security reasons and on certain food products, such as semi-processed meat products, poultry, and fish.

## FISCAL BURDEN OF GOVERNMENT
### Score—Income Taxation: **3**–Stable (moderate tax rates)
### Score—Corporate Taxation: **1.5**–Stable (low tax rates)
### Score—Change in Government Expenditures: **3.5**–Worse (low increase)
### Final Score: **2.4**–Worse (low cost of government)

Lithuania has a flat income tax rate of 33 percent. (Income earned from a primary job is taxed at a flat rate of 33 percent; income earned from a secondary job is taxed progressively from 10 percent to 35 percent.) The top corporate tax rate is 15 percent. Government expenditures as a share of GDP increased 0.6 percentage point to 31.4 percent in 2002, compared to a 1 percentage point decrease in 2001. As a result, Lithuania's fiscal burden of government score is 0.3 point worse this year.

## GOVERNMENT INTERVENTION IN THE ECONOMY
### Score: **2.5**–Worse (moderate level)

Based on data from the International Monetary Fund, the government consumed 20.4 percent of GDP in 2002, up from the 16.2 percent reported in the 2003 Index. As a result,

Lithuania's government intervention score is 0.5 point worse this year. In 2001, according to the IMF, Lithuania received 3.67 percent of its total revenues from state-owned enterprises and government ownership of property.

 **MONETARY POLICY**
Score: **1–Stable** (very low level of inflation)

Data from the International Monetary Fund's *2003 World Economic Outlook* indicate that from 1993 to 2002, Lithuania's weighted average annual rate of inflation was 0.77 percent.

 **CAPITAL FLOWS AND FOREIGN INVESTMENT**
Score: **2–Stable** (low barriers)

Lithuania maintains few barriers to foreign investment. Foreign companies are accorded the same treatment as domestic firms. According to the U.S. Department of State, all sectors of the economy are open to foreign investment, with the exception of the security and defense sectors, and "activities related with the increased danger to human life, health, environment, manufacturing or trade in weapons" require prior permission or a license. Foreigners are allowed to purchase non-agricultural land, and the U.S. Department of State reports that the government is planning to amend the constitution to allow foreigners to purchase agricultural land. Residents may hold foreign exchange accounts; non-residents must obtain approval to hold foreign exchange accounts if the country from which they have come requires approval. There are no controls or restrictions on repatriation of profits, current transfers, or payments for invisible transactions.

 **BANKING AND FINANCE**
Score: **1–Better** (very low level of restrictions)

Lithuania's banking system has recovered from its collapse in 1995 and emerged relatively unscathed from the Russian financial crisis in 1998. The crisis led to consolidation: The number of banks fell from 28 in 1995 to 10 at the end of 2002. Scandinavian banks dominate the banking sector, in which foreign banks own the lion's share of banking capital. Lithuania completed the privatization of Zemes Ukio Bankas (LZUB), its last remaining state-owned bank, on March 19, 2002, increasing foreign ownership of Lithuanian banking capital to 87 percent and virtually removing the government from the banking sector. According to the U.S. Department of State, "Government policies do not interfere in the free flow of financial resources or the allocation of credit." Based on the evidence that the government does not interfere with the banking sector, Lithuania's banking and finance score is 1 point better this year.

 **WAGES AND PRICES**
Score: **2–Stable** (low level of intervention)

Most prices are liberalized. However, according to information provided by the Lithuanian Embassy, price controls remain in effect on electricity, water, and natural gas. According to the Economist Intelligence Unit, the government influences the price of some agricultural goods through subsidies. Lithuania also maintains a minimum wage.

 **PROPERTY RIGHTS**
Score: **3–Stable** (moderate level of protection)

According to the U.S. Department of State, "The Constitution provides for an independent judiciary, and the government generally respected this provision in practice." The European Bank for Reconstruction and Development reports that "weakness of the judicial system is viewed as a deterrent for foreign investors to enforce their rights in local courts." However, the Embassy of Lithuania reports that some laws to improve the judiciary will be passed in 2003. Depending on the effect and enforcement of these laws, Lithuania's property rights score could improve in future editions of the *Index*.

 **REGULATION**
Score: **3–Stable** (moderate level)

Establishing a business is relatively easy; but regulations, though applied evenly in most cases, remain significantly burdensome. According to the U.S. Department of State, "the common problems found in the countries of the former Soviet Union remain. These include government bureaucracy, corruption, and organized crime." Reform in the labor market, reports the Lithuanian Free Market Institute, "does not promise any profound changes." The European Bank for Reconstruction and Development reports that "administrative corruption remains an area of concern."

 **INFORMAL MARKET**
Score: **3–Stable** (moderate level of activity)

Transparency International's 2002 score for Lithuania is 4.8. Therefore, Lithuania's informal market score is 3 this year.

LUXEMBOURG

# LUXEMBOURG

Rank: 4

Score: 1.71

Category: Free

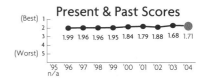

Present & Past Scores

(Best) 1
2
3    1.99  1.96  1.96  1.95  1.84  1.79  1.88  1.68  1.71
4
(Worst) 5

'95  '96  '97  '98  '99  '00  '01  '02  '03  '04
n/a

## QUICK STUDY

### SCORES

| | |
|---|---|
| Trade Policy | 2 |
| Fiscal Burden | 4.1 |
| Government Intervention | 2 |
| Monetary Policy | 1 |
| Foreign Investment | 1 |
| Banking and Finance | 1 |
| Wages and Prices | 2 |
| Property Rights | 1 |
| Regulation | 2 |
| Informal Market | 1 |

**Population:** 455,000

**Total area:** 2,586 sq. km

**GDP:** $25.7 billion

**GDP growth rate:** 1.1%

**GDP per capita:** $56,660

**Major exports:** machinery and transport equipment, manufactured metal products, financial services, travel services, insurance services

**Exports of goods and services:** $29.9 billion

**Major export trading partners:** Germany 24.6%, France 19.6%, Belgium 12.3%, US 3.5% (2001)

**Major imports:** machinery and equipment, chemicals, computer and information, financial services

**Imports of goods and services:** $24.7 billion

**Major import trading partners:** Belgium 34.3%, Germany 25.1%, France 12.8%, US 5.8% (2001)

**Foreign direct investment (net):** –$28.5 billion

2002 Data (in constant 1995 US dollars)

Luxembourg, the smallest member of the European Union, has the world's highest GDP per capita. During the 20th century, it developed from an agrarian society into a manufacturing and services economy and one of the world's richest countries through the rise of the financial services industry, which accounts for about one-third of GDP. With a liberal regulatory framework for financial services and a highly skilled multilingual workforce, Luxembourg is Europe's principal center for mutual funds and a major force in the banking and insurance industries. The coalition government, composed of the Christian Social People's Party (CSV) and Democratic Party (DP), has enacted tax reform as the centerpiece of its domestic policy. The corporate tax, already relatively low, is 30 percent for all corporations, and the top income tax rate declined in 2002. There are no restrictions that apply specifically to foreign investors, the regulatory structure is fair and transparent, the labor force is efficient and productive, and labor strife is minimal. As a result, on a per capita basis, U.S.-sourced foreign direct investment in Luxembourg is the highest in the world outside of North America. Recently, the economy has experienced a significant downturn, and there is little chance that Luxembourg will return to the strong growth rates of the 1990s. GDP increased at a rate of 7.5 percent in 2000, 1 percent in 2001, and 1.1 percent in 2002. In response, the government has stepped up its efforts to promote economic diversification and new sources of foreign direct investment. Luxembourg's fiscal burden of government score is 0.3 point worse this year. As a result, its overall score is 0.03 point worse this year.

###  TRADE POLICY
Score: **2**–Stable (low level of protectionism)

As a member of the European Union, according to the World Bank, Luxembourg had a weighted average tariff rate of 2.6 percent in 2001. The Economist Intelligence Unit reports that Luxembourg "maintains non-tariff barriers common to all EU countries, on television and broadcasting as well as quotas on agricultural products like bananas. In addition, the EU prohibits the importation of hormone-treated beef and all high-value products containing hormone-treated meat." The government requires licenses to import certain industrial products, textiles, and steel.

###  FISCAL BURDEN OF GOVERNMENT
Score—Income Taxation: **3.5**–Stable (high tax rates)
Score—Corporate Taxation: **4**–Stable (high tax rates)
Score—Change in Government Expenditures: **5**–Worse (very high increase)
Final Score: **4.1**–Worse (high cost of government)

Luxembourg's top income tax rate is 38.95 percent (38 percent plus a 2.5 percent surcharge). The top corporate tax rate is 30.38 percent. Government expenditures as a share of GDP increased more in 2002 (5.9 percentage points to 46.1 percent) than they did in 2001 (0.6 percentage point). As a result, Luxembourg's fiscal burden of government score is 0.3 point worse this year.

###  GOVERNMENT INTERVENTION IN THE ECONOMY
Score: **2**–Stable (low level)

According to Luxembourg's statistical agency, the government consumed 18.3 percent of GDP in 2002. In the same year, based on data from the same source, Luxembourg received

3.74 percent of its revenues from state-owned enterprises and government ownership of property.

## MONETARY POLICY
### Score: **1**–Stable (very low level of inflation)

From 1993 to 2002, Luxembourg's weighted average annual rate of inflation was 2.25 percent.

## CAPITAL FLOWS AND FOREIGN INVESTMENT
### Score: **1**–Stable (very low barriers)

Luxembourg has a very open foreign investment regime and actively promotes foreign investment. Foreign and domestic businesses receive equal treatment, and there are no local content requirements. Nearly two-thirds of foreign direct investment involves the banking industry, which has a non-discriminatory policy toward foreign investors. The government restricts investments that directly affect national security, as well as those in some utilities. There are no restrictions or barriers with respect to capital transactions or current transfers, repatriation of profits, purchase of real estate, or access to foreign exchange.

## BANKING AND FINANCE
### Score: **1**–Stable (very low level of restrictions)

The banking system is highly competitive and subject to little government regulation, although banks are restricted in their ability to engage in some financial services, such as real estate. With its bank secrecy laws and no withholding tax on interest, Luxembourg has become an attractive environment in which to do business. However, the Economist Intelligence Unit reports that Luxembourg reached an agreement with EU finance ministers in January 2003 to impose a 15 percent withholding tax on accounts held by non-residents in 2004 (the tax rate will rise to 20 percent in 2007 and 35 percent in 2010) to discourage non-residents from placing money in Luxembourg as a means to avoid paying taxes on interest. According to the EIU, "The state-owned development bank Société nationale de crédit et d'investissement (SNCI) is a major medium- and long-term lender on the domestic market…. It aims to promote the Luxembourg economy and to facilitate both investments and exports through credits and guarantees." Banking is one of Luxembourg's largest industries; its 178 banks from more than 20 countries accounted for approximately 15 percent of GDP in 2000. The government is creating a legal infrastructure to accommodate e-commerce in order to maintain Luxembourg's predominant position as an international finance center.

## WAGES AND PRICES
### Score: **2**–Stable (low level of intervention)

According to the Economist Intelligence Unit, "Price controls are handled by the Price, Competition and Consumer Protection Office (PCCPO), which is part of the Ministry of Economics. The office actively investigates pricing policies throughout Luxembourg's economy. Parliament is in the process of preparing a new law to allow the government to control prices and fix ceilings in emergency situations…." In addition, "The Ministry of Energy fixes energy prices…." Luxembourg affects agricultural prices through its participation in the Common Agricultural Policy, a program that heavily subsidizes agricultural goods. According to Timbro, a Swedish think tank, "EU consumers pay roughly 80–100% more for their food than would be the case in a mature free-market regime." In practice, however, prices for most products are not subject to control. There is a minimum wage.

## PROPERTY RIGHTS
### Score: **1**–Stable (very high level of protection)

Private property is well-protected in Luxembourg. The Economist Intelligence Unit reports that "contractual agreements…are secure, and the country's judiciary and civil service are highly regarded."

## REGULATION
### Score: **2**–Stable (low level)

The process for establishing a business in Luxembourg is relatively simple. The government's one-stop-shopping system for business registration applies to foreign and domestic enterprises alike, and regulations are fair, transparent, and applied evenly in most cases. The Economist Intelligence Unit reports that "strict environmental and planning laws…high wage costs and generous labor protection discourage investment." However, reports the U.S. Department of State, "in comparison with other EU member states, Luxembourg's tax, labor, health, and safety laws are more effective in avoiding distortions…to the efficient mobilization and allocation of investment." Retail businesses (except for some supermarkets) may not operate on Sundays but do not face any unusual difficulties as a result of this policy. Corruption is virtually nonexistent.

## INFORMAL MARKET
### Score: **1**–Stable (very low level of activity)

Transparency International's 2002 score for Luxembourg is 9. Therefore, Luxembourg's informal market score is 1 this year.

# MACEDONIA

Rank: 73

Score: 3.04

Category: Mostly Unfree

Present & Past Scores

(Best) 1
2
3
4
(Worst) 5

3.35  3.23  3.04

'95  '96  '97  '98  '99  '00  '01  '02  '03  '04
n/a n/a n/a n/a n/a n/a n/a n/a

## QUICK STUDY

### SCORES

| | |
|---|---|
| Trade Policy | 4 |
| Fiscal Burden | 2.4 |
| Government Intervention | 3.5 |
| Monetary Policy | 2 |
| Foreign Investment | 3 |
| Banking and Finance | 2 |
| Wages and Prices | 2 |
| Property Rights | 4 |
| Regulation | 4 |
| Informal Market | 3.5 |

**Population:** 2,043,700

**Total area:** 25,333 sq. km

**GDP:** $4.9 billion

**GDP growth rate:** −4.1%

**GDP per capita:** $2,417

**Major exports:** iron and steel, manufactures, food and beverages

**Exports of goods and services:** $2 billion

**Major export trading partners:** Serbia and Montenegro 29.7%, Germany 18.4%, US 8.6%, Italy 7.6%

**Major imports:** foodstuffs, fuels, machinery and equipment, chemicals

**Imports of goods and services:** $2.6 billion

**Major import trading partners:** Greece 17.2%, Germany 11.1%, Serbia and Montenegro 9.4%, Italy 7.6%

**Foreign direct investment (net):** $474.4 million

2001 Data (in constant 1995 US dollars)

In the late spring of 2001, Macedonia dissolved in ethnic conflict. An August 2001 truce averted full-blown civil war, but the prospects for peace and stabilization are still highly uncertain because the fighting has greatly increased inter-ethnic polarization. The present government, a coalition of ethnic Albanian and Macedonian political parties, is scheduled to introduce legislation aimed at achieving significant governmental decentralization in 2003. Under a standby agreement concluded with the International Monetary Fund in 2002, the government is committed to harsh austerity measures, but such a policy could prove destabilizing in a country whose GDP grew at a rate of about 0.3 percent in 2002. Corruption still pervades the economy, and the unemployment rate remains chronically high; only one of every 10 Macedonians receives income from regular work on a regular basis, and an estimated one-quarter of all employees are not paid wages on time. In addition, political instability has had a debilitating effect on foreign investment. Macedonia's fiscal burden of government score is 0.1 point worse this year, and its government intervention score is 0.5 point worse; however, its trade policy score is 1 point better, and its informal market score is 1.5 point better. As a result, Macedonia's overall score is 0.19 point better this year.

## TRADE POLICY
### Score: **4**–Better (high level of protectionism)

The World Bank reports that Macedonia's weighted average tariff rate in 2001 was 13.8 percent, down from the 14.5 percent reported in the 2003 *Index*. As a result, Macedonia's trade policy score is 1 point better this year. Customs corruption acts as a non-tariff barrier. According to the Center for the Study of Democracy, the "customs department [is] seen as [one of the country's] most corrupt institutions...."

## FISCAL BURDEN OF GOVERNMENT
Score—Income Taxation: **1.5**–Better (low tax rates)
Score—Corporate Taxation: **1.5**–Stable (low tax rates)
Score—Change in Government Expenditures: **5**–Worse (very high increase)
### Final Score: **2.4**–Worse (low cost of government)

According to the International Monetary Fund, Macedonia's top income tax rate is 18 percent, down from the 35 percent reported in the 2003 *Index*. The top corporate income tax rate is 15 percent. However, government expenditures as a share of GDP increased 6.2 percentage points to 28 percent in 2001, compared to a 1.2 percentage point decrease in 2000. On net, Macedonia's fiscal burden of government score is 0.1 point worse this year.

## GOVERNMENT INTERVENTION IN THE ECONOMY
### Score: **3.5**–Worse (high level)

According to the World Bank, the government consumed 24.7 percent of GDP in 2001, up from the 18 percent reported in the 2003 *Index*. As a result, Macedonia's government intervention score is 0.5 point worse this year. In 2002, based on data from the Ministry of Finance, Macedonia received 3.28 percent of its total revenues from state-owned enterprises and government ownership of property. This figure, however, should be viewed with caution. As of June 30, 2001, according to the Privatization Agency of the Republic of Macedonia, "privatization [had not been] performed in the following entities: Enterprises

273

and organizations that conduct activities of special national interest; Public utilities and enterprises that conserve water, forests, land and other public goods; Enterprises designated as monopolies, that are to be privatized under separate laws." In June 2003, the Economist Intelligence Unit reported that the government had made limited progress toward selling the country's remaining state-owned enterprises. Based on the apparent unreliability of official figures on revenues from state-owned enterprises, 1 point has been added to Macedonia's government intervention score.

## MONETARY POLICY
### Score: **2**–Stable (low level of inflation)

Data from the International Monetary Fund's *2003 World Economic Outlook* indicate that from 1993 to 2002, Macedonia's weighted average annual rate of inflation was 3.29 percent.

## CAPITAL FLOWS AND FOREIGN INVESTMENT
### Score: **3**–Stable (moderate barriers)

Macedonia's Law on Trading Companies grants foreign and domestic investors equal treatment and permits non-residents to invest in domestic firms, establish new firms, or launch joint ventures without restrictions outside of a few sectors, such as arms manufacturing. Foreign investors are able to acquire state-owned firms slated for privatization. According to the Economist Intelligence Unit, "Of the 84 state companies left for sale, most are categorised as 'strategic' and will be sold to foreign investors." The government controls all real estate transactions involving foreign investment. The International Monetary Fund reports that residents may hold foreign exchange accounts if they were established after 1991, but such accounts may be held abroad only with the government's approval. Non-residents also may hold foreign exchange accounts. Payments and transfers face few controls and restrictions. Most capital and money market activities require the approval of the Ministry of Finance or must be registered with the government.

## BANKING AND FINANCE
### Score: **2**–Stable (low level of restrictions)

The Economist Intelligence Unit reports that the collapse of the former Yugoslavia threw Macedonia's banking system into chaos. When the National Bank of Yugoslavia refused to return the foreign exchange deposits of Macedonian banks, they could not cover such deposits; the Macedonian government assumed these debts, but "foreign-currency deposits held in Macedonian banks were frozen and are now being paid out in installments...." The restrictions on access to savings led to various pyramid schemes that collapsed in 1997. The government is restructuring the banking sector and has sold its bank holdings. Of the 21 banks in Macedonia at the beginning of 2003, six are majority foreign-owned. Overall, the banking system is weak and suffers from a legacy of bad

loans. Legislation passed in July 2000 brought supervisory standards closer to those of the European Union and allows foreign banks to establish branches in the country.

## WAGES AND PRICES
### Score: **2**–Stable (low level of intervention)

In 2000, the Commission of the European Communities reported that "Price liberalization has been essentially completed. Price controls exist for only very few products." The government influences prices through the remaining state-owned sectors; however, many state-owned enterprises have been privatized, and this influence is declining. The Economist Intelligence Unit reports that the government controls the price of oil. Macedonia has a minimum wage that is set by law at two-thirds of the average wage.

## PROPERTY RIGHTS
### Score: **4**–Stable (low level of protection)

Protection of property in Macedonia still needs to be strengthened. According to the U.S. Department of State, "the Constitution provides for an independent judiciary, and the Government respects this provision in practice, although the court system at times was inefficient and subject to political manipulation." The U.S. Agency for International Development reports that "an inefficient judiciary and a lack of rule of law are key impediments to the economic and democratic development of the country."

## REGULATION
### Score: **4**–Stable (high level)

The government has made some effort to establish a regulatory system to promote competitiveness. According to a survey sponsored by Freedom House, "the main problems are state bureaucracy, corruption and unpredictability of laws and regulations."

## INFORMAL MARKET
### Score: **3.5**–Better (high level of activity)

Transparency International's 1999 score for Macedonia is 3.3. Therefore, Macedonia's informal market score is 3.5 this year—1.5 point better than last year.

# MADAGASCAR

Rank: 86

Score: 3.14

Category: Mostly Unfree

**Present & Past Scores**

(Best) 1
2
3
4
(Worst) 5

3.74  3.55  3.44  3.51  3.45  3.39  3.29  3.29  2.85  3.14

'95  '96  '97  '98  '99  '00  '01  '02  '03  '04

Madagascar is still recovering from the civil unrest that followed its December 2001 presidential election. The Economist Intelligence Unit reports that supporters of former President Didier Ratsiraka are still being detained in large numbers. Ratsiraka has close ties to French President Jacques Chirac and is living in France, from which it is doubtful that he will be extradited. As a result of the civil unrest, economic activity was virtually at a standstill for the first half of 2002, and unemployment increased. According to the International Monetary Fund, it is estimated that poverty increased from 69 percent in 2001 to 75 percent in 2002. Further hindering investment and growth is President Marc Ravalomanana's refusal to privatize Sirama, the national sugar producer. Additionally, the EIU notes that non-performing loans are at a high level. The government has established an anti-corruption commission, but it has much more to do if it is to recover from the political crisis and lower the country's high rate of poverty. Madagascar's trade policy and monetary policy scores are 1 point worse this year; in addition, its fiscal burden of government score is 0.4 point worse, and its informal market score is 0.5 point worse. As a result, its overall score is 0.29 point worse this year, causing Madagascar to be classified as a "mostly unfree" economy.

## TRADE POLICY
### Score: **3**–Worse (moderate level of protectionism)

The World Bank reports that Madagascar's weighted average tariff rate in 1995 (the most recent year for which World Bank data are available) was 5.3 percent. According to the World Trade Organization, "Madagascar maintains a limited number of import restrictions. Restrictions currently in force are retained for reasons of health, security or morals, and concern products such as arms, explosives, and radioactive products. Import restrictions also apply to products considered by the Government to be strategic (e.g. vanillin and precious stones). Importation of all these products is either prohibited or requires prior authorization by the relevant Ministry…. A prior authorization is also required for imports of telecommunication items and equipment in order to ensure compatibility with established standards." Based on new evidence of non-tariff barriers, Madagascar's trade policy score is 1 point worse this year.

## FISCAL BURDEN OF GOVERNMENT
### Score—Income Taxation: **3.5**–Stable (high tax rates)
### Score—Corporate Taxation: **4.5**–Stable (very high tax rates)
### Score—Change in Government Expenditures: **5**–Worse (very high increase)
### Final Score: **4.4**–Worse (high cost of government)

According to the International Monetary Fund, Madagascar's top income tax rate is 35 percent. The top corporate income tax rate is 35 percent. Government expenditures as a share of GDP increased more in 2001 (3.7 percentage points to 21.8 percent) than they did in 2000 (0.7 percentage point). As a result, Madagascar's fiscal burden of government score is 0.4 point worse this year.

## GOVERNMENT INTERVENTION IN THE ECONOMY
### Score: **1.5**–Stable (low level)

The World Bank reports that the government consumed 8 percent of GDP in 2001. In the same year, according to the International Monetary Fund, Madagascar received 4.06 percent

275

of its total revenues from state-owned enterprises and government ownership of property.

## MONETARY POLICY
### Score: **4**–Worse (high level of inflation)

From 1993 to 2002, Madagascar's weighted average annual rate of inflation was 13.19 percent, up from the 6.66 percent from 1992 to 2001 reported in the 2003 *Index*. As a result, Madagascar's monetary policy score is 1 point worse this year.

## CAPITAL FLOWS AND FOREIGN INVESTMENT
### Score: **3**–Stable (moderate barriers)

Most sectors of Madagascar's economy are open to 100 percent foreign ownership, and the government has established Export Processing Zones in which export firms enjoy tax advantages. Foreign investors have also gained access to Madagascar through its privatization program. However, President Ravalomanana appears to be taking steps to prevent foreign investors from acquiring the state-owned sugar producer, Sirama. According to the Economist Intelligence Unit, he "has stated categorically that Sirama represents part of the national asset base…and should not, therefore, be handed over to foreign interests." Unofficial barriers such as a large bureaucracy also discourage foreign investment. According to the U.S. Department of State, "Potential foreign investors are compelled to deal with a thicket of bureaucratic obstacles as they seek the necessary permits and approvals." The African Growth and Opportunity Act led to substantial investment in the textile sector, which was prospering before the advent of instability. The International Monetary Fund reports that both residents and non-residents may open foreign exchange accounts subject to certain restrictions. There are no restrictions on payments or transfers, though profits must be repatriated within 30 days. All capital movements with other nations require government authorization.

## BANKING AND FINANCE
### Score: **3**–Stable (moderate level of restrictions)

The political crisis threw the financial system into disarray for the first half of 2002. As a result, reports the Economist Intelligence Unit, the probability that banks will acquire more non-performing loans has increased as many businesses and bank customers' financial positions have been weakened. The government has largely withdrawn from the banking sector. According to the EIU, "All the major commercial banks are now at least part-privatised, with a strong involvement by major French names, whose financial clout should help them to rebuild after the traumatic first half of 2002." The state owns two insurance companies. "For private banks," reports the U.S. Department of State, "financial statements are in compliance with international standards and audits are performed both by local and internationally recognized accounting firms."

## WAGES AND PRICES
### Score: **2**–Stable (low level of intervention)

The government has abolished price controls on virtually all products, although it influences or controls prices for some agricultural products. The Ministry of Civil Service, Labor, and Social Laws enforces wages set by the labor code and supporting legislation.

## PROPERTY RIGHTS
### Score: **3**–Stable (moderate level of protection)

According to the U.S. Department of State, "The Constitution provides for an autonomous judiciary; however, at all levels, the judiciary was susceptible to the influence of the executive and at times susceptible to corruption." In addition, "Investors in Madagascar face a legal environment in which security of private property and the enforcement of contracts are inadequately protected by the judicial system."

## REGULATION
### Score: **3**–Stable (moderate level)

Despite efforts to streamline the regulatory process, lack of transparency and red tape remain problems. "The bureaucratic process for establishing a new enterprise is time consuming and requires considerable maneuvering," reports the U.S. Department of State. "Ministerial overlap and bureaucratic struggles for dominance are serious problems. Often, investors have no idea which ministries to approach, or where to start. While there has been a recent move to simplify, the process is still lacking in transparency and corruption is a persistent problem." According to the Economist Intelligence Unit, "Reform of the civil service, to be piloted in a small number of ministries, has been under discussion for some time but has yet to make substantial progress."

## INFORMAL MARKET
### Score: **4.5**–Worse (Very high level of activity)

Transparency International's 2002 score for Madagascar is 1.7. Therefore, Madagascar's informal market score is 4.5 this year—0.5 point worse than last year.

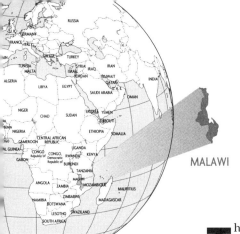

# MALAWI

Rank: 114

Score: 3.46

Category: Mostly Unfree

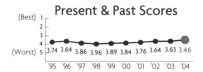

**Present & Past Scores**

(Best) 1
2
3
4
(Worst) 5

| 3.74 | 3.64 | 3.86 | 3.96 | 3.89 | 3.84 | 3.76 | 3.64 | 3.63 | 3.46 |

'95 '96 '97 '98 '99 '00 '01 '02 '03 '04

## QUICK STUDY

### SCORES
| | |
|---|---|
| Trade Policy | 3 |
| Fiscal Burden | 4.1 |
| Government Intervention | 2.5 |
| Monetary Policy | 4 |
| Foreign Investment | 3 |
| Banking and Finance | 4 |
| Wages and Prices | 3 |
| Property Rights | 3 |
| Regulation | 4 |
| Informal Market | 4 |

**Population:** 10,526,300

**Total area:** 118,480 sq. km

**GDP:** $1.7 billion

**GDP growth rate:** −1.5%

**GDP per capita:** $163

**Major exports:** tea, tobacco, sugar, cotton, wood products, coffee

**Exports of goods and services:** $524.9 million

**Major export trading partners:** US 17.7%, Germany 12.9%, South Africa 8.7%, Japan 7.6%

**Major imports:** food, petroleum products, consumer goods, transportation equipment

**Imports of goods and services:** $731.6 million

**Major import trading partners:** South Africa 47.7%, Zambia 13.7%, India 3.9%, UK 2.6%

**Foreign direct investment (net):** $48.4 million

2001 Data (in constant 1995 US dollars)

The ruling United Democratic Front continues to maintain its hold on Malawi in the face of a faction-ridden opposition. The fate of President Bakili Muluzi, however, is uncertain as he approaches the end of his second term. Malawi's constitution prevents a sitting president from seeking a third term. Attempts are underway to amend the constitution ahead of the 2004 elections, but they face widespread opposition. The looming humanitarian disaster fueled by the prevalence of HIV/AIDS and growing food shortages will complicate the president's plans to retain power. Muluzi's successor is likely to be Vice President Justin Malewezi. The overall economic outlook for Malawi is starting to appear more positive despite the threat of famine in parts of the country. The Economist Intelligence Unit projects that real GDP growth will rebound from a contraction in 2002 to 1.6 percent in 2003 and 2.6 percent in 2004. Sustained long-term growth will depend on the implementation of major reforms, among them improving the infrastructure, increasing fiscal discipline and accountability, and diversifying the economy. Malawi's informal market score is 0.5 point worse this year; however, its trade policy and monetary policy scores are 1 point better, and its fiscal burden of government score is 0.2 point better. As a result, Malawi's overall score is 0.17 point better this year.

## TRADE POLICY
### Score: **3**–Better (moderate level of protectionism)

The World Bank reports that Malawi's weighted average tariff rate in 2001 (the most recent year for which World Bank data are available) was 8.2 percent, down from the 11.5 percent reported in the 2003 *Index*. As a result, Malawi's trade policy score is 1 point better this year. Non-tariff barriers include strict import licenses. According to the U.S. Department of State, "Trade licensing covers thirteen import and four export commodities."

## FISCAL BURDEN OF GOVERNMENT
### Score—Income Taxation: **4**–Worse (high tax rates)
### Score—Corporate Taxation: **4.5**–Stable (very high tax rates)
### Score—Change in Government Expenditure: **3.5**–Better (low increase)
### Final Score: **4.1**–Better (high cost of government)

According to the International Monetary Fund, Malawi's top income tax rate is 40 percent, up from the 35 percent reported in the 2003 *Index*. The top corporate tax rate is 35 percent. Government expenditures as a share of GDP increased less in 2001 (0.3 percentage point to 31.9 percent) than they did in 2000 (2.6 percentage points). On net, Malawi's fiscal burden of government score is 0.2 point better this year.

## GOVERNMENT INTERVENTION IN THE ECONOMY
### Score: **2.5**–Stable (moderate level)

The World Bank reports that the government consumed 17.6 percent of GDP in 2001. In the 2001–2002 fiscal year, based on data from the International Monetary Fund, Malawi received 5.3 percent of its total revenues from state-owned enterprises and government ownership of property.

## MONETARY POLICY
### Score: **4**–Better (high level of inflation)

From 1993 to 2002, Malawi's weighted average annual rate of inflation was 19.68 percent, down from the 29.28 percent from 1992 to 2001 reported in the 2003 *Index*. As a result, Malawi's monetary policy score is 1 point better this year.

## CAPITAL FLOWS AND FOREIGN INVESTMENT
### Score: **3**–Stable (moderate barriers)

The government encourages foreign investment in most sectors. According to the U.S. Department of State, "Since industrial licensing in Malawi applies to both domestic and foreign investment, and is only restricted to a short list of products, it does not impede investment, limit competition, protect domestic interests, or discriminate against foreign investors at any stage of investment." The International Monetary Fund reports that residents who regularly receive foreign exchange transfers from abroad may hold foreign exchange accounts, but these accounts may not be held abroad. Non-residents may hold foreign exchange accounts with authorized dealers, and some transactions require government approval. Neither residents nor non-residents may hold offshore accounts of domestic currency. Some payments and transfers, such as those for travel and medical treatment, are subject to quantitative limits. Most capital transactions by non-residents are unrestricted, but most capital transactions by residents—including purchase of foreign capital or money market instruments by residents, credit operations from non-residents to residents, and outward direct investment—require exchange control approval.

## BANKING AND FINANCE
### Score: **4**–Stable (high level of restrictions)

The government exercises a great deal of control over the financial system. According to the U.S. Department of State, "The conglomerate Press Corporation Limited (PCL), in which the government holds a 49% stake, sold [its shares of Commercial Bank of Malawi (CBM)] but increased its holding in rival National Bank of Malawi (NBM)." Together, the CBM and NBM control over 80 percent of the banking market. The government also affects the allocation of credit. According to the Economist Intelligence Unit, "Much bank lending is to the government and parastatals, usually on a short-term basis; there is little lending to private individuals." A foreign presence is allowed; for example, a subsidiary of a Mauritian bank opened in Malawi in 1999, and Fincom is partly owned by the South African Nedbank. In 2000, a U.S. investor, along with two Malawian companies, purchased over 60 percent of Malawi's National Insurance Company Ltd.

## WAGES AND PRICES
### Score: **3**–Stable (moderate level of intervention)

The government has lifted price controls on almost all products, although controls on the prices of some food items and energy remain in effect. According to the U.S. Department of State, "Prices for most goods are generally market-determined. Petroleum and sugar are still subject to some degree of price controls. The Agricultural Development and Marketing Corporation (ADMARC) has intervened in the maize market in the recent past, attempting to stabilize prices. State-provided utilities and services (telephones, water, electricity, etc.) are also subject to varying degrees of government price administration." As most Malawians are active in the agricultural sector, these price restrictions affect a substantial portion of the economy. The Ministry of Labor and Vocational Training sets different urban and rural minimum wages based on recommendations of a tripartite wage board composed of government, labor, and employer representatives.

## PROPERTY RIGHTS
### Score: **3**–Stable (moderate level of protection)

The U.S. Department of State reports that "Malawi has an independent but overburdened judiciary, which derives its procedures from English Common Law. There has been little government interference in the court system, although there have on occasion been allegations of government involvement…. There are also frequent allegations of bribery in civil and criminal cases. Administration of the courts is weak, and due process can be very slow. Serious shortcomings in the judicial system include poor record keeping, a lack of attorneys and trained personnel, heavy caseloads, and insufficient financial resources."

## REGULATION
### Score: **4**–Stable (high level)

Malawi's regulatory environment is significantly burdensome. "No tax, labor, environment, health and safety or other laws distort or impede investment," reports the U.S. Department of State. "However, procedural delays, red tape, and corrupt practices continue to impede the business and investment approval process. These include decision making, which is often neither transparent nor based purely on merit, and required land-access approvals." According to the Economist Intelligence Unit, "Relations with donors have recently been damaged by allegations of corruption surrounding the use of donor funds and significant funding has been withheld. Problems over governance and the rule of law are also viewed with concern and donor scrutiny will remain high."

## INFORMAL MARKET
### Score: **4**–Worse (high level of activity)

Transparency International's 2002 score for Malawi is 2.9. Therefore, Malawi's informal market score is 4 this year—0.5 point worse than last year.

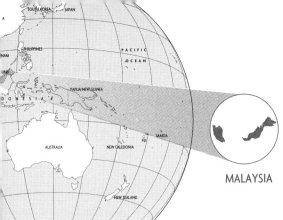

# MALAYSIA

MALAYSIA

Rank: 87

Score: 3.16

Category: Mostly Unfree

**Present & Past Scores**

(Best) 1
2
3
4
(Worst) 5

2.45 2.63 2.85 2.64 2.64 2.76 3.05 3.23 3.14 3.16

'95 '96 '97 '98 '99 '00 '01 '02 '03 '04

In May 2003, Prime Minister Mahathir Mohamad (who retired on October 31, 2003) announced a comprehensive plan to address medium-term economic issues. The package includes relaxing limits on foreign investment in listed companies, encouraging property purchases by foreigners, and cutting red tape. The issue of a cut in the corporate tax rate is not addressed, however, and this could undermine Mahathir's desire to attract foreign capital. Malaysia's economic climate remains relatively benign. Private investment has begun to recover as public consumption revives. Exports of electrical and electronic goods, the drivers of the Malaysian economy, have been falling because of shrinking world demand and the sluggish U.S. economy. Yet the Malaysian economy is steadied by an increase in the global prices of such exports as palm oil, oil and gas, and chemicals. Overall, export growth has eased, but import growth has fallen more rapidly; as a result, the current account remains in surplus. Manufacturing output has lost momentum, and domestic-oriented production has stagnated. In 2002, Malaysia's fiscal deficit rose to 4.7 percent, and 2003 will mark the sixth straight year of budget deficits. Severe Acute Respiratory Syndrome (SARS) has cut domestic tourism by 60 percent, according to the Association of Tour and Travel Agencies. GDP per capita fell from $4,797 in 2000 to $4,708 in 2001, and the GDP growth rate fell from 8.3 percent in 2000 to 0.4 percent in 2001. Malaysia's fiscal burden of government score is 0.2 point worse this year. As a result, its overall score is 0.02 point worse this year.

## QUICK STUDY

### SCORES

| | |
|---|---|
| Trade Policy | 3 |
| Fiscal Burden | 3.6 |
| Government Intervention | 4 |
| Monetary Policy | 1 |
| Foreign Investment | 4 |
| Banking and Finance | 4 |
| Wages and Prices | 3 |
| Property Rights | 3 |
| Regulation | 3 |
| Informal Market | 3 |

**Population:** 23,802,360

**Total area:** 329,750 sq. km

**GDP:** $112.1 billion

**GDP growth rate:** 0.4%

**GDP per capita:** $4,708

**Major exports:** electronics, petroleum, chemicals, palm oil, textiles, clothing, travel services, transportation, financial services, construction

**Exports of goods and services:** $117.6 billion

**Major export trading partners:** US 20.5%, Singapore 17.3%, Japan 13.8%, Hong Kong 4.6%

**Major imports:** capital goods, transport equipment, manufactured goods, insurance services, financial services

**Imports of goods and services:** $98.7 billion

**Major import trading partners:** Japan 19.7%, US 16.2%, Singapore 13.9%, China 5.0%, Thailand 3.9%

**Foreign direct investment (net):** $257 million

2001 Data (in constant 1995 US dollars)

## TRADE POLICY

### Score: **3**–Stable (moderate level of protectionism)

According to the World Bank, Malaysia's weighted average tariff rate in 1997 (the most recent year for which World Bank data are available) was 5.8 percent. The Economist Intelligence Unit reports that "Malaysia's system of import prohibitions and licensing is not fully transparent…. [T]he persistent denial of sanitary certificates for products such as chicken, pork, liquid milk, and eggs effectively acts to prohibit imports…. [I]mport quotas are maintained on some farm products, like unroasted coffee, to protect local producers…."

## FISCAL BURDEN OF GOVERNMENT

Score—Income Taxation: **2.5**–Stable (moderate tax rates)
Score—Corporate Taxation: **3.5**–Stable (high tax rates)
Score—Change in Government Expenditures: **5**–Worse (very high increase)

### Final Score: **3.6**–Worse (high cost of government)

Malaysia's top income tax rate is 28 percent, down from the 29 percent reported in the 2003 *Index*. The top corporate tax rate is 28 percent. Government expenditures as a share of GDP increased more in 2001 (5.6 percentage points to 29.5 percent) than they did in 2000 (1.2 percentage points). As a result, Malaysia's fiscal burden of government score is 0.2 point worse this year.

## GOVERNMENT INTERVENTION IN THE ECONOMY

### Score: **4**–Stable (high level)

The World Bank reports that the government consumed 12.2 percent of GDP in 2001. According to the Economist Intelligence Unit, the government "has gradually reduced its direct participation in enterprises" but "retains very large industrial and commercial holdings. Meanwhile, it has transformed a range of government institutions into profit-oriented corporations, without directly privatizing them." As of April 2003, "there were 35 non-financial public enterprises...or state-run enterprises.... More generally, the government is active in oil, utilities, transport, banking and public services, and it operates more than 200 industrial estates."

## MONETARY POLICY
### Score: 1–Stable (very low level of inflation)

From 1993 to 2002, Malaysia's weighted average annual rate of inflation was 1.77 percent.

## CAPITAL FLOWS AND FOREIGN INVESTMENT
### Score: 4–Stable (high barriers)

Although Malaysia encourages foreign investment in some sectors, such as high-technology and export-oriented manufacturing, the U.S. Department of State reports that it also "retains considerable discretionary authority in approving individual investment projects." According to the same source, the Malaysian Industrial Development Authority screens all manufacturing investment proposals, both foreign and domestic, to determine "whether each project is consistent with the Second Industrial Master Plan (1996–2005) and government strategic and social policies." Malaysia restricts foreign participation in such sectors as banking, telecommunications, and media and requires foreign-owned manufacturing firms with licenses issued before June 17, 2003, to export a certain percentage of their products. The decision-making process in granting foreign investment often lacks transparency. Foreign-controlled companies must get 50 percent of local credit from domestic banks. The government has abolished many onerous restrictions on foreign capital flows. All capital transactions are subject to various limitations and approval requirements.

## BANKING AND FINANCE
### Score: 4–Stable (high level of restrictions)

The government is heavily involved in financial markets. Most recently, it forced the 58 domestic banks to merge into 10 larger financial institutions, after which it recapitalized these institutions and restructured their extensive non-performing loans through the national asset management company, Pengurusan Danaharta Nasional Berhad. In 2001, the Bank Negara Malaysia (the central bank) announced a 10-year plan for strengthening the financial sector that blocks competition from new foreign banks until after 2007. Overall, foreign participation in commercial banking is limited to 30 percent of equity in any single institution. The government also affects the allocation of credit. According to the Economist Intelligence Unit, "An unusual feature of the Malaysian financial sector is that financial institutions are required to provide loans 'at reasonable cost' to priority sectors—all *bumiputera* groups (groups owned by ethnic Malays or other indigenous peoples), low-cost housing and small-scale enterprises. The government also sets lending targets

for the banking sector within an overall macroeconomic framework and threatens sanctions when targets are missed, as has happened in recent years." Foreign insurance companies are not allowed more than 49 percent ownership without approval from the government.

## WAGES AND PRICES
### Score: 3–Stable (moderate level of intervention)

The market determines most wages and prices. According to the Economist Intelligence Unit, "Under the Price Control Act, most prices are market-determined but the Ministry of Domestic Trade and Consumer Affairs controls prices of selected essential foods and commodities and also certain manufactured products (including cement)." In addition, the government is considering new legislation that would "give the Ministry of Domestic Trade and Consumer Affairs the power to intervene in the market if it felt that price increases in certain areas were 'unjust'." Malaysia does not have a national minimum wage, but the U.S. Department of State reports that "the Wage Councils Act provides for a minimum wage in those sectors or regions of the country where market determined wages are insufficient."

## PROPERTY RIGHTS
### Score: 3–Stable (moderate level of protection)

Private property is protected in Malaysia, but the judiciary is subject to political influence. According to the Economist Intelligence Unit, "companies are aware that the application of commercial laws is still sometimes unpredictable in Malaysian courts; decisions depend on the leaning of the judges who often seem divided between upholding justice and protecting their jobs."

## REGULATION
### Score: 3–Stable (moderate level)

Malaysia's regulatory regime is efficient and fairly transparent, but there are restrictions, and the government intervenes in the economy to promote official policies. Both foreign and domestic businesses must have ethnic Malay (Bumiputeras) business partners with a share in the enterprise of at least 30 percent. The Economist Intelligence Unit reports that all firms seeking manufacturing licenses must comply with the National Development Policy, which maintains the spirit of the affirmative action requirements in favor of the country's Bumiputeras. Given the lack of skilled labor, particularly in high-tech industries, investors find the ceiling on workers from other countries a significant deterrent to investing in Malaysia. The government is considering phasing out this requirement.

## INFORMAL MARKET
### Score: 3–Stable (moderate level of activity)

Transparency International's 2002 score for Malaysia is 4.9. Therefore, Malaysia's informal market score is 3 this year.

# MALI

Rank: 102

Score: 3.34

Category: Mostly Unfree

## QUICK STUDY

### SCORES

| | |
|---|---|
| Trade Policy | 3 |
| Fiscal Burden | 4.4 |
| Government Intervention | 4 |
| Monetary Policy | 2 |
| Foreign Investment | 3 |
| Banking and Finance | 4 |
| Wages and Prices | 2 |
| Property Rights | 3 |
| Regulation | 3 |
| Informal Market | 5 |

**Population:** 11,094,340

**Total area:** 1,240,000 sq. km

**GDP:** $3.2 billion

**GDP growth rate:** 1.4%

**GDP per capita:** $292

**Major exports:** gold, cotton, livestock

**Exports of goods and services:** $1.07 billion

**Major export trading partners:** Thailand 17.0%, Brazil 12.5%, Italy 6.0%, South Korea 4.1%

**Major imports:** capital goods, petroleum, foodstuffs, textiles

**Imports of goods and services:** $1.28 billion

**Major import trading partners:** Ivory Coast 17.5%, France 13.9%, Germany 4.5%, Senegal 3.8%

**Foreign direct investment (net):** $61 million

2001 Data (in constant 1995 US dollars)

Mali holds a difficult position on the African continent. Internally, an ever-increasing portion of its land is subject to desertification, drought, and soil degradation, while to the south there is instability in the Ivory Coast. Mali had the first successful transfer of power in its post-colonial history in 2002, and the government of Amadou Toumani Toure must now attempt to deal with the fact that nearly 65 percent of the population lives below the poverty line. Economic support from the International Monetary Fund and World Bank has helped economic liberalization, the fight against corruption, and other internal reforms, but the country's economic limitations complicate these efforts. Mali's reliance on commodity exports makes it highly susceptible to price swings. Growth could match the projected 4 percent, depending on the conflict in the Ivory Coast and a fall in cotton prices. Should peace come to the South however, the Economist Intelligence Unit looks for economic growth approaching 6 percent. Mali's fiscal burden of government score is 0.4 point worse this year, and its banking and finance score is 1 point worse. As a result, Mali's overall score is 0.14 point worse this year.

## TRADE POLICY

### Score: 3–Stable (moderate level of protectionism)

Mali is a member of the West African Economic and Monetary Union (WAEMU), which imposes a common external tariff with four rates: 0 percent, 5 percent, 10 percent, and 20 percent. (The other seven members of the WAEMU are Benin, Burkina Faso, Guinea–Bissau, Ivory Coast, Niger, Senegal, and Togo.) According to the World Bank, Mali's weighted average tariff rate in 2001 (the most recent year for which World Bank data are available) was 9.4 percent. Most import barriers have been lifted, although import licenses are still required.

## FISCAL BURDEN OF GOVERNMENT

### Score—Income Taxation: 4–Stable (high tax rates)
### Score—Corporate Taxation: 4.5–Stable (very high tax rates)
### Score—Change in Government Expenditures: 4.5–Worse (high increase)
### Final Score: 4.4–Worse (high cost of government)

The International Monetary Fund reports that Mali's top income tax rate is 40 percent. The top corporate tax rate is 35 percent. Government expenditures as a share of GDP increased 2.7 percentage points to 26.5 percent in 2001, compared to a 0.5 percentage point decrease in 2000. As a result, Mali's fiscal burden of government score is 0.4 point worse this year.

## GOVERNMENT INTERVENTION IN THE ECONOMY

### Score: 4–Stable (high level)

The World Bank reports that the government consumed 13 percent of GDP in 2001. Through the parastatals, the government is actively involved in marketing, pricing, and coordinating the production of the country's major products, such as cotton and rice. According to the Economist Intelligence Unit, "Mali's cotton industry is currently organised as a vertically integrated system, with CMDT [the cotton parastatal] controlling almost all aspects of production, including the supply of fertilisers, the purchase, transport and ginning of seed cotton, and the marketing of cotton fibre. This structure has been blamed for generating a number of inefficiencies and rent-seeking activities and for constituting an implicit tax burden on cotton farmers.... [T]he government released a reform action plan for the sector in June 2001. This envisages the restructuring of CMDT so that it concentrates on its core activities of ginning and marketing.... Full liberalisation of the sector is planned for 2005." The government also has shares in companies in the mining sector.

## MONETARY POLICY
### Score: 2–Stable (low level of inflation)

From 1993 to 2002, Mali's weighted average annual rate of inflation was 4.36 percent. Mali has benefited from a stable currency—a rarity in sub-Saharan Africa—as a member of the CFA franc zone. Fourteen countries use the CFA franc, a common currency with a fixed parity with the euro. (The other 13 countries are Benin, Burkina Faso, Cameroon, Central African Republic, Chad, Congo [Brazzaville], Equatorial Guinea, Gabon, Guinea–Bissau, Ivory Coast, Niger, Senegal, and Togo.)

## CAPITAL FLOWS AND FOREIGN INVESTMENT
### Score: 3–Stable (moderate barriers)

The government has an established investment code and permits 100 percent foreign ownership of any new business. Foreign investors may purchase privatized state-owned enterprises and invest in most areas of the economy; they must go through the same screening process as domestic investors. According to the U.S. Department of State, foreign investors may face discriminatory treatment by tax collectors. The International Monetary Fund reports that both residents and non-residents may hold foreign exchange accounts with permission of the government and the Banque Centrale des Etats de l'Afrique de l'Ouest (Central Bank of West African States, or BCEAO). Transfers to countries other than France, Monaco, WAEMU members, Central African Economic and Monetary Community members, and Comoros require government approval. Credit and loan operations, and issues and purchases of securities, derivatives, and other instruments, are subject to various requirements, controls, and authorization depending on the transaction. Purchase of real estate requires prior authorization from the Ministry of Finance.

## BANKING AND FINANCE
### Score: 4–Worse (high level of restrictions)

The BCEAO, a central bank common to the eight members of the WAEMU, governs Mali's banking system. Member countries use the CFA franc that is issued by the BCEAO and pegged to the euro. Mali's banking sector is small, underdeveloped, and concentrated in urban areas, leaving rural services to the rapidly increasing number of microfinance lenders. According to the Economist Intelligence Unit, seven commercial banks were operating in Mali in 2002, along with an agricultural bank and a housing bank. "The sector is characterised by heavy government ownership," reports the EIU;

"only three of the nine banks are 100% privately owned. This has led to the availability of only a limited range of financial products and weak intermediation." Commercial banks are permitted to invest in foreign capital markets. Based on the increasing evidence of government domination of the banking sector, Mali's banking and finance score is 1 point worse this year.

## WAGES AND PRICES
### Score: 2–Stable (low level of intervention)

The market determines most wages and prices. The government has adopted a plan to introduce market-determined pricing, including producer prices for cotton, by 2005. The government influences prices through its state-owned enterprises and public utilities and sets a national minimum wage.

## PROPERTY RIGHTS
### Score: 3–Stable (moderate level of protection)

The constitution provides for an independent judiciary, which in practice is subject to political influence. According to the U.S. Department of State, "the rule of law is generally respected, although corruption [is] a significant problem within the judiciary." In addition, "low salaries and inadequate resources impact negatively on the quality of judicial decisions."

## REGULATION
### Score: 3–Stable (moderate level)

Despite government efforts to improve the regulatory structure and reform the civil service, corruption, inconsistent application of regulations, and inefficient bureaucracy continue to present impediments to business. The Economist Intelligence Unit reports that "corruption is most pervasive in government procurement, where lower and middle-ranking civil servants may request bribes to expedite paperwork, but is not a serious impediment to foreign investment."

## INFORMAL MARKET
### Score: 5–Stable (very high level of activity)

Violations of intellectual property rights are common, and there is an informal market in currency and the illegal tapping of water and electricity lines. According to the Economist Intelligence Unit, "Commerce is at the heart of Mali's informal economy. According to official data, trading accounted for 16% of GDP in 2000, but most retailing and trading activity takes place in street markets." Africa News Service reports that most of the labor force works in the informal market.

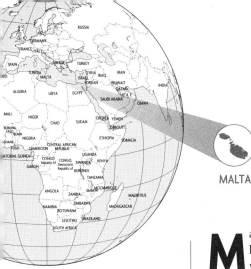

MALTA

# MALTA

Rank: 37
Score: 2.51
Category: Mostly Free

Present & Past Scores

(Best) 1
2
3
4
(Worst) 5

3.44 3.24 3.25 3.15 3.14 3.09 2.84 2.78 2.76 2.51
'95 '96 '97 '98 '99 '00 '01 '02 '03 '04

**M**alta gained its independence from Great Britain in 1964, and its economy since then has depended on tourism, foreign trade, and manufacturing. Malta's well-trained workers, relatively cheap labor costs, and proximity to the European Union market have attracted foreign companies. During negotiations to enter the EU, which Malta is slated to join in 2004, the government has moved to liberalize and deregulate the economy, removing some import tariffs at the start of 2000 and reducing aid for loss-making state-owned shipyards. By May 2004, all barriers to the movement of goods and capital between Malta and the rest of the EU will be removed. However, given the prevailing political and economic culture, further privatization of government-owned assets can be expected to prove politically difficult, as protectionism has been an essential component of the government's policy. Malta's trade policy score is 1 point worse this year, and its fiscal burden of government score is 0.5 point worse; however, its government intervention, banking and finance, wages and prices, and informal market scores are 1 point better. As a result, Malta's overall score is 0.25 point better this year.

### TRADE POLICY
Score: **4**–Worse (high level of protectionism)

According to the World Bank, Malta's average tariff rate in 2000 (the most recent year for which World Bank data are available) was 9.8 percent. The U.S. Department of State reports that the government imposes taxes above normal tariff rates to protect local industries. Health, security, and environment-related products require an import license. Based on the evidence of non-tariff barriers, Malta's trade policy score is 1 point worse this year.

### FISCAL BURDEN OF GOVERNMENT
Score—Income Taxation: **3.5**–Stable (high tax rates)
Score—Corporate Taxation: **4.5**–Stable (very high tax rates)
Score—Government Expenditures: **4**–Worse (moderate increase)
Final Score: **4.1**–Worse (high cost of government)

Malta's top income tax rate is 35 percent. The top corporate tax rate is 35 percent. Government expenditures as a share of GDP increased 1.5 percentage points to 47.4 percent in 2001, compared to a 2.1 percentage point decrease in 2000. As a result, Malta's fiscal burden of government score is 0.5 point worse this year.

### GOVERNMENT INTERVENTION IN THE ECONOMY
Score: **3**–Better (moderate level)

The World Bank reports that the government consumed 20.2 percent of GDP in 2001. In the same year, based on data from Malta's Treasury Department, Malta received 6.64 percent of its total revenues from state-owned enterprises and government ownership of property. Based on newly available data on revenues from state-owned enterprises, Malta's government intervention score is 1 point better this year.

## MONETARY POLICY
### Score: **1**–Stable (very low level of inflation)

From 1993 to 2002, Malta's weighted average annual rate of inflation was 2.38 percent.

## CAPITAL FLOWS AND FOREIGN INVESTMENT
### Score: **3**–Stable (moderate barriers)

Malta seeks to attract foreign investment, at least in selected sectors. According to the International Monetary Fund, "All applications for establishing companies with nonresident participation are subject to [Malta Financial Services Center] approval. However, direct investment by nonresidents is usually permitted in all sectors except real estate, wholesale retail trade, and public utilities. Nonresident participation may not exceed 50% of equity in businesses involved in information technology services." The government prohibits both foreign and domestic investment in the energy sector. Foreign investors may purchase privatized state-owned enterprises. The Business Promotion Act of 2001 provides a number of incentives to promote investment, both foreign and domestic. The IMF reports that both residents and non-residents may hold foreign exchange accounts, subject to maximum amounts for residents and restricted to income earned in Malta for non-residents. Payments, capital transactions and transfers, and repatriation of profits are subject to proper documentation and authorization, maximum amounts, and time limits, depending on the financial activity and residency; non-residents may purchase real estate with permission from the Ministry of Finance.

## BANKING AND FINANCE
### Score: **2**–Better (low level of restrictions)

The financial sector is small but competitive. The government removed ceilings on interest rates and loan maturities in 1994 and then removed some restrictions on inward and outward direct investment flows and further liberalized exchange controls in 2000. The government has largely privatized its state-owned banks. In 1999, according to a November 25, 2002, *Financial Times* article, it sold Mid-Med Bank to HSBC of the United Kingdom. More recently, the government has floated the Bank of Valletta on the Malta stock exchange, although it continues to hold a 24.5 percent stake in the bank and retains the right to appoint its chairman. The *Financial Times* reports that HSBC and the Bank of Valetta dominate Malta's banking sector but face increasing competition from a number of foreign banks. Commercial banks may offer all forms of commercial banking services. Based on the evidence that the government has significantly reduced its holdings in the banking sector and foreign banks do not face significant obstacles to entering the banking market, Malta's banking and finance score is 1 point better this year.

## WAGES AND PRICES
### Score: **2**–Better (low level of intervention)

According to the Economist Intelligence Unit, "The inflation rate in January 2002 stood at 4.6%. This high rate was a result of significant increases in food items, beverages and electricity charges in recent months following the removal of government price controls." However, the government plans to impose price controls in the telecommunications sector, effective January 1, 2004. Based on the evidence that, overall, the government is removing price controls, Malta's wages and prices score is 1 point better this year. The government mandates a minimum wage.

## PROPERTY RIGHTS
### Score: **1**–Stable (very high level of protection)

Malta's judiciary is independent, both under the constitution and in practice. "The Maltese judiciary has a long tradition of independence," reports the U.S. Department of State. The *Financial Times* reports that Malta has "a well-founded legal system [and] respect for the rule of law…." The threat of expropriation is low.

## REGULATION
### Score: **2**–Stable (low level)

Malta's regulatory structure is transparent and largely consistent with those of its European neighbors. Companies are requested to submit a business proposal to the Malta Development Corporation before establishing operations. The U.S. Department of State reports that the government "has adopted transparent and effective policies and regulations to foster competition. It is striving to eliminate unnecessary bureaucratic procedures and has taken steps to revise labor, safety, health and other laws in general to conform to EU standards." According to PricewaterhouseCoopers, "Formation procedure is straightforward, and expenses are nominal" in establishing a business. Companies must obtain a license from the police to begin operations. Corruption is rare.

## INFORMAL MARKET
### Score: **3**–Better (moderate level of activity)

The government has managed to reduce smuggling and other informal market activities to some extent. Protection of intellectual property rights is adequate, although software and video piracy has been cited as a significant problem that led to the closing of Virgin Megastore's operations in 2001. According to the U.S. Department of State, "Companies and trusts are now fairly well regulated…. [A]lternative remittance systems…black market exchanges, and trade-based money laundering, are not a problem in Malta." Based on new evidence with respect to the level of activity, Malta's informal market score is 1 point better this year.

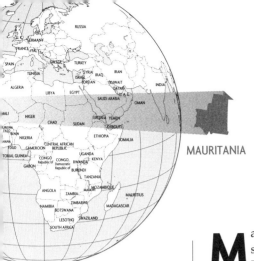

# MAURITANIA

Rank: 67

Score: 2.94

Category: Mostly Free

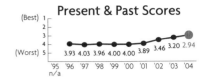

**Present & Past Scores**

(Best) 1
2
3
4
(Worst) 5

3.93 4.03 3.96 4.00 4.00 3.89 3.46 3.20 2.94

'95 '96 '97 '98 '99 '00 '01 '02 '03 '04
n/a

## QUICK STUDY

### SCORES

| | |
|---|---|
| Trade Policy | 3 |
| Fiscal Burden | 2.9 |
| Government Intervention | 2.5 |
| Monetary Policy | 2 |
| Foreign Investment | 2 |
| Banking and Finance | 2 |
| Wages and Prices | 3 |
| Property Rights | 4 |
| Regulation | 4 |
| Informal Market | 4 |

**Population:** 2,749,150

**Total area:** 1,030,700 sq. km

**GDP:** $1.38 billion

**GDP growth rate:** 4.6%

**GDP per capita:** $502

**Major exports:** iron ore, fish

**Exports of goods and services:** $566.9 million

**Major export trading partners:** Italy 15.0%, France 14.9%, Spain 12.4%, Japan 8.0%

**Major imports:** machinery and equipment, petroleum products, foodstuffs

**Imports of goods and services:** $728 million

**Major import trading partners:** France 23.0%, Belgium 8.0%, Spain 5.5%, Algeria 3.7%

**Foreign direct investment (net):** $26.9 million

2001 Data (in constant 1995 US dollars)

Mauritania continues to struggle. Due to a poor harvest and floods that killed thousands of cattle, sheep, and goats, several regions are in dire need of assistance; the Economist Intelligence Unit estimates that 420,000 people are in need of food aid. Mauritania continues to receive significant assistance from various countries and international organizations, including the U.N. World Food Program and World Vision, and has been granted debt relief by the Islamic Development Bank. According to the International Monetary Fund, the country's export base is heavily concentrated, with close to 99 percent of exports consisting of iron ore and fish. Mauritania's key trading partner is the European Union; however, the EIU predicts that exports will remain stagnant since demand in the EU is expected to be depressed. The government remains committed to privatization of the state electricity company, Somelec. Mauritania needs to push ahead with such efforts and privatize the parastatal mining company. The export base also needs to be diversified into areas beyond iron ore and fish to give Mauritanians more opportunities. Mauritania's trade policy score is 1 point better this year; in addition, its fiscal burden of government score is 1.1 point better, and its government intervention score is 0.5 point better. As a result, its overall score is 0.26 point better this year, causing Mauritania to be classified as a "mostly free" economy.

## TRADE POLICY
### Score: **3–Better** (moderate level of protectionism)

The World Bank reports that Mauritania's weighted average tariff rate in 2001 (the most recent year for which World Bank data are available) was 9 percent, down from the 10 percent reported in the 2003 *Index.* As a result, Mauritania's trade policy score is 1 point better this year. Trade restrictions include strict labeling and inspection requirements as well as a sometimes corrupt and inefficient customs agency. According to the U.S. Department of State, "Foreign investors frequently complain of corruption and complexity in customs procedures."

## FISCAL BURDEN OF GOVERNMENT
### Score—Income Taxation: **4–Better** (high tax rates)
### Score—Corporate Taxation: **3–Stable** (moderate tax rates)
### Score—Change in Government Expenditures: **1.5–Better** (high decrease)
### Final Score: **2.9–Better** (moderate cost of government)

The International Monetary Fund reports that Mauritania's top income tax rate is 40 percent, down from the 55 percent reported in the 2003 *Index.* The top corporate tax rate is 25 percent. Government expenditures as a share of GDP decreased 3.6 percentage points to 26.7 percent in 2001, compared to a 4.6 percentage point increase in 2000. On net, Mauritania's fiscal burden of government score is 1.1 points better this year.

## GOVERNMENT INTERVENTION IN THE ECONOMY
### Score: **2.5–Better** (moderate level)

According to the World Bank, the government consumed 15.6 percent of GDP in 2001, down from the 17.3 percent reported in the 2003 *Index.* In the same year, based on data from the International Monetary Fund, Mauritania received 6.95 percent of its total revenues from state-owned enterprises and government ownership of property. Based on the lower rate of government consumption and newly available data on revenues from state-owned enterprises, Mauritania's government intervention score is 0.5 point better this year.

## MONETARY POLICY
### Score: **2**–Stable (low level of inflation)

From 1993 to 2002, Mauritania's weighted average annual rate of inflation was 4.16 percent.

## CAPITAL FLOWS AND FOREIGN INVESTMENT
### Score: **2**–Stable (low barriers)

Mauritania encourages foreign investment in all sectors. "In 2002," reports the Economist Intelligence Unit, "the government adopted a new investment code to encourage local and foreign investors and give them greater security. In particular, foreign investors will be exempted from all customs duties on equipment and goods imported for a start-up, export-oriented project. Also guaranteed is the free transfer of convertible currencies earned from new investments [and] the right to national or international arbitration in the event of a dispute…." Mauritania has set up a one-stop shop for foreign investors to facilitate administrative procedures for dealing with government agencies. The new code, however, does not cover mining and fisheries, Mauritania's most important sectors, which are covered by their own sectoral codes. The privatization process, in which foreign participation is encouraged, also has met with success. The International Monetary Fund reports that both residents and non-residents may hold foreign exchange accounts, but non-resident accounts are subject to some restrictions; capital movements are subject to exchange controls, and payments and transfers are subject to reporting requirements and some restrictions.

## BANKING AND FINANCE
### Score: **2**–Stable (low level of restrictions)

Mauritania's banking sector has been liberalized and is becoming more competitive; however, it remains underdeveloped, with only six commercial banks, three credit agencies, and four insurance companies. According to the U.S. Department of State, the government "has sold its equity stake in commercial banks and insurance companies. Consequently, banks have considerably increased their capital and instituted stricter management. As a result, banks began to receive more customer deposits and make more rational credit decisions…. The banks' financial statements are in compliance with international standards and are annually audited by local accounting firms." The Economist Intelligence Unit reports that a Kuwaiti bank was granted a license to begin operations in Mauritania in 2003.

## WAGES AND PRICES
### Score: **3**–Stable (moderate level of intervention)

The Economist Intelligence Unit reports that the government has removed many price controls. The government maintains a monthly minimum wage and, according to the International Monetary Fund, controls the price of land transportation services. Wages and prices are also distorted through subsidies to businesses and state-owned utilities like electricity. According to the U.S. Department of State, "Privatization…is reducing the economic dominance of state-owned companies."

## PROPERTY RIGHTS
### Score: **4**–Stable (low level of protection)

Mauritania's judicial system is chaotic and corrupt. The U.S. Department of State reports that "impartial application of the law by the Mauritanian judiciary has been a problem for some local companies. Mauritania's banks, for example, have had difficulty getting local courts to enforce banks' right under loan agreements to seize pledged assets from local merchants." In addition, "the executive branch exercises significant pressure on the judiciary through its ability to appoint and influence judges," and "poorly educated and poorly trained judges who are susceptible to social, financial, tribal, and personal pressures limit the judicial system's fairness."

## REGULATION
### Score: **4**–Stable (high level)

In recent years, the government has taken several steps to address Mauritania's burdensome regulatory structure. In 1997, reports the U.S. Department of State, the government created the "Mauritanian Investment Window, a one-stop shop intended to enable investors to comply with Government requirements at a central location. In 1998, this office was renamed the Investment Promotion Office, and its services were expanded." In 2002, the government introduced a new investment code to facilitate economic activity for both local and foreign investors. Lack of transparency and accountability continue in some parts of the bureaucracy. According to the U.S. Department of State, "Corruption exists at all levels of government and society. While Mauritania has laws, regulations, and penalties against corruption, enforcement is very limited. As a result, some wealthy business groups and [government] officials receive favors from authorities. The meager salaries of [government] employees at all levels foster corruption."

## INFORMAL MARKET
### Score: **4**–Stable (high level of activity)

Mauritania's large informal market is confined principally to consumer goods and entertainment products. According to the Economist Intelligence Unit, "The low volume of recorded trade with Senegal and Mali belies substantial cross-border commerce, little of which appears in official statistics."

*2004 Index of Economic Freedom*

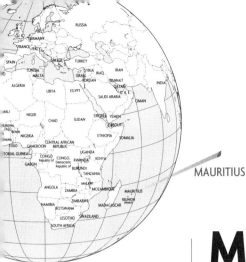

# MAURITIUS

Rank: 71

Score: 2.99

Category: Mostly Free

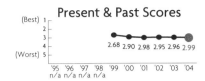

Present & Past Scores

(Best) 1
2
3   2.68 2.90 2.98 2.95 2.96 2.99
4
(Worst) 5

'95 '96 '97 '98 '99 '00 '01 '02 '03 '04
n/a n/a n/a n/a

## QUICK STUDY

### SCORES

| | |
|---|---|
| Trade Policy | 5 |
| Fiscal Burden | 2.9 |
| Government Intervention | 3 |
| Monetary Policy | 2 |
| Foreign Investment | 3 |
| Banking and Finance | 2 |
| Wages and Prices | 4 |
| Property Rights | 2 |
| Regulation | 3 |
| Informal Market | 3 |

**Population:** 1,197,900

**Total area:** 1,860 sq. km

**GDP:** $5.2 billion

**GDP growth rate:** 7.2%

**GDP per capita:** $4,352

**Major exports:** clothing, food, beverages and tobacco, textiles, precious stones, sugar

**Exports of goods and services:** $2.96 billion

**Major export trading partners:** UK 31.3%, US 19.8%, France 18.8%, Germany 3.6%

**Major imports:** textile fiber, machinery and transport equipment, food, beverages, mineral fuels, chemicals

**Imports of goods and services:** $3.3 billion

**Major import trading partners:** South Africa 13.8%, France 9.3%, India 8.0%, UK 3.6%

**Foreign direct investment (net):** $8.9 million

2001 Data (in constant 1995 US dollars)

**M**auritius is an Indian Ocean island nation with a population of 1.2 million led by former Finance Minister Paul Berenger, who became Prime Minister in September 2003. The value-added tax was increased from 12 percent to 15 percent in 2002, yet a large government deficit still looms. The financial services sector is growing and now represents over 9 percent of GDP. The economy grew by 2.6 percent in 2000 and 7.2 percent in 2001. In 2001, the government introduced the Sugar Sector Strategic Plan. The goal of this five-year plan, according to Reuters, is to lower production costs by reducing the number of sugar factories from 14 to seven, modernizing factories, generating more electricity from sugar residues, preparing more land for mechanized production, and introducing a voluntary retirement scheme. In 2002, however, a poor sugar crop caused overall economic growth to decline to 5.3 percent. Europe is the key export market for the country's sugar. Mauritius's fiscal burden of government score is 0.2 point better this year; however, its government intervention score is 0.5 point worse. As a result, Mauritius's overall score is 0.03 point worse this year.

 ## TRADE POLICY
### Score: **5**–Stable (very high level of protectionism)

The World Bank reports that Mauritius's weighted average tariff rate in 1998 (the most recent year for which World Bank data are available) was 24.5 percent. According to the U.S. Department of State, "The State Trading Corporation controls imports of rice, flour, petroleum products, and cement, and the Agricultural Marketing Board controls imports of potatoes, onions, corn, and some spices that compete with locally-grown produce."

 ## FISCAL BURDEN OF GOVERNMENT
### Score—Income Taxation: **2.5**–Stable (moderate tax rates)
### Score—Corporate Taxation: **3**–Stable (moderate tax rates)
### Score—Change in Government Expenditures: **3**–Better (very low decrease)
### Final Score: **2.9**–Better (moderate cost of government)

Mauritius's top income tax rate is 25 percent. The top corporate income tax rate is 25 percent. Government expenditures as a share of GDP decreased 0.9 percentage point to 23.9 percent in 2001, compared to a 1.4 percentage point increase in 2000. As a result, Mauritius's fiscal burden of government score is 0.2 point better this year.

 ## GOVERNMENT INTERVENTION IN THE ECONOMY
### Score: **3**–Worse (moderate level)

The World Bank reports that the government consumed 13 percent of GDP in 2001. In the same year, according to the International Monetary Fund, Mauritius received 10.86 percent of its total revenues from state-owned enterprises and government ownership of property, up from the 8.97 percent reported in the 2003 *Index*. As a result, Mauritius's government intervention score is 0.5 point worse this year.

 ## MONETARY POLICY
### Score: **2**–Stable (low level of inflation)

From 1993 to 2002, Mauritius's weighted average annual rate of inflation was 5.63 percent.

**CAPITAL FLOWS AND FOREIGN INVESTMENT**
Score: **3**–Stable (moderate barriers)

Mauritius generally welcomes foreign investment and has a transparent and well-defined foreign investment code. Foreigners may not own land without prior permission from the Prime Minister and the Minister of Internal Affairs. According to the U.S. Department of State, "The government has no economic or industrial strategy that discriminates against foreign investors. A foreign investor in export-oriented manufacturing is permitted 100% equity, although the government encourages local participation. Foreign participation may be limited to 50% in investments serving the domestic market, and is generally not encouraged in areas where Mauritius has already mastered the technology." The International Monetary Fund reports that both residents and non-residents may hold foreign exchange accounts. There are no controls on payments or transfers, but there are controls on some capital transactions.

 **BANKING AND FINANCE**
Score: **2**–Stable (low level of restrictions)

Mauritius has an open, efficient, and competitive banking system. There are 12 commercial banks, of which eight are foreign-owned. The U.S. Department of State reports that banks may provide "short-term finance, term loans of five to seven years, discounting of export bills, letters of credit, guarantees, and post-shipment finance for exporters at preferential rates." The state-controlled Development Bank of Mauritius Ltd. provides loans to large and medium-sized enterprises and concessionary lending for small-scale enterprises. Eleven offshore banks have taken advantage of Mauritius's efforts to become a regional financial center offering merchant banking, insurance, fund management, and securities services. Mauritius has come under Organisation for Economic Co-operation and Development scrutiny because of suspected money laundering.

 **WAGES AND PRICES**
Score: **4**–Stable (high level of intervention)

According to the U.S. Department of State, the government controls the price of imported products in the agriculture, iron, steel, and petroleum sectors and applies price controls on a number of consumer goods such as appliances, sporting goods, and pharmaceuticals. "In July 1998," reports the same source, "the government passed a new [law] which provides for an extension of price control on several basic commodities, including cornflakes, butter, cheese, cooking oil, canned meat, canned and frozen fish, frozen chicken, milk powder, edible oil, fruit juice and sugar. It also provides for the imposition of maximum markups for goods not currently subject to government control as well as the setting up of a Profiteering Court." The government also controls key utility services and administratively sets a minimum wage that varies according to sector and is indexed to inflation.

 **PROPERTY RIGHTS**
Score: **2**–Stable (high level of protection)

Expropriation of property is unlikely. The judiciary is independent and provides citizens with a fair trial. According to the U.S. Department of State, "The domestic legal system is generally non-discriminatory and transparent." In addition, "corruption exists but is much less than what is encountered elsewhere in Africa."

 **REGULATION**
Score: **3**–Stable (moderate level)

"To streamline the bureaucratic procedures," reports the U.S. Department of State, "the government has recently set up a Board of Investment, which acts as a one-stop-shop for investors." However, regulations are burdensome, and the weight of bureaucracy can cause significant delays. There is some corruption, but the U.S. Department of State reports that it falls below levels seen in the rest of Africa, and the government has made anti-corruption efforts a priority. The government has revised some regulations—for example, in financial services—in an effort to improve the business environment.

 **INFORMAL MARKET**
Score: **3**–Stable (moderate level of activity)

Transparency International's 2002 score for Mauritius is 4.5. Therefore, Mauritius's informal market score is 3 this year.

# MEXICO

Rank: 63

Score: 2.90

Category: Mostly Free

**Present & Past Scores**

(Best) 1
2
3
4
(Worst) 5

3.10 3.31 3.35 3.41 3.25 3.09 3.05 2.96 2.81 2.90

'95 '96 '97 '98 '99 '00 '01 '02 '03 '04

## QUICK STUDY

### SCORES

| | |
|---|---|
| Trade Policy | 2 |
| Fiscal Burden | 4 |
| Government Intervention | 3.5 |
| Monetary Policy | 3 |
| Foreign Investment | 3 |
| Banking and Finance | 2 |
| Wages and Prices | 2 |
| Property Rights | 3 |
| Regulation | 3 |
| Informal Market | 3.5 |

---

**Population:** 102,400,000

**Total area:** 1,972,550 sq. km

**GDP:** $376.8 billion

**GDP growth rate:** 0.9%

**GDP per capita:** $3,679

**Major exports:** manufactures, oil exports, agricultural products, mining products

**Exports of goods and services:** $160.2 billion

**Major export trading partners:** US 89.0%, Latin America and the Caribbean 3.5%, EU 3.3%, Canada 1.7%, Japan 0.3%

**Major imports:** electrical equipment, car parts for assembly, repair parts for motor vehicles, aircraft and aircraft parts, capital goods

**Imports of goods and services:** $190.3 billion

**Major import trading partners:** US 63.5%, EU 9.7%, Japan 5.7%, Latin America and the Caribbean 3.6%, Canada 2.6%

**Foreign direct investment (net):** $12.5 billion

2002 Data (in constant 1995 US dollars)

Mexico is the world's ninth largest economy and the United States' second largest trade partner. Despite a downturn in the global economy, growth has recovered from a decline in 2001. Unemployment is low compared to other Latin American countries, and inflation is 5 percent compared to 18 percent in 1998. Mexico is divided between a relatively prosperous north and a poverty stricken south. More than 50 percent of all Mexicans have an income less than $1,440 and some 23 percent earn less than $720 annually. With Congress divided among three major parties, needed political and economic reforms may not be forthcoming, and police and court reforms have been only partially implemented. Restoring growth means establishing a climate that encourages the creation and growth of small and medium-size businesses. The lack of any visible desire by President Vicente Fox's administration to sell off parts of or privatize the state petroleum monopoly PEMEX sends a powerful negative signal. No doubt the lack of a majority for his National Action Party (PAN) in Congress accounts for some of this weakness. Additionally, both PAN and the rival Institutional Revolutionary Party (PRI) are under investigation for allegations of accepting tainted or foreign campaign funds. Like other leaders in Latin America, Fox will have to work harder to create a better business climate in order to strengthen public confidence in markets and democracy. Mexico's fiscal burden of government score is 0.1 point better this year; however, its government intervention score is 1 point worse. As a result, Mexico's overall score is 0.09 point worse this year.

### TRADE POLICY
**Score: 2–Stable** (low level of protectionism)

Based on data from the Economist Intelligence Unit, Mexico's average tariff rate in 2001 was 1.7 percent (based on import duties as a percent of total imports). According to the Economist Intelligence Unit, "Import controls, including quotas, still apply to many key imports.... All branded patent medicines, toiletries, foodstuffs and drinks must be registered with the Department of Health, and all electrical equipment must meet Mexican safety rules."

### FISCAL BURDEN OF GOVERNMENT
Score—Income Taxation: **3**–Better (moderate tax rates)
Score—Corporate Taxation: **4.5**–Stable (very high tax rates)
Score—Change in Government Expenditures: **4**–Worse (moderate increase)
**Final Score: 4–Better** (high cost of government)

Mexico's top income tax rate is 34 percent, down from 40 percent, and is scheduled to be reduced by 1 percentage point each year until it reaches 32 percent in 2005. The top corporate tax rate is 34 percent, down from 35 percent, and is scheduled to be reduced by 1 percentage point a year until it reaches 32 percent in 2005. Government expenditures increased more in 2002 (1.1 percentage points to 23.7 percent) than they did in 2000 (0.6 percentage point). On net, Mexico's fiscal burden of government score is 0.1 point better this year.

### GOVERNMENT INTERVENTION IN THE ECONOMY
**Score: 3.5–Worse** (high level)

The World Bank reports that the government consumed 11.6 percent of GDP in 2001. In 2000, according to the International Monetary Fund, the government received 9.07 percent of its

289

revenues from state-owned enterprises. This figure, however, does not appear to include government revenues from state-owned companies in the oil sector; in 2001, according to the Bank of Mexico, Mexico received 31.5 percent of its revenues from the state-owned PEMEX oil company and from oil-related non-tax revenues. Based on the higher level of government consumption and the new methodology used to analyze this factor, Mexico's government intervention score is 1 point worse this year.

### MONETARY POLICY
### Score: **3**–Stable (moderate level of inflation)

From 1993 to 2002, Mexico's weighted average annual rate of inflation was 6.34 percent.

### CAPITAL FLOWS AND FOREIGN INVESTMENT
### Score: **3**–Stable (moderate barriers)

Mexico revised its foreign investment law in 1993, and the Economist Intelligence Unit reports that "foreign direct investment (FDI) inflows have been strong and broadly stable" since 1996. Nevertheless, a number of restrictions continue to impede foreign investment. Industries reserved for the government include petroleum and hydrocarbons, petrochemicals, electricity, nuclear energy, radioactive materials, telecommunications, postal service, and control and supervision of ports and airports. State control of the most significant sectors also inhibits investment. Foreign investment in retail trade in gasoline or liquefied gas, broadcasting other than cable television, ground passenger transport, tourism, credit unions, development banks, and certain professional services is prohibited. There are restrictions against majority foreign ownership in over 30 additional businesses. Foreigners may invest in border and coastal property subject to certain restrictions. The EIU reports that foreign investment has been "hindered by a lack of structural reform, [the government's] inability to liberalise further foreign investment legislation (as it lacks a majority in Congress), and the legal uncertainty surrounding foreign investment in the energy sector." Most payments, transactions, and transfers are permissible.

### BANKING AND FINANCE
### Score: **2**–Stable (low level of restrictions)

Mexico's banking sector—40 banks, including five development banks in mid-2002—is becoming more competitive and open to foreign investment. According to the Economist Intelligence Unit, "Foreign financial institutions in mid-2002 controlled or participated in 30 of the 32 private banks operating in Mexico." An April 8, 2003, *Financial Times* article notes that foreign banks control approximately 90 percent of all the assets in Mexico's banking sector. In May 2001, Citigroup acquired Banamex, making it Mexico's largest bank. The government also has increased its transparency and efficiency by adopting U.S. GAAP-based accounting standards and has updated its bankruptcy law to allow companies to use their own capital, such as real estate, machinery,

or a brand name, as a credit guarantee. Commercial banks offer a wide range of services including deposit accounts, consumer and commercial lending, corporate finance, trusts, mutual funds, foreign exchange, and money market trading. The government owns seven development banks that provide financing to specific areas in the economy such as small and medium-size enterprises, public works and infrastructure, agriculture, and foreign trade, but these banks play only a small role in the banking sector. In addition, the government has reduced its bank intervention to three banks as of mid-2002, down from the 13 reported in the 2003 *Index*. The government completed the sale of the state-owned insurance company, Aseguradora Hidalgo, in May 2002 and in September 2001 sold Ban Crecer to the Mexican-owned bank, Banorte, making Banorte the country's fourth largest bank.

### WAGES AND PRICES
### Score: **2**–Stable (low level of intervention)

According to the Economist Intelligence Unit, "Mexico maintains suggested retail prices for medicines and limits increases to a percentage of the amount that producers invest in research and development." The government also controls prices through some state-owned utilities and the energy sector. A government-set minimum wage varies by region.

### PROPERTY RIGHTS
### Score: **3**–Stable (moderate level of protection)

The threat of expropriation is low. President Fox has promised reforms in this area, but progress has been slow. According to the Economist Intelligence Unit, "the [judicial] process remains slow and bureaucratic, and sometimes corrupt. The judiciary branch in Mexico is independent to the point that it can uphold many government decisions…. Contractual agreements are generally upheld in Mexico. The Fox Administration is keen in attracting foreign investment and assuring investors that their investments are safe."

### REGULATION
### Score: 3–Stable (moderate level)

According to the Secretaría de Economía de Mexico (Mexico's Ministry of Economy), people can open a business or request a license in one business day. The primary beneficiaries are businesses carrying out any of the 685 activities officially identified as involving "low public risk." The government estimates that "low risk businesses" entail 80 percent of the most frequent activities carried out by small and medium-size enterprises. The regulatory burden is still significant for larger investments, which have to comply with, for example, more complex environmental impact assessments. Labor legislation is still rigid.

### INFORMAL MARKET
### Score: **3.5**–Stable (high level of activity)

Transparency International's 2001 score for Mexico is 3.6. Therefore, Mexico's informal market score is 3.5 this year.

MOLDOVA

Rank: 79

Score: 3.09

Category: Mostly Unfree

Present & Past Scores

(Best) 1
2
3
4
(Worst) 5

'95 4.10 '96 3.50 '97 3.65 '98 3.48 '99 3.49 '00 3.35 '01 3.75 '02 3.30 '03 3.13 '04 3.09

## QUICK STUDY

### SCORES

| | |
|---|---|
| Trade Policy | 2 |
| Fiscal Burden | 2.4 |
| Government Intervention | 2.5 |
| Monetary Policy | 3 |
| Foreign Investment | 4 |
| Banking and Finance | 3 |
| Wages and Prices | 3 |
| Property Rights | 3 |
| Regulation | 4 |
| Informal Market | 4 |

**Population:** 4,272,519

**Total area:** 33,843 sq. km

**GDP:** $2.9 billion

**GDP growth rate:** 6.1%

**GDP per capita:** $678

**Major exports:** foodstuffs, textiles, vegetable products, machinery and equipment

**Exports of goods and services:** $1.9 billion

**Major export trading partners:** Russia 43.0%, Ukraine 10.1%, Italy 8.1%, Germany 7.2%, Romania 6.7%

**Major imports:** mineral products, machinery and equipment, textiles, chemicals

**Imports of goods and services:** $2.9 billion

**Major import trading partners:** Ukraine 18.0%, Russia 15.1%, Romania 13.1%, Germany 10.5%, Italy 6.4%

**Foreign direct investment (net):** $134.5 million

2001 Data (in constant 1995 US dollars)

Moldova, one of Europe's poorest countries, has been torn between its Romanian roots and Russian ties since winning its independence in 1991. It is the second smallest of the former Soviet Republics and also the most densely populated. In April 2001, in a democratic election, Communist Party chairman Vladimir Voronin was chosen to serve as president. This election brought Moldova and Russia closer but failed to resolve the secession of Transnistria, a communist-dominated enclave plagued by corruption and the smuggling of arms and contraband. The communist government's democratic economic policy and credentials remain suspect. Before the communist takeover, Moldova had steadily increased its macroeconomic stability; nevertheless, it remains one of the region's most heavily indebted countries. Inflation fell from 39 percent in 1999 to 6.4 percent at the end of 2001. Progress in structural reforms resulted in GDP growth of 2 percent in 2000 and 6.1 percent in 2001. The goal of privatizing the energy and agricultural sectors was also achieved with the assistance of the U.S. Agency for International Development. Moldova's capital flows and foreign investment score is 1 point worse this year, and its informal market score is 0.5 point worse; however, its fiscal burden of government score is 0.4 point better, its government intervention score is 0.5 point better, and its monetary policy score is 1 point better. As a result, Moldova's overall score is 0.04 point better this year.

###  TRADE POLICY
### Score: **2**–Stable (low level of protectionism)

The World Bank reports that Moldova's weighted average tariff rate in 2000 (the most recent year for which World Bank data are available) was 2.3 percent. According to the U.S. Department of State, there are significant non-tariff barriers.

### FISCAL BURDEN OF GOVERNMENT
Score—Income Taxation: **2.5**–Stable (moderate tax rates)
Score—Corporate Taxation: **3**–Stable (moderate tax rates)
Score—Change in Government Expenditures: **1**–Better (very high decrease)
### Final Score: **2.4**–Better (low cost of government)

Moldova's top income tax rate is 25 percent. The top corporate tax rate is 25 percent. Government expenditures decreased more in 2001 (4 percentage points to 22.7 percent) than they did in 2000 (1.7 percentage points). As a result, Moldova's fiscal burden of government score is 0.4 point better this year.

###  GOVERNMENT INTERVENTION IN THE ECONOMY
### Score: **2.5**–Better (moderate level)

The World Bank reports that the government consumed 12.3 percent of GDP in 2001. In the same year, according to the International Monetary Fund, Moldova received 7.05 percent of its revenues from state-owned enterprises and government ownership of property, down from the 10.78 percent reported in the 2003 *Index*. As a result, Moldova's government intervention score is 0.5 point better this year.

291

## MONETARY POLICY
Score: **3**–Better (moderate level of inflation)

Between 1993 and 2002, Moldova's weighted average annual rate of inflation was 9.87 percent, down from the 18.13 percent from 1992 to 2001 reported in the 2003 *Index.* As a result, Moldova's monetary policy score is 1 point better this year.

 ## CAPITAL FLOWS AND FOREIGN INVESTMENT
Score: **4**–Worse (high barriers)

Although the Moldovan government does not maintain many formal barriers to foreign investment, there are several informal barriers. According to the Economist Intelligence Unit, "Moldova's modest FDI record reflects its slow progress on privatisation and restructuring in key industrial sectors. In particular, powerful business interests have until recently blocked any attempts to privatize enterprises in wine and tobacco—two of Moldova's most attractive sectors…. Other deterrents include widespread corruption, and slow regulatory and legal reform…. Similarly, critical sectors such as wine, tobacco and fixed-line telecommunications remain in state hands, and FDI inflows into the agricultural sector have remained small." Overall, foreign direct investment in Moldova is among the lowest in the region, behind even Russia and Belarus. The International Monetary Fund reports that both residents and non-residents may hold foreign exchange accounts. Payments and transfers require supporting documentation and approval of the National Bank of Moldova if they exceed specified amounts. Most capital transactions require approval by or registration with the National Bank of Moldova. Based on the evidence of capital controls and informal barriers to foreign investment, Moldova's capital flows and foreign investment score is 1 point worse this year.

 ## BANKING AND FINANCE
Score: **3**–Stable (moderate level of restrictions)

There are no official barriers to founding foreign banks or branches in Moldova. The banking sector is composed of 19 commercial banks, including three foreign bank subsidiaries. One bank—Banca de Economii a Moldovei—is state-controlled. The central bank has been increasing the minimum capital requirements, which could force the consolidation or closure of some smaller banks. Moldova opened its insurance market to foreign competition in 1999. The former state-owned insurance company, Asito, continues to dominate the market with more than 50 percent of commercial business and 90 percent of individual business.

 ## WAGES AND PRICES
Score: **3**–Stable (moderate level of intervention)

The government influences prices through the country's large state-owned sector and, according to the Embassy of Moldova, regulates prices of monopolistic goods and services, energy services, and goods and services tied to basic needs. Moldova has two legal monthly minimum wages— one wage for state employees and another, higher wage for the private sector.

 ## PROPERTY RIGHTS
Score: **3**–Stable (moderate level of protection)

Moldova has passed laws guaranteeing private property and strengthening the judiciary. The U.S. Department of State reports that the "legal system has improved in recent years. Moldova has a documented and consistently applied commercial law." Nevertheless, much more needs to be done: "The Constitution provides for an independent judiciary; however, the executive branch has exerted undue influence on the judiciary. Many observers believe that arrears in salary payments also make it difficult for judges to remain independent from outside influences and free from corruption."

 ## REGULATION
Score: **4**–Stable (high level)

According to the U.S. Department of State, "Bureaucratic procedures are not always transparent and red tape often makes processing unnecessarily long." In addition, Moldova's anti-corruption laws "are not effectively enforced and corruption exists at an advanced level." Labor laws are somewhat rigid, based on a report provided by the Embassy of Moldova.

 ## INFORMAL MARKET
Score: **4**–Worse (high level of activity)

Transparency International's 2001 score for Moldova is 2.1. Therefore, Moldova's informal market score is 4 this year— 0.5 point worse than last year.

# MONGOLIA

Rank: 63

Score: 2.90

Category: Mostly Free

**Present & Past Scores**

(Best) 1
2
3
4
(Worst) 5

3.50 3.60 3.23 3.14 3.18 3.06 3.03 2.98 3.01 2.90

'95 '96 '97 '98 '99 '00 '01 '02 '03 '04

## QUICK STUDY

### SCORES

| | |
|---|---|
| Trade Policy | 2 |
| Fiscal Burden | 4.5 |
| Government Intervention | 2.5 |
| Monetary Policy | 2 |
| Foreign Investment | 3 |
| Banking and Finance | 3 |
| Wages and Prices | 2 |
| Property Rights | 3 |
| Regulation | 4 |
| Informal Market | 3 |

**Population:** 2,421,360

**Total area:** 1,565,000 sq. km

**GDP:** $1 billion

**GDP growth rate:** 1.4%

**GDP per capita:** $430

**Major exports:** livestock, copper, animal products, wool hides

**Exports of goods and services:** $603 million

**Major export trading partners:** China 48.1%, US 30.1%, Russia 6.9%, Italy 3.5%

**Major imports:** machinery and equipment, fuels, food products, chemicals, sugar, tea

**Imports of goods and services:** $752 million

**Major import trading partners:** Russia 42.3%, China 23.8%, South Korea 15.3%, Japan 7.5%

**Foreign direct investment (net):** $56.5 million

2001 Data (in constant 1995 US dollars)

Mongolia remains very much a rural economy with agriculture comprising one-third of GDP. The results of a serious drought and wildfires in the summer of 2002, followed by a harsh winter, continue to hurt growth. The budget deficit, foreign trade deficits, and public debt are major concerns, but inflation has been kept under control. Ulan Bator plans to deal with the budget deficit by reducing tax exemptions rather than by curbing spending. Much-needed privatization has proceeded more slowly than expected, with several large companies, including Mongolia's largest insurance company, and smaller state assets, including buildings, slated for divestiture in 2003. The government is also working to sell farmlands, and poor farmers have organized to buy the lands on which they have worked. Fierce political debate on land privatization is expected. Foreign direct investment in the country's resurgent mining sector has risen in the past two years—a welcome surprise. By 2004, mining will account for one-fifth of GDP. Mongolia's fiscal burden of government score is 0.1 point better this year, and its monetary policy score is 1 point better. As a result, its overall score is 0.11 point better this year, causing Mongolia to be classified as a "mostly free" economy.

## TRADE POLICY
### Score: **2**–Stable (low level of protectionism)

According to the U.S. Department of State, Mongolia has an "across the board import tariff of 5 percent" but no quotas or onerous licensing requirements.

## FISCAL BURDEN OF GOVERNMENT
Score—Income Taxation: **4**–Stable (high tax rates)
Score—Corporate Taxation: **5**–Stable (very high tax rates)
Score—Change in Government Expenditures: **4**–Better (moderate increase)
### Final Score: **4.5**–Better (very high cost of government)

Mongolia's top income tax rate is 40 percent. The top corporate tax rate is 40 percent. Government expenditures as a share of GDP increased less in 2001 (1.8 percentage points to 35.3 percent) than they did in 2000 (2.5 percentage points). As a result, Mongolia's fiscal burden of government score is 0.1 point better this year.

## GOVERNMENT INTERVENTION IN THE ECONOMY
### Score: **2.5**–Stable (moderate level)

The World Bank reports that the government consumed 19.3 percent of GDP in 2001. In the same year, according to the International Monetary Fund, Mongolia received 7.44 percent of its total revenues from state-owned enterprises and government ownership of property.

## MONETARY POLICY
### Score: **2**–Better (low level of inflation)

Data from the International Monetary Fund's 2003 *World Economic Outlook* indicate that from 1993 to 2002, Mongolia's weighted average annual rate of inflation was 3.63 percent, down from the 9.66 percent from 1992 to 2001 reported in the 2003 *Index*. As a result, Mongolia's monetary policy score is 1 point better this year.

**CAPITAL FLOWS AND FOREIGN INVESTMENT**
Score: **3**–Stable (moderate barriers)

Mongolia welcomes foreign investment, and foreign investors are accorded non-discriminatory treatment and may participate in privatization of state-owned property and enterprises. There is no screening of foreign investment, and no sectors are closed. Mongolian law provides for the protection of private property and foreign investments from government expropriation. However, the investment climate is hindered by corruption and a lack of transparency. Foreigners may own land but must register it with the State Real Estate Registry. According to the International Monetary Fund, residents may hold foreign exchange accounts in authorized banks and may use them for any purpose. Non-residents may hold foreign exchange accounts as long as they register with the State Registry. The issuing of capital market securities, money market instruments, collective investment securities, and derivatives is prohibited. Most credit and loan operations must be registered with the central bank.

 **BANKING AND FINANCE**
Score: **3**–Stable (moderate level of restrictions)

Mongolia's underdeveloped financial sector consists of 12 commercial banks, some privately owned and some state-owned. The government is privatizing some of its holdings in the banking sector. The Economist Intelligence Unit reports that the Trade and Development Bank was sold to an international consortium in 2002 and that the Agricultural Bank was sold to a Japanese company in 2003. According to the U.S. Department of State, "Mortgages do not really exist in Mongolia because of the weak banking sector. With annual interest rates of around 35 percent, few want or can take out a mortgage. Many businesses try to use their fixed assets as security for various business transactions. One problem with accepting the deed to property as security is that there is no registry of such liabilities, thus no way to tell whether that property has been offered to someone else as security for some transaction." Several private and savings credit unions are emerging to fill the need for small community banking.

 **WAGES AND PRICES**
Score: **2**–Stable (low level of intervention)

The U.S. Department of State reports that the government of Mongolia intervenes in the market to adjust prices for grain and other commodities. The government liberalized energy prices in 1996 but still controls the price of fuel. A minimum wage that is applied to both public-sector and private-sector employees is enforced by the Ministry of Social Welfare and Labor.

 **PROPERTY RIGHTS**
Score: **3**–Stable (moderate level of protection)

In June 2002, the government passed a land ownership law that allows for the sale of arable land to individuals. The enforcement of laws protecting private property is weak. According to the U.S. Department of State, "The President…has strong influence on the judiciary through the power to appoint members to both the Supreme Court and Constitutional Court." One of "the political problems most affecting business development in Mongolia [is] the need to strengthen the rule of law…. Reform within the legal and judicial sectors that is sorely needed as a foundation for business has been delayed and deferred…. [C]orruption…is increasingly an obstacle to honest business and efficiency." Judges do not fully understand modern business practices.

 **REGULATION**
Score: **4**–Stable (high level)

The vast number of regulations implemented over the past several years, combined with the continuing restructuring of the government, imposes a sizeable burden on business. The U.S. Department of State identifies "corruption in the bureaucracy" as one of the typical problems affecting business development.

 **INFORMAL MARKET**
Score: **3**–Stable (moderate level of activity)

Transparency International's 1999 score for Mongolia is 4.3. Therefore, Mongolia's informal market score is 3 this year.

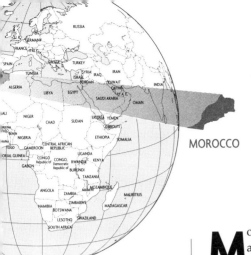

MOROCCO

# MOROCCO

Rank: 66

Score: 2.93

Category: Mostly Free

Present & Past Scores

(Best) 1
2
3
4
(Worst) 5

-3.03 2.89 3.00 3.08 2.95 3.05 2.80 3.15 2.96 2.93

'95 '96 '97 '98 '99 '00 '01 '02 '03 '04

## QUICK STUDY

### SCORES

| | |
|---|---|
| Trade Policy | 5 |
| Fiscal Burden | 3.8 |
| Government Intervention | 2 |
| Monetary Policy | 1 |
| Foreign Investment | 2 |
| Banking and Finance | 3 |
| Wages and Prices | 2 |
| Property Rights | 4 |
| Regulation | 3 |
| Informal Market | 3.5 |

**Population:** 29,170,000

**Total area:** 446,550 sq. km

**GDP:** $41.9 billion

**GDP growth rate:** 6.5%

**GDP per capita:** $1,436

**Major exports:** consumer goods, food, drink, tobacco, minerals

**Exports of goods and services:** $12.1 billion

**Major export trading partners:** France 24.3%, Spain 11.4%, UK 7.0%, Italy 5.6%

**Major imports:** machinery and equipment, consumer goods, semifinished goods

**Imports of goods and services:** $16.3 billion

**Major import trading partners:** France 22.3%, Spain 11.6%, Italy 6.5%, Germany 5.4%

**Foreign direct investment (net):** $2.3 billion

2001 Data (in constant 1995 US dollars)

Morocco is a constitutional monarchy that gained its independence from France in 1956 and has been liberalizing its economy since the early 1980s. King Mohammed VI, who succeeded his father in 1999, remains committed to political and economic reform, privatization, expanded civil rights, and the elimination of corruption. Over the past decade, the government has sold stakes in 62 state enterprises, reined in spending, and reduced trade barriers. The recent appointment of Prime Minister Driss Jettou promises some acceleration of the reform process and a more investor-friendly environment, but full implementation will be difficult because of opposition from vested interests within the political elite that seek to derail the government's divestment schedule and undermine economic reform efforts. Rampant unemployment and widespread poverty—one of every five citizens lives in poverty—remain a burden for the government. In 2002, King Mohammed VI announced that the U.S. and Morocco would begin negotiations toward a free trade agreement. Morocco is blessed with rich resources (including the world's largest phosphate reserves), a booming tourist industry, and a growing manufacturing sector, but agriculture remains the backbone of the economy, accounting for 20 percent of GDP and employing 40 percent of the population. According to the Economist Intelligence Unit, agricultural sector expansion will drive economic growth to 4 percent in 2003, strengthening both real investment and private consumption. Morocco's informal market score is 0.5 point worse this year; however, its fiscal burden of government score is 0.3 point better, and its government intervention score is 0.5 point better. As a result, Morocco's overall score is 0.03 point better this year.

 ## TRADE POLICY
### Score: **5**–Stable (very high level of protectionism)

The World Bank reports that Morocco's weighted average tariff rate in 2001 (the most recent year for which World Bank data are available) was 25.4 percent. Non-tariff barriers largely consist of inconsistent customs procedures. According to the U.S. Department of State, "cumbersome customs administration and procedures…impose costs and delays on firms currently involved in international trade and defer [sic] others potentially interested in entering the trade area."

 ## FISCAL BURDEN OF GOVERNMENT
### Score—Income Taxation: **4**–Stable (high tax rates)
### Score—Corporate Taxation: **4.5**–Stable (very high tax rates)
### Score—Change in Government Expenditures: **2**–Better (moderate decrease)
### Final Score: **3.8**–Better (high cost of government)

Morocco's top income tax rate is 44 percent. The top corporate tax rate is 35 percent. (For banks and insurance companies, the rate is 39.6 percent; the general rate of 35 percent applied to business was used to score this factor.) Government expenditures decreased 2.2 percentage points to 30.5 percent in 2001, compared to a 0.5 percentage point increase in 2000. As a result, Morocco's fiscal burden of government score is 0.3 point better this year.

## GOVERNMENT INTERVENTION IN THE ECONOMY
### Score: **2**–Better (low level)

The World Bank reports that the government consumed 17.9 percent of GDP in 2001. In the same year, based on data from the Economist Intelligence Unit, Morocco received 4.27 percent of its total revenues from state-owned enterprises and government ownership of property, down from the 7.31 percent reported in the 2003 Index. As a result, Morocco's government intervention score is 0.5 point better this year.

## MONETARY POLICY
### Score: **1**–Stable (very low level of inflation)

Between 1993 and 2002, Morocco's weighted average annual rate of inflation was 2.14 percent.

## CAPITAL FLOWS AND FOREIGN INVESTMENT
### Score: **2**–Stable (low barriers)

Morocco treats foreign-owned and locally owned investments equally and permits 100 percent foreign ownership in most sectors. There is no screening requirement for foreign investment, but investment in some sectors is restricted. According to the Economist Intelligence Unit, "The state has a monopoly on phosphate mining and tobacco marketing. Foreigners can invest in the agricultural sector but cannot own agricultural land. Regulations prevent foreign firms from having a majority stake in a Moroccan insurance company." A recent edict by the king established 16 regional investment centers, headed by an appointed wali (governor), to circumvent bureaucratic opposition and stimulate new investment by consolidating the investment process, coordinating land purchases, offering incentives, and providing land with clear title. The International Monetary Fund reports that both residents and non-residents may hold foreign exchange accounts, subject to restrictions and requirements. Personal payments, transfer of interest, and travel payments are subject to limits, documentation requirements, and approval in some cases.

## BANKING AND FINANCE
### Score: **3**–Stable (moderate level of restrictions)

The bank reform law of 1993 clarified lines of responsibility for oversight and supervision of the banking and financial sector, laid out penalties for violating banking regulations, established a depositors guarantee fund, and liberalized credit allocation. The Embassy of Morocco reports that the banking sector consists of 18 banks, of which five are government-owned. According to the U.S. Department of State, "The banking system is still used by the government to channel domestic savings to finance government debt, and the banks are required to hold a part of their assets in bonds paying below market interest rates." The same source reports that two state-owned banks, which account for over 60 percent of non-performing loans in the banking system, are under investigation for bad management and corruption. Foreigners may participate freely in the local stock exchange, but commercial banks must have majority Moroccan ownership. The Economist Intelligence Unit reports that state holdings in Banque nationale pour le développement économique and Crédit immobilier et hotelier are expected to be put up for sale in 2003.

## WAGES AND PRICES
### Score: **2**–Stable (low level of intervention)

According to the Economist Intelligence Unit, "Prices are liberalised with the exception of petrol, vegetable oil, sugar and flour; prices on these are set by the government." The government also influences prices through the country's many state-owned enterprises. Morocco has one minimum wage for the industrial sector and another for the agricultural sector, but they are not observed in the extensive informal sector.

## PROPERTY RIGHTS
### Score: **4**–Stable (low level of protection)

Morocco's constitution provides for an independent judiciary, although ultimate authority rests with the king. The courts are not reliable. According to the Economist Intelligence Unit, "The judiciary has long been criticized by all parties, particularly with regard to business-related litigation. Its weaknesses include: the lack of efficiency and timeliness in the judicial process—resulting in a huge backlog of cases even at the Supreme Court level; the absence of transparency in judicial decision-making and of predictability in judgments; an inability to enforce judgments; and incompetence in matters of commercial law." In addition, "the judiciary is … a tool of the state." A survey among businesses that was conducted by the American Chamber of Commerce in Morocco revealed that corruption in the legal system is regarded as one of the main impediments to doing business. The quality is improving slowly. The government is making efforts to improve the commercial laws.

## REGULATION
### Score: **3**–Stable (moderate level)

Regulations and bureaucracy remain significantly burdensome despite the government's attempts at reform. The Economist Intelligence Unit reports that "permits are slow to be issued and local government permits often require the payment of bribes. Corruption is widespread and affects most levels of the administration." According to the U.S. Department of State, "Deficiencies remain in other areas…such as the labor law, which limits firms' ability to dismiss workers. Even in areas where the regulations are favorable on paper, there are often problems in practice. Government procedures are not always transparent, efficient or quick. Routine permits, especially those required by local governments, can be difficult to obtain." The Embassy of Morocco reports that the government "has launched a new investment policy including the one-stop shop system…in each of the 16 regions of Morocco."

## INFORMAL MARKET
### Score: **3.5**–Worse (high level of activity)

Transparency International's 2002 score for Morocco is 3.7. Therefore, Morocco's informal market score is 3.5 this year—0.5 point worse than last year.

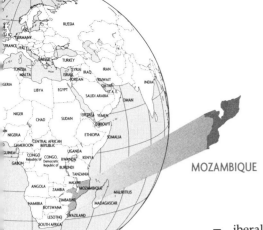

MOZAMBIQUE

# MOZAMBIQUE

Rank: 95
Score: 3.28
Category: Mostly Unfree

Present & Past Scores

(Best) 1
2
3
4
(Worst) 5

'95 4.39  '96 4.11  '97 4.15  '98 4.15  '99 3.95  '00 3.94  '01 3.40  '02 3.15  '03 3.40  '04 3.28

## QUICK STUDY

### SCORES

| | |
|---|---|
| Trade Policy | 4 |
| Fiscal Burden | 3.8 |
| Government Intervention | 2 |
| Monetary Policy | 4 |
| Foreign Investment | 2 |
| Banking and Finance | 2 |
| Wages and Prices | 3 |
| Property Rights | 4 |
| Regulation | 4 |
| Informal Market | 4 |

**Population:** 18,071,160

**Total area:** 801,590 sq. km

**GDP:** $3.8 billion

**GDP growth rate:** 13.9%

**GDP per capita:** $213

**Major exports:** aluminum, prawns, electricity, cotton, manufactures

**Exports of goods and services:** $1.1 billion

**Major export trading partners:** South Africa 15.3%, Zimbabwe 5.3%, Japan 4.2%, Portugal 4.0%

**Major imports:** machinery and equipment, vehicles, transport equipment, fuel, textiles

**Imports of goods and services:** $1.7 billion

**Major import trading partners:** South Africa 40.5%, Portugal 8.4%, US 1.8%, UK 1.1%

**Foreign direct investment (net):** $228.7 million

2001 Data (in constant 1995 US dollars)

L iberalization, privatization, and relative peace and stability have helped make Mozambique a model for economic development and post-war recovery. The Economist Intelligence Unit predicts that real GDP growth, driven by substantial foreign direct investment, will average 9 percent in 2003–2004. U.N. Conference on Trade and Development data show that Mozambique was the fourth largest recipient of FDI in sub-Saharan Africa in 2001, with US$481 million ($228.7 million in net terms); between 1996 and 2001, it received a total of US$1,350 million in FDI. However, roughly 70 percent of the population remains in poverty. The International Monetary Fund lent Mozambique $11 million in 1992 as part of its $113 million Poverty Reduction and Growth Facility (PRGF) for the country, and Italy agreed to cancel $500 million in foreign debt. The drought affecting much of the southern African region has left over half a million Mozambicans in need of food aid, and as much as 14 percent of the population is afflicted with AIDS. Corruption pervades all areas of society, including government, politics, the judiciary, and business. President Joaquim Chissano, who has been in power for 17 years, will step down after the December 2004 general election. His successor as leader of the ruling FRELIMO party, Armando Guebuza, will compete against RENAMO leader Afonso Dhlakama for the presidency. It is doubtful whether Guebuza, known as a more hard-line authoritarian, will continue the reformist agenda pursued by Chissano if he is elected. Mozambique's monetary policy score is 1 point worse this year; however, its fiscal burden of government score is 0.2 point better, and its government intervention score is 2 points better. As a result, Mozambique's overall score is 0.12 point better this year.

###  TRADE POLICY
#### Score: **4**–Stable (high level of protectionism)

According to the World Bank, Mozambique's weighted average tariff rate in 2001 (the most recent year for which World Bank data are available) was 13.8 percent. Customs management was privatized in 1997. "Although the company [managing customs] plans to introduce strict measures to secure the gains made in recent years," reports the Economist Intelligence Unit, "it has admitted that corruption remains a serious problem. According to Crown Agents, the increased risk of getting caught has not been a major deterrent." Imports of pharmaceuticals, firearms, and certain controlled substances are prohibited.

###  FISCAL BURDEN OF GOVERNMENT
#### Score—Income Taxation: **2.5**–Worse (moderate tax rates)
#### Score—Corporate Taxation: **4**–Better (high tax rates)
#### Score—Change in Government Expenditures: **4.5**–Better (high increase)
### Final Score: **3.8**–Better (high cost of government)

According to Ernst and Young, Mozambique's top income tax rate is 27.60 percent, up from the 20 percent reported in the 2003 *Index*. However, the top corporate income tax rate is 32 percent, down from the 35 percent reported in the 2003 *Index*, and government expenditures as a share of GDP increased less in 2001 (2.7 percentage points to 31.1 percent) than they did in 2000 (3.7 percentage points). On net, Mozambique's fiscal burden of government score is 0.2 point better this year.

## GOVERNMENT INTERVENTION IN THE ECONOMY
### Score: **2**–Better (low level)

The World Bank reports that the government consumed 10.4 percent of GDP in 2001. In the same year, based on data from the International Monetary Fund, Mozambique received 1.18 percent of its total revenues from state-owned enterprises and government ownership of property. Based on newly available data on revenues from state-owned enterprises, as well as a lower level of government consumption, Mozambique's government intervention score is 2 points better this year.

## MONETARY POLICY
### Score: **4**–Worse (high level of inflation)

Data from the International Monetary Fund's *2003 World Economic Outlook* indicate that from 1993 to 2002, Mozambique's weighted average annual rate of inflation was 14.06 percent, up from the 9.97 percent from 1992 to 2001 reported in the 2003 *Index.* As a result, Mozambique's monetary policy score is 1 point worse this year.

## CAPITAL FLOWS AND FOREIGN INVESTMENT
### Score: **2**–Stable (low barriers)

Most sectors of Mozambique's economy are open to 100 percent foreign investment, and foreign investors generally receive the same treatment as domestic investors. Some restrictions remain in effect; outright private ownership of land, for example, is prohibited, and mining and management contracts are subject to specific performance requirements. "In the past," reports the U.S. Department of State, "political risk, corruption, bureaucratic red tape, dilapidated infrastructure, and the relatively small size of the market served as strong deterrents to foreign investment. While these issues have not been entirely resolved, they have improved markedly." Mozambique allows 100 percent repatriation of profits and retention of earned foreign exchange in domestic accounts. The International Monetary Fund reports that both residents and non-residents may hold foreign exchange accounts. Payments and transfers are subject to maximum amounts above which they must be approved by the central bank. Capital transactions, money market instruments, and derivatives are subject to controls.

## BANKING AND FINANCE
### Score: **2**–Stable (low level of restrictions)

The government has been dealing with the banking crisis following the insolvency of two banks that accounted for more than half of the banking sector: Banco Comercial de Mozambique (BCM) and Banco Austral (BA). The failures were caused by extensive non-performing loans made to politically connected individuals. BCM merged with the Bank of Mozambique in October 2001, and BA was taken over by the government. The government sold 80 percent of its equity in Bank Austral to a South African bank in 2001 and intends to sell the remaining 20 percent at a later date. Government influence in the banking sector is diminishing and competition is growing as more foreign banks enter the country. After 1992, reports the Economist Intelligence Unit, "Foreign banks were allowed to invest in Mozambique; interest rates were deregulated; and the regulatory and commercial activities of the central bank were separated…. The transformation of the banking sector has been rapid…. Several banks are diversifying their products and services as competition in the market increases." In April 2002, the central bank improved supervision of the sector by requiring commercial banks to report their capital adequacy monthly rather than semiannually. A major weakness of the banking sector is the lack of property rights. According to the U.S. Department of State, "Access to capital in the rural areas is limited as the lack of private ownership of land prevents its use as collateral."

## WAGES AND PRICES
### Score: **3**–Stable (moderate level of intervention)

According to the International Monetary Fund, Mozambique has price controls on water, electricity, passenger taxicab services, and local, national, and international telephone rates and subsidizes such agricultural goods as sugar, tea, and copra. The Economist Intelligence Unit adds that the government controls the price of fuel. A minimum wage for industry and for agriculture is set by ministerial decree based on the advice of annual tripartite (labor unions, government, and employers) meetings.

## PROPERTY RIGHTS
### Score: **4**–Stable (low level of protection)

According to the Economist Intelligence Unit, "State ownership of land is enshrined in the constitution. However, a new land law was passed in 1997, allowing private parties to acquire land-use rights." Property rights are weakly protected, and the judiciary is corrupt. BBC News reports that "Mozambique's attorney general has admitted the entire legal system in the country is plagued by corruption…. [A]ll arms of the legal system, including the judiciary, have been tainted with sleaze….[The attorney general has cited] incompetence, corruption and abuse of power at all levels of the administration of justice—police, attorneys, judges, lawyers and prisons." The U.S. Department of State reports that most commercial disputes are settled privately because of the judicial system's inefficiency.

## REGULATION
### Score: **4**–Stable (high level)

Corruption reportedly continues to characterize Mozambique's regulatory environment. The Economist Intelligence Unit reports that "a 'red tape study' carried out by the World Bank in 1996…uncovered the labyrinthine procedures required for relatively simple private-sector activities such as registering a company. The commercial code, previously based on 19th-century Portuguese law, has now been updated to meet the needs of a modern commercial economy, and harmonized with the codes of neighboring countries. However, implementation of the reform measures…is significantly behind schedule…. The private sector still complains that it faces extensive and opaque regulation; a lack of predictability in determining how long procedures will take, rather than their cost, is the greatest single problem."

 ## INFORMAL MARKET
### Score: **4–Stable** (high level of activity)

Transparency International's 2000 score for Mozambique was 2.2. Therefore, Mozambique's informal market score is 4 this year.

# NAMIBIA

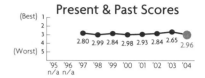

Rank: 70

Score: 2.96

Category: Mostly Free

**Present & Past Scores**

(Best) 1
2
3
4
(Worst) 5

2.80  2.99  2.84  2.98  2.93  2.84  2.65  2.96

'95  '96  '97  '98  '99  '00  '01  '02  '03  '04
n/a  n/a

**Population:** 1,792,060

**Total area:** 825,418 sq. km

**GDP:** $4.3 billion

**GDP growth rate:** 4.6%

**GDP per capita:** $2,383

**Major exports:** diamonds, preserved fish, metal ores, food products, live animals

**Exports of goods and services:** $2.04 billion

**Major export trading partners:** UK 48%, South Africa 23%, Spain 15% (2000)

**Major imports:** transport equipment, chemical products, plastic products, refined petroleum products, machinery and equipment

**Imports of goods and services:** $2.5 billion

**Major import trading partners:** South Africa 80%, US 5%, Germany 3%, Russia 1% (2000)

**Foreign direct investment (net):** $87.9 million

2001 Data (in constant 1995 US dollars)

N amibia has one of sub-Saharan Africa's most stable economies and an enviable record of post-independence racial reconciliation. The Economist Intelligence Unit predicts real GDP growth of 4.5 percent in 2004. The country is rich in mineral wealth, including uranium, gem-quality diamonds, lead, silver, tin, tungsten, and zinc. The land issue, however, has major implications for both the economy and race relations. While mining, manufacturing, and services provide most GDP, a majority of Namibians are employed in subsistence agriculture in the northern part of the country. Poverty and unemployment remain high. President Sam Nujoma, leader of the ruling South West Africa People's Organization (SWAPO) and an increasingly strident supporter of Robert Mugabe's disastrous land seizures in Zimbabwe, has issued warnings against Namibia's 4,000 white farmers, who continue to own roughly half of the arable land, prompting fears of a Zimbabwe-style land redistribution. Nujoma is due to step down at the next presidential election, to be held by the end of 2004, and the future of land reform will be in the hands of his successor, who probably will be Foreign Affairs Minister Hidipo Hamutenya. Namibia's trade policy, banking and finance, and capital flows and foreign investment scores are 1 point worse this year, and its fiscal burden of government score is 0.1 point worse. As a result, Namibia's overall score is 0.31 point worse this year.

## TRADE POLICY
### Score: **4**–Worse (high level of protectionism)

Namibia belongs to the Southern African Customs Union (SACU), a regional trade arrangement with Botswana, Lesotho, South Africa, and Swaziland. According to the World Trade Organization, in 2002 (the most recent year for which WTO data are available), the SACU had an average common external tariff rate of 11.4 percent, up from the 8.5 percent reported in the 2003 *Index*. As a result, Namibia's trade policy score is 1 point worse this year. The WTO reports that "licensing of certain products is non-automatic…and requires a permit from the relevant ministry. Seasonal import bans on maize, maize meal, wheat, and wheat flour ensure the domestic crop is used first." Namibia also has several marketing boards that regulate the trade in controlled cereals and meat.

## FISCAL BURDEN OF GOVERNMENT
### Score—Income Taxation: **3.5**–Stable (high tax rates)
### Score—Corporate Taxation: **4.5**–Stable (very high tax rates)
### Score—Change in Government Expenditures: **4**–Worse (moderate increase)
### Final Score: **4.1**–Worse (high cost of government)

Namibia's top income tax rate is 36 percent. The top corporate tax rate is 35 percent. Government expenditures as a share of GDP increased more in 2001 (1.8 percentage points to 37.4 percent) than they did in 2000 (0.2 percentage point). As a result, Namibia's fiscal burden of government score is 0.1 point worse this year.

## GOVERNMENT INTERVENTION IN THE ECONOMY
### Score: **3**–Stable (moderate level)

The World Bank reports that the government consumed 28.6 percent of GDP in 2001. In the 2001–2002 fiscal year, based on data from the Bank of Namibia, Namibia received 7.07 percent of its total revenues from state-owned enterprises and government ownership of property.

301

## MONETARY POLICY
### Score: **3**–Stable (moderate level of inflation)

From 1993 to 2002, Namibia's weighted average annual rate of inflation was 10.56 percent.

## CAPITAL FLOWS AND FOREIGN INVESTMENT
### Score: **3**–Worse (moderate barriers)

Namibia guarantees foreign investors national treatment for most sectors, the right to international arbitration of disputes between investors and the government, and the right to remit profits and access foreign exchange. According to the Economist Intelligence Unit, "Manufacturing capacity is mainly in the hands of Namibian-owned or based firms, and the government gives preference to investors establishing locally registered companies with Namibian partners." On April 1, 2003, the government began collecting a land tax that discriminates against foreign owners by charging them a higher tax per hectare (the tax begins at 1 percent for foreign owners and 0.75 percent for Namibian owners) on the unimproved site value of each farm. Companies that are 75 percent or more foreign-owned are subject to exchange controls. Residents may hold foreign exchange accounts subject to prior approval and some restrictions. Non-residents may hold foreign currency accounts only if they operate in an export-processing zone. Transactions, transfers, and payments are subject to various restrictions, approvals, and quantitative limits. Based on the evidence of official discrimination against foreign investors, as well as restrictions on capital flows, Namibia's capital flows and foreign investment score is 1 point worse this year.

## BANKING AND FINANCE
### Score: **3**–Worse (moderate level of restrictions)

The banking sector is small but sound and includes the central bank and four private commercial banks, three of which are linked with banking institutions in South Africa. The government owns the Agricultural Bank of Namibia, NamPost, and the Namibia Development Corporation. The 1998 Banking Institutions Act brought Namibia's regulatory and supervisory standards up to international standards. Of increasing concern is the number of government loan guarantees, particularly to state-owned enterprises, over the past six years. The Economist Intelligence Unit reports that the central bank produced data in December 2002 (the first time in a number of years) that loan guarantees amounted to N$3.5bn, equivalent to 11 percent of GDP. The central bank has acknowledged that a number of the loan guarantees have a high risk of default and has advised the government "to review the current procedures for issuing loan guarantees in order to avert a 'potential financial crisis.'" Since 1995, the government has required domestic insurance companies to invest a minimum of 35 percent of assets in specified areas of the local market, as opposed to South Africa where they traditionally were invested. Based on the government's ownership of some financial institutions

and interference with the allocation of credit through the issuance of loan guarantees, Namibia's banking and finance score is 1 point worse this year.

## WAGES AND PRICES
### Score: **2**–Stable (low level of intervention)

The government has abolished most price controls, and the market now sets most wages and prices. The government still controls the prices of petroleum and paraffin, as well as such utilities as electricity, telecommunications, water, and transportation. There is no national minimum wage law. According to the U.S. Department of State, "During the year, representatives of farm owners and managers and the Ministry of Labor agreed upon a minimum wage for farm workers."

## PROPERTY RIGHTS
### Score: **2**–Stable (high level of protection)

The judiciary is independent, and the threat of expropriation is low. According to the U.S. Department of State, "The lack of qualified magistrates, other court officials, and private attorneys has resulted in a serious backlog of criminal cases, which often translates in delays of up to a year or more between arrest and trial."

## REGULATION
### Score: **3**–Stable (moderate level)

The Economist Intelligence Unit reports that "Namibia is burdened by an oversized civil service, which accounts for an unsustainably high proportion of government spending." Despite an anti-corruption bill passed by the National Assembly in November 2001, the U.S. Department of State and other sources continue to cite concerns about corruption. Businesses face burdensome regulations, including health and safety standards and a requirement that businesses submit an environmental impact statement for proposed new investments and construction. According to the EIU, "the government enacted separate investment incentive packages for manufacturing and export-oriented activities alongside a national EPZ [Export Processing Zones] regime rather than adopt the more common geographically limited EPZs."

## INFORMAL MARKET
### Score: **2.5**–Stable (moderate level of activity)

Transparency International's 2002 score for Namibia is 5.7. Therefore, Namibia's informal market score is 2.5 this year.

NEPAL

Rank: 121
Score: 3.53
Category: Mostly Unfree

Present & Past Scores

(Best) 1 2 3 4 (Worst) 5

3.86 3.89 3.67 3.54 3.79 3.60 3.51 3.63 3.53

'95 '96 '97 '98 '99 '00 '01 '02 '03 '04
n/a

## QUICK STUDY

### SCORES

| | |
|---|---|
| Trade Policy | 5 |
| Fiscal Burden | 3.3 |
| Government Intervention | 2 |
| Monetary Policy | 1 |
| Foreign Investment | 4 |
| Banking and Finance | 4 |
| Wages and Prices | 3 |
| Property Rights | 4 |
| Regulation | 4 |
| Informal Market | 5 |

**Population:** 23,584,710

**Total area:** 140,800 sq. km

**GDP:** $5.9 billion

**GDP growth rate:** 5.9%

**GDP per capita:** $248

**Major exports:** garments, woolen carpets, jute goods, vegetables

**Exports of goods and services:** $1.4 billion

**Major export trading partners:** US 30.7%, India 30.2%, Germany 11.6%, Argentina 7.4%

**Major imports:** petroleum products, textiles, gold and silver, vehicles

**Imports of goods and services:** $1.9 billion

**Major import trading partners:** India 36.7%, Argentina 15.5 %, China 13.3%, United Arab Emirates 5.8%

**Foreign direct investment (net):** $17 million

2001 Data (in constant 1995 US dollars)

Prolonged political unrest and violent Maoist insurgencies have plagued Nepal's economy. During the first year of his reign, King Gyanendra added to the turmoil by dissolving parliament, firing the prime minister, and indefinitely postponing parliamentary elections. In 2002, according to the *Far Eastern Economic Review,* Nepal's economy recorded its worst performance in two decades, with GDP shrinking by 0.6 percentage point. The manufacturing sector fell by 10 percent, and excessive rain in the eastern part of the country severely damaged agricultural crops. Trade and tourism fell by 10.8 percent; the number of tourists traveling to Nepal in 2002, as reported by the Nepal Tourism Board, fell by 28 percent. The economy was saved by remittances—estimated to average $90 million per year—from around 700,000 Nepalese working in 19 foreign countries. In February 2003, the government and the Maoist insurgents signed a cease-fire, which was still in place as of May 2003. Although it might help, however, a prolonged cease-fire is not enough to rectify the problems that beset Nepal's economy. The government must institute reforms aimed at creating jobs and encouraging investments; it also must hold the long-overdue elections. With a reported GDP per capita of $248 for 2001, Nepal remains one of the world's poorest countries. GDP growth for 2003 is projected at less than 2 percent. Nepal's fiscal burden of government score is 0.5 point worse this year; however, its government intervention score is 0.5 point better, and its monetary policy score is 1 point better. As a result, Nepal's overall score is 0.1 point better this year.

 ### TRADE POLICY
Score: **5**–Stable (very high level of protectionism)

The World Bank reports that Nepal's weighted average tariff rate in 2000 (the most recent year for which World Bank data are available) was 16.8 percent. According to the U.S. Department of State, "All imports may be brought in without a license except for banned or quantitatively restricted items such as…communications equipment including computers and home entertainment products such as television sets and VCRs; valuable metals and jewelry; and beef and beef products."

 ### FISCAL BURDEN OF GOVERNMENT
Score—Income Taxation: **2.5**–Stable (moderate tax rates)
Score—Corporate Taxation: **3**–Stable (moderate tax rates)
Score—Change in Government Expenditures: **4.5**–Worse (high increase)
Final Score: **3.3**–Worse (moderate cost of government)

The International Monetary Fund reports that Nepal's top income tax rate is 25 percent. The top corporate tax rate is 20 percent for industrial enterprises, 25 percent for other enterprises, and 30 percent for financial institutions. The general enterprise tax of 25 percent has been used to grade this factor. Government expenditures as a share of GDP increased 3 percentage points to 20.4 percent in 2001, compared to a 1.4 percentage point decrease in 2000. As a result, Nepal's fiscal burden of government score is 0.5 point worse this year.

 ### GOVERNMENT INTERVENTION IN THE ECONOMY
Score: **2**–Better (low level)

The World Bank reports that the government consumed 10 percent of GDP in 2001. In the same year, according to the International Monetary Fund, Nepal received 9.15 percent of its total revenues from state-owned enterprises and government ownership of property, down from the 11.01 percent reported in the 2003 *Index.* As a result, Nepal's government intervention score is 0.5 point better this year.

## MONETARY POLICY
### Score: **1**–Better (very low level of inflation)

From 1993 to 2002, Nepal's weighted average annual rate of inflation was 2.90 percent, down from the 3.27 percent from 1992 to 2001 reported in the 2003 *Index.* As a result, Nepal's monetary policy score is 1 point better this year.

## CAPITAL FLOWS AND FOREIGN INVESTMENT
### Score: **4**–Stable (high barriers)

Nepal has streamlined licensing requirements, permitting 100 percent foreign ownership, removing minimum investment requirements, and opening the telecommunications and civil aviation sectors; but many sectors, such as business and management consulting, accounting, engineering, legal services, defense, alcohol and cigarette production, travel and trekking agencies, and retail sales, remain closed. The U.S. Department of State notes, "[T]here is often a wide discrepancy between the letter of the law and law's implementation. Foreign investors constantly complain about complex and opaque government procedures and a working-level attitude that is more hostile than accommodating." The International Monetary Fund reports that residents may hold foreign exchange accounts only in specific instances. Most non-residents may hold foreign exchange accounts. Most payments and transfers are subject to quantitative limitation restrictions. There are numerous restrictions on capital transactions.

## BANKING AND FINANCE
### Score: **4**–Stable (high level of restrictions)

Nepal's financial sector, is in disarray. Two state-owned banks (the fully state-owned Rastriya Banijya Bank and 40.49 percent government-owned Nepal Bank) are technically insolvent—a critical problem as they account for 60 percent of all lending and 50 percent of all deposits. The Nepal Rastra Bank (the central bank) is contracting with two private companies to manage Rastriya Banijya Bank and Nepal Bank and restore them to financial health. Many private-sector banks are also in a questionable state, and the government has issued directives raising capital adequacy and accounting standards, clarifying credit classifications, and increasing reporting transparency. Foreign banks have been permitted to establish joint ventures in Nepal since 1984, but majority ownership was not permitted until 2001.

## WAGES AND PRICES
### Score: **3**–Stable (moderate level of intervention)

The government has eliminated most price controls. "Since 1990," reports the U.S. Department of State, "Nepal has priva-

tized a number of public enterprises, eliminated public monopolies in air transport and hydropower generation, scrapped price controls on most products, [and] reduced consumer subsidies...." The same source notes, however, that "there are special subsidies and preferred credit arrangements for individual public and private companies in select sectors, such as rural electrification, fertilizer importation, and the provision of agricultural credit." The Economist Intelligence Unit reports that the government controls the price of petrol, diesel, kerosene, and liquefied petroleum gas. The government also sets a minimum wage for children from 14 to 16 years old, as well as for unskilled workers, skilled workers, and highly skilled workers.

## PROPERTY RIGHTS
### Score: **4**–Stable (low level of protection)

Nepal's judicial system suffers from corruption and inefficiency. According to the U.S. Department of State, the Supreme Court has demonstrated independence, but "lower level courts remain vulnerable to political pressure and bribery of judges and court staff is endemic." In addition, "property disputes account for half of the current backlog in Nepal's overburdened court system and such cases can take years to be settled.... [L]aws and regulations are unclear, and interpretation can vary from case to case."

## REGULATION
### Score: **4**–Stable (high level)

Nepal's regulatory regime is not transparent. The U.S. Department of State reports that obstacles to investment include "inadequate and obscure commercial legislation and unclear rules regarding labor relations. Policies intended to establish a 'one window policy' and simplify necessary interactions between investor and host government have produced few results. Foreign investors constantly complain about complex and opaque government procedures and a working-level attitude that is more hostile than accommodating." In addition, "Facilities granted under certain Acts or policies are often either contradicted or negated by another set of rules or policies.... Some companies report that the process of terminating unsatisfactory employees is cumbersome.... [I]nvestors have identified pervasive corruption as an obstacle to maintaining and expanding their...investments in Nepal."

## INFORMAL MARKET
### Score: **5**–Stable (very high level of activity)

Both legislation and enforcement of intellectual property protection are inadequate. Nepal's informal market is substantial, especially in consumer goods, labor, construction, currency, and the smuggling of weapons. According the University of Linz, Austria, "1,657,000 people were employed in the informal sector in 1999, an estimated 73.3% of the population." The Economist Intelligence Unit reports that "gold smuggling from Nepal to India is huge."

# THE NETHERLANDS

NETHERLANDS

Rank: 19

Score: 2.04

Category: Mostly Free

Present & Past Scores

(Best) 1
2
3  1.89 1.88 2.03 2.01 2.03 1.84 2.03 2.00 2.04
4
(Worst) 5

'95 '96 '97 '98 '99 '00 '01 '02 '03 '04
n/a

The Netherlands became a driving force in global trade and banking during the 17th and 18th centuries and, despite developing a large, European-style safety net over the years, maintains its traditional openness to the rest of the world. Rotterdam remains the world's largest port as measured by tonnage of goods. Over the past two decades, the Netherlands has been the most successful of the core European Union countries, growing at an average rate of 3 percent per annum since 1982. Much of this success is attributable to a tradition of effective negotiation and consensus among the government, employer federations, and unions; agreements reached by these three groups have led to public spending restraint, labor market reform, and wage moderation. There are few restrictions on foreign direct investment, and the Netherlands is one of the most open to FDI of all the world's countries. The only major problem is hidden rates of unemployment: Official numbers do not include a large number of people categorized as disabled, with nearly 1 million people on the rolls out of a working-age population of 7 million. Following the surprisingly close January 2003 parliamentary election, outgoing Prime Minister Jan Peter Balkenende was narrowly returned to power, ruling in coalition with the conservative People's Party for Freedom and Democracy (VVD) and the centrist Democrats 66 (D66). The new government's biggest challenge will be implementing its program of 13 billion euros in spending cuts, with health care provision and rent subsidies slated for reduction because of the current recession and GDP increasing by only 0.2 percent in 2002. The Netherlands' fiscal burden of government score is 0.1 point better this year; however, its government intervention score is 0.5 point worse. As a result, the Netherlands' overall score is 0.04 point worse this year.

## QUICK STUDY

### SCORES

| | |
|---|---|
| Trade Policy | 2 |
| Fiscal Burden | 4.4 |
| Government Intervention | 3 |
| Monetary Policy | 2 |
| Foreign Investment | 1 |
| Banking and Finance | 1 |
| Wages and Prices | 2 |
| Property Rights | 1 |
| Regulation | 3 |
| Informal Market | 1 |

**Population:** 16,193,000

**Total area:** 41,526 sq. km

**GDP:** $504.4 billion

**GDP growth rate:** 0.2%

**GDP per capita:** $31,149

**Major exports:** chemicals, machinery and equipment, foodstuffs, transportation, travel services, financial services

**Exports of goods and services:** $332.3 billion

**Major export trading partners:** Germany 24.4%, Belgium 11.8%, UK 10.9%, France 10.0%, US 4.9%

**Major imports:** transport equipment, machinery, fuels, clothing, computer and information, financial services

**Imports of goods and services:** $304.3 billion

**Major import trading partners:** Germany 19.4%, Belgium 10.8%, US 8.7%, UK 8.0%

**Foreign direct investment (net):** $2.9 billion

2002 Data (in constant 1995 US dollars)

## TRADE POLICY
### Score: **2**–Stable (low level of protectionism)

As a member of the European Union, according to the World Bank, the Netherlands' weighted average tariff rate in 2001 (the last year for which World Bank data were available) was 2.6 percent. The Economist Intelligence Unit reports that the primary non-tariff barriers are import license requirements, which are based on a quota and therefore are issued until the limit is reached. The Netherlands abides by the common EU antidumping rules.

## FISCAL BURDEN OF GOVERNMENT
### Score—Income Taxation: **5**–Stable (very high tax rates)
### Score—Corporate Taxation: **4.5**–Stable (very high tax rates)
### Score—Change in Government Expenditures: **3.5**–Better (low increase)
## Final Score: **4.4**–Better (high cost of government)

The top income tax rate is 52 percent. The top corporate tax rate is 34.5 percent. Government expenditures as a share of GDP increased less in 2002 (0.9 percentage point to 47.3 percent) than they did in 2001 (1.1 percentage points). As a result, the Netherlands' fiscal burden of government score is 0.1 point better this year.

## GOVERNMENT INTERVENTION IN THE ECONOMY
### Score: **3**–Worse (moderate level)

Based on data from Statistics Netherlands, the government consumed 24.2 percent of GDP in 2002. In 2001, based on data from Statistics Netherlands, the Netherlands received 6.4 percent of its revenues from state-owned enterprises and government ownership of property, up from the 4.07 percent reported in the 2003 *Index*. As a result, the Netherlands' government intervention score is 0.5 point worse this year.

## MONETARY POLICY
Score: **2**–Stable (low level of inflation)

From 1993 to 2002, the Netherlands' weighted average annual rate of inflation was 3.59 percent.

## CAPITAL FLOWS AND FOREIGN INVESTMENT
Score: **1**–Stable (very low barriers)

The Netherlands actively promotes foreign investment. According to the U.S. Department of State, "The Netherlands' trade and investment policy is among the most open in the world." The government requires no approval for investments, and foreign investors receive national treatment, the only exception being air transport. There are no restrictions or barriers on current transfers, repatriation of profits, purchase of real estate, or access to foreign exchange. Capital transactions are not restricted but are subject to reporting requirements under the External Financial Relations Act. The few restrictions that exist apply to investment in defense-related industries, such as the manufacturing of weapons, and a few public and private monopolies that ban investment for both foreign and domestic investors, such as public broadcasting and the railways.

## BANKING AND FINANCE
Score: **1**–Stable (very low level of restrictions)

The Netherlands has been one of Europe's financial and banking centers for centuries, and its banking system operates freely with little government regulation. Banks established in the Netherlands may engage in a variety of financial services, such as buying, selling, and holding securities, insurance policies, and real estate. Three Dutch bank conglomerates—ABN Amro, Rabobank and ING bank—dominate the sector, accounting for approximately 75 percent of lending. Banks are subject to limits on their foreign currency and precious metals position and must submit reports to the government on non-resident assets and liabilities. The government is minimally involved in the banking sector. According to the Economist Intelligence Unit, "The Ministry of Economic Affairs occasionally extends credit to promote technical development in medium-sized ventures."

## WAGES AND PRICES
Score: **2**–Stable (low level of intervention)

Wages and prices in the Netherlands are set primarily by the market. According to the Economist Intelligence Unit, "The Price Control Act gives the government substantial powers to control prices, especially in times of high inflation. These powers have been exercised occasionally since 1973....

Legislation was passed in January 1996 to introduce price controls for medicines." The Netherlands also affects agricultural prices through its participation in the Common Agricultural Policy, a program that heavily subsidizes agricultural goods. According to Timbro, a Swedish think tank, "EU consumers pay roughly 80–100% more for their food than would be the case in a mature free-market regime." The Netherlands maintains a minimum wage.

## PROPERTY RIGHTS
Score: **1**–Stable (very high level of protection)

Private property is secure. The Economist Intelligence Unit reports that "contractual agreements remain very secure in the Netherlands. The judiciary and the civil service are of high quality."

## REGULATION
Score: **3**–Stable (moderate level)

According to the U.S. Department of State, laws and regulations affecting investment are non-discriminatory and applied evenly. In general, starting a business is relatively easy. However, the Economist Intelligence Unit reports that "the Environmental Management Act requires businesses to ensure that their activities do not cause pollution. This might involve registering with local authorities on compliance with environmental regulations or seeking an environmental permit." The Netherlands abides by the "polluter pays" principle. Most available building land is owned by local government, which limits the number of building permits issued. Combined with the scarcity of land and high property prices, this also makes establishing a business more challenging. The government has expanded laws allowing for increased part-time work. *The Economist* reports that "labour laws in the Netherlands, unlike those in France and Germany, are sufficiently flexible to permit job cuts."

## INFORMAL MARKET
Score: **1**–Stable (very low level of activity)

Transparency International's 2001 score for the Netherlands is 9. Therefore, the Netherlands' informal market score is 1 this year.

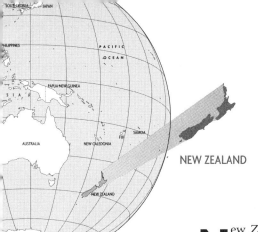

NEW ZEALAND

Rank: 3
Score: 1.70
Category: Free

**Present & Past Scores**

(Best) 1
2
3
4
(Worst) 5

1.74 1.75 1.83 1.71 1.75 1.71 1.68 1.68 1.70

'95 '96 '97 '98 '99 '00 '01 '02 '03 '04
n/a

## QUICK STUDY

### SCORES

| | |
|---|---|
| Trade Policy | 2 |
| Fiscal Burden | 4 |
| Government Intervention | 2 |
| Monetary Policy | 1 |
| Foreign Investment | 1 |
| Banking and Finance | 1 |
| Wages and Prices | 2 |
| Property Rights | 1 |
| Regulation | 2 |
| Informal Market | 1 |

**Population:** 3,942,000

**Total area:** 268,680 sq. km

**GDP:** $73.8 billion

**GDP growth rate:** 3.8%

**GDP per capita:** $18,721

**Major exports:** dairy products, forest products, fruit and vegetables, aluminum, wool

**Exports of goods and services:** $24.7 billion

**Major export trading partners:** Australia 19.6%, US 15.2%, Japan 11.5%, UK 4.9%

**Major imports:** machinery and mechanical appliances, vehicles, electrical machinery and equipment, mineral fuels and oils

**Imports of goods and services:** $24.8 billion

**Major import trading partners:** Australia 22.6%, US 15.0%, Japan 11.4%, UK 3.8%

**Foreign direct investment (net):** $442 million

2002 Data (in constant 1995 US dollars)

New Zealand is a parliamentary democracy with a population just shy of 4 million. With 45 million sheep and nearly 9 million cattle, its lush landscape could be described as a big farm, but Organisation for Economic Co-operation and Development data indicate that it also has the lowest farm subsidies in the world. While exports clearly contribute to growth, according to the Economist Intelligence Unit, strong growth in housing motivated by new migrants, low interest rates, and active job creation has further driven the economy. The EIU also notes that hosting the America's Cup races has called attention to New Zealand as a tourist destination with modern amenities. Even though the government is forecasting higher operating surpluses than previously expected, no tax cuts have been announced. There is a self-enforced cap on extra spending, but the EIU does not appear to have confidence in the government's willingness to observe spending limits if economic growth fails to maintain its current pace. New Zealand's fiscal burden of government score is 0.2 point worse this year. As a result, its overall score is 0.02 point worse this year.

### TRADE POLICY
Score: **2**–Stable (low level of protectionism)

According to the World Bank, New Zealand's weighted average tariff rate in 2000 (the most recent year for which World Bank data are available) was 2.4 percent. The Economist Intelligence Unit reports that New Zealand has "strict health, content, safety and origin-labeling rules for imported and domestically produced goods, and there are stringent animal and plant health requirements.... Foreign suppliers particularly should note the country's restrictions on packaging materials." According to the U.S. Trade Representative, "New Zealand maintains a strict regime of sanitary and phytosanitary (SPS) control for virtually all imports of agricultural products.... [I]n 2001, SPS regulations were tightened."

### FISCAL BURDEN OF GOVERNMENT
Score—Income Taxation: **3.5**–Stable (high tax rates)
Score—Corporate Taxation: **4.5**–Stable (very high tax rates)
Score—Change in Government Expenditures: **3.5**–Worse (low increase)
Final Score: **4**–Worse (high cost of government)

New Zealand's top income tax rate is 39 percent. The top corporate tax rate is 33 percent. Government expenditures as a share of GDP increased 0.4 percentage point to 36.5 percent in 2002, compared to a 1.1 percentage point decrease in 2001. As a result, New Zealand's fiscal burden of government score is 0.2 point worse this year.

### GOVERNMENT INTERVENTION IN THE ECONOMY
Score: **2**–Stable (low level)

The New Zealand Embassy reports that the government consumed 17.8 percent of GDP in 2002. In 2001, according to the International Monetary Fund, New Zealand received 3.51 percent of its total revenues from state-owned enterprises and government ownership of property.

## MONETARY POLICY
### Score: **1**–Stable (very low level of inflation)

From 1993 to 2002, New Zealand's weighted average annual rate of inflation was 2.55 percent.

## CAPITAL FLOWS AND FOREIGN INVESTMENT
### Score: **1**–Stable (very low barriers)

New Zealand generally encourages foreign investment, and practical barriers to investment are minimal. Officially, foreign ownership is restricted in only three areas—fishing, airlines, and real estate—although it is sometimes possible to get approval for the latter. According to the International Monetary Fund, "For foreign investment in certain types of land, the investor must undergo a bona fide test and the investment must be in the national interest. Authorization is required for acquisitions of the following: land exceeding 5 hectares in area or where the consideration exceeds $NZ 10 million; islands or land containing or adjoining reserves, historic, or heritage areas; foreshore or lakes in excess of 0.4 hectares; and effective January 1, 2002, land containing or adjoining foreshore in excess of 0.4 hectares." Foreign investments in businesses or property where foreign ownership is 25 percent or greater and the investment exceeds NZ$50 million require approval from the Overseas Investment Commission (OIC). The Embassy of New Zealand reports that in 2002, the OIC received 347 applications and approved 338 investments (97 percent). There are no restrictions or barriers on current transfers, repatriation of profits, or access to foreign exchange.

## BANKING AND FINANCE
### Score: **1**–Stable (very low level of restrictions)

New Zealand's banking system is deregulated, and foreign banks are welcome; foreigners own or control all but two of New Zealand's registered banks. The government owns one bank, Kiwibank Limited, which began operations in February 2002, but foreign banks dominate the sector. According to the Economist Intelligence Unit, New Zealand has 17 registered banks, and foreign banks control over 90 percent of total bank assets. The Reserve Bank of New Zealand is limited to prudential supervision. The government does not provide deposit insurance for financial institutions; instead, banks provide full disclosure of their financial condition to the public on a quarterly basis. The Labour government has returned control of workplace accident insurance to the state monopoly.

## WAGES AND PRICES
### Score: **2**–Stable (low level of intervention)

The market determines most wages and prices. According to the Economist Intelligence Unit, however, "The Ministry of Economic Development (MED) and Commerce Commission have the power…to control prices in markets where effective competition is absent…." The government imposed price hikes on airfares following its takeover of Air New Zealand. New Zealand has a minimum wage.

## PROPERTY RIGHTS
### Score: **1**–Stable (very high level of protection)

Private property is well-protected in New Zealand. The Economist Intelligence Unit reports that "contracts and court decisions are generally very well respected." According to the U.S. Department of State, "the law provides for an independent judiciary and the Government respects this provision in practice. The Judiciary provides citizens with a fair and efficient judicial process."

## REGULATION
### Score: **2**–Stable (low level)

It is easy to establish a business in New Zealand, and years of substantive reforms have created a relatively light, transparent regulatory regime. According to the Embassy of New Zealand, "a new company can be incorporated online…. [T]here are three steps involved in the registration of a new company: submit application online, fax in consents, and print incorporation certificates." The Resource Management Act of 1991 created a three-layer regulatory system involving national, regional, and local authorities that requires businesses to acquire a resource consent, or permit, for most types of business activity. The result is an inconsistent system in which each of the country's 83 different local authorities interprets the law in its own way and accusations of environmental violations can be filed on a broad-ranging basis. This process can take as much as two years, and the system is overloaded with cases. The government has tried to fine-tune this act to reduce its burden on businesses, but with only marginal results. Labor laws are somewhat rigid but much less so than in other developed countries. In general, New Zealand's business environment is open and competitive.

## INFORMAL MARKET
### Score: **1**–Stable (very low level of activity)

Transparency International's 2002 score for New Zealand is 9.5. Therefore, New Zealand's informal market score is 1 this year.

NICARAGUA

# NICARAGUA

Rank: 67

Score: 2.94

Category: Mostly free

**Present & Past Scores**

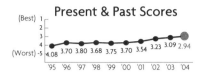

(Best) 1 2 3 4 (Worst) -5

4.08 3.70 3.80 3.68 3.75 3.70 3.54 3.23 3.09 2.94

'95 '96 '97 '98 '99 '00 '01 '02 '03 '04

O btaining international financial assistance and cleaning up corruption left over from the previous administration have consumed the efforts of President Enrique Bolaños Geyer of the Partido Liberal. Meanwhile, powerful Sandinista Party leader Daniel Ortega has been making deals with Bolaños to fight corruption on one hand and reportedly is aiding ex-President Arnoldo Alemán's attempt to return to power on the other. It was with Ortega's help that Alemán manipulated the country's political institutions to hide alleged enrichment schemes, stack the supreme court, and establish unelected seats for himself and Ortega in the National Assembly with immunity from prosecution for any possible crimes; once Alemán was out of office, the Assembly lifted his immunity, and he was subsequently jailed. Nicaragua, however, has more pressing problems. GDP per capita remains the Western Hemisphere's second lowest at about $500. According to the U.S. Agency for International Development, Nicaragua's combined foreign and internal debt is more than three times its GDP, severely restricting public finances. Nicaragua needs to diversify its exports beyond coffee; strengthen property rights; educate its workforce (less than 50 percent of all children attend secondary school); and establish an effective rule of law. Nicaragua's capital flows and foreign investment score is 1 point worse this year; however, its government intervention score is 1.5 point better, and its monetary policy score is 1 point better. As a result, Nicaragua's overall score is 0.15 point better this year, causing Nicaragua to be classified as "mostly free."

## TRADE POLICY
### Score: **2**–Stable (low level of protectionism)

The World Bank reports that Nicaragua's weighted average tariff rate in 2001 (the most recent year for which World Bank data are available) was 3 percent. According to the U.S. Trade Representative, "Importers complain of steep secondary customs costs, including customs declarations form charges and consular fees. In addition, importers are required to employ licensed customs agents, adding further costs." A license is required to import sugar.

## FISCAL BURDEN OF GOVERNMENT
Score—Income Taxation: **2.5**–Stable (moderate tax rates)
Score—Corporate Taxation: **3**–Stable (moderate tax rates)
Score—Change in Government Expenditures: **3**–Stable (very low decrease)
### Final Score: **2.9**–Stable (moderate cost of government)

Nicaragua's top income tax rate is 25 percent. The top corporate tax rate is 25 percent. Government expenditures as a share of GDP remained unchanged at 45.1 percent in 2001, compared to a 0.6 percentage point decrease in 2000. On net, Nicaragua's fiscal burden of government score is unchanged this year.

## GOVERNMENT INTERVENTION IN THE ECONOMY
### Score: **2.5**–Better (moderate level)

The International Monetary Fund reports that the government consumed 20.1 percent of GDP in 2001. In 2000, according to the same source, Nicaragua received 1.69 percent of its revenues from state-owned enterprises and government ownership of property. Based on newly available data with respect to revenues from state-owned enterprises, Nicaragua's government intervention score is 1.5 point better this year.

## MONETARY POLICY
### Score: **2**–Better (low level of inflation)

From 1993 to 2002, Nicaragua's weighted average annual rate of inflation was 5.71 percent, down from the 8.91 percent from 1992 to 2001 reported in the 2003 *Index.* As a result, Nicaragua's monetary policy score is 1 point better this year.

 ## CAPITAL FLOWS AND FOREIGN INVESTMENT
### Score: **3**–Worse (moderate barriers)

The U.S. Department of State reports that the May 24, 2000, Foreign Investment Law "a) assures that foreign and domestic investment receive the same treatment; b) eliminates the need to sign an investment contract; c) abolishes the foreign investment committee; d) eliminates restrictions on the way in which foreign capital can enter the country; e) recognizes the investor's right to own property and use it as he wishes, and in the case of a declaration of eminent domain, receive proper indemnification." The large number of disputes that remain unresolved from the expropriation of property during the 1980s presents unofficial barriers. According to the U.S. Trade Representative, "Poorly enforced property rights and the resulting proliferation of property disputes are among the most serious barriers to investment in Nicaragua…. The resolution of commercial and investment disputes is still unpredictable." "Arbitrary or slow bureaucracy" is another problem, according to the U.S. Department of State. "Doing business in Nicaragua can sometimes mean becoming involved with slow-moving government approvals." The International Monetary Fund reports that both residents and non-residents may hold foreign exchange accounts. There are no controls or restrictions on payments and transfers. There are very few restrictions on capital transactions. Based on the evidence that unofficial barriers continue to deter foreign investment, Nicaragua's capital flows and foreign investment score is 1 point worse this year.

 ## BANKING AND FINANCE
### Score: **2**–Stable (low level of restrictions)

The 1999 reform of the General Banking Law adopted the Basel standard for capital adequacy of 10 percent, created a maximum cap on bank shares held by any one private shareholder, placed limits on loans to any one borrower, and curbed the ability of banks to lend to related companies. In 2000 and 2001, the banking sector suffered a crisis due to mismanagement and fraud in a number banks. The six banks in existence today are all under majority private ownership. One of the most significant outgrowths of the crisis is legislation, passed in December 2000, that guarantees up to US$20,000 per depositor. The government owns an insurance company, but a 1996 law opened the sector to competition, and today four private insurance firms also exist. Although Nicaragua's banking system is weak and underdeveloped, the government has only a minimal presence.

 ## WAGES AND PRICES
### Score: **3**–Stable (moderate level of intervention)

According to the Economist Intelligence Unit, "Nicaragua maintains price controls only on sugar, domestically produced soft drinks, certain petroleum products, and pharmaceuticals." The government also influences prices through state-owned enterprises in utilities and such other areas as construction, insurance, building materials, pharmaceuticals, and agriculture. The minimum wage system applies different rates to different economic sectors. The various rates are set through tripartite negotiations involving business, government, and labor and confirmed by the National Assembly.

 ## PROPERTY RIGHTS
### Score: **4**–Stable (low level of protection)

Protection of property rights is weak. The U.S. Trade Representative reports that "poorly enforced property rights and the resulting proliferation of property disputes are among the most serious barriers to investment in Nicaragua." According to the Economist Intelligence Unit, "The selection of magistrates and judges has always been political and judicial independence from executive and legislative pressures is slight. There is no judicial career (merit) system, the training of judges is highly deficient, and public confidence in the fairness of judicial processes is very low. Corruption and influence-peddling in the judicial branch put foreign investors at a sharp disadvantage in any litigation or dispute." Expropriation is possible.

 ## REGULATION
### Score: **4**–Stable (high level)

"Despite significant streamlining in recent years," reports the U.S. Department of State, "Nicaragua's legal and regulatory framework remains cumbersome. The rules are not fully transparent, and much business is still conducted on a 'who you know' basis…. Although the 1997 tax law eliminated many special tax exonerations, investors still express frustration at a high level of discretion and overcentralized decision making in taxation and customs procedures." Labor laws impose a significant burden on businesses. According to the Economist Intelligence Unit, "employees are entitled to generous medical leave and vacation provisions; maternity leave is also included. When a company terminates an employee's contract, one month salary must be paid for each year worked, up to five months." Both the Economist Intelligence Unit and the U.S. Department of State have characterized corruption as a continuing problem.

 ## INFORMAL MARKET
### Score: **4**–Stable (high level of activity)

Transparency International's 2002 score for Nicaragua is 2.5. Therefore, Nicaragua's informal market score is 4 this year.

# NIGER

NIGER

**Rank:** 111

**Score:** 3.43

**Category:** Mostly Unfree

## QUICK STUDY

### SCORES

| | |
|---|---|
| Trade Policy | 4 |
| Fiscal Burden | 4.3 |
| Government Intervention | 3 |
| Monetary Policy | 1 |
| Foreign Investment | 3 |
| Banking and Finance | 3 |
| Wages and Prices | 3 |
| Property Rights | 4 |
| Regulation | 4 |
| Informal Market | 5 |

**Population:** 11,184,130

**Total area:** 1,267,000 sq. km

**GDP:** $2.3 billion

**GDP growth rate:** 7.6%

**GDP per capita:** $208

**Major exports:** uranium ore, livestock

**Exports of goods and services:** $400.8 million

**Major export trading partners:** France 33.5%, Nigeria 30.5%, South Korea 18.7%, US 5.4%

**Major imports:** consumer goods, machinery, petroleum

**Imports of goods and services:** $475 million

**Major import trading partners:** France 18.6%, US 16.4%, Ivory Coast 9.3%, Germany 9.3%

**Foreign direct investment (net):** $29.6 million

2001 Data (in constant 1995 US dollars)

Relative peace and political stability continued in Niger through the early part of 2003, and the republic celebrated eight years of peace on April 24. Niger still has one of sub-Saharan Africa's highest fertility rates despite the obvious effects of substantial population growth on the country's already weak economic growth. Nearly 90 percent Muslim, Niger differs from neighboring Nigeria in its unwillingness to adopt Islam as its state religion. This, however, has not prevented Islamic influence in such areas as law and education. Economically, Niger continues to rely heavily on subsistence agriculture, which contributes 40 percent of GDP and employs nearly 90 percent of the active population. The remaining 60 percent of GDP is divided between the service sector (40 percent) and industry, mining, and manufacturing (18 percent–20 percent). Niger remains one of the region's poorest countries; a 2001 U.N. human development report ranked it 161st out of 162 countries. Commercial gold mining is set to begin within the few years, but its economic effects could well be undermined by the continued instability of the world gold market. Niger's fiscal burden of government score is 0.2 point worse this year; however, its government intervention and monetary policy scores are 1 point better. As a result, Niger's overall score is 0.18 point better this year.

## TRADE POLICY
### Score: **4**–Stable (high level of protectionism)

Niger is a member of the West African Economic and Monetary Union (WAEMU), which imposes a common external tariff with four rates: 0 percent, 5 percent, 10 percent, and 20 percent. The World Bank reports that Niger's weighted average tariff rate in 2001 (the most recent year for which World Bank data are available) was 13.2 percent. According to the U.S. Department of State, "Importing companies must be listed in the trade and employers registries and possess business and import licenses...." Some goods require further special authorization from the Ministry of Commerce.

## FISCAL BURDEN OF GOVERNMENT
Score—Income Taxation: **4.5**–Stable (very high tax rates)
Score—Corporate Taxation: **4.5**–Better (very high tax rates)
Score—Change in Government Expenditures: **3.5**–Worse (low increase)
### Final Score: **4.3**–Worse (high cost of government)

The International Monetary Fund reports that Niger's top income tax rate is 45 percent. The top corporate tax rate is 35 percent, down from the 42.5 percent reported in the 2003 *Index*. Government expenditures as a share of GDP increased 0.4 percentage point to 16.6 percent in 2001, compared to a 2.3 percentage point decrease in 2000. As a result, Niger's fiscal burden of government score is 0.2 point worse this year.

## GOVERNMENT INTERVENTION IN THE ECONOMY
### Score: **3**–Better (moderate level)

The World Bank reports that the government consumed 12.3 percent of GDP in 2001. In the same year, based on data from the International Monetary Fund, Niger received 3.1 percent of its total revenues from state-owned enterprises and government ownership of property. This figure, however, should be viewed with caution. According to the U.S. Department of State, "Several industrial enterprises are para-statals wholly or partially owned by the government." In addition, reports the Economist Intelligence Unit, the government still owns "the electricity utility, Nigelec, the company that imports petroleum products, Sonidep, and the Gaweye Hotel" as well as "three state-owned financial institutions…and the national postal and savings office…." Based on the apparent unreliability of official figures on revenues from state-owned enterprises, 1 point has been added to Niger's government intervention score. Overall, based on the new methodology used to score this factor, Niger's government intervention score is 1 point better this year.

## MONETARY POLICY
### Score: 1–Better (very low level of inflation)

From 1993 to 2002, Niger's weighted average annual rate of inflation was 2.86 percent, down from the 3.25 percent from 1992 to 2001 reported in the 2003 *Index*. As a result, Niger's monetary policy score is 1 point better this year. Niger has benefited from a stable currency—a rarity in sub-Saharan Africa—as a member of the CFA franc zone.

## CAPITAL FLOWS AND FOREIGN INVESTMENT
### Score: 3–Stable (moderate barriers)

Niger does not screen foreign investment and grants national treatment to foreign investors. According to the U.S. Department of State, "Total foreign ownership is permitted in all sectors except those few restricted for national security." The bureaucracy is cumbersome, and corruption is present. The International Monetary Fund reports that both residents and non-residents may hold foreign exchange accounts with the approval of the Banque Centrale des Etats de l'Afrique de l'Ouest (Central Bank of West African States, or BCEAO). Payments and transfers to countries other than France, Monaco, members of the Central African Economic and Monetary Community, members of the WAEMU, and Comoros are subject to quantitative limits and approval in some cases. Some capital transactions to countries other than members of the WAEMU are subject to authorization. Real estate purchases by non-residents must be declared to the government prior to purchase.

## BANKING AND FINANCE
### Score: 3–Stable (moderate level of restrictions)

The BCEAO, a central bank common to the eight members of the WAEMU, governs Niger's banking system. The banking system remains underdeveloped, and credit is difficult to obtain. The Economist Intelligence Unit reports that "Niger's banking system remains one of the weakest in the [WAEMU], with none of its banks complying with the regional grouping's set of prudential ratios. Some banks have also struggled to meet the reserve requirements set by the regional central bank…." In addition, Banque commercial du Niger has been recapitalized, and its temporary management arrangement with the central bank ended in June 2003; the government is giving funds to Banque Islamique du Niger pour le commerce

et l'investissement to restructure itself; and the government has suspended the operations of Caisse de prets aux collectivités territoriales. Although the government is involved in the financial system, private banks and foreign banks operate freely.

## WAGES AND PRICES
### Score: 3–Stable (moderate level of intervention)

According to the U.S. Department of State, "Prices are set by market forces, not by the government." However, the Economist Intelligence Unit reports that the government controls the price of fuel. The government also sets state-owned utility rates. Minimum wages for salaried workers differ by sector, and Niger's large public sector affects wages and prices.

## PROPERTY RIGHTS
### Score: 4–Stable (low level of protection)

The judicial system is inefficient and subject to outside influence. According to the U.S. Department of State, "Judges sometimes feared reassignment or having their financial benefits reduced if they rendered a decision unfavorable to the government…." The Economist Intelligence Unit reports that "At the end of February the head of the Syndicat autonome des magistrates du Niger (SAMAN) noted that political interference in the affairs of the judiciary was rife and that corruption was partly fuelled by the low salaries received by judges and the lack of adequate training programmes."

## REGULATION
### Score: 4–Stable (high level)

The U.S. Department of State reports that "investors should be prepared for delays caused by the process of acquiring inter-ministerial approvals." Corruption is an admitted problem. The Economist Intelligence Unit, for example, reports that corruption (among other things) is what "brought the economy to its knees." The bureaucracy is also significantly burdensome. According to the EIU, "Public administration in Niger is under-resourced, largely inefficient and a drain on state resources. Cutting the bloated bureaucracy is an enormous challenge…. Transparency is also lacking and financial malpractices are deeply rooted at all levels of public administration."

## INFORMAL MARKET
### Score: 5–Stable (very high level of activity)

According to the Economist Intelligence Unit, "as much as two thirds of all economic activity takes place in the informal sector." The informal market includes the sale of commercial goods, including petroleum, and provides a transit point for drug trafficking. Arms trafficking between Niger and its neighbors is likewise active.

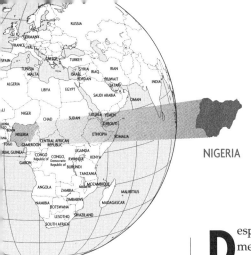

# NIGERIA

NIGERIA

**Rank:** 142

**Score:** 3.95

**Category:** Mostly Unfree

**Present & Past Scores**

(Best) 1
2
3
4
(Worst) 5

3.43 3.53 3.43 3.40 3.40 3.39 3.49 3.79 4.04 3.95

'95 '96 '97 '98 '99 '00 '01 '02 '03 '04

Despite widespread allegations of vote rigging, fraud, and intimidation, Western governments recognized the April 2003 re-election of President Olusegun Obasanjo. Obasanjo faces mounting economic problems as well as sectarian violence in parts of the country. Ethnic and religious tensions remain high, and more than 10,000 people have been killed in religious and ethnic clashes over the past four years. Nigeria has sub-Saharan Africa's largest population and second largest economy, in addition to being the world's sixth largest exporter of oil; yet per capita income remains extremely low, and two thirds of the population are poor. Declining oil revenues and the slow pace of privatization led to suspension of some debt payments in 2002. Only 14 of the 107 state-owned enterprises scheduled for privatization have been fully privatized. Corruption continues to act as a major deterrent to foreign direct investment: According to Transparency International, Nigeria is one of the world's two most corrupt countries. At the same time, however, it has rich resources, an entrepreneurial population, and a productive agricultural sector that would yield significant rewards if economic reform, good governance, and the rule of law were instituted. The Economist Intelligence Unit predicts real GDP growth of 3.1 percent in 2003 and 3.9 percent in 2004. Nigeria's fiscal burden of government score is 0.1 point worse this year; however, its government intervention and informal market scores are 0.5 point better. As a result, its overall score is 0.09 point better this year, although Nigeria is still classified as a "mostly unfree" economy.

## TRADE POLICY
### Score: **5**–Stable (very high level of protectionism)

The World Bank reports that Nigeria's weighted average tariff rate in 1995 (the most recent year for which World Bank data are available) was 20 percent. According to the U.S. Trade Representative, the government bans imports of vehicles over five years old, textiles containing "hazardous chemicals such as chlorides," sorghum, millet, wheat flour, cassava, frozen poultry, vegetable oil, kaolin, gypsum, mosquito repellent coils, used clothing, and bagged cement. Importers "face long [customs] clearance procedures, corruption, high berthing and unloading costs, and uncertain application of customs regulations."

## FISCAL BURDEN OF GOVERNMENT
### Score—Income Taxation: **2.5**–Stable (moderate tax rates)
### Score—Corporate Taxation: **4**–Stable (high tax rates)
### Score—Change in Government Expenditures: **3.5**–Worse (low increase)
### Final Score: **3.5**–Worse (high cost of government)

Nigeria's top income tax rate is 25 percent. The corporate tax rate is 30 percent. Government expenditures as a share of GDP increased 0.5 percentage point to 28.9 percent in 2001, compared to a 0.9 percentage point decrease in 2000. As a result, Nigeria's fiscal burden of government score is 0.1 point worse this year.

## GOVERNMENT INTERVENTION IN THE ECONOMY
### Score: **4.5**–Better (very high level)

The World Bank reports that the government consumed 25.2 percent of GDP in 2001. In 2001, based on data from the International Monetary Fund, Nigeria received 60.31 percent of its total revenues from state-owned enterprises and government ownership of property. Based on the new methodology used to analyze this factor, Nigeria's government intervention score is 0.5 point better this year.

### MONETARY POLICY
### Score: **4**–Stable (high level of inflation)

From 1993 to 2002, Nigeria's weighted average annual rate of inflation was 12.81 percent.

### CAPITAL FLOWS AND FOREIGN INVESTMENT
### Score: **3**–Stable (moderate barriers)

According to the U.S. Department of State, a 1995 decree issued by the Nigerian Investment Promotion Commission "eliminated discriminatory screening processes for foreign investment and allowed 100 percent foreign ownership of any business enterprise except those in the oil sector and in sectors deemed sensitive to national security." The same source reports that "investment in Nigeria also confronts several impediments. They include inconsistent macroeconomic policies, an inefficient national infrastructure, corruption, an unresponsive bureaucracy, lack of skilled labor, and courts and commercial dispute-resolution mechanisms that often prove slow and ineffective." The International Monetary Fund reports that some capital transactions are subject to documentation requirements and restrictions. Most payments and transfers must be conducted through banks, and applications for foreign exchange must be approved by the central bank.

### BANKING AND FINANCE
### Score: **4**–Stable (high level of restrictions)

Foreign banks must acquire licenses from the central bank in order to operate. Since 1999, the government has granted new banking licenses and revoked others to bring the number of banks to 89 in June 2002. However, the U.S. Department of State reports that the five largest banks control approximately 75 percent of total bank deposits. The government maintains 100 percent ownership in the Bank of Industry and the Nigerian Agricultural and Rural Development Bank. It also affects the allocation of credit. According to the U.S. Department of State, "in its Monetary Policy the [Central Bank of Nigeria] in 2001 mandated banks to set aside 10 percent of their gross profit towards financing SME projects." In 2001, Nigeria introduced universal banking, which allowed banks to engage in money market activities, capital market activities, and insurance services. Overall, the banking system is chaotic, prone to small crises, and weak, and the government has demonstrated a strong tendency to intervene.

### WAGES AND PRICES
### Score: **3**–Stable (moderate level of intervention)

According to the Economist Intelligence Unit, "There are no price control laws for manufactured goods and products. However, the government still regulates utility and fuel pricing. The proposed deregulation of utility and fuel pricing remains a sensitive political issue, particularly in light of nation-wide strikes in January 2002 over fuel price increases." The government also influences prices through several state-owned enterprises. Nigeria has a minimum wage.

### PROPERTY RIGHTS
### Score: **4**–Stable (low level of protection)

Property rights are weakly protected. The Economist Intelligence Unit reports that Nigeria's "judicial system is still deeply undermined by corruption and is hugely underfunded. This has resulted in poor administration of justice, including long delays in hearing cases...." According to the U.S. Department of State, "Several factors undermine effective enforcement [of judgements]: the severe lack of available court facilities; hand-written judgements and the lack of computerized systems to facilitate document processing; the arbitrary adjournment of court sessions due to power outages; and easily corrupted court officials and judges. In some instances, decrees have been promulgated and backdated to circumvent court rulings."

### REGULATION
### Score: **4**–Stable (high level)

There is a high regulatory burden in Nigeria. The Economist Intelligence Unit describes the civil service as "bloated, corrupt and inefficient." According to the U.S. Department of State, "The primary problem regarding Nigeria's regulatory system is lax and uneven enforcement." In addition, "corruption is an endemic problem...and permeates all aspects of society, despite laws and penalties on the books. Foreign investors are convenient targets for extortion, bribery, and other corruptive acts since they are viewed as both relatively easy to coerce and profitable."

### INFORMAL MARKET
### Score: **4.5**–Better (very high level of activity)

Transparency International's 2002 score for Nigeria is 1.6. Therefore, Nigeria's informal market score is 4.5 this year— 0.5 point better than last year.

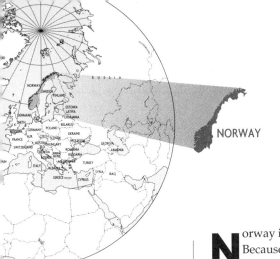

# NORWAY

NORWAY

Rank: 28
Score: 2.35
Category: Mostly Free

Present & Past Scores

(Best) 1
2
3
4
(Worst) 5

2.39 2.39 2.28 2.28 2.25 2.44 2.40 2.28 2.35

'95 '96 '97 '98 '99 '00 '01 '02 '03 '04
n/a

## QUICK STUDY

### SCORES

| | |
|---|---|
| Trade Policy | 2 |
| Fiscal Burden | 4 |
| Government Intervention | 3.5 |
| Monetary Policy | 1 |
| Foreign Investment | 3 |
| Banking and Finance | 3 |
| Wages and Prices | 2 |
| Property Rights | 1 |
| Regulation | 3 |
| Informal Market | 1 |

**Population:** 4,538,423

**Total area:** 324,220 sq. km

**GDP:** $174.6 billion

**GDP growth rate:** 1.0%

**GDP per capita:** $38,478

**Major exports:** crude oil, natural gas and refined petroleum products, machinery, food, beverages and tobacco

**Exports of goods and services:** $71.7 billion

**Major export trading partners:** UK 19.3%, Germany 12.3%, France 11.6%, Netherlands 9.3%, US 8.5%, Sweden 7.3%

**Major imports:** machinery and transport equipment, chemicals, food, beverages and tobacco

**Imports of goods and services:** $62.7 billion

**Major import trading partners:** Sweden 15.4%, Germany 13.1%, Denmark 7.9%, UK 7.3%, US 6.1%

**Foreign direct investment (net):** −$3.5 billion

2002 Data (in constant 1995 US dollars)

Norway is a constitutional monarchy with a population of more than 4.5 million people. Because Norway is a member of the European Free Trade Association and the European Economic Area, the European Union is its biggest trading partner. According to the U.S. Department of State, the economy is centered on the production of energy and energy-based industries, crude oil, natural gas, and metals production. Norway is the world's second wealthiest industrialized country, but increasing budget deficits have caused it to dig deeper into its oil revenues than planned. Like its neighbors, Norway has high taxes and a large welfare state. The Economist Intelligence Unit reports that "some tax cuts and further tax incentives for businesses will be phased in during 2003, and more can be expected in 2004," but the scope of these cuts is expected to be very limited. Norway needs to reduce its massive welfare state and implement large tax cuts. Lowering taxes would attract greater investment, which in turn would offer greater opportunities to the Norwegian people. Norway's fiscal burden of government score is 0.2 point worse this year, and its government intervention score is 0.5 point worse. As a result, Norway's overall score is 0.07 point worse this year.

### TRADE POLICY
Score: **2**–Stable (low level of protectionism)

The World Bank reports that Norway's weighted average tariff rate in 2001 (the most recent year for which World Bank data are available) was 1.6 percent. Non-tariff barriers include quotas and other restrictions on agricultural imports. According to the Economist Intelligence Unit, "Imports from some countries...require a license.... Some items (including certain grains, materials and equipment for the fishing industry and pharmaceuticals) may be imported only by a government monopoly.... Norway also regulates imports of textiles and foodstuffs.... [L]abels and advertisements for pharmaceuticals must be submitted to health authorities...."

### FISCAL BURDEN OF GOVERNMENT
Score—Income Taxation: **4.5**–Stable (very high tax rates)
Score—Corporate Taxation: **3.5**–Stable (high tax rates)
Score—Change in Government Expenditures: **4.5**–Worse (high increase)
Final Score: **4**–Worse (high cost of government)

Norway's top income tax rate is 47.5 percent. The top corporate tax rate is 28 percent. Government expenditures as a share of GDP increased more in 2002 (2.5 percentage points to 46.7 percent) than they did in 2001 (0.7 percentage point). As a result, Norway's fiscal burden of government score is 0.2 point worse this year.

### GOVERNMENT INTERVENTION IN THE ECONOMY
Score: **3.5**–Worse (high level)

According to the Economist Intelligence Unit, the government consumed 22 percent of GDP in 2002, up from the 20 percent reported in the 2003 *Index*. As a result, Norway's government intervention score is 0.5 point worse this year. In the same year, based on data from Norway's National Statistics, Norway received 18.7 percent of its total revenues from state-owned enterprises and government ownership of property.

## MONETARY POLICY
**Score: 1–Stable** (very low level of inflation)

From 1993 to 2002, Norway's weighted average annual rate of inflation was 1.89 percent.

## CAPITAL FLOWS AND FOREIGN INVESTMENT
**Score: 3–Stable** (moderate barriers)

In 1995, Norway adopted European Economic Area rules guaranteeing national treatment for foreign investors and liberalizing regulations that constrain foreign investment in industrial companies. The U.S. Department of State reports that the government still restricts investment in certain sectors, including financial services, mining, hydropower, media, railways, production and distribution of alcohol, and some real estate and land. The government mandates specific conditions in granting petroleum exploration and production licenses and gives preferential treatment to domestic oil companies. The International Monetary Fund reports that both residents and non-residents may hold foreign exchange accounts. There are no restrictions on payments, transfers, or repatriation of profits.

## BANKING AND FINANCE
**Score: 3–Stable** (moderate level of restrictions)

Norway's banking system is becoming more liberalized. "The Finance Ministry," reports the U.S. Department of State, "has abolished remaining restrictions on the establishment of branches by foreign financial institutions including banks, mutual funds and other financial institutions. Under the liberalized regime, branches of U.S. and other foreign financial institutions are granted the same treatment as nationals in Norway." However, "any investor—foreign or domestic— must obtain permission/concession from the Norwegian Finance Ministry to acquire more than 10 percent of the equity in a Norwegian financial institution." The government favors Norwegian investors over foreign investors. Although the government has reduced its holdings in Norway's three largest banks and has sold its stake in the largest (Den Norske Bank), it is still involved in the banking sector. According to the U.S. Department of State, "There are special banks for fisheries, agriculture, shipping, industry, house building, and export finance. The State, to varying degrees, participates in all of these."

## WAGES AND PRICES
**Score: 2–Stable** (low level of intervention)

The government exercises indirect control over some wages and prices. According to the Economist Intelligence Unit, "Indirect price controls and price fixing exist in several industries. Besides the oil-sector cases…the government has defended the right of utilities to practice price discrimination and to refuse to sell power outside of their distribution areas." The Embassy of Norway reports that the government regulates the price of prescription drugs and subsidizes agricultural goods, but that these subsidies have been declining over the past two years. According to the U.S. Department of State, "There is no legislated or specified minimum wage, but wages normally fall within a national scale negotiated by labor, employers and the Government at the local and company level."

## PROPERTY RIGHTS
**Score: 1–Stable** (very high level of protection)

Private property is safe from expropriation. The Economist Intelligence Unit reports that "contractual agreements are secure, with solid legal basis, and Norwegians generally place a high value on meeting these obligations. The civil service and the Judiciary are both of high quality…."

## REGULATION
**Score: 3–Stable** (moderate level)

Some of Norway's economy—especially agriculture and such service industries as telecommunications and transportation—remains heavily regulated. The U.S. Department of State reports that "Norway's market, with the notable exception of agricultural products and ancillary processed foods, is transparent and quite open. Few technical standards exist except in telecommunications equipment, although there are stringent regulations for chemicals and foodstuffs." The pharmaceutical industry is probably the most heavily regulated. According to the U.S. Department of State, "Pharmacies have traditionally been highly regulated in Norway with a virtual monopoly to a privileged few proprietary pharmacists protected by outdated laws and regulations." Building permits are subject to considerable government oversight and can take some time to approve. In July 2002, the government passed a law easing restrictions on the hiring of foreign skilled workers from outside the European Economic Area. When key sectors like the oil and gas industry and transportation are threatened by strikes, the government imposes mandatory wage mediation.

## INFORMAL MARKET
**Score: 1–Stable** (very low level of activity)

Transparency International's 2001 score for Norway is 8.5. Therefore, Norway's informal market score is 1 this year.

OMAN

# OMAN

Rank: 54

Score: 2.80

Category: Mostly Free

**Present & Past Scores**

(Best) 1
2
3
4
(Worst) 5

2.80 2.85 2.79 2.69 2.80 2.93 2.60 2.78 2.75 2.80

'95 '96 '97 '98 '99 '00 '01 '02 '03 '04

## QUICK STUDY

### SCORES

| | |
|---|---|
| Trade Policy | 3 |
| Fiscal Burden | 1.5 |
| Government Intervention | 4.5 |
| Monetary Policy | 1 |
| Foreign Investment | 3 |
| Banking and Finance | 3 |
| Wages and Prices | 4 |
| Property Rights | 3 |
| Regulation | 3 |
| Informal Market | 2 |

**Population:** 2,478,000

**Total area:** 212,460 sq. km

**GDP:** $17.9 billion

**GDP growth rate:** 9.3%

**GDP per capita:** $7,295

**Major exports:** oil, metals, fish, textiles

**Exports of goods and services:** $8.1 billion

**Major export trading partners:** China 22.3%, Japan 18.7%, South Korea 17.6%, Thailand 9.6%

**Major imports:** machinery and electrical equipment, food, beverages and tobacco

**Imports of goods and services:** $6.8 billion

**Major import trading partners:** United Arab Emirates 28.4%, Japan 15.1%, UK 8.2%, US 5.8%

**Foreign direct investment (net):** $43 million

2001 Data (in constant 1995 US dollars)

The Sultanate of Oman is an absolute monarchy that has been ruled by the Al Bu Sa'id family since the middle of the 18th century. The government is politically stable but faces few challenges to its authority. There remains a lingering uncertainty about succession since the heirless Sultan Qaboos announced his plans to defer the decision of his succession to the ruling family following his death. Although Oman is a relatively small oil producer—roughly 850,000 barrels of crude oil per day—the oil industry accounts for 86 percent of export revenues and roughly 43 percent of GDP. At current production rates, its oil reserves are projected to last for 18 years. Recognizing the need to reduce its dependency on oil, the government has made diversification of the economy a priority and seeks to expand development of its gas-based industries. Diminishing oil prices and weak production caused by recent technical problems within the oil sector have added a new impetus to these measures. In 2001, after Oman joined the World Trade Organization, the government launched the sixth in a series of five-year economic development plans designed to boost economic activity, facilitate foreign investment and privatization, and promote private-sector employment. Oman has amended its foreign investment, tax, and intellectual property rights laws and has opened the power and water sectors to private participation, but much more needs to be done. Unemployment remains dangerously high, particularly among Oman's overwhelmingly young population. In response, the government has placed a high priority on "Omanization," a quota program aimed at providing increased economic opportunities to the fast-growing population by replacing foreign workers with Omanis. Oman's fiscal burden of government score is 0.5 point better this year; however, its wages and prices score is 1 point worse. As a result, Oman's overall score is 0.05 point worse this year.

## TRADE POLICY
### Score: **3**–Stable (moderate level of protectionism)

According to the World Bank, Oman's weighted average tariff rate in 1997 (the most recent year for which World Bank data are available) was 4.5 percent. Import licenses are required for all imports, and the U.S. Department of State reports that "customs procedures are complex. There are complaints of sudden changes in the enforcement of regulations."

## FISCAL BURDEN OF GOVERNMENT
### Score—Income Taxation: **1**–Stable (very low tax rates)
### Score—Corporate Taxation: **1**–Stable (very low tax rates)
### Score—Change in Government Expenditures: **3**–Better (very low decrease)
### Final Score: **1.5**–Better (low cost of government)

No income taxes are imposed on individuals. A corporate tax of 30 percent is applied to companies with over 70 percent foreign ownership; the top corporate tax rate for domestic firms, and for companies with foreign ownership under 70 percent, is 12 percent. The latter figure has been used to calculate Oman's corporate taxation score. Government expenditures as a share of GDP decreased 0.7 percentage point to 46.3 percent in 2001, compared to a 4.6 percentage point increase in 2000. As a result, Oman's fiscal burden of government score is 0.5 point better this year.

## GOVERNMENT INTERVENTION IN THE ECONOMY
Score: **4.5**–Stable (very high level)

The Economist Intelligence Unit reports that the government consumed 22.8 percent of GDP in 2001. In the same year, according to the International Monetary Fund, Oman received 65.7 percent of its total revenues from state-owned enterprises and government ownership of property.

## MONETARY POLICY
Score: **1**–Stable (very low level of inflation)

From 1993 to 2002, Oman's weighted average annual rate of inflation was –0.76 percent.

## CAPITAL FLOWS AND FOREIGN INVESTMENT
Score: **3**–Stable (moderate barriers)

When Oman became a member of the World Trade Organization, it adopted a policy of automatic approval of majority foreign ownership up to 70 percent; foreign ownership above 70 percent is allowed with Minister of Commerce and Industry approval. Domestic firms and companies with less than 70 percent foreign participation are taxed at the same rate; firms with more than 70 percent participation are taxed at a substantially higher rate. Entry of new foreign firms in accounting, legal services, engineering, and architecture is not permitted, but the government has announced plans to open its service sector to foreign firms in the next few years. The official "Omanization" requirement that private-sector firms meet quotas for hiring native Omani workers, replacing foreign workers, is an impediment to foreign investment. According to the U.S. Department of State, "the approval process for establishing a business remains slow and subject to multiple government authorities, particularly with respect to land acquisition and labor requirements." Both residents and non-residents may hold foreign exchange accounts. Restrictions on payments, transactions, and transfers generally apply only to Israel.

## BANKING AND FINANCE
Score: **3**–Stable (moderate level of restrictions)

Oman's thriving banking sector includes 15 commercial banks, nine of which are foreign branches. The government operates three specialized banks that provide housing and industrial loans at favorable terms to Omani citizens. The Economist Intelligence Unit reports that the 2000 banking law set "limits on investment in foreign securities and raised the paid-up capital requirements…." According to the U.S. Department of State, "Foreign banks in particular find onerous Central Bank requirements that banks maintain a 12 percent level of capital adequacy and restrict consumer lending to 35 percent of the loan portfolio, as well as the higher taxation rates leveled on non-Omani firms." Investment in the local stock market is limited to Gulf Cooperation Council nationals, although foreign-

ers may take part in mutual funds. In 1999, the government reformed the rules governing the stock market to increase transparency, improve regulations, bring the exchange more in line with accepted international practice, and establish the Capital Markets Authority to regulate the market.

## WAGES AND PRICES
Score: **4**–Worse (high level of intervention)

The government controls the price of many goods and services through subsidies and free services. The Economist Intelligence Unit reports that inflationary pressures "will be largely countered by the maintenance of the government subsidy system, which will continue to hold the price of a range of core goods and services in check." The government also controls the prices of some commodities and affects prices through state-owned monopolies. According to the Economist Intelligence Unit, "The retail price of petroleum products is set by the government, and government monopolies on some services mean that in effect the government sets prices such as water." Oman has a minimum wage. Based on the evidence that the government subsidizes a wide range of goods and services, affects prices through state-owned enterprises, and controls the price of petroleum, Oman's wages and prices score is 1 point worse this year.

## PROPERTY RIGHTS
Score: **3**–Stable (moderate level of protection)

The threat of expropriation is low, although the judiciary is subject to political influence. "The ultimate adjudicator of business disputes within Oman," reports the U.S. Department of State, "is the Commercial Court, which was reorganized in mid-1997 from the former Authority for Settlement of Commercial Disputes (ASCD).… Business representatives generally have found that the former ASCD's use of general principles of equity in deciding cases not directly covered by Omani commercial law was fair. There have been complaints that powerful businessmen utilized their connections to secure an unfair advantage in ASCD rulings." According to the Economist Intelligence Unit, "The legal system has been restructured considerably over the past two years, with most of the changes brought into effect in late 2001 and early 2002. The new judicial system has three tiers, headed by the Supreme Court based in Muscat. Separate lower courts have also been established for civil, commercial, Sharia and criminal matters.… [C]hanges to the legal system have included the creation of about 40 new courts outside the capital. In addition to the reorganisation of the courts, the Public Prosecution Service has been separated from the police, and an independent attorney-general has been appointed."

## REGULATION
Score: **3**–Stable (moderate level)

The U.S. Department of State describes Oman's regulatory system as "not always transparent and sometimes contradictory.... [T]here is no complete body of regulations codifying Omani labor and tax laws and many government decisions are made on an ad hoc basis." The system can be characterized by red tape, confusion, and considerable delay, as the private sector must run a gantlet of government ministries to win approval for business plans. The labor laws, which enforce the "Omanization" requirement that private-sector firms meet quotas for hiring native Omani workers, are similarly burdensome.

 **INFORMAL MARKET**
Score: **2**–Stable (low level of activity)

Oman's informal market is not very large, but piracy is a problem. According to the Business Software Alliance, "In the ...global piracy report for 2002, Oman had the 13th highest software piracy rate. Its piracy rate dropped from 78% in 2000 to 77% in 2001." The U.S. Department of State reports that smuggling "is becoming an increasing concern."

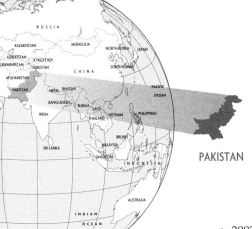

PAKISTAN

PAKISTAN

Rank: 109

Score: 3.40

Category: Mostly Unfree

**Present & Past Scores**

(Best) 1
2
3
4
(Worst) 5

3.34  3.26  3.29  3.31  3.50  3.50  3.50  3.44  3.44  3.40

'95  '96  '97  '98  '99  '00  '01  '02  '03  '04

## QUICK STUDY

### SCORES

| | |
|---|---|
| Trade Policy | 5 |
| Fiscal Burden | 4 |
| Government Intervention | 3 |
| Monetary Policy | 1 |
| Foreign Investment | 3 |
| Banking and Finance | 4 |
| Wages and Prices | 3 |
| Property Rights | 4 |
| Regulation | 3 |
| Informal Market | 4 |

**Population:** 141,450,144

**Total area:** 803,940 sq. km

**GDP:** $73.2 billion

**GDP growth rate:** 2.7%

**GDP per capita:** $517

**Major exports:** textiles (cotton fabrics and yarn, garments), rice

**Exports of goods and services:** $11.5 billion

**Major export trading partners:** US 23.9%, United Arab Emirates 7.4%, UK 6.6%, Germany 5.2%, Hong Kong 5.1%

**Major imports:** machinery, chemicals, minerals, fuels

**Imports of goods and services:** $11.4 billion

**Major import trading partners:** United Arab Emirates 13.1%, Saudi Arabia 11.3%, Kuwait 6.7%, US 5.8%, Japan 5.3%

**Foreign direct investment (net):** $317.4 million

2001 Data (in constant 1995 US dollars)

I n 2002, after governing as self-appointed president for two years, General Pervez Musharraf handed the government over to civilian rule but maintained his position as head of state. The current ruling coalition in parliament is broad and holds a tenuous majority, so populist policies have begun to dilute the government's previous economic reform agenda. In 2002, the economy enjoyed its best performance in three years, meeting the government's official GDP growth target of 4.5 percent. This was largely due to decent agricultural growth; an impressive export sector, particularly in textiles and cotton; and stronger than average remittances from overseas workers. The Karachi Stock Market was also among the best performers, growing by almost 110 percent. All this has given the government enough political capital to restart a flagging privatization program by offering initial public offerings for two major energy firms and selling additional shares of several state-owned enterprises. Because of excessive government intervention into the economy, however, Pakistan continues to forgo enormous economic opportunities. Infrastructure remains abysmal; Pakistan's telephone line-to-user ratio is below the Asian average, and the exorbitant price of electricity reflects the inefficiency of chronically overstaffed state firms. Most important, the continued presence and political influence of anti-Western terrorist groups continue to deter investors. Pakistan's banking and finance score is 1 point worse this year; however, its fiscal burden of government score is 0.4 point better, and its monetary policy score is 1 point better. As a result, Pakistan's overall score is 0.04 point better this year.

### TRADE POLICY
### Score: **5**–Stable (very high level of protectionism)

According to the World Bank, Pakistan's weighted average tariff rate in 2001 (the most recent year for which World Bank data are available) was 14.7 percent. The U.S. Department of State reports that non-tariff barriers include extraneous fees, discriminatory treatment of imported goods, and arbitrary application of customs tariffs. Local content requirements, according to the Economist Intelligence Unit, also act as a non-tariff barrier.

### FISCAL BURDEN OF GOVERNMENT
Score—Income Taxation: **3.5**–Stable (high tax rates)
Score—Corporate Taxation: **5**–Stable (very high tax rates)
Score—Change in Government Expenditures: **2.5**–Better (low decrease)
### Final Score: **4**–Better (high cost of government)

Pakistan's top income tax rate is 35 percent. Ernst and Young reports that the corporate tax rate is 43 percent, down from the 45 percent reported in the 2003 *Index*. Government expenditures as a share of GDP decreased 1.4 percentage points to 21.8 percent in 2001, compared to a 1.2 percentage point increase in 2000. As a result, Pakistan's fiscal burden of government score is 0.4 point better this year.

### GOVERNMENT INTERVENTION IN THE ECONOMY
### Score: **3**–Stable (moderate level)

The World Bank reports that the government consumed 10.3 percent of GDP in 2001. In the same year, according to the International Monetary Fund, Pakistan received 12.64 percent of its total revenues from state-owned enterprises and government ownership of property.

## MONETARY POLICY
### Score: **1–Better** (very low level of inflation)

From 1993 to 2002, Pakistan's weighted average annual rate of inflation was 2.37 percent, down from the 3.92 percent from 1992 to 2001 reported in the 2003 *Index.* As a result, Pakistan's monetary policy score is 1 point better this year.

## CAPITAL FLOWS AND FOREIGN INVESTMENT
### Score: **3–Stable** (moderate barriers)

The only formal restrictions on foreign investment involve defense production, banking, and broadcasting. Officially, domestic and foreign firms are accorded equal treatment. Foreign investment in real estate for business purposes is not restricted. The government favors foreign investments that use local content. The Economist Intelligence Unit reports that Pakistan has a "broad policy favouring the use of local content…. Instead of punishing firms for not meeting local-content goals (a rare occurrence in any event), the government plans to reward enterprises that attain targets for eliminating the use of imported components…." Unofficial barriers include inconsistent application of the law, corruption, and poor infrastructure. According to the Economist Intelligence Unit, "Investors remain discouraged by political instability, the military regime's strengthening hold on the central government, sectarian strife, weak infrastructure and high crime rates." The International Monetary Fund reports that foreign exchange accounts are subject to restrictions. Payments and transfers are subject to approval and some restrictions. Many capital transactions either are not permitted or require approval.

## BANKING AND FINANCE
### Score: **4–Worse** (high level of restrictions)

The government has privatized Allied Bank Limited and Muslim Commercial Bank but retains control of United Bank Ltd.; National Bank of Pakistan; and the country's largest bank, Habib Bank Ltd. The Economist Intelligence Unit reports that state banks account for the majority of deposits. In 2002, 44 banks were operating in Pakistan: 25 domestic and 19 foreign. According to Ernst and Young, banks are taxed at a rate of 47 percent (as opposed to a top corporate tax rate of 43 percent for private firms and 35 percent for public firms). The top rate for banks is scheduled to be reduced to 35 percent by 2007. According to the U.S. Department of State, the government "has pursued a policy of prescribing target levels of lending to certain sectors of the economy to ensure that priority sectors receive adequate credit. The credit targets apply only to state-owned banks." On June 24, 2002, the Supreme Court overturned its earlier ruling that all interest rates were to be outlawed. In July 2002, the central bank capped interest rates at a maximum of 8 percent. Based on evidence that the government dominates the banking system, affects the allocation of credit, and caps interest rates, Pakistan's banking and finance score is 1 point worse this year.

## WAGES AND PRICES
### Score: **3–Stable** (moderate level of intervention)

The government sets some prices and subsidizes some agricultural products. "Provincial and local authorities occasionally set the price of commodities perceived to be in short supply," reports the Economist Intelligence Unit, "and the government effectively fixes prices on locally manufactured goods granted tariff protection. The government fixes prices…for certain products of state-owned firms, including cars, petroleum, and public utilities. The government extends price support to farmers for certain crops (such as rice, cotton, sugarcane and wheat)…. Formal price controls for the private sector, however, are in place only for the pharmaceutical industry." A tripartite national wage council sets minimum wages that takes into account regional differences.

## PROPERTY RIGHTS
### Score: **4–Stable** (low level of protection)

The Economist Intelligence Unit reports that "Pakistan's Judiciary was completely separated from the executive in mid-2001, [but] the legal system still functions poorly, hampered by ineffective implementation of laws, poor security for judges and witnesses, delays in sentencing and a huge backlog of cases…. Investors often cite the laws relating to water and power, labour, food, agriculture and social security as particularly obstructive to private and foreign investment." According to the U.S. Department of State, the judiciary suffers from corruption.

## REGULATION
### Score: **3–Stable** (moderate level)

The government of Pakistan has made some effort to improve its business environment in recent years. The Economist Intelligence Unit reports that, "according to the new Investment Policy announced in mid-2001, official approval is not required for new manufacturing investments…." According to the U.S. Department of State, however, "Policy inconsistency, weak implementation and corruption have dampened investor interest and economic growth in Pakistan."

## INFORMAL MARKET
### Score: **4–Stable** (high level of activity)

Transparency International's 2002 score for Pakistan is 2.6. Therefore, Pakistan's informal market score is 4 this year.

# PANAMA

Rank: 58

Score: 2.83

Category: Mostly Free

**Present & Past Scores**

(Best) 1
2
3
4
(Worst) 5

2.70 2.60 2.54 2.45 2.43 2.56 2.58 2.68 2.59 **2.83**

'95 '96 '97 '98 '99 '00 '01 '02 '03 '04

## QUICK STUDY

### SCORES

| | |
|---|---|
| Trade Policy | 3 |
| Fiscal Burden | 3.8 |
| Government Intervention | 3.5 |
| Monetary Policy | 1 |
| Foreign Investment | 2 |
| Banking and Finance | 2 |
| Wages and Prices | 2 |
| Property Rights | 4 |
| Regulation | 3 |
| Informal Market | 4 |

**Population:** 2,900,589

**Total area:** 78,200 sq. km

**GDP:** $9.4 billion

**GDP growth rate:** 0.3%

**GDP per capita:** $3,243

**Major exports:** bananas, shrimp, sugar

**Exports of goods and services:** $3.3 billion

**Major export trading partners:** US 49.6%, Nicaragua 5.1%, Sweden 4.8%, Costa Rica 3.7%

**Major imports:** capital goods, food products, oil

**Imports of goods and services:** $3.7 billion

**Major import trading partners:** US 32.9%, Ecuador 7.9%, Colombia 5.7%, Mexico 3.9%

**Foreign direct investment (net):** $460 million

2001 Data (in constant 1995 US dollars)

Panama's economy is sustained primarily by an established services sector and international banking, although it depends in part on traffic passing through the Canal and on traditional rural agriculture. Economic growth over the past year has been lackluster and is not likely to improve. Foreign investors are increasingly wary of Panama's weak justice system, which is perceived as serving insider elites and being seriously clogged with cases. There are few adequately trained prosecutors and police investigators relative to the amount of crime. The administration of President Lireya Moscoso has never developed a sound economic development plan in the wake of the U.S. withdrawal. Reverted properties from U.S. military bases still languish. Meanwhile, the Canal watershed remains under assault from encroaching migrant farmers, deforestation, and agricultural and industrial pollution. For the Canal to remain viable, it must expand to accommodate today's larger ships. Violence from Colombia spills into Panama's depopulated Darien region, which has become a transit point for arms and narcotics shipments, an entry point for Colombian refugees, and a hideout for narcoterrorists temporarily fleeing Colombian security forces. Although Panama's socioeconomic indicators are higher than those of most other countries in Latin America, they mask growing poverty and unemployment. Panama's fiscal burden of government score is 0.4 point worse this year; in addition, its government intervention and informal market scores are 0.5 point worse, and its banking and finance score is 1 point worse. As a result, Panama's overall score is 0.24 point worse this year.

 ## TRADE POLICY
### Score: **3**–Stable (moderate level of protectionism)

According to the World Bank, Panama's weighted average tariff rate in 2001 (the most recent year for which World Bank data are available) was 7.1 percent. The U.S. Department of State reports that "Panama continues to obstruct agriculture imports via a slow and arbitrary procedure for issuing phytosanitary permits." In addition, "The Government has erected substantial non-tariff barriers for certain agricultural products including chicken, beef, and some produce and dairy products."

 ## FISCAL BURDEN OF GOVERNMENT
### Score—Income Taxation: **3**–Stable (moderate tax rates)
### Score—Corporate Taxation: **4**–Stable (high tax rates)
### Score—Change in Government Expenditures: **4**–Worse (moderate increase)
### Final Score: **3.8**–Worse (high cost of government)

Panama's top income tax rate is 30 percent. The top corporate tax rate is 30 percent. Government expenditures as a share of GDP increased 1.1 percentage points to 28 percent in 2001, compared to a 1 percentage point decrease in 2000. As a result, Panama's fiscal burden of government score is 0.4 point worse this year.

 ## GOVERNMENT INTERVENTION IN THE ECONOMY
### Score: **3.5**–Worse (high level)

The World Bank reports that the government consumed 15.1 percent of GDP in 2001. In 2000, according to the International Monetary Fund, Panama received 21.09 percent of its total revenues from state-owned enterprises and government ownership of property, up from the

18.49 percent reported in the 2003 *Index*. As a result, Panama's government intervention score is 0.5 point worse this year.

## MONETARY POLICY
### Score: **1**–Stable (very low level of inflation)

Between 1993 and 2002, Panama's weighted average annual rate of inflation was 0.87 percent, primarily because Panama has used the U.S. dollar as its currency since 1904.

## CAPITAL FLOWS AND FOREIGN INVESTMENT
### Score: **2**–Stable (low barriers)

Most sectors of the economy are open to foreign investment, although there are a few restrictions on retail trade, media, and some services, and some professions (such as doctors, certain types of lawyers, and custom brokers) are reserved for Panamanian citizens. Foreign investors have been able to acquire state-owned firms put up for privatization. The International Monetary Fund reports that both residents and non-residents may hold foreign exchange accounts; there are no restrictions or controls on payments, transactions, transfers, or repatriation of profits. Non-residents may purchase real estate except within 10 kilometers of a national border or an island.

## BANKING AND FINANCE
### Score: **2**–Worse (low level of restrictions)

Domestic banking competition is relatively high, and major banks from all over the world are represented. In October 2002, 80 banks were operating in Panama. Offshore banking in the International Banking Center is significant and subject to little financial regulation. Foreign and domestic banks are treated equally. The government issues three types of licenses that determine which services each bank may offer. Domestic banks are permitted to engage in a broad range of services. There are few restrictions on opening banks, and the government exercises little control over the allocation of credit. A 1998 banking reform law further modernized the banking system by requiring banks to adopt international standards and open their books to international auditing firms. This was followed in July 1999 by a law regulating the securities market. Panama does not have a central bank, but the state-owned Banco Nacional de Panama—the largest commercial bank—performs some of the functions of a central bank. The government also owns three other banks. The Economist Intelligence Unit reports that privatization of these banks is unlikely in the near future. Based on the evidence of government involvement in the banking sector, Panama's banking and finance score is 1 point worse this year.

## WAGES AND PRICES
### Score: **2**–Stable (low level of intervention)

The market sets most wages and prices. According to the Economist Intelligence Unit, "The law limits price regulation to those instances where monopolistic practices can be demonstrated to do direct or imminent damage to consumers…. Price regulation is applied only to cooking gas and to medicines…. Rent control, enforced by the Ministry of Housing, applies to residential units renting for less than US$150 per month." The government also imposes a minimum wage that is reviewed every two years.

## PROPERTY RIGHTS
### Score: **4**–Stable (low level of protection)

Panama's constitution provides for an independent judiciary, but the judicial system is inefficient and subject to corruption. The Economist Intelligence Unit reports that "Panama continues to have problems with the judiciary and civil service, which still lack independence and have traditionally been plagued with corruption and scandals."

## REGULATION
### Score: **3**–Stable (moderate level)

Regulations in Panama are generally transparent, but businesses can be hampered by red tape. According to the Economist Intelligence Unit, "since coming to power in 1999 the Moscoso government has made no progress in reducing the red tape that imposes heavy costs on business…. It has done nothing to improve customs services, procurement processes and the regulatory environment, or to modernize the labour code." Labor laws are generally more rigid than in neighboring countries. The EIU reports that "dismissing workers can be difficult, as it often requires permission from the labour ministry…." Corruption is a continuing problem; according to the U.S. Department of State, companies complain that corruption in Panama is a "nuisance" obstacle to doing business.

## INFORMAL MARKET
### Score: **4**–Worse (high level of activity)

Transparency International's 2001 score for Panama is 3. Therefore, Panama's informal market score is 4 this year—0.5 point worse than last year.

PARAGUAY

# PARAGUAY

Rank: 106

Score: 3.39

Category: Mostly Unfree

Present & Past Scores

(Best) 1
2
3
4
(Worst) 5

2.94 2.89 2.91 3.04 3.00 3.01 3.39 3.28 3.40 3.39

'95 '96 '97 '98 '99 '00 '01 '02 '03 '04

## QUICK STUDY

### SCORES

| | |
|---|---|
| Trade Policy | 3 |
| Fiscal Burden | 3.4 |
| Government Intervention | 3 |
| Monetary Policy | 3 |
| Foreign Investment | 3 |
| Banking and Finance | 3 |
| Wages and Prices | 3 |
| Property Rights | 4 |
| Regulation | 4 |
| Informal Market | 4.5 |

**Population:** 5,635,620

**Total area:** 406,750 sq. km

**GDP:** $9.6 billion

**GDP growth rate:** 2.7%

**GDP per capita:** $1,703

**Major exports:** soybeans, cotton, meat, electricity

**Exports of goods and services:** $1.2 billion

**Major export trading partners:** Brazil 37.2%, Uruguay 17.1%, Argentina 3.6%

**Major imports:** vehicles, tobacco, petroleum products

**Imports of goods and services:** $2.5 billion

**Major import trading partners:** Brazil 32.2%, Argentina 20.0%, Uruguay 4.3%

**Foreign direct investment (net):** $130.9 million

2001 Data (in constant 1995 US dollars)

Although the Partido Colorado has ruled since 1947, Paraguay has been freely electing presidents and national representatives since the fall of dictator Alfredo Stroessner some 14 years ago. The government generally respects human rights, protects freedom of speech, and has made steady improvements in its judicial system. Initial democratic reforms have not been enough to overcome poverty and corruption, however. Most workers are subsistence farmers, and dependence on trade with Argentina and Brazil through MERCOSUR has left Paraguay vulnerable to the economic woes of those two countries. Elected by a comfortable margin on April 27, 2003, President Nicanor Duarte Frutos has promised to renegotiate external debt, trim wasteful spending, and bring together opponents in a national dialogue. His predecessor, Luis González Macchi, presided over a stagnant economy and—accused of embezzling funds and buying a stolen car—narrowly escaped removal by the Paraguayan congress near the end of his term. Reliance on short-term loans has increased Paraguay's indebtedness, and growing disenchantment with democracy and liberal markets could pave the way for a return of unsuccessful coup leader General Lino Oviedo, now living in Brazil. Paraguay's fiscal burden of government score is 0.4 point worse this year; however, its informal market score is 0.5 point better. As a result, Paraguay's overall score is 0.01 point better this year.

###  TRADE POLICY
#### Score: 3–Stable (moderate level of protectionism)

As a member of the Southern Cone Common Market (MERCOSUR), Paraguay adheres to a common external tariff that ranges from zero to 23 percent. According to the World Bank, Paraguay's weighted average tariff rate in 2001 (the most recent year for which World Bank data are available) was 12.6 percent. The government maintains no major non-tariff barriers, although it has erected barriers to some agricultural imports such as poultry.

### FISCAL BURDEN OF GOVERNMENT
Score—Income Taxation: **1**–Stable (very low tax rates)
Score—Corporate Taxation: **4**–Stable (high tax rates)
Score—Change in Government Expenditures: **4.5**–Worse (high increase)
#### Final Score: **3.4**–Worse (moderate cost of government)

Paraguay imposes no taxes on income derived from personal work, services provided, or professional services rendered. (The government levies a 30 percent tax on individuals engaged in sole proprietorship, but the impact of this tax is negligible.) The top corporate tax rate is 30 percent. Government expenditures as a share of GDP increased 3 percentage points to 18.5 percent in 2001, compared to a 0.5 percentage point decrease in 2000. As a result, Paraguay's fiscal burden of government score is 0.4 point worse this year.

###  GOVERNMENT INTERVENTION IN THE ECONOMY
#### Score: **3**–Stable (moderate level)

The World Bank reports that the government consumed 9.1 percent of GDP in 2001. In the same year, according to the International Monetary Fund, Paraguay received 27.74 percent of its total revenues from state-owned enterprises and government ownership of property.

325

## MONETARY POLICY
### Score: **3**–Stable (moderate level of inflation)

From 1993 to 2002, Paraguay's weighted average annual rate of inflation was 9.51 percent.

## CAPITAL FLOWS AND FOREIGN INVESTMENT
### Score: **3**–Stable (moderate barriers)

According to the U.S. Department of State, "There are no formal restrictions [on] foreign investment in Paraguay. National treatment of foreign investors is guaranteed, as is full repatriation of capital and profits." Other factors, however, such as the lack of property rights protection and the existence of many government-controlled sectors, impede foreign investment. Foreign investors also still face widespread corruption, bureaucracy, and a lack of transparency. "Government efforts to attract foreign investment through privatization have progressed slowly," reports the U.S. Department of State, "because of residual political opposition and uncertainty about the transparency of the process." The International Monetary Fund reports that both residents and non-residents may hold foreign exchange accounts. Most payments and transfers are permitted. Capital transactions are subject to minimal restrictions.

## BANKING AND FINANCE
### Score: **3**–Stable (moderate level of restrictions)

The banking system remains weak and poorly supervised, and private banks tend to invest abroad rather than in Paraguay. Bank Aleman, the country's third largest bank, collapsed in June 2002, and Multibanco collapsed in April 2003. In both cases, the central bank intervened with infusions of cash to cover small depositors. Non-performing loans constitute 48 percent of the state-owned Banco Nacional de Fomento's total loan portfolio. According to the Economist Intelligence Unit, wholly foreign-owned banks account for over 50 percent of deposits in Paraguay, while majority-owned foreign banks account for another 25 percent. Efforts to merge, reform, or close public-sector banks have met political resistance; this is also a financially difficult issue, as the expense of absorbing large amounts of non-performing loans will be steep. There were 19 banks operating in Paraguay as of June 2003.

## WAGES AND PRICES
### Score: **3**–Stable (moderate level of intervention)

The market sets most prices, but the Economist Intelligence Unit reports that the government controls the price of fuel. The government also affects prices through state-owned enterprises in the rail, petroleum, cement, electricity, water, and telephone sectors (among others) and heavily subsidizes the cotton sector. According to the EIU, "Output prospects this season have been boosted by the government's decision to provide growers with free seed and insecticide, which

together account for 30% of production costs." The Ministry of Justice and Labor sets a private-sector minimum wage.

## PROPERTY RIGHTS
### Score: **4**–Stable (low level of protection)

Expropriation of property is still possible. According to the U.S. Department of State, "Increasing pressure by peasants for land has led to invasions of rural properties and expropriations by the government." The judiciary is corrupt, and property protection is extremely weak. *The New York Times* reports, for example, that "Nintendo brought 36 cases in Paraguayan courts over counterfeiting or smuggling of its goods. None have been resolved yet." The U.S. Department of State reports that "judges are often pressured by politicians and other persons whose interests are at stake…. There is little confidence in the legal system because cases routinely take several years, even as long as a decade, to resolve and because accusations of undue influence on judges are widespread."

## REGULATION
### Score: **4**–Stable (high level)

According to the U.S. Department of State, "Institutionalized corruption is…a significant barrier to investment." In addition, "The Civil Code and law 1,034/83 regulate business and industrial activities…. Under the existing framework, the Ministry of Industry and Commerce is charged with overall industrial policy coordination; the Ministry of Finance handles tax and fiscal policy; and the Central Bank is the principal coordinator of monetary policy." Any would-be business must register with three different agencies in a duplicative process that frequently takes months to conclude.

## INFORMAL MARKET
### Score: **4.5**–Better (very high level of activity)

Transparency International's 2002 score for Paraguay is 1.7. Therefore, Paraguay's informal market score is 4.5 this year— 0.5 point better than last year.

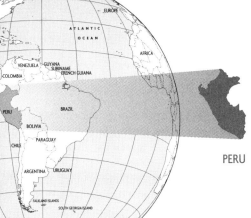

# PERU

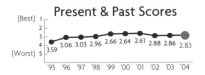

PERU

Rank: 58

Score: 2.83

Category: Mostly Free

## QUICK STUDY

### SCORES

| | |
|---|---|
| Trade Policy | 4 |
| Fiscal Burden | 3.3 |
| Government Intervention | 2.5 |
| Monetary Policy | 1 |
| Foreign Investment | 2 |
| Banking and Finance | 2 |
| Wages and Prices | 2 |
| Property Rights | 4 |
| Regulation | 4 |
| Informal Market | 3.5 |

**Population:** 26,347,990

**Total area:** 1,285,220 sq. km

**GDP:** $60.9 billion

**GDP growth rate:** 0.2%

**GDP per capita:** $2,311

**Major exports:** gold, copper, fish products, petroleum

**Exports of goods and services:** $10.8 billion

**Major export trading partners:** US 25.2%, Switzerland 8.0%, China 6.3%, Japan 5.6%

**Major imports:** transport equipment, machinery, foodstuffs, chemicals

**Imports of goods and services:** $10 billion

**Major import trading partners:** US 23.9%, Chile 8.2%, Colombia 5.8%, Venezuela 5.8%

**Foreign direct investment (net):** $901 million

2001 Data (in constant 1995 US dollars)

Since November 2002, when autocratic President Alberto Fujimori resigned in disgrace, Peru has made a remarkable comeback in rebuilding democratic institutions and promoting a more market-based economy. Economist Alejandro Toledo won the presidency in 2001 in elections that were largely free and fair. Since then, devolution of authority from the national government to district and local levels, reduction of corruption, adoption of a bicameral legislature, and pursuit of free trade with the United States and Mexico have dominated national politics. Over the past year, the economy grew by close to 5 percent, making Peru one of the few South American countries to have a positive growth rate. Per capita income growth, however, remains stagnant at close to 1967 levels, and although President Toledo's ongoing reforms have proved successful, discontented farmers, teachers, and health workers have rocked Peru with a series of strikes. Meanwhile, the Shining Path guerrillas—once nearly defeated after the 1993 capture of their leader, Abimael Guzmán—have reappeared in the Upper Huallaga and Apurímac River valleys as well as other locations. Instead of marauding and pillaging rural communities as they once did, they pay for supplies with drug money and try to portray themselves as friends of rural inhabitants while claiming that the government is the real enemy. Peru's fiscal burden of government score is 0.3 point better this year. As a result, its overall score is 0.03 point better this year.

## TRADE POLICY
### Score: **4**–Stable (high level of protectionism)

The World Bank reports that Peru's weighted average tariff rate in 2001 (the most recent year for which World Bank data are available) was 12.6 percent. According to the U.S. Trade Representative, "the government maintains some 'temporary' tariff surcharges on agricultural goods in an effort to protect local production...." The government also bans imports of "several insecticides, fireworks, used clothing, used shoes, used tires, radioactive waste, cars over five years old, and trucks over eight years old."

## FISCAL BURDEN OF GOVERNMENT
### Score—Income Taxation: **2.5**–Stable (moderate tax rates)
### Score—Corporate Taxation: **4**–Stable (high tax rates)
### Score—Change in Government Expenditures: **2.5**–Better (low decrease)
### Final Score: **3.3**–Better (moderate cost of government)

According to the Peruvian Embassy, Peru's top income tax rate is 27 percent. The corporate tax rate is 27 percent plus a 4.1 percent additional tax on distributed earnings, resulting in a potential corporate tax of 31.1 percent. Government expenditures as a share of GDP decreased 1 percentage point to 18.3 percent in 2001, compared to a 2 percentage point increase in 2000. As a result, Peru's fiscal burden of government score is 0.2 point better this year.

## GOVERNMENT INTERVENTION IN THE ECONOMY
### Score: **2.5**–Stable (moderate level)

The World Bank reports that the government consumed 11.2 percent of GDP in 2001. In the same year, according to the International Monetary Fund, Peru received 5.06 percent of its total revenues from state-owned enterprises and government ownership of property.

327

## MONETARY POLICY
### Score: **1**–Stable (very low level of inflation)

From 1993 to 2002, Peru's weighted average annual rate of inflation was 1.17 percent.

## CAPITAL FLOWS AND FOREIGN INVESTMENT
### Score: **2**–Stable (low barriers)

Foreign investment in Peru is welcomed and encouraged. Equal treatment for foreign and domestic investors is mandated by law, as is automatic investment approval, except in the media and defense sectors. The government has eliminated controls on capital flows, and there are no local content requirements. Foreign ownership of land or water within 50km of the country's borders is prohibited unless the government grants an exception. The International Monetary Fund reports that both residents and non-residents may hold foreign exchange accounts. There are no restrictions or controls on payments, transactions, transfers, or repatriation of profits. Foreign investors must register with the National Commission on Foreign Investment and Technology to guarantee the repatriation of profits, capital, and royalties. Peruvian law limits foreign employees to 20 percent of the workforce and no more than 30 percent of the payroll, but there are numerous exemptions.

## BANKING AND FINANCE
### Score: **2**–Stable (low level of restrictions)

The 1991 Law of Banks, modified in 1996, established a non-discriminatory policy toward foreign banks, opened the country to foreign banks and insurance companies, established capital requirements, and strengthened prudential standards and disclosure requirements. The government has liberalized the banking sector and has privatized most state-owned banks. As of mid-2002, there were 15 commercial banks, 11 of them majority foreign-owned. The government owns two banks: Banco de la Nacion, a deposit-taking bank, and COFIDE, a development bank. In February 1999, the Peruvian Congress passed a law establishing a fund to guarantee deposits in private and corporate savings accounts.

## WAGES AND PRICES
### Score: **2**–Stable (low level of intervention)

The market determines most wages and prices. According to the Economist Intelligence Unit, "Most price controls have been eliminated, including those on fuel (though the government still controls prices set by the state oil company, PetroPerú, which can in turn affect market prices). Different regulatory agencies must approve rate hikes on electricity and telephone calls. Price controls on public water were supposed to be eliminated once the state facilities providing such services were privatised…but the government has held off on water concessions." Peru maintains a minimum wage.

## PROPERTY RIGHTS
### Score: **4**–Stable (low level of protection)

The government does not protect private property effectively. The Economist Intelligence Unit reports that "the justice system is rebuilding after years of intervention during the Fujimori administration." According to the U.S. Department of State, "The judicial branch is antiquated and rife with corruption." The government of Alejandro Toledo has yet to address this problem.

## REGULATION
### Score: **4**–Stable (high level)

Peru remains plagued by an inefficient bureaucracy. According to the U.S. Department of State, "Various procedures—such as obtaining building licenses or certificates of occupancy—require many steps to carry out, and information on necessary procedures is often difficult to obtain. Business people often complain of excessive government red tape…. Peruvian business organizations allege that high government-imposed costs impede investment." In addition, "corruption is a major factor influencing the business climate." The last labor reform, passed in February 2002, increased the labor market's rigidity.

## INFORMAL MARKET
### Score: **3.5**–Stable (high level of activity)

Transparency International's 2001 score for Peru is 4. Therefore, Peru's informal market score is 3.5 this year.

# THE PHILIPPINES

PHILIPPINES

Rank: 74

Score: 3.05

Category: Mostly Unfree

### Present & Past Scores

(Best) 1
2
3
4
(Worst) 5

3.35  3.14  3.06  2.84  2.98  3.00  3.16  3.05  2.95  3.05

'95  '96  '97  '98  '99  '00  '01  '02  '03  '04

## QUICK STUDY

### SCORES

| | |
|---|---|
| Trade Policy | 2 |
| Fiscal Burden | 3.5 |
| Government Intervention | 2 |
| Monetary Policy | 2 |
| Foreign Investment | 3 |
| Banking and Finance | 3 |
| Wages and Prices | 3 |
| Property Rights | 4 |
| Regulation | 4 |
| Informal Market | 4 |

**Population:** 78,317,032

**Total area:** 300,000 sq. km

**GDP:** $91 billion

**GDP growth rate:** 3.4%

**GDP per capita:** $1,165

**Major exports:** electrical and electronic equipment, machinery and transport equipment, garments, and chemicals

**Exports of goods and services:** $33.9 billion

**Major export trading partners:** US 27.9%, EU 19.3%, Japan 15.7%, Netherlands 9.3%, Singapore 7.2%

**Major imports:** semi-processed raw materials, telecommunications equipment, petroleum

**Imports of goods and services:** $37.6 billion

**Major import trading partners:** Japan 20.6%, US 16.9%, EU 9.3%, South Korea 6.6%

**Foreign direct investment (net):** $1.5 billion

2001 Data (in constant 1995 US dollars)

Philippine President Gloria Macapagal Arroyo describes her country as "the oldest democracy in Asia" but also "one of the weakest." Despite an attempt to depoliticize her final two years in office by announcing that she would not run for president in 2004, a divided polity and a lack of political imagination have prevented President Arroyo from launching needed economic reform. The government has delayed scheduled tariff reductions for 2,000 products, including garments, steel, and agricultural goods, and has only narrowly avoided international sanctions for inadequate measures against money laundering. The biggest economic concern is the nearly historic budget deficit, which crashed through three successive targets before settling at 5.3 percent of GDP. As a result, the government had to issue treasury bonds, which kept lending rates from being competitive with the rest of Asia. Government overspending and widespread tax evasion are considered the causes of this massive deficit. The violent radical Muslim insurgency in the south, which spawned several terrorist groups that have peppered the country with terrorist bombings, continues to deter tourists and investors. Through all this, the economy managed to grow by 3.4 percent in 2001, largely on the strength of the agricultural sector and decent export profits. The Philippines' property rights score is 1 point worse this year. As a result, its overall score is 0.1 point worse this year, causing the Philippines to be classified as "mostly unfree."

### TRADE POLICY
Score: **2**–Stable (low level of protectionism)

According to the World Bank, the Philippines' weighted average tariff rate in 2001 (the most recent year for which World Bank data are available) was 4 percent. The Economist Intelligence Unit reports that "the National Food Authority (NFA) remains the sole importer of ordinary rice and continues to be involved in imports of maize…. In addition, 15 tariff lines of agricultural commodities…are now subject to minimum access volume tariff rate quotas…." Private importers of "fancy" rice need an Import Clearance before importing. According to the EIU, "importers have complained that processing of import shipments [was] delayed on a number of occasions by disputes over the valuation of goods."

### FISCAL BURDEN OF GOVERNMENT
Score—Income Taxation: **3**–Stable (moderate tax rates)
Score—Corporate Taxation: **4**–Stable (high tax rates)
Score—Change in Government Expenditures: **3**–Stable (very low decrease)
Final Score: **3.5**–Stable (high cost of government)

The Philippines' top income tax rate is 32 percent. The top corporate tax rate is also 32 percent. Government expenditures as a share of GDP decreased slightly less in 2001 (0.1 percentage point to 19.4 percent) than they did in 2000 (0.3 percentage point). On net, the Philippines' fiscal burden of government score is unchanged this year.

### GOVERNMENT INTERVENTION IN THE ECONOMY
Score: **2**–Stable (low level)

The World Bank reports that the government consumed 12.2 percent of GDP in 2001. In the same year, according to the International Monetary Fund, the Philippines received 4.53 percent of its total revenues from state-owned enterprises and government ownership of property.

329

## MONETARY POLICY
### Score: **2**–Stable (low level of inflation)

From 1993 to 2002, the Philippines' weighted average annual rate of inflation was 4.12 percent.

## CAPITAL FLOWS AND FOREIGN INVESTMENT
### Score: **3**–Stable (moderate barriers)

The Philippines maintains barriers to many foreign investments. Either 100 percent or majority Filipino ownership is required in over 25 specified industries, including mass media, retail trade, most professional services, use of marine resources, weapons, advertising, public utilities, commercial fishing, most manufacturing, and development of natural resources. Foreign equity in real estate is limited to 40 percent and is subject to provisions in the constitution. According to the U.S. Department of State, "Kidnappings and violence by separatist bandits and communist guerrillas throughout the archipelago... have driven away potential investors across all sectors...." The International Monetary Fund reports that both residents and non-residents may hold foreign exchange accounts, although non-residents may do so only with foreign currency deposits or proceeds from conversions of property in the Philippines. Payments, transactions, and transfers are subject to numerous restrictions, controls, quantitative limits, and authorizations.

## BANKING AND FINANCE
### Score: **3**–Stable (moderate level of restrictions)

The banking sector is weak and is still trying to recover from the 50 percent devaluation in the Philippine peso in 1997 and non-performing loans that, according to the U.S. Department of State, have "ballooned by 474.5% from the mid-1997 level to equal 13.8% of total banking sector assets [as of March 2003]." A law passed in January 2003 encourages the establishment of private asset-management companies to dispose of non-performing loans and allows banks to write off their losses on these debts against their taxes. The General Banking Law of 2000 allows an unlimited number of foreign banks to fully own domestic banks until May 2007 (after which foreign investments will be limited to a 60 percent stake). As of December 2001, the banking sector included 43 commercial banks, 17 of them foreign-controlled. The Embassy of the Philippines reports that the government wholly owns three banks and partially owns two banks. The banking system still suffers from insufficient supervision and periodic government intervention.

## WAGES AND PRICES
### Score: **3**–Stable (moderate level of intervention)

The market sets most wages and prices, but the Economist Intelligence Unit reports that the government controls or influences the price of "electricity distribution, water, telephone charges, public-transport fares, port charges and road tolls." In addition, "The president can also impose price con-

trols to check inflation or ease social tension." The Embassy of the Philippines reports that the government regulates the prices of "basic necessities" (primarily food items and basic household items) and "prime necessities" (primarily fruits, meats, and basic household items). The Philippine Wage Rationalization Act created regional tripartite (government, labor, and employer) wage and productivity boards to fix minimum wages—enforced by fines and jail sentences—for regions, provinces, or industries.

## PROPERTY RIGHTS
### Score: **4**–Worse (low level of protection)

The Economist Intelligence Unit reports that "the country has a slow judicial system, hampered by lack of funding and an insufficient number of judges to handle court cases. The courts are therefore ill suited to cope with the proliferating corporate disputes involving multinational firms and their local partners." The EIU also reports that the Supreme Court recently "upheld the government's cancellation of two major contracts." According to the U.S. Department of State, "The judiciary is independent, but suffers from inefficiency and corruption.... The court system remains susceptible to the influence of the wealthy and powerful." In addition, "both foreign and domestic investors have expressed concern about the propensity of courts to issue temporary restraining orders and to stray beyond matters of legal interpretation into policymaking functions." Based on increasing evidence of weak protection of property rights, the Philippines' property rights score is 1 point worse this year.

## REGULATION
### Score: **4**–Stable (high level)

The Philippine government's regulatory agencies lack transparency, and regulations are enforced haphazardly. The U.S. Department of State reports that "investors find business registration, customs, immigration, and visa procedures in the Philippines burdensome and a source of frustration. Some agencies (such as the Securities and Exchange Commission, Board of Investment, Department of Foreign Affairs) have established express lanes or 'one-stop shops' to reduce bureaucratic delays, with varying degrees of success...." Labor laws are somewhat rigid. According to the Economist Intelligence Unit, "regulations require that the Department of Labour and Employment be given a one-month notice of the termination of employee services." Corruption continues up to the highest levels of government. The U.S. Department of State reports that corruption in the bureaucracy is extensive.

## INFORMAL MARKET
### Score: **4**–Stable (high level of activity)

Transparency International's 2002 score for the Philippines is 2.6. Therefore, the Philippines' informal market score is 4 this year.

POLAND

# POLAND

Rank: 56

Score: 2.81

Category: Mostly Free

Present & Past Scores

(Best) 1
2
3
4
(Worst) 5

3.46 3.24 3.09 2.91 2.83 2.84 2.64 2.60 2.83 **2.81**

'95 '96 '97 '98 '99 '00 '01 '02 '03 '04

## QUICK STUDY

### SCORES

| | |
|---|---|
| Trade Policy | 3 |
| Fiscal Burden | 3.6 |
| Government Intervention | 2 |
| Monetary Policy | 2 |
| Foreign Investment | 3 |
| Banking and Finance | 2 |
| Wages and Prices | 3 |
| Property Rights | 3 |
| Regulation | 3 |
| Informal Market | 3.5 |

**Population:** 38,610,000

**Total area:** 312,685 sq. km

**GDP:** $166.8 billion

**GDP growth rate:** 1.3%

**GDP per capita:** $4,320

**Major exports:** machinery and transport equipment, miscellaneous manufactured goods, food and live animals

**Exports of goods and services:** $55.8 billion

**Major export trading partners:** Germany 34.4%, France 5.4%, Italy 5.4%, UK 5.0%

**Major imports:** machinery and transport equipment, mineral fuels and lubricants, chemicals

**Imports of goods and services:** $56.9 billion

**Major import trading partners:** Germany 23.9%, Russia 8.8%, Italy 8.2%, France 6.8%

**Foreign direct investment (net):** $7.9 billion

2002 Data (in constant 1995 US dollars)

At the beginning of the 1990s, Poland became the first country in post-communist Europe to embrace rapid economic liberalization—a goal implemented by both center–right and center–left governments. Years of economic transformation have led to deep structural change and have made Poland's economy one of the most successful and open in Central Europe. Banking has been almost completely privatized, with foreign institutions owning 70 percent of total assets. Despite pressures from the Union of Labor and the Peasants Party (populist coalition partners in the ruling Democratic Left Alliance) to loosen monetary policies, the government has maintained its commitment to monetary discipline. The government's ambitious program to return the country to a path of sustained economic growth, announced in October 2001, is focused on three major components: job creation for young professionals, support of medium and small enterprises, and infrastructure development. Exports depend largely on European Union markets; Germany alone accounted for nearly 35 percent of exports in 2001. Therefore, joining the EU has become the overall political and economic priority for Poland, which is also a member of the World Trade Organization and NATO. In June 2003, Poles voted in a referendum to join the EU. Poland's property rights score is 1 point worse this year; however, its fiscal burden of government score is 0.2 point better, and its monetary policy score is 1 point better. As a result, Poland's overall score is 0.02 point better this year.

## TRADE POLICY
### Score: 3–Stable (moderate level of protectionism)

According to the World Bank, Poland's weighted average tariff rate in 2000 (the most recent year for which World Bank data are available) was 7.3 percent. The government maintains non-tariff barriers through its issuance of import permits on a growing number of products. The U.S. Department of State reports that these permit requirements "hamper import prospects for certain bulk products that might otherwise be shipped in larger quantities on ocean-going vessels."

## FISCAL BURDEN OF GOVERNMENT
Score—Income Taxation: **4**–Stable (high tax rates)
Score—Corporate Taxation: **3.5**–Stable (high tax rates)
Score—Change in Government Expenditures: **3.5**–Better (low increase)
### Final Score: **3.6**–Better (high cost of government)

Poland's top income tax rate is 40 percent. The top corporate tax rate is 27 percent, down from the 28 percent reported in the 2003 *Index*, and is scheduled to fall to 24 percent in 2004. Government expenditures as a share of GDP increased less in 2002 (0.8 percentage point to 43.2 percent) than they did in 2001 (1.7 percentage points). As a result, Poland's fiscal burden of government score is 0.2 point better this year.

## GOVERNMENT INTERVENTION IN THE ECONOMY
### Score: **2**–Stable (low level)

Based on data from the Organisation for Economic Co-operation and Development, the government consumed 15 percent of GDP in 2002. In 2001, according to the International Monetary Fund, Poland received 3.96 percent of its total revenues from state-owned enterprises and government ownership of property.

331

## MONETARY POLICY
### Score: **2–Better** (low level of inflation)

From 1993 to 2002, Poland's weighted average annual rate of inflation was 3.82 percent, down from the 7.17 percent from 1992 to 2001 reported in the 2003 *Index.* As a result, Poland's monetary policy score is 1 point better this year.

## CAPITAL FLOWS AND FOREIGN INVESTMENT
### Score: **3–Stable** (moderate barriers)

Polish law allows 100 percent foreign ownership of domestic businesses with such notable exceptions as broadcasting, insurance, and aviation services. The government lifted the cap on foreign ownership of telecommunications on January 1, 2001. Foreign purchase of land over a set area requires government approval. According to the U.S. Department of State, foreign and domestic investors face considerable red tape. All public procurement bids must contain a 50 percent domestic material and labor content minimum clause, and the U.S. Department of State reports that foreign firms "face potential discrimination in public procurement contracts." The International Monetary Fund reports that both residents and non-residents may hold foreign exchange accounts, subject to certain restrictions. Payments, transactions, and transfers over a specified amount must be conducted through a domestic bank. Most capital transactions require foreign exchange permits or central bank approval.

## BANKING AND FINANCE
### Score: **2–Stable** (low level of restrictions)

Until the late 1980s, Poland's banking system was geared to supporting the state-run economy. The National Bank of Poland was established as the central bank in 1989 and oversaw the creation of nine independent regional banks, which subsequently were privatized and joined by a number of new private banks in the 1990s. The banking sector is now open and competitive. There are 83 private banks, and foreign banks account for 70 percent of assets. The Economist Intelligence Unit reports that the government retains control of four state-owned banks and intends to hold "a majority share in any sale involving PKO BP [the largest Polish bank], raising concerns that PKO BP will be used by the authorities to direct credit to chosen, 'strategic' sectors." Nevertheless, according to the U.S. Department of State, "The majority of Polish banks have been privatized.... The majority of the Polish banking sector's assets, deposits, and equity are in the hands of the private sector. Foreign companies do not have special restrictions on access to local finance as long as funds are used for activities in Poland." The insurance sector is still dominated by the communist-era monopoly provider, which is now partially privatized.

## WAGES AND PRICES
### Score: **3–Stable** (moderate level of intervention)

The government has removed a number of price controls but continues to influence the prices of some products. According to the Economist Intelligence Unit, "Official prices apply under the following conditions and products: (1) to goods or services when there are substantial threats to the proper functioning of the economy as specified by the Council of Ministers; (2) to pharmaceutical and medical materials that are covered by health insurance; and (3) to prices for taxi services.... [U]tility prices [are subject to] supervision if the provider is market dominating...." A mandated minimum wage is adjusted every three months through negotiations involving the government, the unions, and employers.

## PROPERTY RIGHTS
### Score: **3–Worse** (moderate level of protection)

The threat of expropriation is low, but recent corruption scandals have revealed serious weaknesses in Poland's judicial system. The transformation from communism to democracy, reports the *Financial Times,* did not guarantee that democratic institutions would function properly. "Institutions were imported from the west without making sure they could function. For example, the courts are nominally independent, but, in practice, underpaid officials are often subject to corrupt influences." According to the U.S. Department of State, "Many investors—foreign and domestic—complain about the slowness of the judicial system.... [I]nvestors often voice concern about frequent or unexpected issuance of or changes in laws and regulations." Based on new evidence of corruption in the judiciary, Poland's property rights score is 1 point worse this year.

## REGULATION
### Score: **3–Stable** (moderate level)

According to the U.S. Department of State, "The government acknowledges that its policies are not as transparent as they ought to be and that bureaucratic requirements continue to impose a burden on investors.... [U]neven and unpredictable regulatory treatment and a generally high level of administrative 'red tape' are recurring complaints of investors...." In addition, "investors must comply with a variety of laws concerning...taxation, labor practices, health and safety, and the environment. Complaints about these laws, especially the tax system, center on the lack of clarity and often-draconian penalties for minor errors."

## INFORMAL MARKET
### Score: **3.5–Stable** (high level of activity)

Transparency International's 2001 score for Poland is 4. Therefore, Poland's informal market score is 3.5 this year.

PORTUGAL

# PORTUGAL

Rank: 31

Score: 2.38

Category: Mostly Free

PORTUGAL

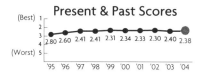

Present & Past Scores

(Best) 1
2
3
4
(Worst) 5

2.80 2.60 2.41 2.41 2.31 2.34 2.33 2.30 2.40 2.38

'95 '96 '97 '98 '99 '00 '01 '02 '03 '04

## QUICK STUDY

### SCORES

| | |
|---|---|
| Trade Policy | 2 |
| Fiscal Burden | 3.8 |
| Government Intervention | 2 |
| Monetary Policy | 2 |
| Foreign Investment | 2 |
| Banking and Finance | 3 |
| Wages and Prices | 2 |
| Property Rights | 2 |
| Regulation | 3 |
| Informal Market | 2 |

**Population:** 10,411,600

**Total area:** 92,391 sq. km

**GDP:** $132.5 billion

**GDP growth rate:** 0.5%

**GDP per capita:** $12,722

**Major exports:** machinery, clothing and footwear, chemicals

**Exports of goods and services:** $46.3 billion

**Major export trading partners:** Spain 20.2%, Germany 18.4%, France 12.6%, UK 10.5%, US 5.8%

**Major imports:** transport equipment, petroleum, textiles, agricultural products

**Imports of goods and services:** $59.1 billion

**Major import trading partners:** Spain 28.1%, Germany 15.0%, France 10.2%, Italy 6.5%, UK 5.2%, US 2.2%

**Foreign direct investment (net):** $752 million

2002 Data (in constant 1995 US dollars)

Upon winning a close parliamentary election in April 2002, Prime Minister Jose Durao Barroso, leader of a center–right coalition headed by his Social Democratic Party, found that the previous government, by overestimating tax revenues and underestimating public spending, had woefully understated Portugal's projected deficit at 2 percent of GDP: Unless the government acted immediately, the real deficit was likely to be a staggering 4.5 percent of GDP. Durao Barroso, against all odds, has not wavered in implementing the government's tough austerity program of deep spending cuts coupled with privatization of the government-owned telecommunications network. This has brought the deficit down to 2.8 percent of GDP, in line with the government's promises to meet the EU stability pact limit of 3 percent. Given the anemic growth rate in the wake of budget tightening, with growth reaching about 0.5 percent of GDP in 2002, it seems certain that further tough times lie ahead. However, this has not deterred the Portuguese government from pushing ahead with further reforms, such as a law passed in 2003 to curtail the power of local governments to increase government debt. The shock of Portugal's perilous economic situation has stimulated genuine and desperately needed economic liberalization. Portugal's fiscal burden of government score is 0.2 point better this year. As a result, its overall score is 0.02 point better this year.

## TRADE POLICY
### Score: **2–Stable** (low level of protectionism)

As a member of the European Union, in 2001 (the most recent year for which World Bank data are available), Portugal had a weighted average tariff rate of 2.6 percent. Portugal applies the same non-tariff barriers as the rest of the European Union, including quotas on certain products and dumping protection. Bureaucratic customs procedures also act as non-tariff barriers.

## FISCAL BURDEN OF GOVERNMENT
### Score—Income Taxation: **4–Stable** (high tax rates)
### Score—Corporate Taxation: **4–Stable** (high tax rates)
### Score—Change in Government Expenditures: **3–Better** (very low decrease)
### Final Score: **3.8–Better** (high cost of government)

Portugal's top income tax rate is 40 percent. The top corporate tax rate is 30 percent. Government expenditures as a share of GDP decreased 0.2 percentage point to 46.1 percent in 2002, compared to a 1.1 percentage point increase in 2001. As a result, Portugal's fiscal burden of government score is 0.2 point better this year.

## GOVERNMENT INTERVENTION IN THE ECONOMY
### Score: **2–Stable** (low level)

Based on data from the Ministry of Finance, the government consumed 20 percent of GDP in 2002. In the same year, based on data from the same source, Portugal received 4.87 percent of its total revenues from state-owned enterprises and government ownership of property.

333

## MONETARY POLICY
### Score: **2**–Stable (low level of inflation)

From 1993 to 2002, Portugal's weighted average annual rate of inflation was 3.65 percent.

## CAPITAL FLOWS AND FOREIGN INVESTMENT
### Score: **2**–Stable (low barriers)

Portugal has opened most of its industries to foreign investment and has liberalized the bureaucratic process for foreign investors. The government does not discriminate against foreign investments by favoring domestic investors. Investments are permitted in all sectors except those closed to private enterprise (postal services, armaments, water and sewage services, port operations, and certain industrial activities). Non-EU ownership of civil aviation, television, and telecommunications is limited. Both residents and non-residents may hold foreign exchange accounts. There are no controls or restrictions on repatriation of profits, current transfers, payments for invisible transactions, or real estate transactions. Foreign employees from non-EU countries may comprise no more than 10 percent of the workforce in businesses with more than five employees.

## BANKING AND FINANCE
### Score: **3**–Stable (moderate level of restrictions)

Extensive privatization since the late 1980s has left Caixa Geral do Depositos (CGD) as Portugal's only remaining state financial services firm, as well as its largest. According to the Economist Intelligence Unit, "[CGD] is still the largest financial group and has on several occasions served as an instrument of government intervention in the economy, usually as a defence against unwanted takeover bids from foreign investors." The government influences the allocation of credit through a program designed to assist small and medium enterprises (SMEs); according to the U.S. Department of State, "Portugal's Institute for Supporting Small and Medium-sized Enterprises and Investment (IAPMEI) has a program of mutual guarantees so that SME's do not have to use their assets or those of shareholders to collateralize debt." The Bank of Portugal (for the EU) or the Ministry of Finance (non-EU) must authorize both the establishment or acquisition of new credit institutions or finance companies and the establishment of subsidiaries.

## WAGES AND PRICES
### Score: **2**–Stable (low level of intervention)

The government has eliminated almost all price controls. According to the Economist Intelligence Unit, "The state continues to administer the prices of certain energy sources, including petrol and diesel … electricity, basic foodstuffs … and most public transportation." Portugal also affects agricultural prices through its participation in the Common Agricultural Policy, a program that heavily subsidizes agri-

cultural goods. According to Timbro, a Swedish think tank, "EU consumers pay roughly 80–100% more for their food than would be the case in a mature free-market regime." A mandated minimum wage applies to all full-time workers, rural workers, and domestic employees.

## PROPERTY RIGHTS
### Score: **2**–Stable (high level of protection)

The judiciary is independent, and the threat of expropriation is low. The court system, however, can be inefficient. The Economist Intelligence Unit reports that "the judiciary is independent and provides a fair legal process but is somewhat backlogged and inefficient."

## REGULATION
### Score: **3**–Stable (moderate level)

Regulation in Portugal is burdensome, and red tape abounds. "Decision-making tends to be overly centralized," reports the U.S. Department of State, "and obtaining government approvals or permits can be time-consuming and costly, particularly for small- and medium-sized foreign investors and entrepreneurs. [Firms] report substantial delays and red tape in accomplishing such basic tasks as registering companies, filing taxes, receiving value-added tax refunds, and importing vehicles." The government has created a one-stop "Formality Center" to address the bureaucratic problem. Portuguese labor law tends to be rigid. According to the Economist Intelligence Unit, however, "A new labor law, which took effect in January 2002, radically overhauls Portugal's immigration laws, giving legal status to undocumented workers…who present a valid work contract…. [This law] is the EU's most liberal in terms of labor immigration."

## INFORMAL MARKET
### Score: **2**–Stable (low level of activity)

Transparency International's 2002 score for Portugal is 6.3. Therefore, Portugal's informal market score is 2 this year.

QATAR

# QATAR

Rank: 60

Score: 2.86

Category: Mostly Free

**Present & Past Scores**

(Best) 1
2
3
4
(Worst) 5

3.11  3.18  3.18  3.03  2.78  2.86

'95  '96  '97  '98  '99  '00  '01  '02  '03  '04
n/a  n/a  n/a  n/a

## QUICK STUDY

### SCORES

| | |
|---|---|
| Trade Policy | 3 |
| Fiscal Burden | 3.1 |
| Government Intervention | 4.5 |
| Monetary Policy | 1 |
| Foreign Investment | 3 |
| Banking and Finance | 3 |
| Wages and Prices | 2 |
| Property Rights | 3 |
| Regulation | 4 |
| Informal Market | 2 |

**Population:** 597,550

**Total area:** 11,437 sq. km

**GDP:** $13.4 billion

**GDP growth rate:** 5.2%

**GDP per capita:** $22,359

**Major exports:** petroleum products, fertilizers, steel

**Exports of goods (fob):** $9.8 billion

**Major export trading partners:** Japan 43.5%, South Korea 18.0%, Singapore 4.9%, US 4.1%

**Major imports:** machinery and transport equipment

**Imports of goods (fob):** $3 billion

**Major import trading partners:** France 17.9%, US 9.1%, Italy 8.6%, Japan 8.1%, Germany 7.8%

**Foreign direct investment (net):** $190 million

2001 Data (in constant 1995 US dollars)

The energy-rich Persian Gulf emirate of Qatar has been ruled by the al-Thani family since gaining its independence from Great Britain in 1971. Its robust economy is dominated by the oil and gas industry, which accounts for 30 percent of GDP, roughly 80 percent of export revenues, and 67 percent of government revenues. At current production rates, its oil reserves are projected to last for 23 years. Qatar has 3.7 billion barrels of proven oil reserves, and its natural gas reserves are among the largest in the world, accounting for approximately 5 percent of the world's total proven reserves. Although Qatar's economy will remain heavily dependent on the oil industry, the government recognizes the need for diversification and seeks to expand development of its offshore natural gas reserves. Amir Sheikh Hamad bin Khalifa al-Thani, who came to power in 1995 after ousting his father in a bloodless coup, has undertaken a bold program of economic reform to encourage economic growth and foreign investment through accelerated privatization and private-sector development. Under its democratization program, the government also has liberalized the political system; given women the right to vote; enacted new laws and regulations for foreign trade and intellectual property rights; and nurtured an independent television station, al-Jazira, that has acquired a wide audience throughout the Arab world. In April 2003, by nationwide referendum, the country approved a new constitution to replace the provisional one that had been in place since 1971. The new constitution allows for the establishment of a 45-member parliament with significant legislative powers, to be chosen in elections scheduled for 2004, and includes provisions for freedom of the press and religion. Qatar's fiscal burden of government score is 0.3 point worse this year, and its government intervention score is 0.5 point worse. As a result, Qatar's overall score is 0.08 point worse this year.

## ⚓ TRADE POLICY

### Score: 3–Stable (moderate level of protectionism)

According to Ernst & Young, the majority of goods are subject to a 4 percent ad valorem customs duty; however, "certain goods which compete with locally manufactured products are subject to a higher customs duty tariff as a protectionist measure." There is no clear information regarding Qatar's average tariff rate, although the evidence provided by Ernst & Young indicates that it is clearly above 4 percent. The U.S. Department of State reports that non-tariff barriers include strict licensing requirements, import bans, and quotas.

##  FISCAL BURDEN OF GOVERNMENT

### Score—Income Taxation: 1–Stable (very low tax rates)
### Score—Corporate Taxation: 4.5–Stable (very high tax rates)
### Score—Change in Government Expenditures: 2.5–Worse (low decrease)
### Final Score: 3.1–Worse (moderate cost of government)

The government does not impose income taxes on individuals. Qatar has a progressive tax regime on corporate profits that starts at 0 percent and is capped at 35 percent. This tax does not apply to corporate entities wholly owned by Qatari nationals or to Qatari shares in the profits of corporate bodies; if a business is 40 percent foreign-owned, for example, taxes are applied to 40 percent of its profits. For purposes of scoring this factor, the top corporate tax rate is 35 percent. Government expenditures as a share of GDP decreased less in 2001 (1.6 percentage points to 29.9 percent) than they did in 2000 (6.9 percentage points). As a result, Qatar's fiscal burden of government score is 0.3 point worse this year.

335

## GOVERNMENT INTERVENTION IN THE ECONOMY
### Score: **4.5**–Worse (very high level)

The World Bank reports that the government consumed 24.2 percent of GDP in 2001. In the same year, based on data from the International Monetary Fund, Qatar received 67.39 percent of its total revenues just from state-owned oil companies. Based on new evidence with respect to the level of revenues from state-owned enterprises, Qatar's government intervention score is 0.5 point worse this year.

## MONETARY POLICY
### Score: **1**–Stable (very low level of inflation)

From 1993 to 2002, Qatar's weighted average annual rate of inflation was 1.67 percent.

## CAPITAL FLOWS AND FOREIGN INVESTMENT
### Score: **3**–Stable (moderate barriers)

An October 2000 investment law permits majority and full foreign ownership of businesses in agriculture, industry, health, education, and tourism. Most sectors are capped at 49 percent foreign ownership. The law still requires foreign businesses to employ a local agent. Foreign nationals may not buy land, but 50-year leases are available. The U.S. Department of State reports that government "procurement regulations favor Qatari and [Gulf Cooperation Council] nationals." The government screens all major foreign investment projects in the oil and gas industry; according to the Economist Intelligence Unit, "No foreign company has a majority stake in any of Qatar's existing hydrocarbon ventures, and this is unlikely to change." Unofficial barriers also impede foreign investment. "In general," reports the EIU, "the foreign investment climate retains its lack of transparency. Many of the incentives on offer to foreign investors, such as tax breaks and customs-duty waivers, are only available on an ad hoc basis. As such, there is no 'level playing field'." The International Monetary Fund reports that both residents and non-residents may hold foreign exchange accounts. There are no controls or restrictions on payments and transfers.

## BANKING AND FINANCE
### Score: **3**–Stable (moderate level of restrictions)

The government influences the banking sector and owns 50 percent of the country's largest bank—which also accounts for 50 percent of total banking assets—but foreign banks are able to operate, and the regulatory system is transparent and up to international standards. The banking sector consists of 14 commercial banks, of which six are domestically owned and six are foreign-owned. According to the Economist Intelligence Unit, "Loans to the government…account for the majority of commercial bank loans." The Doha Securities Market is very small, with only 24 listings, and restricted to Qatari citizens. Qatar has 12 insurance companies, seven of which are foreign-

owned, but the Qatar Insurance Company, in which the government has a 20 percent stake, dominates the market and manages the government's insurance business.

## WAGES AND PRICES
### Score: **2**–Stable (low level of intervention)

There are few official price controls. According to the Economist Intelligence Unit, "The government does not actively intervene to set prices of key goods, but it does enjoy a monopoly in the distribution of certain key goods and services and, as such, sets prices. These include power and water provision, telecommunications and petrol retailing." The government does not mandate a minimum wage, but it does influence wages through its extensive employment of Qatari citizens.

## PROPERTY RIGHTS
### Score: **3**–Stable (moderate level of protection)

Expropriation of property is not likely. The judiciary, however, is subject to inefficiencies and influence from the executive. "Contracts are generally secured in Qatar," reports the Economist Intelligence Unit, but "the domestic legal process has a reputation for being long and bureaucratic…. [T]he Qatari system is regarded as adequate in the field of commercial law." According to the U.S. Department of State, "The judiciary is nominally independent, but most judges are foreign nationals who hold residence permits granted by the civil authorities and thus hold their positions at the Government's pleasure…. The legal system is biased in favor of citizens and the Government."

## REGULATION
### Score: **4**–Stable (high level)

The government enforces some regulations more rigorously on foreign companies and those engaged in joint ventures. "In the past," reports Ernst & Young, "the government has pursued the principle of reserving most business activities for Qataris. The new investment law enacted in 2000, allows for majority owned foreign investments in specific projects in the health, tourism, education, agriculture, power and manufacturing sectors." Government businesses are often exempt from some regulations, leaving private companies to bear a greater regulatory burden. The overall regulatory burden is therefore significant.

## INFORMAL MARKET
### Score: **2**–Stable (low level of activity)

Overall, Qatar's informal market is small. According to the Business Software Alliance, however, the rate of piracy in 2001 was 84 percent for software and 30 percent for motion pictures.

# ROMANIA

**Rank:** 129

**Score:** 3.66

**Category:** Mostly Unfree

Present & Past Scores

(Best) 1
2
3
4
(Worst) 5

3.60  3.40  3.30  3.21  3.20  3.20  3.59  3.78  3.71  3.66

'95 '96 '97 '98 '99 '00 '01 '02 '03 '04

Romania's economic development has been constrained by the centralized economy inherited from the former communist regime. Free-market, reformist policies have clashed with populist pressure from the center–left. Former President Emil Constantinescu initiated privatization programs and structural changes, and Socialist President Ion Iliescu, re-elected in 2000, has vowed to continue on the path of economic reform. Iliescu's record, however, makes Romania's economic future uncertain. The result was the European Union's decision not to invite Romania to join in the wave of new members in 2004. In 2003, Romania was invited to join NATO, partly because of its strategic position and access to the Black Sea. The government has implemented privatization, and the parliament approved improvements in land restitution in March 2002. A July 2001 law on the promotion of investment granted tax exemptions for greenfield projects that exceed US$1 million. Romania receives technical and financial assistance from the United States, the EU, and other industrial nations. It has also received assistance from such other sources as the World Bank, International Monetary Fund, European Bank for Reconstruction and Development, and U.S. Agency for International Development. Romania's capital flows and foreign investment score is 1 point worse this year; however, its government intervention score is 1.5 point better. As a result, Romania's overall score is 0.05 point better this year.

## TRADE POLICY
### Score: **4**–Stable (high level of protectionism)

According to the World Bank, Romania's weighted average tariff rate in 2001 (the most recent year for which World Bank data are available) was 13.7 percent. Both the U.S. Trade Representative and the U.S. Department of State cite customs corruption as an obstacle to trade.

## FISCAL BURDEN OF GOVERNMENT
### Score—Income Taxation: **4**–Stable (high tax rates)
### Score—Corporate Taxation: **3**–Stable (moderate tax rates)
### Score—Change in Government Expenditures: **2.5**–Stable (low decrease)
### Final Score: **3.1**–Stable (moderate cost of government)

Romania's top income tax rate is 40 percent. The top corporate income tax rate is 25 percent. Government expenditures as a share of GDP decreased by the same percentage in 2001 (1.7 percentage points to 33.7 percent) as they did in 2000 (also 1.7 percentage points). As a result, Romania's fiscal burden of government score is unchanged this year.

## GOVERNMENT INTERVENTION IN THE ECONOMY
### Score: **2.5**–Better (moderate level)

The World Bank reports that the government consumed 6.3 percent of GDP in 2001, down from the 12.5 percent reported in the 2003 *Index*. In 2000, according to the International Monetary Fund, Romania received 1.22 percent of its revenues from state-owned enterprises and government ownership of property. According to the Economist Intelligence Unit, however, "state-owned enterprises [continue] to account for a significant share of economic activity [and] play a major role in many sectors of the economy, including utilities, finance and manufacturing." Based on the apparent unreliability of the figure for revenues from state-owned enterprises, 1 point has been added to Romania's government intervention score. Based on the decrease in the level of government consumption, Romania's government intervention score is 1.5 point better this year.

## MONETARY POLICY
### Score: 5–Stable (very high level of inflation)

From 1993 to 2002, Romania's weighted average annual rate of inflation was 29.08 percent.

## CAPITAL FLOWS AND FOREIGN INVESTMENT
### Score: 4–Worse (high barriers)

Economic reform legislation passed between 1999 and 2001 opened more sectors to foreign investment, guaranteed foreign investors national treatment and removed caps on their involvement in commercial enterprises. The U.S. Department of State reports that projects involving the privatization of large firms "frequently become stymied by vested political and economic interests and bogged down by inaction within and lack of coordination among governmental ministries." The Economist Intelligence Unit reports that Romania is one of the most difficult countries in the region in which to do business without resorting to bribery." The International Monetary Fund reports that foreign exchange accounts are subject to government approval. All payments and transfers must be documented. Most capital transactions between residents and non-residents require central bank approval. The foreign exchange market was liberalized in 1997. Based on the evidence that unofficial barriers such as bureaucracy and corruption continue to undermine foreign investment, Romania's capital flows and foreign investment score is 1 point worse this year.

## BANKING AND FINANCE
### Score: 3–Stable (moderate level of restrictions)

Romania's banking sector consists of 42 commercial banks, of which 24 have majority-foreign capital and eight are subsidiaries of foreign banks. The government privatized Bank Agricola in 2001 and plans to sell its stake in the country's largest bank, Banca Comerciala Romana, which accounted for 32 percent of total assets in 2002. Specifically, it plans to sell a joint 25 percent stake to the European Bank for Reconstruction and Development and to the International Finance Corporation, and to reach full privatization by 2006. The Economist Intelligence Unit reports that the government's market share in the banking system declined from 75 percent in 1998 to 42.8 percent in 2002. Supervision of the banking sector has improved significantly since the 1990s. According to the Economist Intelligence Unit, "The clean-up and closure of problem banks, including the removal of bad and dubious loans, has greatly reduced the vulnerability of the banking sector. The share of non-performing loans had been reduced from 71.7% at end-1998 to 2.8% in June 2002. However, despite these advances the financial system remains highly underdeveloped and cannot yet provide effective intermediation between savers and investors."

## WAGES AND PRICES
### Score: 3–Stable (moderate level of intervention)

Some prices are set through Romania's extensive state-owned enterprises, which include (but are not limited to) enterprises in the energy, utilities, chemical plants, transportation, and metal sectors. The U.S. Department of State reports that the government owns nearly two-thirds of all industrial assets. According to the Economist Intelligence Unit, "Price controls still affect some 20% of the consumption basket." In January, Romania increased the minimum wage by 43 percent.

## PROPERTY RIGHTS
### Score: 4–Stable (low level of protection)

According to the U.S. Department of State, "Property and contractual rights are recognized, but enforcement through Romanian courts is difficult. Foreign companies engaged in trade or investment in Romania often express concerns with respect to the international commercial experience of Romanian courts. Judges generally have little experience in the functioning of a market economy, international business methods, or the application of new Romanian commercial laws." The Economist Intelligence Unit reports that "successive reports by the European Commission have raised serious questions about the political neutrality of the Judiciary [and] the low level of training and qualifications of personnel in the judicial system."

## REGULATION
### Score: 4–Stable (high level)

The *Financial Times* reports, based on a U.S. Agency for International Development study, that "it takes anything from 49 to 102 days to register a new company: 83 pages of forms have to be completed, weighing half a kilo.... Small to medium-sized enterprises have between 11 and 23 inspections a year.... A business start-up needs between 23 and 29 authorisations and approvals." According to the U.S. Department of State, "Cumbersome and non-transparent bureaucratic procedures are a major problem in Romania. Foreign investors point to the excessive time it takes to secure necessary zoning permits, property titles, licenses, and utility hook-ups.... [R]egulations change frequently, sometimes literally overnight, often without advance notice. These changes...can significantly add to the costs of doing business [and] make it difficult for investors to develop effective business plans." According to the Embassy of Romania, a "one-stop shop" will streamline the process for registering a business, but the *Financial Times* reports that this reform applies only to "investors with more than [US]$10 m[illion]."

## INFORMAL MARKET
### Score: 4–Stable (high level of activity)

Transparency International's 2002 score for Romania is 2.6. Therefore, Romania's informal market score is 4 this year.

# RUSSIA

Rank: 114

Score: 3.46

Category: Mostly Unfree

**Present & Past Scores**

(Best) 1
2
3
4
(Worst) 5

3.55  3.65  3.83  3.54  3.60  3.75  3.79  3.74  3.54  3.46

'95  '96  '97  '98  '99  '00  '01  '02  '03  '04

Since being elected president in April 2000, Vladimir Putin has concentrated on consolidating his political power and promoting economic reform. In May 2002 the Russia–NATO Council was established, giving Russia a voice in the Alliance's policymaking. In 2002, Putin presented balanced budgets, enacted a flat personal income tax, and reduced the corporate and small business tax. Over the past several years, the ruble has rapidly appreciated as a result of large current account surpluses. Russia has been able both to meet its foreign debt and to make large advance payments to the IMF. To promote retirement of the remaining debt, G–8 countries at the June 2002 summit agreed to explore the cancellation of past Soviet debt in exchange for safeguarding nuclear materials that could be used by terrorists. The government has stated that joining the World Trade Organization is a major priority, but it is not likely to meet the accession standards, which include eliminating subsidies through artificially low energy prices, creating a non-discriminatory environment for foreign goods and services, protecting intellectual property rights, and reforming the financial and banking sectors before 2004–2005. Russia also needs to fight corruption and strengthen the rule of law and the court system, which are still deficient. In his 2003 State of the Federation address, Putin called for a doubling of GDP within 10 years. Although the main portion of capital spending is financed by profits from increased oil and gas exports, bank lending accounts for only 3 percent of investment. Without significant foreign competition, financial companies lack proper incentives to improve their operations. Russia's fiscal burden of government score is 0.2 point worse this year; however, its trade policy score is 1 point better. As a result, Russia's overall score is 0.08 point better this year.

## TRADE POLICY

### Score: **3**–Better (moderate level of protectionism)

The World Bank reports that Russia's weighted average tariff rate in 2001 (the most recent year for which World Bank data are available) was 8.4 percent, down from the 11.3 percent reported in the 2003 *Index*. As a result, Russia's trade policy score is 1 point better this year. According to the U.S. Department of State, "frequent and unpredictable changes in Russian customs regulations" are a major non-tariff barrier. In addition, there is a burdensome licensing regime, particularly for products containing alcohol.

## FISCAL BURDEN OF GOVERNMENT

Score—Income Taxation: **1.5**–Stable (low tax rates)
Score—Corporate Taxation: **3**–Stable (moderate tax rates)
Score—Change in Government Expenditures: **3**–Worse (very low decrease)

### Final Score: **2.6**–Worse (moderate cost of government)

Russia has reformed its tax code and has adopted a flat income tax of 13 percent. The top corporate tax rate is 24 percent. Government expenditures as a share of GDP decreased less in 2001 (0.3 percentage point to 34.1 percent) than they did in 2000 (2.8 percentage points). As a result, Russia's fiscal burden of government score is 0.2 point worse this year.

## GOVERNMENT INTERVENTION IN THE ECONOMY

### Score: **2**–Stable (low level)

The World Bank reports that the government consumed 14.3 percent of GDP in 2001. In the same year, according to the International Monetary Fund, Russia received 4.2 percent of its

total revenues from state-owned enterprises and government ownership of property.

## MONETARY POLICY
### Score: **5**–Stable (very high level of inflation)

From 1993 to 2002, Russia's weighted average annual rate of inflation was 20.16 percent.

## CAPITAL FLOWS AND FOREIGN INVESTMENT
### Score: **3**–Stable (moderate barriers)

Russia updated its foreign investment code in June 1999 by identifying criteria for the types of investment projects that may receive favorable treatment and granting national treatment to foreign investors except in sectors involving national security or to protect the constitution, public morals and health, and the rights and lawful interests of other persons. According to the U.S. Department of State, "High costs in complying with Russian tax authorities, inconsistent government regulation, the inability of some investors to obtain redress through the legal system, and crime and corruption all dissuade investors." Foreigners may establish wholly owned companies in most sectors—although the registration process can be cumbersome—and may take part in the privatization process. Foreigners remain banned from buying agricultural land but may lease agricultural land for 49 years and purchase non-agricultural land and property. The government limits foreign ownership in "strategic" sectors, which include gas and power monopolies, banking, insurance, mass media, diamond mining, and civil aviation. The International Monetary Fund reports that residents may hold foreign exchange accounts, but the use of foreign exchange proceeds from capital transactions requires a central bank license in most cases. Non-residents may maintain four types of foreign exchange accounts, categorized by purpose. Transactions involving capital and money market instruments, derivatives, and credit operations are subject to central bank authorization in many cases. In June 2002, Russia announced that it would loosen restrictions on repatriation of foreign funds frozen during the 1998 financial crisis.

## BANKING AND FINANCE
### Score: **4**–Stable (high level of restrictions)

Russia's 1998 financial crisis sent the entire financial system into chaos. Many banks became insolvent and shut down; others were taken over by the government and heavily subsidized. The banking sector consists of 1,331 banks, many of which are undercapitalized, and is dominated by two state-owned banks, Sberbank and Vneshtorgbank, which account for 30 percent of total banking assets. In March 2003, the central bank and the Ministry of Finance issued their plan for reforming the banking sector, but the Economist Intelligence Unit reports that "it has little to say about the future of Sberbank, the dominant position of which is one of the main impediments to the development of a competitive banking

sector." The EIU also reports that banks still do "not fulfill [their] main function, that of channelling household savings into industrial investments." In 2002, banks financed less than 5 percent of private-sector investment—significantly less than the 50 percent share in developed countries. In late 2002, the government abolished the restriction that had limited foreign investment in banking to 12 percent of total banking sector capital. There is a 49 percent cap on foreign ownership of life insurance firms, and total foreign assets in the sector are capped at 15 percent.

## WAGES AND PRICES
### Score: **3**–Stable (moderate level of intervention)

The government of Russia has liberalized most prices. According to the Economist Intelligence Unit, "The major exceptions are the tariffs charged by the utility companies (gas, electricity and telecoms), and also railways, local transport and communal services…. As in most countries, government regulators set utility prices, but there is no clear formula for doing so in Russia, which increases the sway of such things as political lobbying and the demands of government counter-inflation policy." The government also keeps a list of companies that dominate Russian industry; currently, it consists of 300 legal entities, of which 60 are medium-sized companies. "Placing companies on the list," reports the EIU, "does not mean the state will intervene in their business activities, but price ceilings are specified for these companies, and they are not allowed to exceed them without special consent from the federal control body." Russia has a minimum wage.

## PROPERTY RIGHTS
### Score: **4**–Stable (low level of protection)

Protection of private property in Russia is weak. The Economist Intelligence Unit reports that "the country's judicial system is still weak and subject to abuses and influence…. [I]f carefully drawn up and followed, contracts have become more secure; however, some investors have found that winning a favourable decision in court does not mean it will be implemented or that there will be anything to recover. Thus, many businesses prefer to have some kind of practical leverage to ensure that their partners follow through contracts." Corruption in the judiciary is a serious problem. The U.S. Department of State reports that "U.S. firms have identified corruption as a pervasive problem, both in number of instances and in the size of bribes sought." Land ownership is legal, but the purchase of farmland by businesses and foreigners is prohibited.

## REGULATION
### Score: **4**–Stable (high level)

Bureaucracy, lack of transparency, and red tape continue to present significant impediments to business in Russia. According to *The Wall Street Journal*, a recent World Bank survey revealed that "laws designed to help small businesses had increased, rather than reduced red tape." The Economist Intelligence Unit reports that "corruption is so widespread in Russia that bribes...amount[ed] to an estimated 4 percent of gross domestic product in 2001...." According to the U.S. Department of State, "The legal system in Russia is in flux, with various parts of the government struggling to create new laws on a broad array of topics. In this environment, negotiations and contracts for commercial transactions are complex and protracted.... Keeping up with legislative changes, presidential decrees and government resolutions is a challenging task. Uneven implementation of laws creates further complications; various officials, branches of government and jurisdictions interpret and apply regulations with little consistency and the decisions of one may be overruled or contested by another."

 ## INFORMAL MARKET
### Score: **4–Stable** (high level of activity)

Transparency International's 2002 score for Russia is 2.7. Therefore, Russia's informal market score is 4 this year.

RWANDA

# RWANDA

**Rank:** 103

**Score:** 3.36

**Category:** Mostly Unfree

**Present & Past Scores**

(Best) 1
2
3
4
(Worst) 5

4.70  4.70  4.29  4.28  3.94  3.73  3.93  3.36

'95  '96  '97  '98  '99  '00  '01  '02  '03  '04
n/a  n/a

## QUICK STUDY

### SCORES

| | |
|---|---|
| Trade Policy | 3 |
| Fiscal Burden | 4.6 |
| Government Intervention | 2 |
| Monetary Policy | 1 |
| Foreign Investment | 4 |
| Banking and Finance | 3 |
| Wages and Prices | 3 |
| Property Rights | 4 |
| Regulation | 4 |
| Informal Market | 5 |

**Population:** 8,690,550

**Total area:** 26,338 sq. km

**GDP:** $2.2 billion

**GDP growth rate:** 6.7%

**GDP per capita:** $253

**Major exports:** tea, coffee, hides

**Exports of goods and services:** $228.6 million

**Major export trading partners:** Germany 39.4%, China 21.3%, US 8.1%, Netherlands 7.4%, Belgium 2.8%

**Major imports:** capital goods, machinery and equipment, foodstuffs

**Imports of goods and services:** $453.5 million

**Major import trading partners:** Kenya 25.7%, Belgium 9.0%, US 7.7%, Germany 3.7%

**Foreign direct investment (net):** $7.2 million

2001 Data (in constant 1995 US dollars)

The successful implementation of a new constitution in June 2003 is an important step in Rwanda's attempts to put 10 years of bloodshed behind it. Though open political activity may once again be a reality, however, this will not prevent the ruling Rwandan Patriotic Front from restricting the activities of other parties to maintain its hold on the government. Externally, the increasingly volatile situation between Rwanda and neighboring Uganda seems ready to deteriorate into war. The countries have accused one another of backing insurgent groups, and several prominent Rwandan politicians have defected to Uganda. Economically, given its recent bloody history and a lack of natural resources, one might expect very little in terms of growth and development; yet in 2002, an improved agricultural infrastructure, friendly weather, and a strong manufacturing sector led to a 9.7 percent increase in real GDP, the third highest on the continent. Estimates for 2003 should fall short of the previous year; the Economist Intelligence Unit projects a 6.5 percent increase in real GDP with moderate inflation of 5 percent. After two impressive years, and with a third more than likely, Rwanda should continue to receive favorable assessments by the International Monetary Fund, which in 2002 granted Rwanda entry into the poverty reduction and growth facility (PRGF). Rwanda's fiscal burden of government score is 0.3 point worse this year; however, its trade policy and government intervention scores are 2 points better, and its monetary policy and regulation scores are 1 point better. As a result, Rwanda's overall score is 0.57 point better this year.

## TRADE POLICY
### Score: **3**–Better (moderate level of protectionism)

According to the World Bank, Rwanda's weighted average tariff rate in 2001 (the most recent year for which World Bank data are available) was 8.1 percent, down from the 25.5 percent reported in the 2003 *Index*. As a result, Rwanda's trade policy score is 2 points better this year. The U.S. Department of State reports that "customs procedures…are complex, bureaucratic and fraught with corruption."

## FISCAL BURDEN OF GOVERNMENT
### Score—Income Taxation: **4**–Stable (high tax rates)
### Score—Corporate Taxation: **5**–Stable (very high tax rates)
### Score—Change in Government Expenditures: **4.5**–Worse (high increase)
### Final Score: **4.6**–Worse (very high cost of government)

According to the International Monetary Fund, Rwanda's top income tax rate is 40 percent. The top corporate tax rate is 40 percent. Government expenditures as a share of GDP increased 2.3 percentage points in 2000, compared to a 0.9 percentage point decrease in 1999. As a result, Rwanda's fiscal burden of government score is 0.3 point worse this year.

## GOVERNMENT INTERVENTION IN THE ECONOMY
### Score: **2**–Better (low level)

The World Bank reports that the government consumed 11.7 percent of GDP in 2001. In 2002, based on data from the same source, Rwanda received 4.91 percent of its total revenues from state-owned enterprises and government ownership of property. Based on newly available data for revenues from state-owned enterprises and the use of a new methodology to grade

343

this factor, Rwanda's government intervention score is 2 points better this year.

## MONETARY POLICY
### Score: 1–Better (very low level of inflation)

From 1993 to 2002, Rwanda's weighted average annual rate of inflation was 2.50 percent, down from the 3.33 percent from 1992 to 2001 reported in the 2003 *Index*.

## CAPITAL FLOWS AND FOREIGN INVESTMENT
### Score: 4–Stable (high barriers)

Rwanda continues to have difficulty attracting foreign investment because of the looting and damage done to investments during the 1994 genocide, ongoing concern about latent political instability, and existing political instability in neighboring countries. The government relaxed some restrictions on foreign investment in June 2000 and adopted a floating exchange rate in July 2000. The International Monetary Fund reports that both residents and non-residents may hold foreign exchange accounts, but only if they provide supporting documentation. Payments and transfers are subject to authorizations and maximum allowances and limits. Nearly all capital transactions require the central bank's approval. The South African energy company Engen, which had taken over BP Fina's Rwandan fuel sector assets in 1998, sold them to a Rwandan business at a loss in 2001 after charging the government with bureaucratic harassment, corruption, and undisclosed past-due tax obligations.

## BANKING AND FINANCE
### Score: 3–Stable (moderate level of restrictions)

Rwanda's small banking sector has become more competitive since 1994. Five of the country's nine commercial banks have been established since 1994. The Economist Intelligence Unit reports that in April 2003, the government authorized the sale of the country's largest bank, Banque Commercial du Rwanda. The sale was scheduled to take place in August 2003, but the EIU reports that this date will likely be missed. The government also plans to sell its stake in Banque Rwandaise de Développement, and Sonarwa, the largest insurance company. The government has made an effort to improve banking supervision, and all commercial banks were audited in 1999. The country also has increased its capital requirements. Although the government remains involved in some domestic banks, there is private banking, and a Belgian bank operates in Rwanda.

## WAGES AND PRICES
### Score: 3–Stable (moderate level of intervention)

The government affects the price of tea and many other goods and services, particularly utilities, through state-owned enterprises. Though privatization is scheduled for many of these industries, it has met with many delays. The government sets minimum wages that vary by type of job; more important, it sets wages as the country's largest employer.

## PROPERTY RIGHTS
### Score: 4–Stable (low level of protection)

Property rights have improved in Rwanda since the genocide in 1994 and 1995, although there is still uncertainty regarding the protection of private property. "Land ownership is a sensitive issue," reports the Economist Intelligence Unit, "and the government is preparing new legislation with extreme caution." Overall, protection of property is weak. According to the U.S. Department of State, "the…law provides for an independent judiciary; however, the government did not respect this provision fully; the judiciary is subject to executive influence and also suffers from inefficiency, a lack of resources, and some corruption. There were occasional reports of bribery of officials, ranging from clerks to judges."

## REGULATION
### Score: 4–Better (high level)

Rwanda's government has made efforts to establish a consistent regulatory regime following the civil unrest of earlier years, but it still has a long way to go. According to the U.S. Department of State, "A private sector regulatory law was passed by the National Assembly in 2001. This law created a regulatory board to regulate the utility sectors in Rwanda, including telecommunications, electricity, gas and water. A new regulatory agency provides guidance on granting licenses, enforcing regulations, addressing anti-competitive activities, and implementing standards. The law also provides incentives for investment in Rwanda's utility sector. The labor code was revised in 2000 to eliminate gender discrimination, restrictions on the mobility of labor, and wage controls. The law allows for economic layoffs. A new insurance law is being prepared." Corruption is a burden to businesses. The Economist Intelligence Unit reports that "some local manufacturers and import-exporters insist that graft has worsened and that unofficial payments to state officials are a major impediment to their profitability." Based on the evidence of increasing reforms to allow private-sector activity, Rwanda's regulation score is 1 point better this year.

## INFORMAL MARKET
### Score: 5–Stable (very high level of activity)

Most economic activity occurs informally. The U.S. Department of State reports that the volume of smuggling between Rwanda and Burundi is huge. Animal trafficking and medicine smuggling are also prominent.

SAUDI
ARABIA

# SAUDI ARABIA

Rank: 74

Score: 3.05

Category: Mostly Unfree

## QUICK STUDY

### SCORES

| | |
|---|---|
| Trade Policy | 4 |
| Fiscal Burden | 2 |
| Government Intervention | 4.5 |
| Monetary Policy | 1 |
| Foreign Investment | 4 |
| Banking and Finance | 4 |
| Wages and Prices | 2 |
| Property Rights | 3 |
| Regulation | 3 |
| Informal Market | 3 |

**Population:** 21,408,470

**Total area:** 1,960,582 sq. km

**GDP:** $142 billion

**GDP growth rate:** 1.2%

**GDP per capita:** $6,614

**Major exports:** crude oil, oil products

**Exports of goods and services:** $70.1 billion

**Major export trading partners:** US 18.3%, Japan 17.4%, South Korea 10.2%, Singapore 5.4%

**Major imports:** machinery and transport equipment, chemical products

**Imports of goods and services:** $40.8 billion

**Major import trading partners:** US 17.7%, Japan 10.4%, Germany 7.9%, UK 6.5%

**Foreign direct investment (net):** $18 million

2001 Data (in constant 1995 US dollars)

Saudi Arabia, the largest of the Persian Gulf monarchies, owns the world's largest proven oil reserves, with over 260 billion barrels of oil, and is the world's foremost oil exporter, which gives it a dominant role in the Organization of Petroleum Exporting Countries (OPEC). The petroleum sector accounts for about 90 percent of export earnings, 45 percent of GDP, and about 80 percent of budget revenues. Although Saudi Arabia has enormous oil wealth, it also faces a rapidly growing population, water shortages, and political challenges from Islamic extremists, including Osama bin Laden. The government has sought to diversify the economy to reduce dependence on oil exports and strengthen the private sector, which makes up about 25 percent of the economy. Crown Prince Abdallah, who has become the de facto ruler because of King Fahd's declining health, has undertaken cautious economic reforms, which include encouraging foreign investment and privatizing some public-sector companies. In December 2002, the government sold 30 percent of its shares in the Saudi Telecommunications Company, worth an estimated $4 billion. However, privatization is likely to proceed at a slow pace because of opposition from the state-owned energy monopoly, Saudi Aramco, and several senior members of the royal family who object to offering stakes in key Saudi industries to foreign investors. Saudi Arabia's capital flows and foreign investment score is 1 point worse this year; however, its fiscal burden of government score is 1.4 points better. As a result, Saudi Arabia's overall score is 0.04 point better this year.

##  TRADE POLICY
### Score: 4–Stable (high level of protectionism)

According to the World Bank, Saudi Arabia's weighted average tariff rate in 2000 (the most recent year for which World Bank data are available) was 10.5 percent. The Economist Intelligence Unit reports that "imports of alcohol and of non-medical drugs are banned, as are most non-Islamic religious materials.... [W]eapons and electronic equipment are tightly controlled for security reasons.... [In 1994] the government banned the import of television satellite dishes...." The U.S. Department of State reports that other non-tariff barriers include "preferences for national and [Gulf Cooperation Council] products in government procurement" and "a requirement that foreign contractors obtain their imported goods and services exclusively through Saudi agents...."

##  FISCAL BURDEN OF GOVERNMENT
### Score—Income Taxation: 1–Stable (very low tax rates)
### Score—Corporate Taxation: 1–Better (very low tax rates)
### Score—Change in Government Expenditures: 5–Worse (very high increase)
### Final Score: 2–Better (low cost of government)

Saudi Arabia has no income tax rate for residents. The top corporate tax rate is 0 percent, down from the 30 percent reported in the 2003 *Index*. (Foreign companies are assessed a tax rate of 30 percent; this is taken into account in the capital flows and foreign investment factor.) Government expenditures as a share of GDP increased more in 2001 (3.2 percentage points to 36.5 percent) than they did in 2000 (2.8 percentage points). Based on the lower corporate tax rate, Saudi Arabia's fiscal burden of government score is 1.4 points better this year.

345

## GOVERNMENT INTERVENTION IN THE ECONOMY
Score: **4.5**–Stable (very high level)

According to the World Bank, the government consumed 27 percent of GDP in 2001. In the same year, based on data from the International Monetary Fund, Saudi Arabia received 80.43 percent of its total revenues from state-owned oil companies.

## MONETARY POLICY
Score: **1**–Stable (very low level of inflation)

From 1993 to 2002, Saudi Arabia's weighted average annual rate of inflation was –0.55 percent.

## CAPITAL FLOWS AND FOREIGN INVESTMENT
Score: **4**–Worse (high barriers)

In April 2000, the government updated its investment code by guaranteeing repatriation of profits and capital, allowing foreign investment without a Saudi partner, and creating the General Investment Authority, which has jurisdiction over approving new investment projects. In February 2001, the government developed a "negative list" of 22 sectors off-limits to foreign investors, including such sectors as upstream oil exploration, real estate investment in Mecca and Medina, education, telecommunications, distribution services, and land and air transportation services. In February 2003, the government removed insurance, power transmission and distribution, education, and pipeline services from the "negative list." "However," reports the Economist Intelligence Unit, "permission does not necessarily equal practice, nor, more fundamentally, the creation of a business environment attractive to foreign investors." Foreign workers and companies are subject to a 30 percent tax rate. According to the U.S. Department of State, "disincentives to investment [include] an absence of accurate data, a government requirement that companies hire Saudi nationals [private companies are required to increase their percentage of Saudi nationals by 5 percent per year], slow payment of government contracts...a restrictive visa policy for all workers...enforced segregation of the sexes in most business and social settings...." The EIU reports that "Saudi Arabia has consistently favored domestic vested interests over foreign capital; domestic and Gulf Co-operation Council (GCC) bids are favored in government procurement.... [A]n offset programme requires reinvestment of a portion of the value of large contracts in the local economy...." The International Monetary Fund reports that residents may hold foreign exchange accounts but that approval is required for non-residents. There are no controls or restrictions on payments and transfers. Only Saudi Arabian nationals may engage in portfolio investment in listed Saudi Arabian companies, and non-residents must have permission to issue securities, bonds, or money market instruments. Based on the evidence that the government does not accord foreign investors national treatment and restricts foreign investors from its

major industries, Saudi Arabia's capital flows and foreign investment score is 1 point worse this year.

## BANKING AND FINANCE
Score: **4**–Stable (high level of restrictions)

The Saudi central bank maintains tight control of the banking system, which is composed of 10 Saudi banks and two GCC banks: the Bahrain-based Gulf International Bank and Dubai-based Emirates Bank International. According to the Economist Intelligence Unit, "the Saudi banking sector rests heavily on the fortunes of oil on the international markets and the state of the government's finances. The ten domestic commercial banks are heavily exposed to the government and to contractors dependent on government payments." Most banks are joint ventures with foreign banks, and only three are wholly Saudi-owned. Foreigners may own no more than 49 percent of domestic banks. Saudi Arabia's largest bank in terms of assets, the National Commercial Bank, sold 50 percent of its shares to the government in 1999. These shares are supposed to be sold back to the private sector; according to the Economist Intelligence Unit, however, "The prospect of the Public Investment Fund (PIF) selling some or all of its stake in National Commercial Bank (NCB) remains but is somewhat remote...." According to the U.S. Department of State, "Credit is available from several government credit institutions, such as the Saudi Industrial Development Fund (SIDF), which allocates credit based on government-set criteria rather than market conditions."

## WAGES AND PRICES
Score: **2**–Stable (low level of intervention)

The market determines most wages and prices. According to the Economist Intelligence Unit, "Price controls are considered contrary to Islamic law and, as such, are illegal in Saudi Arabia. This only applies to goods supplied by the private sector, however; public-sector goods such as power and water are often heavily subsidised. As pressure on government finances increased over the second half of the 1990s, many of these subsidies were eased, including those on agricultural products, fuels, telecommunications and power. Nevertheless, an element of subsidy continues on many basic food commodities, utilities, medicines, cement and other goods." There is no legal minimum wage.

## PROPERTY RIGHTS
Score: **3**–Stable (moderate level of protection)

According to the U.S. Department of State, the judiciary is not independent and is influenced by other branches of government. The Economist Intelligence Unit reports that "the enforcement of contracts [is] hampered by the complex nature, lengthy process and questionable neutrality of the Saudi Judiciary. Many businessmen in the kingdom complain that the workings of the commercial courts are slow and opaque; others suggest that the courts routinely favour Saudi parties in disputes with foreign firms or individuals, particularly those with connections to the ruling elite and royal family."

## REGULATION
### Score: **3**–Stable (moderate level)

Regulations are not transparent in Saudi Arabia, and bureaucracy poses a substantial hurdle for would-be businesses. Implementation of laws can be inconsistent. The official "Saudiisation" policy of promoting employment of Saudi nationals creates an additional burden. According to the U.S. Department of State, "Foreign firms have identified corruption as an obstacle to investment in Saudi Arabia.... Bribes, often disguised as 'commissions,' are reputed to be commonplace." The state has taken some action, albeit slowly; the Economist Intelligence Unit reports that "structural reform has gained the full backing of Crown Prince Abdullah—the kingdom's most powerful political actor—and real progress has been made."

## INFORMAL MARKET
### Score: **3**–Stable (moderate level of activity)

Saudi Arabia's informal market is growing. The Business Software Alliance reports that Saudi Arabia had a piracy rate of 52 percent in 2001. According to the U.S. Department of State, "Manufacturers of consumer products and automobile spare parts are particularly concerned about the widespread availability of counterfeit products in Saudi Arabia. Anticounterfeiting laws exist, and the U.S. Government has urged the Saudi authorities to step up enforcement actions against perpetrators. In some popular consumer goods, manufacturers estimate that as much as 75% of the entire Saudi market is counterfeit."

# SENEGAL

**Rank:** 72

**Score:** 3.00

**Category:** Mostly Unfree

### Present & Past Scores

(Best) 1
2
3
4
(Worst) 5

3.81 3.64 3.51 3.41 3.34 3.33 3.45 3.33 3.00

'95 '96 '97 '98 '99 '00 '01 '02 '03 '04
n/a

## QUICK STUDY

### SCORES
| | |
|---|---|
| Trade Policy | 3 |
| Fiscal Burden | 4.5 |
| Government Intervention | 2 |
| Monetary Policy | 1 |
| Foreign Investment | 3 |
| Banking and Finance | 3 |
| Wages and Prices | 3 |
| Property Rights | 3 |
| Regulation | 4 |
| Informal Market | 3.5 |

**Population:** 9,769,448

**Total area:** 196,190 sq. km

**GDP:** $6.1 billion

**GDP growth rate:** 5.7%

**GDP per capita:** $628

**Major exports:** fish, groundnuts (peanuts), petroleum products, phosphates, cotton

**Exports of goods and services:** $2.1 billion

**Major export trading partners:** India 18.0%, France 15.6%, Italy 9.0%, Mali 5.9% (2000)

**Major imports:** foods and beverages, consumer goods, capital goods, petroleum products

**Imports of goods and services:** $2.4 billion

**Major import trading partners:** France 27.4%, Nigeria 18.9%, Germany 5.3%, Italy 3.6% (2000)

**Foreign direct investment (net):** $99.5 million

2001 Data (in constant 1995 US dollars)

Senegal continues to face many challenges, including poverty, illiteracy, poor health care, and policies that inhibit growth. According to the Organisation for Economic Co-operation and Development, "A survey on the perception of poverty by Senegalese in 2001 showed that 94.5 percent thought the standard of living would improve if the government managed to stamp out corruption throughout the country." Standard & Poors reports that Senegal's general government debt was an estimated 71.3 percent of GDP in 2002. The OECD notes that investment is hindered by high taxes and the lack of a national land register. The electricity sector is in desperate need of reform; the country continues to experience power shortages because there is not enough power to go around, and the government's efforts to privatize Senelec have failed. Senegal has West Africa's lowest rate of HIV/AIDS, and infant mortality is lower than in neighboring countries; yet life expectancy is only 54 years. The government aims to increase vaccination coverage and access to health care. Primary education remains substandard, with low enrollment and a high rate of illiteracy, despite the fact that Senegal spends more on education than other sub-Saharan countries, according to OECD reports. Senegal needs to lower taxes, register land, and fight corruption to attract investment, and the government needs to allocate more of its education budget to primary education. Senegal's fiscal burden of government score is 0.2 point worse this year; however, its trade policy score is 1 point better, its government intervention score is 2 points better, and its informal market score is 0.5 point better. As a result, Senegal's overall score is 0.33 point better this year.

## TRADE POLICY
### Score: **3–Better** (moderate level of protectionism)

Senegal is a member of the West African Economic and Monetary Union, which imposes a common external tariff with four rates: 0 percent, 5 percent, 10 percent, and 20 percent. (The other seven members of the WAEMU are Benin, Burkina Faso, Guinea–Bissau, Ivory Coast, Mali, Niger, and Togo.) The World Bank reports that Senegal's weighted average tariff rate in 2001 (the most recent year for which World Bank data are available) was 8.5 percent, down from the 12 percent reported in the 2003 *Index*. As a result, Senegal's trade policy score is 1 point better this year. Customs corruption acts as a non-tariff barrier. According to the U.S. Department of State, "Corruption can range from large-scale customs fraud, including invoice under-valuation, to bribe taking by officials."

## FISCAL BURDEN OF GOVERNMENT
Score—Income Taxation: **5–Stable** (very high tax rates)
Score—Corporate Taxation: **4.5–Stable** (very high tax rates)
Score—Change in Government Expenditures: **4–Worse** (moderate increase)
### Final Score: **4.5–Worse** (very high cost of government)

Senegal's top income tax rate is 50 percent. The top corporate tax rate is 35 percent. Government expenditures as a share of GDP increased 1.7 percentage points to 21.7 percent in 2001, compared to a 0.8 percentage point decrease in 2000. As a result, Senegal's fiscal burden of government score is 0.2 point worse this year.

349

## GOVERNMENT INTERVENTION IN THE ECONOMY
### Score: **2**–Better (low level)

The World Bank reports that the government consumed 10.1 percent of GDP in 2001. In the same year, based on data from the International Monetary Fund, Senegal received 2.29 percent of its total revenues from state-owned enterprises and government ownership of property. Based on newly available data on revenues from state-owned enterprises and the application of a new methodology to score this factor, Senegal's government intervention score is 2 points better this year.

## MONETARY POLICY
### Score: **1**–Stable (very low level of inflation)

From 1993 to 2002, Senegal's weighted average annual rate of inflation was 2.25 percent. Senegal has benefited from a stable currency—a rarity in sub-Saharan Africa—as a member of the CFA franc zone. Fourteen countries use the CFA franc, a common currency with a fixed parity with the euro. (The other 13 countries are Benin, Burkina Faso, Cameroon, Central African Republic, Chad, Congo [Brazzaville], Equatorial Guinea, Gabon, Guinea–Bissau, Ivory Coast, Mali, Niger, and Togo.) Monetary policy is set by the Central Bank of West African States.

## CAPITAL FLOWS AND FOREIGN INVESTMENT
### Score: **3**–Stable (moderate barriers)

There is no legal discrimination against foreign investors, and 100 percent foreign ownership of businesses is permitted in most sectors, except in the electricity, telecommunications, and water sectors. The U.S. Department of State reports that "administrative regulations combined with high factor costs have been obstacles to potential investors." According to the International Monetary Fund, the government must approve most capital transfers to countries other than members of the West African Economic and Monetary Union. Other transfers are subject to numerous requirements, controls, and authorization depending on the transaction. Residents and non-residents must receive approval from the Banque Centrale des Etats de l'Afrique de l'Ouest (Central Bank of West African States, or BCEAO) and the Senegalese government to hold foreign exchange accounts. Most capital transactions require approval of or declaration to the government.

## BANKING AND FINANCE
### Score: **3**–Stable (moderate level of restrictions)

The BCEAO, a central bank common to the eight members of the WAEMU, governs Senegal's banking system. Member countries use the CFA franc that is issued by the BCEAO and pegged to the euro. The banking system consists of 14 banks, and the government holds a stake of 25 percent or more in three banks, including a majority share in Caisse Nationale de Credit Agricole Sénégalais (Agricultural Bank). Three privately owned banks hold approximately two-thirds of total deposits.

## WAGES AND PRICES
### Score: **3**–Stable (moderate level of intervention)

Senegal's large state-owned sector (the country's largest employer) influences wages and prices, and the International Monetary Fund reports that the government directly controls the prices of charcoal, gas, pharmaceutical products, water, electricity, and transportation services. Senegal has a monthly minimum wage.

## PROPERTY RIGHTS
### Score: **3**–Stable (moderate level of protection)

Expropriation of private property is unlikely. The U.S. Department of State reports that Senegal's judiciary, while independent, is "subject to influence and pressure. Magistrates are vulnerable to outside pressures due to low pay, poor working conditions, and family and political ties." In addition, "The investment code provides for settlement of disputes via due process of the law prescribed in the cumbersome Senegalese judicial system. In order to overcome the weaknesses of the judicial system in the dispute settlement area and to speed the settlement process, Senegal established, in 1998, an arbitration center administered by the Dakar Chamber of Commerce." The government is training judges in commercial law.

## REGULATION
### Score: **4**–Stable (high level)

Competition is constrained by the state's dominant role in the economy. Regulatory and enforcement agencies are characterized by red tape. A cumbersome regulatory environment and corruption in the bureaucracy are significantly burdensome. According to the U.S. Department of State, "The potential for corruption is a significant obstacle for economic development and competitiveness in Senegal, in spite of laws, regulations, penalties, and agencies to combat it. Credible allegations of corruption have been made concerning government procurement, dispute settlement, and regulatory and enforcement agencies."

## INFORMAL MARKET
### Score: **3.5**–Better (high level of activity)

Transparency International's 2002 score for Senegal is 3.1. Therefore, Senegal's informal market score is 3.5 this year—0.5 point better than last year.

SERBIA AND
MONTENEGRO

# SERBIA AND MONTENEGRO

Rank: Suspended

Score: n/a

Category: n/a

Present & Past Scores

(Best) 1
2
3
4
(Worst) 5

4.21 4.28

'95 '96 '97 '98 '99 '00 '01 '02 '03 '04
n/a n/a n/a n/a n/a n/a n/a          n/a

Serbia, the dominant republic in Yugoslavia, along with a restive and largely autonomous Montenegro, is worse off economically than almost all of the other transition economies of Central and Eastern Europe. The devastation caused by a series of wars culminating in the Kosovo campaign of 1999, which involved the bombing of Yugoslavia by NATO, was exacerbated by the chronic mismanagement and corruption that characterized the regime of Slobodan Milosevic. Under reformist Serbian Prime Minister Zoran Djindjic, Milosevic has been sent to the Hague to be tried for war crimes, and foreign aid to Belgrade has been resumed. In March 2002, Serbia and Montenegro agreed, at least temporarily, to resolve their constitutional dispute over whether Montenegro should remain part of a broader Yugoslavia. A new political entity, to be called Serbia and Montenegro rather than Yugoslavia, allows both entities to run their own economies, currencies, and customs unions while remaining part of a decentralized state. The Serbian government is committed to far-reaching reforms. In June 2001, the Serbian parliament passed privatization legislation to sell 4,000 enterprises in the next four years, and the government has both streamlined registration and inspection requirements for businesses and loosened constraints on access to financing and foreign investment. The assassination of Prime Minister Djindjic by members of the Zemun drug cartel demonstrated that, despite government efforts to break up networks of gangsters, Belgrade's underground power structure remains in the grip of war criminals, corrupt security chiefs, and ultra-nationalist politicians. It will be up to Djindjic's reformist heir, Prime Minister Zoran Zivkovic, to complete Serbia's perilous economic transition. Grading of Serbia and Montenegro is suspended this year, both because the differing policies in Serbia and Montenegro make it impossible to assign a grade to the individual factors and because insufficient information is available to grade Serbia and Montenegro separately.

## QUICK STUDY

### SCORES

Trade Policy                        n/a
Fiscal Burden                       n/a
Government Intervention  n/a
Monetary Policy                 n/a
Foreign Investment          n/a
Wages and Prices             n/a
Banking and Finance        n/a
Property Rights                 n/a
Regulation                         n/a
Informal Market               n/a

**Population:** 10,651,000

**Total area:** 102,350 sq. km

**GDP:** $13.8 billion

**GDP growth rate:** 5.5%

**GDP per capita:** $1,302

**Major exports:** manufactured goods, food and live animals, raw materials

**Exports of goods and services:** $2.5 billion

**Major export trading partners:** Bosnia and Herzegovina 14.5%, Italy 14.5%, Germany 10.7%, Macedonia 9.1%

**Major imports:** machinery and transport equipment, fuels and lubricants, manufactured goods, chemicals, food and live animals, raw materials

**Imports of goods and services:** $4.6 billion

**Major import trading partners:** Russia 12.5%, Germany 13.1%, Italy 10.3%, Greece 4.4%

**Foreign direct investment (net):** $147.9 million

2001 Data (in constant 1995 US dollars)

## TRADE POLICY
### Score: Not graded

According to the International Monetary Fund, Serbia's average tariff rate in 2000 was 10 percent. No reliable information on Montenegro's average tariff rate or the "Serbia and Montenegro" union is available.

## FISCAL BURDEN OF GOVERNMENT
### Score—Income Taxation: Not graded
### Score—Corporate Taxation: Not graded
### Score—Change in Government Expenditures: Not graded
## Final Score: Not graded

Serbia and Montenegro's top income tax rate is 20 percent. The top corporate tax rate is also 20 percent. Government expenditure data for Serbia and Montenegro are not available; therefore, government consumption as a share of GDP was used as a proxy for government expenditure as a share of GDP this year. Government consumption as a share of GDP decreased less in 2001 (1 percentage point to 18 percent) than it did in 2000 (10 percentage points).

## GOVERNMENT INTERVENTION IN THE ECONOMY
### Score: Not graded

The World Bank reports that the government of Yugoslavia consumed 18.4 percent of GDP in 2001. (No data on either Serbia's or Montenegro's level of government consumption are available.) According to the Economist Intelligence Unit, "Official data [for Serbia] show that privatisation inflows up to September 2002 amounted to around US$250m. Some 54 state companies were privatised in the first nine months of 2002, with the Serbian Ministry of Economy and Privatisation indicating that it planned to sell a further 400–600 enterprises before the end of 2002, although this is not likely to be achieved owing to the lack of time." In Montenegro, half of the economy had been privatized by mid-2002. However, according to the EIU, "The Montenegrin government has been less successful in its attempts to sell…Telekom Crne Gore, the KAP aluminium plant, Jugopetrol and others. A wide range of assets in the tourist industry are to be put on the market."

## MONETARY POLICY
### Score: Not graded

Between 1993 and 2002, Serbia and Montenegro's weighted average annual rate of inflation was 38.10 percent. This figure, however, is somewhat misleading since Montenegro has adopted the more stable euro as its currency while Serbia remains wedded to the dinar.

## CAPITAL FLOWS AND FOREIGN INVESTMENT
### Score: Not graded

The foreign investment climate in Serbia and Montenegro is improving. According to the European Bank for Reconstructions and Development, "the investment climate is gradually improving in both republics…. The most impressive achievements include a highly practical and 'deal-oriented' privatisation law, the dismantling of old and unduly restrictive labour laws and the introduction of a foreign investment law which underlines the essentially equal status of foreign and domestic investors. However, the short-term political risks remain significant. These include the possibility of destabilizing internal rivalries within each republic…. Corruption is seen by the public in both Republics as one of the most serious problems facing society today." The International Monetary Fund reports that both residents and non-residents may hold foreign exchange accounts with permission from the central bank. Payments and transfers are subject to restrictions, and most capital transactions are subject to controls.

## BANKING AND FINANCE
### Score: Not graded

Serbia and Montenegro's banking system is underdeveloped, inefficient, and undercapitalized. According to the European Bank for Reconstruction and Development, "Most banks in [Serbia and Montenegro] do not function properly. Savings rates are extremely low and lending to enterprises is almost non-existent or, at best, on a very limited short term basis. The Serbian authorities have prepared a rehabilitation strategy for the sector and have already taken decisive action,

including the closure of the four largest state-owned banks in January 2002 (representing 60 percent of banking system assets). Montenegro, meanwhile, has implemented very strict controls on banks which has limited their ability to make loans…. A 100 per cent reserve requirement on local deposits was recently reduced to 80 per cent. The reserve requirement is expected to be gradually reduced further to 45 per cent over the next year…."

## WAGES AND PRICES
### Score: Not graded

According to the Institute for Strategic Studies and Prognoses, an independent economic institute in Montenegro, the government controls the price of electricity, oil, and communal services. According to the G17 Institute, a social science think tank in Serbia, the government controls the price of electricity, oil, utilities, coal production, liquid gas, and textbooks. Serbia and Montenegro has a minimum wage.

## PROPERTY RIGHTS
### Score: Not graded

The Economist Intelligence Unit reports that Serbia and Montenegro's judicial system "comprises courts of general jurisdiction at the federal and republican levels within a uniform system…. Economic or trade matters come under the jurisdiction of economic courts. Judges are elected or removed by the republican assemblies or the federal assembly. The system is overburdened and inefficient; judges need retraining to keep up with recent developments and low levels of pay are an invitation to corruption."

## REGULATION
### Score: Not graded

In Serbia, according to KPMG, "government regulation makes it difficult for business to conduct business activities." The International Monetary Fund (still reporting on the Federal Republic of Yugoslavia) indicates that the authorities are taking steps to deregulate the bureaucracy, including removing "onerous registration and inspection requirements, inefficiencies in the domestic payments system, and constraints on access to financing for investment and working capital."

## INFORMAL MARKET
### Score: Not graded

Transparency International's 2001 score for Yugoslavia (Serbia and Montenegro) is 1.3. Therefore, Yugoslavia's (Serbia and Montenegro's) informal market score is 4.5 this year.

# SIERRA LEONE

Rank: 134

Score: 3.73

Category: Mostly Unfree

**Present & Past Scores**

(Best) 1
2
3
4
(Worst) 5

3.90  3.65  3.79  3.70  3.96  4.04          3.95  3.73

'95  '96  '97  '98  '99  '00  '01  '02  '03  '04
n/a  n/a

## QUICK STUDY

### SCORES

| | |
|---|---|
| Trade Policy | 5 |
| Fiscal Burden | 4.3 |
| Government Intervention | 2 |
| Monetary Policy | 1 |
| Foreign Investment | 4 |
| Banking and Finance | 4 |
| Wages and Prices | 2 |
| Property Rights | 5 |
| Regulation | 5 |
| Informal Market | 5 |

**Population:** 5,133,380

**Total area:** 71,740 sq. km

**GDP:** $810.7 million

**GDP growth rate:** 5.4%

**GDP per capita:** $158

**Major exports:** diamonds, cocoa, coffee, fish

**Exports of goods and services:** $13.8 million

**Major export trading partners:** Greece 32.1%, Belgium 28.2%, US 6.3%, UK 5.9%

**Major imports:** foodstuffs, fuel, machinery and transport equipment, manufactured goods

**Imports of goods and services:** $114 million

**Major import trading partners:** UK 25.3%, Netherlands 10.3%, US 7.9%, Germany 6.3%

**Foreign direct investment (net):** n/a

*2001 Data (in constant 1995 US dollars)*

For most of the past decade, Sierra Leone, diamond-rich but plagued by a brutal civil war and political instability, remained one of the world's poorest countries. However, the successful British-led military intervention in 2000 and the subsequent U.N. peacekeeping operation brought a measure of hope. The civil war ended in early 2002, and President Ahmad Tejan Kabbah was re-elected for a new five-year term in May 2002. He faces a huge challenge in rebuilding his shattered nation and convincing international donors that he is committed to building a stable democracy and thriving market economy free of the scourge of corruption. There are positive signs of renewed economic confidence. Diamond exports have soared in the past two years, and the Economist Intelligence Unit forecasts real GDP growth of 6 percent–7 percent in 2003–2004. However, according to the EIU, that figure will need to grow to 15 percent per annum over a five-year period for poverty to be significantly reduced. Political stability will be assisted by the continuing British military presence and by the establishment of a South African–style Truth and Reconciliation Commission, which will hear testimony from hundreds of combatants and victims of the civil war and will operate in conjunction with a Special Court for War Crimes. Sierra Leone's fiscal burden of government score is 0.2 point better this year, and its monetary policy score is 2 points better. As a result, Sierra Leone's overall score is 0.22 point better this year.

## TRADE POLICY
### Score: **5**–Stable (very high level of protectionism)

The World Bank reports that Sierra Leone's average tariff rate in 1995 (the most recent year for which World Bank data are available) was 21 percent. This figure should be viewed with caution, however. According to the Economist Intelligence Unit, "Official trade figures have been unreliable in recent years, as a result of the civil war."

## FISCAL BURDEN OF GOVERNMENT
Score—Income Taxation: **4**–Stable (high tax rates)
Score—Corporate Taxation: **4.5**–Stable (very high tax rates)
Score—Change in Government Expenditures: **4**–Better (moderate increase)
### Final Score: **4.3**–Better (high cost of government)

Sierra Leone's top income tax rate is 40 percent. The top corporate tax rate is 35 percent. Government expenditures as a share of GDP increased less in 2001 (1.9 percentage points to 30.6 percent) than they did in 2000 (6.7 percentage points). As a result, Sierra Leone's fiscal burden of government score is 0.2 point better this year.

## GOVERNMENT INTERVENTION IN THE ECONOMY
### Score: **2**–Stable (low level)

The World Bank reports that the government consumed 17.2 percent of GDP in 2001. In 2000, based on data from the Bank of Sierra Leone, Sierra Leone received 1.06 percent of its total revenues from state-owned enterprises and government ownership of property. (There are no new revenues statistics.) It should be noted that civil unrest interrupted normal business in 2000 and that revenues should increase as economic activity resumes.

353

**MONETARY POLICY**
Score: **1**–Better (very low level of inflation)

From 1993 to 2002, Sierra Leone's weighted average annual rate of inflation was –0.06 percent, down from the 9.68 percent from 1992 to 2001 reported in the 2003 *Index*. As a result, Sierra Leone's monetary policy score is 2 points better this year.

 **CAPITAL FLOWS AND FOREIGN INVESTMENT**
Score: **4**–Stable (high barriers)

The government has little choice but to welcome foreign investment, as it lacks the resources necessary to rebuild its industry and infrastructure, much less meet public demand, in the aftermath of the civil war. However, the risky political environment, rampant corruption, and uncertain laws and legal enforcement hinder investment. According to the Economist Intelligence Unit, "Measures to improve governance and the legal and judicial systems are also needed to improve the climate for private investment." The International Monetary Fund reports that residents and non-residents are permitted to hold foreign exchange accounts subject to some restrictions. Payments and transfers are generally permitted but face quantitative limits and approval requirements in some instances. Most capital transactions involving capital and money market instruments, credit operations, and purchase of real estate abroad require approval by the Bank of Sierra Leone.

 **BANKING AND FINANCE**
Score: **4**–Stable (high level of restrictions)

The civil war between the government and rebel forces led to the collapse of the financial system, but the recent peace and elections have led to its revival. The Banking Act of 2000, the Banking Regulations of 2001, and the Other Financial Services Act of 2001 established capital adequacy ratios and bank licensing regulations in addition to clarifying the powers and responsibilities of the central bank. The banking system suffers from a large number of non-performing and underperforming loans. In March–April 2003, the government appointed James Rogers as governor of the central bank to replace James Sanpha Koroma, who is alleged to have mismanaged the bank and engaged in corrupt activities. According to the Economist Intelligence Unit, "The appointment of Mr Rogers as governor is questionable. Although a trained economist, he is seen as a political appointee without the necessary experience of running such an organisation." The government-owned Sierra Leone Commercial Bank and government-controlled Rokel Commercial Bank currently dominate the banking system, which is undergoing the transition to a functioning post-conflict system.

 **WAGES AND PRICES**
Score: **2**–Stable (low level of intervention)

The government sets few prices and wages, but it does influence the price of utilities through state-owned firms and through subsidies. A minimum wage was established by law in 1997 and has not been adjusted since then.

 **PROPERTY RIGHTS**
Score: **5**–Stable (very low level of protection)

Property is not secure in Sierra Leone. According to the U.S. Department of State, "The Constitution provides for an independent Judiciary…. [H]owever, the judiciary functioned only in part of the country…. [T]here is evidence that corruption has influenced some cases. Traditional justice systems continued to supplement extensively the central government judiciary in cases involving family law, inheritance, and land tenure, especially in rural areas." According to the Economist Intelligence Unit, "The efforts of the [Anti Corruption Commission] to rein in corrupt officials are being hindered by political interference as well as the near total venality of the judiciary."

 **REGULATION**
Score: **5**–Stable (very high level)

According to the Economist Intelligence Unit, "The government of Ahmad Tejan Kabbah hopes to encourage investment by developing a range of incentives (including tax exemptions) for export- and resource-based industries, as well as for new investors, but weak local demand and foreign-exchange shortages are continuing to inhibit industrial expansion, while foreign companies are reluctant to invest in a country with such high levels of political risk." The same source reports that "Even before the insurgency the economy had suffered from decades of corruption and mismanagement."

 **INFORMAL MARKET**
Score: **5**–Stable (very high level of activity)

Civil unrest and war have devastated the formal economy, and most economic activity occurs in the informal sector. The diamond trade accounts for a significant portion of Sierra Leone's informal market.

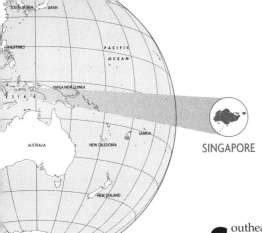

# SINGAPORE

SINGAPORE

Rank: 2

Score: 1.61

Category: Free

### Present & Past Scores

(Best) 1
2
3
4
(Worst) 5

1.68  1.63  1.68  1.54  1.54  1.59  1.66  1.69  1.61  1.61

'95  '96  '97  '98  '99  '00  '01  '02  '03  '04

Southeast Asia is a politically volatile region, and Singapore's relative stability is reassuring to foreign investors and U.S. security interests. The People's Action Party (PAP) retains its overwhelming control of the parliament, holding 82 of 84 seats and garnering more than 75 percent of the vote in the last election. Singapore is one of the world's least corrupt countries, and the rule of law is strong, thus protecting contracts. Nevertheless, stability has come at a price. The Singapore government censors the media and limits the distribution of foreign publications, even business-oriented publications such as the *Asian Wall Street Journal* that do not submit to Singapore censorship. Self-censorship in order to avoid the appearance of criticizing the government is a common practice among Singaporeans, and this inevitably has a chilling effect on the marketplace of ideas in the tiny city-state. Government-linked companies (GLCs) are a prominent method of political control of the economy; for example, all Singapore media are owned by a GLC. The GLCs are regarded as competently run but risk-averse and subject to making investments directed by the government rather than the marketplace. Singapore's politicians also use defamation suits to intimidate the media and opposition politicians. The judiciary's remarkable record of siding with prominent politicians calls into question the true extent of its neutrality in any contract dispute involving a politically sensitive issue.

## QUICK STUDY

### SCORES

| | |
|---|---|
| Trade Policy | 1 |
| Fiscal Burden | 2.6 |
| Government Intervention | 3.5 |
| Monetary Policy | 1 |
| Foreign Investment | 1 |
| Banking and Finance | 2 |
| Wages and Prices | 2 |
| Property Rights | 1 |
| Regulation | 1 |
| Informal Market | 1 |

**Population:** 4,163,700

**Total area:** 647.5 sq. km

**GDP:** $113.1 billion

**GDP growth rate:** 2.2%

**GDP per capita:** $27,172

**Major exports:** machinery and equipment, chemicals, mineral fuels, electronics, travel services, transportation, financial and insurance services

**Exports of goods and services:** $126.4 billion

**Major export trading partners:** Malaysia 17.4%, US 14.7%, Hong Kong 9.2%, Japan 7.1%, Taiwan 5.5%

**Major imports:** machinery and equipment, mineral fuels, oil, chemicals, foodstuffs, financial and insurance services

**Imports of goods and services:** $116.5 billion

**Major import trading partners:** Malaysia 18.2%, US 14.2%, Japan 12.5%, China 7.6%, Thailand 4.6%

2002 Data (in constant 1995 US dollars)

###  TRADE POLICY
### Score: **1**–Stable (very low level of protectionism)

According to the World Bank, Singapore's weighted average tariff rate in 2001 (the most recent year for which World Bank data are available) was approximately 0 percent. The same source reports that 0.2 percent of imports are subject to specific tariffs. According to the Economist Intelligence Unit, the government prohibits "the import of chewing gum, certain cigarette lighters, firecrackers and rhinoceros horns." It takes just two days to obtain import licenses. Customs corruption is virtually nonexistent.

###  FISCAL BURDEN OF GOVERNMENT
Score—Income Taxation: **2**–Stable (low tax rates)
Score—Corporate Taxation: **2.5**–Stable (moderate tax rates)
Score—Change in Government Expenditures: **3.5**–Stable (low increase)
### Final Score: **2.6**–Stable (moderate cost of government)

Singapore's top income tax rate is 22 percent. The corporate tax rate is 22 percent. According to the Embassy of Singapore, the government is planning to reduce the top corporate tax rate to 20 percent by 2005. (The government gave a 5 percent rebate on corporate taxes and a 10 percent rebate on income taxes in 2002 and has given varying rebates since 1980. The variation in the amounts of these rebates makes it impractical to incorporate them into this score.) Government expenditures as a share of GDP increased slightly more in 2002 (0.8 percentage point to 18.9 percent) than they did in 2001 (0.3 percentage point). On net, Singapore's fiscal burden of government score is unchanged this year.

###  GOVERNMENT INTERVENTION IN THE ECONOMY
### Score: **3.5**–Stable (high level)

Based on data from Singapore's Department of Statistics, the government consumed 12.9 percent of GDP in 2002. In 2001, according to the International Monetary Fund, Singapore received 23.3 percent of its revenues from state-owned enterprises and government ownership of property. The *Financial Times* reports that "Temasek's [the government's investment arm] seven top state companies had a market capitalisation of S$72bn ($41bn) at the end of May [2002], or 21 percent of Singapore Exchange's total capitalisation."

 ## MONETARY POLICY
### Score: 1–Stable (very low level of inflation)

From 1993 to 2002, Singapore's weighted average annual rate of inflation was 0.11 percent.

 ## CAPITAL FLOWS AND FOREIGN INVESTMENT
### Score: 1–Stable (very low barriers)

Singapore's investment laws are clear and fair, and they pose few problems for business. The government makes it a priority to foster investment; foreign and domestic businesses are treated equally, and there are no production or local content requirements. According to the Economist Intelligence Unit, "The prominent position of foreign multinationals in many sectors is a major determinant of economic policy. Simple statistics make clear the importance of foreign investment—78% of investment commitments in manufacturing came from abroad in 2002...." Foreign investment in broadcasting, news media, domestic retail banking, some professional services, and some sectors dominated by government-linked companies remains restricted. There are no controls or requirements on current transfers, capital transactions, or repatriation of profits.

 ## BANKING AND FINANCE
### Score: 2–Stable (low level of restrictions)

The Monetary Authority of Singapore has shown greater willingness to grant Qualifying Full Bank (QFB) licenses—six foreign banks since 1999—and restricted bank licenses over the past few years to foreign banks. "Despite liberalization," reports the U.S. Trade Representative, "foreign banks in the domestic retail banking sector still face significant restrictions and are not accorded national treatment. Aside from the limit on the number of foreign QFBs and their customer service locations, the foreign QFBs are not allowed to access the local ATM network. Local retail banks do not face similar constraints." According to the same source, "Officials say they want local banks' share of total resident deposits to remain above 50 percent." The government maintains significant holdings in the Development Bank of Singapore, which is the largest bank in Southeast Asia. All banks are limited to 25 percent of capital base in lending to a single borrower or group of borrowers.

 ## WAGES AND PRICES
### Score: 2–Stable (low level of intervention)

The market sets almost all wages and prices. According to the Economist Intelligence Unit, "the Ministry of Trade and

Industry can impose controls as it deems necessary. Rice and live pigs are now the only two price-controlled items under the Price Control Act, administered by the Ministry. The act also empowers the price controller to regulate the import and export of such items." The National Wage Council (a tripartite body of government, business, and labor) annually reviews wage and economic trends and provides wage increase guidelines for implementation by companies and unions. "Although the government is keen not to be seen to set wages directly," reports the EIU, "it undoubtedly wields influence on settlements made by large government-linked companies (GLCs). Obviously, it also controls most civil service pay.... A longer-standing method of controlling wage costs for lower-grade workers is through the manipulation of the restrictions on the hiring of foreign labour."

 ## PROPERTY RIGHTS
### Score: 1–Stable (very high level of protection)

The court system is very efficient and strongly protects private property, and there is no threat of expropriation. The constitution authorizes an independent judiciary. According to the U.S. Department of State, however, "there has been a perception that it reflects the views of the executive in politically sensitive cases as government leaders historically have utilized court proceedings successfully, in particular defamation suits, against political opponents and critics." Despite reports of political influence, the legal system is sound and enforces contracts effectively. The Economist Intelligence Unit reports that "contractual agreements in Singapore are secure, and the professionalism and efficiency of key agencies are widely acknowledged."

 ## REGULATION
### Score: 1–Stable (very low level)

Regulations in Singapore are straightforward and simple, and the procedures for obtaining licenses and permits are generally transparent and not burdensome. According to the U.S. Department of State, "With the exception of restrictions in the financial services, professional services, and media sectors, Singapore maintains an open investment regime.... The Singapore Government promotes its regulatory environment as business-friendly, with transparent and clear regulations. Tax, labor, banking and finance, industrial health and safety, arbitration, wage and training rules and regulations are formulated and reviewed with the interests of foreign investors and local enterprises in mind, and the Government is usually open to comments from interested businesses." Most observers and business persons regard Singapore's government as clean and corruption-free.

 ## INFORMAL MARKET
### Score: 1–Stable (very low level of activity)

Transparency International's 2002 score for Singapore is 9.3. Therefore, Singapore's informal market score is 1 this year.

SLOVAK
REPUBLIC

# SLOVAK REPUBLIC

Rank: 35
Score: 2.44
Category: Mostly Free

**Present & Past Scores**

(Best) 1
2
3
4 2.88 3.18 3.18 3.31 3.38 3.18 2.85 2.76 2.71 2.44
(Worst) 5

'95 '96 '97 '98 '99 '00 '01 '02 '03 '04

The reformist government of Prime Minister Mikulas Dzurinda and President Rudolf Schuster that came to power in September 1998 after defeating nationalists led by Vladimir Meciar has improved transparency and pursued European integration. It also has liberalized prices, reduced taxes, accelerated privatization, and begun the restructuring of the banking sector. The economy exceeded expectations in 2000–2001. Foreign investment has risen, progress has been achieved in macroeconomic stabilization, and privatization is nearly complete. In 2001, the government reduced personal and corporate income tax rates and removed its 3 percent surcharge on imports. In December 2001, the cabinet eliminated 10 of the 12 off-budget government funds, placing expenditures under the control of the Finance Ministry and improving transparency. The banking sector is dominated by foreign capital. The greatest challenge facing the economy is the high levels of unemployment that are typical for post-communist transitions. Unemployment stands at about 20 percent, having increased from 17.2 percent in 2002. Slovakia was admitted to the Organisation for Economic Co-operation and Development in the second half of 2000. Based on the success of its economic and democratic reforms, it also has been invited to join both the European Union and NATO. The Slovak Republic's fiscal burden of government score is 0.3 point worse this year; however, its monetary policy, banking and finance, and wages and prices scores are 1 point better. As a result, the Slovak Republic's overall score is 0.27 point better this year.

## TRADE POLICY
### Score: **3**–Stable (moderate level of protectionism)

According to the World Trade Organization, the Slovak Republic's average tariff rate in 2001 was 6.1 percent. The U.S. Department of State reports that the "licensing system is Slovakia's primary non-tariff measure."

## FISCAL BURDEN OF GOVERNMENT
Score—Income Taxation: **3.5**–Stable (high tax rates)
Score—Corporate Taxation: **3**–Stable (moderate tax rates)
Score—Change in Government Expenditures: **2**–Worse (moderate decrease)
### Final Score: **2.9**–Worse (moderate cost of government)

The Slovak Republic's top income tax rate is 38 percent. The top corporate tax rate is 25 percent. According to the Economist Intelligence Unit, the Ministry of Finance has announced that the top income and corporate tax rates will be reduced to 20 percent at the beginning of 2004. Government expenditures as a share of GDP decreased less in 2002 (2.5 percentage points to 50.6 percent) than they did in 2001 (5.7 percentage points). As a result, the Slovak Republic's fiscal burden of government score is 0.3 point worse this year.

## GOVERNMENT INTERVENTION IN THE ECONOMY
### Score: **2**–Stable (low level)

Based on data from the International Monetary Fund, the government consumed 19.9 percent of GDP in 2002. In 2001, according to the IMF, the Slovak Republic received 4.66 percent of its total revenues from state-owned enterprises and government ownership of property.

## MONETARY POLICY
### Score: **2**–Better (low level of inflation)

From 1993 to 2002, the Slovak Republic's weighted average annual rate of inflation was 5.27 percent, down from the 8.67 percent from 1992 to 2001 reported in the 2003 *Index*. As a result, the Slovak Republic's monetary policy score is 1 point better this year.

## CAPITAL FLOWS AND FOREIGN INVESTMENT
### Score: **2**–Stable (low barriers)

The Dzurinda government has made attracting foreign investment a priority. Incentives include tax breaks and elimination of tariffs on imports of new manufacturing machinery. There is no screening process for foreign investment, and both 100 percent foreign ownership and repatriation of profits are permitted. New policies on allowing "strategic privatisation" in formerly restricted sectors have further liberalized the foreign investment regime. The law requires that the state retain 51 percent ownership in privatized utilities, but this has not prevented intense interest by foreign investors in 49 percent of the natural gas company, the energy sector, and oil pipeline. According to the U.S. Department of State, "The state must still retain ownership of the railroad rights of way, postal services, water supplies (but not suppliers) and forestry companies." The International Monetary Fund reports that residents may establish foreign exchange accounts when staying abroad or with permission of the National Bank of Slovakia; non-residents may not hold foreign exchange accounts. Foreign purchase of real estate is restricted to inheritance, diplomatic presence, acquisition through marriage or family, exchange of properties of equivalent value, use in the core activities of a foreign-owned business, or a few other restricted circumstances.

## BANKING AND FINANCE
### Score: **1**–Better (very low level of restrictions)

The Slovak Republic has implemented an aggressive privatization program for its state-owned banks. Interest rates have been completely liberalized, and credit limits have been abolished. The government has privatized its larger and medium-sized state-owned banks and retains control of two small banks, Postova Banka and Banka Slovakia, both of which are up for privatization. According to the Economist Intelligence Unit, "Foreign capital already controls nearly 100% of banking assets." On January 1, 2003, the Slovak Republic introduced new rules that make it easier for companies to offer collateral (intellectual property and trademarks) in order to obtain loans. Based on the evidence of negligible government involvement and the dominant role played by foreign banks, the Slovak Republic's banking and finance score is 1 point better this year.

## WAGES AND PRICES
### Score: **2**–Better (low level)

The Slovak Republic has removed a number of price controls. According to the Economist Intelligence Unit, "Inflation is expected to accelerate in 2003…mainly as a result of the liberalisation of administered prices, particularly for energy, as most controls must be lifted ahead of EU accession in 2004." The government mandates a minimum wage. Based on the evidence that the government is removing price controls, the Slovak Republic's wages and prices score is 1 point better this year.

## PROPERTY RIGHTS
### Score: **3**–Stable (moderate level of protection)

Expropriation is unlikely in the Slovak Republic, but the country has a somewhat weak and inefficient judicial system. "The legal system enforces property and contractual rights," reports the U.S. Department of State, "but decisions may take years, thus limiting the utility of courts for dispute resolution…. The commercial code seems to be applied consistently. A bankruptcy law exists but has not been as effective as needed." Corruption is a problem. According to the U.S. Department of State, "Sixty percent of the population [in a survey] blamed the courts and prosecution offices for being the most problematic institutions that prevent a more efficient fight against corruption."

## REGULATION
### Score: **3**–Stable (moderate level)

The government has reduced the level of regulation, and most businesses do not need a license. Lack of transparency, the persistence of red tape, and excessive and inefficient bureaucracy continue to present problems. The U.S. Department of State reports that "transparency and predictability have been a problem on many issues involving investors…. Investors also complain that the purchase of land and granting of building permits is a long, unpredictable process that can delay projects." In addition, "the public continues to perceive corruption as a significant problem and business leaders claim that corruption is endemic," despite the government's efforts to combat it. The Economist Intelligence Unit reports that "the persistence of high unemployment also reflects rigidities in the labour market."

## INFORMAL MARKET
### Score: **3.5**–Stable (high level of activity)

Transparency International's 2002 score for the Slovak Republic is 3.7. Therefore, the Slovak Republic's informal market score is 3.5 this year.

SLOVENIA

# SLOVENIA

Rank: 52
Score: 2.75
Category: Mostly Free

Present & Past Scores

(Best) 1
2
3
4
(Worst) 5

3.74  3.45  3.15  3.05  3.20  3.01  3.25  2.86  2.75

'95  '96  '97  '98  '99  '00  '01  '02  '03  '04
n/a

Slovenia, the richest of the eight formerly communist countries likely to join the European Union in 2004 (its GDP per capita makes it about as rich as Greece), has pursued a gradualist approach to economic development. The establishment has never accepted the need for radical economic reform, maintaining that the country's relatively high regional level of economic development—the Economist Intelligence Unit, for example, projects that the economy will grow at the healthy rate of 3.1 percent of GDP in 2003—renders such drastic change irrelevant. For several years, the sale of key assets to foreigners has encountered widespread hostility; foreign direct investment has been modest because of the high level of bureaucratic red tape and the small size of the Slovene market. In addition, Slovenia has endured a persistently high rate of inflation, about which the government has done little until recently. In May 2002, however, the government completed the sale of a minority stake in Slovenia's largest bank to a Belgian financial institution. All the main political parties in Slovenia have supported final preparations for entry into the EU in May 2004, and Slovenia has experienced relative political stability for the past decade. Slovenia's trade policy score is 1 point better this year, and its fiscal burden of government score is 0.1 point better. As a result, Slovenia's overall score is 0.11 point better this year.

## QUICK STUDY

### SCORES

| | |
|---|---|
| Trade Policy | 3 |
| Fiscal Burden | 3.5 |
| Government Intervention | 2.5 |
| Monetary Policy | 3 |
| Foreign Investment | 3 |
| Banking and Finance | 3 |
| Wages and Prices | 2 |
| Property Rights | 3 |
| Regulation | 2 |
| Informal Market | 2.5 |

**Population:** 1,995,033

**Total area:** 20,253 sq. km

**GDP:** $24.7 billion

**GDP growth rate:** 3.2%

**GDP per capita:** $12,363

**Major exports:** machinery and transport equipment, manufactures, chemicals, food and live animals

**Exports of goods and services:** $16.4 billion

**Major export trading partners:** Germany 24.8%, Italy 12.2%, Croatia 8.7%, Austria 7.1%

**Major imports:** machinery and transport equipment, chemicals, manufactures, mineral fuels and lubricants

**Imports of goods and services:** $16.7 billion

**Major import trading partners:** Germany 19.2%, Italy 17.9%, France 10.3%, Austria 8.3%, Croatia 3.6%

**Foreign direct investment (net):** $1.6 billion

2002 Data (in constant 1995 US dollars)

## TRADE POLICY
### Score: **3–Better** (moderate level of protectionism)

According to the World Bank, Slovenia's weighted average tariff rate in 2001 (the most recent year for which World Bank data are available) was 9.9 percent, down from the 11.4 percent reported in the 2003 *Index*. As a result, Slovenia's trade policy score is 1 point better this year. Non-tariff barriers include quotas for textiles and import licenses. The U.S. Department of State reports that "import quotas restrict a few categories of goods, and in some sectors permits or licenses restrict importation."

## FISCAL BURDEN OF GOVERNMENT
### Score—Income Taxation: **5–Stable** (very high tax rates)
### Score—Corporate Taxation: **3–Stable** (moderate tax rates)
### Score—Change in Government Expenditures: **3–Better** (very low decrease)
### Final Score: **3.5–Better** (high cost of government)

Slovenia's top income tax rate is 50 percent. The top corporate tax rate is 25 percent. Government expenditures as a share of GDP remained unchanged at 44.5 percent in 2002, compared to a 0.3 percentage point increase in 2001. As a result, Slovenia's fiscal burden of government score is 0.1 point better this year.

## GOVERNMENT INTERVENTION IN THE ECONOMY
### Score: **2.5–Stable** (moderate level)

Based on data from the International Monetary Fund, the government consumed 20.5 percent of GDP in 2002. In 2001, according to the IMF, Slovenia received 2.77 percent of its total revenues from state-owned enterprises and government ownership of property.

**MONETARY POLICY**
Score: **3**–Stable (moderate level of inflation)

From 1993 to 2002, Slovenia's weighted average annual rate of inflation was 7.80 percent.

 **CAPITAL FLOWS AND FOREIGN INVESTMENT**
Score: **3**–Stable (moderate barriers)

Slovenia updated its foreign investment code in 2001 by opening most business activities to foreign investment. Foreign investors are accorded national treatment, restrictions on portfolio investment have been abolished, and the government has streamlined the investment process. Certain restrictions remain on foreign ownership in the broadcasting, communications, insurance, and rail and air transport sectors. The U.S. Department of State reports that "a number of practical impediments to increased FDI inflows persist.... [T]he legal framework regulating corporate activities is incomplete, with continued administrative barriers to business.... [S]ecuring land and business premises, especially for industrial use, remains difficult.... [T]he failure to begin a comprehensive restructuring process has prevented recently privatized companies from searching for strategic partners.... [A]mbiguous signals as to Slovenia's attitude toward FDI continue.... [A]n aggressive FDI policy has yet to materialize." The International Monetary Fund reports that residents and non-residents may hold foreign exchange accounts after proving their identity. There are no restrictions on payments and transfers. Issue of foreign debt securities and investment securities is subject to approval by the Ministry of Finance, and the Bank of Slovenia sets conditions for the purchase, sale, or issue of money market instruments.

 **BANKING AND FINANCE**
Score: **3**–Stable (moderate level of restrictions)

The International Monetary Fund reports that foreign banks, insurance companies, and stock brokering companies may open branches in Slovenia. As a result of this increased foreign competition, the financial sector is consolidating. The government maintains a significant presence. According to the Economist Intelligence Unit, there were 20 banks and two savings institutions in Slovenia in January 2003. The EIU reports that the government has sold a 34 percent stake in the country's largest bank, Nova Ljubljanksa, which accounts for 35 percent of the country's banking sector. However, the government still retains a 33 percent stake in the company. The EIU also reports that in late 2002, the government decided to retain the second largest bank for the time being. The government has a 85 percent stake in the largest insurance firm, but the EIU reports that a February 2003 Constitutional Court ruling should open up the possibility for privatization and restructuring in the insurance sector.

 **WAGES AND PRICES**
Score: **2**–Stable (low level of intervention)

According to the U.S. Department of State, "Prices are generally determined by the market. The price of gasoline is set through a pricing model, which adjusts to world prices every two weeks. The government sets the price of energy, natural gas, railway transport, telecommunications, milk, and some other products. The government may also influence the pricing policies of companies under its direct or indirect control." Price controls do not represent a large portion of national output, and the Embassy of Slovenia reports that the share of administered prices in the consumer price index has fallen from 23 percent in 1995 to 12.6 percent in 2003. The government mandates a minimum wage.

 **PROPERTY RIGHTS**
Score: **3**–Stable (moderate level of protection)

Private property is guaranteed by Slovenia's constitution. According to the Economist Intelligence Unit, "Judges are appointed by the executive branch...but are generally politically neutral." However, "The Slovenian court system is marred by inadequate staffing and slow procedural progress and is in need of further reform." According to the U.S. Department of State, a number of laws have been passed to strengthen the legal framework that supports Slovenia's private sector, but "progress has been somewhat halting." The same source reports that the European Union Commission has criticized "Slovenia's lack of progress in reforming the public administration and the judiciary."

 **REGULATION**
Score: **2**–Stable (low level)

It is becoming easier to establish a business as the government has undertaken regulatory reform, although an entrenched and sometimes inefficient bureaucracy continues to hinder business development. Deregulation of the labor market has not progressed. According to the Economist Intelligence Unit, "the labour market remains relatively inflexible and over-protected, and pay scales in public service are very complicated and do not reward performance." The government has made progress in reforming public administration and identifying and reducing red tape. The U.S. Department of State reports that the government has the authority to establish market restrictions in cases of natural disasters, epidemics, goods shortages, and other states of emergency. The same source reports that corruption exists on a "minor scale."

 **INFORMAL MARKET**
Score: **2.5**–Stable (moderate level of activity)

Transparency International's 2002 score for Slovenia is 6. Therefore, Slovenia's informal market score is 2.5 this year.

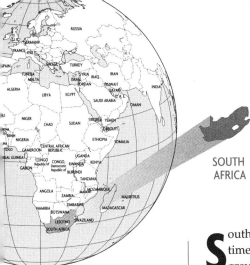

# SOUTH AFRICA

SOUTH
AFRICA

**Rank:** 53

**Score:** 2.79

**Category:** Mostly Free

**Present & Past Scores**

(Best) 1
2
3
4
(Worst) 5

3.23 3.25 2.99 2.88 2.98 3.01 3.00 2.79 2.58 2.79

'95 '96 '97 '98 '99 '00 '01 '02 '03 '04

## QUICK STUDY

### SCORES

| | |
|---|---|
| Trade Policy | 4 |
| Fiscal Burden | 3.9 |
| Government Intervention | 2 |
| Monetary Policy | 3 |
| Foreign Investment | 2 |
| Banking and Finance | 2 |
| Wages and Prices | 2 |
| Property Rights | 3 |
| Regulation | 3 |
| Informal Market | 3 |

**Population:** 43,240,000

**Total area:** 1,219,912 sq. km

**GDP:** $175.9 billion

**GDP growth rate:** 2.2%

**GDP per capita:** $4,068

**Major exports:** metal and metal products, gold, diamonds, machinery and transport equipment

**Exports of goods and services:** $46.2 billion

**Major export trading partners:** Germany 15.2%, US 11.4%, UK 8.6%, Japan 5.8%

**Major imports:** machinery and appliances, mineral products, chemicals, transport and equipment

**Imports of goods and services:** $41.9 billion

**Major import trading partners:** Germany 15.2%, US 11.4%, UK 8.6%, Japan 5.8%

**Foreign direct investment (net):** $448.4 million

2001 Data (in constant 1995 US dollars)

South Africa remains Africa's economic powerhouse, with a per capita GDP that is two times greater than Egypt's and six times greater than Nigeria's or Kenya's. Real GDP grew by 3 percent in 2002 and is expected to rise to 3.5 percent by 2004. The rand has begun to stabilize and in 2002 reversed the preceding year's 38 percent fall in value. Despite this relative success, however, the economy faces major obstacles to long-term growth and stability. A report by investment bank Goldman Sachs revealed that South Africa will need to double its growth rate in the coming years if it is to reduce its staggeringly high unemployment rate of 30 percent. The African National Congress–led government has stated its commitment to flexible labor markets and privatization, but powerful unions continue to oppose these goals and have managed to slow their implementation. Restrictive labor regulations have aggravated the unemployment problem. An extremely high crime rate, a soaring incidence of AIDS, and a growing number of corruption scandals also have undermined long-term prospects for investment and growth. The political crisis in neighboring Zimbabwe threatens to have a major destabilizing effect on South Africa and the region. An estimated 2 million Zimbabweans have fled to South Africa, and regional instability has acted as a major deterrent to foreign investors, but there is little sign that the government is willing to deal with the crisis. President Thabo Mbeki has come under increasing criticism for his controversial policy of "silent engagement" with Zimbabwe and is seemingly content to pursue a strategy of appeasement toward the dictatorship of Robert Mugabe. South Africa's trade policy and monetary policy scores are 1 point worse this year, and its fiscal burden of government score is 0.1 point worse. As a result, South Africa's overall score is 0.21 point worse this year.

### TRADE POLICY
**Score: 4–Worse** (high level of protectionism)

South Africa belongs to the Southern African Customs Union (SACU), a regional trade arrangement with Botswana, Lesotho, Namibia, and Swaziland. According to the World Trade Organization, in 2002 (the most recent year for which WTO data are available), the SACU had an average common external tariff rate of 11.4 percent, up from the 8.5 percent reported in the 2003 *Index*. As a result, South Africa's trade policy score is 1 point worse this year. The U.S. Trade Representative reports that some products still require an import license. Some companies have begun to use antidumping claims to gain trade protection.

### FISCAL BURDEN OF GOVERNMENT
**Score—Income Taxation: 4–Stable** (high tax rates)
**Score—Corporate Taxation: 4–Stable** (high tax rates)
**Score—Change in Government Expenditures: 3.5–Worse** (low increase)
**Final Score: 3.9–Worse** (high cost of government)

South Africa has a progressive tax system. The top income tax rate is 40 percent, down from the 42 percent reported in the 2003 *Index*. The corporate tax is 30 percent. Government expenditures as a share of GDP increased by 0.5 percentage point to 26.9 percent in 2001, compared to a 0.2 percentage point decrease in 2000. As a result, South Africa's fiscal burden of government score is 0.1 point worse this year.

361

## GOVERNMENT INTERVENTION IN THE ECONOMY
### Score: **2**–Stable (low level)

The World Bank reports that the government consumed 19 percent of GDP in 2001. In the same year, according to the International Monetary Fund, South Africa received 2.52 percent of its total revenues from state-owned enterprises and government ownership of property.

## MONETARY POLICY
### Score: **3**–Worse (moderate level of inflation)

From 1993 to 2002, South Africa's weighted average annual rate of inflation was 8.12 percent, up from the 5.71 percent from 1992 to 2001 reported in the 2003 *Index*. As a result, South Africa's monetary policy score is 1 point worse this year.

## CAPITAL FLOWS AND FOREIGN INVESTMENT
### Score: **2**–Stable (low barriers)

The government does not require approval for investment, and foreign investors in most cases are subject to the same laws as domestic investors. Only a few areas of the economy are reserved for South Africans, and foreign investors are free to acquire land. Foreign-controlled firms are subject to domestic borrowing restrictions. The state continues to control a significant portion of the economy despite some slow, partial privatization, and this necessarily limits foreign involvement. The Economist Intelligence Unit reports that the main impediments to foreign investment include a "high overall tax burden, a heavy regulatory environment, the dominance of some markets by large conglomerates and a lack of real incentives." The International Monetary Fund reports that both residents and non-residents may establish foreign exchange accounts through authorized dealers but face quantitative limits on investments abroad. Payments, transactions, and transfers are subject to some restrictions, controls, quantitative limits, and prior approval, although most exchange controls have been phased out.

## BANKING AND FINANCE
### Score: **2**–Stable (low level of restrictions)

South Africa's banking system is the most developed in sub-Saharan Africa, and foreign financial institutions are largely free of restrictions. According to the Economist Intelligence Unit, the four largest banks control 69.1 percent of the banking sector (measured by deposit base and assets). Racial tensions are reflected in demands by black empowerment groups for government-set ratios of assets that must be invested in black enterprises, but the government has resisted these policies. The EIU reports that South Africa's parliament is considering a Community Reinvestment Bill that would require banks to provide financing for low-income borrowers.

## WAGES AND PRICES
### Score: **2**–Stable (low level of intervention)

Prices are set by the market with the exception of petroleum products, coal, paraffin, and utilities. South Africa does not have a legally mandated minimum wage; however, the Economist Intelligence Unit reports that the Basic Conditions of Employment Act "empowers the minister of labour to make sectoral determinations; they may include setting the basic remuneration level." On March 1, 2003, the Minister of Labor introduced a minimum wage for agricultural workers.

## PROPERTY RIGHTS
### Score: **3**–Stable (moderate level of protection)

The threat of expropriation is low. The judiciary is independent, and contractual arrangements are generally secure. According to the U.S. Department of State, "High rates of violent crime make it difficult for South African criminal and judicial entities to dedicate adequate resources to anti-corruption efforts.... During the last few years, violent crime has been a more serious problem and impediment to and a cost of doing business in South Africa."

## REGULATION
### Score: **3**–Stable (moderate level)

Even though the government has moved to increase transparency in the regulatory framework through a series of legislative and other reforms, regulation of economic activity can be burdensome. Labor regulations are onerous. According to the Economist Intelligence Unit, "the main regulatory risk for companies is complying with black empowerment legislation and meeting other related goals, which can raise the cost of implementing a commercial strategy. These regulations may also be changed on short notice." In addition, "Owing to South Africa's dearth of skilled labor, concerns exist over the capacity of the bureaucracy at the various levels of government, and performance is mixed. A further problem has been co-ordination and co-operation between different government departments and different tiers of government.... In provincial and local governments (outside the three main metropolitan areas) these problems tend to be worse."

## INFORMAL MARKET
### Score: **3**–Stable (moderate level of activity)

Transparency International's 2002 score for South Africa is 4.8. Therefore, South Africa's informal market score is 3 this year.

SPAIN

# SPAIN

Rank: 27

Score: 2.31

Category: Mostly Free

## QUICK STUDY

### SCORES

| | |
|---|---|
| Trade Policy | 2 |
| Fiscal Burden | 4.1 |
| Government Intervention | 2 |
| Monetary Policy | 2 |
| Foreign Investment | 2 |
| Banking and Finance | 2 |
| Wages and Prices | 2 |
| Property Rights | 2 |
| Regulation | 3 |
| Informal Market | 2 |

**Population**: 41,837,894

**Total area:** 504,782 sq. km

**GDP:** $737.2 billion

**GDP growth rate:** 2.0%

**GDP per capita:** $17,620

**Major exports:** raw materials, machinery, capital goods, energy products, consumer goods

**Exports of goods and services:** $225.5 billion

**Major export trading partners:** France 19.2%, Germany 11.6%, UK 9.7%, Italy 9.4%, US 4.4%

**Major imports:** machinery and equipment, fuels, chemicals, consumer goods

**Imports of goods and services:** $241.9 billion

**Major import trading partners:** France 16.5%, Germany 16.4%, Italy 8.9%, UK 6.4%, US 4.1%

**Foreign direct investment (net):** $3.6 billion

2002 Data (in constant 1995 US dollars)

Upon joining the European Union in 1986, Spain undertook a program of privatization that significantly reduced the size of government and helped open the economy. This trend continued throughout the 1990s, especially under the government of Prime Minister Jose Maria Aznar, with liberalization of the banking, energy, and telecommunications sectors and a decline in public spending as a percentage of GDP. During his seven years in office, Aznar has cut unemployment, cracked down on Basque terrorism, won a landslide re-election, and presided over an economic and cultural boom. Spain has enjoyed both economic growth and job creation, with GDP increasing by 2 percent in 2002—the fastest rate of growth among the larger EU countries. Likewise, unemployment decreased from 22.9 percent in 1995 to around 12.7 percent in 2001. Following the June 2000 elections, Aznar embarked on an ambitious plan to open the gas and electricity markets, a process that met with success in January 2003. The main area still awaiting reform is the labor market; Spain's dismissal laws remain among the strictest within the EU, and 68.5 percent of Spanish workers have lifetime contracts or the promise of generous nationally mandated redundancy payments.

## TRADE POLICY
### Score: **2**–Stable (low level of protectionism)

The World Bank reports that, as a member of the European Union, Spain had a weighted average tariff rate of 2.6 percent in 2001. According to the Economist Intelligence Unit, Spain implements "EU dumping levels against third-country imports.... All foodstuff imports must qualify under [the] 1975 foodstuff law.... The Ministry of Economy...sets annual global quotas for some items from non-EU countries (for example, cars and textiles).... Licenses are...necessary (and difficult to obtain) to import used machinery...."

## FISCAL BURDEN OF GOVERNMENT
Score—Income Taxation: **4.5**–Stable (very high tax rates)
Score—Corporate Taxation: **4.5**–Stable (very high tax rates)
Score—Change in Government Expenditures: **3**–Stable (very low decrease)
### Final Score: **4.1**–Stable (high cost of government)

Spain has reduced its top income tax rate from 48 percent to 45 percent (although this reduction is not substantial enough to affect its income taxation score). The top corporate rate is 35 percent. Government expenditures as a share of GDP decreased less in 2002 (0.1 percentage point to 39.8 percent) than they did in 2000 (0.3 percentage point). On net, Spain's fiscal burden of government score remains unchanged this year.

## GOVERNMENT INTERVENTION IN THE ECONOMY
### Score: **2**–Stable (low level)

Based on data from the Banco de España, the government consumed 17.57 percent of GDP in 2002. In the same year, based on data from the Ministry of Economy, Spain received 4.5 percent of its total revenues from state-owned enterprises and government ownership of property.

**MONETARY POLICY**
Score: **2**–Stable (low level of inflation)

From 1993 to 2002, Spain's weighted average annual rate of inflation was 3.18 percent.

 **CAPITAL FLOWS AND FOREIGN INVESTMENT**
Score: **2**–Stable (low barriers)

Spain maintains few restrictions on foreign investment. The government allows up to 100 percent foreign ownership in most sectors and is liberalizing regulations on capital movements. For the most part, prior investment approval is not required. Foreign investment in the air transport, radio, minerals, mining, television, gambling, telecommunications, private security, and national defense sectors faces some restrictions. The government does employ its power to restrict unwanted investment. According to the Economist Intelligence Unit, "The government demonstrated in May 2000 that it was willing to use its 'golden share' in formerly state-owned public services to block foreign investment: it prevented a planned merger between the now-privatised Telefónica and KPN, a Dutch telecoms firm in which the Dutch government held a 43.25% stake. The golden share gives the government the right to intervene in operations that it considers of national interest." There are no restrictions or controls on resident or non-resident foreign exchange accounts, repatriation of profits, and proceeds from invisible transactions. Current transfers are not restricted but must be declared to deposit institutions. The Bank of Spain requires reporting on most credit and lending activities.

 **BANKING AND FINANCE**
Score: **2**–Stable (low level of restrictions)

Spain's banking and financial sectors are diverse, modern, and fully integrated into international financial markets. Integration into the European Union has forced Spain to open its banking system to banks from other EU members. The government has also made progress in opening the banking system to foreign competition by removing restrictions on investments from non-EU investors, but foreign competitors face substantial challenges from competitive domestic rivals and low margins. Spain's retail banking sector is dominated by the Banco Bilbao Vizcaya Argentaria (BBVA) and Banco Santander Central Hispano groups, which account for almost 80 percent of banking assets. Foreign firms are governed by the same conditions that apply to domestic interests with regard to access to the financial system. The government provides financing through the Official Credit Institute for industrial restructuring and to smaller firms. Spain's stock market has developed rapidly, and Madrid now has the European Union's fifth largest stock market.

 **WAGES AND PRICES**
Score: **2**–Stable (low level of intervention)

The government has removed most price controls. According to the Economist Intelligence Unit, "Price fixing has all but disappeared except in sectors still controlled by the national government: farm insurance, stamps, public transport, electricity, natural gas/butane/propane and medicines. Regional governments also control a few prices locally." Spain also affects agricultural prices through its participation in the Common Agricultural Policy, a program that heavily subsidizes agricultural goods. According to Timbro, a Swedish think tank, "EU consumers pay roughly 80–100% more for their food than would be the case in a mature free-market regime." The government mandates a minimum wage.

 **PROPERTY RIGHTS**
Score: **2**–Stable (high level of protection)

Property is relatively safe from government expropriation. The judiciary is independent in practice, but bureaucratic obstacles at the national and state levels are significant. The Economist Intelligence Unit reports that "contractual agreements are secured although the legal system can be painfully slow, and enforcement becomes a tortuous process when contracts are not honored. Out-of-court settlements are common."

 **REGULATION**
Score: **3**–Stable (moderate level)

Although the government has streamlined its regulatory regime, the Economist Intelligence Unit reports that "bureaucratic steps are considerable both at the national and state levels, and many civil servants are un-cooperative, though generational change is helping make dealings with the public sector somewhat more agile." Spain has the full array of European Union environmental regulations but does not enforce them effectively. One key area needing reform is the labor market, which is known for its rigidity. According to the EIU, "Despite the loosening of labour restrictions, chiefly by lowering the cost of dismissals, a recent study found that Spanish dismissal compensation was still by far the most generous [among]…the countries surveyed. In all, payments approached 200% of basic annual compensation."

 **INFORMAL MARKET**
Score: **2**–Stable (low level of activity)

Transparency International's 2002 score for Spain is 7.1. Therefore, Spain's informal market score is 2 this year.

# SRI LANKA

Rank: 76

Score: 3.06

Category: Mostly Unfree

Present & Past Scores

(Best) 1
2
3
4  3.06 2.94 2.61 2.76 2.81 2.91 2.84 2.89 3.05 3.06
(Worst) 5

'95 '96 '97 '98 '99 '00 '01 '02 '03 '04

S ri Lanka's GDP grew by 3.2 percent in 2002, recovering from the previous year's contraction of 1.4 percent. Growth was fueled partly by optimism arising from the progress of peace talks between the government and the Liberation Tigers of Tamil Eelam (LTTE). After six rounds of Norwegian-mediated negotiations, both sides have made unprecedented concessions: The LTTE have agreed to consider autonomy rather than insist on independence, and the Sri Lankan government has agreed to give them interim administrative control over the northeast, which the LTTE claim as their homeland. Nevertheless, Sri Lanka's economic performance was well below expectations, convincing many that more economic reform is necessary. The government has begun to whittle away Sri Lanka's regulatory framework in preparation for deeper reforms. It also has begun to streamline the convoluted tax code by establishing a single revenue collection agency. A major concern is Sri Lanka's cumbersome budget deficit, currently at 8.9 percent of GDP, the only positive upshot of which has been the forced sale of state-owned enterprises to balance the economy. Sri Lanka also suffers from massive public debt, which is 105.3 percent of GDP. Sri Lanka's fiscal burden of government score is 0.4 point better this year; however, its informal market score is 0.5 point worse. As a result, Sri Lanka's overall score is 0.01 point worse this year.

## TRADE POLICY

### Score: 3–Stable (moderate level of protectionism)

According to the World Bank, Sri Lanka's weighted average tariff rate in 2001 (the most recent year for which World Bank data are available) was 7.2 percent. The *Financial Times* reports that Sri Lanka maintains one of the world's toughest bans on genetically modified food. According to the U.S. Department of State, the government controls certain imports, such as meat, drugs, firearms, pesticides, used air conditioners, and remote-controlled toys, with license requirements. In addition, "Corruption is a persistent problem in customs clearance and enables wide-scale smuggling."

## FISCAL BURDEN OF GOVERNMENT

Score—Income Taxation: **3–Better** (moderate tax rates)
Score—Corporate Taxation: **4–Better** (high tax rates)
Score—Change in Government Expenditures: **3.5–Stable** (low increase)
### Final Score: **3.6–Better** (high cost of government)

Sri Lanka's top income tax rate is 30 percent, down from the 35 percent reported in the 2003 *Index*, and its top corporate tax rate is 30 percent, down from the 35 percent reported in the 2003 *Index*. As a result, Sri Lanka's fiscal burden of government score is 0.4 point better this year. Government expenditures as a share of GDP increased by the same percentage in 2001 (0.7 percentage point to 26.3 percent) as they did in 2000 (0.7 percentage point).

## GOVERNMENT INTERVENTION IN THE ECONOMY

### Score: **2.5–Stable** (moderate level)

The World Bank reports that the government consumed 10.1 percent of GDP in 2001. In the same year, according to the International Monetary Fund, Sri Lanka received 6.86 percent of its total revenues from state-owned enterprises and government ownership of property.

**MONETARY POLICY**
Score: **3**–Stable (moderate level of inflation)

From 1993 to 2002, Sri Lanka's weighted average annual rate of inflation was 10.29 percent.

 **CAPITAL FLOWS AND FOREIGN INVESTMENT**
Score: **3**–Stable (moderate barriers)

Legislation liberalizing foreign investment rules took effect on April 19, 2002. Foreign investment up to 100 percent is allowed in most sectors, and foreign firms receive the same treatment as domestic firms. Foreign investments in travel agencies, freight forwarding, fishing, timber, and various agricultural sectors when foreign ownership exceeds 49 percent are screened and require government approval. Foreign investment is prohibited in non-bank lending, pawnbroking, retail trade with a capital investment of less than $1 million (some exceptions are permitted), coastal fishing, and education of Sri Lankan citizens under the age of 14. The International Monetary Fund reports that residents may hold foreign exchange accounts; non-residents may hold foreign exchange accounts provided they originate from specified activities. There are strict reporting requirements on payments, transactions, and transfers, and capital transactions are subject to many restrictions, controls, and reporting requirements. Repatriation of profits is permitted.

 **BANKING AND FINANCE**
Score: **3**–Stable (moderate level of restrictions)

Sri Lanka has liberalized its financial services sector by raising foreign-equity limits to 100 percent in commercial banks, insurance services, and stockbroking. Wholly-owned foreign banks are allowed to operate without restrictions. The state owns the two largest banks—Bank of Ceylon and People's Bank. According to the U.S. Department of State, "Despite a gradual loss in market share, the two state-owned commercial banks…still dominate banking, making up a little over half of all assets and liabilities…. The World Bank and the IMF have identified the dominance of the inefficient state banks as a main constraint for development of the financial sector." The Economist Intelligence Unit reports that the government has ruled out privatization of the two-state-owned banks but is planning to restructure them. The government has largely withdrawn from the insurance sector with sale of Sri Lanka Insurance Corporation in April 2003.

 **WAGES AND PRICES**
Score: **3**–Stable (moderate level of intervention)

"The state continues to control the price of (basic) bread, flour, petroleum, bus and rail fares, telecom rates, water and electricity," reports the U.S. Department of State. The Economist Intelligence Unit reports that the government subsidizes utilities, fertilizer, and petrol. Sri Lanka does not have a national minimum wage, but the law provides for and enforces the decisions of wage boards for specific sectors and industries.

 **PROPERTY RIGHTS**
Score: **3**–Stable (moderate level of protection)

The judiciary is constitutionally independent but, in practice, is weak and subject to political influence. According to the U.S. Department of State, "Settlement through the Sri Lankan court system is subject to extremely protracted and inexplicable delay. Aggrieved investors (especially those dealing with the Government of Sri Lanka on projects) have frequently pursued out-of-court settlements, which offer the possibility—not frequently realized—of speedier resolution of disputes."

 **REGULATION**
Score: **3**–Stable (moderate level)

Sri Lankan regulations can be difficult to decipher, in addition to which enforcement can be deficient and transparency is sometimes lacking. The U.S. Department of State reports that "some of the laws and regulations are not freely available and are difficult to access. Foreign and domestic investors often complain that the regulatory system allows far too much leeway for bureaucratic discretion…." The Economist Intelligence Unit reports that "labour laws are archaic and the sacking of employees requires permission of a labour commission." Corruption can be an obstacle to doing business.

 **INFORMAL MARKET**
Score: **3.5**–Worse (high level of activity)

Transparency International's 2002 score for Sri Lanka is 3.7. Therefore, Sri Lanka's informal market score is 3.5 this year—0.5 point worse than last year.

SUDAN

# SUDAN

Rank: Suspended

Score: n/a

Category: n/a

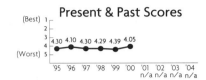

Present & Past Scores

(Best) 1
2
3
4
(Worst) 5

4.30  4.10  4.30  4.29  4.39  4.05

'95  '96  '97  '98  '99  '00  '01  '02  '03  '04
                                n/a n/a n/a n/a

S udan's increased cooperation in the war on terrorism is considered a sign of progress, but the practice of slavery continues unabated. The relative cease-fire between the government and the rebel Sudanese People's Liberation Army (SPLA), though fragile, has continued. This positive development, however, does not seem to have affected the state of emergency ordered by President Omar Hassan Ahmed, which will continue into next year. Hassan has full executive authority over the country, and there is little that can be done to offset his power. Economically, Sudan's healthy reserves of oil provide a strong foundation for future development. The Economist Intelligence Unit projects that an increase in productivity both inside and outside of the oil industry will drive growth to 5.6 percent of GDP. In addition to its tenuous relationship with Amnesty International, Sudan remains under the ever-watchful eye of the International Monetary Fund. Specifically, the government's ability to balance its budget by cutting down on expenditures will factor into the IMF's decision as to whether it should provide future loans. Early indications suggest that the 2003 budget may fall short of that goal, as the EIU estimates real spending to increase "significantly." Of further concern are signs of rising prices and an increase in the supply of currency. Taken together, they signal a troubling future for the people of Sudan.

### TRADE POLICY
#### Score: Not graded

According to the World Bank, Sudan's weighted average tariff rate in 1996 (the most recent year for which World Bank data are available) was 4.4 percent. The government has eliminated import and export licenses but continues to ban the importation of some 30 items. Corruption pervades the customs service.

### FISCAL BURDEN OF GOVERNMENT
#### Score—Income Taxation: Not graded
#### Score—Corporate Taxation: Not graded
#### Score—Change in Government Expenditures: Not graded
### Final Score: Not graded

According to the United Nations Development Programme, Sudan's top income tax rate is 30 percent, and the top corporate tax rate is 40 percent. Government expenditures as a share of GDP increased 0.5 percentage point to 12.4 percent in 2000, compared to a 3.5 percentage point increase in 1999.

### GOVERNMENT INTERVENTION IN THE ECONOMY
#### Score: Not graded

The World Bank reports that the government consumed an estimated 6 percent of GDP in 2001. In the same year, based on data from the International Monetary Fund, Sudan received 40.46 percent of its total revenues from state-owned enterprises and government ownership of property.

## MONETARY POLICY
### Score: Not graded

Data from the International Monetary Fund's *2002 World Economic Outlook* indicate that from 1993 to 2002, Sudan's weighted average annual rate of inflation was 6.80 percent.

 ## CAPITAL FLOWS AND FOREIGN INVESTMENT
### Score: Not graded

Foreign investment in Sudan is restricted by cumbersome regulations, political instability, and corruption. The government is seeking foreign investment, especially in connection with the privatization of state-owned enterprises. According to the Economist Intelligence Unit, however, "The poor state of the SOEs has discouraged potential private operators, who are not only unwilling to take on the companies' debts, but are also aware of the substantial investment many of the companies require after years of neglect.... In addition, accusations of corruption have dogged the privatisation programme, with government officials alleged to have demanded payments...." The International Monetary Fund reports that all residents (except the government, public institutions, and public enterprises) are permitted to hold foreign exchange accounts. Non-residents may also hold foreign exchange accounts, but only with government approval.

 ## BANKING AND FINANCE
### Score: Not graded

Sudan's banking sector includes 25 commercial banks, 16 of which are wholly or majority owned by the private sector. State-owned banks dominate the banking sector. According to the Economist Intelligence Unit, "A number of measures have been introduced to strengthen the system, notably the tightening of capital adequacy ratios and the establishment of new paid-in capital minimums.... The sector has also been liberalized, most notably through the relaxation of strict credit allocation rules that had previously required the commercial banks to focus new lending on areas designated for 'priority development' by the government."

 ## WAGES AND PRICES
### Score: Not graded

Although Sudan has liberalized some prices, price controls on foodstuffs remain in effect, and many goods are subsidized. The Economist Intelligence Unit reports that fuel subsidies were cut at the end of 2001. The Ministry of Labor enforces Sudan's minimum wage.

 ## PROPERTY RIGHTS
### Score: Not graded

There is little respect for private property in Sudan. According to the U.S. Department of State, "The judiciary is not independent and is largely subservient to the Government." In addition, "The authorities do not ensure due process, and the military forces summarily tried and punished citizens. The Government infringed on citizens' privacy rights."

 ## REGULATION
### Score: Not graded

Sudan's regulatory burden is heavy and inefficient. Businesses often find it difficult to obtain licenses to operate, and business owners may be harassed by corrupt bureaucrats. One example of the effect of Sudan's burdensome regulations is the agricultural sector, which accounts for more than 80 percent of employment. The Economist Intelligence Unit cites corruption as an "endemic" problem.

 ## INFORMAL MARKET
### Score: Not graded

Rationing has led to an informal market in many items, including petroleum and sugar, and the ban on some imports encourages smuggling.

SURINAME

# SURINAME

Rank: 143

Score: 3.96

Category: Mostly Unfree

Present & Past Scores

(Best) 1
2
3
4
(Worst) 5

4.20  4.00  4.10  4.08  3.98  3.98  4.03  4.06  3.96

'95  '96  '97  '98  '99  '00  '01  '02  '03  '04
n/a

## QUICK STUDY

### SCORES

| | |
|---|---|
| Trade Policy | 5 |
| Fiscal Burden | 3.6 |
| Government Intervention | 4 |
| Monetary Policy | 5 |
| Foreign Investment | 3 |
| Banking and Finance | 4 |
| Wages and Prices | 3 |
| Property Rights | 3 |
| Regulation | 4 |
| Informal Market | 5 |

**Population:** 419,660

**Total area:** 163,270 sq. km

**GDP:** $434.7 million

**GDP growth rate:** 5.9%

**GDP per capita:** $1,036

**Major exports:** alumina, shrimp, crude oil, rice

**Exports of goods and services:** $92.5 million

**Major export trading partners:** US 30.9%, Norway 18.8%, Netherlands 9.2%

**Major imports:** petroleum, foodstuffs, cotton

**Imports of goods and services:** $94 million

**Major import trading partners:** US 58.5%, Netherlands 27.6%, Trinidad and Tobago 21.5%

**Foreign direct investment (net):** n/a

2001 Data (in constant 1995 US dollars)

Suriname, a former Dutch colony, became a fully independent republic in 1975. Relations with the Netherlands remained good until the Netherlands charged Desi Bouterse, who served as president during the period of military government, with illegal drug trafficking and the murder of 15 opposition leaders during his tenure. In September 2002, according to the Economist Intelligence Unit, Bouterse was tried *in absentia* for illegal drug trafficking at The Hague after attempts to extradite him had failed. The court sentenced Bouterse to 16 years in prison, but he is protected against extradition by the Surinamese constitution. Suriname is rich in natural resources, especially timber and minerals; there are reserves of bauxite, gold, nickel, silver, and other minerals. According to the EIU, mining accounted for 13.8 percent of GDP in 2000. Agriculture accounts for 8.6 percent of GDP. The large public sector is the primary employer, with half of the labor force on its rolls. Despite its large natural resource endowment, however, Suriname is one of South America's poorest countries, with about 85% of households living below the official poverty line. Fiscal deficits have been the country's most pressing economic problem. Suriname's trade policy score is 1 point worse this year; however, its fiscal burden of government and government intervention scores are 1 point better. As a result, its overall score is 0.1 point better this year.

###  TRADE POLICY
#### Score: **5**–Worse (very high level of protectionism)

As a member of the Caribbean Community and Common Market (CARICOM), Suriname has a common external tariff rate that ranges from 5 percent to 20 percent. According to the World Bank, Suriname's average tariff rate in 1999 (the most recent year for which reliable data are available) was 15.3 percent, up from the 9.1 percent reported in the 2003 *Index*. As a result, Suriname's trade policy score is 1 point worse this year. The U.S. Department of State reports that the government maintains a "complicated import/export licensing system, and extensive paperwork requirements [that] create…delays and frustration to be considered by some a form of trade barrier."

###  FISCAL BURDEN OF GOVERNMENT
#### Score—Income Taxation: **3.5**–Stable (high tax rates)
#### Score—Corporate Taxation: **5**–Stable (very high tax rates)
#### Score—Change in Government Expenditures: **1**–Better (very high decrease)
#### Final Score: **3.6**–Better (high cost of government)

Suriname's top income tax rate is 38 percent. The top corporate tax rate is 36 percent. According to the Economist Intelligence Unit, government expenditures as a share of GDP decreased 7.5 percentage points to 34.1 percent in 2001, compared to a 7.3 percentage point increase in 2000. As a result, Suriname's fiscal burden of government score is 1 point better this year.

###  GOVERNMENT INTERVENTION IN THE ECONOMY
#### Score: **4**–Better (high level)

The World Bank reports that the government consumed 18.9 percent of GDP in 2001, down from the 32.8 percent reported in the 2003 *Index*. As a result, Suriname's government intervention score is 1 point better this year. The level of government involvement in the economy is significant. According to the Economist Intelligence Unit, "There is a large state sector, accounting for 17.4% of GDP, which employs about half the workforce."

## MONETARY POLICY
Score: **5**–Stable (very high level of inflation)

From 1993 to 2002, Suriname's weighted average annual rate of inflation was 29.94 percent.

## CAPITAL FLOWS AND FOREIGN INVESTMENT
Score: **3**–Stable (moderate barriers)

Despite improvement, foreign investors in Suriname still face such deterrents as administrative barriers and red tape. Licensing requirements are particularly cumbersome. The government updated its investment code in December 2001 to replace legislation that had governed foreign investment since 1960. According to the U.S. Department of State, "Now companies…no longer need to negotiate directly with the Surinamese government on concessions, licenses and hiring. Suriname is working on other investment law updates to make granting concessions less quixotic and more immune to patronage and favoritism. However, there has been little effort to implement this law." Progress in liberalizing the economy has attracted foreign investment in gold, oil, and forestry. The International Monetary Fund reports that residents may hold foreign exchange accounts provided that the funds come from sales of real estate in Suriname or from exports. Non-residents may open foreign exchange accounts in U.S. dollars and with the approval of the Foreign Exchange Commission. Payments and transfers face various quantitative limits and approval requirements. The IMF reports that capital transactions involving outward remittances of foreign exchange require the approval of the Foreign Exchange Commission.

## BANKING AND FINANCE
Score: **4**–Stable (high level of restrictions)

Suriname's banking legislation is out of date, although a new law is under consideration, and the central bank does not provide adequate oversight of the banking system. A minimum capital reserve requirement was passed in May 2001. The government remains active in the banking sector. According to the U.S. Department of State, "Suriname's banking system consists of three major commercial banks…. The government owns at least some interest in most banks." The Economist Intelligence Unit reports that the government maintains a 51 percent stake in Hakrinbank, one of the country's major banks.

## WAGES AND PRICES
Score: **3**–Stable (moderate level of intervention)

According to the U.S. Department of State, "Price controls remain on a few of [sic] consumption goods. In addition, there is an old law still on the books which makes overpricing of goods illegal. However, this law is only rarely enforced in cases where prices are truly excessive." In 2003, the government reduced subsidies on gasoline and bread, primarily because it could no longer afford them. The government intervenes in prices through state-owned enterprises, agricultural producers, and utilities. In addition, although there is no official minimum wage, the government influences wages as a major employer. "Of Suriname's 100,000 strong formal-sector labor force," reports the U.S. Department of State, "roughly half is employed in the public sector."

## PROPERTY RIGHTS
Score: **3**–Stable (moderate level of protection)

Private property is not well-protected. The judicial process is inefficient. According to the U.S. Department of State, "the judiciary has a significant shortage of judges…. Surinamese law provides for the right of an individual or company to hold land, buildings and equipment. Settlement of ownership disputes or damage to property, buildings or equipment can be an extremely long process in the undermanned, overworked, legal system."

## REGULATION
Score: **4**–Stable (high level)

Suriname's state-owned sector plays a considerable role in the economy and impedes private enterprise. Moreover, the regulatory regime is burdensome and lacks transparency. "Favoritism, especially for the political/ethnic/business elite, remains common in business and government," reports the U.S. Department of State, and "bureaucratic delays and red tape are a constant irritation." In addition, although a new investment law is designed to ease the burden of doing business in Suriname, "bureaucratic delays have prohibited it from taking effect."

## INFORMAL MARKET
Score: **5**–Stable (very high level of activity)

Piracy of television programs, music, and videos is common. Suriname has an extensive informal labor market, particularly in the gold mining business. Smuggling between Suriname and Guyana is extensive.

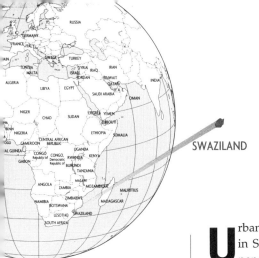

# SWAZILAND

Rank: 89

Score: 3.18

Category: Mostly Unfree

**Present & Past Scores**

(Best) 1
2
3
4
(Worst) 5

3.16  3.30  3.31  3.13  3.06  3.16  3.05  3.21  3.00  3.18

'95  '96  '97  '98  '99  '00  '01  '02  '03  '04

## QUICK STUDY

### SCORES

| | |
|---|---|
| Trade Policy | 4 |
| Fiscal Burden | 3.8 |
| Government Intervention | 2 |
| Monetary Policy | 3 |
| Foreign Investment | 3 |
| Banking and Finance | 3 |
| Wages and Prices | 3 |
| Property Rights | 3 |
| Regulation | 3 |
| Informal Market | 4 |

**Population:** 1,068,052

**Total area:** 17,360 sq. km

**GDP:** $1.6 billion

**GDP growth rate:** 1.6%

**GDP per capita:** $1,475

**Major exports:** sugar, wood pulp, cotton yarn, refrigerators, citrus and canned fruit

**Exports of goods and services:** $967.5 million

**Major export trading partners:** South Africa 59.7%, US 8.8%, EU 8.0%, Mozambique 6.2%

**Major imports:** motor vehicles, machinery, transport equipment, foodstuffs, petroleum products, chemicals

**Imports of goods and services:** $1.3 billion

**Major import trading partners:** South Africa 95.6%, EU 0.9%, Japan 0.9%, Singapore 0.3%

**Foreign direct investment (net):** $58.3 million

2001 Data (in constant 1995 US dollars)

U rban opposition to the monarchy has increased the likelihood of constitutional reform in Swaziland. Political parties were banned in 1973 when the constitution was suspended by then-King Sobhuza. That act and the monarchy's authority over all matters in the kingdom remain unchanged, at least for the time being. During the recent constitutional rewrite, the state acknowledged the existence of human rights; it also, however, denied that those same rights are "absolute," once again leaving all power in the hands of the monarchy. A landlocked nation that owes much of its export business to neighboring South Africa, Swaziland seems indifferent to South African pleas for political reform, although that does not seem to have prevented either country from benefiting economically from the other. The kingdom is highly dependent on its agriculture and agro-industry business. Its principal export in 2001 was soft drink concentrate, followed by a healthy sugar business. The Economist Intelligence Unit projects growth of 4.5 percent in 2003, in part from the opening of a new zinc mine and a refinery in April. This number could be revised, however, should the people decide to carry out their own constitutional reforms. Swaziland's government intervention score is 0.5 point better this year; however, its trade policy score is 2 points worse, and its fiscal burden of government score is 0.3 point worse. As a result, Swaziland's overall score is 0.18 point worse this year.

## TRADE POLICY

### Score: **4**–Worse (high level of protectionism)

Swaziland belongs to the Southern African Customs Union (SACU), a regional trade arrangement with Botswana, Lesotho, Namibia, and South Africa. According to the World Trade Organization, in 2002 (the most recent year for which WTO data are available), the SACU had an average common external tariff rate of 11.4 percent, up from the 8.5 percent reported in the 2003 *Index*. According to Swaziland's central bank, a National Marketing Board regulates imports of grain (maize, flour, sorghum, millet, and others) through quotas. Based on newly available evidence of non-tariff barriers and the increase in the average common external tariff rate, Swaziland's trade policy score is 2 points worse this year.

## FISCAL BURDEN OF GOVERNMENT

Score—Income Taxation: 3–Stable (moderate tax rates)
Score—Corporate Taxation: 4–Stable (high tax rates)
Score—Change in Government Expenditures: 4–Worse (moderate increase)

### Final Score: **3.8**–Worse (high cost of government)

Swaziland's top income tax rate is 33 percent. The top corporate tax rate is 30 percent. Government expenditures as a share of GDP increased 1.6 percentage points to 31.7 percent in 2001, compared to a 0.6 percentage point decrease in 2000. As a result, Swaziland's fiscal burden of government score is 0.3 point worse this year.

## GOVERNMENT INTERVENTION IN THE ECONOMY

### Score: **2**–Better (low level)

The World Bank reports that the government consumed 19.6 percent of GDP in 2001, down from the 20.4 percent reported in the 2003 *Index*. As a result, Swaziland's government intervention score is 0.5 point better this year. In the same year, based on data from the

371

International Monetary Fund, the government received 4.44 percent of its total revenues from state-owned enterprises and government ownership of property.

## MONETARY POLICY
### Score: **3**–Stable (moderate level of inflation)

From 1993 to 2002, Swaziland's weighted average annual rate of inflation was 10.82 percent.

## CAPITAL FLOWS AND FOREIGN INVESTMENT
### Score: **3**–Stable (moderate barriers)

Swaziland prohibits the nationalization of foreign-owned property, and foreign firms receive national treatment. The economy depends largely on export production run by foreign majority–owned firms in such industries as wood pulp, sugar, and soft drink concentrate. The Central Bank of Swaziland reports that foreign businesses must seek its approval to make investments. According to the International Monetary Fund, both residents and non-residents may hold foreign exchange accounts, but residents face quantitative limits. Payments and transfers are subject to controls but are not usually restricted. The IMF also reports that, except for equity investments by non-residents, the central bank must approve all inward capital transfers. Most other capital transactions require documentation, are controlled, are prohibited, or face quantitative limits. Real estate transactions by non-residents must be approved.

## BANKING AND FINANCE
### Score: **3**–Stable (moderate level of restrictions)

Banks in Swaziland are relatively free of government control. According to the International Monetary Fund, the banking system consists of four banks. The government owns the Swaziland Development and Savings Bank, which accounted for 15 percent of total deposits and 4 percent of total loans as of June 2002. Banks may not invest more than 25 percent of their bank capital in a single investment. "In a small market like Swaziland," reports the central bank, "this places significant constraints on the funding of larger infrastructure and development projects." The Economist Intelligence Unit reports that the government owns 41 percent of the Swaziland Royal Insurance Corporation, which has a monopoly in the insurance sector. Parliament is considering a bill, first introduced in 1993, that would open the insurance industry to competition. According to the EIU, "Several South African companies have indicated that they would enter if the market were liberalised."

## WAGES AND PRICES
### Score: **3**–Stable (moderate level of intervention)

According to the Central Bank of Swaziland, "A majority of goods and services, particularly those used by the poor are subjected to government price control. Public transport, fuel, energy, sugar, bread and grains are among the controlled products." The International Monetary Fund reports that administered prices account for approximately 16 percent of the consumer price index. "[Government] Subsidies have a significant presence in the Swazi economy," reports the central bank. "The major services industries like electricity, telecommunications, railways, and water services are controlled by the state and government makes transfers to these parastatals to control the prices. Direct subsidies are present in a limited number of agricultural inputs including seed, fertilisers, dipping chemicals and services." Swaziland has a legally mandated minimum wage that varies according to type of work.

## PROPERTY RIGHTS
### Score: **3**–Stable (moderate level of protection)

Property is legally protected against government expropriation. The U.S. Department of State reports that "Swaziland has a dual legal system…[that] can be confusing and has, at times, presented problems for foreign-owned business…." In addition, "a lack of an independent court budget, lack of trained manpower, inadequate levels of salary remuneration and managing case work remain problems for the judiciary…. [D]elays in trials are common." According to the Economist Intelligence Unit, "The legal system has been plunged into disarray after government statements that it would ignore Court of Appeal rulings. This follows a number of court decisions that have gone against the government." Although this crisis has undermined the image of judicial protection in Swaziland, it also represents an opportunity for the country to demonstrate the strength of law enforcement and judicial independence.

## REGULATION
### Score: **3**–Stable (moderate level)

"Despite inadequate legislation," reports the U.S. Department of State, "starting a business in Swaziland can be relatively simple process." The Bank of Swaziland reports that businesses must provide a healthy work environment and must submit an environmental impact assessment. According to the Economist Intelligence Unit, the "Trade and Business Facilitation Bill, which aims to attract investment and enhance industrial competitiveness by making it possible to obtain a trading license over the counter," should be passed this year. Some government regulations (especially those dealing with safety conditions) are applied erratically, and this can lead to uncertainty and confusion. The Bank of Swaziland reports that "Corruption in the bureaucracy is on the high side."

## INFORMAL MARKET
### Score: **4**–Stable (high level of activity)

Swaziland has an active informal market, primarily in the supply of labor, transportation service, the construction industry, and computer software. The Economist Intelligence Unit reports "high levels of illegal crossborder trade."

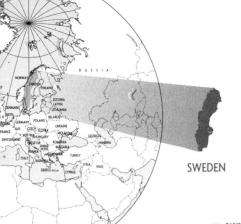

# SWEDEN

Rank: 12

Score: 1.90

Category: Free

SWEDEN

**Present & Past Scores**

(Best) 1
2
3
4
(Worst) 5

2.63 2.53 2.25 2.24 2.20 2.15 2.03 1.88 1.88 1.90

'95 '96 '97 '98 '99 '00 '01 '02 '03 '04

## QUICK STUDY

### SCORES
| | |
|---|---|
| Trade Policy | 2 |
| Fiscal Burden | 4 |
| Government Intervention | 3 |
| Monetary Policy | 1 |
| Foreign Investment | 1 |
| Banking and Finance | 1 |
| Wages and Prices | 2 |
| Property Rights | 1 |
| Regulation | 3 |
| Informal Market | 1 |

**Population:** 8,940,788

**Total area:** 449,964 sq. km

**GDP:** $299 billion

**GDP growth rate:** 1.9%

**GDP per capita:** $33,442

**Major exports:** machinery and transport equipment, chemicals, financial and insurance services, travel services

**Exports of goods and services:** $143.9 billion

**Major export trading partners:** US 11.5%, Germany 10.1%, Norway 8.8%, UK 8.2%, Denmark 6.2%, Finland 5.8%

**Major imports:** machinery and transport equipment, chemical, mineral fuels, travel services, financial and insurance services

**Imports of goods and services:** $135.5 billion

**Major import trading partners:** Germany 18.6%, Denmark 9.2%, UK 8.7%, Norway 7.9%, Netherlands 6.8%

**Foreign direct investment (net):** $193.8 million

2002 Data (in constant 1995 US dollars)

S weden is a constitutional monarchy and the third largest country by area in Western Europe. Its population is just under 9 million, and half of the land is covered by forest. In true Scandinavian fashion, Sweden has high taxes and a large welfare state. The level of unemployment is low, but workers take excessive sick leave; according to the Economist Intelligence Unit, an average of 430,000 employees, or 10 percent of the workforce, are on sick leave at any given time. Despite these drawbacks, as was pointed out in the 2003 *Index*, the economic landscape of Scandinavia is changing. Economic freedom in Sweden has grown with the implementation of policies that increase opportunity and attract investment through low trade barriers, stable money, open domestic financial markets, an openness to foreign investment, reduced regulation, market-determined wages and prices, and relatively little informal market activity. In addition, Sweden's history of political stability, strong rule of law, and protection of property rights provides fertile ground for such policies to take root. Sweden's fiscal burden of government score is 0.2 point worse this year. As a result, its overall score is 0.02 point worse this year.

###  TRADE POLICY
Score: **2–Stable** (low level of protectionism)

As a member of the European Union, according to the World Bank, Sweden had a weighted average tariff rate of 2.6 percent in 2001. The Economist Intelligence Unit reports that import restrictions on agricultural products are strongly applied. A license is required for the importation of meat, pharmaceuticals, and weapons.

###  FISCAL BURDEN OF GOVERNMENT
Score—Income Taxation: **5–Stable** (very high tax rates)
Score—Corporate Taxation: **3.5–Stable** (high tax rates)
Score—Change in Government Expenditures: **4–Worse** (moderate increase)
Final Score: **4–Worse** (high cost of government)

Sweden's tax burden is one of the heaviest among the world's industrialized economies: a 60 percent top income tax rate and a 28 percent top corporate tax rate. Government expenditures as a share of GDP increased 1.4 percentage points to 58.3 percent in 2002, compared to a 0.5 percentage point decrease in 2000. As a result, Sweden's fiscal burden of government score is 0.2 point worse this year.

###  GOVERNMENT INTERVENTION IN THE ECONOMY
Score: **3–Stable** (moderate level)

Based on data from the International Monetary Fund, the government consumed 28 percent of GDP in 2002. In 2001, according to the IMF, Sweden received 6.7 percent of its total revenues from state-owned enterprises and government ownership of property.

###  MONETARY POLICY
Score: **1–Stable** (very low level of inflation)

From 1993 to 2002, Sweden's weighted average annual rate of inflation was 2.03 percent.

## CAPITAL FLOWS AND FOREIGN INVESTMENT
### Score: **1**–Stable (very low barriers)

Sweden presents few barriers to foreign investment, maintaining restrictions only on investments in companies involved in national security–related sectors. Both domestic and foreign investors are prohibited from investing in the retail sale of pharmaceuticals and alcoholic beverages, in which the government maintains a monopoly. The government does not require investors to obtain prior approval of acquisitions, and corporate taxes are among the lowest in Europe. As a result of deregulation in the early 1990s, there are no controls or requirements on current transfers, access to foreign exchange, or repatriation of profits. The International Monetary Fund reports that a permit may be required for the purchase of real estate.

## BANKING AND FINANCE
### Score: **1**–Stable (very low level of restrictions)

Most commercial banks in Sweden are privately owned and operated. The Economist Intelligence Unit reports that the government reacted to the banking crisis of the early 1990s by taking over a number of banks, which have since been privatized. Banks are allowed to offer a full range of services. According to the U.S. Department of State, "Regulation on foreign ownership in financial services has been liberalized. Now foreign banks, insurance companies, brokerage firms, and cooperative mortgage institutions are permitted to establish branches in Sweden on equal terms with domestic firms even if a permit is required." The EIU reports that deregulation has paved the way for foreign banks to operate in Sweden and that, as of August 2002, 19 foreign banks had operations in the country. Net foreign exchange positions of financial institutions as a percentage of their capital base are limited by government guidelines.

## WAGES AND PRICES
### Score: **2**–Stable (low level of intervention)

The market sets most prices for goods and services. The Economist Intelligence Unit reports that "price-setting in Sweden is generally by market forces. An exception is the case of monopolies such as the state-owned chain of liquor stores. Another is the state-owned chemist chain, Apotek, which has the only license to sell medicines." Sweden also affects agricultural prices through its participation in the Common Agricultural Policy, a program that heavily subsidizes agricultural goods. According to Timbro, a Swedish think tank, "EU consumers pay roughly 80–100% more for their food than would be the case in a mature free-market regime." There is no national minimum wage law, but social welfare entitlement programs substantially augment wages. Wages are set through collective bargaining agreements that traditionally apply to all workers regardless of union affiliation.

## PROPERTY RIGHTS
### Score: **1**–Stable (very high level of protection)

Sweden has a well-developed and efficient legal system. The judiciary is independent and provides citizens with a fair judicial process. According to the Economist Intelligence Unit, "contractual agreements are generally highly respected in Sweden, not just from a legal stand point but morally as well. The quality of the judiciary and civil service is high, and the country's legal code is well developed."

## REGULATION
### Score: **3**–Stable (moderate level)

The process for opening a business in Sweden is relatively easy and straightforward. According to the Economist Intelligence Unit, "A local commercial bank, law or accounting office can handle the formalities [to open a new business] within a week…." The regulatory regime, while complex, is also relatively transparent. The EIU reports that Swedish business rules and practices include "annual submission of company accounts [and] employee representation on boards of directors." The high cost of labor, both in terms of payroll taxes and legislation, is one of the biggest deterrents to doing business. The U.S. Department of State reports that "a number of practical impediments to investment remain in Sweden. These include a fairly extensive, though non-discriminatory, system of permits and authorizations needed to engage in many activities and the dominance of few, very large players in certain sectors, e.g. construction and food wholesaling." Environmental law continues to become increasingly stringent, surpassing even European Union standards.

## INFORMAL MARKET
### Score: **1**–Stable (very low level of activity)

Transparency International's 2002 score for Sweden is 9.3. Therefore, Sweden's informal market score is 1 this year.

SWITZERLAND

# SWITZERLAND

Rank: 9

Score: 1.84

Category: Free

Present & Past Scores

(Best) 1
2
3        1.94  1.91  1.91  1.88  1.91  1.89  1.80  1.88  1.84
4
(Worst) 5

'95  '96  '97  '98  '99  '00  '01  '02  '03  '04
n/a

## QUICK STUDY

### SCORES

| | |
|---|---|
| Trade Policy | 2 |
| Fiscal Burden | 3.4 |
| Government Intervention | 2 |
| Monetary Policy | 1 |
| Foreign Investment | 2 |
| Banking and Finance | 1 |
| Wages and Prices | 2 |
| Property Rights | 1 |
| Regulation | 3 |
| Informal Market | 1 |

**Population:** 7,320,900

**Total area:** 41,290 sq. km

**GDP:** $340.6 billion

**GDP growth rate:** 0.1%

**GDP per capita:** $46,530

**Major exports:** chemicals, machinery and electronic devices, watches, precision instruments, financial services, travel services, insurance services

**Exports of goods and services:** $130.2 billion

**Major export trading partners:** Germany 20.8%, US 11.0%, France 9.2%, Italy 8.3%, UK 4.9%

**Major imports:** machinery and electronic devices, vehicles, financial services

**Imports of goods and services:** $101.7 billion

**Major import trading partners:** Germany 32.3%, Italy 10.8%, France 10.4%, US 5.3%, UK 4.7%

**Foreign direct investment (net):** −$2.2 billion

2002 Data (in constant 1995 US dollars)

With its stable currency and politics, relatively low taxes, and secure banking system, as well as its federal and cantonal incentives for new investors, Switzerland is an attractive investment location, particularly for small manufacturing. In most areas of business, there are no overall restrictions on the percentage of equity that foreign firms may hold; some cantons waive taxes on new firms for up to 10 years. Larger businesses are highly competitive and international, although smaller businesses—particularly those related to agriculture—are highly protected. Switzerland has two of Europe's five largest banks. The economy was broadly stagnant in 2002, and the Economist Intelligence Unit estimates that it will grow only at around 0.7 percent of GDP in 2003. Switzerland still has one of the world's highest incomes per capita and a political system that obliges the federal government to call for a popular referendum on major changes in policy. In 1992, for example, the Swiss voted against joining the European Economic Area, a free trade area consisting of members of the European Union and other European countries that have not joined the EU; in May 1999, however, 67 percent of the voters approved closer trading ties with the EU. The Swiss are involved in negotiations over this bilateral agreement with Brussels, but full EU accession remains unlikely. As a result, the Swiss have improved their ties with the EU's single market while shunning some of the excessive regulation that has impaired EU countries' rates of growth. One initiative under this enhanced relationship involves permitting the eventual free movement of labor between Swiss and EU nationals, with the Swiss being able to roam freely in the EU beginning in 2003 and EU nationals being accorded the same privilege by 2013. Switzerland's fiscal burden of government score is 0.1 point worse this year; however, its government intervention score is 0.5 point better. As a result, Switzerland's overall score is 0.04 point better this year.

### TRADE POLICY
Score: **2**–Stable (low level of protectionism)

According to the World Bank, Switzerland's weighted average tariff rate in 2001 (the most recent year for which World Bank data are available) was approximately 0 percent. The government maintains import quotas, high tariffs, and import licenses on agricultural products.

### FISCAL BURDEN OF GOVERNMENT
Score—Income Taxation: **1.5**–Stable (low tax rates)
Score—Corporate Taxation: **4**–Stable (high tax rates)
Score—Change in Government Expenditures: **4**–Worse (moderate increase)
Final Score: **3.4**–Worse (moderate cost of government)

Switzerland's top federal income tax rate is 11.5 percent. The top corporate tax rate is 30 percent. Government expenditures as a share of GDP increased more in 2002 (1.3 percentage points to 39.9 percent) than they did in 2001 (1 percentage point). As a result, Switzerland's fiscal burden of government score is 0.1 point worse this year.

### GOVERNMENT INTERVENTION IN THE ECONOMY
Score: **2**–Better (low level)

The Economist Intelligence Unit reports that the government consumed 15.2 percent of GDP in 2002. In the same year, according to the Swiss Federal Finance Administration,

Switzerland received 1.2 percent of its total revenues from state-owned enterprises and government ownership of property, down from the 8.42 percent reported in the 2003 *Index*. As a result, Switzerland's government intervention score is 0.5 point better this year.

## MONETARY POLICY
### Score: **1**–Stable (very low level of inflation)

From 1993 to 2002, Switzerland's weighted average annual rate of inflation was 0.79 percent.

## CAPITAL FLOWS AND FOREIGN INVESTMENT
### Score: **2**–Stable (low barriers)

Switzerland is generally open to foreign investment and grants foreign investors national treatment. Formal approval is not required for foreign direct investment and is not under the auspices of any one government office. The government restricts investment in utilities and other sectors considered essential to national security (such as hydroelectric and nuclear power plants, operation of oil pipelines, operation of airlines and marine navigation, and the transportation of explosive materials). Visas and work permits for foreign workers are strictly controlled. The International Monetary Fund reports that both residents and non-residents may hold foreign exchange accounts. There are no restrictions on repatriation of profits, payments for invisible transactions, or current transfers. Purchases of real estate by non-residents must be approved by the canton in which the property is located.

## BANKING AND FINANCE
### Score: **1**–Stable (very low level of restrictions)

Switzerland's banking system is one of the world's freest and most competitive. Banks may offer a wide range of financial services with virtually no government interference. Establishing a foreign bank requires a permit from the Swiss Federal Banking Commission, which supervises 369 financial institutions. Two banks—UBS and Credit Suisse—accounted for 50 percent of total bank assets in 2002. Foreign financial institutions are accorded national treatment, and foreign banks accounted for about 40 percent of Swiss banking institutions and about 9 percent of total bank assets in 2001. Credit is allocated on market terms.

## WAGES AND PRICES
### Score: **2**–Stable (low level of intervention)

The market sets wages and most non-agricultural prices. According to the Economist Intelligence Unit, "Permanent price and margin controls apply to all agricultural goods and their by-products that are subsidized or protected by the government…. An official surveyor examines price increases for changes that exploit consumers, especially in monopolistic…sectors such as oil and food…. Companies that refuse to adjust prices voluntarily can be ordered to do so." The U.S.

Department of State reports that Swiss farmers are among the world's most highly subsidized producers. Switzerland has no minimum wage.

## PROPERTY RIGHTS
### Score: **1**–Stable (very high level of protection)

Switzerland may be one of the world's best protectors of property rights. The judiciary is independent, and the government respects this independence in practice. The Economist Intelligence Unit reports that "contractual arrangements are completely secure in Switzerland, and the judiciary and civil service are of high quality."

## REGULATION
### Score: **3**–Stable (moderate level)

Regulations are extensive, particularly at the local level, but the government applies them evenly and transparently in most cases. According to the U.S. Department of State, "Indirect [government] involvement is evident in the extensive number of government regulations…. Building codes, regulated hours of establishment, labor laws, zoning ordinances, environmental regulation (for instance, garbage control), noise codes and administered prices are examples of areas where rules and regulations are…pervasive…." The Economist Intelligence Unit reports that "companies have relative freedom in hiring and firing. Nevertheless there are usually generous social plans for those who lose their jobs." In addition, "strict limits on the entry of foreign workers rule out the entry of firms in labor-intensive industries."

## INFORMAL MARKET
### Score: **1**–Stable (very low level of activity)

Transparency International's 2002 score for Switzerland is 8.5. Therefore, Switzerland's informal market score is 1 this year.

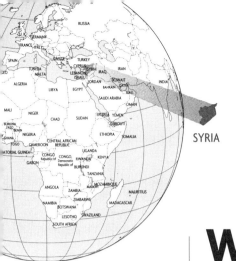

SYRIA

# SYRIA

Rank: 138

Score: 3.88

Category: Mostly Unfree

Present & Past Scores

(Best) 1
2
3
4
(Worst) 5

4.15  4.14  4.01  4.04  4.05  4.00  4.11  3.88 3.88
'95   '96   '97   '98   '99   '00   '01   '02  '03  '04
n/a

## QUICK STUDY

### SCORES

| | |
|---|---|
| Trade Policy | 4 |
| Fiscal Burden | 3.3 |
| Government Intervention | 4.5 |
| Monetary Policy | 1 |
| Foreign Investment | 4 |
| Banking and Finance | 5 |
| Wages and Prices | 4 |
| Property Rights | 4 |
| Regulation | 4 |
| Informal Market | 5 |

**Population:** 16,593,210

**Total area:** 185,180 sq. km

**GDP:** $13.2 billion

**GDP growth rate:** 2.8%

**GDP per capita:** $796

**Major exports:** crude oil and petroleum products, food and live animals, textiles and textile fibers, raw cotton

**Exports of goods and services:** $6.2 billion

**Major export trading partners:** France 20.6%, Italy 17.8%, Turkey 9.7%, Lebanon 5.0%

**Major imports:** machinery and transport equipment, food, live animals, beverages and tobacco, chemicals, manufactured products

**Imports of goods and services:** $4.5 billion

**Major import trading partners:** Italy 8.6%, Germany 7.1%, France 6.2%, Turkey 5.2%

**Foreign direct investment (net):** n/a

2001 Data (in constant 1995 US dollars)

When he came to power after the June 2000 death of his father, Hafez al-Assad, Syrian President Bashar al-Assad pledged to undertake cautious economic reforms. To consolidate his power, however, he has reached an accommodation with the old guard generals, intelligence chiefs, and politicians who were the mainstays of his father's regime and remain opposed to radical economic reform. Bashar's economic reform agenda also has been blocked by the deeply rooted corruption that flourishes in Syria's statist economic system. These factors have constrained his government's efforts to reform the economy, which desperately needs liberalization and restructuring. Foreign and private investments are urgently needed to modernize Syria's outmoded technological base and inadequate infrastructure, but potential investors remain deterred by cumbersome legal, regulatory, and bureaucratic structures. Assad's regime seeks to attract investment from Syrian expatriates and has passed a law to allow private banks to operate in Syria, albeit under strict terms. But the regime's attempt to follow a Syrian version of the "Chinese model," which permits limited economic reforms without threatening the supremacy of the Baath Party, means that economic growth will continue to be retarded by various government bureaucracies.

## TRADE POLICY
### Score: **4**–Stable (high level of protectionism)

Based on data from the World Bank, Syria's average tariff rate in 1999 (the most recent year for which World Bank data are available) was 11.2 percent (based on international trade taxes as a percent of total imports). According to the U.S. Department of State, "Customs procedures are cumbersome, tedious, and time-consuming because of complex regulations. Producers often complain that it may take up to six months to import spare parts for their plant."

## FISCAL BURDEN OF GOVERNMENT
Score—Income Taxation: **1.5**–Stable (low tax rates)
Score—Corporate Taxation: **5**–Stable (very high tax rates)
Score—Change in Government Expenditures: **1.5**–Stable (high decrease)
### Final Score: **3.3**–Stable (moderate cost of government)

According to data from the International Monetary Fund, Syria's top income tax rate is 15 percent, but War Effort Surtaxes increase this to 17.25 percent. The top corporate tax rate is 45 percent, but War Effort Surtaxes raise this to 58 percent, down from the 60.3 percent reported in the 2003 *Index*. The adjusted rates were used to score this factor. Government expenditures as a share of GDP decreased slightly less in 2000 (3.6 percentage points to 27.5 percent) than they did in 1999 (3.9 percentage points). On net, Syria's fiscal burden of government score is unchanged this year.

## GOVERNMENT INTERVENTION IN THE ECONOMY
### Score: **4.5**–Stable (very high level)

The World Bank reports that the government consumed 10.9 percent of GDP in 2001. In 1999, according to the International Monetary Fund, Syria received 23.62 percent of its total revenues from state-owned enterprises and government ownership of property. According to the U.S. Department of State, however, "The government continues to control all 'strategic' industries such as oil production, oil refining, port operation, telecommunications, air transport, power generation/distribution, and water distribution...." In addition, reports the Economist Intelligence Unit, "The overstaffed and inefficient public sector continues to act as a drain on the economy, soaking up government expenditure, foreign exchange and capital investment." Based on the apparent unreliability of the reported figure for government consumption, 1 point has been added to Syria's government intervention score.

## MONETARY POLICY
### Score: 1–Stable (very low level of inflation)

From 1993 to 2002, Syria's weighted average annual rate of inflation was 0.97 percent. It is likely that the official inflation figures underestimate the true rate, however, as Syria influences prices both through direct price controls and through subsidies administered by state-owned enterprises.

## CAPITAL FLOWS AND FOREIGN INVESTMENT
### Score: 4–Stable (high barriers)

Syria has made some efforts to attract foreign investment. Foreigners now may own 100 percent of a company and the land on which a business is located. In May 2000, the investment law was amended to increase incentives. According to the U.S. Department of State, "Almost all sectors are open to foreign direct investment except for power generation and distribution, air transport, port operation, water bottling, telephony, and oil and gas production and refining." Foreign investment remains encumbered by a bureaucratic approval process, excessive regulation, and the lack of a strong legal structure. The U.S. Department of State reports that the government "has not fully adopted the strong legal and regulatory framework demanded by both foreign and Syrian investors.... [M]ost observers continue to find Syria's business environment a difficult one, plagued by ambiguous regulations and arbitrary government enforcement. Economic reforms in the recent past have been largely symbolic and have done little to improve Syria's overall investment climate." Many capital transactions are subject to controls.

## BANKING AND FINANCE
### Score: 5–Stable (very high level of restrictions)

The government owns Syria's major banks, and most banks lend only to the public sector. The U.S. Department of State reports that the banking system consists of the central bank and five specialized banks that are highly restricted. According to the Economist Intelligence Unit, "Lending priority is given to the public sector, with many loans often insufficiently serviced by public institutions. Private companies often find it difficult to obtain loans through the banks.... There are no investment banks or private insurance companies, and no foreign banks yet operate in the country, although five were given licenses to set up in December 2002." A law enacted in April 2001 permits private banking, which had been prohibited for 30 years. The government has granted licenses to three private banks, but they are not expected to begin operations until late 2003 or early 2004. The EIU reports that "strict rules still govern their operation, the main one being that the majority stake (at least 51%) must be Syrian owned."

## WAGES AND PRICES
### Score: 4–Stable (high level of intervention)

"Both the Ministry of Industry and the Ministry of Supply control product pricing for many goods," reports the U.S. Department of State. "The pricing regime has relaxed slightly from the rigidity of previous years, but Syrian consumers remain very price conscious and prices are not allowed to fluctuate greatly." The government also continues to intervene in agriculture, which is the largest sector of the economy. According to the Economist Intelligence Unit, "The authorities have designated this sector as 'strategic', which has led to significant state intervention. This has taken the form of pricing, subsidies and marketing controls, but not ownership." The U.S. Department of State reports that "The Minister of Labor and Social Affairs is responsible for enforcing minimum wage levels in the public and private sectors."

## PROPERTY RIGHTS
### Score: 4–Stable (low level of protection)

Protection of property rights is weak. According to the U.S. Department of State, "there is considerable government interference in the court system and judgments by foreign courts are generally accepted only if the verdict favors the Syrian government. Although a written bankruptcy law exists, it is not applied fairly and creditors may or may not salvage their investment." The same source reports that judicial independence is enshrined in the constitution, but "political connections and bribery can influence verdicts."

## REGULATION
### Score: 4–Stable (high level)

A cumbersome and inefficient bureaucracy overburdens Syria's regulatory system. According to the U.S. Department of State, "Fiscal and welfare regulations, such as tax, labor, safety, and health laws, appear to be enforced without systemic discrimination—when they are actually enforced. Bureaucratic procedures for licensing and necessary documentation move slowly and require official approval from many levels within the government. Under-the-table payments are often required, as corruption is endemic at nearly all levels of government."

## INFORMAL MARKET
### Score: 5–Stable (very high level of activity)

Syria's informal market is extensive. Many goods are smuggled. The University of Linz, Austria, reports that informal labor represents about 50 percent of non-agricultural employment. Piracy of books, computer software, and videos is extensive. According to the U.S. Department of State, "Motion picture industry contacts estimate the home video market in Syria to be 100 percent pirated...."

TAJIKISTAN

# TAJIKISTAN

Rank: 146

Score: 4.15

Category: Repressed

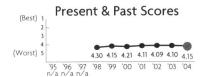
## QUICK STUDY

### SCORES

| | |
|---|---|
| Trade Policy | 3 |
| Fiscal Burden | 3.5 |
| Government Intervention | 4 |
| Monetary Policy | 5 |
| Foreign Investment | 4 |
| Banking and Finance | 5 |
| Wages and Prices | 4 |
| Property Rights | 4 |
| Regulation | 4 |
| Informal Market | 5 |

**Population:** 6,244,730

**Total area:** 143,100 sq. km

**GDP:** $2.6 billion

**GDP growth rate:** 10.2%

**GDP per capita:** $420

**Major exports:** cotton, vegetables, textiles, electricity, oil

**Exports of goods and services:** $603.6 million

**Major export trading partners:** Netherlands 29.8%, Russia 16.1%, Uzbekistan 13.3%, Switzerland 7.9%

**Major imports:** foodstuffs, machinery and equipment, petroleum, electricity

**Imports of goods and services:** $718.4 million

**Major import trading partners:** Uzbekistan 21.9%, Russia 18.8%, Kazakhstan 12.9%, Azerbaijan 4.9%

**Foreign direct investment (net):** n/a

2001 Data (in constant 1995 US dollars)

ajikistan is one of the poorest countries in Central Asia. Its geopolitical location and proximity to Afghanistan have brought international development assistance, which has the potential to create jobs and increase long-term stability. Tajikistan has joined NATO's Partnership for Peace and is in the early stages of seeking membership in the World Trade Organization. The Islamic Renaissance Party of Tajikistan, which formerly spearheaded an armed rebellion, is the only Islamic group in Central Asia that has parliamentary and cabinet-level representation. The regime, however, continues to suppress other opposition movements, thereby increasing the likelihood of popular support for violence. Russian military forces continue to patrol Tajikistan's long border with Afghanistan. The economy is still half the size it was in 1991, and inflation remains high. Tajikistan depends heavily on foreign revenue from cotton. External debt and poor implementation of structural reforms have had a negative effect on macroeconomic performance. Tajikistan's government intervention score is 0.5 point worse this year. As a result, its overall score is 0.05 point worse this year.

## TRADE POLICY
### Score: **3**–Stable (moderate level of protectionism)

According to the International Monetary Fund, Tajikistan's average tariff rate in 1999 (the most recent year for which reliable data are available) was 8 percent. Customs corruption is the most significant non-tariff barrier.

## FISCAL BURDEN OF GOVERNMENT
Score—Income Taxation: **2**–Better (low tax rates)
Score—Corporate Taxation: **4**–Stable (high tax rates)
Score—Change in Government Expenditures: **4**–Worse (moderate increase)
### Final Score: **3.5**–Stable (high cost of government)

According to the International Monetary Fund, Tajikistan's top income tax rate is 20 percent, down from the 40 percent reported in the 2003 *Index*. The top corporate tax is 30 percent. Government expenditures as a share of GDP increased 1.1 percentage points to 15.3 percent in 2001, compared to a 2.4 percentage point decrease in 2000. On net, Tajikistan's fiscal burden of government score is unchanged this year.

## GOVERNMENT INTERVENTION IN THE ECONOMY
### Score: **4**–Worse (high level)

The World Bank reports that the government consumed 8.8 percent of GDP in 2001. In the same year, according to the International Monetary Fund, Tajikistan received 5.47 percent of its total revenues from state-owned enterprises and government ownership of property, up from the 3.43 percent reported in the 2003 *Index*. According to the U.S. Department of State, however, "Government revenue depends highly on state-controlled cotton production [and] the level of medium to large scale privatization is [low at] approximately 16 percent…." The Economist Intelligence Unit reports that "many of the enterprises in the…construction, transport, communications and agricultural sectors are still largely state-owned…. [M]ost of the labour force is still employed by the government…." Based on the apparent unreliability of reported figures for government consumption and total revenues, 2 points have been added to Tajikistan's government intervention score. Based on the higher reported percent-

379

age of revenues from state-owned enterprises, Tajikistan's government intervention score is 0.5 point worse this year.

## MONETARY POLICY
### Score: 5–Stable (very high level of inflation)

Data from the International Monetary Fund's *2003 World Economic Outlook* indicate that from 1993 to 2002, Tajikistan's weighted average annual rate of inflation was 22.5 percent.

## CAPITAL FLOWS AND FOREIGN INVESTMENT
### Score: 4–Stable (high barriers)

The government has opened some of the economy to foreign investment and has made some efforts to promote increased investment—for example, by offering two-year tax holidays on profits—but the bureaucratic procedure is arbitrary and restrictive. According to the Economist Intelligence Unit, "Although a few foreign entities have invested in Tajikistan, political and economic instability…have discouraged substantial amounts of foreign direct investment (FDI). Investors are deterred by corruption and the lack of democratic reforms, while the slow pace of the privatization process—in particular of medium- and large-scale enterprises—has also kept investment inflows low. Other factors deterring investors include limited access to finance and the weakness of the public administration." The International Monetary Fund reports that both residents and non-residents may hold foreign exchange accounts, although residents may hold them abroad only with the central bank's approval. Restrictions on payments and transfers include quantitative limits on wages for foreign workers and requirements on repatriation. Many capital transactions require the central bank's approval.

## BANKING AND FINANCE
### Score: 5–Stable (very high level of restrictions)

The Economist Intelligence Unit reports that Tajikistan's banking system is weak and consists of the central bank and 16 commercial banks. Commercial banks have focused generally on channeling credit from the central bank to state-owned enterprises in the agricultural and industrial sectors. The state controls most of the financial system's assets. According to the EIU, "The combined capital of the banking sector was less than US$10m in March 2001, with most banks insolvent and hampered by non-performing loans. The three main private banks are Agroinvestbank, Orienbank, and Tojiksodirotbonk…with Sberbank being the only remaining state-owned bank. Although in theory most banks are privatised (having been transformed into joint-stock companies), they are still closely controlled by the state through the shareholdings of state-owned enterprises." The banking system is largely ineffective, and increasing numbers of people conduct business—including financial activities—in the shadow economy.

## WAGES AND PRICES
### Score: 4–Stable (high level of intervention)

Wages and prices are greatly influenced by the large government sector. "Prices in many areas rose strongly in January–March 2003," reports the Economist Intelligence Unit. "This was attributable partly to the fact that the government is progressively raising fuel and energy tariffs in order to bring them more closely into line with world rates and to reduce the energy sector deficit—which the IMF has calculated as being some 5.5% of GDP." The government influences prices through extensive socialist-era collectives and state farms and state-owned industries and utilities. Since agriculture and electricity are the major economic output, such government intervention is significant. According to the U.S. Department of State, "The President, on the advice of the Ministry of Labor and in consultation with trade unions, sets the minimum monthly wage…."

## PROPERTY RIGHTS
### Score: 4–Stable (low level of protection)

Protection of private property is weak in Tajikistan. According to the U.S. Department of State, "the Constitution provides for an independent judiciary; however, in practice judges do not function independently of the executive branch and the judicial system is subject to the influence of executive authorities. In many instances, armed paramilitary groups directly influence judicial officials…. Judges at all levels have extremely poor access to legal reference materials. Bribery of prosecutors and judges appears to be a common practice."

## REGULATION
### Score: 4–Stable (high level)

The procedure for establishing a business in Tajikistan can be both tedious and time-consuming. *The Washington Post* reports that "corruption, overregulation, senseless tax policies and inertia have frustrated the development of a private sector beyond retail trade and simple services, according to business people, bankers and diplomats [there]." According to Freedom House, "Corruption is reportedly pervasive throughout the government…. Barriers to private enterprise, including limited access to commercial real estate and the widespread practice of bribe payments, continue to restrict equality of opportunity."

## INFORMAL MARKET
### Score: 5–Stable (very high level of activity)

Informal market activity is present everywhere in Tajikistan, and despite laws to protect intellectual property rights, significant piracy of such goods continues. According to *The Washington Post*, it is calculated that drug smuggling represents about "a third of gross domestic product."

# TANZANIA

TANZANIA

**Rank: 98**

**Score: 3.29**

**Category: Mostly Unfree**

**Present & Past Scores**

(Best) 1
2
3
4
(Worst) 5

3.79 3.73 3.46 3.48 3.36 3.58 3.65 3.56 3.54 3.29

'95 '96 '97 '98 '99 '00 '01 '02 '03 '04

Tanzania may be one of Africa's most stable countries, but it also remains one of the poorest. The World Bank estimates a per capita income of about $277 per year; the issue of poverty is therefore likely to find its way into the 2005 election, which could result in the displacement of the ruling Chama Cha Mapinuzi. The recent terrorist strikes in Mombasa, Kenya, have revived memories of the Dar es Salaam attack in August of 1998; increasing religious tensions and an ongoing political conflict in Zanzibar have citizens worried that a similar strike may occur in the future. The Economist Intelligence Unit estimates that the economy will grow by 5 percent this year, partly because of progress in stabilizing the macroeconomic environment, which has also had a positive effect in reducing poverty. Agriculture continues to be the most important market, accounting for nearly 85 percent of exports and 45 percent of GDP. In recent years, a flood of foreign investment in the mining sector has enabled Tanzania to become one of the world's largest producers of gold. Despite these efforts, however, there has been little improvement in the average Tanzanian's standard of living. Whether this will change will depend on the government's ability to follow through with its reforms. Tanzania's fiscal burden of government score is 0.5 point worse this year; however, its government intervention, monetary policy, and banking and finance scores are 1 point better. As a result, Tanzania's overall score is 0.25 point better this year.

## QUICK STUDY

### SCORES

| | |
|---|---|
| Trade Policy | 5 |
| Fiscal Burden | 3.9 |
| Government Intervention | 2 |
| Monetary Policy | 2 |
| Foreign Investment | 3 |
| Banking and Finance | 2 |
| Wages and Prices | 3 |
| Property Rights | 4 |
| Regulation | 4 |
| Informal Market | 4 |

**Population:** 34,449,620

**Total area:** 945,087 sq. km

**GDP:** $6.7 billion

**GDP growth rate:** 5.7%

**GDP per capita:** $197

**Major exports:** manufactured goods, minerals, tobacco, coffee

**Exports of goods and services:** $1.49 billion

**Major export trading partners:** India 15.4%, Germany 7.8%, Belgium 6.7%, Japan 6.7%, UK 6.5%

**Major imports:** machinery and transportation equipment, crude oil

**Imports of goods and services:** $2.2 billion

**Major import trading partners:** South Africa 13.3%, UK 6.3%, Kenya 6.2%, India 5.9%, Japan 5.3%

**Foreign direct investment (net):** $333.6 million

2001 Data (in constant 1995 US dollars)

## TRADE POLICY
### Score: **5**–Stable (very high level of protectionism)

The World Bank reports that Tanzania's weighted average tariff rate in 2000 (the most recent year for which World Bank data are available) was 14.5 percent. According to the U.S. Department of State, "the customs department and the port authorities are the greatest hindrance to importers throughout Tanzania…. Corruption is a serious problem…. These hindrances can also cause unpredictable delays when importing goods into the country."

## FISCAL BURDEN OF GOVERNMENT
Score—Income Taxation: **3**–Stable (moderate tax rates)
Score—Corporate Taxation: **4**–Stable (high tax rates)
Score—Change in Government Expenditures: **4.5**–Worse (high increase)
### Final Score: **3.9**–Worse (high cost of government)

Tanzania's top income tax rate is 30 percent. The top corporate tax rate is 30 percent. Government expenditures as a share of GDP increased 2.2 percentage points to 20.6 percent in 2001, compared to a 1.9 percentage point decrease in 2000. As a result, Tanzania's fiscal burden of government score is 0.5 point worse this year.

## GOVERNMENT INTERVENTION IN THE ECONOMY
### Score: **2**–Better (low level)

The World Bank reports that the government consumed 6.3 percent of GDP in 2001. In the July 2001–June 2002 fiscal year, based on data from the International Monetary Fund, Tanzania received 9.72 percent of its total revenues from state-owned enterprises and government ownership of property. Based on newly available data for revenues from state-owned enterprises and the use of a new methodology to grade this factor, Tanzania's government intervention score is 1 point better this year.

## MONETARY POLICY
### Score: **2–Better** (low level of inflation)

From 1993 to 2002, Tanzania's weighted average annual rate of inflation was 5.11 percent, down from the 6.03 percent from 1992 to 2001 reported in the 2003 *Index*. As a result, Tanzania's monetary policy score is 1 point better this year.

## CAPITAL FLOWS AND FOREIGN INVESTMENT
### Score: **3–Stable** (moderate barriers)

Tanzania officially welcomes foreign investment under the investment regime established by the 1997 Tanzania Investment Act, which established the Tanzania Investment Center, identified investment priorities, overhauled the company registration process, and established investor rights and incentives. Investors must be licensed and must meet minimum capital requirements. The U.S. Department of State reports that informal barriers to foreign investment "include bureaucratic intransigence, corruption and poor infrastructure." According to the International Monetary Fund, residents may hold foreign exchange accounts only with central bank approval and that accounts held abroad are subject to restrictions. Non-residents may hold foreign exchange accounts subject to restrictions. Documentation is required to purchase foreign exchange, payments for travel face quantitative limits, and other payments require documentation. The IMF reports that all transfers of foreign currency from residents to non-residents must be approved by the central bank. Most capital transactions face restrictions and reporting requirements. Foreign purchase of real estate must have the consent of the Commissioner for Lands.

## BANKING AND FINANCE
### Score: **2–Better** (low level of restrictions)

Until 1991, private banks had been illegal in Tanzania for nearly 25 years; since then, the government has made great strides toward privatizing the sector. The Economist Intelligence Unit reports that 20 banks were licensed to operate in Tanzania as of June 2001 and that most international banks with a presence in Africa were represented. The government sold a majority stake in the National Commercial Bank to a South Africa banking group in March 2000 and has privatized the Cooperative and Rural Development Bank. According to the U.S. Trade Representative, Tanzania is privatizing its remaining state-owned financial institutions, the National Micro Finance Bank Limited and National Insurance Corporation. PricewaterhouseCoopers reports that several foreign insurance companies have undertaken operations in Tanzania since the government opened the insurance sector to competition in 1996. There are 11 non-bank financial institutions. A stock exchange was launched in March 1998, but only five companies are listed. Based on the evidence that the government is divesting itself from the banking and finance sector, Tanzania's banking and finance score is 1 point better this year.

## WAGES AND PRICES
### Score: **3–Stable** (moderate level of intervention)

According to the U.S. Department of State, "The Tanzanian government has eliminated most price controls; however, the government still regulates the price of gasoline, diesel fuel and kerosene." The government affects agricultural prices through marketing boards for its main export crops. Tanzania has a legal monthly minimum wage.

## PROPERTY RIGHTS
### Score: **4–Stable** (low level of protection)

"The Constitution provides for an independent judiciary," reports the U.S. Department of State; "however, the judiciary is corrupt, inefficient and subject to executive influence." In addition, "Clerks took bribes to decide whether or not to open cases and to hide or misdirect the files of those accused of crimes." The same source reports that "the Government…established a Commercial Court (CC) in September 1999. The Commercial Court…in principle, provides a place for speedy, efficient and commercially aware litigation of commercial disputes."

## REGULATION
### Score: **4–Stable** (high level)

Tanzania's bureaucracy is still burdensome, and corruption reportedly is rampant. According to the U.S. Department of State, "Tanzania has an antiquated and burdensome [system of] regulations on trade, commerce, employment, and resource utilization. Many of these regulations date from the colonial era, or the post-independence socialist period and have yet to be adjusted to serve the needs of a liberal market-based economy." Despite specific investment incentives, reports the *Financial Times*, "businessmen continue to complain of endless daily bureaucratic obstacles, including petty corruption."

## INFORMAL MARKET
### Score: **4–Stable** (high level of activity)

Transparency International's 2002 score for Tanzania is 2.7. Therefore, Tanzania's informal market score is 4 this year.

# THAILAND

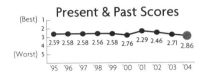

Rank: 60

Score: 2.86

Category: Mostly Free

**Present & Past Scores**

(Best) 1
2
3
4
(Worst) 5

2.59 2.58 2.58 2.56 2.58 2.76 2.29 2.46 2.71 2.86

'95 '96 '97 '98 '99 '00 '01 '02 '03 '04

THAILAND

**QUICK STUDY**

**SCORES**

| | |
|---|---|
| Trade Policy | 4 |
| Fiscal Burden | 3.6 |
| Government Intervention | 2.5 |
| Monetary Policy | 1 |
| Foreign Investment | 3 |
| Banking and Finance | 3 |
| Wages and Prices | 2 |
| Property Rights | 3 |
| Regulation | 3 |
| Informal Market | 3.5 |

**Population:** 61,183,900

**Total area:** 514,000 sq. km

**GDP:** $174.7 billion

**GDP growth rate:** 1.8%

**GDP per capita:** $2,853

**Major exports:** machinery and mechanical appliances, electrical apparatus for circuits, computer parts, and electrical appliances

**Exports of goods and services:** $94.6 billion

**Major export trading partners:** US 20.3%, Japan 15.3%, Singapore 8.1%, Hong Kong 5.1%, Malaysia 4.2%

**Major imports:** capital goods, raw materials, fuel and lubricants

**Imports of goods and services:** $72.7 billion

**Major import trading partners:** Japan 16.0%, US 11.6%, China 6.0%, Singapore 6.0%, Malaysia 5.0%

**Foreign direct investment (net):** $3.2 billion

2001 Data (in constant 1995 US dollars)

After two years in office, Prime Minister Thaksin Shinawatra has delivered on most of his ambitious campaign promises. His populist spending programs have included a $23,000 endowment for every village in the country, a socialized medicine program, and a debt moratorium for farmers. In addition, despite a promise to rein in spending to mollify credit rating agencies, he has unveiled even more ambitious programs, including a nearly $2 billion program to build a million new homes for low-income families and a $650 million project to make the southern city of Chiang Mai into an aviation hub. There is even talk of building a canal through Thailand to shorten trans-Pacific shipping routes. Prime Minister Thaksin's fiscal stimulus programs have boosted domestic demand and pushed GDP growth to 4.9 percent. Meanwhile, strong corporate earnings and more efficient tax collection have helped keep the deficit to a manageable 2.3 percent of GDP. Regrettably, the government's spending spree has not reignited the cycle of private investment necessary for sustained growth, and the lingering problem of nonperforming loans has been overlooked. The strong economy has also weakened the impetus for privatization, and scheduled public offerings for several state-controlled companies have been postponed. Thailand's government intervention score is 0.5 point worse this year, and its property rights score is 1 point worse. As a result, Thailand's overall score is 0.15 point worse this year.

## TRADE POLICY
### Score: **4**–Stable (high level of protectionism)

According to the World Bank, Thailand's weighted average tariff rate in 2000 (the most recent year for which World Bank data are available) was 9.7 percent. Non-tariff barriers include a strict import licensing system for products in direct competition with Thai products, as well as customs controls, duties, taxes, and currency controls.

## FISCAL BURDEN OF GOVERNMENT
### Score—Income Taxation: **3.5**–Stable (high tax rates)
### Score—Corporate Taxation: **4**–Stable (high tax rates)
### Score—Change in Government Expenditures: **3**–Stable (very low decrease)
### Final Score: **3.6**–Stable (high cost of government)

Thailand's top income tax rate is 37 percent. The top corporate tax rate is 30 percent. Government expenditures as a share of GDP remained unchanged at 15.2 percent in 2001, compared to a 0.6 percentage point decrease in 2000. On net, Thailand's fiscal burden of government score is unchanged this year.

## GOVERNMENT INTERVENTION IN THE ECONOMY
### Score: **2.5**–Worse (moderate level)

The World Bank reports that the government consumed 11.6 percent of GDP in 2001, up from the 9.4 percent reported in the 2003 *Index*. As a result, Thailand's government intervention score is 0.5 point worse this year. In the same year, according to the International Monetary Fund, Thailand received 7.01 percent of its total revenues from state-owned enterprises and government ownership of property.

## MONETARY POLICY
### Score: **1**–Stable (very low level of inflation)

From 1993 to 2002, Thailand's weighted average annual rate of inflation was 1.04 percent.

## CAPITAL FLOWS AND FOREIGN INVESTMENT
### Score: **3**–Stable (moderate barriers)

The government has opened nearly all service and manufacturing sectors to foreign investment and has relaxed restrictions on land and the financial sector. The law permits 100 percent foreign ownership except in 32 restricted service occupations. Foreign investors are limited to a 49 percent-ownership share in the agriculture, animal husbandry, fisheries, mineral exploration, mining, and services sectors. Residents may hold foreign exchange accounts, subject to approval and maximum limits in some cases, and non-residents must receive approval to sell foreign currencies for baht. The International Monetary Fund reports that some foreign exchange transactions, repatriation, some outward direct investments, and transactions involving capital market securities, bonds, debt securities, money market instruments, real estate, and short-term money securities are regulated. Non-Thai businesses and citizens must receive permission to own land except in government-approved industrial areas.

## BANKING AND FINANCE
### Score: **3**–Stable (moderate level of restrictions)

The banking sector consists of 13 domestic banks and 18 fully licensed foreign banks. The government also maintains several banks that provide credit for specific sectors of the economy. "The public financial sector," reports the U.S. Department of State, "includes several 'specialized' government banks, namely the Government Savings Bank for small savings deposits, the Bank for Agriculture and Agricultural Cooperatives for farm credits, the Government Housing [B]ank for middle and low income housing mortgages, the Industrial Finance Corporation of Thailand for industrial development projects, and the Export Import Bank for importers and exporters." The banking sector suffers from a large number of non-performing loans. According to a December 6, 2002, *Financial Times* article, "Fitch Ratings says bad loans still account for 20 per cent of the banks' total loans, while another 25 per cent are restructured loans which remain vulnerable to any downturn." In October 2001, the government set up the Thai Asset Management Corporation to help reduce the number of non-performing loans.

## WAGES AND PRICES
### Score: **2**–Stable (low level of intervention)

The market determines most wages and prices. According to the Economist Intelligence Unit, "Under the Price Maintenance on Goods and Services Act...the Department of Internal Trade in the Ministry of Commerce administers price controls…. Since 1997 the ministry has ended the practice of directly controlling the price of goods. Nevertheless, it reserves the right to intervene in some sectors with a high degree of public interest—notably bottled water and passenger cars smaller than 1,600 cu cm." In February 2003, the government capped fuel prices. There is a minimum wage.

## PROPERTY RIGHTS
### Score: **3**–Worse (moderate level of protection)

Thailand generally protects private property, but there are some indications of inefficiency and corruption. According to the Economist Intelligence Unit, "private property rights are generally protected, though vested interests continue to intervene, especially in legal judgments." The EIU also reports that, "owing to widespread corruption and political influence, PERC [Political & Economic Risk Consultancy] rated Thailand's police and judicial system among the worst in Asia in its June 2002 survey…." Based on increasing evidence of corruption in the judiciary, Thailand's property rights score is 1 point worse this year.

## REGULATION
### Score: **3**–Stable (moderate level)

Thailand has extensive legislation, especially to protect the environment and labor. According to the U.S. Department of State, "consistent and predictable enforcement of government regulations remains an obstacle to investment in Thailand. Gratuity payment to civil servants responsible for regulatory oversight and enforcement unfortunately remains a common practice. Through such payments, regulations can often be by-passed or ignored and approval processes expedited."

## INFORMAL MARKET
### Score: **3.5**–Stable (high level of activity)

Transparency International's 2002 score for Thailand is 3.2. Therefore, Thailand's informal market score is 3.5 this year.

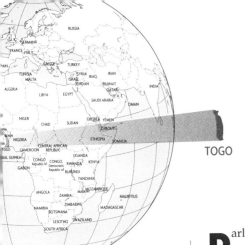

TOGO

# TOGO

Rank: 134

Score: 3.73

Category: Mostly Unfree

Present & Past Scores

(Best) 1 –
2 –
3 –
4 –
(Worst) 5 –

4.14  4.05  4.00  3.88  3.86  3.73

'95  '96  '97  '98  '99  '00  '01  '02  '03  '04

## QUICK STUDY

### SCORES

| | |
|---|---|
| Trade Policy | 3 |
| Fiscal Burden | 4.3 |
| Government Intervention | 3 |
| Monetary Policy | 2 |
| Foreign Investment | 4 |
| Banking and Finance | 4 |
| Wages and Prices | 3 |
| Property Rights | 4 |
| Regulation | 5 |
| Informal Market | 5 |

**Population:** 4,653,400

**Total area:** 56,785 sq. km

**GDP:** $1.5 billion

**GDP growth rate:** 2.7%

**GDP per capita:** $322

**Major exports:** cotton, coffee, cocoa

**Exports of goods and services:** $443.9 million

**Major export trading partners:** Benin 13%, Nigeria 9%, Ghana 5%, Colombia 4%

**Major imports:** petroleum products, machinery and equipment, foodstuffs

**Imports of goods and services:** $722.5 million

**Major import trading partners:** Ghana 35%, France 10%, China 8%, Ivory Coast 8%

**Foreign direct investment (net):** $36.8 million

2001 Data (in constant 1995 US dollars)

Parliament's approval of several amendments to the 1992 constitution helped to guarantee President Gnassingbe Eyadema's re-election in the latter half of 2003. With Eyadema in full control, Togo's poor human rights record is likely to continue. The government's increasingly arrogant posture and reluctance even to consider calls for democracy will cause Western financial support to diminish. Given this short-term hurdle, the close relationship between Eyadema and French President Jacques Chirac could translate into increased assistance from the European Union, but this does not mean that Togo can write off the potential for support from the International Monetary Fund. Togo's economic policy will reflect this recognition, albeit passively, and the Economist Intelligence Unit predicts entry into the poverty reduction and growth facility (PRGF) by the end of 2003. A moderate recovery in Togo's principal export—cotton—should help to elevate 2002's 2.9 percent gain in GDP. The EIU projects 3.5 percent growth in 2003 and 4 percent in 2004, provided that the country meets its potential for outside assistance. Togo's fiscal burden of government score is 0.3 point better this year, and its government intervention score is 1 point better. As a result, Togo's overall score is 0.13 point better this year.

## TRADE POLICY

Score: **3**–Stable (moderate level of protectionism)

Togo is a member of the West African Economic and Monetary Union (WAEMU), which imposes a common external tariff with four rates: 0 percent, 5 percent, 10 percent, and 20 percent. According to the World Bank, Togo's weighted average tariff rate in 2001 was 12.6 percent. (The other seven members of the WAEMU are Benin, Burkina Faso, Guinea–Bissau, Ivory Coast, Mali, Niger, and Senegal.) The government does not require any import licenses and has eliminated its quotas.

## FISCAL BURDEN OF GOVERNMENT

Score—Income Taxation: **5**–Stable (very high tax rates)

Score—Corporate Taxation: **5**–Stable (very high tax rates)

Score—Change in Government Expenditures: **2**–Better (moderate decrease)

Final Score: **4.3**–Better (high cost of government)

Ernst & Young reports that Togo's top income tax rate is 55 percent. The top corporate tax rate is 40 percent. Government expenditures as a share of GDP decreased 2.9 percentage points to 16.3 percent in 2001, compared to a 0.4 percentage point increase in 2000. As a result, Togo's fiscal burden of government score is 0.3 point better this year.

## GOVERNMENT INTERVENTION IN THE ECONOMY

Score: **3**–Better (moderate level)

The World Bank reports that the government consumed 9.3 percent of GDP in 2001, down from the 10.8 percent reported in the 2003 *Index*. As a result, Togo's government intervention score is 1 point better this year. According to the Economist Intelligence Unit, "the privatisation agenda [which includes 15 companies] has been delayed by the freeze in external assistance since 1998 and the poor financial condition of many of the targeted parastatals." The government also owns four banks and the telecommunications company.

## MONETARY POLICY
### Score: **2**–Stable (low level of inflation)

From 1993 to 2002, Togo's weighted average annual rate of inflation was 3.08 percent. Togo has benefited from a stable currency—a rarity in sub-Saharan Africa—as a member of the CFA franc zone. Fourteen countries use the CFA franc, a common currency with a fixed parity with the euro.

## CAPITAL FLOWS AND FOREIGN INVESTMENT
### Score: **4**–Stable (high barriers)

According to the U.S. Department of State, "Investor interest fell sharply in the early 1990's, a period of overt political unrest in Togo. The 1990 investment code includes local content restrictions and requirements on hiring Togo citizens, and there is an overall lack of administrative transparency. Investment is permitted only in certain sectors of the economy and are subject to minimum capital requirements and are screened on a case-by-case basis, and Togolese citizens must receive at least 60 percent of the payroll. The International Monetary Fund reports that both residents and non-residents may hold foreign exchange accounts after obtaining approval of the government and the Banque Centrale des Etats de l'Afrique de l'Ouest (Central Bank of West African States, or BCEAO). Payments and transfers to countries other than France, Monaco, members of the Central African Economic and Monetary Community, members of the West African Economic and Monetary Union, and Comoros are subject to authorization and quantitative limits in some cases. Purchases of real estate by non-residents for purposes other than business are subject to controls. Capital transfers abroad and most other capital transactions require government approval.

## BANKING AND FINANCE
### Score: **4**–Stable (high level of restrictions)

The BCEAO, a central bank common to the eight members of the WAEMU, governs Togo's banking system. Member countries use the CFA franc that is issued by the BCEAO and pegged to the euro. Government involvement in banking and lending decisions has caused the banking sector to deteriorate in recent years. The banking system suffers from a large number of non-performing loans, particularly within the four state-owned banks. The Economist Intelligence Unit reports that the government partially privatized three state-owned banks and one wholly owned bank in 1997 but that progress since then has been slow because of the poor financial health of the remaining banks. In April 2002, BNP-Paribus, a French bank, increased its stake in the state-owned bank BTCI to 48 percent; however, according to the Economist Intelligence Unit, BNP-Paribus pulled out of Togo in November 2002 because the bank "did not gain majority control as expected, leaving BNP-Paribus vulnerable to government interference." The government privatized the state-owned insurance company in December 2000. Although heavy government involvement has led the banking sector to the brink of collapse, the system (including participation by foreign banks) continues to function.

## WAGES AND PRICES
### Score: **3**–Stable (moderate level of intervention)

Togo lifted most price controls in the late 1980s. According to the U.S. Department of State, "Price control and profit margin regulations have been largely eliminated with electricity, water, and telecommunications the only sectors still subject to administrative price controls." The government continues to intervene in agricultural markets, particularly cotton. According to the Economist Intelligence Unit, "To…promote recovery in the sector Sotoco [the state-owned cotton company] raised farm-gate prices…and has maintained them at this level despite a further downturn in world prices in 2001–02." The government sets minimum wages from unskilled workers through professional positions.

## PROPERTY RIGHTS
### Score: **4**–Stable (low level of protection)

The judicial system does not protect private property sufficiently and is subject to the influence of the executive. The U.S. Department of State reports that "the court system remained overburdened and understaffed." In addition, "Lack of transparency and predictability of the judiciary is a serious obstacle in enforcing property and judgment rights, and similar difficulties apply to administrative procedures."

## REGULATION
### Score: **5**–Stable (very high level)

Togo's regulatory system lacks transparency. The U.S. Department of State reports that "establishing an office in Togo is in theory relatively simple, but administrative obstacles and delays are common." In addition, corruption "has spread as a business practice in recent years…. Bribes, whether to private or government officials, are considered crimes…but [corruption] cases are relatively rare, and appear mostly to [involve] those who have in some way lost official favor."

## INFORMAL MARKET
### Score: **5**–Stable (very high level of activity)

Togo has a large informal market in such pirated intellectual property as computer software and video and cassette recordings. According to the U.S. Department of State, "The size of the [Togolese] market is difficult to estimate because so much of the trade is informal."

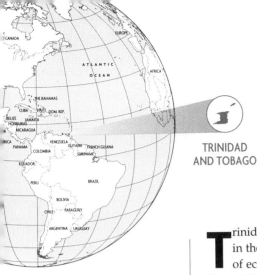

# TRINIDAD AND TOBAGO

TRINIDAD
AND TOBAGO

Rank: 36
Score: 2.45
Category: Mostly Free

**Present & Past Scores**

(Best) 1
2
3  2.69 2.68 2.60 2.49 2.48 2.64 2.54 2.54 2.45
4
(Worst) 5
'95 '96 '97 '98 '99 '00 '01 '02 '03 '04
n/a

rinidad and Tobago was the first member of the British Commonwealth to have a seat in the Organization of American States as well. It also has experienced lengthy periods of economic growth in the years since 1962, when it gained its independence from the United Kingdom. While it relies heavily on tourism, Trinidad and Tobago has diversified and strengthened such other sectors of its economy as petroleum and petrochemicals production, which has expanded with the construction of new natural gas plants. Energy now accounts for 25 percent of government revenues. On February 14, 2003, Maxwell Richards was elected president to replace Arthur Robinson, who had completed his term of office. Patrick Manning of the People's National Movement (PNM) remained in place as prime minister. Currently, the PNM has a 20 to 16 majority in Congress, ending the deadlock that existed two years ago when the PNM and the United National Congress (UNC) each held 18 seats. Trinidad and Tobago's fiscal burden of government score is 0.6 point worse this year, and its informal market score is 0.5 point worse; however, its trade policy score is 2 points better. As a result, Trinidad and Tobago's overall score is 0.09 point better this year.

## TRADE POLICY
### Score: **2**–Better (low level of protectionism)

As a member of the Caribbean Community and Common Market (CARICOM) trade bloc, Trinidad and Tobago has a common external tariff rate that ranges from 5 percent to 20 percent. According to the World Bank, Trinidad and Tobago's weighted average tariff rate in 2001 (the most recent year for which World Bank data are available) was 4.6 percent, down from the 17 percent reported in the 2003 *Index*. As a result, Trinidad and Tobago's trade policy score is 2 points better this year. The U.S. Department of State reports that only a few items require an import license and that "standards, labeling, testing and certification rarely hinder U.S. exports."

## FISCAL BURDEN OF GOVERNMENT
### Score—Income Taxation: **3.5**–Stable (high tax rates)
### Score—Corporate Taxation: **4.5**–Stable (very high tax rates)
### Score—Change in Government Expenditures: **3.5**–Worse (low increase)
### Final Score: **4**–Worse (high cost of government)

Trinidad and Tobago's top income tax rate is 35 percent. The top corporate tax rate is 35 percent. Government expenditures as a share of GDP increased 0.1 percentage point to 24.7 percent in 2001, compared to a 4.1 percentage point decrease in 2000. As a result, Trinidad and Tobago's fiscal burden of government score is 0.6 point worse this year.

## GOVERNMENT INTERVENTION IN THE ECONOMY
### Score: **2.5**–Stable (moderate level)

The World Bank reports that the government consumed 11 percent of GDP in 2001. In 2002, based on data from the central bank, Trinidad and Tobago received 6.87 percent of its total revenues from state-owned enterprises and government ownership of property.

**MONETARY POLICY**
Score: **2**–Stable (low level of inflation)

From 1993 to 2002, Trinidad and Tobago's weighted average annual rate of inflation was 4.42 percent.

 **CAPITAL FLOWS AND FOREIGN INVESTMENT**
Score: **2**–Stable (low barriers)

Trinidad and Tobago is open to foreign investment. Government screening takes place only to determine an investment's environmental impact and whether the investment qualifies for incentives, although bureaucracy can delay the process. Foreign investment in private business is not subject to limitations, but a foreigner must obtain a license to purchase more than 30 percent of a publicly held business. Foreign ownership of land is limited to one acre for residential purposes and five acres for trade purposes. The U.S. Department of State reports that "waivers on corporate equity and land ownership restrictions have been freely granted." According to the International Monetary Fund, both residents and non-residents may hold foreign exchange accounts. There are no restrictions or controls on payments, transactions, transfers, or repatriation of profits.

 **BANKING AND FINANCE**
Score: **2**–Stable (low level of restrictions)

The banking system is open and well-developed. There are six commercial banks, including one state-owned bank. There are no restrictions on foreign banks, although government approval is required for the establishment of new foreign banks. Banks are free to engage in a wide range of services. The International Monetary Fund reports that in 2001, the government lowered the reserve requirement on domestic currency deposits to 18 percent from 21 percent. The government requires a liquid asset ratio of 25 percent on foreign currency deposits.

 **WAGES AND PRICES**
Score: **2**–Stable (low level of intervention)

The market sets most wages and prices, but the government determines prices on sugar, schoolbooks, and pharmaceuticals. The government subsidizes some agricultural goods and mandates a minimum wage.

 **PROPERTY RIGHTS**
Score: **2**–Stable (high level of protection)

The judiciary is independent and provides a fair judicial process. However, the judicial process can be long. According to the U.S. Department of State, "At present there is a several year backlog of cases waiting to be heard."

 **REGULATION**
Score: **3**–Stable (moderate level)

Regulations and bureaucratic red tape are burdensome. According to the U.S. Department of State, "Bureaucratic delays in approval of investment packages can be frustrating for investors.... Environmental approval for large industrial projects can also be extremely time consuming, and many projects begin with only outline approval." Investors complain about "a perceived lack of delineation of authority for final investment approvals between the various ministries which may be involved in a project...." There are reports of moderate corruption, but this has not seriously undermined business operations.

 **INFORMAL MARKET**
Score: **3**–Worse (moderate level of activity)

Transparency International's 2002 score for Trinidad and Tobago is 4.9. Therefore, Trinidad and Tobago's informal market score is 3 this year—0.5 point worse than last year.

# TUNISIA

TUNISIA

**Rank: 67**

**Score: 2.94**

**Category: Mostly Free**

Present & Past Scores

(Best) 1
2
3
4  2.98 2.83 2.89 2.90 3.01 2.94 3.04 2.89 2.91  2.94
(Worst) 5

'95 '96 '97 '98 '99 '00 '01 '02 '03 '04

## QUICK STUDY

### SCORES

| | |
|---|---|
| Trade Policy | 5 |
| Fiscal Burden | 3.9 |
| Government Intervention | 2.5 |
| Monetary Policy | 1 |
| Foreign Investment | 3 |
| Banking and Finance | 3 |
| Wages and Prices | 2 |
| Property Rights | 3 |
| Regulation | 3 |
| Informal Market | 3 |

**Population:** 9,673,600

**Total area:** 163,610 sq. km

**GDP:** $24.8 billion

**GDP growth rate:** 4.9%

**GDP per capita:** $2,562

**Major exports:** textiles, electrical equipment, leather, petroleum

**Exports of goods and services:** $11.7 billion

**Major export trading partners:** France 28.8%, Italy 22.5%, Germany 12.5%, Spain 5.0%

**Major imports:** machinery, textiles, electrical equipment

**Imports of goods and services:** $12.5 billion

**Major import trading partners:** France 28.0%, Italy 19.8%, Germany 10.4%, Spain 4.6%

**Foreign direct investment (net):** $435.8 million

2001 Data (in constant 1995 US dollars)

Tunisia is one of the Arab world's most modern, stable, and cosmopolitan countries. Although it developed a socialist economy under President Habib Bourguiba, who ruled from independence in 1956 until 1987, it has undertaken substantial free market economic reforms under the leadership of President Zine al-Abedine Ben Ali, who was re-elected to a third term in 1999. Tunisia's diverse economy includes important agricultural, mining, energy, tourism, and manufacturing sectors; and its association agreement with the European Union, which entered into force in 1998, was the first such agreement between the EU and a Maghreb country. In recent years, expanding trade and tourism have helped to yield steady economic growth, although the tourism industry has been hurt by post–September 11 worries about Islamist terrorism in the region. Fueled by a major influx of foreign investment, the economy grew by an average of 5.2 percent annually from 1997–2001. The government has taken a gradualist approach to economic reform. Its privatization program focused on small loss-making state-owned firms from 1987 to 1994. Privatization accelerated in 1995, but it was not until 1998 that the government began to sell off large profit-making businesses. The pace of privatization slowed in 2001, but the government listed 26 state-owned firms for sale in 2002, despite political resistance. Tunisia's fiscal burden of government score is 0.2 point better this year; however, its informal market score is 0.5 point worse. As a result, Tunisia's overall score is 0.03 point worse this year.

## TRADE POLICY
### Score: **5**–Stable (very high level of protectionism)

According to the World Bank, Tunisia's weighted average tariff rate in 1998 (the most recent year for which World Bank data are available) was 26.3 percent. Non-tariff barriers include import licenses and quotas, particularly on consumer goods and motor vehicles.

## FISCAL BURDEN OF GOVERNMENT
Score—Income Taxation: **3.5**–Stable (high tax rates)
Score—Corporate Taxation: **4.5**–Stable (very high tax rates)
Score—Change in Government Expenditures: **3**–Better (very low decrease)
### Final Score: **3.9**–Better (high cost of government)

Tunisia's top income tax rate is 35 percent. The top corporate tax rate is 35 percent. Government expenditures as a share of GDP decreased 0.4 percentage point to 32.3 percent in 2001, compared to a 1.4 percentage point increase in 2000. As a result, Tunisia's fiscal burden of government score is 0.2 point better this year.

## GOVERNMENT INTERVENTION IN THE ECONOMY
### Score: **2.5**–Stable (moderate level)

The World Bank reports that the government consumed 15.7 percent of GDP in 2001. In 2000, according to the International Monetary Fund, Tunisia received 6.79 percent of its total revenues from state-owned enterprises and government ownership of property.

## MONETARY POLICY
Score: **1**–Stable (very low level of inflation)

From 1993 to 2002, Tunisia's weighted average annual rate of inflation was 2.59 percent.

## CAPITAL FLOWS AND FOREIGN INVESTMENT
Score: **3**–Stable (moderate barriers)

Tunisia is open to foreign investment generally but does restrict it in some sectors. According to the U.S. Department of State, "The Tunisian Government screens potential foreign investment to minimize the impact of the investment on domestic competitors and employment, and to minimize foreign currency outflows." All real estate transactions require approval, and foreigners may not own agricultural land, although leasing (up to 40 years) is allowed. Foreign investment in "strategic" sectors like finance, petroleum refining and production, the national airline, electricity, water, and telecommunications is prohibited. Foreign investors are allowed to participate in Tunisia's privatization program; as of August 2002, according to *African Economic Outlook,* foreign capital constituted 75 percent of Tunisia's revenue from its sale of state-owned enterprises. The International Monetary Fund reports that certain residents may hold foreign exchange accounts subject to restrictions. There are some controls and restrictions on payments, transactions, and transfers. There are many restrictions and controls on capital transactions—including derivatives, capital and money market instruments, purchases abroad by residents, repatriation, and direct investment—and many of these transactions require official approval.

## BANKING AND FINANCE
Score: **3**–Stable (moderate level of restrictions)

"The banking system remains inefficient, state-dominated and burdened by nonperforming loans (NPLs)," reports the Economist Intelligence Unit. "However, the system is slowly being restructured through a series of bank mergers aimed at replacing the large number of specialist banks with a smaller number of stronger, more efficient multi-purpose institutions for the opening of the sector to foreign competition under agreements with the World Trade Organization (WTO) and the EU." The government sold its 52 percent stake in the commercial Union Internationale de Banques (UIB) in October 2002 and is attempting to privatize its stake in Banque du Sud (BS). According to the Economist Intelligence Unit, "The sale of BS would leave just three commercial banks out of 14 under state control...." However, Tunisia's largest bank, Société Tunisienne de Banque, is still government-owned, and the EIU reports that "the government is understood to see the two other banks as playing such important roles—financing agriculture and housing respectively—that they will not be sold in the foreseeable future." According to the Ministry of Development and International Cooperation, foreign banks must obtain a license from the Ministry of Finance and must meet a minimum capital requirement of 10 million TND.

## WAGES AND PRICES
Score: **2**–Stable (low level of intervention)

The market determines most wages and prices. According to the Ministry of Development and International Cooperation, market forces determine approximately 87 percent of prices at the production level and 80.6 percent of prices at the distribution level. The government mandates a minimum wage.

## PROPERTY RIGHTS
Score: **3**–Stable (moderate level of protection)

The executive branch is the supreme arbiter of events in the cabinet, government, judiciary, and military. According to the U.S. Department of State, "Local legal experts assert that courts are susceptible to political pressure.... In general, complaints about the Tunisian legal system from the commercial sector concern the length and the complexity of unfamiliar legal procedures." The Economist Intelligence Unit reports that "in July 2001, [a senior judge]...said judges were harassed and intimidated to make them pronounce judgements decided in advance by the authorities."

## REGULATION
Score: **3**–Stable (moderate level)

The bureaucracy can be a considerable impediment to business. According to the Economist Intelligence Unit, "Tunisian bureaucracy can still be slow and lacking in transparency, and work permits can take weeks to obtain.... [D]espite some reform, labor law is still relatively rigid, with high add-on costs and cumbersome regulations governing the hiring and dismissal of employees." The U.S. Department of State reports that "firms may need to complete a wide range of regulatory, licensing and logistical procedures before bringing their products or services to the market." Corruption is reportedly an obstacle to doing business in Tunisia.

## INFORMAL MARKET
Score: **3**–Worse (moderate level of activity)

Transparency International's 2002 score for Tunisia is 4.8. Therefore, Tunisia's informal market score is 3 this year—0.5 point worse than last year.

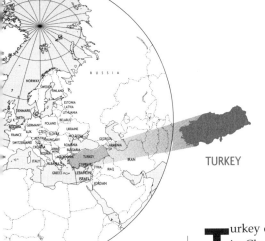

# TURKEY

TURKEY

**Rank:** 106

**Score:** 3.39

**Category:** Mostly Unfree

Present & Past Scores

(Best) 1
2
3
4
(Worst) 5

2.95 3.00 2.70 2.66 2.80 2.73 2.93 3.33 3.50 3.39

'95 '96 '97 '98 '99 '00 '01 '02 '03 '04

## QUICK STUDY

### SCORES

| | |
|---|---|
| Trade Policy | 3 |
| Fiscal Burden | 3.9 |
| Government Intervention | 2.5 |
| Monetary Policy | 5 |
| Foreign Investment | 3 |
| Wages and Prices | 3 |
| Banking and Finance | 3 |
| Property Rights | 3 |
| Regulation | 4 |
| Informal Market | 3.5 |

**Population:** 69,626,000

**Total area:** 780,580 sq. km

**GDP:** $204.7 billion

**GDP growth rate:** 7.8%

**GDP per capita:** $2,940

**Major exports:** textiles and clothing, metals, motor vehicles and parts, agricultural products, food and beverages

**Exports of goods and services:** $57.1 billion

**Major export trading partners:** Germany 16.6%, US 9.2%, UK 8.5%, Italy 6.4%

**Major imports:** chemicals, crude oil and gas, machinery and equipment, transport equipment

**Imports of goods and services:** $68.9 billion

**Major import trading partners:** Germany 13.7%, Italy 8.1%, Russia 7.6%, US 6.0%

**Foreign direct investment (net):** $367.7 million

2002 Data (in constant 1995 US dollars)

Turkey experienced a severe financial crisis in the spring of 2001. The Minister of State in Charge of the Treasury at the time, Kemal Dervis, pledged that the government would pass 15 laws to recapitalize state-owned and private banks, make the central bank more independent of political control, allow the lira to float freely, decrease government spending, and arrange for the further privatization of state-owned banks and some companies. The International Monetary Fund has warned Ankara that it will not receive further assistance if this latest overhaul fails; no bilateral aid was offered to augment the multilateral institutions' loans, and disbursement of the tranches was tied to successful implementation of the Dervis plan. The Islamist Justice and Development Party (AKP), which won the November 2002 parliamentary election by an overwhelming margin, has proved itself inexperienced in dealing with matters of state. Most tellingly, despite its majority, by failing to shepherd a bill through parliament that would have allowed U.S. troops to attack Iraq from the north, it caused Turkey to forfeit $24 billion in promised loans and grants from the United States; the next day, the stock market in Istanbul lost one-quarter of its value. The AKP also has granted government increases in civil service pensions and wages without explaining how these increases are to be funded. In general, however, the government of Prime Minister Recep Tayyip Erdogan has embraced the basic tenets of the Dervis–IMF plan. This is vital for Turkey, which will need to roll over a staggering $93.5 billion in debt repayments in 2003. Turkey's fiscal burden of government score is 0.6 point better this year, and its government intervention score is 0.5 point better. As a result, Turkey's overall score is 0.11 point better this year.

## TRADE POLICY
### Score: **3**–Stable (moderate level of protectionism)

The World Bank reports that Turkey's weighted average tariff rate in 1999 (the most recent year for which World Bank data are available) was 5.4 percent. According to the U.S. Trade Representative, "Non-tariff barriers result in costly delays, demurrage charges and other uncertainties that stifle trade for many agricultural products...."

## FISCAL BURDEN OF GOVERNMENT
### Score—Income Taxation: **4**–Stable (high tax rates)
### Score—Corporate Taxation: **4.5**–Stable (very high tax rates)
### Score—Change in Government Expenditures: **2.5**–Better (low decrease)
### Final Score: **3.9**–Better (high cost of government)

Turkey's top income tax rate is 40 percent. The top corporate tax rate is 30 percent, but a surtax of 10 percent is applied to this rate, yielding a total corporate income tax rate of 33 percent. Government expenditures as a share of GDP decreased 1.1 percentage points to 41.7 percent in 2002, compared to a 6.3 percentage point increase in 2001. As a result, Turkey's fiscal burden of government score is 0.6 point better this year.

## GOVERNMENT INTERVENTION IN THE ECONOMY
### Score: **2.5**–Better (moderate level)

Based on data from the International Monetary Fund, the government consumed 14 percent of GDP in 2002. In 2001, according to the IMF, Turkey received 5.71 percent of its total revenues from state-owned enterprises and government ownership of property, down from the 10.13 percent reported in the 2003 *Index*. As a result, Turkey's government intervention score is 0.5 point better this year.

## MONETARY POLICY
### Score: **5**–Stable (very high level of inflation)

From 1993 to 2002, Turkey's weighted average annual rate of inflation was 49.37 percent.

## CAPITAL FLOWS AND FOREIGN INVESTMENT
### Score: **3**–Stable (moderate barriers)

Turkey welcomes foreign investment but maintains a number of formal and informal barriers. Foreign equity is restricted to 20 percent in broadcasting companies and 49 percent in aviation, maritime transportation, and value-added telecommunications services companies. According to the U.S. Department of State, legislation passed in June 2003 eliminated minimum capital requirements for foreign investors, provided national treatment to foreign investors purchasing real estate, and replaced the screening of foreign investment with a notification system; however, implementing regulations have not been enacted. The same source notes that obstacles to investment include "high inflation, political and macroeconomic uncertainties, excessive bureaucracy, weaknesses in the judicial system, high and inconsistently collected taxes, weakness in corporate governance, arbitrary decisions taken at the municipal level, and frequent, sometimes unclear changes in the legal and regulatory environment." The International Monetary Fund reports that both residents and non-residents may hold foreign exchange accounts. There are virtually no restrictions on payments and transfers. Some restrictions and reporting requirements apply to capital transactions.

## BANKING AND FINANCE
### Score: **3**–Stable (moderate level of restrictions)

Supervision of the banking sector has improved. The Economist Intelligence Unit reports that "since 1999, short foreign-exchange positions have been limited to 20% of capital, and new rules have been introduced to limit in-group exposure and ensure credit risk diversification. Banks have been required to set up internal risk management systems and to provision more thoroughly for bad loans. In the first half of 2002, all banks were subjected to a special audit to ensure that they matched up to a new 8% capital adequacy requirement." The government, however, continues to play a dominant role. According to the EIU, "The high level of borrowing required by the state has resulted in dwindling resources for investment. Government borrowing is the direct consequence of an inefficient tax system.... The state has traditionally been the banks' biggest client, leaving few resources for others." According to the Embassy of Turkey, there are three state-owned commercial banks, which are being privatized, and three state-owned development and investment banks. Foreign banks face no barriers to entry; the government has sought foreign banks to take over troubled domestic banks, and 18 foreign banks are now operating in the country.

## WAGES AND PRICES
### Score: **3**–Stable (moderate level of intervention)

"Despite talk of allowing the enterprises to set their own prices," reports the Economist Intelligence Unit, "the government primarily sets prices of goods produced by state-owned firms.... In general, the government sets annual prices for a range of crops. The municipalities fix ceilings on the price of bread. The Ministry of Health controls drug prices." The Embassy of Turkey reports that the government adjusts petroleum prices based on changes in the exchange rate and world prices of petroleum products. The Ministry of Labor is required by law to adjust the minimum wage at least every two years based on the advice of the Minimum Wage Determination Commission, a tripartite body composed of government, labor, and employer representatives.

## PROPERTY RIGHTS
### Score: **3**–Stable (moderate level of protection)

The U.S. Department of State reports that "Turkey's...court system is overburdened...sometimes resulting in slow decisions and judges lacking sufficient time to grasp complex issues. Judgments of foreign courts need to be reconsidered by local courts before they are accepted and enforced." According to the Economist Intelligence Unit, "the judicial process can be...subject to political interference in high-profile cases."

## REGULATION
### Score: **4**–Stable (high level)

Turkish regulations are moderately burdensome. Establishing a business is relatively simple, but obtaining permits can be difficult. According to the U.S. Department of State, "bureaucratic 'red tape' remains a significant problem.... Obtaining the approval of both national and local officials for essential permits is a time consuming and often frustrating process." The U.S. Department of State and other sources report that corruption is a significant impediment to doing business.

## INFORMAL MARKET
### Score: **3.5**–Stable (high level of activity)

Transparency International's 2002 score for Turkey is 3.2. Therefore, Turkey's informal market score is 3.5 this year.

TURKMENISTAN

# TURKMENISTAN

Rank: 150

Score: 4.31

Category: Repressed

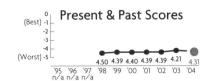

Present & Past Scores

(Best) 0, -1, -2, -3, -4, (Worst) -5

4.50 4.39 4.40 4.39 4.39 4.21 4.31
'95 '96 '97 '98 '99 '00 '01 '02 '03 '04
n/a n/a n/a

2001 Data (in constant 1995 US dollars)

## QUICK STUDY

### SCORES

| | |
|---|---|
| Trade Policy | 5 |
| Fiscal Burden | 3.1 |
| Government Intervention | 5 |
| Monetary Policy | 4 |
| Foreign Investment | 4 |
| Banking and Finance | 5 |
| Wages and Prices | 4 |
| Property Rights | 4 |
| Regulation | 4 |
| Informal Market | 5 |

**Population:** 5,435,000

**Total area:** 488,100 sq. km

**GDP:** $8.6 billion

**GDP growth rate:** 20.5%

**GDP per capita:** $1,587

**Major exports:** gas, crude and refined oil, textiles

**Exports of goods and services:** $2.77 billion

**Major export trading partners:** Iran 20.4%, Ukraine 15.4%, Azerbaijan 10.4%, Kazakhstan 5.9%, Italy 5.5%

**Major imports:** foodstuffs, machinery and equipment

**Imports of goods and services:** $2.8 billion

**Major import trading partners:** US 17.6%, Ukraine 15.4%, United Arab Emirates 10.2%, Russia 9.8%, Germany 9.1%

**Foreign direct investment (net):** n/a

Turkmenistan possesses the world's fifth largest reserves of natural gas and is among the world's top 10 producers of cotton. Its communist-era leader, President Saparmurat Niyazov, known as "Turkmenbashi" (Leader of All Ethnic Turkmens), was voted president for life in December 1999 and promotes an ostentatious cult of personality. In November 2002, he used allegations of a coup to incarcerate opposition leaders, including former Foreign Minister Boris Shikhmuradov. He also has stripped the Russian minority of citizenship, causing tens of thousands to flee, and has cracked down on religious freedom. Key industries are still owned by the state, and over-regulation of the economy limits the incentives for foreign investment. In addition, the currency is not fully convertible. GDP growth in 2001 was due to increased export of hydrocarbons and higher oil and gas prices. The reported 20.5 percent growth rate is suspect and cannot be substantiated. The government announced the budget deficit for 2001 as a surplus by ignoring expenditures by massive state-run extra-budgetary funds. Corruption is rampant, and investors rely on bribes to top officials to ensure support for their projects. In April 2003, Turkmenbashi signed the "deal of the century" committing to export of all Turkmen gas via Russia at half of the global market price over the next 25 years. Turkmenistan's fiscal burden of government score is 1 point worse this year. As a result, its overall score is 0.10 point worse this year.

## TRADE POLICY
### Score: **5**–Stable (very high level of protectionism)

According to the World Bank, Turkmenistan's weighted average tariff rate in 1998 (the most recent year for which World Bank data are available) was 0 percent, but this figure does not accurately reflect the extent of the country's tariff regime. The European Bank for Reconstruction and Development reports that the government imposes excise taxes, ranging from 10 percent to 100 percent, on a large number of imports. The U.S. Department of State reports that "Turkmenistan maintains a significant number of non-tariff barriers to trade…. In addition, the government sets price requirements that lead to the import of products and services of low quality."

## FISCAL BURDEN OF GOVERNMENT
### Score—Income Taxation: **1.5**–Stable (low tax rates)
### Score—Corporate Taxation: **3**–Stable (moderate tax rates)
### Score—Change in Government Expenditures: **5**–Worse (very high increase)
### Final Score: **3.1**–Worse (moderate cost of government)

Turkmenistan's top income tax rate is 12 percent, up from the 11 percent reported in the 2003 *Index*. The top corporate tax rate is 25 percent. Government expenditures as a share of GDP increased 9.8 percentage points to 29.2 percent in 2000, compared to a 5.2 percentage point decrease in 1999. As a result, Turkmenistan's fiscal burden of government score is 1 point worse this year.

## GOVERNMENT INTERVENTION IN THE ECONOMY
### Score: **5**–Stable (very high level)

The World Bank reports that the government consumed 14.7 percent of GDP in 2001. According to the Economist Intelligence Unit, however, "Official fiscal data…hide a large structural deficit in off-budget accounts, debts and arrears." In addition, "Turkmenistan has one of the lowest private sector/GDP ratios in the region…. Privatisation has centred almost entirely on small enterprises in the services sector." The government guarantees employment for every Turkmen citizen. Based on the apparent unreliability of reported figures for government consumption, 1 point has been added to Turkmenistan's government intervention score. Another point has been added based on the level of state-owned enterprise.

### MONETARY POLICY
### Score: **4**–Stable (high level of inflation)

From 1993 to 2002, Turkmenistan's weighted average annual rate of inflation was 17.32 percent.

### CAPITAL FLOWS AND FOREIGN INVESTMENT
### Score: **4**–Stable (high barriers)

Turkmenistan's government controls most of the economy and allows little foreign participation. The International Monetary Fund reports that investments by "juridical persons" are permitted for all sectors in theory, but authorization from the government (at the highest level for investments over $500,000) is mandatory. The state restricts investment in a number of "strategic" sectors, such as utilities and oil and gas. According to the Economist Intelligence Unit, "Despite the government's expressions of support for foreign investment, it has failed to introduce the political and macroeconomic reforms necessary to ensure a favourable business environment…. All foreign investment must be approved by the State Agency for Foreign Investment (SAFI)—a time consuming and bureaucratic process—while the maintenance of many price and currency controls is a further disincentive to foreign investors." The IMF reports that foreign exchange accounts require government approval. All payments and transfers require the approval of the exchange control authorities. Inward and outward capital transactions require central bank approval.

### BANKING AND FINANCE
### Score: **5**–Stable (very high level of restrictions)

The government of Turkmenistan owns most of the commercial banks and controls almost all of the financial system's assets. According to the Economist Intelligence Unit, "Turkmenistan's financial system remains firmly under state control, with the financial sector dominated by state-owned or state-influenced institutions…. An estimated 95% of all loans continue to go to state enterprises. Directed credits from the state-owned Daikhan bank to agriculture at subsidized interest rates (nominal rates of 1% per year) are set to persist…. As a result of growing inter-enterprise arrears, negative real interest rates and chronic late payment on debts owed to banks, many of Turkmenistan's banks are insolvent by international standards." The only non-bank financial institution is the state-owned insurance monopoly.

### WAGES AND PRICES
### Score: **4**–Stable (high level of intervention)

In Turkmenistan's command economy, the government controls prices and most wages through widespread price controls, subsidies, and the extensive state-owned sector. According to the European Bank for Reconstruction and Development, "Households have free access to electricity, water and gas up to certain relatively generous limits…. Rents and public transport are also subsidised…. Fuel is sold domestically at around 4 cent/litre…which may not even cover fully the cost of production and certainly does not account for any investment in road maintenance. Telecommunications remain tightly controlled by the government…. Total domestic subsidies in the oil and gas sector alone were estimated by the World Bank at around US$ 600 million in 2000 (21 per cent of GDP)." According to the U.S. Department of State, there is no minimum wage, but the government influences wages as a major employer.

### PROPERTY RIGHTS
### Score: **4**–Stable (low level of protection)

The U.S. Department of State reports that "there is no legal system in place for the effective enforcement of property and contractual rights. Therefore, disputes must be worked out directly between the Turkmen Government and the investor." Moreover, "The President's power to select and dismiss judges subordinates the judiciary to the Presidency." According to the Economist Intelligence Unit, "The judiciary is badly trained and open to bribery…. The provision in the constitution for the private ownership of land, Article 9, has yet to be implemented in practice."

### REGULATION
### Score: **4**–Stable (high level)

Since the government controls much of the economy, Turkmenistan's business climate is necessarily constrained. According to the U.S. Department of State, "The government's desire to regulate economic and commercial transactions creates impediments to investment. Personal relations with Government officials often play a decisive role in acquiring a contract or running a successful business. Since investment contracts are concluded on a case by case basis, it is difficult for the investor to identify a clear set of rules that apply and that will apply over the term of the investment."

### INFORMAL MARKET
### Score: **5**–Stable (very high level of activity)

Smuggling is rampant, and there is an informal market in currency. About 7 percent of the population worked informally in 1999 (the most recent year for which data are available). The Business Software Alliance estimates that in 2000, the rate of computer software piracy was 90 percent.

*2004 Index of Economic Freedom*

# UGANDA

Rank: 48

Score: 2.70

Category: Mostly Free

## QUICK STUDY

### SCORES
| | |
|---|---|
| Trade Policy | 3 |
| Fiscal Burden | 3 |
| Government Intervention | 2 |
| Monetary Policy | 1 |
| Foreign Investment | 3 |
| Banking and Finance | 2 |
| Wages and Prices | 2 |
| Property Rights | 3 |
| Regulation | 4 |
| Informal Market | 4 |

**Population:** 22,788,000

**Total area:** 236,040 sq. km

**GDP:** $8.1 billion

**GDP growth rate:** 4.6%

**GDP per capita:** $355

**Major exports:** coffee, tea, gold, cotton, fish products

**Exports of goods and services:** $1.3 billion

**Major export trading partners:** Belgium 14.3%, Netherlands 14.1%, Germany 7.5%, US 6.0%, Spain 5.7%

**Major imports:** vehicles, petroleum, medical and pharmaceutical products, cereals

**Imports of goods and services:** $2.3 billion

**Major import trading partners:** Kenya 43.2%, India 6.8%, UK 5.6%, US 3.7%, Japan 2.9%

**Foreign direct investment (net):** $200.9 million

2001 Data (in constant 1995 US dollars)

U ganda continues to benefit from strong economic growth, declining poverty, low inflation, and rising per capita income. The Economist Intelligence Unit expects real GDP growth of 5.6 percent in 2003 and 6.5 percent in 2004. Government statistics reported by the Organisation for Economic Co-operation and Development show that the proportion of the population living below the official poverty line of $1 per day fell from 56 percent in 1992 to 35 percent in 2001. During a decade of privatization that has significantly benefited the economy, 74 businesses have been taken out of state hands and another 85 have been slated for privatization. The Ugandan government has led the way in Africa in combating the spread of AIDS; the HIV rate of infection actually fell from 6.9 percent in 1999 to 6.1 percent in 2002. Overall, however, nearly a million Ugandans died of the disease between 1982 and 2002, reducing life expectancy to just 38 years by 1997. Foreign direct investment and donor confidence are likely to benefit from wide-ranging political reforms in the next year. A 17-year ban on multiparty politics is expected to end in 2004 following a referendum on the issue. However, it is expected that President Yoweri Museveni will seek to amend the current constitution, which limits the number of terms a president can serve. Museveni, who has been in power since 1986, is widely expected to contest the 2006 presidential election. Civil war remains Uganda's biggest problem. A cease-fire signed in March 2003 between the Ugandan government and the Lord's Resistance Army (LRA), led by Joseph Kony, failed to end the conflict. An estimated 600,000 Ugandans have been displaced by the violence in the north of the country. Uganda's fiscal burden of government and banking and finance scores are 1 point better this year, and its informal market score is 0.5 point better. As a result, Uganda's overall score is 0.25 point better this year.

 ## TRADE POLICY
### Score: **3**–Stable (moderate level of protectionism)

According to the World Bank, Uganda's weighted average tariff rate in 2001 (the most recent year for which World Bank data are available) was 6.9 percent. Many imports require an import certificate (license), valid for 6 months. The World Trade Organization reports that imports are subject to an import license commission of 2 percent as well as other taxes.

 ## FISCAL BURDEN OF GOVERNMENT
### Score—Income Taxation: **3**–Stable (moderate tax rates)
### Score—Corporate Taxation: **4**–Stable (high tax rates)
### Score—Change in Government Expenditures: **1**–Better (very high decrease)
### Final Score: **3**–Better (moderate cost of government)

Uganda's top income tax rate is 30 percent. The corporate tax rate is 30 percent. Government expenditures as a share of GDP decreased 5.2 percentage points to 20.2 percent in 2001, compared to a 7.1 percentage point increase in 2000. As a result, Uganda's fiscal burden of government score is 1 point better this year.

 ## GOVERNMENT INTERVENTION IN THE ECONOMY
### Score: **2**–Stable (low level)

The World Bank reports that the government consumed 12.5 percent of GDP in 2001. In 2000, according to the International Monetary Fund, Uganda received 2.92 percent of its total rev-

395

enues from state-owned enterprises and government owner-ship of property.

## MONETARY POLICY
### Score: **1**–Stable (very low level of inflation)

From 1993 to 2002, Uganda's weighted average annual rate of inflation was 0.75 percent.

## CAPITAL FLOWS AND FOREIGN INVESTMENT
### Score: **3**–Stable (moderate barriers)

Uganda is fairly open to foreign investment. According to the U.S. Department of State, "Foreign investors may form 100 percent foreign-owned companies and majority or minority joint ventures with local investors with no restrictions." The government allows foreign investment in privatized indus-tries, including the partially privatized telecommunications sector. Most barriers to foreign investment, such as corrup-tion, an inefficient bureaucracy, and inconsistent application of regulations, are informal. "The investment code provides fewer advantages to foreigners as compared with nationals of Uganda," reports the U.S. Department of State. "For example, licensing authorities may apply performance obligations on foreign investors, to which nationals are not subject…." The International Monetary Fund reports that both residents and non-residents may hold foreign exchange accounts. There are no restrictions or controls on payments, transactions, or transfers. Resident foreign nationals may purchase land, but non-resident foreign nationals may only lease land for up to 99 years.

## BANKING AND FINANCE
### Score: **2**–Better (low level of restrictions)

Aside from the central Bank of Uganda (BOU), there are 16 commercial banks and two development banks. An April 2003 International Monetary Fund report gave Uganda's banking system a positive assessment, based primarily on the closure of insolvent banks in 1998–1999, the partial privatiza-tion of the Uganda Commercial Bank, increased supervision, and the increasing presence of foreign banks. "The main rea-son for the improvement," reports the Economist Intelligence Unit, "was found to be the closure of four local banks in 1998/99, and the fact that the system is now dominated by large reputable foreign banks that appear to be well capi-talised and resilient." According to the International Monetary Fund, "Banking supervision has been increasingly more vigorous, with on-site inspections being stepped up substantially…. New capital requirements came into effect on January 1, 2003, raising the minimum paid-up capital to U Sh 4.0 billion. As a result of these actions, the performance indi-cators for the banking system have continued to improve. The ratio of nonperforming loans to total loans declined from 9.8 percent in December 2000 to 3.6 percent in June 2002…." Based on the evidence of a reduced government presence, increasing supervision, and an expanded presence by foreign banks, Uganda's banking and finance score is 1 point better this year.

## WAGES AND PRICES
### Score: **2**–Stable (low level of intervention)

The government dismantled price controls in January 1994, and the abolition of coffee, cotton, and other government monopolies has allowed the market to set wages and prices in these important sectors. Uganda maintains a minimum wage, but most wages are set through negotiation among individuals, unions, and employers; the government is involved only if it is the employer.

## PROPERTY RIGHTS
### Score: **3**–Stable (moderate level of protection)

The judicial system is not fully independent and lacks resources. According to the U.S. Department of State, "the President has extensive legal powers that influence the exer-cise of [judicial] independence." The government is compen-sating individuals for property that was confiscated in the past.

## REGULATION
### Score: **4**–Stable (high level)

Doing business in Uganda is still difficult, particularly for local small businesses. Obstacles include corruption, ineffi-cient government services, and mismanagement. According to the National Center for Policy Analysis, "in Uganda, a 1998 private sector survey revealed that, on average, 15 percent of management time was consumed by regulatory compliance activity, with some firms reporting as much as 40 percent." The same source reports that "bribery has an adverse effect on firms' growth more than three times greater than that of taxation."

## INFORMAL MARKET
### Score: **4**–Better (high level of activity)

Transparency International's 2002 score for Uganda is 2.1. Therefore, Uganda's informal market score is 4 this year—0.5 point better than last year.

# UKRAINE

UKRAINE

Rank: 117

Score: 3.49

Category: Mostly Unfree

**Present & Past Scores**

(Best) 1
2
3
4
(Worst) 5

4.05  3.75  3.83  3.83  3.75  3.75  3.88  3.84  3.59 3.49

'95  '96  '97  '98  '99  '00  '01  '02  '03  '04

## QUICK STUDY

### SCORES

| | |
|---|---|
| Trade Policy | 3 |
| Fiscal Burden | 3.9 |
| Government Intervention | 3 |
| Monetary Policy | 3 |
| Foreign Investment | 4 |
| Banking and Finance | 3 |
| Wages and Prices | 3 |
| Property Rights | 4 |
| Regulation | 4 |
| Informal Market | 4 |

**Population:** 49,093,000

**Total area:** 603,700 sq. km

**GDP:** $48.4 billion

**GDP growth rate:** 9.1%

**GDP per capita:** $986

**Major exports:** metals, minerals, electronics, chemicals, vegetables

**Exports of goods and services:** $31.6 billion

**Major export trading partners:** Russia 17.8%, Turkey 6.9%, Italy 4.6%, Germany 4.2%, China 3.9%

**Major imports:** minerals, electronics, transport equipment, metals

**Imports of goods and services:** $29.2 billion

**Major import trading partners:** Russia 37.2%, Turkmenistan 11.1%, Germany 9.8%, Poland 3.2%, US 2.8%

**Foreign direct investment (net):** $671.6 million

2001 Data (in constant 1995 US dollars)

Ukraine's political system is gripped by maneuvering to succeed President Leonid Kuchma, who has ruled since 1995. The March 2002 parliamentary elections did not lead to the formation of a majority coalition, and the opposition remains divided between the center–right and left. Ukraine has become embroiled in corruption scandals. President Kuchma has been implicated in scandals involving the disappearance and death of Hrihory Gongadze, an investigative journalist, as well as the surreptitious taping of conversations in his office. Former Prime Minister Pavlo Lazarenko has been indicted for money laundering and corruption in both the United States and Switzerland. Ukraine depends almost entirely on energy imports from Russia, and the Kremlin has been using this dependence to gain political influence. However, there has been moderate progress on economic reforms, including land reform, price liberalization, and reducing barriers to trade, and tax reform is expected in 2003. Rising industrial outputs and falling inflation also have contributed to the recent improvement in GDP growth. Most Western observers are hoping for the formation of a pro-reform cabinet following presidential elections in 2004. Ukraine has expressed an interest in joining the European Union and has been an active member of the NATO Partnership for Peace program. In May 2002, it announced that it planned to move away from its position of neutrality and intends to apply formally to join NATO. Ukraine's monetary policy score is 1 point better this year. As a result, its overall score is 0.10 point better this year.

## TRADE POLICY
### Score: **3**–Stable (moderate level of protectionism)

According to the World Bank, Ukraine's weighted average tariff rate in 1997 (the most recent year for which World Bank data are available) was 5.3 percent. Non-tariff barriers include non-transparent standards, cumbersome procedures for phytosanitary certification, and import licenses.

## FISCAL BURDEN OF GOVERNMENT
### Score—Income Taxation: **4**–Stable (high tax rates)
### Score—Corporate Taxation: **4**–Stable (high tax rates)
### Score—Change in Government Expenditures: **3.5**–Stable (low increase)
### Final Score: **3.9**–Stable (high cost of government)

Ukraine's top income tax rate is 40 percent. The top corporate tax rate is 30 percent. In May 2003, the parliament passed legislation that will replace the current progressive tax code with a 13 percent flat rate starting in 2004; because the cut-off date for any new policy changes is June 30, 2003, the 13 percent flat tax rate will be reflected in next year's *Index*. Government expenditures as a share of GDP increased less in 2001 (0.2 percentage point to 36.6 percent) than they did in 2000 (0.3 percentage point). On net, Ukraine's fiscal burden of government score is unchanged this year.

## GOVERNMENT INTERVENTION IN THE ECONOMY
### Score: **3**–Stable (moderate level)

The World Bank reports that the government consumed 22.5 percent of GDP in 2001. In the same year, according to the International Monetary Fund, Ukraine received 9.62 percent of its total revenues from state-owned enterprises and government ownership of property.

## MONETARY POLICY
### Score: **3**–Better (moderate level of inflation)

Data from the International Monetary Fund's *2003 World Economic Outlook* indicate that from 1993 to 2002, Ukraine's weighted average annual rate of inflation was 7.52 percent, down from the 18.88 percent from 1992 to 2001 reported in the 2003 *Index.* As a result, Ukraine's monetary policy score is 1 point better this year.

## CAPITAL FLOWS AND FOREIGN INVESTMENT
### Score: **4**–Stable (high barriers)

Although foreign investment in most types of businesses is permitted, foreign investment is impeded by a number of formal and informal barriers. According to the U.S. Department of State, legislation passed in October 2001 "places a 20-year moratorium on land sales to foreigners, although foreigners are permitted to own land plots on which company facilities have been built." Apart from the general lack of transparency in Ukraine's privatization program, foreign investors may participate only in the privatization of "strategic" sectors, which include radio, television, radio, and insurance. Foreign equity shares in television, radio, and publishing companies are restricted to 30 percent. The International Monetary Fund reports that resident and non-resident foreign exchange accounts are subject to restrictions. Payments and transfers are subject to various licensing requirements and quantitative limits. Some capital transactions, including credit operations, are subject to controls and licenses.

## BANKING AND FINANCE
### Score: **3**–Stable (moderate level of restrictions)

Ukraine's banking sector is underdeveloped and undercapitalized. The Economist Intelligence Unit reports that "total capitalization of the banking sector is less than US$2bn, or roughly the size of one large bank in central Europe. Moreover, with around 150 registered banks, the sector remains excessively fragmented." The government owns two banks, and they are among the largest in the country. The Financial Action Task Force, an anti–money laundering watchdog organization, has kept Ukraine on its list of countries that are not doing enough to combat money laundering.

## WAGES AND PRICES
### Score: **3**–Stable (moderate level of intervention)

The government controls some prices. According to the U.S. Department of State, "The cabinet of Ministers of Ukraine has price-setting authority with products, goods, and services in certain sectors. These lists include basic tariffs (e.g., electricity, telecommunications, transportation, utilities), and some crucial products such as sugar, grain, gas, oil, etc. Government regulated prices and tariffs may change as a result of changes in production and sale conditions." Ukraine has a minimum wage.

## PROPERTY RIGHTS
### Score: **4**–Stable (low level of protection)

Protection of property is weak in Ukraine. According to the U.S. Department of State, "the Constitution provides for an independent judiciary; however, in practice, the judiciary is subject to considerable political interference from the executive branch and also suffers from corruption and inefficiency." In addition, "Organized crime is alleged to influence court decisions."

## REGULATION
### Score: **4**–Stable (high level)

There are significant obstacles to doing business in Ukraine. The U.S. Department of State reports that "private investment (including U.S. investment) is greatly hampered by rampant corruption, overregulation, lack of transparency, high business taxes, and inconsistent application of local law…. The bureaucratic procedures for obtaining various permits, licenses, etc., are complex and unpredictable, burdensome and duplicative; they create confusion, significantly raise the cost of doing business in Ukraine, provide opportunities for corruption, and drive much activity into the burgeoning 'shadow' economy."

## INFORMAL MARKET
### Score: **4**–Stable (high level of activity)

Transparency International's 2002 score for Ukraine is 2.4. Therefore, Ukraine's informal market score is 4 this year.

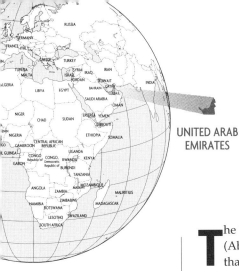

# UNITED ARAB EMIRATES

Rank: 42

Score: 2.60

Category: Mostly Free

**Present & Past Scores**

(Best) 1
2
3
4
(Worst) 5

2.40 2.35 2.35 2.30 2.20 2.16 2.28 2.20 **2.60**

'95 '96 '97 '98 '99 '00 '01 '02 '03 '04
n/a

## QUICK STUDY

### SCORES

| | |
|---|---|
| Trade Policy | 2 |
| Fiscal Burden | 2 |
| Government Intervention | 4 |
| Monetary Policy | 1 |
| Foreign Investment | 3 |
| Banking and Finance | 4 |
| Wages and Prices | 3 |
| Property Rights | 2 |
| Regulation | 3 |
| Informal Market | 2 |

**Population:** 2,976,290

**Total area:** 82,880 sq. km

**GDP:** $51.8 billion

**GDP growth rate:** 3.5%

**GDP per capita:** $17,422

**Major exports:** natural gas, crude oil

**Exports of goods and services:** $43 billion

**Major export trading partners:** Japan 31.1%, India 10.2%, South Korea 5.2%, Singapore 3.6%

**Major imports:** machinery, manufactured goods, fuel, foodstuffs

**Imports of goods and services:** $36 billion

**Major import trading partners:** Japan 6.9%, US 6.7%, UK 6.6%, Italy 6.4%

**Foreign direct investment (net):** n/a

2001 Data (in constant 1995 US dollars)

The United Arab Emirates (UAE), an oil-rich federation of seven small Arab monarchies (Abu Dhabi, Ajman, Dubai, Fujairah, Ras Al-Khaimah, Sharjah, and Umm al-Qaiwain) that gained its independence from Great Britain in 1971, controls roughly 10 percent of the world's oil supply and nearly 5 percent of the world's proven natural gas reserves. Oil and gas production provides about one-third of GDP, and energy reserves are expected to last for more than 100 years at current rates of production. Because the country's national income is closely tied to the rise and fall of prices on the volatile international oil market, the federal government has been forced to look for ways to diversify the economy, particularly in Dubai, where oil reserves are dwindling. Dubai has taken the lead in encouraging foreign investment initiatives, focusing on the development of its service sector and non-industrial base; Abu Dhabi, which accounts for about 90 percent of oil production, is spearheading the privatization of utilities and seeking foreign investment in the power and water sectors to bring in modern technology and management techniques and reduce costs. UAE nationals continue to rely heavily on a bloated public sector for employment, subsidized services, and government handouts. The extensive welfare system also continues to provide rich incentives for the country's large expatriate population, which constitutes more than 80 percent of the population and 93 percent of the workforce. The UAE is the world's third most active re-export center after Singapore and Hong Kong. The UAE's fiscal burden of government, banking and finance, wages and prices, and informal market scores are 1 point worse this year. As a result, the UAE's overall score is 0.40 point worse this year.

### TRADE POLICY

Score: **2**–Stable (low level of protectionism)

According to the U.S. Department of State, the UAE's highest custom duty in 2000 (the most recent year for which data are available) was 4 percent. The same source reports that imports require an import license and that the government sets "restrictive agency/sponsorship/distributorship requirements, and restrictive shelf-life requirements for food stuffs."

### FISCAL BURDEN OF GOVERNMENT

Score—Income Taxation: **1**–Stable (very low tax rates)
Score—Corporate Taxation: **1**–Stable (very low tax rates)
Score—Change in Government Expenditures: **5**–Worse (very high increase)
Final Score: **2**–Worse (low cost of government)

The UAE has no income tax, no corporate tax, and no other significant taxes. Government expenditures as a share of GDP increased 4.3 percentage points to 36.9 percent in 2001, compared to a 4 percentage point decrease in 2000. As a result, the UAE's fiscal burden of government score is 1 point worse this year.

### GOVERNMENT INTERVENTION IN THE ECONOMY

Score: **4**–Stable (high level)

According to the Economist Intelligence Unit, the government consumed 17 percent of GDP in 2001. In the same year, based on data from the EIU, the United Arab Emirates received 58.83 percent of its total revenues just from public enterprises in the hydrocarbon sector.

399

## MONETARY POLICY
### Score: 1–Stable (very low level of inflation)

Data from the International Monetary Fund's *2003 World Economic Outlook* indicate that from 1993 to 2002, the UAE's weighted average annual rate of inflation was 2.51 percent.

## CAPITAL FLOWS AND FOREIGN INVESTMENT
### Score: 3–Stable (moderate barriers)

Foreign investment in the UAE is restricted, and foreigners do not receive national treatment. According to the Economist Intelligence Unit, "In many parts of the Emirates foreigners are allowed to own property and businesses, particularly in Dubai. However, these rights are only available in specially designated areas. In most areas of the country foreign ownership of property is not allowed, and all businesses must be at least 51% owned by a UAE national. Furthermore, UAE negotiators have told counterparts at the World Trade Organisation (WTO) that they will not open several strategic sectors to foreign investment." Foreign investment is restricted in the banking, telecommunications, and petroleum sectors. There are no controls or requirements on current transfers, access to foreign exchange, or repatriation of profits. Foreign ownership of land and stock is restricted.

## BANKING AND FINANCE
### Score: 4–Worse (high level of restrictions)

There are 21 domestic banks, 14 of which have some federal or local government ownership, and 26 foreign banks. The government remains involved in the banking sector through loan guarantees. According to the Economist Intelligence Unit, "Most major projects involve some level of government backing, making the risk of default relatively low and attracting the participation of international investment banks." The UAE has no corporate income tax, but there is a 20 percent tax on foreign bank profits. As a condition of membership in the World Trade Organization, the UAE is required to end the current restriction on allowing new foreign banks into the country. The government is seeking to replace foreign workers in the banking sector with UAE nationals through a policy called "Emiratisation." "Of the 47 banks operating in the UAE," reports the EIU, "only 19 achieved the stated target of 4% growth in Emiratisation quotas. Banks that miss their target are forced to pay into a fund for the training and development of nationals." Commercial banks operating in the UAE are not allowed to engage in non-banking activities. Banks may not lend more than 7 percent of their capital to any single foreign institution or invest more than 25 percent of bank funds in commercial bonds or shares. Non-residents are prohibited from owning over 20 percent of the shares in UAE national banks. Based on the evidence of a dominant government role in the banking sector, the United Arab Emirates' banking and finance score is 1 point worse this year.

## WAGES AND PRICES
### Score: 3–Worse (moderate level of intervention)

The government affects prices through extensive government subsidies. According to the Economist Intelligence Unit, "More broadly, inflation will be constrained by the emirates' extensive system of subsidies, which restricts scope for price increases on a range of core goods and services." The government also influences the domestic price of oil. Price setting for the domestic market does not extend to oil exports. There is no minimum wage. The U.S. Department of State reports that, "according to the Ministry of Labor and Social Affairs, there is an unofficial, unwritten minimum wage rate, which afford[s] a worker and family a minimal standard of living." Based on evidence that the government subsidizes a wide range of goods and services, the United Arab Emirates' wages and prices score is 1 point worse this year.

## PROPERTY RIGHTS
### Score: 2–Stable (high level of protection)

Private property is generally well-protected in the UAE. According to the U.S. Department of State, the judiciary's "decisions are subject to review by the political leadership." In addition, "codified law based on modern norms is new and still evolving, as are practices based on the law, such as court and other legal procedures…. [D]ispute resolution can be difficult and uncertain…. Enforcing judgments has not always been easy, and judicial proceedings can often go on several years." All land in Abu Dhabi, the largest of the UAE's seven emirates, is owned by the government.

## REGULATION
### Score: 3–Stable (moderate level)

Establishing a business in the UAE is easy if the business is not to compete directly with state-owned concerns. The government requires a license only for opening a place of business in the UAE, not for companies exporting to the emirates. Licenses available include trade, industrial, service, professional, and construction licenses. Special bylaws apply to business practice in the free zones. The U.S. Department of State reports that "private sector institutions, including banks and foreign oil companies, are not allowed to disseminate statistics to the public." In addition, "corruption is a concern for U.S. firms seeking to do business in the UAE."

## INFORMAL MARKET
### Score: 2–Worse (low level of activity)

In 2000, according to University of Linz, Austria, the informal economy was about 26.4 percent of GNP. Software piracy levels, while high by global standards, are the lowest in the region. The U.S. Department of State reports a high level of smuggling. Based on newly available data, the UAE's informal market score is 1 point worse this year.

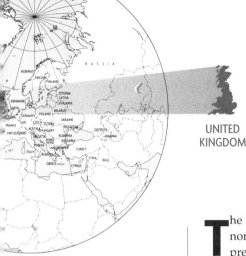

UNITED
KINGDOM

# UNITED KINGDOM

Rank: 7

Score: 1.79

Category: Free

Present & Past Scores

(Best) 1
2
3 1.75 1.85 1.95 1.85 1.76 1.85 1.78 1.83 1.88 1.79
4
(Worst) 5

'95 '96 '97 '98 '99 '00 '01 '02 '03 '04

## QUICK STUDY

### SCORES

Trade Policy                     2
Fiscal Burden                    3.9
Government Intervention          2
Monetary Policy                  1
Foreign Investment               2
Banking and Finance              1
Wages and Prices                 2
Property Rights                  1
Regulation                       2
Informal Market                  1

**Population:** 60,100,000

**Total area:** 244,820 sq. km

**GDP:** $1.35 trillion

**GDP growth rate:** 1.8%

**GDP per capita:** $22,544

**Major exports:** manufactured goods, oil and other fuels, food, travel services, financial and insurance services, transportation, computer and information

**Exports of goods and services:** $348.9 billion

**Major export trading partners:** US 15.2%, Germany 11.8%, France 10.0%, Ireland 8.2%, Netherlands 7.5%

**Major imports:** finished manufactures, semi-manufactures, food, oil, financial services, communications

**Imports of goods and services:** $391.3 billion

**Major import trading partners:** US 13.7%, Germany 11.3%, France 8.5%, Netherlands 6.8%

**Foreign direct investment (net):** –$13.3 billion

2002 Data (in constant 1995 US dollars)

The United Kingdom has a long tradition of a strong rule of law and political and economic freedom. The Labour government, first elected in 1997, has largely continued the previous Conservative government's pattern of support for privatization, deregulation, and competition. During Labour's first term in office, Chancellor of the Exchequer Gordon Brown avoided aggravating the economic cycle by affording the Bank of England more independence, further insulating monetary policy from political influence. Britain's privatized pension system, which allows workers to invest their own Social Security taxes, is in sharp contrast to the underfunded retirement systems of other European governments that will require crippling tax increases or massive cuts in benefits. Such structural reforms and New Labour's insistence on not undoing the Thatcher revolution continue to pay dividends. However, while the UK weathered the global economic slowdown better than most developed countries, its rate of growth dipped to 1.8 percent in 2002, its slowest rate since 1992. Labour's priority in its second term—a once-in-a-generation boost to public-sector funding that is designed to transform the quality of public services, especially education and the National Health Service—is more indicative of the "Old Labour," whose past tax-and-spend policies proved ruinous. As a result, the UK's deficit is likely to be greater than 3 percent in 2004. A saving grace is that the ratio of government debt to GDP remains low. The United Kingdom's fiscal burden of government score is 0.4 point better this year, and its informal market score is 0.5 point better. As a result, the United Kingdom's overall score is 0.09 point better this year.

## TRADE POLICY
### Score: **2**–Stable (low level of protectionism)

As a member of the European Union, according to the World Bank, the United Kingdom was subject to a common EU weighted average external tariff of 2.6 percent in 2001. The UK's import licenses and other non-tariff measures are subject to EU regulations, including restrictions on textiles and clothing, as well as agricultural, horticultural, and livestock products.

## FISCAL BURDEN OF GOVERNMENT
Score—Income Taxation: **4**–Stable (high tax rates)
Score—Corporate Taxation: **4**–Stable (high tax rates)
Score—Change in Government Expenditures: **3.5**–Better (low increase)
### Final Score: **3.9**–Better (high cost of government)

The United Kingdom's top income tax rate is 40 percent. The top corporate tax rate is 30 percent. Government expenditures as a share of GDP increased less in 2002 (0.5 percentage point to 40.9 percent) than they did in 2001 (3.4 percentage points). As a result, the United Kingdom's fiscal burden of government score is 0.4 point better this year.

## GOVERNMENT INTERVENTION IN THE ECONOMY
### Score: **2**–Stable (low level)

According to the Economist Intelligence Unit, the government consumed 20 percent of GDP in 2002. In the April 2001–March 2002 fiscal year, based on data from Her Majesty's Treasury, the United Kingdom received 1.15 percent of its total revenues from state-owned enterprises and government ownership of property.

**MONETARY POLICY**
Score: **1**–Stable (very low level of inflation)

From 1993 to 2002, the United Kingdom's weighted average annual rate of inflation was 1.82 percent.

 **CAPITAL FLOWS AND FOREIGN INVESTMENT**
Score: **2**–Stable (low barriers)

The United Kingdom welcomes foreign investment, and foreign investors receive the same treatment as domestic businesses. More non–European Union businesses establish themselves in the UK than in any other European country. "There are only a few exceptions to national treatment," reports the U.S. Department of State. "For example, foreign (non-EU or non-EFTA [European Free Trade Area]) ownership of UK airlines is limited by law to 49%. Registration of shipping vessels is limited to UK citizens or nationals of EU/EFTA member states resident in the UK." According to the Economist Intelligence Unit, "The main regulatory hazards for direct investors, especially those planning acquisitions, stem from Brussels, not London." The International Monetary Fund reports that both residents and non-residents are permitted to hold foreign exchange accounts. Payments and proceeds on invisible transactions and current transfers face no restrictions, profits can be repatriated freely, and there are no controls on real estate transactions.

 **BANKING AND FINANCE**
Score: **1**–Stable (very low level of restrictions)

The London Stock Exchange is one of the world's largest exchanges. The UK has a well-developed, competitive system of universal banking in which banking institutions are permitted to sell securities and insurance products, as well as invest in industrial firms. The Economist Intelligence Unit reports that regulatory oversight of the banking and finance sector has been transferred from the Bank of England to a Financial Services Authority, which will oversee all aspects of the sector, including banking, insurance, and securities and investments. According to the EIU, "The most important [advantage] is that it will allow closer supervision of markets and institutions at a time when the traditional distinctions between banks, investment houses and insurance companies are becoming blurred. Critics of the new regime…fear the new regime will be excessively unwieldy and rigid and will hence stifle financial innovation. However, there is little evidence that this is happening…."

 **WAGES AND PRICES**
Score: **2**–Stable (low level of intervention)

The market sets most prices in the United Kingdom. According to the Economist Intelligence Unit, "The government, either directly or through regulatory agencies, has permanent price-control powers over matches, milk, most public utilities and London taxi fares…." The Office of Telecommunications has introduced price controls on British Telecom (BT) in the residential market, beginning August 2002. The United Kingdom also affects agricultural prices through its participation in the Common Agricultural Policy, a program that heavily subsidizes agricultural goods. According to Timbro, a Swedish think tank, "EU consumers pay roughly 80–100% more for their food than would be the case in a mature free-market regime." The United Kingdom has a minimum wage.

 **PROPERTY RIGHTS**
Score: **1**–Stable (very high level of protection)

Property rights in the United Kingdom are well-secured. The Economist Intelligence Unit reports that "contractual agreements are generally secure in the UK. There is no discrimination against foreign companies in court. The judiciary is of high quality when dealing with commercial cases."

 **REGULATION**
Score: **2**–Stable (low level)

Opening a business in the United Kingdom is easy, and the regulatory system, though somewhat burdensome, is better those of most other industrialized countries. Companies may self-regulate their industries. Businesses subscribe voluntarily to a code of conduct that, if violated, causes them to be penalized by consumers using free market competition. Nonetheless, businesses complain about an increasingly burdensome regulatory environment due to the UK's compliance with EU regulations. According to *The Economist*, a British Chamber of Commerce survey revealed that business must cut jobs to adjust for higher insurance contributions, a higher minimum wage, and increasing parental employment rights.

 **INFORMAL MARKET**
Score: **1**–Better (very low level of activity)

Transparency International's 2002 score for the United Kingdom is 8.7. Therefore, the United Kingdom's informal market score is 1 this year—0.5 point better than last year.

# UNITED STATES

Rank: 10

Score: 1.85

Category: Free

**Present & Past Scores**

(Best) 1
2
3 | 1.99 1.94 1.88 1.89 1.89 1.88 1.79 1.84 1.86 1.85
4
(Worst) 5

'95 '96 '97 '98 '99 '00 '01 '02 '03 '04

## QUICK STUDY

### SCORES

| | |
|---|---|
| Trade Policy | 2 |
| Fiscal Burden | 4 |
| Government Intervention | 2 |
| Monetary Policy | 1 |
| Foreign Investment | 2 |
| Banking and Finance | 1 |
| Wages and Prices | 2 |
| Property Rights | 1 |
| Regulation | 2 |
| Informal Market | 1.5 |

**Population:** 288,600,000

**Total area:** 9,629,091 sq. km

**GDP:** $9.2 trillion

**GDP growth rate:** 2.4%

**GDP per capita:** $31,830

**Major exports:** industrial supplies, consumer goods, automotive goods, food and beverages, travel services, financial and insurance services, computer and information

**Exports of goods and services:** $1.08 trillion

**Major export trading partners:** Canada 23.2%, Mexico 14.1%, Japan 7.4%, UK 4.8%

**Major imports:** Crude oil, refined petroleum products, automobiles, consumer goods, industrial raw materials, financial and insurance services

**Imports of goods and services:** $1.6 trillion

**Major import trading partners:** Canada 18.1%, Mexico 11.6%, China 10.8%, Japan 10.4%

**Foreign direct investment (net):** −$83.8 billion

2002 Data (in constant 1995 US dollars)

The U.S. Constitution provides strong protections for private property, and the vibrancy and dynamism of the U.S. economy are testimony to these constitutionally protected economic liberties. In the post–World War II period, the United States generally took a strong leadership position in expanding global trade through lower tariff barriers. In the 1980s, economic growth reflected deregulation and tax cuts. In the 1990s, a stable monetary policy and a wave of technological innovation, buttressed by strong protection of intellectual property rights, continued the growth trend. In 2001, that trend was interrupted by a recession. With the uncertainties of the Iraq war clarified, the prolonged economic weakness seems to be dissipating in 2003. In addition, the Administration of George W. Bush has taken a leadership role in both free trade and reducing domestic tax rates. With signed free trade agreements with both Singapore and Chile, ongoing negotiations with Morocco, Australia, and the Central American countries, and overtures to other countries throughout the world, global free trade once again has become a viable possibility. Domestically, the top marginal tax rates for individuals have been reduced several percentage points, and the partial elimination of double taxation on dividends leaves corporations less reliant on debt financing, and therefore less vulnerable to economic downturns. Inflation is almost nonexistent, and interest rates are the lowest in half a century. Overall, the United States remains one of the world's freest and most vibrant economies. The United States' fiscal burden of government score is 0.1 point better this year. As a result, its overall score is 0.01 point better this year.

## TRADE POLICY
### Score: **2**–Stable (low level of protectionism)

The World Bank reports that the United States' weighted average tariff rate in 2001 (the most recent year for which World Bank data are available) was 1.8 percent. According to the Economist Intelligence Unit, the government imposes non-tariff barriers, including quotas, tariff rate import quotas, antidumping provisions, countervailing duties, and licensing requirements, on a number of goods.

## FISCAL BURDEN OF GOVERNMENT
Score—Income Taxation: **3.5**–Stable (high tax rates)
Score—Corporate Taxation: **4.5**–Stable (very high tax rates)
Score—Change in Government Expenditures: **3.5**–Better (low increase)
### Final Score: **4**–Better (high cost of government)

The United States' top federal income tax rate is 35 percent, down from the 39.1 percent reported in the 2003 *Index*. (This decrease is not substantial enough to affect the United States' income taxation score, however.) The top corporate tax rate is 35 percent. Government expenditures as a share of GDP increased less in 2002 (0.7 percentage point to 35.6 percent) than they did in 2001 (1.3 percentage points). As a result, the United States' fiscal burden of government score is 0.1 point better this year.

## GOVERNMENT INTERVENTION IN THE ECONOMY
### Score: **2**–Stable (low level)

Based on data from the U.S. Bureau of Economic Analysis, the government consumed 15.5 percent of GDP in 2002. In 2001, according to the International Monetary Fund, the United

States received 3.11 percent of its total revenues from state-owned enterprises and government ownership of property.

## MONETARY POLICY
### Score: **1**–Stable (very low level of inflation)

From 1993 to 2002, the United States' weighted average annual rate of inflation was 2.05 percent.

## CAPITAL FLOWS AND FOREIGN INVESTMENT
### Score: **2**–Stable (low barriers)

The United States welcomes foreign investment. Foreign and domestic enterprises are treated equally under the law; foreign investors are not required to register with or seek approval from the federal government; and there are no local content requirements or ownership restrictions on most industries. The government continues to restrict foreign investment in nuclear energy, maritime and air shipping and transport, broadcast licenses, and communications. It also restricts foreign acquisitions that threaten to impair national security. Restrictions on financial transactions with Cuba and Cuban nationals, Burma, Iran, Iraq, Libya, Sudan, the Taliban, specified terrorist groups, and specified drug traffickers are strict and enforced. There are no controls or requirements on current transfers, access to foreign exchange, or repatriation of profits. Purchase of real estate is unrestricted on a national level, although purchase of agricultural land by foreign nationals or companies with at least 10 percent foreign ownership must be reported to the U.S. Department of Agriculture; some states impose restrictions on purchases of land by foreign nationals.

## BANKING AND FINANCE
### Score: **1**–Stable (very low level of restrictions)

Federal and state governments share regulatory responsibility for banks. In recent years, there has been substantial deregulation of banking. Reform of the Glass–Steagall Act and the 1956 Bank Holding Company Act in 1999 eliminated barriers to entry into U.S. financial markets and removed prohibitions against the purchase of banks by insurance and securities companies. This has facilitated both the creation of universal financial services companies and the competitiveness of U.S. banking, as well as further consolidation of the financial services industry, enabling U.S. firms to compete more effectively in global markets. According to the Economist Intelligence Unit, "The US has the largest, deepest and most sophisticated capital markets in the world. Access to funds for both foreign and domestic investors is excellent." A troubling development during the 1990s was the growing nationalization of mortgage risk through the growth of government-sponsored enterprises focused on housing finance. However, the overall trend in financial services is toward more competition and continued product innovation. Foreign banking and securities firms generally compete on an equal footing with domestic firms.

## WAGES AND PRICES
### Score: **2**–Stable (low level of intervention)

Overall, the market sets wages and prices. According to the Economist Intelligence Unit, "Price controls do exist for some regulated monopolies (like utilities and the postal service), and certain states and localities control residential rents. The most recent imposition of price restrictions was approved on May 2nd 2002, when the state legislature of Hawaii approved price caps on petrol prices, which have historically been higher than in any other US state." The federal government continues to influence prices on some goods and services by purchasing excess production, closing borders to imports, and manipulating prices through subsidies to companies like Amtrak. The government also influences prices of some dairy products by subsidizing dairy farmers. Under the recently enacted Farm Security and Rural Investment Act of 2002, agricultural spending and subsidies will rise by more than 80 percent (from $100 billion to $180 billion) over the next 10 years, with subsidies for corn, soybeans, wheat, rice, and cotton increasing by 70 percent. While these subsidy amounts are immense, so is the U.S. agricultural sector (and the economy in general, of which agriculture accounts for only 2 percent), and this reduces the overall impact of agricultural subsidies on prices. The federal government imposes a minimum wage.

## PROPERTY RIGHTS
### Score: **1**–Stable (very high level of protection)

The United States does very well in most measures of property rights protection, including an independent judiciary, a sound commercial code and other laws for the resolution of property disputes between private parties, and the recognition of foreign arbitration and court rulings. However, the concerns outlined in the 2003 *Index* linger. Uncompensated government expropriations of property remain highly unlikely, but local governments' abuse of eminent domain power with the seizure of private land (with some compensation) and its transfer to another party for a non-public or quasi-public use has become more common—despite some successful legal challenges to that practice. An even more serious problem is that governments at all levels impose numerous regulatory and land-use controls that diminish the value and enjoyment of private property. Examples include extensive "growth controls"; unreasonable zoning hurdles; facility permitting regimes; and far-reaching environmental, wetlands, and habitat restrictions on the use and development of real estate. Thus, the protections for private property are undermined by a vast bureaucracy that has the power to interfere substantially with many property rights. The level of protection for property in the United States may eventually turn on whether the courts place clear limits on bureaucratic power or require cost-effective remedies for property owners whose rights have been affected. In recent years, the Supreme Court's performance in such government "takings" cases has been decidedly mixed. The past year was a disappointment, with the Court reversing itself in *Brown v. Legal Foundation of Washington* and holding that states may seize the interest from certain attorney–client trust accounts and not pay compensation.

## REGULATION
### Score: **2**–Stable (low level)

Establishing a business is easy. "Through a fairly simple procedure," reports the Economist Intelligence Unit, a firm "can then set up offices, plants or other permanent establishments under the corporation laws of other states…. Firms may choose a location on the basis of which state's laws offer greater flexibility." The U.S. labor market is one of the world's most flexible. According to the EIU, few federal laws inhibit investment by either foreign or domestic firms. Regulations are applied evenly and consistently. However, many regulations—for example, the Americans with Disabilities Act, various civil rights regulations, environmental laws, health and product safety standards, and food and drug labeling requirements—although well-intentioned, can be onerous. Electronic commerce is minimally regulated. By global standards, the level of regulation in the United States is low.

## INFORMAL MARKET
### Score: **1.5**–Stable (low level of activity)

Transparency International's 2002 score for the United States is 7.7. Therefore, the United States' informal market score is 1.5 this year.

URURUGUAY

# URUGUAY

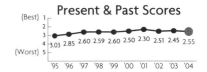

Rank: 39

Score: 2.55

Category: Mostly Free

Present & Past Scores

(Best) 1
2
3
4
(Worst) 5

3.03  2.85  2.60  2.59  2.60  2.50  2.30  2.51  2.45  2.55

'95  '96  '97  '98  '99  '00  '01  '02  '03  '04

After a decade of steady economic growth, debt reduction, and market liberalization, Uruguay's economic fortunes continue to be tied to troubled neighbors Argentina and Brazil in the Southern Cone Common Market (MERCOSUR). Argentina's devaluation wiped out much of that country's wealth, forcing Argentines to cut back sharply on their net consumption. Consequently, the market for Uruguay's products shrank. Nor could Uruguay rely instead on Brazil's economy, which also has not been growing. In 2002, Uruguayan President Jorge Batlle announced his country's intention to break out of MERCOSUR's restricted markets by seeking a free trade agreement (FTA) with the United States; but Uruguay has had to get in line behind the U.S.–Chile FTA and the U.S.–Central America Free Trade Agreement (CAFTA) now being negotiated. In the meantime, Argentines have withdrawn millions from Uruguayan banks, local consumer spending has declined, and Uruguay has allowed its own peso to float in order to keep its exports competitive. Nonetheless, Uruguay seems to have weathered the worst of the storm. To move forward, it will have to continue diversifying its export base away from agriculture, reduce the size of its public sector, and reform labor laws that, while providing an extensive social safety net, reward non-productivity. Uruguay's trade policy score is 1 point better this year, and its government intervention core is 0.5 point better; however, its fiscal burden of government score is 0.5 point worse this year, and its monetary policy and banking and finance scores are 1 point worse. As a result, Uruguay's overall score is 0.10 point worse this year.

## TRADE POLICY
### Score: **2–Better** (low level of protectionism)

As a member of the Southern Cone Common Market (MERCOSUR), Uruguay adheres to a common external tariff that ranges from zero to 23 percent. According to the World Bank, Uruguay's weighted average tariff rate in 2001 (the most recent year for which World Bank data are available) was 6.6 percent, down from the 13 percent reported in the 2003 *Index*. As a result, Uruguay's trade policy score is 1 point better this year. Few other restrictions on imports remain in effect. Import licenses are easy to obtain and do not serve to restrict imports. In addition, a "de-bureaucratization" commission has reduced bureaucratic delays in getting goods through customs.

## FISCAL BURDEN OF GOVERNMENT
### Score—Income Taxation: **1–Stable** (very low tax rates)
### Score—Corporate Taxation: **4.5–Worse** (very high tax rates)
### Score—Change in Government Expenditures: **4–Worse** (moderate increase)
### Final Score: **3.5–Worse** (high cost of government)

There is no income tax in Uruguay. The top corporate tax rate is 35 percent, up from the 30 percent reported in the 2003 *Index*. Government expenditures as a share of GDP increased 1.8 percentage points to 33.3 percent in 2001, compared to a 0.3 percentage point decrease in 2000. Based on the increase in the top corporate tax rate and government expenditures as a share of GDP, Uruguay's fiscal burden of government score is 0.5 point worse this year.

407

## GOVERNMENT INTERVENTION IN THE ECONOMY
### Score: **2**–Better (low level)

The World Bank reports that the government consumed 13.4 percent of GDP in 2001. In the same year, according to the International Monetary Fund, Uruguay received 3.87 percent of its total revenues from state-owned enterprises and government ownership of property, down from the 5.54 percent reported in the 2003 *Index*. As a result, Uruguay's government intervention score is 0.5 point better this year.

## MONETARY POLICY
### Score: **3**–Worse (moderate level of inflation)

From 1993 to 2002, Uruguay's weighted average annual rate of inflation was 10.73 percent, up from the 5.17 percent from 1992 to 2001 reported in the 2003 *Index*. As a result, Uruguay's monetary policy score is 1 point worse this year.

## CAPITAL FLOWS AND FOREIGN INVESTMENT
### Score: **2**–Stable (low barriers)

In 1998, Uruguay updated its foreign investment code. According to the U.S. Department of State, "The main aspects of the law are that foreign and national investments are treated alike, that investments are allowed without prior authorization or registration, that the Government does not prevent the establishment of investments in the country, and that investors may freely transfer abroad their capital and profits from the investment." Uruguay permits full foreign ownership of domestic concerns except for the so-called national security industries that require authorization; these include electricity, hydrocarbons, railroads, some minerals, port administration, and telecommunications, although the government is deregulating the telecommunications sector. According to the International Monetary Fund, both residents and non-residents may hold foreign exchange accounts; there are no restrictions or controls on payments, transactions, transfers, or repatriation of profits; and non-residents may purchase real estate.

## BANKING AND FINANCE
### Score: **3**–Worse (moderate level of restrictions)

Problems in neighboring Argentina led to a run on Uruguay's banks as Argentine depositors raided their Uruguayan deposits. The Argentine crisis led to withdrawal of 45 percent of deposits in Uruguayan banks by September 2002, and the Uruguayan government was forced to intervene in three local banks. The government has used the assets of these three banks to establish a new state-owned bank, Nuevo Banco Comercial. It also owns three banks, including the Banco de la República Oriental del Uruguay (BROU). According to the U.S. Department of State, "BROU is Uruguay's largest bank, and offers loans at the lowest rates and best terms. As of November 2002, it held 40% of overall private sector deposits

and had provided over one-third of total credits to the resident private sector." In August 2002, BROU froze all dollar-denominated deposits and established a repayment schedule over a three-year period. The state-owned BSE insurance company had a monopoly on all insurance until the automobile insurance market was opened to private competition in 1994; the government is considering liberalization of other portions of the insurance sector. Based on the evidence of increased government intervention in the banking sector, Uruguay's banking and finance score is 1 point worse this year.

## WAGES AND PRICES
### Score: **2**–Stable (low level of intervention)

"Although Uruguay has eliminated most price controls," reports the Economist Intelligence Unit, "the executive branch continues to fix prices on certain basics, including milk, fuels, electricity, water supply and telephone services. It also adjusts the monthly fees of collective medical-care institutions...and the annual increase of housing and office rents." The government mandates a minimum wage.

## PROPERTY RIGHTS
### Score: **2**–Stable (high level of protection)

Private property is generally secure in Uruguay, and expropriation is unlikely. Judicial proceedings tend to be slow but also, as reported by the Economist Intelligence Unit, to be based on sound legal grounds. Bureaucracy in the court system lends itself to varied interpretations, making appeals the norm rather than the exception. As an alternative to civil suits, the government has established a Settlement and Arbitration Center to improve investment relations.

## REGULATION
### Score: **3**–Stable (moderate level)

Establishing a business can involve a lengthy process because of the number of applicable regulations. According to the U.S. Department of State, although firms "have not encountered major obstacles in Uruguay's investment climate, some have been frustrated by the length of time it takes to complete bureaucratic procedures and by the numerous changes in rules or new taxes since 2001." The Economist Intelligence Unit reports that "employer–employee relations are governed by hundreds of regulations scattered among various laws and decrees...." There have been investigations of corruption, but it is not considered an impediment to business.

## INFORMAL MARKET
### Score: **3**–Stable (moderate level of activity)

Transparency International's 2002 score for Uruguay is 5.1. Therefore, Uruguay's informal market score is 3 this year.

UZBEKISTAN

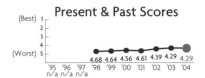

Rank: 149

Score: 4.29

Category: Repressed

**Present & Past Scores**

(Best) 1
2
3
4
(Worst) 5

4.68  4.64  4.56  4.61  4.39  4.29  4.29
'95  '96  '97  '98  '99  '00  '01  '02  '03  '04
n/a  n/a  n/a

UZBEKISTAN

## QUICK STUDY

### SCORES
| | |
|---|---|
| Trade Policy | 5 |
| Fiscal Burden | 2.9 |
| Government Intervention | 4 |
| Monetary Policy | 5 |
| Foreign Investment | 4 |
| Banking and Finance | 5 |
| Wages and Prices | 4 |
| Property Rights | 4 |
| Regulation | 5 |
| Informal Market | 4 |

**Population:** 25,068,000

**Total area:** 447,400 sq. km

**GDP:** $12.8 billion

**GDP growth rate:** 4.5%

**GDP per capita:** $512

**Major exports:** machinery and equipment, chemicals, food, beverage, and agricultural products, fuel and energy

**Exports of goods and services:** $4.2 billion

**Major export trading partners:** Russia 21.5%, Turkey 5.9%, Italy 4.9%, Germany 4.2%

**Major imports:** fuel and energy, machinery and equipment, chemicals

**Imports of goods and services:** $3.2 billion

**Major import trading partners:** Russia 34.4%, Turkmenistan 9.8%, Germany 8.2%, Italy 2.4%

**Foreign direct investment (net):** $63.7 million

2001 Data (in constant 1995 US dollars)

Uzbekistan's large population, unique location, and significant armed forces make it one of Central Asia's most important countries. The state continues to suppress the media and the political opposition, and President Islam Karimov, a Soviet-era leader, holds all the power as chief executive. A January 2002 referendum, which was boycotted by international observers, extended the presidential term from five to seven years. With his regime threatened by the Islamic Movement of Uzbekistan (IMU), an organization that has been closely linked with al-Qaeda, Karimov quickly joined the U.S.-led coalition in the war on terrorism, allowing approximately 1,000 U.S. troops to be deployed in support of the war in Afghanistan. The U.S. has expanded aid by over 50 percent, but Karimov is still under pressure to put an end to human rights violations. Though rich in gold, natural gas, oil, coal, silver, and copper, Uzbekistan remains underdeveloped. A recent European Bank for Reconstruction and Development conference in Uzbekistan criticized Karimov's track record and called for expanding economic reforms. Uzbekistan's import-substitution industrialization has failed; the country remains primarily an exporter of raw materials and low value added goods. Living conditions continue to deteriorate; in 2001, the average monthly wage in agriculture was just US$9, a 30 percent decrease from 2000. To secure US$100 million in loans and assistance, the government has vowed to implement an International Monetary Fund program that involves major economic reforms.

###  TRADE POLICY
**Score: 5–Stable** (very high level of protectionism)

The International Monetary Fund reports that in 2001, Uzbekistan's average tariff rate was 29 percent (based on import duties as a percent of total imports). According to the U.S. Department of State, Uzbekistan "restricts imports in many ways, including…requirements for certificates of origin for imported products, licensing requirements for importers and wholesale traders…and limited access to hard currency."

###  FISCAL BURDEN OF GOVERNMENT
Score—Income Taxation: **3**–Stable (moderate tax rates)
Score—Corporate Taxation: **2**–Better (low tax rates)
Score—Change in Government Expenditures: **4.5**–Worse (high increase)
**Final Score: 2.9–Stable** (moderate cost of government)

The Economist Intelligence Unit reports that Uzbekistan has reduced tax rates in an effort to boost compliance. Uzbekistan's top income tax rate has been lowered to 32 percent from the 33 percent reported in the 2003 *Index*, and the top corporate tax rate has been reduced to 20 percent from the 24 percent reported in the 2003 *Index*. However, government expenditures as a share of GDP increased 2.8 percentage points to 33 percent in 2001, compared to a 1.8 percentage point decrease in 2000. On net, Uzbekistan's fiscal burden of government score is unchanged this year.

###  GOVERNMENT INTERVENTION IN THE ECONOMY
Score: **4**–Stable (high level)

The World Bank reports that the government consumed 18.4 percent of GDP in 2001. "To date," reports the U.S. Department of State, "no major state owned enterprises in the telecommunications, energy, or mining sectors have been privatized." According to the Economist Intelligence Unit, "The government is hostile to allowing the development of an independent private sector, over which it would have no control."

## MONETARY POLICY
### Score: **5**–Stable (very high level of inflation)

Data from the International Monetary Fund's *2003 World Economic Outlook* indicate that from 1993 to 2002, Uzbekistan's weighted average annual rate of inflation was 42.77 percent.

## CAPITAL FLOWS AND FOREIGN INVESTMENT
### Score: **4**–Stable (high barriers)

Officially, the government of Uzbekistan welcomes foreign investment. In practice, however, foreign investors must contend with numerous unofficial barriers. According to the U.S. Department of State, "Direct foreign investors are granted a host of incentives on a case-by-case basis.… However, legislative requirements for these benefits are ambiguous, processes and procedures are cumbersome, and the regulatory environment is capricious. While these conditions provide opportunities to companies in a position to turn special decrees and privileges to their advantage, most potential investors are deterred. As a result, Uzbekistan has so far attracted less foreign direct investment per capita than any other CIS country despite its strategic location and considerable economic potential." The International Monetary Fund reports that the central bank must approve most foreign exchange accounts. Various limits apply to payments and transfers, including limits and bona fide tests. Nearly all capital transactions, including capital and money market instruments, derivatives, credit operations, and real estate transactions, are subject to controls.

## BANKING AND FINANCE
### Score: **5**–Stable (very high level of restrictions)

According to the U.S. Department of State, "The banking system is…dominated by large state-owned banks and marked by a lack of openness and competition, presence of non-performing loans, relatively high degrees of concentration.… Furthermore, the banking system remains the primary conduit for the [government's] directed credits to state-owned enterprises at negative real interest rates.… The largest bank in the country is the state-owned National Bank for Foreign Economic Activity of Uzbekistan (NBU). NBU controls most of the commercial bank loan portfolio and 66 percent of Uzbekistan's foreign exchange business." The government also maintains numerous restrictions on banking activities. According to the U.S. Department of State, "All inter-firm transactions must be conducted by bank transfer. Cash withdrawals by legal entities are only permitted for payment of wages and travel expenses. Cash receipts must be deposited on the same day they are received." Private banks are few and very small.

## WAGES AND PRICES
### Score: **4**–Stable (high level of intervention)

The government directly controls prices on a large number of goods and services. According to the Economist Intelligence Unit, the use of price controls helps keep inflation far below the officially reported rate. The government affects the price of agricultural goods, particularly in the cotton sector, which is the largest export earner and employer. The U.S. Department of State reports that "the state determines what crops will be grown on what land, provides farms with the needed inputs at subsidized prices, and buys half of the crop at a state-determined price, generally far below its market value. As a result, production of cotton and grain is inefficient, and probably far below potential." The Ministry of Labor sets the minimum wage in consultation with the Council of the Federation of Trade Unions.

## PROPERTY RIGHTS
### Score: **4**–Stable (low level of protection)

Protection of property is weak in Uzbekistan. According to the Economist Intelligence Unit, "The judiciary is subordinate to the government, since it is appointed by the executive. Judicial procedures fall a long way short of international standards and corruption is widespread." Expropriation is frequent. The U.S. Department of State reports that the government "has also been known to frequently take property from local businesses and individuals with inadequate compensation. Agricultural enterprises are particularly vulnerable to expropriation of land."

## REGULATION
### Score: **5**–Stable (very high level)

The process for establishing a business is highly burdensome. "Lack of transparency in the regulatory system is a major concern," reports the U.S. Department of State. "Sudden legislative and regulatory changes are common; many decrees have secret provisions. The involvement of state bodies in commerce, including those with regulatory authority, produces inherently anti-competitive pressures." According to the Economist Intelligence Unit, "Corruption is a serious and all-pervasive problem in Uzbekistan that weakens the effectiveness of the state and creates considerable popular discontent. The political elite dominates business."

## INFORMAL MARKET
### Score: **4**–Stable (high level of activity)

Transparency International's 2002 score for Uzbekistan is 2.9. Therefore, Uzbekistan's informal market score is 4 this year.

# VENEZUELA

Rank: 147

Score: 4.18

Category: Repressed

**Present & Past Scores**

(Best) 1
2
3
4
(Worst) 5

'95 3.28 '96 3.63 '97 3.58 '98 3.43 '99 3.48 '00 3.43 '01 3.78 '02 3.88 '03 3.71 '04 4.18

VENEZUELA

President Hugo Chávez has succeeded in strangling Venezuela's private sector—the source of much of his opposition. Already weakened by a lengthy national strike that Venezuelan entrepreneurs undertook to force him from power, Chávez retaliated with foreign exchange controls that, combined with the reduction in oil exports when state oil company workers struck in January, could result in a 20 percent economic contraction by the end of 2003. Venezuela reportedly suffered a 35 percent drop in GDP in the first quarter of this year, and Chávez has been advising citizens to plant vegetable gardens to make up for lost food imports. Detractors claim that his ultimate goal is to punish domestic business critics with exchange controls and to replace Venezuela's already debilitated private sector with foreign businesses that will not oppose him. Negotiations continue for a referendum to recall Chávez from office; but despite the requisite number of signatures and encouragement from the Organization of American States, Chávez seems determined to block any attempt at removal, even if it means ignoring the constitution he promulgated in 1999 to help ensure his longevity in power. Venezuela's economic slide also has affected such neighboring countries as Colombia, which used to export up to $2 billion in goods to this troubled nation, and the disappearance of a market economy in Venezuela could depress economies elsewhere in the region. Venezuela's fiscal burden of government score is 0.2 point worse this year; in addition, its government intervention is 0.5 point worse, its monetary policy and banking and finance scores are 1 point worse, and its capital flows and foreign investment score is 2 points worse. As a result, its overall score is 0.47 point worse this year, causing Venezuela to be classified as "repressed."

## TRADE POLICY
### Score: **4**–Stable (high level of protectionism)

According to the World Bank, Venezuela's weighted average tariff rate in 2000 (the most recent year for which World Bank data are available) was 13.5 percent. The U.S. Department of State reports that Venezuela restricts imports of certain agricultural products (including wheat, grains, rice, pork, poultry, oilseeds, edible oils, oilseed meals, and milk) through the Andean Community's price band mechanism; in addition, the government arbitrarily decides not to allow imports under the tariff-rate quota agreement once the quota is met.

## FISCAL BURDEN OF GOVERNMENT
Score—Income Taxation: **3**–Stable (moderate tax rates)
Score—Corporate Taxation: **4.5**–Stable (very high tax rates)
Score—Change in Government Expenditures: **5**–Worse (very high increase)
### Final Score: **4.3**–Worse (high cost of government)

Venezuela's top income tax rate is 34 percent. The top corporate tax rate is 34 percent. Government expenditures as a share of GDP increased more in 2001 (3.7 percentage points to 25.1 percent) than they did in 2000 (2.1 percentage points). As a result, Venezuela's fiscal burden of government score is 0.2 point worse this year.

## GOVERNMENT INTERVENTION IN THE ECONOMY
### Score: **3.5**–Worse (high level)

The World Bank reports that the government consumed 8 percent of GDP in 2001. In the same year, according to the International Monetary Fund, Venezuela received 42.07 percent of its total revenues from state-owned enterprises and government ownership of property, up from the 33.64 percent reported in the 2003 *Index*. As a result, Venezuela's government intervention score is 0.5 point worse this year.

## MONETARY POLICY
### Score: **5**–Worse (very high level of inflation)

From 1993 to 2002, Venezuela's weighted average annual rate of inflation was 20.06 percent, up from the 15.98 percent from 1992 to 2001 reported in the 2003 *Index*. As a result, Venezuela's monetary policy score is 1 point worse this year.

## CAPITAL FLOWS AND FOREIGN INVESTMENT
### Score: **5**–Worse (very high barriers)

The political and economic changes that have marked the Chávez administration generate uncertainty among prospective investors. The International Monetary Fund reports that mass media, communications, Spanish-language newspapers, and professional services are reserved for national ownership. New investments must be registered with the government. Foreign investment in the petroleum and iron sectors is restricted. A lack of transparency in the regulatory system and government intervention in the economy continue to concern foreign investors. In February 2003, Chávez introduced exchange controls, which the Economist Intelligence Unit reports will "continue to be used as a weapon against the government's opponents in the private sector." The EIU explains the effects of these controls: "Starved of vital inputs and components, many companies have had to curtail their production drastically, while others have had to shut down temporarily and some have been forced out of business altogether." Based on the evidence that the government's exchange controls are making it extremely difficult for foreign and domestic businesses to operate, Venezuela's capital flows and foreign investment score is 2 points worse this year.

## BANKING AND FINANCE
### Score: **4**–Worse (high level of restrictions)

The banking sector is still recovering from the mid-1990s financial crisis, which was caused by lax supervision, directed lending, and poor credit practices and is estimated to have cost Venezuela at least 15 percent of GDP. The government permits 100 percent foreign ownership in banking and financial services. It also is increasing its presence in the banking sector. According to the Economist Intelligence Unit, "Heavy domestic borrowing by the government since 1999–2000 has been crowding out private borrowing in a shallow market." The government influences the allocation of credit. "At the end of April," reports the EIU, "a tripartite agreement was signed between the government, the Central Bank and the banking system. The key feature of the accord is that the banks promise to lend at least Bs500bn (US$300m, representing around 6% of their outstanding loan portfolio) to the private sector over the next year at a preferential interest rate.

The preferential rate is set at 85% of the average lending rate of the country's six largest banks. The agreement is a victory for Mr Chávez who had long been demanding sweeping interest rate controls." As a result, Venezuela's banking and finance score is 1 point worse this year.

## WAGES AND PRICES
### Score: **4**–Stable (high level of intervention)

The government has the authority to control most prices. According to the Economist Intelligence Unit, "Venezuela has a long history of using price controls, but had removed many of them between 1996 and 1998. Restrictions remained on a few agricultural products, some medicines, and petrol." The same source notes that "Venezuela put in place sweeping price controls for foodstuffs, toiletries, and a variety of basic services in February 2003. These rules for over 200 items were published in the Official Gazette on February 11th–12th. They set maximum permissible prices that were far below actual market prices, and often under wholesale or import costs. They apply to some 60% of all goods sold in supermarkets, according to industry sources."

## PROPERTY RIGHTS
### Score: **4**–Stable (low level of protection)

Protection of private property in Venezuela is weak. According to the Economist Intelligence Unit, "business groups argue that a land law throws private property rights into question." In addition, "the government still appears prone to back away from inconvenient contractual agreements on populist grounds or to seek more favorable terms, particularly in the oil sector."

## REGULATION
### Score: **4**–Stable (high level)

Regulation can be applied arbitrarily. According to the Economist Intelligence Unit, "investors complain that regulators are often poorly equipped, trained and staffed and that decisions are based on political rather than technical criteria." The U.S. Department of State reports that "Venezuelan laws are complicated, even more so since many activities are regulated, not only by laws, but also by presidential decrees or specific regulations. The bureaucracy and paperwork are often complicated." Labor laws are burdensome, and bureaucratic corruption is extensive.

## INFORMAL MARKET
### Score: **4**–Stable (high level of activity)

Transparency International's 2002 score for Venezuela is 2.5. Therefore, Venezuela's informal market score is 4 this year.

VIETNAM

# VIETNAM

Rank: 141

Score: 3.93

Category: Mostly Unfree

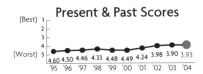

Present & Past Scores

(Best) 1
2
3
4
(Worst) 5

4.60 4.50 4.46 4.33 4.48 4.49 4.24 3.98 3.90 3.93
'95 '96 '97 '98 '99 '00 '01 '02 '03 '04

2001 Data (in constant 1995 US dollars)

## QUICK STUDY

### SCORES

| | |
|---|---|
| Trade Policy | 5 |
| Fiscal Burden | 4.3 |
| Government Intervention | 4 |
| Monetary Policy | 1 |
| Foreign Investment | 4 |
| Banking and Finance | 4 |
| Wages and Prices | 3 |
| Property Rights | 5 |
| Regulation | 5 |
| Informal Market | 4 |

**Population:** 79,526,050

**Total area:** 329,560 sq. km

**GDP:** $31 billion

**GDP growth rate:** 6.8%

**GDP per capita:** $390

**Major exports:** crude oil, fisheries products, textiles and garments, rice, footwear

**Exports of goods and services:** $16 billion

**Major export trading partners:** Japan 17.1%, Australia 7.6%, China 7.5%, US 7.2%, Germany 6.9%

**Major imports:** refined petroleum, steel, cloth, computer and electronic goods

**Imports of goods and services:** $16.7 billion

**Major import trading partners:** Singapore 13.6%, China 11.9%, Japan 11.6%, South Korea 11.2%, Thailand 5.1%

**Foreign direct investment (net):** $1.2 billion

Since the signing and implementation of the U.S.–Vietnam Bilateral Trade Agreement (BTA), trade between the two countries has skyrocketed. From 2001 to 2002, Vietnam's exports to the United States increased by 109 percent, from $863 million to $1.8 billion. Despite the slow recovery of the global economy, Vietnam's real GDP growth for 2002 is reported at 7 percent, and industrial output has grown by 14.4 percent. Robust domestic private consumption and investment drive the economy. Vietnam, with support from the European Union and the U.S., continues negotiations to join the WTO by the 2005 deadline. It also has become more stringent in dealing with corruption—a sign that the government is beginning to recognize that rule of law is necessary for economic prosperity. Overall, economic trends appear to be positive. However, the government seems ambivalent toward reform of Vietnam's state-owned enterprises, and equitization (privatization) continues to advance only at a slow pace. Investors remain concerned about issues of transparency, investment, and protection of intellectual property rights, all criteria that, while included in the BTA, Vietnam has yet to fully implement. Although Vietnam has committed to certain provisions toward resolving these issues, it has yet to reinforce them effectively. Recently, the government has attempted to block Internet sites and closely monitor Internet cafes. Easy access to information is crucial to compete in the global economy, and such interventionist government policies can only serve to impede trade relations abroad. Vietnam's fiscal burden of government score is 0.2 point better this year; however, its government intervention score is 0.5 point worse. As a result, Vietnam's overall score is 0.03 point worse this year.

## TRADE POLICY
### Score: **5**–Stable (very high level of protectionism)

According to the World Bank, Vietnam's weighted average tariff rate in 2001 (the most recent year for which World Bank data are available) was 15.1 percent. The Economist Intelligence Unit reports that the government controls trade through a licensing system. Other restrictions include quotas, excise taxes, reference prices, or direct import bans. "In practice," reports the U.S. Department of State, "customs valuation remains non-transparent and is highly discretionary."

## FISCAL BURDEN OF GOVERNMENT
Score—Income Taxation: **5**–Stable (very high tax rates)
Score—Corporate Taxation: **4**–Stable (high tax rates)
Score—Change in Government Expenditures: **4**–Better (moderate increase)
### Final Score: **4.3**–Better (very high cost of government)

Vietnam's top income tax rate is 50 percent. The top corporate tax rate is 32 percent. (This is the top rate for companies with no foreign-owned capital; Vietnam taxes companies with foreign-owned capital at a top rate of 25 percent.) Government expenditures as a share of GDP increased less in 2001 (1.1 percentage points to 24.9 percent) than they did in 2000 (5.9 percentage points). As a result, Vietnam's fiscal burden of government score is 0.2 point better this year.

## GOVERNMENT INTERVENTION IN THE ECONOMY
### Score: **4**–Worse (high level)

The World Bank reports that the government consumed 6.2 percent of GDP in 2001. In 2000, according to the International Monetary Fund, Vietnam received 7.6 percent of its total revenues from state-owned enterprises and government ownership of property, up from the 4.49 percent reported in the 2003 *Index*. According to the Economist Intelligence Unit, however, Vietnam has over 5,000 state-owned enterprises, and "The state-owned sector generates 41% of industrial output...." The state is involved in the finance, telecommunications, energy, and manufacturing sectors. The EIU also reports that "the state-owned sector is often given preferential treatment over the private sector in areas like tendering for public projects or access to tax breaks...." Based on the apparent unreliability of the foregoing figures, 2 points have been added to Vietnam's government intervention score: 1 point for questionable data on government consumption and 1 point for questionable data on revenues from state-owned enterprises. Based on the increase in revenues from state-owned enterprises, Vietnam's government intervention score is 0.5 point worse this year.

## MONETARY POLICY
### Score: **1**–Stable (very low level of inflation)

Data from the International Monetary Fund's *2003 World Economic Outlook* indicate that from 1993 to 2002, Vietnam's weighted average annual rate of inflation was 2.56 percent.

## CAPITAL FLOWS AND FOREIGN INVESTMENT
### Score: **4**–Stable (high barriers)

The government permits up to 30 percent foreign ownership in companies not owned by the state in 35 different sectors of the economy. The International Monetary Fund reports that both residents and non-residents may hold foreign exchange accounts with government approval and provided the foreign exchange used to open the accounts originated outside of Vietnam; all transactions require individual authorization from the Ministry of Finance, except for payments involving authorized imports. Controls apply to all transactions in money market and capital instruments, derivatives, commercial credits, and direct investments. Foreigners may not own land. The U.S. Department of State reports that "investors [cite] official corruption as a significant problem in establishing and running their business."

## BANKING AND FINANCE
### Score: **4**–Stable (high level of restrictions)

Since the central bank ended its commercial activity and assumed a supervisory role, the banking sector has assumed an increased market orientation. The four state-owned banks continue to dominate the sector, accounting for 72 percent of

loans outstanding as of mid-2001. Vietnam's banks do not adhere to the Basel capital accords, are not audited by reputable auditing firms, and remain overexposed to the state sector. In June 2002, the government removed interest rate controls on dong and U.S. dollar lending. However, the government still affects the allocation of credit. According to the Economist Intelligence Unit, "Banks are regularly directed to offer preferential interest rates and debt relief to farmers, and...at least two-thirds of bank lending goes to SOEs."

## WAGES AND PRICES
### Score: **3**–Stable (moderate level of intervention)

The government controls prices to stem inflation. According to the Economist Intelligence Unit, "The government continues to set rates for electricity, petrol, telecommunications, water, and fares for train and air travel. In most of these areas, the rates have traditionally been higher for foreigners, although harmonization is underway." Vietnam has a minimum wage.

## PROPERTY RIGHTS
### Score: **5**–Stable (very low level of protection)

Property is not well-protected in Vietnam. "Interference in the legal process and the bribing of judges to serve particular interests is common," reports the Economist Intelligence Unit. "Contractual arrangements are backed by the force of law but the legal system is complicated. Contractual disputes often involve a prolonged period of negotiation preceding any attempt to resolve the matter in court." In addition, "Because of the lack of faith in the Vietnamese legal system, many foreign investors include clauses in their contracts allowing disputes to be dealt with by the Singapore Court of Arbitration."

## REGULATION
### Score: **5**–Stable (very high level)

The U.S. Department of State reports that investors face "poorly developed infrastructure, underdeveloped and cumbersome legal and financial systems, an unwieldy bureaucracy, non-transparent regulations, high start-up costs, arcane land acquisition and transfer regulations and procedures, and shortage of trained personnel. Issuance of investment licenses and implementation of projects often is a lengthy process during which the investment environment in areas such as taxes and procedures frequently changes." According to the Political and Economic Risk Consultancy, "Civil servants in Vietnam can be some of the most difficult to work with in Asia [and] can still be very obstructionist."

## INFORMAL MARKET
### Score: **4**–Stable (high level of activity)

Transparency International's 2002 score for Vietnam is 2.4. Therefore, Vietnam's informal market score is 4 this year.

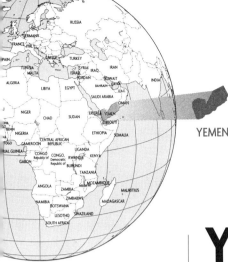

YEMEN

# YEMEN

Rank: 131

Score: 3.70

Category: Mostly Unfree

**Present & Past Scores**

(Best) 1
2
3
4
(Worst) 5

3.79  3.88  3.95  4.15  4.19  3.94  3.98  3.74  3.73  3.70
'95  '96  '97  '98  '99  '00  '01  '02  '03  '04

---

## QUICK STUDY

### SCORES
| | |
|---|---|
| Trade Policy | 3 |
| Fiscal Burden | 4 |
| Government Intervention | 4 |
| Monetary Policy | 3 |
| Foreign Investment | 3 |
| Banking and Finance | 4 |
| Wages and Prices | 3 |
| Property Rights | 4 |
| Regulation | 4 |
| Informal Market | 5 |

**Population:** 18,045,750

**Total area:** 527,970 sq. km

**GDP:** $5.7 billion

**GDP growth rate:** 3.1%

**GDP per capita:** $316

**Major exports:** minerals, fuels and lubricants, food and livestock, machines and transport equipment

**Exports of goods and services:** $2.2 billion

**Major export trading partners:** China 18.6%, Thailand 15.9%, India 17.5%, South Korea 10.2%, Singapore 8.7%

**Major imports:** food and livestock, machinery and transport equipment, chemicals, minerals, fuels and lubricants

**Imports of goods and services:** $2.1 billion

**Major import trading partners:** Saudi Arabia 12.6%, United Arab Emirates 9.1%, US 7.4%, France 6.1%, Italy 3.6%

**Foreign direct investment (net):** −$183.4 million

2001 Data (in constant 1995 US dollars)

---

**Y**emen, a poor country with few resources, is located on the Red Sea coast of the Arabian Peninsula. In 1990, North and South Yemen united after two decades of political and civil turmoil. A southern secessionist movement that erupted again in 1994 was quickly subdued, but not before it undermined the limited progress that had been made toward economic liberalization. Yemen remains a cauldron of political intrigue with an economy that remains hamstrung by rampant unemployment, frequent water shortages, high population growth rates, and an often-corrupt bureaucracy that has permeated all levels of the government, including the judiciary. President Ali Abdallah Saleh, who led Northern Yemen before the merger, faces strong opposition from southern Yemeni political parties, autonomous tribes, and Islamic radicals who oppose the government's economic reform program and seek to obstruct private-sector initiatives. Future economic development will be closely tied to the level of the government's adherence to the International Monetary Fund's structural adjustment program. Although the administration has adopted marginal measures to reduce state intervention in commercial activities and government spending, more needs to be done, particularly in the areas of economic diversification, civil service reform, and attracting foreign investment. However, because recurring violence and an uncertain security environment have the potential to undermine foreign investor confidence in the economy, the government is not likely to retreat from its economic reform efforts as this would jeopardize its fragile relationship with international donors. Yemen's fiscal burden of government score is 0.3 point better this year. As a result, its overall score is 0.03 point better this year.

### TRADE POLICY
Score: **3–Stable** (moderate level of protectionism)

Based on data from the Yemeni central bank, Yemen's average tariff rate in 2000 was 7.4 percent (based on import duties as a percent of total imports). According to the U.S. Department of State, "The government prohibits importation of seven items: pork and pork products, coffee, alcohol, narcotics, some types of fresh fruits and vegetables during their local production season…and rhinoceros horns." The Economist Intelligence Unit reports that "excessively complex customs procedures" act as a trade barrier.

### FISCAL BURDEN OF GOVERNMENT
Score—Income Taxation: **3.5–Stable** (high tax rates)
Score—Corporate Taxation: **4.5–Stable** (very high tax rates)
Score—Change in Government Expenditures: **3.5–Better** (low increase)
Final Score: **4–Better** (high cost of government)

Yemen's top income tax rate is 35 percent. The top corporate tax rate is also 35 percent. Government expenditures as a share of GDP increased less in 2001 (0.8 percentage point to 35.7 percent) than they did in 2000 (2.8 percentage points). As a result, Yemen's fiscal burden of government score is 0.3 point better this year.

### GOVERNMENT INTERVENTION IN THE ECONOMY
Score: **4–Stable** (high level)

The World Bank reports that the government consumed 14.1 percent of GDP in 2001. In the same year, based on data from the Economist Intelligence Unit, Yemen received 71.46 percent of its total revenues from state-owned enterprises and government ownership of property.

 ## MONETARY POLICY
### Score: **3**–Stable (moderate level of inflation)

From 1993 to 2002, Yemen's weighted average annual rate of inflation was 11.94 percent.

 ## CAPITAL FLOWS AND FOREIGN INVESTMENT
### Score: **3**–Stable (moderate barriers)

Yemen has streamlined its investment laws and procedures in an attempt to attract more foreign investment and permits foreign investment in most sectors. A new policy grants equal treatment to all investors, both domestic and foreign. Foreign investment in the exploration for and production of oil, gas, and minerals is subject to production-sharing agreements. Foreign investment is not permitted in the arms and explosive materials industries, banking and money exchange, industries that could cause environmental disasters, or wholesale and retail imports. Other barriers to foreign investment are ongoing security concerns and the lack of infrastructure. The International Monetary Fund reports that foreign exchange accounts are permitted. There are no restrictions on payments and transfers.

 ## BANKING AND FINANCE
### Score: **4**–Stable (high level of restrictions)

According to the Economist Intelligence Unit, Yemen's "banking system is comprised of the Central Bank of Yemen, 15 commercial banks and two specialized state-owned development banks. Of the 15 commercial banks, nine are private domestic banks (including four Islamic banks), four are private foreign banks and two are majority state-owned…. The largest commercial bank in the country is the National Bank of Yemen, which is fully state-owned and targeted for privatization." The EIU also reports that the state-owned Yemen Bank for Reconstruction and Development is being restructured with a view to eventual privatization, although it suffers from a large number of non-performing loans and is undercapitalized, and that the inadequacy of the legal system discourages loans to other than certain preferred clients.

 ## WAGES AND PRICES
### Score: **3**–Stable (moderate level of intervention)

The government of Yemen affects some prices, particularly in the agriculture and fisheries sectors. According to the Economist Intelligence Unit, "The Agriculture and Fisheries Production and Promotion Fund (AFPPF) was launched to protect the livelihoods of the poorest members of the fishing and farming communities after diesel subsidies were reduced. While the AFPPF is still a system based on subsidies, it subsidises agricultural inputs and equipment rather than diesel. Nevertheless, diesel is still subsidized by the government—and this acts as an important crutch for those in the fishing and farming communities, as it powers their irrigation pumps and fishing boats." Yemen's labor law specifies that the minimum wage for a private-sector worker may not be less than the minimum wage for a civil servant.

 ## PROPERTY RIGHTS
### Score: **4**–Stable (low level of protection)

According to the Economist Intelligence Unit, "The judiciary is generally under-trained, inefficient and seen as corrupt." The U.S. Department of State reports that enforcement of laws and contracts "remains problematic at best and nonexistent at worst." Also, "in cases involving interest, most judges use Shari'a (Islamic) law as the guideline, under which claims for interest payments due are almost always rejected."

 ## REGULATION
### Score: **4**–Stable (high level)

Bureaucratic inefficiency and corruption present serious impediments to business. Yemeni ministries are hugely overstaffed, and reforming the civil service remains a promise unfulfilled. Regulations are applied haphazardly. According to the U.S. Department of State, "While Yemen has fundamentally sound investment laws…transparency of implementation and enforcement is elusive."

 ## INFORMAL MARKET
### Score: **5**–Stable (very high level of activity)

According to the Economist Intelligence Unit, "Smuggling forms a large and unrecorded part of trade…." Protection of intellectual property in Yemen is weak, and piracy of such products is substantial. In 2000, according to the University of Linz, Austria, the informal economy was approximately 22 percent of GDP.

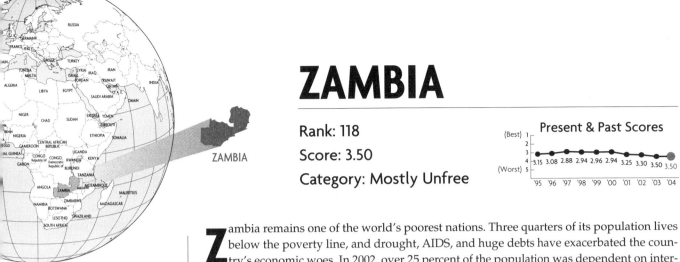

# ZAMBIA

Rank: 118

Score: 3.50

Category: Mostly Unfree

Present & Past Scores

(Best) 1
2
3
4
(Worst) 5

3.15  3.08  2.88  2.94  2.96  2.94  3.25  3.30  3.50  3.50

'95  '96  '97  '98  '99  '00  '01  '02  '03  '04

Zambia remains one of the world's poorest nations. Three quarters of its population lives below the poverty line, and drought, AIDS, and huge debts have exacerbated the country's economic woes. In 2002, over 25 percent of the population was dependent on international food aid. Lusaka's refusal to accept genetically modified grain was heavily criticized by the United States, one of the country's largest aid donors. Anglo–American PLC's decision to quit the Zambian copper industry was also a major blow for the economy. Mining of copper and cobalt is the economic mainstay, supplying over 75 percent of exports; but production has been declining since the 1970s, and the country's rich mines are struggling to remain profitable as international prices decline. Corrupt politicians, chronic mismanagement, and unproductive labor have eroded the value of the mines and caused investors to be skeptical. Rising trade union opposition has slowed the government's economic liberalization program, under which 251 of 287 state-owned companies were either privatized or liquidated. Failure to proceed with the privatization program could jeopardize an agreement with the International Monetary Fund to relieve Zambia's $6 billion debt burden. President Levy Mwanawasa's Movement for Multiparty Democracy remains in a powerful position, even though its former leader Frederick Chiluba has been charged with 60 counts of corruption.

## TRADE POLICY
### Score: 4–Stable (high level of protectionism)

According to the World Bank, Zambia's weighted average tariff rate in 1997 (the most recent year for which World Bank data are available) was 13.1 percent. The government requires "import certificates" for such items as meat, poultry, plants, pharmaceuticals, and firearms and ammunition. It also bans the importation of ivory.

## FISCAL BURDEN OF GOVERNMENT
### Score—Income Taxation: 3–Stable (moderate tax rates)
### Score—Corporate Taxation: 4.5–Stable (very high tax rates)
### Score—Change in Government Expenditures: 4–Stable (moderate increase)
### Final Score: 4–Stable (high cost of government)

Zambia's top income tax rate is 30 percent. The top corporate tax rate is 35 percent. Government expenditures as a share of GDP increased slightly less in 2001 (1.2 percentage points to 32 percent) than they did in 2000 (2 percentage points). On net, Zambia's fiscal burden of government score is unchanged this year.

## GOVERNMENT INTERVENTION IN THE ECONOMY
### Score: 2–Stable (low level)

The World Bank reports that the government consumed 13 percent of GDP in 2001. In 2000, based on data from the Ministry of Finance and Economic Development, Zambia received less than 1 percent of its total revenues from state-owned enterprises and government ownership of property.

417

## MONETARY POLICY
### Score: **5**–Stable (very high level of inflation)

From 1993 to 2002, Zambia's weighted average annual rate of inflation was 22.66 percent.

## CAPITAL FLOWS AND FOREIGN INVESTMENT
### Score: **3**–Stable (moderate barriers)

Zambia welcomes foreign investment. An investment board screens all proposed foreign investment, but the process is open to appeal, and the board reportedly reaches decisions within 30 days. Foreign investors receive national treatment, and there are no local content, equity, financing, employment, or technology transfer requirements. Foreign investors have been able to participate in Zambia's privatization program. However, a number of informal barriers deter foreign investment. According to the U.S. Department of State, "High transaction costs, poor infrastructure and political risk create an uncertain business and commercial environment." The same source notes that "Governmental corruption and bureaucratic inefficiency are continuing problems that affect the business environment." The International Monetary Fund reports that both residents and non-residents are permitted to hold foreign exchange accounts. There are no controls on payments, transfers, capital transactions, or repatriation of profits.

## BANKING AND FINANCE
### Score: **3**–Stable (moderate level of restrictions)

Zambia's commercial banking sector includes private international banks, private domestic banks, and state-owned banks. The Bank of Zambia, which is the central bank and reports to the Ministry of Finance, supervises the banking sector. There are four international banks and one government-owned bank. The government has received no bids for its 35 percent share of the state-owned Zambia National Commercial Bank (Zanaco), which is wracked by huge non-performing loans.

## WAGES AND PRICES
### Score: **3**–Stable (moderate level of intervention)

The government affects prices in the agricultural sector through the Food Reserve Agency (FRA), which buys and sells agricultural products from the private sector. The Economist Intelligence Unit reports that "over time the FRA became used for a host of very different functions, including purchasing large stocks of maize or fertiliser and distributing it at subsidised prices, and thus undercutting the private sector." In May 2003, the government set a price floor on maize. Since agriculture is one of the most important economic sectors, influencing its prices significantly distorts the economy. There is a minimum wage for non-unionized workers.

## PROPERTY RIGHTS
### Score: **3**–Stable (moderate level of protection)

Zambia's judicial system, though fairly independent, suffers from inefficiency and a lack of resources and may be weakening. According to the Economist Intelligence Unit, "The 1996 constitution circumscribes the power of the judiciary to pronounce legislation as unconstitutional and also empowers the president to remove High Court judges if he decides they have committed 'gross misconduct'." The U.S. Department of State reports that "contractual and property rights are weak and final court decisions can take a long time."

## REGULATION
### Score: **4**–Stable (high level)

Business in Zambia is hampered by outdated laws that do not reflect, and therefore cannot be applied effectively to, current business practice. Acquiring a business license involves complex procedures and delays. An investment board screens domestic investment. According to the U.S. Department of State, "Governmental corruption and bureaucratic inefficiency are continuing problems that affect the business environment."

## INFORMAL MARKET
### Score: **4**–Stable (high level of activity)

Transparency International's 2002 score for Zambia is 2.6. Therefore, Zambia's informal market score is 4 this year.

# ZIMBABWE

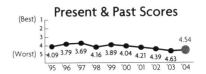

ZIMBABWE

Rank: 153

Score: 4.54

Category: Repressed

**Present & Past Scores**

(Best) 1
2
3
4
(Worst) 5

4.09  3.79  3.69  4.16  3.89  4.04  4.21  4.39  4.63  **4.54**

'95  '96  '97  '98  '99  '00  '01  '02  '03  '04

**Population:** 12,820,650

**Total area:** 390,580 sq. km

**GDP:** $7.2 billion

**GDP growth rate:** −8.4%

**GDP per capita:** $559

**Major exports:** tobacco, gold, textiles and clothing

**Exports of goods and services:** $3 billion

**Major export trading partners:** South Africa 14.1%, Japan 6.6%, Germany 6.5%, UK 6.0%

**Major imports:** transport equipment and machinery, chemicals, manufactures, petroleum products

**Imports of goods and services:** $2.98 billion

**Major import trading partners:** South Africa 44.5%, Mozambique 4.6%, UK 4.1%, Germany 3.5%, US 3.4%

**Foreign direct investment (net):** $8.9 million

2001 Data (in constant 1995 US dollars)

**Z**imbabwe, once the breadbasket of Africa, is unable to feed its own population. Government confiscation of white-owned farmland without compensation has led to a man-made famine of historic proportions, with 5 million Zimbabweans facing starvation. Unemployment stands at 80 percent, and inflation is running at over 200 percent. The Economist Intelligence Unit expects the economy to contract further in the next two years. Real GDP is forecast to decline by 8.8 percent in 2003 and 4.7 percent in 2004. President Robert Mugabe has earned his reputation as Africa's most brutal dictator. His Zimbabwe African National Union–Patriotic Front (ZANU–PF) rules with an iron fist, suppressing political opposition and quashing dissent. The United States, Great Britain, and other leading Western nations refuse to recognize Mugabe as the country's legitimate ruler, and the ruling elite remain the target of stringent U.S. and European Union "smart sanctions." Despite his advanced age (79), Mugabe is expected to cling to power, driving the nation into further ruin, rather than step down. The opposition Movement for Democratic Change (MDC), led by Morgan Tsvangirai, continues to enjoy widespread support despite a massive campaign of intimidation against its supporters. Polls suggest that the MDC would win a huge majority if free and fair elections were to be held. Zimbabwe's wages and prices score is 1 point worse this year; however, its fiscal burden of government score is 0.9 point better, and its government intervention score is 1 point better. As a result, Zimbabwe's overall score is 0.09 point better this year.

## TRADE POLICY
### Score: **5**–Stable (very high level of protectionism)

The World Bank reports that Zimbabwe's weighted average tariff rate in 2001 (the most recent year for which World Bank data are available) was 15.6 percent. According to the U.S. Department of State, the government "maintains a 'negative list' of prohibited items that require special permission from the government to import." The same source reports that customs corruption acts as a non-tariff barrier. The government also restricts trade through foreign exchange controls.

## FISCAL BURDEN OF GOVERNMENT
Score—Income Taxation: **4.5**–Worse (very high tax rates)
Score—Corporate Taxation: **4**–Stable (high tax rates)
Score—Change in Government Expenditures: **1**–Better (very high decrease)
### Final Score: **3.4**–Better (high cost of government)

Zimbabwe's top income tax rate is 45 percent, up from the 40 percent reported in the 2003 *Index*. The top corporate income tax rate is 30 percent. Government expenditures as a share of GDP decreased 11.9 percentage points to 38.1 percent in 2001, compared to a 12.7 percentage point increase in 2000. On net, Zimbabwe's fiscal burden of government score is 0.9 point better this year.

## GOVERNMENT INTERVENTION IN THE ECONOMY
### Score: **4**–Better (high level)

The World Bank reports that the government consumed 19.3 percent of GDP in 2001, down from the 24 percent reported in the 2003 *Index*. As a result, Zimbabwe's government inter-

419

vention score is 1 point better this year. According to the U.S. Department of State, "Regarding privatization of Zimbabwe's parastatal companies, progress has been very slow in the decade since it was identified as a priority, with only six organizations out of the 57 earmarked making the transition."

## MONETARY POLICY
### Score: 5–Stable (very high level of inflation)

From 1993 to 2002, Zimbabwe's weighted average annual rate of inflation was 113.46 percent. According to a July 31, 2003, *Economist* article, "Bad governments, when they run out of money, print more. But Zimbabwe's government has run out of the ink and special paper needed to print enough notes to keep pace with inflation, currently 365% and rising."

## CAPITAL FLOWS AND FOREIGN INVESTMENT
### Score: 5–Stable (very high barriers)

The government will consider foreign investment up to 100 percent in high-priority projects but applies pressure for eventual majority ownership by Zimbabweans. A new foreign investment code was enacted in 1998, but significant restrictions on foreign participation remain in effect. According to the U.S. Department of State, "There is growing hostility to foreign investment; priority is given to economic nationalism over competitiveness, resulting in the rise of cronyism and corruption in government and the private sector." The government re-imposed exchange controls in November 2002. According to the U.S. Trade Representative, "The Government of Zimbabwe has also placed severe restrictions on exporters, who are required to remit 50 percent of their foreign currency earnings to the Central Bank for exchange at the official rate." The official exchange rate is Z\$55 to \$1, but the parallel exchange rate is Z\$1,500 to \$1. Virtually all capital transactions between residents and non-residents are subject to controls and government approval.

## BANKING AND FINANCE
### Score: 5–Stable (very high level of restrictions)

Zimbabwe's relatively sophisticated financial system, developed under British colonial rule, has been squandered in recent years as the government has become ever more involved in the financial sector. The Reserve Bank of Zimbabwe has allowed the government to use it to finance deficit spending and direct loans to state-owned enterprises. Rising debt has exacerbated the instability of an already shaky sector and could lead to the collapse of the system. The Economist Intelligence Unit reports that "one of Leonard Tsumba's last actions as governor of the Reserve bank was to warn the country's commercial banks that the Reserve Bank was considering withdrawing their licenses or imposing heavy fines if they are found to have breached exchange control regulations."

## WAGES AND PRICES
### Score: 5–Worse (very high level of intervention)

The government is expanding its use of price controls. According to the International Monetary Fund, "the government in 2001 established a Price Surveillance and Monitoring Unit…. [I]ts tasks are to closely monitor prices of basic consumption items, recommend reasonable increases, and identify businesses that deviate from these prices…. [T]he government introduced direct price controls in October 2001 on a number of items, such as bread, maize meal, sugar, cooking oil, margarine, salt, washing powder, bar soap, milk, meat, and generic drugs…. Producers have to make their case for price increases to the Ministry of Industry and International Trade (MIIT) with profit margins not exceeding 20 percent…." Approximately 70 percent of the items in the consumer price index were subject to price controls in 2002. Zimbabwe maintains a minimum wage. Based on the evidence of widespread and expanding use of price controls, Zimbabwe's wages and prices score is 1 point worse this year.

## PROPERTY RIGHTS
### Score: 5–Stable (very low level of protection)

According to the U.S. Department of State, "[judicial] cases involving high or prominent ruling party or government officials usually do not reach court, regardless of the magnitude or egregiousness of the offense." The Economist Intelligence Unit reports that the government ended its land reform program—a program that consisted of expropriating commercial farmland from white owners to give it to black peasants—at the end of 2002. Apart from being a massive violation of property rights, this program led to massive starvation since the peasants do not have the means to work the land. Since June 2000, reports the U.S. Department of State, "the Government has orchestrated a campaign of violence and intimidation against the judiciary…."

## REGULATION
### Score: 4–Stable (high level)

Businesses face considerable impediments in Zimbabwe. The bureaucracy is extremely arbitrary and not transparent. The U.S. Department of State reports that "many bureaucratic functions in this still heavily controlled economy are less than fully transparent and can by no means be considered streamlined. Corruption within the regulatory system is increasingly worrisome."

## INFORMAL MARKET
### Score: 4–Stable (high level of activity)

Transparency International's 2002 score for Zimbabwe is 2.7. Therefore, Zimbabwe's informal market score is 4 this year.

# Appendix

# Per Capita Income Throughout the World
## (Expressed in Purchasing Power Parity and in Constant 1995 U.S. Dollars)

This table is provided for those readers interested in per capita income measured in terms of purchasing power parity compared to per capita income measured in constant U.S. dollars.

| Country | 2001 per capita GDP (measured in purchasing power parity*) | 2001 per capita GDP (measured in 1995 constant U.S. dollars**) | Country | 2001 per capita GDP (measured in purchasing power parity*) | 2001 per capita GDP (measured in 1995 constant U.S. dollars**) |
|---|---|---|---|---|---|
| Albania | $3,738 | $1,032 | Equatorial Guinea | 23,086 | 1,578 |
| Algeria | 5,328 | 1,616 | Estonia | 10,959 | 4,707 |
| Angola | 1,815 | 525 | Ethiopia | 701 | 121 |
| Argentina | 11,544 | 7,468 | Fiji | 5,105 | 2,763 |
| Armenia | 2,598 | 1,068 | Finland | 25,333 | 32,121 |
| Australia | 26,864 | 24,203 | France | 25,749 | 30,492 |
| Austria | 28,150 | 33,172 | Gabon | 6,066 | 4,378 |
| Azerbaijan | 2,824 | 460 | Gambia, The | 1,761 | 382 |
| Bahamas, The | 16,800 | 13,481 | Georgia | 2,053 | 526 |
| Bahrain | 16,593 | 11,060 | Germany | 26,146 | 32,813 |
| Bangladesh | 1,613 | 386 | Ghana | 1,985 | 421 |
| Barbados | 16,024 | 8,610 | Greece | 17,406 | 13,669 |
| Belarus | 5,052 | 1,494 | Guatemala | 3,894 | 1,554 |
| Belgium | 26,412 | 31,218 | Guinea | 1,977 | 613 |
| Belize | 5,786 | 3,189 | Guinea–Bissau | 860 | 206 |
| Benin | 998 | 424 | Guyana | 4,109 | 942 |
| Bolivia | 2,338 | 944 | Haiti | 1,611 | 354 |
| Bosnia and Herzegovina | 5,345 | 1,584 | Honduras | 2,508 | 712 |
| Botswana | 7,954 | 4,130 | Hong Kong, China | 25,393 | 24,505 |
| Brazil | 7,571 | 4,633 | Hungary | 12,656 | 5,540 |
| Bulgaria | 6,625 | 1,630 | Iceland | 29,715 | 32,060 |
| Burkina Faso | 976 | 250 | India | 2,493 | 477 |
| Burma | 1,500 | 152 | Indonesia | 3,020 | 1,034 |
| Burundi | 602 | 141 | Iran, Islamic Rep. | 6,094 | 1,707 |
| Cambodia | 1,591 | 317 | Iraq | 2,500 | N/A |
| Cameroon | 1,688 | 696 | Ireland | 32,397 | 29,401 |
| Canada | 27,883 | 23,080 | Israel | 20,000 | 16,576 |
| Cape Verde | 4,657 | 1,550 | Italy | 25,181 | 21,144 |
| Central African Republic | 1,155 | 344 | Ivory Coast | 1,557 | 715 |
| Chad | 928 | 230 | Jamaica | 3,754 | 2,171 |
| Chile | 9,354 | 5,385 | Japan | 25,672 | 44,458 |
| China | 4,135 | 878 | Jordan | 3,957 | 1,639 |
| China, Republic of (Taiwan) | 17,200 | 12,597 | Kazakhstan | 5,225 | 1,720 |
| Colombia | 6,050 | 2,277 | Kenya | 996 | 325 |
| Congo, Dem. Rep. | 629 | 85 | Korea, North | 1,000 | N/A |
| Congo, Rep. | 991 | 792 | Korea, South | 15,528 | 13,502 |
| Costa Rica | 8,543 | 3,900 | Kuwait | 16,328 | 13,345 |
| Croatia | 9,462 | 5,355 | Kyrgyz Republic | 1,598 | 417 |
| Cuba | 2,300 | N/A | Lao PDR | 1,641 | 465 |
| Cyprus | 17,725 | 14,592 | Latvia | 8,241 | 2,816 |
| Czech Republic | 14,495 | 5,583 | Lebanon | 4,217 | 2,890 |
| Denmark | 29,386 | 38,710 | Lesotho | 2,131 | 563 |
| Djibouti | 2,018 | 777 | Libya | 7,600 | 4,625 |
| Dominican Republic | 5,998 | 2,077 | Lithuania | 9,324 | 2,308 |
| Ecuador | 3,357 | 1,478 | Luxembourg | 56,022 | 56,382 |
| Egypt, Arab Rep. | 3,600 | 1,229 | Macedonia, FYR | 6,232 | 2,417 |
| El Salvador | 4,614 | 1,757 | Madagascar | 848 | 253 |

# Per Capita Income Throughout the World
## (Expressed in Purchasing Power Parity and in Constant 1995 U.S. Dollars)

This table is provided for those readers interested in per capita income measured in terms of purchasing power parity compared to per capita income measured in constant U.S. dollars.

| Country | 2001 per capita GDP (measured in purchasing power parity*) | 2001 per capita GDP (measured in 1995 constant U.S. dollars**) | Country | 2001 per capita GDP (measured in purchasing power parity*) | 2001 per capita GDP (measured in 1995 constant U.S. dollars**) |
|---|---|---|---|---|---|
| Malawi | 582 | 163 | Sierra Leone | 480 | 158 |
| Malaysia | 8,725 | 4,708 | Singapore | 22,456 | 27,118 |
| Mali | 824 | 292 | Slovak Republic | 11,781 | 4,405 |
| Malta | 16,817 | 10,098 | Slovenia | 17,137 | 11,984 |
| Mauritania | 1,727 | 502 | South Africa | 9,916 | 4,068 |
| Mauritius | 10,090 | 4,352 | Spain | 20,279 | 17,595 |
| Mexico | 8,738 | 3,739 | Sri Lanka | 3,234 | 876 |
| Moldova | 1,346 | 678 | Sudan | 1,735 | 328 |
| Mongolia | 1,572 | 430 | Suriname | 3,500 | 1,036 |
| Morocco | 3,628 | 1,436 | Swaziland | 4,405 | 1,475 |
| Mozambique | 900 | 213 | Sweden | 24,924 | 31,627 |
| Namibia | 6,274 | 2,383 | Switzerland | 28,204 | 47,064 |
| Nepal | 1,328 | 248 | Syrian Arab Republic | 3,332 | 796 |
| Netherlands | 27,228 | 31,333 | Tajikistan | 850 | 420 |
| New Zealand | 20,204 | 18,425 | Tanzania | 532 | 197 |
| Nicaragua | 2,500 | 474 | Thailand | 6,452 | 2,853 |
| Niger | 772 | 208 | Togo | 1,438 | 322 |
| Nigeria | 871 | 257 | Trinidad and Tobago | 8,914 | 5,553 |
| Norway | 35,433 | 38,298 | Tunisia | 6,501 | 2,562 |
| Oman | 13,247 | 7,295 | Turkey | 5,790 | 2,873 |
| Pakistan | 1,916 | 517 | Turkmenistan | 4,104 | 1,587 |
| Panama | 6,146 | 3,243 | Uganda | 1,291 | 355 |
| Paraguay | 4,643 | 1,703 | Ukraine | 4,459 | 986 |
| Peru | 4,699 | 2,311 | United Arab Emirates | 21,100 | 17,422 |
| Philippines | 3,919 | 1,165 | United Kingdom | 25,141 | 22,697 |
| Poland | 10,021 | 3,716 | United States | 34,322 | 31,592 |
| Portugal | 17,595 | 13,109 | Uruguay | 12,801 | 5,870 |
| Qatar | 21,200 | 22,359 | Uzbekistan | 1,561 | 512 |
| Romania | 6,024 | 1,393 | Venezuela, RB | 5,763 | 3,326 |
| Russian Federation | 7,653 | 2,609 | Vietnam | 2,103 | 390 |
| Rwanda | 1,143 | 253 | Yemen, Rep. | 779 | 316 |
| Saudi Arabia | 11,516 | 6,614 | Zambia | 790 | 405 |
| Senegal | 1,528 | 629 | Zimbabwe | 2,322 | 559 |
| Serbia and Montenegro | 2,250 | 1,302 | | | |

**Note:** * Purchasing power parity (PPP) GDP is adjusted for inflation (real GDP) and converted to U.S. dollars using current PPP exchange rates. PPP exchange rates are a ratio of the current year's price levels in two countries.
** GDP in constant U.S. dollars is adjusted for inflation and exchange rate changes. GDP in constant 1995 U.S. dollars is converted from real GDP in national currencies using 1995 official market exchange rates.

**Sources:** World Bank, *World Development Indicators Online*, available at *www.worldbank.org/data* by subscription, and Central Intelligence Agency, *World Factbook 2002*.

## Foreign Aid

| Country | **USAID (in millions of US dollars) | | World Bank (***IDA: International Development Association) (in millions of US dollars) | |
|---|---|---|---|---|
| | Aid in 2002 | Cumulative Aid (since 1997) | Loans in 2002 | Cumulative Loans (since 1997) |
| Albania | 36.7 | 215 | 87.5 | 384.3 |
| Algeria | 2.0 | 2.7 | 0 | 0 |
| Angola | 48.0 | 288.8 | 0 | 38 |
| Armenia | 94.4 | 529.8 | 39.2 | 447.5 |
| Azerbaijan | 49.4 | 184.7 | 69.5 | 366.3 |
| Bangladesh | 81.1 | 523.3 | 321.4 | 2,761.2 |
| Belarus | 9.0 | 42.6 | 0 | 0 |
| Benin | 22.0 | 118.9 | 41 | 174.4 |
| Bolivia | 74.6 | 453.1 | 83 | 580.7 |
| Bosnia–Herzegovina | 60.4 | 962.4 | 102 | 801.2 |
| Brazil | 13.7 | 84.1 | 0 | 0 |
| Bulgaria | 33.7 | 203.0 | 0 | 0 |
| Burkina Faso | 10.3 | 80.6 | 121.6 | 392.2 |
| Burma | 6.5 | 25.4 | 0 | 0 |
| Burundi | 9.1 | 40.1 | 36 | 130.5 |
| Cambodia | 42.4 | 145.4 | 48.2 | 298.6 |
| Cameroon | 0.3 | 7.1 | 5.5 | 357.4 |
| Cape Verde | 3.8 | 18.1 | 24 | 110.6 |
| Central African Republic | 0 | 0 | 17 | 45 |
| Chad | 3.7 | 9.3 | 64.6 | 285.5 |
| China | 0 | 1.0 | 0 | 1041 |
| Colombia | 6.6 | 19.2 | 0 | 0 |
| Congo, Democratic Republic of | 41.0 | 113.7 | 500 | 500 |
| Congo, Republic of | 0 | 0 | 89.7 | 89.7 |
| Croatia | 47.5 | 160.0 | 0 | 0 |
| Cyprus | 14.0 | 74.9 | 0 | 0 |
| Djibouti | 1.1 | 3.1 | 25 | 74 |
| Dominican Republic | 18.3 | 100.4 | 0 | 2.2 |
| Ecuador | 25.4 | 103.7 | 0 | 0 |
| Egypt | 891.3 | 4,531.2 | 0 | 452 |
| El Salvador | 96.9 | 307.9 | 0 | 0 |
| Ethiopia | 98.7 | 657.1 | 210 | 876.8 |
| Gambia | 0.1 | 9.3 | 31 | 46 |
| Georgia | 91.8 | 470.3 | 2.7 | 455.9 |
| Ghana | 43.6 | 319.6 | 330.5 | 946.4 |
| Guatemala | 60.8 | 352 | 0 | 0 |
| Guinea | 29.3 | 140 | 145 | 319.4 |
| Guinea–Bissau | 1.3 | 5.6 | 26 | 196 |
| Guyana | 4.1 | 20.9 | 0 | 17.5 |
| Haiti | 53.8 | 507.6 | 0 | 0 |
| Honduras | 36.6 | 228 | 40.4 | 631.9 |
| Hungary | 0 | 28.3 | 0 | 0 |
| India | 177.5 | 884.1 | 1,296.5 | 5,314.4 |
| Indonesia | 124.5 | 598.8 | 70.5 | 535.9 |
| Iraq (Northern) | 0 | 8.1 | 0 | 0 |
| Israel | 720 | 5,987.2 | 0 | 0 |
| Ivory Coast | 0.0 | 1.3 | 212 | 753.3 |
| Jamaica | 15.1 | 73.1 | 0 | 0 |
| Jordan | 234.8 | 835.1 | 0 | 0 |
| Kazakhstan | 51.4 | 244.5 | 0 | 0 |
| Kenya | 63.5 | 327.6 | 16.5 | 366.7 |
| Kyrgyzstan | 64.5 | 189.3 | 15 | 307.9 |

## Foreign Aid (continued)

| Country | **USAID (in millions of US dollars)** Aid in 2002 | Cumulative Aid (since 1997) | World Bank (***IDA: International Development Association) (in millions of US dollars) Loans in 2002 | Cumulative Loans (since 1997) |
|---|---|---|---|---|
| Laos | 2.5 | 4.8 | 44.8 | 86.5 |
| Latvia | 0 | 6.9 | 0 | 0 |
| Lebanon | 10.7 | 91.2 | 0 | 0 |
| Lesotho | 0 | 2.4 | 0 | 46.6 |
| Lithuania | 0 | 16.9 | 0 | 0 |
| Macedonia | 0 | 147.9 | 35 | 84.9 |
| Madagascar | 25.4 | 141.6 | 43.8 | 840.5 |
| Malawi | 43.6 | 203.8 | 0 | 361.9 |
| Mali | 36.2 | 222.3 | 113.5 | 486.6 |
| Malta | 59.2 | 59.2 | 0 | 0 |
| Mauritania | 3.2 | 14.3 | 122.5 | 308.8 |
| Mexico | 26.8 | 99.6 | 0 | 0 |
| Moldova | 36.7 | 248.2 | 45.5 | 55.5 |
| Mongolia | 12 | 68 | 28.7 | 170.4 |
| Morocco | 12.1 | 78.8 | 0 | 0 |
| Mozambique | 58.2 | 390.3 | 270.5 | 762.1 |
| Namibia | 10.7 | 54.9 | 0 | 0 |
| Nepal | 35.7 | 137.4 | 22.6 | 240.5 |
| Nicaragua | 42.4 | 212.9 | 32.6 | 625.7 |
| Niger | 10.2 | 32.3 | 108.7 | 414.9 |
| Nigeria | 83.4 | 235.2 | 427.3 | 681.6 |
| North Korea | 0 | 131.5 | 0 | 0 |
| Pakistan | 626.2 | 647.4 | 800 | 1,174.3 |
| Panama | 8.5 | 28.8 | 0 | 0 |
| Paraguay | 9.6 | 44 | 0 | 0 |
| Peru | 90.7 | 590.5 | 0 | 0 |
| Philippines | 69.6 | 263.8 | 0 | 0 |
| Poland | 37.9 | 133.3 | 0 | 0 |
| Romania | 0 | 199.4 | 0 | 0 |
| Russia | 153.1 | 914.4 | 0 | 0 |
| Rwanda | 36.8 | 242.8 | 25 | 378.6 |
| Senegal | 30.2 | 143 | 44.7 | 849.9 |
| Serbia and Montenegro**** | 1.7 | 47.8 | 171.8 | 171.8 |
| Sierra Leone | 38.5 | 161.5 | 65 | 133.6 |
| Slovakia | 0 | 29.9 | 0 | 0 |
| South Africa | 58.2 | 361.4 | 0 | 0 |
| Sri Lanka | 12.2 | 33.3 | 75 | 371.6 |
| Sudan | 78.4 | 327.5 | 0 | 0 |
| Tajikistan | 74.8 | 148.2 | 40.8 | 297.1 |
| Tanzania | 27.9 | 216.5 | 402 | 1,089.2 |
| Thailand | 1.2 | 6.5 | 0 | 0 |
| Turkey | 199.9 | 238.1 | 0 | 0 |
| Turkmenistan | 10.5 | 40.8 | 0 | 0 |
| Uganda | 82 | 426.5 | 180.7 | 1,160.5 |
| Ukraine | 173.8 | 1,099.4 | 0 | 0 |
| Uzbekistan | 99.7 | 199 | 20 | 20 |
| Venezuela | 0 | 0.5 | 0 | 0 |
| Vietnam | 11.1 | 30.9 | 593 | 2,560.7 |
| Yemen | 0 | 0 | 77.7 | 741 |
| Zambia | 54.5 | 188.6 | 6.7 | 890 |
| Zimbabwe | 39.7 | 106.4 | 0 | 148.6 |
| **Total** | **6,150.3** | **30,707.9** | **7,869.2** | **35,253.8** |

**Note:** * 103 countries that are covered by the *Index* and for which aid data (either USAID or IDA) are available.

** Economic assistance only. Selection of recipients of USAID economic assistance reflects the priorities and interests of United States foreign policy.

*** The International Development Association (IDA) provides the world's poorest countries with credits, which are loans at zero interest with a 10-year grace period and maturities of 35 to 40 years. The operational cutoff for IDA eligibility for FY 2004 is $865 in GNI per capita. Currently, 81 countries are eligible for IDA credits.

**** Data include U.S. aid to Kosovo.

**Sources:** U.S. Agency for International Development, *Congressional Budget Presentation*, FY 2004, FY 2002, FY 2000, and FY 1998, at *http://www.usaid.gov/policy/budget/*; World Bank, *Annual Report*, 2002, 2001, 2000, 1999, 1998, and 1997, at *http://web.worldbank.org/WBSITE/EXTERNAL/EXTABOUTUS/0,,contentMDK:20042527~menuPK:34633~pagePK:43912~piPK:44037,00.html.*

# Major Works Cited

The following sources provided the basis for the country factor analyses in the 2004 *Index of Economic Freedom*. In addition, the authors and analysts of the various elements of the *Index* relied on supporting documentation and information from various government agencies and sites on the Internet, news reports and journal articles, and official responses to inquiries. These sources are cited in each chapter where appropriate. All statistical and other information received from government sources was verified with independent, internationally recognized nongovernmental sources as well.

African Development Bank, *ADB Statistics Pocketbook 2003*; available at *http://www.afdb.org/knowledge/publications/pdf/statistics_pocket_book2003.pdf*.

Asian Development Bank, *Key Indicators of Developing Asian and Pacific Countries 2002*, Vol. XXXIII; available at *http://www.adb.org/Documents/Books/Key_Indicators/2002/default.asp*.

Country statistical agencies, central banks, and ministries of finance, economy, and trade; available at *http://www.un.org/Depts/unsd/gs_natstat.htm*, *http://www.census.gov/main/www/stat_int.html*, *http://www.centralbanking.co.uk/links/mof.htm*, *http://www.bis.org/cbanks.htm*, and *http://dir.yahoo.com/Government/Statistics/*.

Economist Intelligence Unit Limited, *Country Profile*, London, U.K., 2002 and 2003.

———, *EIU Country Report*, London, U.K., 1996 to 2003.

———, *Country Commerce*, London, U.K., 2002 and 2003.

Ernst & Young International, Ltd., *The Global Executive*, New York, N.Y., 2003.

———, *Worldwide Corporate Tax Guide*, New York, N.Y., 2003.

———, direct correspondence with Country Office.

European Bank for Reconstruction and Development, *Country Strategies*, 2002 and 2003; available at *http://www.ebrd.org/about/strategy/index.htm*.

Inter-American Development Bank, at *http://www.iadb.org*.

International Monetary Fund, *Annual Report on Exchange Arrangements and Exchange Restrictions 2002*, Washington, D.C., 2002.

————, *Government Finance Statistics Yearbook*, Vol. XXVI (2002), Washington, D.C., 2002.

————, *International Financial Statistics*, Vol. LV (2002), Washington, D.C., June 2003.

————, *International Financial Statistics Online*, Washington, D.C., 2003; available by subscription at *http://ifs.apdi.net/imf/logon.aspx*.

————, *Selected Issues and Statistical Appendix*, various countries, Washington, D.C., 2001 to 2003.

————, *World Economic Outlook: Growth and Institutions*, Washington, D.C., April 2003; available at *http://www.imf.org/external/pubs/ft/weo/2003/01/index.htm*.

————, *Country Information*; available at *http://www.imf.org/external/country/index.htm*.

O'Driscoll, Gerald P., Jr., Edwin J. Feulner, and Mary Anastasia O'Grady, *2003 Index of Economic Freedom* (Washington, D.C.: The Heritage Foundation and Dow Jones & Company, Inc., 2002).

Organisation for Economic Co-operation and Development, *OECD Economic Outlook* No. 73, June 2003.

————, OECD on-line; available at *http://www.oecd.org/statsportal/0,2639,en_2825_293564_1_1_1_1_1,00.html*.

Standard & Poor's, *Sovereigns Ratings Analysis*, New York, N.Y., 2003; available at *http://www2.standardandpoors.com/NASApp/cs/ContentServer?pagename=sp/Page/FixedIncomeBrowsePg&r=1&l=EN& b=2&s=17&f=3*.

Transparency International, *The Corruption Perceptions Index*, 2002, 2001, 2000, and 1999, Berlin, Germany, 2002, 2001, 2000, and 1999; available at *http://www.transparency.org/cpi/index.html#cpi*.

United States Department of State, *Country Reports on Human Rights Practices for 2002*, released by the Bureau of Democracy, Human Rights, and Labor, March 2003; available on U.S. Department of State Internet site, at *http://www.state.gov/g/drl/rls/hrrpt/2002/index.htm*.

United States Departments of State and Commerce, *Country Commercial Guides*, Washington, D.C., 2002 and 2003; available at *http://www.buyusainfo.net/adsearch.cfm?search_type=int&loadnav=no*.

United States Trade Representative, Office of the, *2003 National Trade Estimate Report on Foreign Trade Barriers* (Washington, D.C.: U.S. Government Printing Office, 2003); available at *http://www.ustr.gov/reports/nte/2003/index.htm*.

World Bank, *World Bank World Development Indicators on CD–ROM 2003*, Washington, D.C., 2003.

————, *World Development Indicators 2003*; available by subscription at *http://publications.worldbank.org/WDI/*.

World Economic Forum, *The Global Competitiveness Report 2002–2003*, Oxford University Press, 2003.

World Trade Organization, *Trade Policy Reviews*, 1995 to 2003; available at *http://www.wto.org/english/tratop_e/tpr_e/tpr_e.htm*.

/